CW00515823

Stay on a farm

BWRDD CROESO CYMRU
WALES TOURIST BOARD

First published in 1992
by Charles Letts & Co Ltd
Letts of London House, Parkgate Road, London SW11 4NQ

in association with the Farm Holiday Bureau (UK) Ltd, the English Tourist
Board and the National Tourist Boards of Scotland, Wales and Northern
Ireland
© Farm Holiday Bureau UK 1992
National Agricultural Centre, Stoneleigh, Warwickshire CV8 2LZ

All our rights reserved. No part of this publication may be reproduced,
stored in a retrieval system, or transmitted, in any form or by any means,
electronic, mechanical, photocopying, recording or otherwise, without the
prior permission in writing of the publishers.

ISBN 1 85238 369 0

'Letts' is a registered trademark of Charles Letts & Co Limited

The information contained in this Guide has been published in good faith
on the basis of the details submitted by the proprietors of the premises
listed. These proprietors are current members of the Farm Holiday Bureau
and have paid for their entries in this Guide. Whilst every effort has been
made to ensure accuracy in this publication, neither the publisher, the
Farm Holiday Bureau nor the National Tourist Boards can guarantee the
accuracy of the information in this Guide and accept no responsibility for
any error or misrepresentation. All liability for loss, disappointment,
negligence or other damage caused by reliance on the information
contained in this Guide, or in the event of bankruptcy, or liquidation, or
cessation of trade of any company, individual or firm mentioned is hereby
excluded.

The Farm Holiday Bureau of the United Kingdom gratefully acknowledges
the continuing assistance and advice offered by the National Tourist
Boards, the Agricultural Development Advisory Service of the Ministry of
Agriculture, the Scottish Agricultual Organisations Society Ltd, and all
those who seek to maintain a balance in the rural community.

Produced by The Pen and Ink Book Company Limited, Huntingdon

Maps provided by Lovell Johns Ltd., Oxford

Cover photographs kindly provided by Gloucestershire County Council
(*front*), Countryside Commission and The English Tourist Board (*back*).

Printed and bound in Great Britain

Contents

The Farm Holiday Bureau

The Farm Holiday Bureau is a national network of farming families offering value for money, good food and a warm welcome in quality self-catering and bed and breakfast accommodation.

Both types of accommodation are widely available, with some farms offering camping and caravanning sites as well. Where evening meals are provided, you can expect good country fare, often using local or even home-grown produce.

High standards prevail throughout this guide. All accommodation must be inspected by the National Tourist Boards, whose classification and grading schemes assess quality as well as quantity of facilities.

All members belong to one of 81 Farm Holiday Groups. The groups also inspect potential new members and provide another stringent quality control, guided by the Farm Holiday Bureau. Collectively the 81 groups form the co-operative which is the Farm Holiday Bureau (UK) Ltd.

The Bureau helps guide the industry as well as promoting it. Training, advice and communication with Government and national authorities on behalf of the membership are part of our national brief as well as marketing and promotion in Britain and overseas. The Bureau works closely with the National and Regional Tourist Boards as well as Agricultural Development Advisory Service (ADAS) and Scottish Agricultural Organisations Society (SAOS) and is continually grateful for all their help and support.

Agriculture is a continually changing industry. Today we have some members whose accommodation varies from the traditional working farm experience, but they still possess the knowledge, experience and sympathy with the countryside and farming practices that are so important to our visitors.

There is no better way of discovering the countryside than by staying on a farm.

Farm Holiday Bureau (UK) Ltd
National Agriculture Centre
Stoneleigh Park
Warwickshire
CV8 2LZ
☎ 0203 696909
Fax 0203 696630

Your real chance to discover the countryside

Where to go

The Farm Holiday Bureau has 81 local Groups, each of which has a section in this guide. The maps show the location of each Group and their position in the countries. Page numbers are indicated in *italic*.

Scotland
1 Highlands & Islands *37*
2 Grampian *42*
3 Angus and Perthshire *45*
4 Fife *48*
5 Heart of Scotland *50*
6 Clyde Valley *54*
7 Bonnie Galloway & Stinchar
   Valley *56*
8 Dumfriesshire (Annandale) *60*
9 Scottish Borders *63*

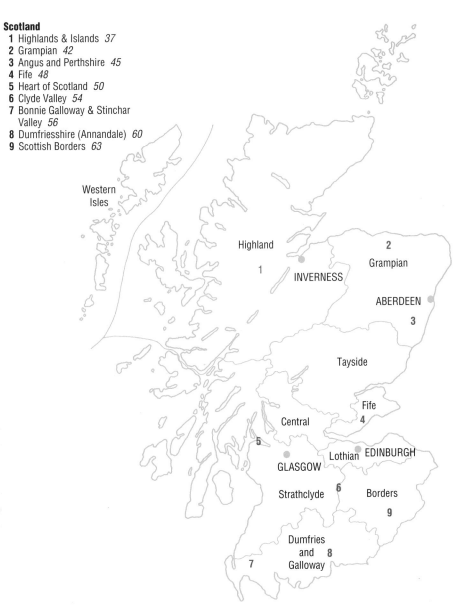

Western
Isles

Highland

1   INVERNESS

2
Grampian

ABERDEEN

3

Tayside

Fife
4

Central

5

GLASGOW
Lothian EDINBURGH

Strathclyde 6   Borders

9

Dumfries
and 8
Galloway

7

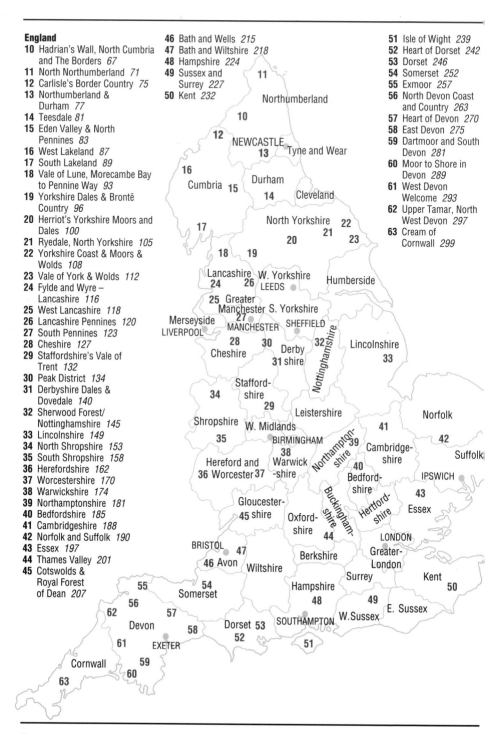

Wales

Northern Ireland

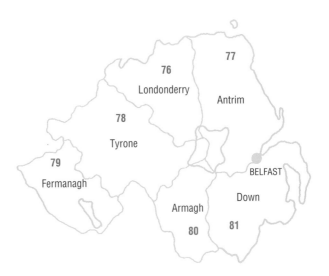

The best welcome to Britain's countryside

The provision of farmhouse and self-catering accommodation has moved from strength to strength over the years. Today, you can enjoy a top quality experience at unbeatable value.

Farm Holiday Bureau members are proud to be able to contribute to such an industry – not only can they offer the best of countryside accommodation, but they can also provide a depth of rural knowledge and environmental understanding which will really help you make the most of your stay on a farm.

Farming families have grown up on the land and have moulded its very formation. They are a part of the history of the countryside. Their intimate knowledge of the landscape, the country way of life and all the attractions it has to offer is unsurpassed. They will tell you all there is to know about the best (and often quietest) places to go. This, combined with their warm welcome and friendly help throughout your stay will give you your real chance to discover the countryside.

By staying on a farm, though, you will not only enjoy your holiday, you will provide a valuable contribution to the whole rural economy – which is such an important part of Britain's heritage. By supporting local industries you will be helping ensure that future generations can also enjoy Britain's countryside. Through staying on a farm, you will be helping those people who live in the countryside in their role as custodians of the environment.

It is not only the holiday makers who can make this valuable contribution, as many farms now cater for business people. A warm and comfortable welcome at the end of a long day means so much more to the weary traveller. Many of our members can now also cater for small meetings. What better way to concentrate on major decisions and long term policy than to spend a day in a farmhouse – where peace, quiet, seclusion, security and anonymity can be guaranteed? Not only that, but you can also guarantee to be well fed from the best of local produce.

Farming families are flexible. You can get up early or arrive late and always be assured of a welcoming smile. The farmer and his family regard your custom as an important part of their businesses. Farmers are busy people though, and farmyards can be large, so it is worth waiting those few extra minutes on the phone when making a booking.

Today, it is also worth booking your holidays well in advance. Farmhouse accommodation is now enormously popular and it is advisable to book ahead, especially for summer holidays. However, off-peak or out of season holidays are becoming increasingly sought after, especially for retired people, and may be booked at relatively short notice. What better way to discover the countryside than in the peace and tranquillity that an out of season short break offers?

If you feel energetic and want to return home to your farm tired, relaxed and ready to enjoy a satisfying meal, we can also help. Many farms can cater for activity holidays – indeed, many activities are a way of life for the farmer and his family. In this year's guide, new symbols indicate those farms which can offer waymarked footpaths on their land, coarse or game fishing and riding. There are many more activities besides – from clay pigeon shooting to bread making. All you have to do is ask!

So if you want fun and games or serious contemplation, or if you just want to enjoy the very best of the British countryside – Farm Holiday Bureau members will be delighted to welcome you.

Come with us, stay on a farm and discover the countryside.

Further information

These official Tourist Boards will be happy to supply you with further general information on their areas.

National Tourist Boards

English Tourist Board
Thames Tower, Black's Road, Hammersmith,
London W6 9EL
081-846 9000

Northern Ireland Tourist Board
59 North Street
Belfast
BT1 1ND
(0232) 231221

Scottish Tourist Board
23 Ravelstone Terrace, Edinburgh EH4 3EU
(031) 332 2433

Wales Tourist Board
Brunel House, 2 Fitzalan Road, Cardiff CF2 1UY
(0222) 499909

Regional Tourist Boards

Cumbria Tourist Board
(covering the county of Cumbria)
Ashleigh, Holly Road, Windermere, Cumbria
LA23 2AQ
(05394) 44444

Northumbria Tourist Board
(covering the counties of Cleveland, Durham,
Northumberland, Tyne & Wear)
Aykley Heads, Durham DH1 5UX
(091) 384 6905

North West Tourist Board
(covering the counties of Cheshire, Greater
Manchester, Lancashire, Merseyside and the
High Peak District of Derbyshire)
Swan House, Swan Meadow Road,
Wigan Pier, Wigan WN3 5BB
(0942) 821222

Yorkshire and Humberside Tourist Board
(covering the counties of North Yorkshire, South
Yorkshire, West Yorkshire and Humberside)
312 Tadcaster Road, York, North Yorkshire YO2
2HF
(0904) 707961

Heart of England Tourist Board
(covering the counties of Gloucestershire,
Hereford & Worcester, Shropshire, Staffordshire,
Warwickshire and West Midlands)
Woodside, Larkhill, Worcester, Hereford &
Worcester WR5 2EF (0905) 763436

East Midlands Tourist Board
(covering the counties of Derbyshire,
Leicestershire, Lincolnshire, Northamptonshire
and Nottinghamshire)
Exchequergate, Lincoln, Lincolnshire LN2 1PZ
(0522) 531521

East Anglia Tourist Board
(covering the counties of Cambridgeshire,
Essex, Norfolk and Suffolk)
Toppesfield Hall, Hadleigh, Suffolk IP7 5DN
(0473) 822922

London Tourist Board
(covering the Greater London area)
26 Grosvenor Gardens, London SW1W 0DU
(071) 730 3488

West Country Tourist Board
(covering the counties of Avon, Cornwall, Devon,
Dorset (parts of), Somerset, Wiltshire and Isles
of Scilly)
60 St Davids Hill, Exeter EX4 4SY
(0392) 76351

Southern Tourist Board
(covering the counties of Hampshire, Eastern
and Northern Dorset and Isle of Wight)
40 Chamberlayne Road, Eastleigh, Hampshire
SO5 5JH
(0703) 620006

South East England Tourist Board
(covering the counties of East Sussex, Kent,
Surrey and West Sussex)
The Old Brew House, Warwick Park, Tunbridge
Wells, Kent TN2 5TU
(0892) 540766

Tourist Information Centres

 There are over 800 Tourist Information Centres throughout the United Kingdom and they are there for you to use both before your holiday and during it. Look in your local telephone directory under 'Tourist Information' to find your nearest centre. TICs can give you details about local attractions, events and accommodation and many will even be able to book it for you. Look out for the information sign.

MAP OF GREAT BRITAIN

KEY TO MAP SECTIONS

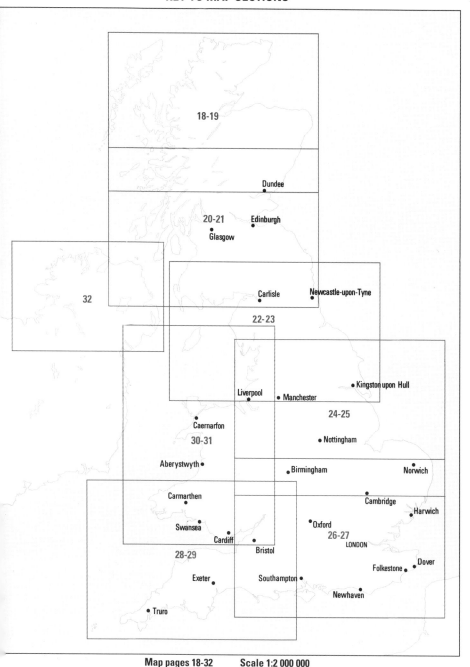

Map pages 18-32   Scale 1:2 000 000

GRID REFERENCE

To locate grid reference position of farms read

1) Eastings (i.e. figures west to east along top and bottom of the page)
2) Northings (i.e. figures south to north up the side of the page)

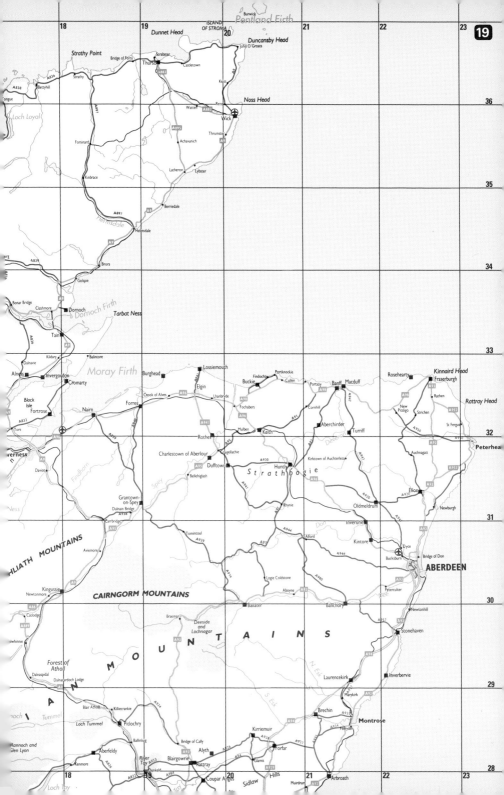

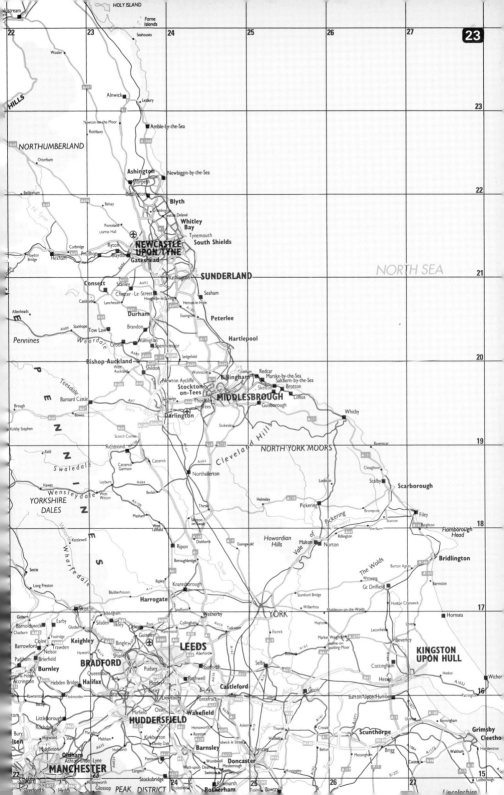

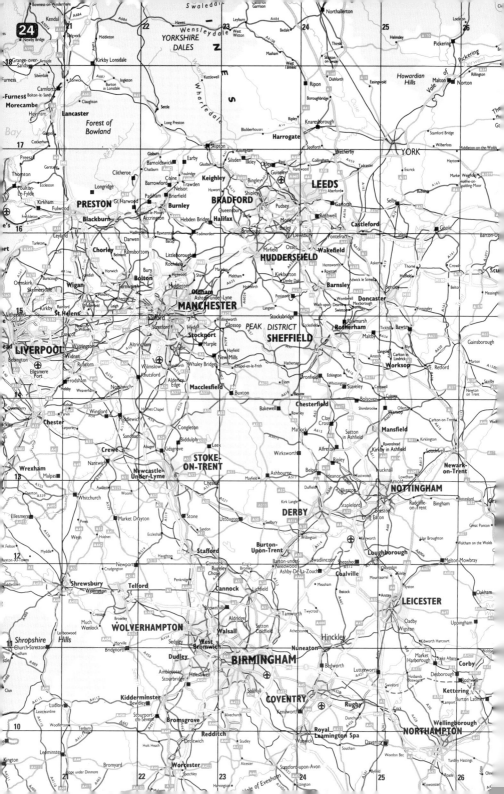

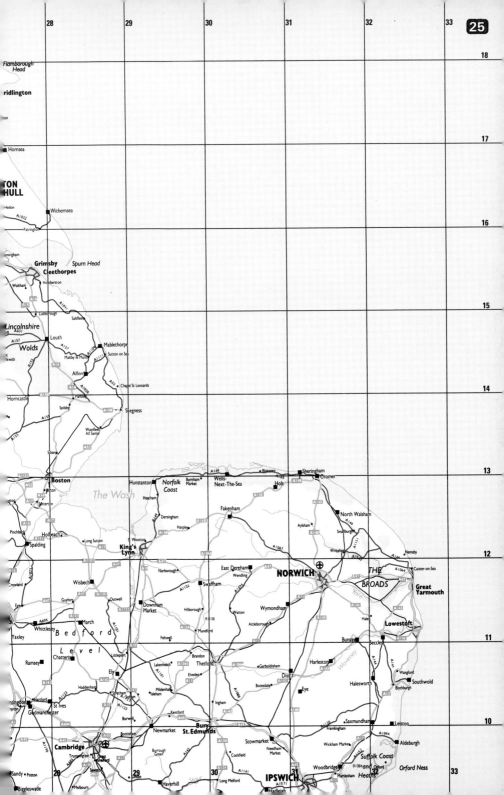

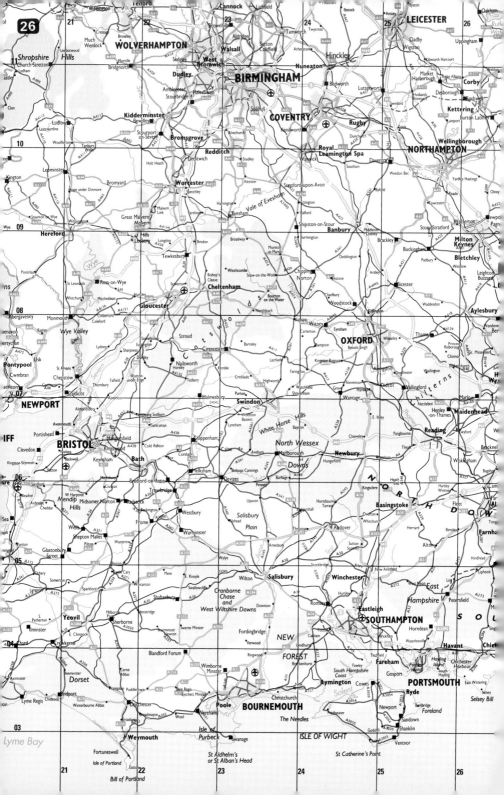

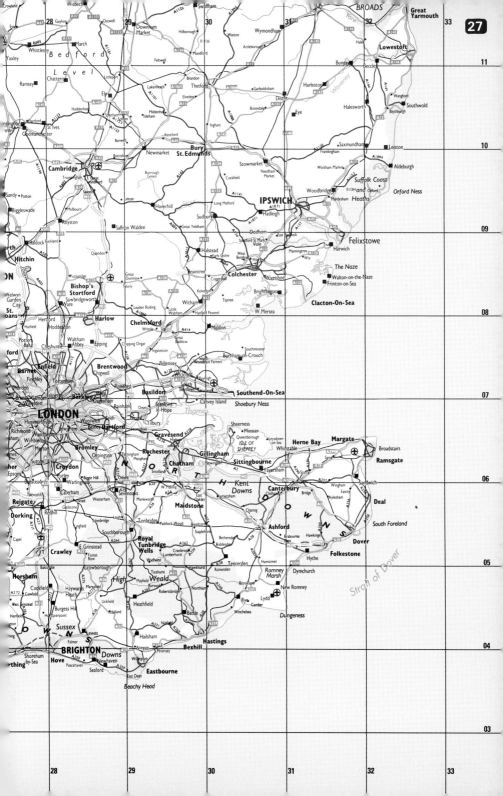

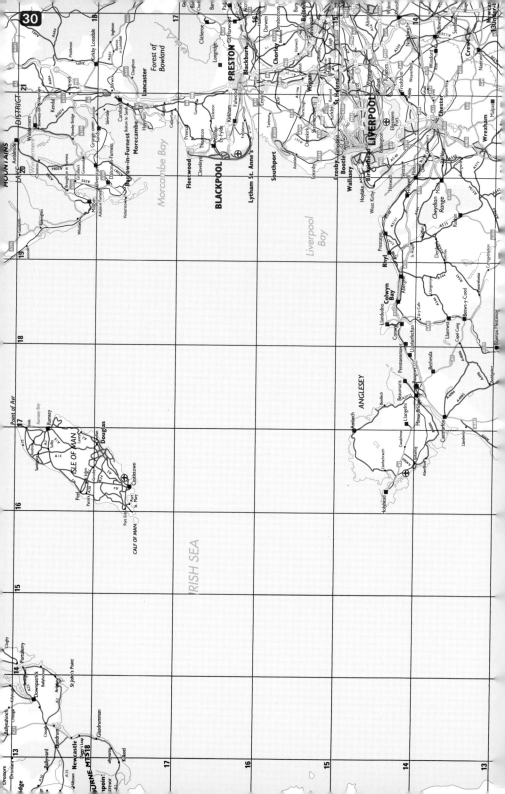

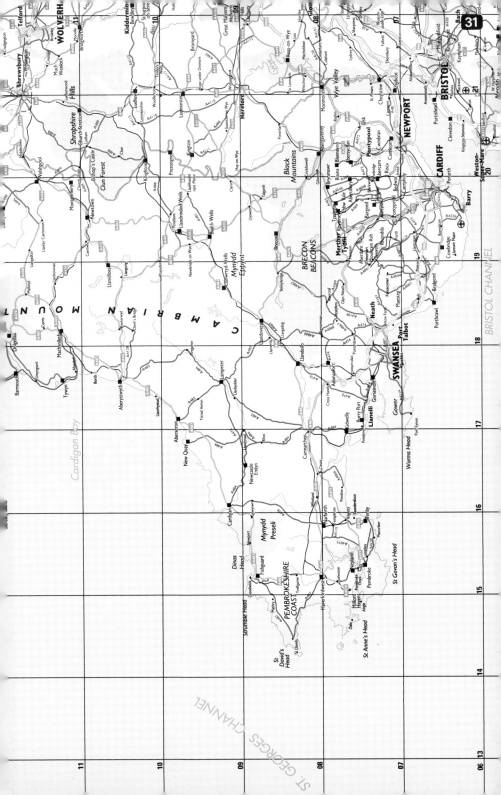

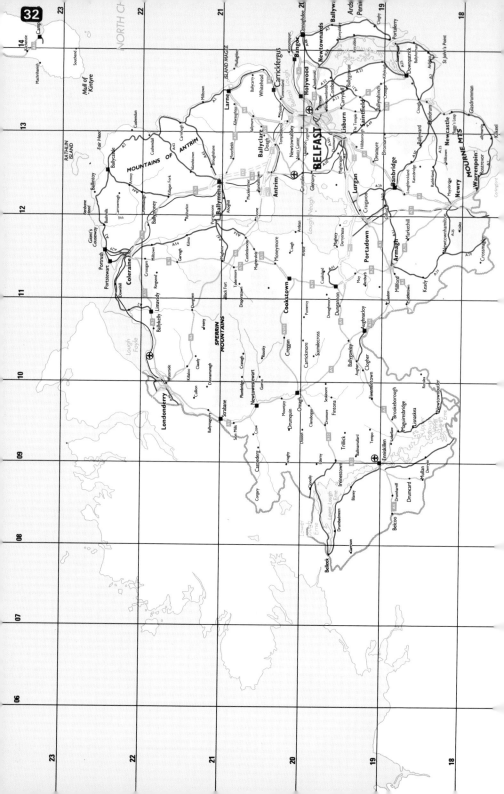

Accommodation classification and grading

Farm Holiday Bureau members are inspected by their Groups to ensure that a high standard of cleanliness, courtesy and service is maintained. All members must also be inspected by their National Tourist Board, agree to meet the Tourist Board Minimum Standards and observe the Tourist Board's Code of Conduct.

Listed

Crown classification and grading scheme for serviced accommodation

The National Tourist Boards for England, Scotland and Wales operate a common classification and grading scheme for serviced accommodation including farmhouses. Each member has a thorough annual inspection by the Tourist Board and is classified, according to the range of facilities provided, within 6 bands from 'Listed' and then from 1–5 Crowns. The more Crowns, the more extensive range of facilities.

Classified establishments can apply to be assessed for a separate quality commendation of 'Approved' ('Merit' in Wales), 'Commended', 'Highly Commended' or 'De Luxe'. When granted, the quality commendation appears alongside the classification. In Wales, members who offer superior standards and have completed a tourism training course also have the 'Award' sign indicating that they are in receipt of the Wales Tourist Board's Farmhouse Award.

Self-catering holiday homes

All Bureau members who offer self-catering accommodation must have been inspected by the Tourist Boards or have applied for an inspection.

England
Scotland
Dragon   Wales

Those inspected in England and Scotland are classified according to the range of facilities they provide (1–5 Keys in England, 1–5 Crowns in Scotland). Holiday Homes with higher quality standards have the term 'Approved', 'Commended' or 'Highly Commended' alongside the classification. In Wales quality standards are indicated on a scale of 1–5 Dragons.

Northern Ireland

The Northern Ireland Tourist Board registers and grades all accommodation under a statutory system. All the farms listed offer a high standard and are inspected annually. Grades are 'Grade A', 'Grade B' and 'Approved'.

British graded holiday parks scheme

✓
✓ ✓
✓ ✓ ✓
✓ ✓ ✓ ✓
✓ ✓ ✓ ✓ ✓

The National Tourist Boards for England, Scotland and Wales operate a common quality grading scheme for holiday caravan, camping and chalet parks. The scheme grades parks according to the relative quality of what is offered, in a range of 1–5 ✓s. The more ✓s the higher the quality.

How to use the guide . . .

The Guide lists all the members of the Farm Holiday Bureau (UK) Limited in the countries of Scotland, England, Wales and Northern Ireland. Within each country's section, each chapter comprises a local FHB Group, as listed and indexed on pages 7–9 with a key map, description of the area and a Group Contact. The Group Contacts can help you find suitable accommodation if you wish.

Properties in each chapter are listed alphabetically under Bed and Breakfast, Self-catering and Camping and Caravanning. Each property has a map reference which corresponds with the colour maps at the beginning of the guide.

An index appears at the back of the guide, showing all members who offer facilities for disabled visitors. A new index showing those farms who welcome business breaks is also located there.

PLEASE REMEMBER TO MENTION 'STAY ON A FARM' WHEN MAKING A BOOKING

How to book . . .

All you have to do is telephone the farm of your choice. If the accommodation you want is not available, the owner will be happy to refer you to similar alternative FHB accommodation. **Alternatively, the Group Contact will be happy to help you find the right accommodation, and can usually provide you with a local group leaflet.**

Many members also offer a 'book a bed ahead' service to their guests. If you are touring, just tell your host where you wish to visit next, and he or she can make the booking for you.

When making a booking . . .

• Mention the guide.

• Specify your planned arrival and departure dates.

• Specify accommodation needed and any particular requirements, eg. twin beds, family room, private bath, ground floor, cot.

• Specify terms required, eg. B&B, evening meal etc. Evening meal times vary and high tea may be available for children. Farms offering evening meals do not necessarily do so all year round so do check.

• Specify special requirements, eg. special diets, facilities for disabled people, arrangements for children, dogs.

• Check prices and any reductions that may be offered.

• Check whether a deposit is payable and, if so, what charges will apply if the booking is cancelled (see 'Cancellations' on page 36).

• Check method and date of payment.

• Check whether B&B access is restricted through the day. Many farms are happy for visitors to stay in the house all day, but on some farms this is not practical and guests are asked to be out of the farmhouse between 10.30am and 4.30pm. Remember, it is essential that children are carefully supervised at all times on and around the farm.

• Check the best time to arrive and ask for directions to the farm. When you are near your destination, look out for the Farm Holiday Bureau member sign at the end of the drive. Your host will be glad to direct you by phone if you get lost.

• Give your name, address and telephone number

NB We recommend that, time permitting, all telephone bookings are confirmed in writing, specifying exactly what you have booked and the price you expect to pay.

Symbols

Symbol	Explanation	French	German
ⓖⓝ	Country house, not a working farm	Manoir (pas une) exploitation agricole)	Landhaus, kein aktiver Bauernhof
Å	Camping facilities	Camping	Camping-Einrichtungen
⚠	Caravanning facilities	Caravaning	Caravan-Einrichtungen
⋔	Dogs by arrangement	Chiens autorisés sous réserve d'accord préalable	Hunde nach Vereinbarung
♿	Facilities for the disabled/less able people (check for details)	Aménagements pour handicapés (Détails à confirmer)	Einrichtungen für Behinderte/weniger agile Menschen (Einzelheiten prüfen)
⚭	No smoking	Non fumeurs de préférence	Nichtraucher vevorzugt
☜ (3)	Children welcome (minimum age)	Enfants bienvenus (âge minimum)	Kinder willkomen (Mindestalter)
💳	Credit card	Cartes de crédit acceptées	Kreditkarten werden akzeptiert
🛄	Business breaks	Business breaks	Geschaftsreisen
🚶	Farm trail (walking)	Piste fermièr (à pied)	Farm-Lehrpfad (zu Fu)
🗣	Foreign language spoken	Langues étrangères parlés	Man spricht Fremdsprachen
🐎	Riding	Randonnée à poney ou équitation	Reiten auf Ponys oder Pferden
🎣	Fishing	La pêche à la ligne	Angeln
🏅	Classification (see p.33)	Classification (voir p.33)	Klassifikation (p.33)
Commended	Grading	Catégorie	Einstufung
⚷ ⚷ ⚷	Self-catering classification (England)	Classification de la location	Klassifizierung für Selbstversorgung
✓ ✓ ✓	Camping and caravan parking classification	Classification du terrain de camping	Campingpltaz-Klassifizierung

	Prices	Prix	Preise
B&B	price per person per night for bed and breakfast	Prix par personne par nuit pour chambre + petit déjeuner	Pries pro Person pro Nacht für Bett und Frühstück
EM	price per person for evening meal	Prix par personne pour repas du soir	Preis pro Person für Abendessen
SC	price per unit per week self-catering	Prix par location par semaine	Preis pro Einheit pro Woche bei Selbstversorgung
Tents	price per tent pitch per night	Prix par tente par nuit	Preis pro Zeltaufstellung pro Nacht
Caravans	price per caravan pitch per night	Prix par caravane par nuit	Preis Pro Caravanaufstellung pro Nacht
	All prices include VAT and service charge if any.	Tous les prix tiennent compete de la TVA et du service, le cas échéant.	Alle Preise inklusive MWSt und Bedienungsgeld, wenn überhaupt

Camping and Caravanning

The index on page 363 shows which farms are listed as offering camping and caravanning facilities

Business Men Welcome

The index on page 363 shows those farms which welcome business travellers, and which can provide meeting rooms.

Payment and deposits

For reservations made in advance a deposit is usually payable and this will be deducted from the total bill. When you book please check when and how payment should be made.

Cancellations

Once a booking has been agreed, on the telephone or by letter, a legally binding contract has been made with the host. If you cancel a reservation fail to take up the accommodation or leave prematurely (regardless of the reasons), the host may be entitled to compensation if it cannot be relet for all or a good part of the booked period. If a deposit has been paid it is likely to be forfeited and an additional payment may be demanded.

Insurance

Travel and holiday insurance protection policies can be taken out to safeguard visitors in the event of cancellation or curtailment. Insurance of personal property can also be sought. Hosts cannot accept liability for any loss or damage to visitors' property, however caused. Do make sure that your valuables are covered by your household insurance before you take them away.

1 Highlands & Islands

'Ceud mìle fàilte', – a hundred thousand welcomes – to the Highlands and Islands, the last great open space in Europe, a spectacular land mass and myriad islands covering nearly 15,000 square miles of unsurpassed scenic beauty. A land of mountains, glens, lochs, lonely sandy beaches and rugged coastline that is changeless and unspoilt.

Contrasting Highland landscapes provide an unrivalled backdrop for holiday activities. Enthusiasts of boating, fishing, golf, walking, birdwatching and geology are well catered for. In the land where deer and eagle roam free, wildlife lovers can also observe seals, ospreys and otters in their natural habitat. Old castles, battlefield monuments and folk museums testify to a past rich in history, culture and folklore. Land use ranges from small west coast crofts to larger hill sheep farms and to beef and grain producing units further east.

The region is easily accessible on superb new roads from the south and you can also travel by improved rail services, or by aeroplane. However you come and wherever you spend your holiday, you are assured of the clean air, peace and freedom which make life worth living and of the traditional Highland welcome famed throughout the world. 'Haste ye back.'

Group Contacts: ⊞ **Margaret Pottie** ☎ **0667 62213/462213**
　　　　　　　　 ⊞ **Jessie Masheter** ☎ **0463 782433**

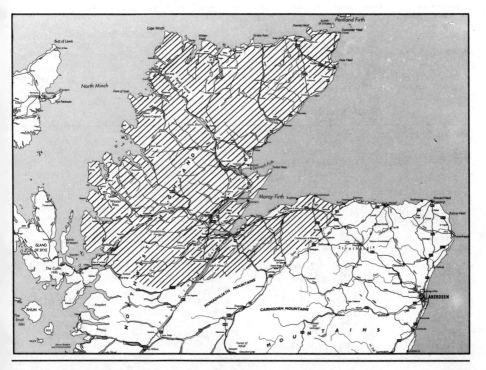

Bed and Breakfast (and evening meal)

Balaggan Farm, Culloden Moor, By Inverness, Inverness-shire IV1 2EL

Mrs Phyllis Alexander
☎ 0463 790213
BB From £13
EM From £8
Sleeps5
🐕 🐈 ⬤
Listed Commended

This comfortable farmhouse set in quiet, peaceful countryside, close to Clava Cairns and standing stones, central for touring Highlands. 1 family and 1 twin bedroom. Relax in front of open peat fire in sitting room with colour TV. Sample the warm hospitality and the good home cooking offered at this small stock rearing farm of 90 acres. Dogs by arrangement. Open Apr–Oct. Map ref: 178 219

"Benview", Morness, Rogart, Sutherland IV28 3XG

Mrs Johan Corbett
☎ 0408 641222
BB From £12.50
EM From £6.50
🐕 🐈
Listed Commended

Traditional country farmhouse offering peace and quiet, comfort, good food and friendly, personal attention. An ideal base for day trips to the north, west and east coasts. Also ideal for hill-walking, golfing, fishing, wildlife, birdwatching. Open 11 May–Nov. Map ref: 176 341

Borlum Farmhouse, Drumnadrochit, Inverness, Inverness-shire IV3 6XN

Vanessa MacDonald-Haig
☎ and fax 045 62 358
BB From £15.50
Sleeps 15
Tents £3 Caravans £4
🐕 ⊞ ⬤ 🐴 ⬤ 🐈 🏇 🅰 ⬤
🖓 🐈
♨ ♨ Commended

This traditional farmhouse commands a spectacular view over Loch Ness. Each year visitors worldwide are delighted with the fresh rooms, food and friendly atmosphere. Borlum is a working hill farm stocking sheep and suckler cows, with its own BHS approved riding centre, making it the ideal place for a riding holiday. Weekend breaks. Please send SAE for colour brochure. Open Mar–Nov. Map ref: 170 313

Clachan Farm, Lochbroom, Ullapool, Ross-shire IV23 2RZ

Mrs Isobel Renwick
☎ 0854 85 209
BB From £12
Sleeps 5
🖓 🐈 🏇
♨ ♨ Commended

A warm welcome awaits you at this very comfortable modern farmhouse, 7 miles south of Ullapool and 2 minutes from the A835. Three-course breakfast, electric blankets, TV lounge available all day. The area has walking, climbing, birdwatching, loch and sea fishing, pony trekking and pleasure cruising. The exotic Inverewe Gardens, Corrieshalloch Gorge and Nature Reserves are all within easy reach. Open March–Nov (no Sunday enquiries please). Map ref: 157 335

Daviot Mains Farm, Daviot, Nr Inverness, Inverness-shire IV1 2ER

Margaret & Alex Hutcheson
☎ and fax 0463 772215
BB From £14
EM From £9
Sleeps 8
🐕 🖓 🐈 (3)
♨ ♨
Highly Commended

Comfortable early 19th century listed farmhouse in quiet situation near Inverness. Relax in the warm atmosphere of this friendly home where delicious meals are thoughtfully prepared for you and where log fires burn in both sitting and dining rooms. En-suite/private facilities available. The perfect base for exploring the Scottish Highlands. Recommended by "Taste of Scotland". Open all year. Map ref: 178 317

Easter Dalziel Farm, Dalcross, Inverness, Inverness-shire IV1 2JL

Bob & Margaret Pottie
☎ 0667 62213/462213
BB From £14
EM From £9
Sleeps 6
🐕 🐈 🐎
♨ ♨
Highly Commended

A friendly Highland welcome awaits the visitor to our 210-acre stock/arable farm. Delightful accommodation in early Victorian farmhouse, log fire, colour TV. Delicious home cooking and baking, choice of breakfasts offered. Lovely garden for guests' use. Sometimes lambs and chicks to feed. Ideal base for exploring the scenic Highlands, locally are Cawdor Castle, Culloden, Fort George, Loch Ness and nearby Castle Stuart. SAE or telephone for details. Open Mar–Nov. Map ref: 181 320

Leanach Farm, Culloden Moor, By Inverness, Inverness-shire IV1 2EJ

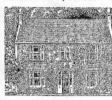

Iain & Rosanne Mackay
☎ 0463 791027
BB From £14
Sleeps 6
♿ 🐕 🐎 🐈 ♨
Listed Commended

An attractive farmhouse, beautifully situated in historic surroundings, 5 miles from Inverness. Culloden battlefield and Clava Cairns within 2 miles. 1 double bedroom and 1 twin bedroom upstairs, 1 twin bedroom downstairs (all with washbasin). Comfortable accommodation, emphasis is placed on a warm welcome and good home baking/cooking. Open Jan–Dec. Map ref: 180 319

Milton of Gollanfield, Ardersier, Inverness, Inverness-shire IV1 2QT

Mrs L MacBean
☎ 0667 462207
BB From £12
Sleeps 6
🐈 🐎 ♨
♨ ♨ **Commended**

For a peaceful, relaxing holiday, a Victorian farmhouse tastefully decorated and furnished for your comfort on a 350-acre working arable farm. Breakfast a speciality. 2 double bedrooms, 1 twin bedroom, all with washbasin, tea/coffee-making facilities and radio. Lounge, dining room, toilet, bathroom and shower room are for the exclusive use of guests. AA listed. Please telephone for brochure. Open May–Nov. Map ref: 180 323

Rheindown Farm, By Beauly, Inverness-shire IV4 7AB

Mrs S. Margaret Ritchie
☎ 0463 782461
BB From £13.50
EM From £8
Sleeps 4 + 2
🐕 🐎
♨ **Commended**

A small livestock farm overlooking the village of Beauly. Outstanding views of river and surrounding hills. 2 bedrooms with washbasin and tea/coffee-making facilities. Usually pet lambs to feed, and hand-reared calf. Evening egg collection from small flock of hens. Golf, fishing, pony trekking, hill-walking, birdwatching also available. Ideal location for touring north and west coasts. Open March–Oct. Map ref: 172 320

The Sycamores, Balintore, Tain, Ross-shire IV20 1XW

Andrew & Nicky Arthur
☎ 0862 832322
BB From £13
EM From £10
Sleeps 5–6
♿ 🐕 🐎
♨ ♨ **Commended**

Enjoy a traditional welcome at our small, friendly farm by the Moray Firth. Help to feed young stock, collect eggs and milk cows and goats. Relax in comfort or try the local activities: golf, pony trekking, birdwatching and sea-fishing all available. Visits to distilleries, gardens and castles also available. Village and sandy beaches within 5 minutes. Open all year. Map ref: 180 333

"Taransay", Lower Muckovie Farm, Inverness, Inverness-shire IV1 2BB

Mrs Aileen Munro
☎ 0463 231880
BB From £14
Sleeps 4
🐈 🐎 🐕
♨ ♨ **Commended**

A warm and friendly welcome awaits you at this comfortable, well-appointed bungalow on a quiet dairy farm. 2 miles south of Inverness, on the old A9, close to Drumrossie Hotel. 1 twin bedroom (en-suite facilities) and 1 double bedroom . Close to Culloden battlefield, Cawdor Castle and golf courses. Good restaurants nearby. Open March–Nov. Map ref: 178 318

Upper Latheron Farm, Latheron, Caithness KW5 6DT

Mrs Camilla Sinclair
☎ 05934 224
BB From £12
EM From £8
Sleeps 6
🐎 🐕 🐈
Listed Commended

Idyllically situated with breathtaking views of coastline and mountains. Either relax in a peaceful atmosphere or use as an excellent base for touring northern highlands, visiting castles, gardens, nature trails. Also ideal for visits to John O'Groats, highland games or sheepdog trials, day trips to the Orkneys, or viewing puffins and seals at Duncansby. Riding/pony trekking available at our own STRA-approved stables. New-born foals offer an additional attraction. Open May–Sept. Map ref: 196 354

Woodside Farm, Kinloss, Forres, Morayshire IV36 0UA

Mrs Alma Rhind
☎ and fax 0309 690258
BB From £13
Sleeps 6
♿ 🐕 🐎
♛ ♛ **Commended**

A warm welcome, comfortable accommodation and delicious breakfasts await you at Woodside, a family farm specialising in production of seed potatoes, cereals and vegetables; also pure-bred herd of Aberdeen Angus cattle. Farm shop sells home-produced potatoes, eggs and vegetables. Only 2 miles from sandy beach at Findhorn; distilleries, golf courses and many amenities nearby. Open Apr–Oct. Map ref: 190 325

Self-Catering

SC

Borlum Farm, Drumnadrochit, Inverness, Inverness-shire IV3 6XN

**Mrs Vanessa
MacDonald-Haig**
☎ and fax 04562 358
SC From £157–£395
♿ 🐕 (by arrangement)
🐎 ⊞ ⚓ ◑ ☂
♛ ♛ ♛ ♛ **Commended**

Borlum Farm is a working hill farm with its own BHS-approved riding centre. The self-catering cottages are spacious, comfortable, and tastefully furnished, with splendid views overlooking Loch Ness. All are excellently equipped, including microwave cookers, hair driers and even hot water bottles! Oil-fired central heating also available if required in colder periods. Open all year. Map ref: 170 313

Culligran Cottages, Glen Strathfarrar, Struy, Nr Beauly, Inverness-shire IV4 7JX

**Frank & Juliet
Spencer-Nairn**
☎ 046 376 285
SC From £99–£339
Sleeps 5/7
🐕 🐎 ◑
♛ ♛ ♛ **Commended to
Highly Commended**

A regular? You soon could be. So don't delay – send for a brochure! This is your opportunity to stay on a deer farm within the beautiful Strathfarrar Nature Reserve. Watch the wild deer from your window and feed the farm deer during a conducted tour. Choice of chalet or cottage. Bikes for hire. Salmon and trout fishing. Hotel and inn nearby. Open 20 Mar–20 Nov. Map ref: 165 317

Easter Dalziel Farm, Dalcross, Inverness, Inverness-shire IV1 2JL

Bob & Margaret Pottie
☎ 0667 462213
SC From £120–£340
Sleeps 4/6
🐎 🐕
♛ ♛ ♛ **Commended–
Highly Commended**

Three traditional stonebuilt cottages, situated midway between Inverness and Nairn on our stock/arable farm. The surrounding rich habitat is a haven for wildlife. Sometimes pet lambs and chicks to feed. Centrally placed for touring the highlands. Locally are Cawdor Castle, Culloden, Fort George, Loch Ness and nearby Castle Stuart. Aviemore 30 miles. Sporting facilities at Inverness and Nairn. Short off-season breaks also available. Open all year. Map ref. 181 320

Flowerburn Holiday Homes, Fortrose, Ross and Cromarty, IV10 8SL

Alisdair Fraser
☎ 0381 21069
SC From £140–£410
🐾 🐴
👑 👑 👑 👑 **Commended to Highly Commended**

Four lodges and two cottages, all with central heating, set in private groups two miles from Rosemarkie on the Black Isle. Our accommodation provides comfort and seclusion for you to enjoy a relaxing holiday. Easy walking, visitor attractions and sports all to be found nearby. Colour brochure available. Open all year. Map ref. 179 323

Greenhill Farmhouse, Mid-Clyth, Lybster, Highland

Mrs Camilla Sinclair
☎ 05934 224
SC From £120–£350
🐾 🐴
👑 👑 👑 👑 👑 **Highly Commended**

Farmhouse overlooking the sea (½ mile away), tastefully decorated, exceptionally well-equipped with all home comforts including dishwasher, washing machine, tumble dryer, fridge/freezer, payphone, microwave, hair dryer, all linen. Ideal for country walks/ picnics. Archeological cairn ib farm. Golf, fishing, pony trekking nearby. Perfect centre for touring North of Scotland. Opean all year. Map ref: 196 354

Mains of Aigas, By Beauly, Inverness-shire IV4 7AD

Mrs Jessie Masheter
☎ 0463 782423
SC From £180–£400
🐾 ♿ 🐾 **Guide dogs only**
👑 👑 👑 – 👑 👑 👑 👑 **Highly Commended**

One house, one cottage, three apartments on livestock farm nestling in the hills overlooking the beautiful Beauly river valley. Very comfortably furnished and equipped to a high standard, colour TV, nightstore heaters, games room, laundry facilities. Area rich in bird, animal and plant life, perfect base for touring/walking or just relaxing. Open all year. Map ref: 170 319

Scatwell Farm, Comrie, Contin, Strathpeffer, Ross-shire IV14 9EN

Margaret Cuthbert
☎ 09976 234
SC From £100–£250
🐾 🐴 🐾
👑 👑 **Approved to Commended**

Three comfortable cottages in a quiet location in beautiful Strathconon. Ideal for fishing, hill walking, bird-watching and as a touring base yet only 25 miles north of Inverness. Come and see the Red deer, salmon, eagles and abundant wildlife. Electric heating, well equipped kitchens, TV's, cot available. Prices include linen, electricity on meter, laundry on site. Fishing arranged. Illustrated brochure on request. Map ref: 168 323

PRICES

Prices include VAT and service charge (if any) and are:
B&B per person per night
EM per person
SC per unit per week
Tents and caravans per pitch per night

FARM HOLIDAY BUREAU

2 Grampian

The eagle soaring in the sky over a vastness of magnificent scenery sets the stage on this beautiful part of Scotland where the air is pure, time is of the essence, and the welcome is from the heart. On your travels relish the heather-clad mountains – a skiers' paradise in winter, the walker's and hill-climber's paradise in summer, and home of the red deer. Sample the delights of the unspoilt north-east where farming and fishing go hand in hand. Follow the long winding rivers of the Spey and Dee renowned for salmon and trout and meander through the rich agricultural land famed for its quality stock and crops. Along the coastline are numerous, picturesque fishing villages and harbours, interspersed with quiet award winning beaches. Attend the many agricultural shows and famous Highland Games held throughout the summer. Enhance your knowledge of the area by exploring Royal Deeside and the 'Trails' – choose from either the Castle, Whisky, Coastal or Victorian Heritage. If golf is your forte there are umpteen championship courses to try out. There are also numerous facilities for pony trekking, fishing, shooting and watersports to suit all standards.

Whatever your interest, there is ample to wet your appetite and give you a holiday to remember.

Group Contacts: BB Mrs Jenny Rae ☎ 0888 62469
SC Mrs Rhona Cruickshank ☎ 04644 229

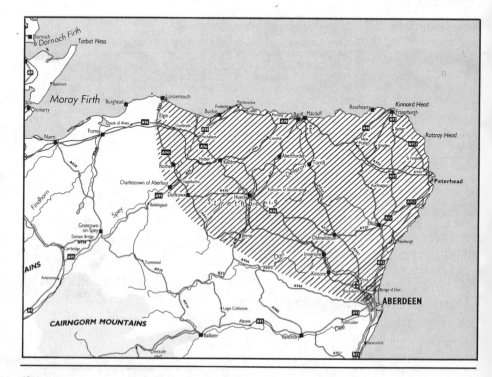

Bed and Breakfast (and evening meal)

Chapelhill Croft, Grange by Keith, Banffshire AB55 3LQ

Mrs Eileen Fleming
☎ 05425 302
🅱 From £12
EM From £7
Sleeps 6
🐾 🐕 ♨
Applied

A warm welcome awaits guests at our rural croft which is ideally situated for fishermen, golfers, walkers or anyone who enjoys the wildlife associated with countryside and coast. We take a pride in our cooking and can provide evening meals and packed lunches on request. Tea/coffee-making facilities available. Open all year. Map ref: 207 323

Meikle Camaloun, Fyvie, Aberdeenshire AB53 8JY

Mrs Marjory Wyness
☎ 0651 891319
🅱 From £12.50
🐾 🐕
♛ ♛ Commended

Large farmhouse in quiet rural location off the main road overlooking Fyvie Castle. Private facilities. Personal attention on the castle trail and 40 minutes from Aberdeen. Home baking and friendly atmosphere. Open Mar–Nov. Map ref: 216 318

Meikle Cantly, Grange, Keith, Banffshire AB55 3LJ

Valerie Fairbairn
☎ 054 25 230
🅱 From £14
EM From £9
Sleeps 4
🐾
♛ ♛ Commended

Set on Balloch's slope near Keith and Huntly, and overlooking the River Isla Valley, this welcoming farm offers peace, comfort and excellent facilities; good farmhouse cooking, baking and home produce; walking, fishing and birdwatching, with golf nearby. It's on the whisky trail, near the castle trail, and close to the Moray Firth's sandy beaches. En-suite facilities. Open Apr–Oct. Map ref: 207 321

Silverwells Farm, St Mary'sWell, Turriff, Aberdeenshire AB53 8BS

Mrs Jenny Rae
☎ 0888 62469
🅱 From £12
EM From £7.50
Sleeps 6
🍴 🐾 🐕
♛ Commended

A warm and friendly welcome awaits you at this 100-acre working stock farm. Traditional sandstone farmhouse set in beautiful countryside with extensive views. Comfortable accommodation comprising 1 double and 2 twin bedded rooms with washbasins, tea/coffee making facilities and TV. Golf, fishing, pony trekking available nearby. Ideal for touring Whisky/Castle/Victorian heritage trails and stunning N.E. coastline. Open all year. Map ref: 216 321

LET THE TELEPHONE RING!
Some farmhouses are big places. Let the telephone ring long enough to give the owner time to answer it.

FARM HOLIDAY BUREAU

Self-Catering

The Beeches Chalet, Linkwood, Elgin, Moray IV30 3RD

Ann Robertson
☎ 0343 542355
⌕ From £125–£295
Sleeps 6
⌂ 🐾
♨ ♨ ♨ Commended

This comfortable chalet is centrally heated, double glazed, has an overbath shower, washing machine, TV, video and sleeps up to 6 (+ cot). In a peaceful setting with lovely views it is within easy reach of Elgin, the highlands. Many local attractions and activities, some of which can be arranged for you. Open mid-Dec to mid-Nov. Map ref: 196 325

Logie Newton, Huntly, Aberdeenshire AB54 6BB

Mrs Rhona Cruickshank
☎ 04644 229
Fax 04644 277
⌕ From £125–£300
Sleeps 4/6
🐾 🦮
♨ ♨ ♨ ♨ Commended
to Highly Commended

Come and relax on our family-run farm in Aberdeenshire. Ideally situated for exploring north east Scotland, including the Whisky and Castle Trails. Various sports available locally, including golf, fishing and pony trekking. Two cottages, each fully modernised to a high standard yet retaining their traditional character. Log fires (logs provided). Brochure available. Open all year. Map ref: 214 318

Strocherie Cottage, Strocherie Farm, King Edward, Banff, Aberdeenshire AB45 3PL

Mrs Winifred Anderson
☎ 0888 551220
⌕ From £100–£260
Sleeps 4
🐾 🦮 (3) ☞
♨ ♨ ♨ ♨ Commended

Enjoy a holiday in our secluded cosy 2-bedroomed farm cottage. Well furnished and equipped. Log fire (logs provided). Fish pond and clay pigeon shooting on farm. Bird watching and wildlife at your doorstep. Riding, beach and golf courses nearby . Open all year. Map ref: 217 324

FARM HOLIDAY BUREAU

BUREAU ACCOMMODATION IS RELIABLE

This Guide lists **Farm Holiday Bureau** members only. They are all inspected by the National Tourist Board for standards (see introduction pages) and by fellow members to maintain a high quality.

3   Angus and Perthshire

Whatever you seek in Scotland, you'll find in Angus, where the Braes of Angus meet the valley of Strathmore. From the glens with their gushing waterfalls to the numerous sandy beaches and bays along the east coast.

Visit Glamis Castle, former home of Queen Elizabeth the Queen Mother and birthplace of Princess Margaret, or Kirriemuir, birthplace of poet J.M. Barrie (Peter Pan). National Trust places of interest include the House of Dun (Adam), the Angus Folk Museum and many others.

Many sports are available, including hill-walking, birdwatching, riding, bowls, swimming, sailing and leisure centre sports. You can fish on the shores and banks of rivers and lochs, or hire a boat and fish the sea. Golf is Angus' most famous sport and can be enjoyed on a wide variety of courses: you can play a different course each day!

The Heritage Trail is a must for the visitor to our area, and Arbroath Abbey, Brechin Cathedral, Restenneth Priory and various Pictish standing stones and hill forts should be seen.

Angus is famous for its wonderful Scottish fayre, ranging from soft fruit, Forfar bridies, Arbroath smokies, Kirriemuir rock and, of course, Angus beef.

Angus is also an ideal touring base for a day visit to either Aberdeen, Dundee, Perth, St. Andrews, Edinburgh or Balmoral.

All Angus members are holders of Food Hygiene Certificates.

Group Contacts: Angus: Mrs Deanna Lindsay ☎ 0307 62887
Perthshire: Mr Nigel Bruges ☎ 0350 724241

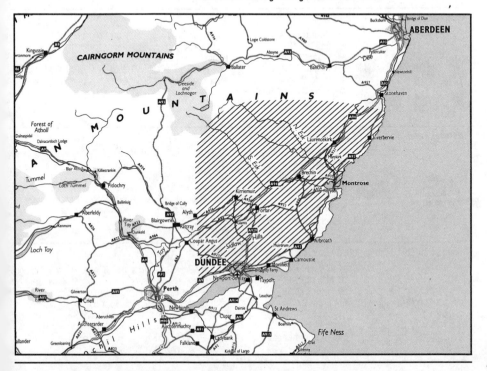

Bed and Breakfast
(and evening meal)

Blibberhill Farm, Blibberhill, Brechin, Angus, Tayside DD9 6TH

Margaret Stewart
☎ 0307 83225
[BB] From £13
EM From £8
Sleeps 6
Highly Commended

Situated in peaceful surroundings, between Angus Glens and coast, near Glamis Castle, 1 hour's drive from Royal Deeside and St Andrews and central to many golf courses, fishing and hill-walking. 1 twin/double room with bath en-suite, 1 twin with shower en-suite, 1 double with washbasin. All bedrooms tastefully decorated and furnished, with tea/coffee-making facilities. A warm welcome is extended , with home cooking, baking, marmalade and jams. Evenin' dinner optional. AA selected. Open all year. Map ref: 208 285

Nether Finlarg, By Forfar, Angus DD8 1XQ

John & Nici Rymer
☎ 030 782 250
[BB] From £15–£18
EM From £7.50
Sleeps 4
Commended

We'll give you a warm welcome with good cuisine at our attractive farmhouse on an award winning conservation farm. Set in stunning scenery, midway between Dundee and Forfar and close to Glamis Castle. Located down a quiet country road 1mile off the A929. Ground floor accommodation comprises of 1 twin, 1 double both with washbasin and shared private bathroom! Open all year. Map ref: 205 280

Purgavie Farm, Lintrathen, Kirriemuir DD8 5HZ

Mrs Moira Clark
☎ 05756 213
[BB] From £12.50
EM From £7
Commended

A warm welcome in homely accommodation on our farm set in peaceful countryside and providing traditional Scottish fayre. Fishing on Lintrathen loch, pony trekking and hill-walking in Glen Isla. Glamis Castle 10 miles. Located 7 miles from Kirriemuir, follow the B951 to Glen Isla; farm signposted at roadside. Open all year. Map ref: 200 285

Wemyss Farm, Montrose Road, Forfar, Angus DD8 2TB

Mrs Deanna Lindsay
☎ 0307 62887
[BB] From £12.50
EM From £7
Sleeps 6
Listed Commended

190-acre mixed farm situated on the B9113 with a wide variety of animals. Glamis Castle nearby. Shooting, fishing, golf, swimming, etc., all in the area. Bedrooms overlooking beautiful countryside. Children made welcome, reduced rates. Evening dinner, optional packed lunches. Ideal base for touring. Quiet and peaceful, yet within easy reach of all amenities. Food hygiene certificate held. Open all year. Map ref: 208 284

Wood of Auldbar, Aberlemno, By Brechin, Angus, Tayside DD9 6SZ

Jean Stewart
☎ 030 783 218
[BB] From £12.50
EM From £7
Sleeps 6
Listed Commended

Wood of Auldbar is a family farm of 187 acres with lovely farmhouse in first class condition. Very central for touring the Angus Glens, Royal Deeside, Balmoral, Glamis; many more castles within easy reach. Beaches, nature walks, birdwatching, fishing, golf, leisure facilities all near at hand. Standing stones and lovely churches. Excellent farmhouse cooking in award-winning farmhouse. Food hygiene certificate held. Tea facilities in all bedrooms. A warm welcome awaits you. Open all year. Map ref: 208 285

Self-Catering

Purgavie Farm, Lintrathen, Kirriemuir DD8 5HZ

Mrs Moira Clark
☎ 05756 213
▣ From £100–£353
🏇 🐎

🐾 🐾 🐾 🐾 –
🐾 🐾 🐾 🐾
**Commended to Highly
Commended**

New Swedish log house also bungalow in lovely Angus glen. Wonderful views of the Valley of Strathmore. Pony trekking in Glen Isla and fishing in Lintrathen loch. Both houses sleep 6; all linen supplied. Loghouse has 3 bedrooms, dishwater and shower. Both properties have fridge freezer, washer, dryer, payphone and microwave. Located 7 miles from Kirriemuir, follow B591 signposted at roadside. Open all year.
 Map ref: 200 285

Wester Riechip, Laighwood, Butterstone, Dunkeld, Perthshire PH8 0HB

W. & W.I. Bruges
☎ 0350 724241
▣ From £300–£476
Sleeps 8
🐕 🐈

🐾 🐾 🐾 🐾
Highly Commended

Wester Riechip has been constructed from the west wing of a 19th century shooting lodge to create a luxurious detached holiday house with superb modern facilities. Comfortably accommodates 8. Spectacular views over surrounding hills and lochs. An ideal base for touring, golfing and birdwatching. Shooting and fishing available on our family-run hill farm. Open all year. Map ref: 192 282

FARM HOLIDAY BUREAU

FOLLOW THE COUNTRY CODE

Leave nothing but footprints,

Take nothing but photographs,

Kill nothing but time!

FINDING YOUR ACCOMMODATION

FARM HOLIDAY BUREAU

The Group contacts at the beginning of each section can always help you find a vacancy in your chosen area.

4 Fife

The Kingdom of Fife as it has traditionally been called has much to entertain visitors. The picturesque fishing villages of East Neuk offer an interesting contrast to the elegant towns of Fife. Boats with sails billowing against a backdrop of fine sandy beaches and white painted, stepped gabled fisher houses all lend an air of enchantment to this peaceful area of Scotland. St Andrews is the home of the Royal and Ancient Golf Course, the oldest in the world and dating back to the 15th century. Golf is a popular sport in Scotland and, with a choice of 30 courses within 30 miles of St Andrews, this is the place to play!

There are many fine places to visit in Fife; the Norman church at Leuchars; at Newport on Tay the second longest road bridge in Europe takes you over the Tay to Dundee via 42 spans. Nearby, at Wormit, is the 2-mile rail bridge which replaces the one that collapsed so tragically in gales in 1879. Pittenweem has some charming old houses grouped round the harbour and a picturesque church tower. Nearby Kellie Castle, of the National Trust for Scotland, is well worth a visit. Dunfermline, ancient capital of Scotland and birthplace of Andrew Carnegie, has a beautiful Abbey; Robert Bruce is buried here. Ceres is reputed to be the prettiest village in Scotland; old cottages surround a green and a medieval bridge and church complete the picture. The farming families of Fife warmly welcome you to their enchanting corner of Scotland.

Group Contact: Mrs Isobel Steven ☎ 0337 28414

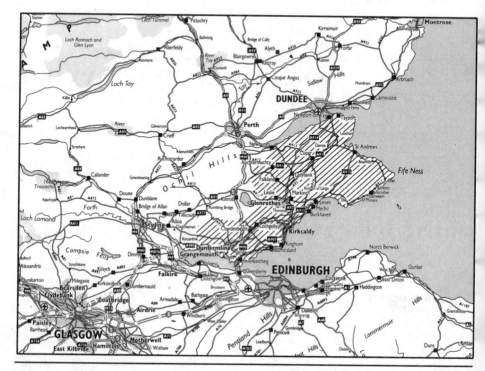

Bed and Breakfast (and evening meal)

Ardchoille Farm Guesthouse, Dunshalt, Nr Auchtermuchty, Fife KY14 7EY

Isobel Steven
☎/Fax 0337 28414
BB From £22
EM From £12.50
Sleeps 6
🐎 🛶 🎿 🖾
👻 👻 👻 Highly
Commended

Donald and Isobel Steven welcome you to Ardchoille, where guests are assured of every comfort. 2 twin and 1 twin/family rooms all with private facilities, colour TV and tea/coffee tray with homemade butter shortbread daily. Substantial breakfasts and four-course dinners. "Taste of Scotland" recommended. Family ponies to ride; golf and tennis 1 mile. Access to house at all times. Edinburgh 1 hr, Perth 20 mins. AA QQQ Farmhouse RAC Highly acclaimed. Open all year. Map ref: 198 271

Cambo House, Kingsbarns, St Andrews, Fife KY16 8QD

Peter Erskine
☎ 0333 50313
BB From £25
EM From £17
Sleeps 2
CH 🐓
👻 👻 👻 Commended

Come and lose yourselves in a glorious four-poster bed in our magnificent Victorian family home.. Set in parkland and woods that meander down to an unspoilt coastline with a fine sweeping beach. Only 10 minutes from St. Andrews. Open mid-Jan to mid-Dec. Map ref: 208 269

Self-Catering

Cambo House, Kingsbarns, St Andrews, Fife KY16 8QD

Peter Erskine
☎ 0333 50313
SC From £165–£385
EM From £17
Sleeps 2
CH 🐓
👻 👻 👻 Commended

We offer the perfect family holiday in self contained self-catering apartments and cottages on a beautiful, traditional wooded coastal estate, only 10 minutes from St. Andrews. At the heart of the estate is a magnificent Victorian mansion with plenty of facilities from a tennis court to a sauna for all the family. Open June–September. Map ref: 208 269

Mountquhanie Holiday Homes, Cupar by St Andrews, Fife KY15 4QJ

Felicity & Andrew Wedderburn
☎ 0826 24252
SC From £155–£555
Sleeps 4/12
🐓
👻 👻 👻 👻 – 👻 👻 👻 👻
Commended-Deluxe

Quality cottages and farmhouses in tranquil traditional countryside, or quality apartments in Georgian mansion, with all the ambience of country house living. Set in hundreds of acres of parkland with mature ancient trees. Experience harmonious integration of farming, forestry and conservation in action. Super for families, kids and pets. Magic for golfers – packages arranged. Open all year. Map ref: 204 270

---

5   Heart of Scotland

Discover the Heart of Scotland, with its wealth of contrasting scenery and interesting places to visit – plus the friendliness of the people. The area lies between the main towns of Edinburgh, Glasgow and Stirling, with easy access from the motorways. Visit Edinburgh Castle, Prince's Street Gardens, The Royal Mile and Palace of Holyrood House, the Scottish residence of the Royal Family; Glasgow's Museums and Art Galleries, plus the world famous Burrell Collection and People's Palace. The historic town of Stirling 'the Gateway to the Highlands', with its magnificent Castle and University is a must – also Doune Motor Museum and Castle nearby. Explore the beautiful mountains and lochs of the 'Trossachs', sail on Loch Lomond, drive through the lovely Carron Valley, follow the Mill Trail, along the foot of the Ochil Hills.

Take the children to Falkirk's Mariner Leisure Centre, Callander Park or to Bo'ness and Kinneil Steam Railway Museum, then on to Linlithgow Palace (birthplace of Mary, Queen of Scots), also Hopetoun House near the famous Forth Bridges. Enthusiasts of golf, pony trekking, hill walking, fishing, swimming, etc. are all well catered for, plus ten pin bowling at Falkirk and Stirling. Various water sports can also be enjoyed.

A warm welcome awaits you. Do come and enjoy good food, comfortable farmhouses and Scottish hospitality at its best.

Group Contacts: Mrs Jean Morton ☎ 0324 822778
Mrs Sheila Taylor ☎ 0324 812459

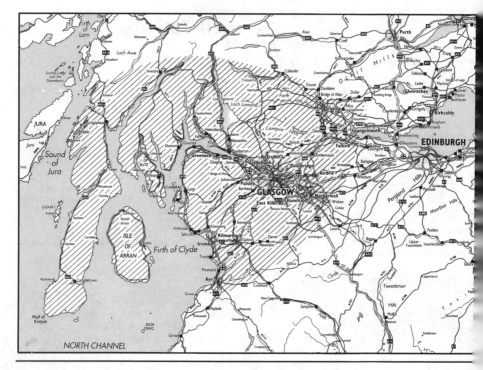

Bed and Breakfast (and evening meal)

Bandominie Farm, Walton Road, Bonnybridge FK4 2HP

Jean Forrester
☎ 0324 840284
🅱🅱 From £13–£14
Sleeps 4
♿ 🐕
Listed Commended

A working farm located 2 miles from the A80 at Castlecary (B816). Easy access from Glasgow and Edinburgh. Lovely view with a homely atmosphere. Central heating, TV lounge. Ample parking. Open all year. Map ref: 183 257

Belsyde Farm, Linlithgow, West Lothian EH49 6QE

Mrs Nan Hay
☎ and fax 0506 847611
🅱🅱 From £15
♿ 🐕
👑 👑 Commended

An 18th century farmhouse located in large, secluded gardens with panoramic views over the Forth estuary. Golfing and fishing available locally. All bedrooms have washbasin (hot & cold), tea/coffee-making facilities, colour TV, central heating, 1 bedroom en-suite. AA listed. Located close to M8, M9 and M90 and to Edinburgh airport. Follow A706 south-west from Linlithgow (1 ½ miles); farmhouse is first entrance on left after crossing Union Canal. Open all year. Map ref: 190 255

Craigruie Farmhouse, Balquhidder, By Lochearnhead, Perthshire FK19 8PQ

Mr Malcolm Marshall
☎ 08774 262
🅱🅱 From £15
EM From £6
♿ 🐕 👤 ♨ 🐾
Sleeps 6
Listed Commended

Craigruie farmhouse lies in a beautiful setting amid the Braes of Balquhidder, overlooking Loch Voil. Comfortable accommodation with excellent Scottish fayre. Salmon, trout and deer-stalking rights owned by the farm. Ideally situated for ramblers, hill-walkers, climbers and countryside lovers. Turn off the A84, past Strathyre, towards Balquhidder. Open all year. Map ref: 174 274

Easter Glentore Farm, Greengairs, Airdrie, Lanarkshire ML6 7TJ

Mrs Elsie Hunter
☎ 0236 830243
🅱🅱 From £16
EM From £9.50
Sleeps6
♿ (5)
👑 👑 Commended

Farm dates back to 1705, located in scenic setting on the B803, mid-way between the villages of Greengairs and Slamannan. Panoramic views. All bedrooms on ground floor, 1 en-suite, all with washbasin, tea/coffee facilities and radio alarms. Central heating throughout. Lounge with colour TV. Warm friendly atmosphere with home baking and cooking. Best B&B award winner. Provides an excellent touring base, 25 minutes to Glasgow or Stirling. Open all year. Map ref: 181 253

Lochend Farm, Carronbridge, Denny, Stirlingshire FK6 5JJ

Jean & Andrew Morton
☎ 0324 822778
🅱🅱 From £15
Sleeps 6
👑 👑 Commended

Peace, panoramic view and good wholesome food – all may be enjoyed at Lochend. Delightfully situated overlooking Loch Coulter in unspoiled countryside, yet only 5 miles from M9/M80 (jct 9). A perfect base for exploring this beautiful part of Scotland. Farmhouse centrally-heated, traditionally furnished. 2 double bedrooms with washbasin, radio, tea-making facilities; also guests' own bathroom, dining room and lounge with colour TV. Open all year. Map ref: 181 258

Lower Tarr Farm, Ruskie, Port of Menteith, Stirling FK8 3LG

Mrs Effie Bain
☎ 0786 850202
ⓑⓑ From £15
EM From £7
Sleeps 6 + cot
🐕 🐎 ♨ ℘
♨ ♨ **Commended**

A mixed arable farm with clear panoramic views, peaceful situation and pretty garden, with Ruskie burn running past. There are cattle, sheep and hens to be seen, plus lots of interesting wildlife. Good home cooking and baking using fresh local produce where possible. Central for touring the Trossachs, Loch Lomond, Stirling and Edinburgh. En-suite rooms. Open all year. Map ref: 174 264

Monachyle Mhor, Balquhidder, Lochearnhead, Perthshire FK19 8PQ

Robert & Jean Lewis
☎ 08774 622
ⓑⓑ From £19.50
EM From £12.50
Sleeps 8
🐕 ⊞ 🏃 ⚒ ℘ ♨
♨ ♨ ♨ **Commended**

Monachyle Mhor is an award winning 18th century farmhouse/hotel located in its own 2000 acre estate. All rooms are en-suite and have magnificent views overlooking lochs Voil and Doine. The hotel is delightfully furnished with family antiques and country fabrics. Fully licensed restaurant serving interesting dishes including game and herbs from our own estate. Taste of Scotland and AA listed private fishing and stalking to guests. Open all year. Map ref: 173 272

The Topps, Fintry Road, Denny, Stirlingshire FK6 5JF

Mrs Jennifer Steel
☎ 0324 822471
ⓑⓑ From £16
EM From £13
Sleeps 18
🐕 🐎 ⚒ ♨ ℘ ♨
♨ ♨ ♨ **Commended**

A chalet farmhouse in a beautiful hillside location with stunning, panoramic views. Family, double or twin-bedded rooms available, all en-suite with tea-making facilities and TV. Food a speciality ("Taste of Scotland" listed). Easy access to all major tourist attractions, or spend your day on the farm with Alistair and Finlay (the dog). Your enjoyment is our aim and pleasure! Open all year (closed 25th Dec & 1st Jan). Map ref: 183 258

Wester Carmuirs Farm, Larbert, Stirlingshire FK5 3NW

Mrs Sheila Taylor
☎ 0324 812459
ⓑⓑ From £15
Sleeps 6
🐕 ℘
♨ **Commended**

A traditional Scottish farmhouse in a spacious garden on an arable/beef farm. Comfortable twin/double/family rooms, all with washbasins, tea/coffee-making facilities. Guests' own bathroom, shower room, dining room and TV lounge. An ideal centre to visit Loch Lomond, the Trossachs, Stirling and Edinburgh. Situated on the A803, near Falkirk (M9/A80). Open all year. Map ref: 185 258

Wester Dullatur Farm, Dullatur, Glasgow G68 0AA

Mrs Eleanor Duncan
☎ 0236 723218
ⓑⓑ From £14
EM From £8
Sleeps 4
🐕 🐎
Listed Approved

Easily accessible, in a peaceful setting, overlooking the Forth and Clyde canal to the Kilsyth hills, offering comfortable accommodation in a friendly atmosphere. 2 miles from motorway routes to Stirling, Glasgow and Edinburgh. An ideal base for scenic tours of surrounding villages or to see the 'city sights'. Open all year. Map ref: 179 255

West Plean, Denny Road, Stirling FK7 8HA

Mrs Moira Johnston
☎ 0786 812208
ⓑⓑ From £16
Sleeps 6
🐕 🐎 ♨ ℘ ♨
Listed Commended

Enjoy warm Scottish farming hospitality in an oasis of peace, with sweeping lawns, walled garden, extensive woodland walks, surrounded by our mixed farm. We offer quality food, spacious comfort, bedrooms en-suite, hot drink facilities and attentive hosts. Located onthe A872 Denny road, 2 minutes from M9/M80 (jct 9). Open Feb–Nov. Map ref: 183 258

Self-Catering

Shemore Cottage, Shantron Farm, Luss, Alexandria, Dunbartonshire G83 8RH

Mrs Anne M Lennox
☎ 038 985 231
⑤ From £110–£250
Sleeps 6
☞

♔ ♔ ♔ ♔
Commended

Regulars often return to this traditional stone cottage attractively situated on a hill sheep farm, 300 ft above Loch Lomond, over which the cottage has magnificent views. The farm has often been filmed for 'Take the High Road' TV series. 3 miles south of picturesque village of Luss. Edinburgh, Oban, Fort William, Ayr – 1½ hours. Ideal for hillwalking, fishing, watersports. Children love to feed lambs. Open all year.
Map ref: 165 261

BUREAU ACCOMMODATION IS RELIABLE

This Guide lists **Farm Holiday Bureau** members only. They are all inspected by the National Tourist Board for standards (see introduction pages) and by fellow members to maintain a high quality.

DISABLED VISITORS

members offering suitable accommodation to disabled/less able visitors. Please do check the extent of the facilities before booking.

6   Clyde Valley

The Romans were the first to cultivate 'Y Strad Cluyd' – the warm valley – where even today the Clyde Valley's many garden centres show the area to be one of Scotland's most fertile. In all, the valley boasts 23 golf courses, including Scotland's highest at 1,400ft in the Lowther Hills at Leadhills, and where gold and lead mines first worked by the Romans have been restored and serve as a unique museum to the industry.

Then 'Follow the Wallace' through Biggar, with its wide, sweeping main street, its four museums, and home to the internationally-famous Purves Puppets. It was here, in 1297, that Scottish patriot William Wallace, disguised as a beggar, hid from the English troops. Moving on to Lanark, pass Tinto Hill, Clyde Valley's highest point at 2320ft, and topped by a large Bronze Age cairn where Druids once held fertility rites. A most rewarding view for the very fit! Nestling in a gorge by the famous 'Falls of Clyde' is the cotton mill village of New Lanark, built in the 18th century, but now a living museum with working spinning looms, visitors' centre and magical history tour.

The Clyde Valley is steeped in history, from Blantre's David Livingstone Centre, which traces the explorer's journeys through Africa, to Chatelherault Country Park, a William Adam 18th century hunting lodge of the Dukes of Hamilton. Bothwell Castle on the banks of the Clyde is the 13th century former stronghold of the Black Douglas family, while Craignethan Castle, where Mary, Queen of Scots, after escaping from Loch Leven Castle, lived happily before her disastrous journey south. Indeed, some claim she still appears there from time to time!

By the way, you fishermen – don't forget to pack your rod and tackle, because with 40 miles of fishing on the Clyde, on lochs and reservoirs, you may stay longer than planned!

Group Contact: Mrs Janet Pitchford ☎ 0899 21257

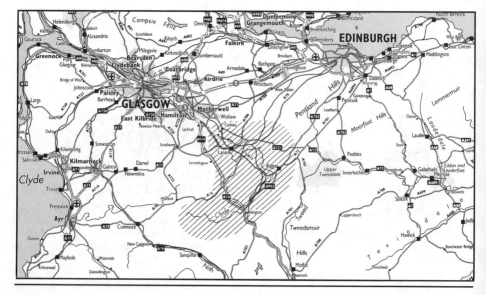

Bed and Breakfast (and evening meal)

Cormiston Farm, Biggar, Lanarkshire ML12 6NS

Mrs Janet Pitchford
☎ 0899 21257
BB From £12
Sleeps 6
🐕 🐎 (8) ♨ 🏕 ⚁ 🐟 ⚓
⚲

Listed Commended

A spacious 19th century farmhouse standing at 800ft above sea level; outstanding views over the local hills. Farm extends to 150 acres, including 1/2 mile of River Clyde. Extensive gardens with rhododendrons and wild flower areas. Situated west of Biggar, on unclassified road to Thankerton. Open Jan–Dec (closed April). Map ref: 192 241

Walston Mansions Farmhouse, Walston Carnwath, Lanark ML11 8NF

Mrs Margaret Kirby
☎ 089981 338
BB From £11
En-suite £13
EM From £6.50
Sleeps 6
🐕 🐎 ♨

👑 👑 👑 **Commended**

A very pleasant family home situated 5 miles from Biggar. A friendly and relaxed atmosphere; children most welcome. Good home cooking with home-produced meat, eggs and organic vegetables. Guest lounge with log fire, TV/video and children's games. An ideal base for touring Strathclyde, Lothian and the Borders; Lanark, Edinburgh and Glasgow only a short drive away. Open all year. Map ref: 193 245

Self-Catering

Carmichael Country Cottages, Carmichael Estate Office, Westmains, Carmichael, Biggar, Lanarkshire ML12 6PG

Richard Carmichael of Carmichael
☎ 089 93 336
Fax 089 93 481
SC From £130–£320
Sleeps 2/7
🐕 ♿ 🐎 📺 ♨ 🎿

👑👑👑–👑👑👑👑👑
Commended to Highly Commended

These 200-year-old stone cottages nestle among the woods and fields of our 700-year-old family estate. You will enjoy our private tennis court and fishing loch. We guarantee comfort, warmth and a friendly welcome in an accessible, unique rural and historic time capsule. We farm deer, cattle and sheep and sell meats and tartan – Carmichael, of course. Breakfast and evening meal available. Open all year. Map ref: 192 241

LET THE TELEPHONE RING!
Some farmhouses are big places. Let the telephone ring long enough to give the owner time to answer it.

7 Bonnie Galloway & Stinchar Valley

You will find plenty of space on our quiet roads and wide rolling countryside. With lush farmlands and miles of beautiful coastline the scenery is enhanced by golden sunsets.

Thanks to our mild climate, many subtropical plants bloom around Port Logan (just one of the many gardens in the area). South west Scotland is a golfer's paradise, with courses wherever you go, both links and inland.

Fishermen will find plenty of opportunities for river, loch and sea fishing, while the hill climber or gentle walker may even be lucky enough to see the golden eagle, an inhabitant of the area for many years.

The area is also rich in historical and Christian heritage. A visit to the archaeological dig at Whithorn, where St. Ninian founded the first Christian church, is a must. Nearby, Culzean Castle with its famous Adam ceilings and superb furnishings is just one of the many castles to be explored in the area. Only the most discerning visitors choose this area of Scotland, and they are always amply rewarded.

Group Contact: Mrs Margaret Hewitson ☎ 0671 2035

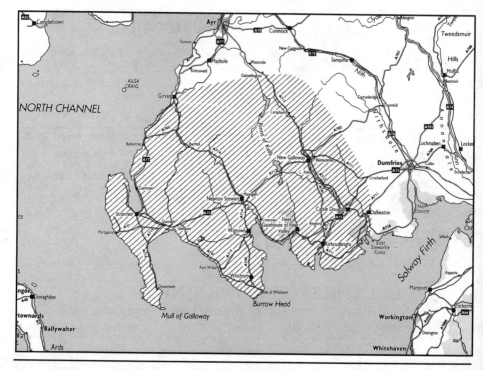

Bed and Breakfast (and evening meal)

Airds Farm, Crossmichael, Castle Douglas, Kirkcudbrightshire DG7 3BG

Barbara McBride
☎ 055 667 418
🅱 From £14
EM From £7.50
Sleeps 10
🐕 🐎
👑 👑 Commended

Airds farmhouse overlooks lovely Loch Ken, 4 miles from Castle Douglas on the A713. All bedrooms tastefully decorated, heated, with wash handbasins, electric blankets and self service tea and coffee facilities. Private lounge and dining room with colour TV. Fire certificate held. Payphone available. Guests are assured a comfortable stay with good home cooking and baking. Open Mar–Nov. Map ref: 181 213

Auchenleck Farm, Newton Stewart, Wigtownshire DG8 7AA

Margaret Hewitson
☎ 0671 2035
🅱 From £15
Sleeps 6
🐎
👑 👑 Commended

Original shooting lodge now comfortable, well-equipped farmhouse in Glentrool National Park. Ideal for hill and forest walking. CH throughout. 2 double rooms, 1 twin all with private bathrooms and WC. Shaver points, electric blankets, tea/coffee-making facilities, radio alarms. Comfortable lounge with Teletext TV, board games, books. Stock rearing farm. Home baking. Payphone. Smoking in lounge only. Open Easter–end Oct. Map ref: 168 209

Bankfield Farm, Glenluce, Newton-Stewart, Wigtownshire

Mrs Margaret-Stewart
☎ 0581 3281
🅱 From £12
EM From £6
Sleeps 6
🚭 🐎
👑 Commended

A warm welcome awaits you at Bankfield farm. H&C and tea/coffee facilities in all rooms. Good home cooking. Golf and pony trekking 1 mile. Games room, bowling green. 5 minutes walk from Farm to Motor Museum. ¾ mile local walks. The farm is on the edge of the A75. Open April–Oct.Map ref: 168 209.

Blair Farm, Barrhill, Girvan, Ayrshire KA26 0RD

Mrs Elizabeth Hughes
☎ 046 582 247
🅱 From £13
EM From £7
Sleeps 6
🐎 🐕 🐝
👑 👑 Commended

Blair is a family run beef and sheep farm situated on the A714, 1 mile south of the village of Barrhill. Guests are assured of a warm friendly welcome, comfortable spacious rooms and a high standard of home cooking and baking. Central heating throughout 1 family and 1 double room both with wash basin and tea/coffee-making facilities. Lounge with colour TV. Fishing available. Open Easter–Oct. Map ref: 161 218.

Blairinnie Farm, Crossmichael, Castle Douglas, Kirkcudbrightshire DG7 3BJ

Janetta McMorran
☎ 055 667 268
🅱 From £12
EM From £7
🚭 🐎 (6)
Listed Commended

Enjoy the best of Scottish hospitality, where guests are assured of a high standard of comfort and food on this family-run hill farm in the Loch Ken valley. 2 double rooms (1 with washbasin), tea/coffee-making facilities. Lounge with colour TV, coal fire on colder evenings. Picturesque walking area, forest walks and sporting activities all nearby. Payphone available. 2 1/2 miles from Crossmichael. SAE or phone for brochure. Open Easter–Oct. Map ref: 181 213

Burnfoot Farm, Colmonell, Girvan, Ayrshire KA26 0SQ

Grace & David
Shankland
☎ 046 588 220/265
🅱 From £13
EM £7
Sleeps 6
🐕 ⅄ 🐈 ⌣ 📠
♨ ♨ Commended

A warm welcome awaits you at Burnfoot, a family-run mixed farm nestling in the beautiful Stinchar Valley. Ideal place to 'get away from it all' and hear the birds sing in peace. 1 family/double room, 1 family suite (2 rooms combined) – a great asset for families. Comfort and cleanliness guaranteed. Home cooking and baking a speciality, using fresh fruit and vegetables from the garden. Open Mar–Oct. Map ref: 158 225

Clugston Farm, Newton Stewart, Wigtownshire DG8 9BH

Janet Adams
☎ 067 183 338
🅱 From £12
EM From £7
Sleeps 6
♿ 🐈 (5) 📠
Listed Commended

Our 400-acre family farm of sheep and cattle is ideally situated for hill walking and golf and fishing which can be arranged. Only 15 minutes to reach the beaches. We offer a high standard of home cooking using our own free range eggs, local beef, lamb and salmon. Varied baking and preserves are a speciality. Double room and twin room, both with washbasin and downstairs next to bathroom. Access for wheelchair users with assistance. Open Mar–Nov. Map ref: 168 209

Collin Hill, Auchencairn, Castle Douglas, Kirkcudbrightshire DG7 1QN

Frances Cannon
☎ 055 664 242
🅱 From £17
Sleeps 4
🐈 🕮
♨ ♨ Highly
Commended

Spend a relaxing holiday at Collin Hill, a tastefully furnished house with every comfort and spectacular views over the Solway Firth to the Cumbrian Hills. Sea and village within walking distance. Many leisure activities within easy reach; bowling green in village. Both bedrooms en-suite with sea views, tea/coffee making facilities and hairdriers. Open Feb–Nov. Map ref: 183 207

Glengennet Farm, Barr, Girvan, Ayrshire KA26 9TY

Vera Dunlop
☎ 046 586 220
🅱 From £15
Sleeps 4
🐈 (10)
♨ ♨ Commended

19th century Victorian farmhouse with lovely views over the Stinchar valley and neighbouring Galloway Forest Park. One double and twin bedded room, 1 room with private bathroom, both with washbasins and tea trays. Guests lounge/dining room with colour TV. Two miles from Barr village where good meals are available. Good base for forest walking/cycling, golf, Ayrshire coast, Burns country, Culzean Castle and Glentrool National Park. Open May–Oct Map ref: 158 225

Hawkhill Farm, Old Dailly, Girvan, Ayrshire KA26 9RD

Mrs Isobel Kyle
☎ 0465 87232
🅱 From £16
Sleeps 4/5
🐈 🐕 🕮 🐎
♨ ♨ Highly
Commended

Superior farmhouse hospitality in spacious 17th-century coaching inn where the emphasis is on comfort and good food. Two delightful bedrooms with private facilities. Visitors' lounge, central heating, log fires, tea tray. Peaceful setting perfect for exploring south west Scotland, Culzean Castle, Galloway Forest Park, Ayr and Burns country. Golf, fishing, pony trekking. Brochure. Open Mar–Oct Map ref: 160 225

High Park Farm, Balmaclellan, Castle Douglas, Kirkcudbrightshire DG7 3PT

Mrs Jessie Shaw
☎ 06442 298
🅱 From £12.50
EM From £6.50
Sleeps 6
♿ 🐕 🐈 ⌣
♨ Commended

Enjoy a holiday amidst beautiful scenery while staying at our comfortable farmhouse situated by Loch Ken. High Park is a family-run dairy, beef and sheep farm. 1 family room, 1 twin bedroom (upstairs), 1 double bedroom (ground floor); all rooms have washbasin, shaver point, tea/coffee-making facilities. Central heating, home baking. Comfort, cleanliness and good food guaranteed. Open Easter–Oct. Map ref: 181 211

Rascarrel Cottage, Rascarrel Farm, Auchencairn, Castle Douglas, Kirkcudbrightshire DG7 1RJ

Ellice Hendry
☎ 055 664 214
BB From £15
Sleeps 6
♛♛ Highly Commended

Excellent, peaceful accommodation is offered at this beautiful cottage 500 yards from the sea. Enjoy panoramic views of our farm and the Solway Firth. Pleasant coastal and forest walks. Bird watching, golfing and fishing nearby. Only 2 miles from Auchencairn village where good meals are available. One twin with private bathroom, 1 double, 1 twin, all with H&C (two on groundfloor). Tea/coffee facilities. Shower room, central heating. Open Mar–Oct. Map ref: 183 207

Self-Catering

Barncrosh Farm, Castle Douglas, Kirkcudbrightshire DG7 1TX

Liz & Ronnie Ball
☎ 055 668 216
Fax 055 668 442
SC From £85–£320
Sleeps 2/8
♛ – ♛♛♛♛
Approved to Commended

Situated amongst rolling Galloway countryside on working farm of 500 acres are 4 modernised houses and 8 self-contained flats converted from the old Stable Block. We offer peace and quiet for that 'get-away' holiday. An ideal touring base for historic south west Scotland within easy reach of the M6. Forestry and moorland walks with abundant wildlife and birdwatching. Open for short breaks in the off-season. Open all year. Map ref: 181 213

FARM HOLIDAY BUREAU

CONFIRM BOOKINGS

Disappointments can arise by misunderstandings over the telephone. Please write to confirm your booking.

8 Dumfriesshire (Annandale)

A peaceful, undiscovered, easily accessible part of south-west Scotland. Take time to explore the countryside and sample the tranquility.

From the beaches of the Solway coast to the rugged Moffat Hills, with the spectacular 'Grey Mare's Tail' and the striking 'Devil's Beef Tub', here is a variety of scenery unmatched in Britain. Quiet lanes winding through lush green countryside, busy small towns with a variety of interesting shops, numerous challenging golf courses, excellent fishing and much, much more. The county town of Dumfries contains the excellent Robert Burns Centre which documents the many links Scotland's foremost poet has with the area. Moffat is a most attractive town with tennis courts, bowling green, woollen mill and many craft shops. Lockerbie, with its bustling cattle market, is well worth a visit. So, whether you enjoy birdwatching or hill walking, swimming or horseriding, sailing or just relaxing with friendly people, you will find everything you want in Dumfriesshire.

Group Contact: Mrs Marjorie Rae ☎ 05766 248

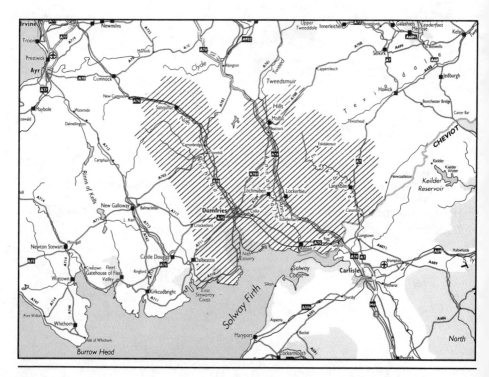

Bed and Breakfast (and evening meal)

Broomlands Farm, Beattock, Moffat, Dumfriesshire DG10 9PQ

Kate Miller
☎ 06833 320
BB From £16
Sleeps 5
🐾 🛏
🐚 🐚 Highly
Commended

A lovely spacious farmhouse 2 miles from the tourist town of Moffat offering a very high standard of accommodation to guests. Double/room, twin/room and single/room all have beautiful en-suite facilites. Central heating. Tea/coffee-making facilites, electric blankets, clock/radios, colour TV in lounge. Enjoy a choice farmhouse breakfast using free range eggs. Ideal base to tour South West Scotland and Borders. Golf, fishing, walking tours horseriding, etc can be arranged. Open Mar–Oct. Map ref: 193 227

Cogries Farm, Beattock, Moffat, Dumfriesshire DG10 9PP

Freda Bell
☎ 057 64 320
BB From £13
EM From £8
Sleeps 12
🚬 🐾 🐕
🐚 Commended

You are offered a warm welcome, good food and a comfortable and relaxed stay at Cogries where you may enjoy the lovely view and peaceful surroundings of the Annandale Valley. We are only ½ mile from the A74 and 5 miles from the spa town of Moffat. This is an ideal base to tour the southwest of Sctoalnd. Double, twin and family rooms all with washbasins and tea/coffee making facilities. Open Feb–Nov. Map ref: 193 227

Corehead Farm, Annanwater, Moffat, Dumfriesshire DG10 9LT

Berenice C Williams
☎ 0683 20973/21087
BB From £20
EM From £12
Sleeps 4
🛏 🚬 🐎
🐚 🐚 🐚 Highly
Commended

Nestling in the Devil's Beef Tub amidst the magnificent Moffat Hills, this traditional 2500-acre hill farm is an ideal centre for exploring Dumfries and Galloway. Guests return year after year to enjoy tranquility and sample tasty soups, succulent roasts and mouthwatering desserts. Comfortable lounge with woodburner. Tastefully decorated bedrooms all en-suite, TV and tea/coffee facilities. 'Taste of Scotland' recommended. Farmhouse Cook of the Year Award. Open Easter–Oct. Map ref: 194 228

Coxhill Farm, Old Carlisle Rd, Moffat, Dumfriesshire DG10 9QN

Mrs Sandra Long
☎ 0683 20471
BB From £14
EM From £9
Sleeps 6
🚬 🐾
🐚 🐚 Highly
Commended

A new farmhouse set in 70 acres of unspoilt countryside with outstanding views, beautiful rose gardens and ample parking. 2 double, 1 twin bedrooms, all with washbasins, tea/coffee-making facilities and central heating. Situated 1 mile south of the charming town of Moffat, and 14 mile from Southern Upland Way. Excellent base for golf, tennis, fishing and touring SW Scotland. Open Mar–Oct. Map ref: 194 228

Ericstane, Moffat, Dumfrieshire DG10 9LT

Robert Jackson
☎ 0683 20127
BB From £14
Sleeps 4/6
🐚 🐚 Commended

Come and enjoy the comforts of our tastefully renovated period farmhouse, situated in attractive grounds. 4 miles from Moffat in the peaceful Annan Water Valley. Twin- and double-bedded rooms with washbasin, TV, tea/coffee-making facilities. Central heating. Ideal base for hill walking and exploring the area. Open all year. Map ref: 194 228

Longbedholm Farm, Beattock, nr Moffat, Dumfriesshire DG10 9SN

Mrs Val Wilson
☎ 06833 414
🅱 From £15
EM From £8
♨ ♞ ↫
🛏 Approved

Set in 37 acres in the Evan valley on the A74, within easy access of Glasgow and Edinburgh. Three Miles from Moffat. There is a 1½ mile trout and salmon river running through the property. Golf, riding and fishing available locally. Meals using local produce available by arrangement. Open all year (closed Christmas). Map ref: 193 227

Nether Boreland, Boreland, Lockerbie, Dumfriesshire DG11 2LL

Mrs Marjorie Rae
☎ 05766 248
🅱 From £18–£20
Sleeps 6
⅍ (10)
🛏 🛏 Commended

Enjoy Scottish hospitality, peaceful friendly surroundings and hearty breakfasts. The spacious and friendly farmhouse has two en-suite bedrooms and one with private bathroom, tea/coffee-making facilities, hairdryers and clock radios. The sitting room has log fires on cold evenings, and colour TV. Enjoy local golf, fishing, pony trekking or leisurely sightseeing. Farmhouse Award winner. Please send for brochure. Open Mar–Nov. Map ref: 196 224

Self-Catering

Broomlands Bungalow, Beattock, Moffat, Dumfriesshire DG10 9PQ

Katie Miller
☎ 06833 320
🆂🅲 From £200–£280
Sleeps 5
♨ ♞
🛏 🛏 🛏 🛏
Highly Commended

Only 2 miles from Moffat, Broomlands Bungalow is a superior self-cating property beautifully furnished and equipped. Colour TV, video, automatic washing machine, fridge/freezer, tumble dryer, etc. Lovely bedrooms and bathroom with shower. Enclosed garden and parking. Excellent touring and walking area. Fishing, golf, horseriding can be arranged. Send for brochure. Open Mar–Oct. Map ref: 193 227

THE 1000+ BUREAU MEMBERS OFFER A UNIQUE LINK TO CUSTOMERS ACROSS THE UK

All Bureau members belong to a local Group. Each member can refer you to an equally high quality member within his Group . . . or across the UK: England, Northern Ireland, Scotland, Wales.

9 Scottish Borders

The Scottish Borders – Sir Walter Scott country – stretch from the Berwickshire coast in the east to west of Peebles and from the Cheviot Hills in the south to Edinburgh in the north.

This is an area of great beauty renowned for its abbeys at Kelso, Melrose, Jedburgh, and Dryburgh. Some of the loveliest of Scotland's great houses are to be found at Bowhill, Abbotsford, Floors and Traquair, to mention but a few.

The lowlands contain some of the best farming land in Britain and this rises to the Cheviot Hills where all you will have for company are the sheep, the birds and perhaps wild goats. The Pennine Way runs along the top of the Cheviots or there is the Southern Upland Way stretching from coast to coast for those who wish to have a walking holiday.

For the fisherman there is fine fishing to be had in the waters of the Tweed or sea fishing on the east coast. Golfers can plan a trip in the region where they can play a different course every day! Rugby is a popular sport here and in the spring and autumn you can watch the 'sevens'.

Horseriding is a passion in this region – trekking through this lovely area is very popular with visitors and, for those who wish only to observe, the larger Border towns have their 'common ridings' during the summer which are supported by hundreds of riders. A magnificent sight; only one of many in this lovely land.

Group Contact: Simon Ashby ☎ 0361 83665

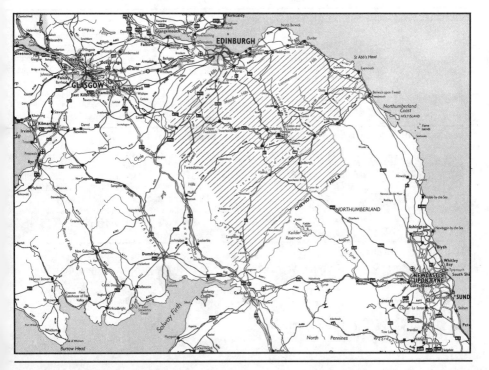

Bed and Breakfast (and evening meal)

Barney Mains, Haddington, East Lothian EH41 3SA

Katie Kerr
☎ 062 088 310
BB From £14
Listed Commended

Beautiful Georgian farmhouse with spectacular views of lovely East Lothian countryside, traditionally furnished and has open fires. Within 20 minutes drive of Edinburgh, close to many golf courses, fine beaches, historic houses and castles and heather-covered hills. Nice walks on the farm which is mostly arable with some cattle. Open Mar–Nov. Map ref: 209 255

Broomhouse Mains, Duns, Berwickshire TD11 3PP

Simon & Tracey Ashby
☎ 0361 83665
BB From £18
EM From £9
Sleeps 6
Highly Commended

Broomhouse Mains is beautifully situated on a 200-acre arable farm, offering commanding views of the Lammermuir Hills and quality accommodation. All rooms have private facilities. Private river frontage with salmon and trout fishing. Ideal base for touring or relaxing. Excellent home cooking in farmhouse kitchen. 15 minutes from coast; 1 hour from Edinburgh, Newcastle or Metro Centre. Treat yourself! Brochure available. Open all year. Map ref: 218 247

Cliftonhill, Kelso, Roxburghshire TD5 7QE

Archie & Maggie Stewart
☎ 0573 25028
Fax 0573 326416
BB From £15
EM From £11
Sleeps 6
Listed Approved

A warm welcome is assured at Cliftonhill. A traditional farmhouse set in the beautiful unspoiled Border country, the farm is 2 miles from Kelso, and an ideal centre for exploring, walking or just relaxing. The River Eden meanders through th farm attracting interesting wildlife. Pools for fishing and swimming. Home-made bread. Beautiful double en-suite, 2 twins sharing bathroom. Seaside ½-hours drive, Edinburgh 1 hour. Open all year. Map ref: 218 239

Cockburn Mill, Duns, Berwickshire TD11 3TL

Mrs A M Prentice
☎ 0361 82811
BB From £16
EM From £8
Sleeps 4

A comfortable riverside farmhouse offering 2 twin bedrooms with luxurious en-suite bathrooms, within sight of River Whiteadder. Electric blankets and tea/coffee-making facilities. Home baking and farm produce. Water from hillside spring. Trout fishing included. Abundant plant and bird life. Ideal for hill-walking, birdwatching, cycling or just relaxing. Hens, ducks, donkeys and pet lambs. Open Mar–Nov. Map ref: 218 247

Lyne Farm, Peebles EH45 8NR

Mrs Arran Waddell
☎ 0721 740255
BB From £14
Sleeps 6
Listed Commended

A large, comfortable farmhouse and garden, in quiet rural are of scenic beauty. Outstanding south-facing views over the Manor and Stobo Valleys. 4 miles west of Peebles on the A72 Easy access to Edinburgh (23 miles). Ideal base for touring, hill walking, fishing, golfing, mountain-biking, riding. Open all year. Map ref: 199 242

Overlangshaw Farm, Langshaw, Galashiels, Selkirkshire TD1 2PE

Sheila Bergius
☎ 0896 86244
BB From £14–£16
⛺ ☃ 🏕
Listed Approved

Situated only 4 miles from Galashiels and Melrose. A welcoming, centrally heated home amidst rolling hills and shady woods. Delicious Scottish cooking with emphasis on quality home produce and preserves. Children welcome. Also dogs by arrangement. Roomy bedrooms, 1 family with private bathroom, 1 double with en-suite. Southern upland way nearby. Map ref: 209 240

Wiltonburn Farm, Hawick, Roxburghshire TD9 7LL

Mrs Sheila Shell
☎ 0450 72414/78000
Fax 0450 78545
BB From £13
Sleeps 6
⛺ ☃ 🏕 ⬛ ▪ 🏇 ♨
Applied

Wiltonburn is a friendly, working, mixed farm situated in a sheltered valley and surrounded by fields, hills and a small stream. Relax in the garden, or use the local facilities, including fishing, riding, swimming, golf, squash, tennis or hill-walking. An ideal base for visiting castles, museums and stately homes, or for buying knitwear. Good selection of eating places nearby. Open all year. Map ref: 209 233

Self-Catering

SC

Bailey Mill, Bailey, Newcastleton, Roxburgh TD9 0TR

Pamela Copeland
☎ 069 78 617
SC From £68–£398
Sleeps 2/10
♿ ⛺ ☃ 🏕 🏇 ♨ ▪
🎠🎠 – 🎠🎠🎠 **Approved**

A warm welcome awaits you from Pam and Ian on this small farm holiday complex nestling on the Roxburgh/Cumbria border. The five superior self-contained apartments include heating (oil), electricity and linen in rent. Colour TV and microwave in each apartment. On site sauna, solarium, gym equipment, games room, laundry, farm kitchen and horseriding. Babysitting service. Breakfast and evening meal available. Brochure. Open all year. Map ref: 205 217

Carter's Cottage, Cockburn Mill, Duns, Berwickshire TD11 3TL

Ann Prentice
☎ 0361 82811
SC From £100–£170
Sleeps 5
⛺ ☃ 🏕
🎠🎠

Stone-built Carter's Cottage within sight and sound of River Whiteadder. Children welcome. Barbecue, dinghy, colour TV available. Overnight storage heating included. Trout fishing included. Water from hillside spring. Abundant plant and bird life. Chicks, donkeys, ducklings and pet lambs. Coast, beaches, Edinburgh, Border keeps and abbeys within easy reach on quiet roads. Dogs by arrangement only. Open all year. Map ref: 218 247

Cherry Tree Cottage, Lochton, Coldstream, Berwickshire TD12 4NH

Mrs Rosalind Aitchison
☎ 0890 830205
Fax 0890 830210
SC From £100–£200
Sleeps 5
☃ 🏕 ♨
🎠🎠 🎠 **Commended**

A warm welcome awaits guests at this traditional refurbished farm cottage, cosy, clean and comfortable. Wonderful views across the Tweed Valley to the Cheviot Hills. Relax in the peaceful environment, see the farm and wildlife, fish for trout in the Tweed. An ideal base to explore the Borders and beyond. Golf packages available. Brochure on request. Open all year. Map ref: 222 242

Craggs Cottage, Cliftonhill, Kelso, Roxburghshire TD5 7QE

Archie & Maggie Stewart
☎ 0573 225028
Fax 0573 226416
🆂 From £75–£300
Sleeps 7
🐾 🐎
🐚 🐚 🐚 **Approved to Commended**

A terraced sandstone cottage, lovingly restored, maintaining its character and charm. One double room – large and luxurious, 1 bedroom with 3 single beds and single bedroom. Large comfortable kitchen with Rayburn cooker. Central heating. Sitting room with log fire and colour TV. Enclosed colourful garden, garden furniture. Delightful restaurant 3 miles. Coast 18 miles, Edinburgh 35 miles. Enquire about our special winter break offer. Open all year. Map ref: 218 239

Easter Deans and Glenrath, Glenrath Farm, Kirkton Manor, Peebles, Tweeddale EH45 9JW

Catherine Campbell
☎ 07214 221
🆂 From £117.50–£500
Sleeps 4/8
🐾 ♿ 🐎
🐚 🐚 🐚 –
🐚 🐚 🐚 🐚 🐚
Up to Commended

We have five very attractive properties ranging from a luxury farmhouse to a 2 bedroom cottage. All centrally heated. Situated on a working hill farm in the county of Tweeddale. The farmhouse is only 25 mins from Edinburgh and the town of Peebles is only 15 mins from any of the properties. Coarse fishing and hill walking. Pets welcome. Ideal for children. Open all year. Map ref: 199 242

Kerchesters, Kelso, Roxburghshire TD5 8HR

Mrs J. Clark
☎ 0573 224321
🆂 From £100–£290
Sleeps 5/7
🐾 🐎 🐕
🐚 🐚 🐚 🐚 **Commended**

Cockerlaw and Todrig cottages are warm, welcoming terraced cottages on a working farm. Well appointed and peacefully situated with good views and ample play areas. Cockerlaw has separate sitting room and shower room. Three miles east of Kelso. Well placed for touring Borders and Northumbria. Edinburgh 1 hour, beach 30 minutes. Local golf, swimming, fishing, riding. Linen included. Brochure on request. Open all year. Map ref: 218 239

Little Swinton Cottages, Little Swinton, Coldstream, Berwickshire TD12 4HH

Sue Brewis
☎ 0890 86 280
🆂 From £160–£220
Sleeps 4–7
🐾 🐎
🐚 🐚 🐚 – 🐚 🐚 🐚 🐚

A row of quiet refurbished, well equipped one storey stone cottages all with open fires, night store heating, colour TV, washing machine, etc. Linen provided. Large enclosed grass play area. Ample parking. Children and pets welcome. Beaches, hills, historic houses, Edinburgh, Newcastle, all within reach. Open all year. Map ref: 223 244

Lyne Farm Cottage, Peebles EH45 8NR

Mrs Arran Waddell
☎ 0721 740255
🆂 From £100–£290
Sleeps 4/6
🐾 🐎
Applied

A warm welcome awaits you at Lyne Cottage situated on a 1300-acre mixed farm overlooking Stobo Valley. The spacious cottage has colour TV, washing machine, microwave and the garden has furniture. Rent includes linen and fuel. Ideal for touring, walking, fishing, riding. Only 4 miles from Peebles and 25 miles from Edinburgh. Open all year. Map ref: 199 24?

NO ANSWER?
Farmers are mostly out and about during the day.
Try to telephone before 9.30am or after 4pm.

10 Hadrian's Wall
North Cumbria & The Borders

Discover the Border Country, a wild wonderland of moors, tarns and loughs, wooded river valleys and rich pastureland. Wildlife abounds with peace and quiet for all who seek it. This is an exciting area for the heritage enthusiast with Roman sites and the world famous Hadrian's Wall, Lanercost Priory, Hexham Abbey, Carlisle, Naworth and Heritage Castles. The historic city of Carlisle with its gem of a cathedral has an excellent Lanes shopping centre of large and small shops.
Whether walking, golfing, fishing, birdwatching or gently touring our quiet roads you will find this area has so much to offer – lots of country inns, market towns, woollen and tweed mills, local craft and agricultural shows and, most important of all, friendly people. Kielder Water is on our doorstep offering many water activities, birdwatching and magnificent forest surroundings. Once you have enjoyed the peace, freedom and our North Country hospitality, you will most certainly wish to return to this unspoilt area.

Group Contact: Mrs Sheila Stobbart ☎ 06977 46668

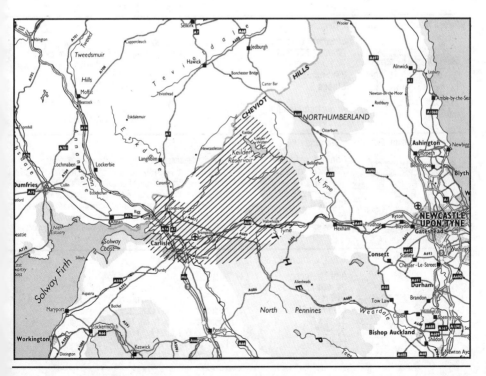

Bed and Breakfast (and evening meal)

Cracrop Farm, Kirkcambeck, Brampton, Cumbria CA8 2B

Marjorie Stobart
☎ 06978 245/06977 48245
BB **From £17**
EM From £12
Sleeps 6
♨ ⚘ ☂ 🛍
♨ ♨ ♨
Highly Commended

Superior holidays on working dairy/sheep farm. Friendly personal service. Large rooms tastefully decorated to high standard. All bedrooms en-suite, colour TV, tea/coffee-making facilities and full CH. Superb views. Excellent for birdwatching and walking (Prize-winners in wildlife and farm competitions). Best English cooking. Relax in spa bath or sauna. Games room. Near Roman Wall, Scottish Borders, 1 mile from B6318. Open all year. Map ref: 210 213

High Rigg, Walton, Brampton, Cumbria CA8 2AZ

Margaret Mounsey
☎ 069 77 2117
BB **From £14**
EM From £7.50
Sleeps 4
♨ ⚘ ⚘ ☂ ⚘
♨ **Approved**

A friendly welcome to our 144-acre mixed farm, prize winning cattle and sheep. Help feed calves, lambs, hens. An 18th-century listed farmhouse on the roadside 1 mile from Walton, near the Roman Wall. Panoramic views over the Pennines and Lakes. Patio, garden, childrens play area, pool/snooker table. Bedrooms have washbasins, tea/coffee-making facilities. Lounge and dining room. Many local walks. Open all year (closed Christmas and New Year). Map ref: 209 213

Howard House Farm, Gilsland, Carlisle, Cumbria CA6 7AN

Elizabeth Woodmass
☎ 0697 747 285
BB **From £14–£17**
EM From £8
Sleeps 6
⚘
♨ ♨ **Commended**

A warm welcome and comfortable accommodation await you on beef/sheep farm. Situated on an elevated site enjoying magnificent views over 2 counties inthe heart of Roman wall country. Guests lounge, colour TV, tea/coffee-making facilities. Dinner by arrangement or bar meals nearby. Discount on 3 night stay. Open all year. Map ref: 214 213

Hullerbank, Talkin, Brampton, Cumbria CA8 1LB

Sheila Stobbart
☎ 06977 46668
BB **From £17**
EM From £10
Sleeps 6
♨
♨ ♨ ♨ **Commended**

Georgian farmhouse with grounds and orchard. A small working sheep farm near Talkin Tarn, Brampton Golf Course and Geltsdale Bird Reserve. Beautiful walks. Convenient Hadrian's Wall, Borders and Lake District. 9 miles Carlisle. Friendly hospitality, excellent cooking using homegrown produce including home produced lamb CH. Open fire, electric blankets, tea-trays. 1 double with private bathroom, 2 twin en-suite. Sorry, no smoking. Open all year (closed Christmas & New Year). Map ref: 208 209

Low Rigg Farm, Walton, Brampton, Cumbria CA8 2DX

Ann Thompson
☎ 06977 3233
BB **From £13**
EM From £8
Sleeps 6
⚘ ⚘
Listed

A family dairy with comfortable farmhouse, 3 miles Brampton market town, 9 miles Carlisle. Ideal base for walking or touring. Many amenities nearby include pony trekking, golf. Bedroom with washbasin, tea/coffee-making facilities. Lounge/dining room with TV. Home cooking, preserves and cakes; packed lunches on request. Reductions for children. Large garden, ample parking. Open all year (closed Christmas & New Year). Map ref: 208 209

Newpallyards, Hethersgill, Carlisle, Cumbria CA6 6HZ

Georgina Elwen
☎ 0228 577308
BB From £17
EM From £9.50
Sleeps 6
🛏 ᵬ ⚘
⚘⚘⚘ **Commended**

Gold Award Winner Peak of Perfection Salon Culinaire Great British Breakfast. A wonderful area and base for Lakes, Scottish Borders and Hadrian's Wall. Filmed for BBC TV. Bowls, putting, etc. Tea-making facilitles. Family double/twin/single double en-suite rooms. Children and disabled welcome. For personal and friendly service., Telephone for brochure. Open all year. Map ref: 207 215

White Craig Farm, Shield Hill, Haltwhistle, Northumberland NE49 9NW

Isobel Laidlow
☎ 0434 320565
BB From £18.50
Sleeps 6
ᵬ ✂ ▣ ♣
⚘⚘
Highly Commended

17th century croft-style farmhouse, clean and comfortable, on western edge of Northumberland's National Park, 1 mile Hadrian's Wall, ½ mile A69. Small working sheep farm with other interesting animals. Magnificent touring/walking area. 1 hr Metro Centre and Lakes. Many local attractions. Nearby inn (food highly recommended). 1 twin, 2 doubles, (all en-suite), tea-making facilities, colour TV, CH, etc. AA QQQ. Phone for brochure. Open all year (closed Christmas & New Year). Map ref: 217 214

Self-Catering

Arch View, Riggfoot, Roadhead, Carlisle, Cumbria CA6 6PF

Mrs Jean James
☎ 06978 213
SC From £120–£360
Sleeps 2/8
⚘ 🛏 ᵬ ⚘ ♔
♪ ♪ **Up to Highly**
Commended

Luxury detached barn conversion and cottage situated in the peaceful Lyne Valley, overlooking beautiful border countryside on a 280-acre working farm. Guests are welcome to join in or just look on. See different breeds of animals. The perfect place to escape to and discover country pleasures, scenic walks, fishing, central for touring, Hadrian's Wall, Scottish borders, Carlisle, Kielder and Lake District. Map ref: 209 218

Bailey Mill, Bailey, Newcastleton, Roxburgh TD9 0TR

Pamela Copeland
☎ 069 78 617
SC From £68–£398
Sleeps 2/10
🛏 ᵬ ⚘ ✂ ⚔ ⚘ ♞
♔ ♣
♪ ♪ – ♪ ♪ ♪
Approved

A warm welcome awaits you from Pam and Ian on this small farm holiday complex nestling on the Roxburgh/Cumbria border. The five superior self-contained apartments include heating (oil), electricity and linen in rent. Colour TV and microwave in each apartment. On-site sauna, solarium, jacuzzi, gym equipment, games room, laundry, farm kitchen and horse riding. Baby sitting service. Breakfast and evening meal available. Brochure. Open all year. Map ref: 205 217

Cracrop Cottage, Cracrop Farm, Kirkcambeck, Brampton, Cumbria CA8 2BW

Marjorie Stobart
☎ 06978 245/
06977 48245
SC From £120–£250
Sleeps 4/6 + cot
🛏 ᵬ ♔ ♣
♪ ♪ ♪ ♪ **Approved**

A delightful cottage, in its own large garden, on working dairy and sheep farm. Surrounded by green fields and woodland. Centrally heated and tastefully furnished with many extras. Ideal for touring Cumbria, Hadrian's Wall, Scottish Borders, Northumberland and Lake District. Farm trail. Birdwatching, fishing, riding, golf and sailing nearby. Suitable for disabled and ideal for children. Cot available. Dogs by arrangement. Open all year. Map ref: 210 213

Long Byres, Talkin Head, Brampton, Cumbria CA8 1JR

Mrs Susan Dean
☎ 06977 46262
⑤ From £80–£225
🐾 ⌖ ⌖
♟ – ♟ ♟ ♟
Commended

Situated on a small North Pennine hill farm, within RSPB Geltsdale reserve. 1 mile from Talkin village (Post Office and eating out). Specialist, fully equipped holiday accommodation; five 2-bedroom houselets (sleep 4/5); two single bedroom (sleep 2/3). Freshly home-cooked meals. Facilities for golf, boating, fishing within 2 miles. Open all year.
Map ref: 211 213

Meadow View, Newpallyards, Hethersgill, Carlisle, Cumbria CA6 6HZ

Georgina Elwen
☎ 0228 577308
⑤ From £60–£320
Sleeps 2/8
🐾 ♿ ⌖
♟ ♟ ♟ – ♟ ♟ ♟ ♟
Commended

Good quality self-catering in 1 bungalow. Modern 3 bedroom bungalow accommodates 2–8 with every home comfort: dishwasher, washer/dryer, etc. Central heating from open fire and gas, fully carpeted and well furnished. One self-contained ground floor apartment, double and cabin bed, shower, WC, lounge/diner, kitchen. Plus 2 holiday cottages recently converted from barn. Gold Award winning proprietor.
Map ref: 207 215

White Craig Farm Cottages, White Craig Farm, Shield Hill, Haltwhistle, Northumberland NE49 9NW

Isobel Laidlow
☎ 0434 320565
⑤ From £90–310
Sleeps 3/8 cot
🅿 🐎 🐾 ⌖ 🐕 ⌂
♟ ♟ ♟ – ♟ ♟ ♟ ♟
Up to Highly Commended

Comfortable 1 and 3 bedroomed farm cottages, very well furnished and equipped to be your holiday home from home. Personally maintained. Inn/restaurant ½ mile; heated pool, squash, bowls, soft play 1 mile, golf 3½ miles. Central section Hadrian's Wall nearby. Excellent area for country pursuits. Dogs by arrangement only. Brochure available on request. Open all year. Map ref: 217 214

FARM HOLIDAY BUREAU

DISABLED VISITORS

members offering suitable accommodation to disabled/less able visitors. Please do check the extent of the facilities before booking.

FARM HOLIDAY BUREAU

THOSE LITTLE EXTRAS

For advice on farms that can offer 'extras' such as four-poster beds, special diets, farm trails, fishing rights – even stabling and trekking arrangements if you are bringing your own horse – ring the Farm Holiday Bureau on (0203) 696909.

11 North Northumberland

North Northumberland is an area of great beauty still little known to many people. There are miles of heritage coastline dotted with castles such as Lindisfarne, Bamburgh and Dunstanburgh and further inland a wealth of historic homes including Alnwick Castle and Cragside. Holy Island (Lindisfarne) is accessible by car at low tide and boats run daily in the summer months to the Farne Islands, famous for their colonies of seals and seabirds.

The Northumberland National Park offers wonderful opportunities for those wishing to walk and explore in peace and solitude. Berwick-upon-Tweed and Alnwick are two busy country towns which still have weekly street markets. Scotland's capital city, Edinburgh to the north and Newcastle with its much acclaimed Metro Shopping Centre to the south are within easy reach by car, train or bus.

Our group offers a wide variety of holiday accommodation of a high standard based on working farms in this unspoilt corner of England's most northerly county.

Group Contact: Mrs Sally Lee ☎ 0665 74 2777

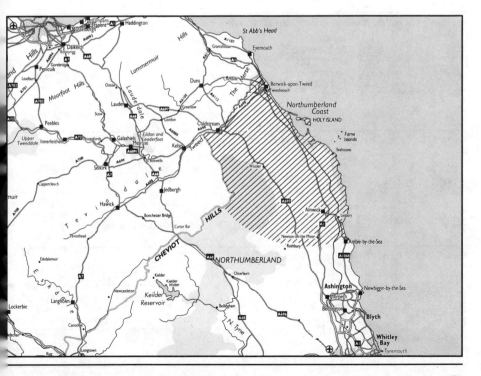

Bed and Breakfast (and evening meal)

Alndyke Farmhouse, Alnwick, Northumberland NE66 3PB

Mrs Anne Davison
☎ 0665 602193
BB From £17
EM From £10
Sleeps 6
✂ ⚒
♛ ♛ **Highly Commended**

Listed Georgian farmhouse standing in own grounds with panoramic views. Over open countryside furnished to a high standard. Bedrooms have washbasins, clock/radio, hairdryers, TV and hot drink facilities. Guest lounge with log fire separate dining room, bathroom and two toilets. Twin room en-suite. Alndyke offers a warm and friendly welcome, where guests return year after year. Recommended in the book *Best Bed and Breakfast in the World*. Open May–Oct. Map ref: 236 232

Bilton Barns, Alnmouth, Alnwick, Northumberland NE66 2TB

Dorothy Jackson
☎ 0665 830427
BB From £17
EM From £9
Sleeps 6
🐎
♛ ♛

Spacious farmhouse in lovely countryside with magnificent views over Alnmouth and Warkworth bays. An excellent centre for many splendid walks, beaches and castles that Northumberland can offer. Full central heating, guests' lounge and dining room. Bedrooms have washbasins, TV and tea/coffee-making facilities. Brian is pleased to take interested guests on a farm walk. Included in *Best Bed and Breakfast in the World*. Open Easter–Oct. Map ref: 238 232

Brandon White House, Powburn, Alnwick, Northumberland NE66 4JE

Janet Dods
☎ 066578 252
BB From £14
Sleeps 4
🐓 🐦 ⚱
Listed

This attractive old farmhouse with a self-contained guest wing, sits at the entrance to the Ingram Valley. The bedrooms, a family double and a twin, are large with hot drink facilities and the guest's sitting-room has a TV. Water comes from a Cheviot hillside spring. A variety of eating places are nearby. Open Easter–Oct. Map ref: 232 234

Doxford Farmhouse, Doxford Farm, Chathill, Northumberland NE6 75DY

Audrey & Douglas Turnbull
☎ 066 579 235
BB From £14
EM From £8
Sleeps 10
🐓 ✂ 🐦
♛ ♛ **Commended**

A peaceful Georgian farmhouse with large garden set in wooded countryside between the hills and the beautiful coastline. Guests are welcome to come on our farm walk and follow the newly created nature trail. Trout fishing and boat on nearby lake, and a squash court. Delicious home cooking and homemade bread. We happily welcome children and pets. Open all year (closed Christmas and New Year). Map ref: 181 233

Earle Hill Head Farm, Wooler, Northumberland NE71 6RH

Sylvia Armstrong
☎ 0668 81243
BB From £15
Sleeps 6
🐓 🐦
Listed

Earle Hill Farm is 2 miles from Wooler at the foot of the Cheviot Hills. We have a 4,000-acre stock farm in the National Park. Lovely walks and a warm welcome will await you in our comfortable farmhouse. Wooler is a perfect centre for the coast, castles and Scottish Borders. Household and Farming Museum. Local nature trails and conducted tours. Open May–Oct. Map ref: 227 237

Elford Farmhouse, Elford, Seahouses, Northumberland NE68 7UT

Mrs M. Robinson
☎ 06657 20 244
⬚ From £14
Sleeps 6
⛌ (12) ⬚ ⅍
Listed

An old stone farmhouse of great character on an arable farm near the villages of Bamburgh and Seahouses. One and a half miles from the sea. Nearby are beautiful beaches, castles, golf, riding and boat trips to the Farnes and Holy Island. Good local restaurants. Comfortable bedrooms with central heating, colour TV and tea/coffee making facilities, elegant dining room. Garden with tennis court. Some use of outdoor heated swimming pool in summer. Open Mar–Oct. Map ref: 236 238

Hipsburn Farm, Lesbury, Alnwick, Northumberland NE66 3PY

Hilda Tulip
☎ 0665 830 206
⬚ From £16
Sleeps 6
⅍
Listed

A spacious farmhouse situated ½ mile from Alnmouth, overlooking the Aln estuary. Rooms centrally-heated, dining room, lounge. Tea/coffee-making facilities in bedrooms. Ideal base for golfers – many courses nearby. Open May–Oct. Map ref: 237 232

Lumbylaw Farm, Edlingham, Alnwick, Northumberland NE66 2BW

Mrs Sally Lee
☎ 0665 74 277
⬚ From £16
Sleeps 6
⅍ ⛌ ⬚ ⅍ ▪
⬚

Friendly hospitality in a comfortable stone farmhouse on a beef and sheep farm. 6 miles between Alnwick and Rothbury. Outstanding views of the 13th century Edlingham Castle and Victorian railway viaduct in the farm grounds. Two twin bedrooms, 1 double bedroom (all with washbasins; one with en-suite shower). Guests' bathroom, central heating throughout. Excellent local eating places available. Open May–Oct. Map ref: 233 230

Shiel Dykes Farmhouse, Newton-on-the-Moor, nr Felton, Morpeth, Northumberland NE55 9LS

Mrs Sheilah Robinson
☎ 0665 575 242
⬚ From £14
Sleeps 5
⅍ ⛌ (5) ⬚ ⅍
Listed

A large traditional farmhouse on an extensive stock farm. 4 miles from A1 and A697 in unspoilt countryside. Spacious bedrooms, tea/coffee-making facilities and lovely views. Guests' dining room and sitting room (with TV). Large sheltered garden. Only 20 mins from coast and castles. Good eating places nearby. Forty minutes from airport. Open all year. Map ref: 234 228

Shiel Dykes Farmhouse, Whittingham, Alnwick, Northumberland NE66 4RZ

Phyllis Campbell
☎ 066 574 220
⬚ From £14
Sleeps 4
⅍ ⛌ (1) ⅍
Listed

A warm welcome awaits you on this 600-acre mixed farm. Thrunton is ideal for a country holiday having magnificent views across Whittingham Vale to the Cheviots and being central for the county's numerous beauty spots and places of interest. Thrunton Woods are popular with walkers and nature lovers. Good food is served in the guests' dining room. TV lounge. Open May–Sept. Map ref: 231 232

FARM HOLIDAY BUREAU

NO ANSWER?
Farmers are mostly out and about during the day.
Try to telephone before 9.30am or after 4pm.

Self-Catering

Firwood Bungalow and Humphreys House, Earle Hill Head Farm, Wooler, Northumberland NE71 6QJ

S. E. Armstrong
☎ 0668 81243
ⓈⒸ From £200–£500
Sleeps 6–12
🐾 🐕
🔑 🔑 🔑 – 🔑 🔑 🔑 🔑
Up to Highly Commended

Firwood and Humphreys have been recently created from Firwood, an attractive and generously proportioned Victorian bungalow with landscaped gardens and fine views over Glendale. They are situated at the foot of Cheviot Hills in Middleton Hall hamlet, 2 miles from Wooler. Walking on our 4,000-acre farm in the National Park. Open fires. Central heating included in rent. Very well equipped. Map ref: 227 237

---

4 Grindon Farm, Berwick-upon-Tweed, Northumberland TD15 2NN

Mrs Audrey Barr
☎ 02893 82212
ⓈⒸ From £100–£250
Sleeps 4
🐕
🔑 🔑 🔑 🔑 **Commended**

Situated in the quiet hamlet of Grindon equidistant from the coast at Berwick-upon-Tweed and Coldstream. Surrounded by arable farmland, there are pleasant walks along the country lanes. Grindon makes a good base for visiting the Scottish borders, Edinburgh, and the fishing villages and beautiful beaches of the Northumbrian coast. Golf, fishing and riding available nearby. Shops and pub 1 mile. Open Mar–Nov. Map ref: 224 244

Lumbylaw Cottage, Edlingham, Northumberland NE66 2BW

Mrs Sally Lee
☎ 0665 74 277
ⓈⒸ From £100–£350
Sleeps 2/6
✂ 🐕 🐄
🔑 🔑 **Commended**

Non smokers. Extensive hill views. The two cottages are situated on our working farm with its own ruined castle and viaduct, providing easy walking along the disused railway line. Both cottages centrally heated. Recently renovated, are prettily decorated, furnished and equipped to a high standard. All fuel and power, bed linen and towels included in rent. Sorry no pets. Brochure available. Open all year. Map ref: 233 230

The Old Smithy, Brackenside, Bowsden, Berwick-upon-Tweed, Northumberland TD15 2TQ

John & Mary Barber
☎ 0289 88293
ⓈⒸ From £160–£320
Sleeps 6
🐾 🐕 ♿
🔑 🔑 🔑 🔑 **Commended**

The high standards of this attractive conversion of a smithy and stable to a comfortable home makes an ideal setting for a peaceful and relaxing holiday. Explore the farm, discover the woodland and conservation areas. See the cows and calves, sheep, lambs and crops (some organic). Table tennis. Bike hire and riding nearby. Gas central heating makes for a perfect winter break. Open all year. Map ref: 227 245

No. 2 and 3 Cottages, Titlington Hall Farm, Alnwick, Northumberland NE66 2EB

Mrs Vera Purvis
☎ 066578 253
ⓈⒸ From £195–£295
🐾 🐕 📺 ⛺ 🛢
🔑 🔑 🔑 **Commended**

Two lovely country cottages available for holiday lets and short breaks. They are beautifully situated and well furnished with TV, fridge, microwave and washing machine. Also central heating. One sleeps 4/5, the other 6/7. There are two inner doors which can be removed making one cottage sleeping 10/12. Open all year. Map ref: 235 232

12 Carlisle's Border Country

The country to the north east of Carlisle is one of the last truly peaceful places in England. It was not always so for here the Border Reivers once rode and it was called the Debateable Land because Scotland and England each claimed parts of it. Now the only debate you will have is which of the many beautiful and historic places you will visit during your stay. Will it be Carlisle itself with its cathedral, castle and city walls dating back many hundreds of years? Or moving to more modern times in the city what about Tullie House, the Museum of the Border, only recently reopened and already the winner of several awards? Will it be wild Liddesdale on the Scots side with the looming mass of Hermitage Castle reminding the visitor of dark deeds of the past? Will it be the Solway coast world renowned for its birdlife? Or will you just drive quiet country lanes where there are fewer cars than there are walkers on the footpaths in other parts of the country?

All our farms are only a short drive from the M6 and so ideal for the stopover on the way to and from Scotland and Northern Ireland but they are also magnificently placed for you to go south to the Lake District, Hadrian's Wall and the Eden Valley, north into Scotland and all the delights of the Borders – even Edinburgh is only a couple of hours drive away, or east to Northumberland and Kielder Water, and west to Carlisle, Gretna Green and the Solway coast. A haven of peace with enough to keep you involved for many more holidays because once you have been welcomed for the first time in one of Carlisle's Border Country farms you will certainly want to come back . . .

Group Contact: Dorothy Downer ☎ 06978 644

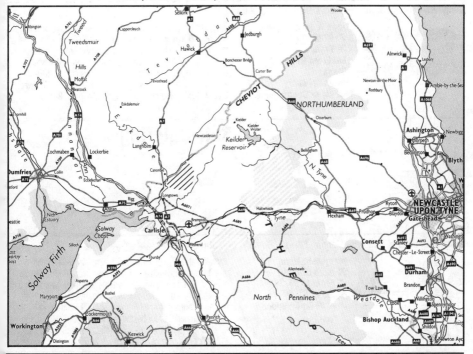

Bed and Breakfast (and evening meal)

Bank End Farm, Roadhead, Carlisle, Cumbria CA6 6NU

Dorothy Downer
☎ 069 78 644
BB From £17.50
EM From £10
Sleeps 2
✎
♥ ♥ ♥ Commended

Relax in peace in our luxurious self-contained suite (twin bedroom, private sitting room, bathroom with shower) on small sheep farm close to the Scottish border. Friendly atmosphere, delicious home cooking, meal times and packed lunches by arrangement. Marvellous centre for walking, fishing, touring; naturalist's paradise. B6318 ½ mile. Phone for brochure with colour photo. Ask for travel directions. Open 1 Mar–30 Nov. Map ref: 209 218

Bessiestown Farm, Catlowdy, Penton, Carlisle, Cumbria CA6 5QP

Margaret Sisson
☎ 0228 577219
BB From £19
EM From £9
Sleeps 8
♿ ♞ ♨ 🍴
♥ ♥ ♥
Highly Commended

One of the nicest B&B to be found, peaceful and quiet. Warm comfortable pretty bedrooms. TV lounge, bar lounge. Delicious food. Indoor heated swimming pool (May–Sept). Ideal touring base. Stop off Scotland and Northern Ireland. M6 exit 44, then A7 to Longtown; right at Bush Hotel 7 miles to T-junction,1½ miles to Bessiestown. Open all year. 10% discount FHB Members. Map ref: 206 217

Craigburn Farm, Catlowdy, Penton, Carlisle, Cumbria CA6 5QP

Jane & Jack Lawson
☎ 0228 577214
BB From £17
EM From £10
Sleeps 10
🐕 ♞ ♨ 🍴 🍴
♥ ♥ ♥ Commended

Enjoy the delights of beautiful Cumbrian countryside and life on our 250-acre working farm. Relax in the peace and quiet of the farmhouse, with delicious farmhouse cooking. Distinction in cookery held. Special breeds animals. Stay here when travelling to and from Scotland. Four-poster bed. 20% off weekly bookings. Weekend break, 10% discounts. Midweek breaks, 15% discount. Open all year. Map ref: 206 217

Self-Catering

Bessiestown Farm, Catlowdy, Penton, Carlisle, Cumbria CA6 5QP

Margaret Sisson
☎ 0228 577 219
SC From £100–300
♿ ♞ 🍴
🔑 🔑 🔑 Commended

Three attractively converted oak beam cottages situated around courtyard with extensive views over Scottish Border country. Spacious warm comfortable and furnished/decorated to high standard. 2 ground floor bedrooms with wash/hand basins. Ground floor bath/shower room. First floor lounge/kitchen. Indoor heated swimming pool (May–Sept). Ideal "away-from-it-all" touring holiday. Out of season breaks. Phone for colour brochure. Map ref: 206 217

13   Northumberland and Durham

Northumbria covers the four most northerly counties of England – Cleveland, Durham, Northumberland and Tyne and Wear. Visitors can escape on traffic-free roads to open countryside and vast, deserted beaches; a great contrast to the modern cities where shopping and entertainment are of a high standard. Old and new complement each other with some of Britain's finest heritage such as Hadrian's Wall, Durham Cathedral, Beamish Museum, Holy Island and new developments like Newcastle upon Tyne's Eldon Square and the Metro Centre at Gateshead.

The region also boasts some of England's finest countryside – the North Pennines designated as an 'Area of Outstanding Natural Beauty' and the Northumberland National Park – retreats from the pressures of modern life.

Visitors to Northumbria can be assured of a warm and hospitable welcome seldom equalled in other areas of the country.

Group Contact: Mrs M.E. Anderson ☎ 0388 527361

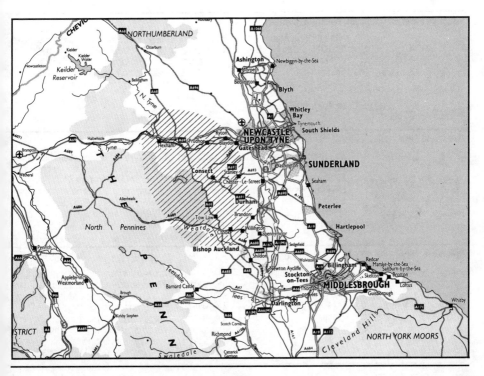

Bed and Breakfast (and evening meal)

Bee Cottage Farm, Castleside, Consett, Co Durham DH8 9HW

Liz Lawson
☎ 0207 508224
BB From £16
EM From £10.50
Sleeps 30
🐕 ♿ ⛵
Listed Commended

A working farm in lovely surroundings with unspoilt views, situated 1½ miles west A68 between Tow Law and Castleside. Visitors may participate in all farm activities, feeding calves, milking goats, bottle feeding lambs, etc. Quiet country walks. Fire certificate. No smoking in farmhouse. Ideally located for Beamish Museum, Metro Centre, Durham Cathedral or a break on a journey between England and Scotland. Open all year. Map ref: 231 207

Cornhills, Cornhills, Kirkwhelpington, Northumberland NE19 2RE

Lorna Thornton
☎ 0830 40232
BB From £16
Sleeps 6
✗ ⛵ 🎍
Listed

A large Victorian farmhouse standing in an acre of garden. An ideal retreat. Within the stock farm's boundaries is the ancient village of West Welpington, for which we hold the reports and maps of the excavation by Professor Jarrett. Ideal location for fishing (Sweethope Lough), walking and sightseeing. 1 mile from the A696. Open May–March. Map ref: 230 219

Friarside Farm, Wolsingham, Weardale, Co Durham DL13 3BH

Mrs Marjorie Anderson
☎ 0388 527361
BB From £14
EM From £8
Sleeps 4
🐕 ⛵ ✗
🦢 **Approved**

Friarside is a working hill farm, with dairy cows, sheep and a small acreage of barley and potatoes. Guests are made to feel at home and, when convenient, are entertained with music and poetry. Meals are taken in a conservatory which affords fantastic views over the Wear Valley. Open all year. Map ref: 231 205

Gairshield Farm, Whitley Chapel, Hexham, Northumberland NE47 0HS

Mrs Hilary Kristensen
☎ 0434 673562
BB From £13.50
EM From £8
Sleeps 2
✗ ⛵ ⚘
Listed

A comfortable 17th century farmhouse on a quiet hill farm (1,000 ft above sea level), with superb views over open countryside. 20 mins south of Hexham. Ideal for touring Hexham and surrounding region. Perfect walking and horse-riding area; horses very welcome. Large attractive family bedroom. Guests' dining room/lounge with TV and tea/coffee making facilities. Open Apr–Oct. Map ref: 225 213

Greenwell Farm, Tow Law, Bishop Auckland, Co Durham DL13 4PH

Mike & Linda Vickers
☎ 0388 527248
BB From £15
EM From £9
Sleeps 6
✗ ⛵ ♿ ♟ ☕ 🎍
🦢🦢
Commended

Enjoy a warm welcome in our charming farmhouse dating back 300 years. On the 280-acre mixed stock and arable farm we have developed our own walks and nature reserve with a wide variety of wildlife. Comfortable and attractive rooms, quality food. Bedrooms with private bathrooms. An excellent base for touring, county cricket and visiting the numerous attractions of the North Pennines and Durham City. Open all year (closed Christmas and New Year). Map ref: 233 204

Low Urpeth Farm, Ouston, Chester Le Street, Co Durham DH2 1BD

Hilary Johnson
☎ 091 410 2901
Fax 091 410 0081
BB From £15
Sleeps 6
🐕 🏡 💼
Listed Commended

Traditional farmhouse accommodation in spacious and comfortably furnished rooms with TV/beverage facilities, one double with washbasin, 2 twin en-suite. Within easy reach of Beamish open air museum, Metro Centre, Durham. Directions – leave A1(M) Chester Le Street, follow A693, at 2nd mini roundabout fork right through Ouston down hill, turn left at 'Trees Please'. Open all year. Map ref: 238 208

Manor House Farm, Ninebanks, Hexham, Northumberland NE47 8DA

Mrs M. I. Lee
☎ 0434 345 236
BB From £14
🐕 🐄 🎠
🏆 Commended

Working farm with cattle and sheep. Georgian farmhouse situated in the beautiful West Allen valley, a designated area of outstanding natural beauty. Ideal overnight stop for Scotland, close to Hadrians Wall. Guests' lounge/dining room. Central heating, tea making facilities, washbasins, radios and hairdriers. Open all year (except Christmas). Map ref: 219 208

Mount Escob Farm, Beamish Woods, Stanley, Co Durham DH9 0SA

Mrs Pamela Bovill
☎ 091 370 0289
BB From £14
Sleeps 4
🐕 (5) 🐄 🍴 🎠 🐎
Listed

A 12-acre grassland holding with that 'heart of the country' feel, yet less than 10 mins from the A1(M)! Close to Beamish Open Air Museum. The house is on the site of a former paper mill, beside Beamish Burn, with the surrounding hills and woods bearing much evidence of small industries of a byegone age. Our horses and youngstock thrive on their visitors' attention! A short drive takes you to either Durham city or to the Metro Centre. Open all year. Map ref: 236 210

Rye Hill Farm, Slaley, Nr Hexham, Northumberland NE47 0AH

Elizabeth Courage
☎ 0434 673259
BB From £17
EM From £9
Sleeps 15
🐕 🐄 🍴 🚸 💼
🏆 🏆 🏆
Commended

We are a small family-run livestock farm set in beautiful countryside with 360-degree panoramic views. We have recently converted some of the old byres into superb modern guest accommodation. We aim for high but simple standards with a homely atmosphere, ideal for your 'get away from it all' break or holiday. Good, fresh, homemade cooking. Well mannered children and pets welcome. Open all year. Map ref: 227 213

Self-Catering

SC

Arbour House Bungalow, Crossgate Moor, Co Durham DH1 4TQ

JW & R Hunter
☎ 091 384 2418
Fax 091 388 0738
SC From £160–£400
♿ 🐕 💼
🍎 🍎 🍎 Approved

A comfortable, modern bungalow on a working farm. Central heating, phone, colour TV, microwave, cooker, washer, fridge/freezer. Sleeps 4/6. Panoramic views of countryside and historic city of Durham. Visit Durham cathedral and castle, Beamish Museum, Metro Centre. Shopping and sports available. Country walks in Weardale. Close to Sunderland, Tyne & Wear, Newcastle-upon-Tyne. Open all year. Map ref: 238 205

Bail Hill, Allenshields, Blanchland, Consett, Co Durham DH8 9PP

Jennifer Graham
☎ 0434 675274
sc From £100–£200
Sleeps 5
ॐ ⌂ ⚱
ℱ ℱ ℱ **Approved**

Centrally heated, 2-bedroomed farmhouse with breathtaking views to Derwent Reservoir near Blanchland. Enjoy the peaceful surroundings of a typical hill farm or use as a central location for Tynedale, Durham and N E Coast. Blanchland is one of the most picturesque of Northumbrian historic villages with Abbey, pub and post office. Open fire and well-equipped kitchen. Enclosed garden and parking outside the house. Open all year. Map ref: 230 208

Bradley Burn Holiday Cottages, Wolsingham, Weardale, Co Durham DL13 3JH

Mrs Judith Stephenson
☎ 0388 527285
sc From £110–£280
ﻉ ﹁ ﺡ
ℱ ℱ ℱ – ℱ ℱ ℱ ℱ
Up to Commended

Four cottages, well-designed conversions of redundant farm buildings, preserving the traditional stone exteriors but incorporating all modern comforts indoors. Rural situation, close to a pretty stream. 2 miles east of former market town of Wolsingham. Centrally placed for sightseeing in Durham, Northumberland and North Yorkshire. Send for brochure. Open all year. Map ref: 231 205

Friarside Farm, Wolsingham, Weardale, Co Durham DL13 3BH

Mrs Marjorie Anderson
☎ 0388 527361
sc From £85–£90
Sleeps 5
ॐ ﹁
Approved

A holiday caravan (27' x 10') in an exclusive ½ acre paddock on a working family farm. 1 double bedroom plus 1 double bed/single if required. Gas heating/cooking (included in rent), shower, fridge, flush toilet. Crockery, cutlery, pans, blankets, pillows included; sheets, pillowcases, towels must be brought. Patio with table/chairs; swing. Pleasant views of valleys and hills. Children have access to animals and may help on farm. Dogs by arrangement. Open all year. Map ref: 231 205

Greenwell Hill Stables and Greenwell Hill Byre, c/o Greenwell Farm, Tow Law, Co Durham DL13 4PH

Linda Vickers
☎ 0388 527248
sc From £120–£285
Sleeps 4/6
ॐ ﹁ ﹀ ⚱ ▪
ℱ ℱ ℱ ℱ **Commended**

Enjoy a relaxing stay in one of two quality cottages. This is a traditional farm in peaceful countryside. Marvellous views, pleasant walks and our own nature trail with conservation area. The larger cottage has a four poster bed, dishwasher and en-suite bedrooms. Both are well equipped with gas central heating, double glazing, natural beams, pine furniture, fitted carpets and comfy chintzy suites. Evening meals available. Open all year. Map ref: 233 204

The Herdsman Cottage, Cornhills, Kirkwhelpington, Northumberland NE19 2RE

Lorna Thornton
☎ 0830 40232
sc From £120–260
Sleeps 5
﹀ ॐ ⚱
ℱ ℱ ℱ **Commended**

A beamed 19th century farm cottage, provides comfortable accommodation for 5 people (double, twin, single). The fully fitted kitchen is equipped with fridge, washing machine, night storage heaters, open fire in winter. Bed linen provided. Enjoy the peace on our stock farm, in the centre of Northumberland. Open May–Feb. Map ref: 230 219

"Isaac's Cottage", Lowsinshope Shield Farm, Sparty Lea, Hexham, Northumberland NE47 9HJ

Heather M Robson
☎ 0434 685312
sc From £100–£280
ॐ ⌂
ℱ ℱ ℱ **Commended**

Beautiful stone cottage adjoining farmhouse, overlooking meadowland and small hamlet of Spartylea. Very warm and cosy, oil central heating. OPen log fire, double glazing, beamed ceilings, quality carpets, colour TV. Garden, ample parking. Two double bedrooms, 1 twin bedroom, bathroom, separate WC, shower. Bed linen provided, also cot/highchair. Ideal for walking, riding, fishing, golf, touring, skiing. Welcome tea. Hexham 16 miles, Allendale 6, Alston 10. Open all year. Map ref: 225 213

14 Teesdale

Teesdale with its wealth of history and outstanding scenery lies south-west of Durham city. Its gentle dales and rolling moorland abound with features of geological and historical interest. The River Tees itself rises at Cross Fell and courses down the valley and includes the impressive 'High Force', England's highest waterfall with a dramatic 70ft drop over Great Whin Sill. Ancient stone quarries and disused lead mines in the upper dale mark industries dating back to Roman times and the many public footpaths in the dale include a magnificent scenic stretch of the well known Pennine Way. Teesdale makes an excellent base for exploring the nearby Yorkshire Dales, the Roman wall, Northumberland and the Lake District, all of which are within an hour's drive. For the holidaymaker interested in castles and museums, there are plenty to choose from: Barnard Castle dating back to the 12th century, the famous French style Bowes Museum and the historic Raby Castle, seat of Lord Barnard. A little further across the county is the now famous Beamish Open Air Museum and many other interesting places too numerous to list.
Visit Teesdale to discover its scenic beauty and historic sights for yourself.

Group Contact: Mrs June Dent ☎ 0833 40349

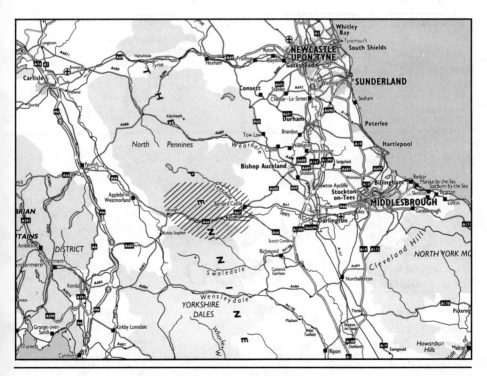

Bed and Breakfast (and evening meal)

East Mellwaters Farm, Bowes, Barnard Castle, Co Durham DL12 9RH

Patricia Milner
☎ 0833 28269
BB From £16.50
EM From £10
Sleeps 6

Half a mile off the A66 you'll approach our farm over an attractive humpback bridge straddling the Greta with fishing and walks. You may well be greeted by the aroma of bread baking. You'll dine under oak beams by an open fire on fresh good homemade fare and then retire to our comfortable en-suite rooms with TV, etc., to decide to explore on foot or by car our lovely area. Send for brochure for a break or holiday. Open all year. Map ref: 225 197

Grassholme Farm, Lunedale, Middleton-in-Teesdale, Barnard Castle, Co Durham DL12 0PR

Mrs Alison Sayer
☎ 0833 40494
BB From £12
EM From £7
Sleeps 4

Listed

A warm welcome awaits you at Grassholme Farm, a typical Dales hill farm in Lunedale, with beef cattle and Swaledale sheep. The farm is 1 mile off the B6276 Middleton-Brough road with the Pennine Way passing through the property. A good base for walking; trout fishing in Grassholme reservoir. Good plain farmhouse cooking and baking. Open March–Oct. Map ref: 225 197

Wythes Hill Farm, Lunedale, Middleton-in-Teesdale, Co Durham DL12 0NX

Mrs June Dent
☎ 0833 40349
BB From £13
EM From £7
Sleeps 6

Wythes Hill is a working stock-rearing farm with panoramic views from all rooms. Situated on the Pennine Way route with many picturesque walks in Teesdale. Visit the Bowes Museum, Raby Castle and High Force Waterfall. Good plain cooking. Two double bedrooms and 1 twin bedroom, all with H&C. All rooms with tea/coffee-making facilities. Lounge with coal fire. Open Easter–end Oct. Map ref: 225 197

FARM HOLIDAY BUREAU

GOOD FOOD

Nearly all Bureau members now hold a certificate in Essential Food Hygiene.

15 Eden Valley & North Pennines

The highest point of this area is Alston, the centre of the North Pennines which was the sbuject of David Bellamy's book "England's Last Wilderness". Alston is a quaint little market town, the highest in England, with cobbled streets. It was once the centre of a thriving lead mining industry, the reamins of which are now being carefully restored under the watchful eyes of the North Pennines Heritage Trust so that the visitors may see for themselves how the people of the area lived and worked, harnessing their natural assets of water power to assist them at places like Kilhope. This unique and beautiful upland landscape was recently designated an Area of Outstanding Natural Beauty and the morrs, which are home to Lapwing. Curlew, Buzzard and the occasional using pack horse roads or even by motor car. Then following along the Pennine range to Kirby Stephen, "crossroad of the Dales", it follows the River Eden as it gradually descends, gaining size along the way from its many tributaries, toward the Solway Plain and the historic city of Carlisle. A short way down the valley we find Appleby, a sleepy market town straddling the Eden which for two weeks every year is host to the largest Gypsy gathering and horse fair in the country, a sight not to be missed! Truly a "Garden of Eden" the area has lush vegetation, wildlife in plenty and a wealth of footpaths. The visitor can enjoy a guided walk or simply obtain a leaflet explaining the route and set off unaccompanied. For those less energetic there are tours around historic houses and sites travelling onthe local minibus, the Fellrunner.

The famous Carlisle to Settle railway runs right through Eden with stations at Armathwait,. Lazonby, Langwathby and Appleby: an ideal way to view the magnificent scenery!

Group Contacts: 🅱🅱 **Pat Dent ☎ 0434 381383**
🆂🅲 **Mrs Anne Ivinson ☎ 069 96 230/Fax 069 96 523**

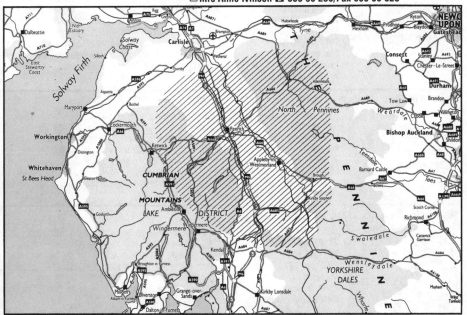

Bed and Breakfast (and evening meal)

Augill House Farm, Brough, Kirkby Stephen, Cumbria CA17 4OX

Jeanette Atkinson
☎ 07683 41305
🅱 From £16
EM From £8.50
Sleeps 6
✗ ⌂ (12)
😊 😊 Commended

Enjoy Cumbrian cooking in our Georgian farmhouse. Super breakfasts and delicious 5 course dinners served in our lovely conservatory overlooking the garden. Bedrooms en-suite or private bath. Colour TV, coffee/Tea making facilities. Ideal for the Lakes, Yorkshire Dales and Northern Pennines. AA approved. Open all year (closed Christmas & New Year). Map ref: 220 224

Ivy House Farm, Garrigill, Alston, Cumbria CA9 3DU

Helen Dent
☎ 0434 382079
🅱 From £12
EM From £8
Sleeps 6
✗ ⌂ ♞
Listed

A warm welcome awaits you when you visit our 256-acre hill farm with grazing cattle and sheep. Situated in the picturesque village of Garrigill on the Pennine Way. Ideal for walking/touring – our 17th century listed farmhouse has 2 bedrooms with handbasins and tea making facilities. Good farmhouse breakfast and excellent food available in village. Open all year (closed Christmas & April). Map ref: 217 206

Low Cornriggs Farm, Cowshill, Upper Weardale, Co Durham DH13 1AQ

Alston Moor & Kilhope Riding Centre
☎ 0388 537600
🅱 From £15.50
EM From £8.50
Sleeps 6
⌂ (5) ♞ ⚘ ☕ ☂ ♨
😊 😊 Commended

Cornriggs farmhouse has undergone extensive refurbishments which have returned it to its former glory but with 20th century comforts. Situated on a traditional organic working farm with stables (Fell and Highland ponies). Magnificent views of Weardale; famous for flora (registered SSSI). Homemade bread, good home cooking and a warm welcome awaits every guest. Open Mar–Dec. Map ref: 219 206

Meaburn Hill Farm, Meaburn Hill, Maulds Meaburn, Penrith, Cumbria CA10 3HN

Ruth Tuer
093 715205
🅱 From £17
Sleeps 6
🅰 ⌂ ✗ ⌂ ☂
Listed Commended

Relax at our beautifully restored 16th century farmhouse, quietly situated in a hidden valley near Appleby. Lovely antique furnished rooms overlooking tranquil river and village green. 2 double rooms and 1 twin room, all with private facilities. Award winning farmhouse breakfasts and afternoon teas. Guests are welcome to explore our 200-acre suckler beef/sheep farm. A warm welcome awaits you. Open Mar–Dec. Map ref: 213 195

Meadow Ing Farm, Crackenthorpe, Appleby, Cumbria CA16 6AE.

Mrs Yvonne Dent
☎ 07683 52543
🅱 From £14
EM From £8
Sleeps 6
⌂ ✗ ♞ ☕ ♨
Listed Commended

Attractive sandstone farmhouse on progressive pedigree dairy farm. Situated in the Eden Valley, near Appleby. Excellent views of Lakeland and Pennine Hills. Antique furnished rooms, oak beams, oak and pine doors. Interesting craft work. Open fire in guests' lounge. Colour TV. Guests' private bathroom. Wholesome food. Fishing on the River Eden. Open all year. Map ref: 216 196

Middle Bayles Farm, Alston, Cumbria CA9 3BS

Mrs Pat Dent
☎ 0434 381383
🅱 From £14
EM From £8
Sleeps 6
🛇 🛏 ⅄ ⚱
🕸 🕸 **Commended**

A 300-acre hill farm with cattle and sheep where visitors are welcome to wander. Ideal walking/touring area. Warm, comfortable 17th century farmhouse, tastefully furnished, with superb views overlooking South Tyne Valley. 1 double/twin en-suite, 1 family room with private bathroom, electric blankets. Tea-making facilities, full CH. Good home cooking including our own bread, warm welcome. Reductions under 14s. Closed Christmas & April. Map ref: 217 206

Park House Farm, Dalemain, Penrith, Cumbria CA11 0HB

Mrs Mary Milburn
☎ 07684 86212
🅱 From £13
Sleeps 6
🛇 ⚱ 🛆
🕸

Spend a secluded, peaceful holiday where you can unwind and enjoy the stunning views of our Lakeland fells. Our sheep farm is situated behind Dalemain Mansion. Only 3 miles from Penrith and Ullswater on the A592. Cumbrian hospitality is assured from a welcome 'cuppa' with home baking to a generous breakfast. Evening meal available locally. One double bedroom, 1 family room each with washbasin, shaver point, heater, tea/coffeemaking facilities. Bathroom and shower room. TV lounge (fire on cold evenings). Open Apr–Oct. Map ref: 211 201

Tymparon Hall, Newbiggin, Stainton, Penrith, Cumbria CA11 0HS

Mrs Margaret Taylor
☎ 07684 83236
🅱 From £14.50
EM From £7.50
Sleeps 6
🛏 🛇 🕮
Listed Approved

A spacious farmhouse and large garden situated on a 150-acre sheep farm in a peaceful rural area. Good home cooking. Tea/coffee-making facilities, electric blankets in bedrooms. Open fire in lounge. A Shetland pony for small children to ride. Reduction for under-12s; no charge for cot. 4 miles from M6 (jct. 40). Open March–Oct. Map ref: 210 200

Self-Catering

Ghyll Burn Cottage, Hartside Nursery Garden, nr Alston, Cumbria CA9 3BL

Mrs Susan Huntley
☎ 0434 381372
🆂🅲 From £135–£320
Sleeps 4/6
🛇 🄴 🛆
🐾 🐾 🐾 **Commended**

Recently renovated farm buildings dating back to 1630 offer spacious and comfortable accommodation for 4/6 people. Kitchen/diner, large lounge with oak beams and wood burning stove on first floor. Attractive twin and double bedrooms, bathroom, are downstairs. Full gas central heating. The cottage is set in a secluded valley with small nursery garden. Ideal for bird wildlife and gardening enthusiasts. Open all year. Map ref: 217 206

Green View Lodges, Green View, Welton, Nr Dalston, Carlisle, Cumbria CA5 7ES

Anne Ivinson
☎ 06996 230 (06974 76230)/Fax 06974 76523
🆂🅲 From £145–£380
Sleeps 4/6
🐾 🛇 🛆 🛆 🕮 ✗
🐾 🐾 🐾–🐾 🐾 🐾
Up to Highly Commended

Three peacefully situated Scandinavian pine lodges new 1984. Set in our large garden in tiny picturesque hamlet, typical Scandinavian specification. CH, telephones, south facing verandahs, not overlooked. 3 bedroom units have second WC. Unspoilt views of rolling farmland to the Caldbeck Fells 3 miles away. Fishing, golf 3/5 miles. 30 minutes' drive to Lake Ullswater, Keswick or Gretna Green. Also 3 cottages with open fire, beams, sleeping 2–7. Open all year. Map ref: 205 208

Hill View, Augill House Farm, Brough, Kirkby Stephen, Cumbria CA17 4DX

Jeanette Atkinson
☎ 07683 41305
ⓢⓒ **From £100–£160**
Sleeps 3
� (5) 🌂
🔑 🔑 🔑 🔑 **Commended**

This lovely chalet situated on our farm is very comfortable. Bathroom , lounge with colour TV. Nice kitchen with gas cooker and microwave. Electric heating. Washing facilities. All linen included in the price. Dinner available in the farmhouse. Also one bedroomed flat with same facilities. Open all year. Map ref: 220 224

Skirwith Hall Cottage, Skirwith Hall, Skirwith, Penrith, Cumbria CA10 1RH

Mrs Laura Wilson
☎ 0768 88241
ⓢⓒ **From £125–£290**
Sleeps 4–8
🐕(by arrangement) ☒
🔑 🔑 🔑 🔑 **Approved**

Georgian farmhouse wing built of local red sandstone overlooking large pleasant garden and stream on 400-acre mixed dairy farm. Exposed beams and open fire in lounge, nightstore heaters, washing machine, colour TV. Two double rooms and one with twin beds and bunks. Cot and high chair. Handy for Lakes or north Pennines. Ideal fishing, walking or simply enjoying idyllic rural surroundings. Open all year, short breaks available in low season. Map ref: 215 205

Smithy Cottage, c/o Skirwith Hall, Skirwith, Penrith, Cumbria CA10 1RH

Mrs Laura Wilson
☎ 0768 88241
ⓢⓒ **From £92–£210**
Sleeps 4
🐕 (by arrangement) ☒
☒ 🛢
🔑 🔑 🔑 **Approved**

Originally the home of the village blacksmith. Situated on the outskirts of an unspoilt village in the shadow of Crossfell. Equipped to a high standard, 1 twin bedded and 1 double room. Nightstore heaters and open fire (coal provided). Colour TV, telephone, washing machine. Shop 2 miles. Handy for Lakes, Yorkshire Dales and Scottish Borders. Golf, riding, fishing nearby. Ideal fell walking, birdwatching or touring. Open all Easter–Nov. Map ref: 215 205

West View Cottages, West View Farm, Winskill, Penrith, Cumbria CA10 1PD

Mr & Mrs A. J. Grave
☎ 0768 881356
ⓢⓒ **From £100–£270**
Sleeps 2–5
☒🐕☒🐾
🔑 🔑 🔑 **Commended**

A roomy cottage and 2 barn conversions on a mixed working farm. All units have central heating, TV, modern kitchen, washing facilities, and linen provided. Ideally situated for touring and within easy reach of the lakes, North Pennines and Scotland. Local facilities include children's play area, open air swimming pool, walking. Sleeps 2/4/5. Short breaks available in low season. Brochure sent on request. Open all year. Map ref: 215 204

THOSE LITTLE EXTRAS

For advice on farms that can offer 'extras' such as four-poster beds, special diets, farm trails, fishing rights – even stabling and trekking arrangements if you are bringing your own horse – ring the Farm Holiday Bureau on (0203) 696909.

FARM HOLIDAY BUREAU

16 West Lakeland

Our hospitality and the warmth of our welcome are renowned. If it is home comforts and peace and tranquility you are after, then this is the place for you.

To most people the Lakes begin and end at Windermere but just venture a little further and you will discover a whole new experience. See the Border City of Carlisle with its chequered history of Romans, Picts and Scots, or the wild, untamed fells of Wasdale. View the hunting grounds of John Peel at Caldbeck, walk around Cockermouth, home of John Dalton, Fletcher Christian and William Wordsworth. Visit Whitehaven, the site of the last invasion of Britain by John Paul Jones, founder of the American Navy. Take the whole family for a ride on 'laal ratty', the miniature steam railway at Ravenglass. Trace the footsteps of the 'Maid of Buttermere' with the help of Melvyn Bragg, son of Wigton, or take the road to the future and spend a day at the British Nuclear Fuels Exhibition Centre at Sellafield. The energetic may like to discover the secrets of our Lakes – Ennerdale, Crummock and Buttermere – and enjoy walking, boating, sea, river or lake fishing. We are the ideal base for touring anywhere in Cumbria – then it's home to the relaxing atmosphere with your friendly farmhouse hosts.

Group Contact: Mrs Alison Hewitson ☎ 0900 823875

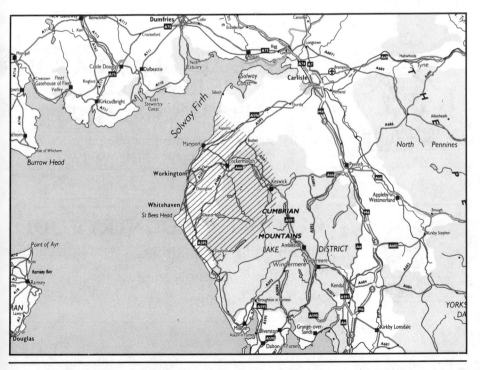

Bed and Breakfast (and evening meal)

Crag End Farm, Rogerscale, Cockermouth, Cumbria CA13 0RG

Mrs Margaret Ann Steel
☎ 0900 85658
BB From £15
EM From £7
Sleeps 6
🐕 🐎 🎣 💼
Listed

Friendly family farmhouse accommodation in comfortable old oak-beamed house dated 1732. Log fire in separate lounge. Good home cooking in guests' own dining room. We are a 250-acre farm looking up Lorton Valley. 4 bedrooms with handbasins, 2 bathrooms (1 with shower), 2 toilets. Easy reach of the Lakes. Open all year. Map ref: 195 201

High Stanger Farm, Cockermouth, Cumbria CA13 9TS

Alison Hewitson
☎ 0900 823875
BB From £14
EM From £7.50
Sleeps 6
🐕 🐕
Listed

A warm welcome to our 17th century farmhouse in the beautiful Lorton Valley, with breathtaking views of the fells. A comfortable lounge with log fire, spacious bedrooms, good cooking in a pleasant dining room. Activities to suit everyone within easy reach. In fact everything for the perfect family holiday. Very quiet location. Special rates for children. Open all year. Map ref: 196 198

BUREAU ACCOMMODATION IS RELIABLE

This Guide lists **Farm Holiday Bureau** members only. They are all inspected by the National Tourist Board for standards (see introduction pages) and by fellow members to maintain a high quality.

FOLLOW THE COUNTRY CODE

Leave nothing but footprints,

Take nothing but photographs,

Kill nothing but time!

17 South Lakeland

Find true country hospitality on a farm in this most beautiful corner of England. South Lakeland centres on the town of Kendal, which, in time, has developed into the focal point of the local community and the 'southern gateway' to the Lake District.

There's plenty to do – you can visit the award-winning Abbot Hall art gallery and Museums of Lakeland Life and Industry and Natural History and Archeology – or even the 'K' shoe factory and shop! There are also many National Trust properties and, especially for the children, the new Beatrix Potter exhibition!

If you're feeling active, Windermere and Bowness – where you can stroll by the lakeside, take a cruise on the 'Teal' or 'Swan', or ride on the steam train to Haverthwaite – are only a few minutes drive away. The fell walking is great too – whether in the valleys of Longsleddale or Kentmere, or on Scout Scar.

The seasons come and go in South Lakeland. Springtime here is a photographer's delight, with rhododendrons, azaleas, and daffodils – so immortalised by Wordsworth – while new-born lambs frolic in the pastures. Yet in autumn, the rich golds of the bracken and leaves contrast with the blue sky – a sightseer's delight.

Group Contact: Mrs Olive Simpson ☎ 0539 83682 (0539 823682)

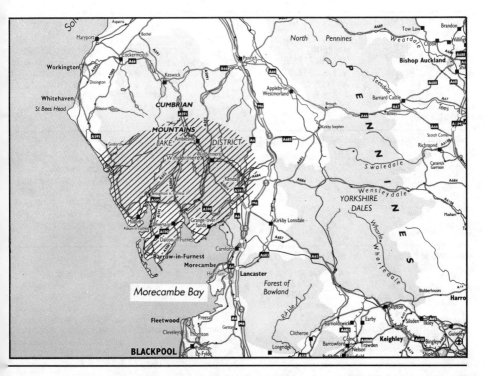

Bed and Breakfast (and evening meal)

Garnett House Farm, Burneside, Kendal, Cumbria LA9 5SF

Mrs Sylvia Beaty
☎ 0539 724542
BB From £13
EM From £6.50
Sleeps 10

AA/RAC recommended 15th century farmhouse on working farm. Only ½ from A591 to Windermere road – down country road with its hedges, wildflowers and birds. Bedrooms have colour TV, washbasins and tea making facilities. BAth and shower rooms and en-suite. Oak panelled lounge, dining room with separate tables with choice for breakfast and 5 course dinners. Child reductions. Easy to find and good parking. Open all year. Map ref: 209 187

Gateside Farm, Windermere Road, Kendal, Cumbria LA9 5SE

Mrs June Ellis
☎ 0539 722036
BB From £13
EM From £7.00
Sleeps 10

Listed Commended

AA/RAC recommended. Traditional lakeland farm, 2 miles north of Kendal on A591. Easily accessible from M6 (jct 36). 16th century farmhouse, fully modernised. Fire certificate. All bedrooms have colour TV, handbasins, tea/coffee-making facilities and heating, some en-suite. Separate bath and shower rooms, separate dining tables, short or weekly stays welcome. Good home cooked breakfasts and evening meals. Good parking facilities. Open all year (closed Christmas and New Year). Map ref: 210 186

Low Hundhowe Farm, Burneside, Kendal, Cumbria LA8 9AB

Jennie & Marjorie Hoggarth
☎ 0539 722060
BB From £12.50
EM From £6.50
Sleeps 6
(2)

This 360-year-old farmhouse nestling in the hillside below Potter Fell is a peaceful retreat, yet only minutes away from A591 and M6 motorway. The ideal base from which to explore the magnificent countryside of the Lake District. Low Hundhowe offers comfort and hospitality, good food and a warm welcome to all our guests. Packed lunches. SAE for brochure. Open all year (closed Christmas). Map ref: 210 186

Low Plain Farm, Brigsteer, Kendal, Cumbria LA8 8AX

Stella & John Dicker
☎ 05395 68323
BB From £15
Sleeps 6

Approved

A small farm incorporating a 'farm park' with a variety of animals and birds set in the beautiful Lyth valley with lovely walks and views. Spacious well appointed bedrooms all with colour TV, H&C, tea/coffee-making facilities, 2 bedrooms en-suite, central heating throughout, guest lounge with colour TV, dining room, telephone. Reductions for weekly bookings and children sharing. Evening by arrangement. Open Feb–Nov. Map ref: 210 186

Murthwaite Farm, Longsleddale, Kendal, Cumbria LA8 9BA

Nancy Waine
☎ 053 983 634 changing to 0539 823634
BB From £12
EM From £6
Sleeps 6

Listed

A warm, friendly welcome awaits you at Murthwaite, our working farm nestling in Longsleddale, one of the Lakeland's loveliest valleys. Quiet and peaceful, yet only 1½ miles from the A6, this 17th century stone-built farmhouse has been tastefully modernised. Full central heating. Tea/coffee-making facilities in bedrooms. Bath/shower room for guests' sole use, colour TV, lounge, separate dining room. Home cooked meals. Packed lunches available. Open Mar–Nov. Map ref: 210 186

Patton Hall Farm, Kendal, Cumbria LA8 9DT

Mrs Margaret Hodgson
☎ 0539 721590
BB From £12.50
EM From £5
Sleeps 6
🛏 ⛄ (2) 🌂
🍽🍽

Friendly farmhouse accommodation is offered on this 200-acre working farm in rural position overlooking Kendal, 1½ miles from A6 (Kendal-Shap road). Good food and comfort assured. Guests free to wander the farmland, with private fishing in River Mint. Two double, 1 twin, washbasins, guest bathroom and separate toilet, tea/coffee-making facilities, lounge, colour TV and dining room. Children over two years welcome. Map ref: 210 186

Riverbank House, Garnett Bridge, Kendal, Cumbria LA8 9AZ

Julia Thom
☎ 053 983 254
BB From £12
EM From £6
Sleeps 6
🐱 🛏 ✗ ⛄
🍽🍽

This lovely country house is situated at the foot of the beautiful valley of Longsleddale. 4½ miles north of Kendal just off the A6. Standing at the head of 20 acres of pastureland beside the River Sprint providing private fishing. Comfortable bedrooms with washbasins, tea/coffee-making facilities. Guests' sitting room, TV and open log fire, background CH. Excellent home cooking and a warm welcome are assured. Open all year (closed Christmas and New Year). Map ref: 210 186

Stockbridge Farm, Staveley, Kendal, Cumbria LA8 9LP

Mrs Betty Fishwick
☎ 0539 821580
BB From £13
Sleeps 11
🐱 ⛄ ♨
Listed

A comfortable, modernised 17th century farmhouse on edge of bypassed village just off A591 Kendal-Windermere road, 15 minutes M6 (jct 36). All bedrooms have fitted washbasins and shaver points, bath/shower room, separate WC. Fire certificate. Full central heating. Separate tables, full English breakfast, bedtime drink. Friendly, personal service. Good parking facilities. On Dalesway Footpath. Open Mar–Oct. Map ref: 210 187

Tranthwaite Hall, Underbarrow, Nr Kendal, Cumbria LA8 8HG

Mrs D Swindlehurst
☎ 05395 68285
BB From £13
Sleeps 4
✗ ⛄ 🌂 ♨
Listed

This magnificent olde worlde farmhouse dates back to the 11th century. Beautiful oak beams, doors and rare antique fire range. Tastefully modernised with full central heating, bath, shower room, colour TV lounge, separate dining room. This dairy/sheep farm has an idyllic setting in a small, picturesque village between Kendal and Windermere. Walking, golf, pony trekking. Many good pubs and inns nearby. SAE for brochure. Open all year. Map ref: 210 186

Please mention **Stay on a Farm** when booking

FARM HOLIDAY BUREAU

DISABLED VISITORS

members offering suitable accommodation to disabled/less able visitors. Please do check the extent of the facilities before booking.

Self-Catering

High Swinklebank Farm, Longsleddale, Nr Kendal, Cumbria LA8 9BD

Mrs Olive Simpson
☎ 053 983 682 changing to 0539 823682
SC From £100–£160
Sleeps 4
🐴 ⛵ 🎾
🔑 🔑 🔑 Commended

High Swinklebank is near the head of the beautiful Longsleddale Valley with lovely views and walking. A very recent conversion which is well appointed includes fitted carpets throughout. Comprising lounge with electric fire, TV, lovely kitchen, shower room, 2 bedrooms – double and bunk. Children welcome with baby listening. Linen provided. Weekends available. Cleanliness and personal attention assured. Open all year. Map ref: 210 187

Preston Patrick Hall Cottage, Preston Patrick Hall, Milnthorpe, Cumbria LA7 7NY

Stephen & Jennifer Armitage
☎ 05395 67200
SC From £95–£240
Sleeps 2/6
🐴 ⛵ 🎾
🔑 🔑 🔑 Approved

Cosy wing of 14th century farmhouse near Crooklands, ideal centre for Lakes and Dales. Oak beamed rooms tastefully modernised to sleep 2 or 3 (further bedroom sleeping 3 optional extra). Fitted kitchen with dishwasher and fridge. Sitting room with log fire and colour TV. Bedroom with antique brass beds and additional 2' 6" bed (linen, electric blankets and cot available). Use of swimming pool and table tennis table. Brochure available. Open all year. Map ref: 209 184

Woodside, Hollin Crag, Garth Row, Underbarrow, Nr Kendal, Cumbria LA8 8AY

Valerie O'Loughlin
☎ 05395 68655
SC From £70–£160
Sleeps 2
🐴 (2) 🐴
🔑 🔑 Commended

Woodside is situated in Lyth Valley just 3 miles from Kendal and 6 miles from Bowness on Windermere. This detached single storey cottage with its own garden comprises lounge/kitchenette with electric fire, colour TV, fridge and electric cooker. 1 bedroom sleeps 2 adults. Shower room. Storage heaters. Bed linen provided. Electricity by 50p meter. Open all year. Map ref: 208 186

FARM HOLIDAY BUREAU

NO ANSWER?

Farmers are mostly out and about during the day.
Try to telephone before 9.30am or after 4pm.

FARM HOLIDAY BUREAU

GOOD FOOD

Nearly all Bureau members now hold a certificate in Essential Food Hygiene.

---

18 Vale of Lune, Morecambe Bay to Pennine Way

Rising in the hills of Cumbria, the Lune flows through richly pastoral countryside. One of its first ports of call is Kirkby Lonsdale, an attractive and unspoilt market town with its 13th century church and Devils Bridge. To the south east lies the busy moorland market town of High Bentham with its Wednesday cattle market and Ingleton, famous for its show caves and spectacular waterfall glens. To the north west lie the unique Limestone Crags of Arnside and Silverdale with its many splendid coastal walks.

The area is a haven for birdwatchers with the R.S.P.B. bird sanctuary at Leighton Moss and for railway enthusiasts 'Steam Town' at Carnforth will take you back in time. The Lune then flows down to the Roman city of Lancaster with its castle and museums including the newly opened Maritime Museum, Museum of Childhood and the Judges Lodgings. At the end of the Lune Valley lies glorious Morecambe Bay. The River Wyre starts its journey to the sea high in the fells of the ancient hunting Forest of Bowland and flows down through unspoilt villages such as Marshaw, Abbeystead and Dolphinholme to the market town of Garstang. Beacon Fell Country Park is on the doorstep and well worth a visit. Both the River Lune and the Wyre offer plenty of opportunities for coarse fishing.

Group Contact: Mrs Jean Fowler ☎ 0995 602140

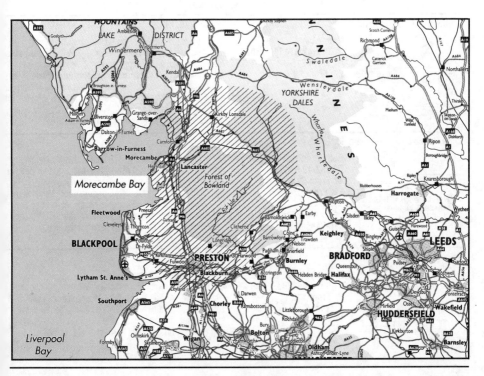

Bed and Breakfast (and evening meal)

Cotestones Farm, Sand Lane, Warton, Carnforth, Lancashire LA5 9NH

Gillian Close
☎ 0524 732418
BB From £12
Sleeps 6
🐕 🐎 ⌨ 🎣 ♿
Listed

Situated on the North Lancashire coast near to the M6 Junction 35 on the Carnforth to Silverdale road, this is a 150-acre family-run dairy farm which adjoins Leighton Moss RSPB Reserve. Also very near to Steamtown Railway Museum. Lying between Lancaster, Morecambe and the Lake District, it is an ideal place for touring the area. Tea/coffee-making facilities and washbasins in all rooms. Reductions for children. Open all year (closed Christmas). Map ref: 212 182

Fowgill Park Farm, High Bentham, Nr Lancaster, North Yorkshire LA2 7AH

Shirley Metcalfe
☎ 052 42 61630
BB From £12
EM From £7
Sleeps 6
🐕 🐎
♨ ♨ Commended

Fowgill is a stock rearing farm, ideal for those who wish to stay where it is quiet. Guests enjoy panoramic views of the Dales and Fells. A good centre for visiting the Lakes, Dales, coast, waterfalls and caves. Beamed bedrooms have washbasins, shaver points and tea/coffee-making facilities; two bedrooms en-suite. Comfortable beamed lounge with television. Separate dining room. Bedtime drink included. Open May–Sept. Map ref: 216 177

Gatehouse Farm, Far Westhouse, Ingleton, Carnforth, Lancashire LA6 3NR

Nancy Lund
☎ 052 42 41458/41307
BB From £15
EM From £8
Sleeps 6
🐕 🐎
♨

Bryan and Nancy (formerly Lund Holme), welcome you to our dairy and sheep farm built in 1740, rooms with old oak beams in elevated position enjoying panoramic views over open countryside in the **Yorkshire Dales National Park**. Guests dining room, and lounge with colour TV. Bedroom with private facilities and tea trays. Welcome drink on arrival. 15 miles exit 34 M6, 1½ miles west of Ingleton just off A65. Open all year (closed Christmas and New Year). Map ref: 218 179

Lane House Farm, Bentham, Nr Lancaster, North Yorkshire LA2 7DJ

Betty Clapham
☎ 052 42 61479
BB From £13
EM From £7
Sleeps 6
🐕 🐎 ⌨ (£2.50) static caravans 🏕
♨ ♨ Commended

Enjoy a relaxing break at our 17th century beamed farmhouse, within ½ mile of the Forest of Bowland, with beautiful views of the Yorkshire Dales. 1 mile from the market town of High Bentham, ½ hour from M6. Ideal for caves, waterfalls, touring the Lakes. Bedrooms have washbasins and tea-making facilities. Bathroom and shower. Two separate toilets. Guests' lounge with colour TV. Separate dining room. Open Mar–Nov. Map ref: 219 178

Stirzakers Farm, Barnacre, Garstang, Preston, Lancashire PR3 1GE

Ruth Wrathall
☎ 0995 603335
BB From £12
Sleeps 6
🐎
Listed Highly Commended

Welcome to our dairy farm where you can relax in the peace and quiet of the beautiful countryside. We have double, family and single rooms in our old stone, beamed farmhouse. CH, separate lounge with colour TV. Two visitors' bathrooms and showers. Tea-making facilities. Children half price. Open all year (closed Christmas and New Year). Map ref: 208 164

Self-Catering

Garden Cottage, High Snab, Gressingham, Lancaster LA2 8LS

Mrs Margaret Burrow
☎ 05242 21347
Ⓢⓒ From £120–£220
Sleeps 4 + cot
🐕 ♨
🔑🔑🔑 Commended

Garden cottage, with its own private drive and garden, adjoins our farmhouse on a working dairy and sheep farm in a quiet location. Ideal for touring lakes, dales and coast. Recently converted. Well equipped kitchen/oak beamed lounge. Two bedrooms, 1 double, 1 twin, π snooker table, bathroom with shower. Central heating from farmhouse cot/high chair available. Electric and linen included. Five miles junction35 M6. Brochure available. Map ref: 212 177

The Granary, Moss Edge Farm, Cockerham, Lancaster, Lancashire LA2 0ER

Frances M Holmes
☎ 0253 790274
Ⓢⓒ From £120–£190
Sleeps 5
🐕 🖼 ♨ 💼
🔑 🔑 🔑 🔑
Commended

Our comfortable 1st floor self-catering flat on our 85-acre working farm is central for Blackpool, Morecambe; Lake District within easy reach. Panoramic views. Gas, CH, cooking facilities. Cot/highchair available. Walking, canal cruising, golf, bowling greens, horse riding, fishing, Steamtown Railway Museum, university amenities all within easy reach. Stabling and cycle hire. Visa/Access/Eurocard. Midweek/weekend bookings accepted. Open all year. Map ref: 208 170

Greenhalgh Cottage, c/o Greenhalgh, Castle Farm, Castle Lane, Garstang, Preston, Lancashire PR3 1RB

Mrs Jean Fowler
☎ 0995 602140
Ⓢⓒ From £110–£250
Sleeps 4
🐕
🔑 🔑 🔑 🔑

Cosy 17th century cottage, traditionally furnished and very well equipped. Situated down quiet country lane, yet only minutes' walk from small country town. Small paved garden with unrestricted views of Bowland Fells. Good centre for touring/walking with fishing and sports facilities locally. Gas central heating. Fuel and linen included. Leaflet on request. SAE please. Open all year. Map ref: 208 167

Keepers Cottage and the Old Stables Cottages, Brackenthwaite Farm, Yealand Redmayne, Carnforth, LA5 9TE

Susan Clarke
☎ 053 95 63276
Ⓢⓒ From £80–£300
Sleeps 4/6
🐎 🐕 📺
🔑🔑🔑 – 🔑🔑🔑🔑
Commended

Brackenthwaite is situated between Lancaster and Kendal with good access to coast, Lakes and Dales. Lovely walks near nature reserves. Access to farm and woodland. We have many interesting animals and an adventure playground. The Old Stables Cottages have been recently converted to a high standard retaining many features. Keepers Cottage has all rooms on ground level. Not suitable for wheelchairs. Laundry facilities available. Open all year. Map ref: 208 179

LET THE TELEPHONE RING!
Some farmhouses are big places. Let the telephone ring long enough to give the owner time to answer it.

19 Yorkshire Dales – Brontë country!

This beautiful region extends from picturesque Kettlewell in the north of the Dales down to Bradford in the south with the National Photographic Museum, the recently refurbished Alhambra Theatre and Mill Shops to explore. Those keen to do their exploring on foot will head for the footpaths in and around the National Park, the Pennine Way and the Dales with their lovely valleys, deep woods, clear streams and waterfalls.

For history and heritage the Brontë Parsonage at Haworth, Harwood House and Skipton with its castle and enchanting Tudor courtyard are a must, as are the semi-ruined abbeys at Bolton and Fountains (reputed to be the most beautiful and certainly the largest of the ruined abbeys in Britain). For a real touch of nostalgia take a ride on the Keighley and Worth Valley or the Yorkshire Dales Railways, or visit Five Rise Locks on the Leeds/Liverpool Canal near Bingley.

Or simply enjoy the beautiful Dales and their villages – Kettlewell, Brunsall, Lothersdale or Malham with its Cove, limestone 'pavements' and Gordale Scar, a ravine with a magnificent succession of waterfalls.

Group Contact: Anne Pearson ☎ 0756 791579

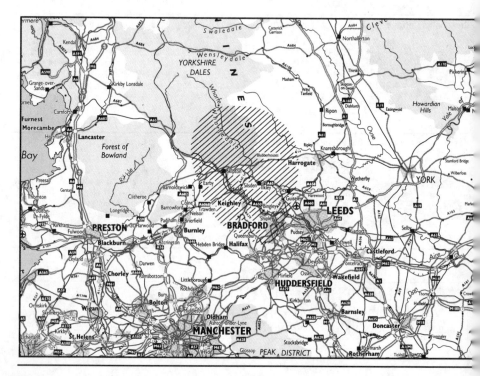

Bed and Breakfast (and evening meal)

Bowes Green Farm, Bishop Thornton, Ripley. Harrogate, North Yorkshire HG3 3JX

Mrs Bridget Sowray
☎ 0423 770114
▥ From £16
EM From £7.50
Sleeps 6
⏍ (12) ♨
⚘ Commended

17th century grade II listed secluded farmhouse with all modern comforts set in the midst of the Yorkshire Dales on a 350-acre mixed farm once farmed by the monks of nearby Fountains Abbey. Large sun garden. Best of fresh farm produce served and cooked on the Aga. Situated ½ mile out of village down a private tarmac road in open countryside. Open Easter–Oct. Map ref: 237 172

Brow Top Farm, Baldwin Lane, Clayton, Bradford, West Yorkshire BD14 6PS

Margaret Priestley
☎ 0274 882178
▥ From £14
Sleeps 4
⏍ ▥
⚘ ⚘ Commended

Visitors are most welcome to our family dairy and beef farm. The farmhouse has recently been modernised to a very high standard with central heating throughout. 1 double, 1 twin and 1 family room all with private bathroom, colour TV and tea/coffee-making facilities. Conveniently situated for visiting the Dales and Brontë Country. Plenty of good eating places in the area. Open all year (closed Christmas). Map ref: 234 163

Fold Farm, Kettlewell, Skipton, North Yorkshire BD23 5RJ

Barbara Lambert
☎ 0756 760886
▥ From £16
Sleeps 6
⏍ (10) ♨
⚘ ⚘ Commended

Fold Farm is a hill sheep farm situated in a quiet backwater of Kettlewell, within easy walking distance of all village amenities. The house dates back to the 15th century and some of its original beams are still in evidence. There are tea-making facilities in all bedrooms, one of which has a private bathroom, and there is a separate guests' sitting room. Open Easter–Oct. Map ref: 227 175

Langber Country Guest House, Ingleton, via Carnforth LA6 3DT

Mrs Mollie Bell
☎ 05242 41587
▥ From £14
EM From £5
Sleeps 14
⏍⏍⏍ ▥
⚘ ⚘

A hilltop position with panoramic views of mountains and farmland. Comfortable accommodation, en-suite facilities available. Friendly, personal service, wholesome, home-cooked meals. Ideal base for touring the Lakes, Dales and coast. Most sports catered for in vicinity. Turn off A65 at crossroads (between 'Mason's Arms and car park). 'Langber' is on left, 1 mile down side road (Tattenhorne Lane) travelling south towards Bentham. Open all year (except Christmas). Map ref: 218 176

Manor House, Rylstone, Skipton, North Yorkshire BD23 6LH

Mary Caygill
☎ 0756 730226
▥ From £20
Sleeps 4
🅰 ⏍ ⏍ (12) ♨
Applied

Visitors are most welcome to our dairy and sheep farm 6 miles from Skipton (B6265) in the village of Rylstone. Spacious country house and garden, beautiful dales setting. Twin and double rooms, both with bathroom en-suite. Tea/coffee making facilities, colour TV. Award winning pub and restaurant within a mile.. Open all year. Map ref: 228 172

Miresfield Farm, Malham, Skipton, North Yorkshire BD23 4DA

Vera Sharp
☎ **0729 830 414**
BB **From £18**
EM From £8
Sleeps 30

Miresfield Farm stands in a beautiful garden bordering the village green and stream. We welcome visitors to our listed farmhouse which has 14 bedrooms, 12 of which are en suite. There are 2 well-furnished lounges and a large conservatory for guests' use. We are becoming well-known for our excellent food, all of which is freshly prepared. Central heating throughout. Tea/coffee-making facilities in all rooms. Open all year. Map ref: 226 174

Scaife Hall Farm, Blubberhouses, Otley, West Yorkshire LS21 2PL

Christine Ryder
☎ **0943 880354**
BB **From £14.50**
Sleeps 6

Commended

Scaife Hall is a working farm set in peaceful countryside, halfway between Harrogate and Skipton (just off A59). Guests are free to roam and take part in seasonal activities, such as lambing. Cosy bedrooms, guests' private bathroom and lounge with log fires on chilly nights. Central heating. Local inns provide excellent evening meals. Open all year. Map ref: 236 168

Self-Catering

SC

Balcony Cottage, Balcony Farm, Dimples Lane, Haworth, West Yorkshire BD22 8QR

Julie Raine
☎ **0535 643627**
SC **From £110–£220**
Sleeps 4 + cot

Highly Commended

Balcony farm and cottage are set in an enviable position, being a 5 minute pleasant stroll to either the cobbled streets of Haworth village or miles of open moorland. Sleeping 4, it has large gardens, including playground and patio furniture. One double, one twin plus cot room and luxury bathroom. Open all year. Map ref: 230 165

Bottoms Farm Cottages, Bottoms Farm, Laycock, nr Keighley, West Yorkshire BD22 0QD

Mrs J. Parr
☎ **0535 607720**
SC **From £110–£250**
Sleeps 2/5

Highly Commended

Bottoms Farm is a rural 35-acre sheep farm situated on the south side of a beautiful valley with spectacular views. Howarth 4 miles, Skipton 7 miles. These luxury cottages have been recently converted to the highest standard from 200 years mistal/barn. Fully equipped. Heating and linen included. Sorry no pets. Open all year. Map ref: 230 166

Cawder Hall Cottages, c/o Cawder Hall, Cawder Lane, Skipton, North Yorkshire BD23 2QQ

Anne Pearson
☎ **0756 791579**
SC **From £120–£290**
Sleeps 2/6

Commended

Enjoy the peace and quiet of our luxury cottages, yet only be 1 mile from the medieval castle and market town of Skipton. Each cottage has been newly converted and is suitable for disabled guests. The cottages are heated and have colour TV, video, fridge and microwave. There is a garden, barbeque, payphone and laundry room. All linen, gas and electricity are included as are cots and high chairs if required. Open all year. Map ref: 228 170

Hole Farm, Dimples Lane, Haworth, Keighley, Yorkshire BD22 8QS

Mrs Janet Milner
☎ 0535 644755
Sleeps 8
🐎 ✂ ⬚ ⛄ 🍴 ♿ 🐴 ↩
🎪 🎒 ✂
⚷ ⚷ ⚷ ⚷ ⚷ **Highly Commended**

Superbly converted barn on small mixed farm, 10 minutes walk to Bronte Museum and 2 minutes from moors. Unrivalled views over Haworth. The cottage sleeps maximum 9. Two double rooms with en-suite, 2 twin and main bathroom. Central heating, dishwasher, washer, dryer, microwave, colour TV, video and stereo. There is a children's play area.
Map ref: 230 165

Lodge Farm Cottage, Providence Lane, Oakworth, Nr Keighley, West Yorkshire BD22 7QS

Glennys Wilkins
☎ 0535 642633
Ⓢ **From £120–£250**
Sleeps 5 + cot
🐎 ↩
⚷ ⚷ ⚷ **Commended**

A 17th century cottage with garden, refurbished to a very high standard, on a 13-acre small-holding. Open views of steam railway and Brontë country. Inglenook fireplace, exposed beams. Colour TV, microwave, washing machine. Animals include horses (from Shires to miniatures), sheep, cows and goats. Also hatchery and antique machinery, harness, blacksmith and textile tools. Own show dray. Open all year.
Map ref: 231 166

Westfield Farm Cottages, c/o Westfield Farm, Tim Lane, Haworth, West Yorkshire BD22 7SA

Wendy Carr
☎ 0535 644568
Ⓢ **From £100–£260**
Sleeps 2/6
🐎 ⛄ ✂ ↩ ⬚ ↩ 🎪 🎒
✂
⚷ ⚷ ⚷ – ⚷ ⚷ ⚷ ⚷
Highly Commended

Enjoy the comforts of home in one of our delightful cottages. 100-acre hill farm with suckler cows and sheep. ½ mile from Haworth. Cottages to sleep 2 to 6 people. Cottage for 2 disabled people. Beautiful south-facing aspect. Colour TV, automatic washer, microwave in each. Dogs by arrangement. Farm-trail and safe river for fishing or play. Open all year.
Map ref: 229 165

FARM HOLIDAY BUREAU

THOSE LITTLE EXTRAS

For advice on farms that can offer 'extras' such as four-poster beds, special diets, farm trails, fishing rights – even stabling and trekking arrangements if you are bringing your own horse – ring the Farm Holiday Bureau on (0203) 696909.

20 Herriot's Yorkshire Moors and Dales

Take a trip around North Yorkshire and sample for yourself the delights of this area as portrayed in James Herriot's 'All Creatures Great and Small'.

Start with the ancient city of York and wander through narrow streets to the Minster, ride upriver to the Bishop's Palace or visit the Railway Museum and Jorvik Centre. Or drive from Helmsley, over Sutton Bank – a favourite for hang-gliders – to the market town of Thirsk where James Herriot still practises. A day all the family will enjoy is a visit to the Lightwater Valley Theme Park where modern farming exhibits combine with an adventure play area. Or maybe you prefer the peace and tranquility of the romantic abbeys, stately homes, gardens and deer parks found here.

In Wensleydale, home of the famous cheese, you can fish or picnic by the waterfalls and enjoy real ale in friendly village pubs. Locally, many craftsmen display their skills, the most famous being the Mouseman of Kilburn.

Walkers can follow the Pennine Way past the Buttertubs, through panoramic Swaledale where shepherd and sheepdog work the hills, to the cobbled streets and Norman castle of Richmond, towering over the river below.

Whatever the weather, whatever your interest, you are spoilt for choice. There is something for everyone in North Yorkshire!

Group Contact: Mrs Jean Wallis ☎ 0748 823712

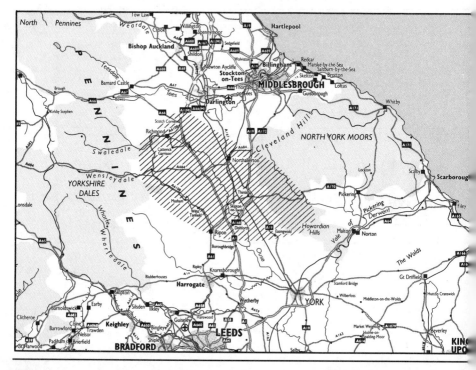

Bed and Breakfast (and evening meal)

Ainderby Myers Farm, Nr Hackforth, Bedale, North Yorkshire DL8 1PF

Mrs Valerie Anderson
☎ 0609 748668
BB From £14.50
EM From £8.50
Sleeps 6
✂ ❄ ☘ ☂
♕ Approved

Historical manor house set amidst moors and dales with origins going back to the 10th century. Terrific atmosphere. Once farmed by the monks of Jervaulx Abbey. Sheep, cattle, crops, pastures and a stream. Walk the fields and discover the wildlife. Visit castles and abbeys. Excellent base for walkers. Pony trekking and fishing by arrangement. Traditional Yorkshire breakfasts. Picnic facilities. Open all year. Map ref: 238 185

Bay Tree Farm, Aldfield, Nr Fountains Abbey, Ripon, North Yorkshire HG4 3BE

Valerie Leeming
☎ 0765 620394
BB From £14
EM From £8
Sleeps 8
♞ ☃ ☂ ☙
♕ Commended

This traditional farmhouse commands peaceful views over open fields towards Fountains Abbey – a World Heritage sight – 1 mile away. Ideal for touring Dales, Moors, York 35 minutes. Routes and advice always at hand. Light, fresh rooms 2 en-suite in barn conversion. Colour TV, tea/coffee facilities, log fire, central heating. Private parking. Home economics trained. Children welcome. Personal attention and kettle always on the boil! Open all year. Map ref: 236 181

Carr House Farm, Shallowdale, Ampleforth, York, North Yorkshire YO6 4ED

Mrs Anna Taylor
☎ 03476 526 (0347 868526–Feb 1993)
BB From £11–£15
EM From £7.50
Sleeps 6
✂ ☃ (7) ☙ ☂
♕ ♕

16th century farmhouse filled with memorabilia. Part of 400-acre family farm for 5 generations. Internationally recommended, "fresh air fiend's dream! Good food, walking, warm welcome". Romantic four-poster bedroom en-suite. Relaxing, peaceful, informal – "heartbeat country". **½ hour York**. See the things dreams are made of – make your holiday memorable – Highland cattle, north country sheep, ponds, orchards, green fields, wild flowers. Open all year (closed Christmas and New Year). Map ref: 251 182

Elmfield House, Arrathorne, Bedale, North Yorkshire DL8 1NE

Edith & Jim Lillie
☎ 0677 50558
BB From £19–£25
EM From £10
Sleeps 20
☺ ♿ ☃ ⊡ ♨
♕ ♕ ♕ Commended

Situated between Richmond and Bedale. Superb views of surrounding countryside, relaxed friendly atmosphere in luxurious country house. 9 spacious bedrooms (all en-suite) including a four-poster bed, twin and family rooms. 2 bedrooms equipped for disabled. All with colour TV (satellite channel), radio, phone, tea/coffee-making facilities, CH. Lounge and bar (residential licence), dining room, games room, solarium. Excellent home cooking. Open all year. Map ref: 234 188

Haregill Lodge, Ellingstring, Masham, Ripon, North Yorkshire HG4 4PW

Mrs Rachel Greensit
☎ 0677 60272
BB From £15–£18
EM From £8.50
Sleeps 6
♘ ☃
♕ ♕ Commended

This attractive 18th century stone farmhouse is set on a family working mixed farm. One bedroom en-suite. Large games room. Secluded garden with children's play area, in peaceful surroundings overlooking the Hambleton Hills. Good base to explore the Dales and Herriot Country. Good home cooking with supper tray for all guests. Fishing and trekking nearby. A warm welcome awaits you. Open all year (closed Christmas and New Year). Map ref: 236 181

Lamb Hill, Masham, Ripon, North Yorkshire HG4 4DJ

Mrs Rosemary Robinson
☎ 0765 689274
🄱🄱 From £13.50
EM From £9
Sleeps 6
🐾
Listed Commended

Come, enjoy a carefree holiday with good food and good service on our beef and arable farm A spacious comfortable old farmhouse with views of the Dales. Ideally situated for walking and exploring abbeys, castles and towns. Pony trekking, fishing nearby. (Masham 2 miles, A1 5 miles, York 45 minutes). Pretty bedrooms, tea/coffee making facilities. TV lounge, open fires, central heating. Garden, farm walks, ample parking. 1 en-suite, 1 guests' bathroom + 1 separate toilet and hand basin. Open Mar–Nov. Map ref: 236 181

Laskill Farm, Hawnby, Nr Helmsley, North Yorkshire YO6 5NB

Sue Smith
☎ 043 96 268
🄱🄱 From £16.50–£20
EM From £10
Sleeps 10
🐎♿🐕🐴🐈🎋🛍

Amidst beautiful North Yorkshire Moors, in heart of James Herriot Country. Attractive farmhouse with own lake/large walled garden for visitors' use. High standard of food and comfort. 2 double rooms, 1 single, 1 twin with handbasin, and 1 twin and 1 double en-suite with colour TV. Ideal centre, for surrounding places of interest and scenic beauty, or simply enjoy peace and tranquillity in idyllic surroundings. Open all year. Map ref: 252 184

Lovesome Hill Farm, Lovesome Hill, Northallerton, North Yorkshire DL6 2PB

Mrs Mary Pearson
☎ 0609 772311
🄱🄱 From £13
EM From £8
Sleeps 4
🐕🎋
🍽🍽 Approved

We welcome you to our period, 165-acre livestock and arable farm. The house offers homely accommodation with every modern convenience, yet retains its character. Guests' lounge looks onto patio and croquet lawn. All home cooking where possible, using local or home-grown produce. Twixt Dales and Moors, this makes a perfect holiday base. Open Easter–Oct. Map ref: 243 190

Mill Close Farm, Patrick Brompton, Bedale, North Yorkshire DL8 1JY

Mrs Patricia Knox
☎ 0677 50257
🄱🄱 From £14–£16
EM From £10
Sleeps 4
🐕🎋🛍
🍽🍽 Commended

Mill Close is an 18th century working farm surrounded by beautiful rolling countryside at the foothills of the Yorkshire Dales and Herriot Country. Situated 2 miles from the A1(M). Spacious rooms, furnished to high standard. Guests' private bathrooms, dining and sitting room with colour TV. A relaxing, peaceful atmosphere with large garden and open fires. Open Easter–Oct. Map ref: 238 185

Mount Pleasant Farm, Whashton, Richmond, North Yorkshire DL11 7JP

Christine Chilton
☎ 0748 822784
🄱🄱 From £14–£15
EM From £8
Sleeps 6
♿🐕🎋
🍽🍽 Approved

The tired business man, a couple touring, or the family with children can all enjoy Mount Pleasant. A working farm, 3 miles from the market town of Richmond. En-suite rooms in a converted stable, each with its own front door. Good farmhouse food. Residential licence. A real Yorkshire welcome! Open all year. Map ref: 231 188

Oxnop Hall, Low Oxnop, Gunnerside, Richmond, North Yorkshire DL11 6JJ

Annie Porter
☎ 0748 86253/86504
🄱🄱 From £18
EM From £11
Sleeps 9
🎋 (5) 🎋
🍽

Stay with us on our working hill farm with beef cattle and Swaledale sheep. Oxnop Hall is of historical interest and has recently been extended with all en-suite rooms. Ideal walking and touring. We are in the Yorkshire Dales National Park, Herriot Country, an Environmentally Sensitive Area which is renowned for its stone walls, barns and flora. Good farmhouse food. Tea/coffee-making facilities. Open all year (closed Christmas). Map ref: 231 188

Walburn Hall, Downholme, Richmond, North Yorkshire DL11 6AF

Diana Greenwood
☎ 0748 822152
BB From £18
Sleeps 5
✕ ♂ ⊞
Listed

Walburn Hall is one of the few remaining working farms with a fortified farmhouse, an enclosed cobbled courtyard and terraced garden. For guests' comfort there is a separate lounge and dining room with beamed ceilings, stone fireplaces and log fires (when required). Centrally heated. Double/twin or family rooms (en-suite) with tea/coffee-making facilities. Ideally situated between Richmond and Leyburn for exploring the Dales. Open Mar–Nov. Map ref: 231 188

Wellfield House Farm, North Otterington, Northallerton, North Yorkshire DL7 9JF

Dorothy Hill
☎ 0609 772766
BB From £14
EM From £9
Sleeps 6
🐕 ♿ 🐎 ⋏ 🔌 🏺
👑 👑

Comfortable farmhouse, (part dates back to 17th century), on sheep/arable working farm. High standard of furnishing. Large garden with patio, goldfish ponds and croquet lawn. Unspoilt views. Coarse fishing available free. Ideally situated for Herriot Country, Moors, Dales, stately homes. Centrally heated. Family, double and twin-bedded rooms with handbasins and 1 en-suite. Visitors' lounge. Home cooking and warm welcome await you. Open all year. Map ref: 244 185

Whashton Springs Farm, Richmond, North Yorkshire DL11 7JS

Fairlie Turnbull
☎ 0748 822884
BB From £19.50
EM From £11
Sleeps 18
🐎 (5) 🏺
👑 👑 👑 Highly
Commended

400-acre beef/sheep, family working farm in heart of Herriot Country. Delightful Georgian farmhouse, featured on 'Wish You Were Here', 1988 AA 'Farmhouse of the North' Award, unusual bay windows, overlooking lawns sloping to a sparkling stream. Real Yorkshire breakfast. Home cooking using local produce. All 8 bedrooms have en-suite baths/showers, TV, phone. One 4-poster bedroom. Historic Richmond 3 miles away. Open all year (closed Christmas & New Year). Map ref: 234 189

Self-Catering

Bridge Cottage, Boville Park, Osmotherley, Northallerton, North Yorkshire DL6 3PZ

Mrs Jean Lamb
☎ 0609 883 208
SC From £100–£275
Sleeps 2/4
🐕 ♿ 🐎 ✦
♪ ♪ ♪ ♪
Commended

Cosy cottage in beautiful open farmland with trout stream. Within National Park and offering complete relaxation. 1 mile Osmotherley village shops and post office. Open fires, CH, well equipped, cots and highchair. Linen provided, towels available. Yorkshire Moors, popular walks, birdwatching, wildlife. Pony trekking locally. Cottage gardens, barbecues, en-tout-cas tennis court. Bring your pets (even ponies). Fish in stream. Open all year (closed Christmas & New Year). Map ref: 246 188

Hardstyles Cottage, Park Top, Marske, Richmond, North Yorkshire DI11 7LS

Mrs Jean Wallis
☎ 0748 823712
SC From £100–£180
Sleeps 6/7
🐕 ♿ 🐎 🎋
♪ ♪ ♪ Approved

Bungalow-type cottage with spacious rooms, situated at the gateway to Swaledale. Detached property in own grounds, ½ mile from village yet within easy reach of historical venues, eating houses and beautiful Dales scenery. Ideal base for walking and touring. Pony trekking centre nearby. Open coal fire if desired, linen provided. Suitable for disabled. Open all year. Map ref: 234 188

1 St Ceadda, Keldholme, Kirkbymoorside, c/o Laskill Farm, Hawnby, Helmsley, North Yorkshire YO6 5NB

Mrs Susan Smith
☎ 04396 268
🆂🅲 From £180–£230
Sleeps 5
🏕
🔑 🔑 🔑 **Approved**

A delightful cottage with every comfort, in the peaceful hamlet of Keldholme, just off the attractive market town of Kirkbymoorside. Well appointed with central heating, colour television, washing machine etc. 2 bedrooms (1 twin bedded and 1 double bedded), dining room, lounge and fully fitted kitchen. Linen included. Central for coast, moors or nearby York. Many places of tranquil beauty with breathtaking scenery. Open all year. Map ref: 252 184

Stanhow Farm Bungalow, Great Langton, c/o Otterington Hall, Northallerton, North Yorkshire DL7 9HW

Lady Mary Furness
☎ 0609 772061/748614
🆂🅲 From £100–£275
Sleeps 6
🏕 ♿ 🐎 🎣 🏛
🔑 🔑 🔑 🔑 **Commended**

Enjoy the comforts of our peaceful detached farm bungalow with lovely views. Well appointed with heating, colour TV, microwave, automatic washer. Lounge with open fire. I double, 2 twin bedrooms. Personally maintained. Level garden, garage. Enjoy the 230-acre farm, see sheep, birds, flowers and conservation areas. Central for touring Dales and Moors and northern heritage. Good local hospitality and recreations. Open all year. Map ref: 238 187

Trips Cottage, Bay Tree Farm, Aldfield, Nr Fountains Abbey, Ripon, North Yorkshire HG4 3BE

Valerie Leeming
☎ 0765 620394
🆂🅲 From £95–£150
Sleeps 2
🏕 🐎 🏛
🔑 🔑 🔑 **Commended**

A newly-converted stable which sleeps 2, to the left of the farmhouse. Fine panoramic views over Fountains Abbey. Tasteful conversion consists of lobby, shower, toilet, fitted kitchen (microwave/electric cooker), lounge/diner (with colour TV). Double bedroom, bed linen and storage heater provided. Electricity £1 meter. Phone 100 yards. Shops at Ripon (3 miles), eating 2 miles. Private parking and gardens. Ideal for touring Dales, Moors and York. Local walks. Open all year. Map ref: 236 181

Whashton Springs Farm, Richmond, North Yorkshire DL11 7JS

Fairlie Turnbull
☎ 0748 822884
🆂🅲 From £150–£250
Sleeps 4–5
🏕 💼
🔑 🔑 🔑 🔑
Highly Commended

The Coach House offers luxury accommodation on our 400-acre working family farm near Richmond, gateway to the Dales. This warm spacious house sleeps 4–5 in double and twin bedrooms. Beamed lounge and well equipped kitchen with washer, freezer, microwave, etc. Heating and bed linen included in tariff. Good local hospitality. Open all year. Map ref: 234 189

Wren Cottage, c/o Street House Farm, Little Holtby, Northallerton, North Yorkshire DL7 9LN

Mrs Jennifer Pybus
☎ 0609 748622
🆂🅲 From £95–£215
Sleeps 4
🏕 🐕 🐥
🔑 🔑 🔑 **Approved**

This cosy cottage for four set in Kirkby Fleetham in the heart of Herriot Country, overlooks the village green where cricket is played in the summer. Nearby is a well-stocked village shop and a local pub providing both bar snacks and full restaurant meals. The cottage with its traditional oak beams and open fire in the lounge has a fully equipped kitchen. Open all year. Map ref: 238 187

Please mention **Stay on a Farm** when booking

21 Ryedale, North Yorkshire

Upper Ryedale is the western part of the North Yorkshire Moors National Park, where the efforts of man to wring a living from the hillsides has enhanced the natural beauty of the classical glacial valleys. It is a place which appeals particularly to the walker.

There are two nationally famous walks passing through the area, the Lyke Wake Walk and the Cleveland Way, but, for those who want to see the abundant wildlife, the network of unnamed footpaths, through woods and over wild moorland, will be more inviting. There is also trout fishing in the Rye.

The area also has three well known monastery ruins and several stately homes, headed by Castle Howard. York, with its magnificent selection of museums, historic Minster and its encircling walls, is an hour away by car. Literary pilgrimages can be made to Coxwold, where Lawrence Sterne preached, or to Thirsk, where James Herriot has his practice. Music lovers can take advantage of Ryedale Festival in Helmsley for the first week in August.

The seaside towns of Scarborough, Whitby and Filey are within reach. Close by are Lightwater Valley and Flamingoland, plus the slightly more sedate pleasures of a ride on the North Yorkshire Moors Steam Railway.

Group Contacts: ⒝ Brenda Johnson ☎ 043 96 278
ⓈⒸ Mrs Susan Garbutt ☎ 043 96 264

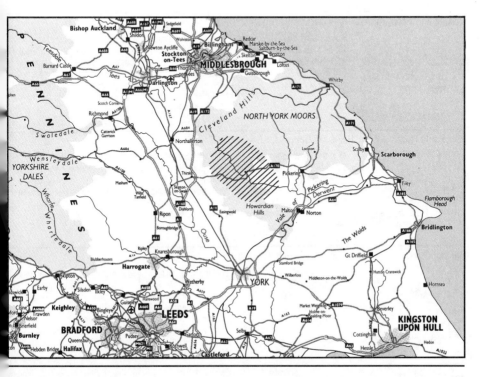

Bed and Breakfast (and evening meal)

Banniscue Farm, Hawnby, Helmsley, North Yorkshire YO6 5QL

Ann Wood
☎ 04396 271
BB From £11
EM From £6
Sleeps 5
🐕 🐎
Listed

A warm welcome awaits you in an old, comfortable, secluded farmhouse in the lovely York National Park. Ideal walking, touring, riding, plus good food. Tea/coffee facilities and washbasins in all bedrooms. Open Mar–Oct. Map ref: 252 184

Barn Close Farm, Rievaulx, Helmsley, North Yorkshire YO6 5HL

Joan Milburn
☎ 043 96 321
BB From £16
EM From £10
Sleeps 6
🐕 🐎 ♿
👑 👑 👑

Comfortable, relaxed atmosphere at Barn Close Farm set in an idyllic wooded valley of outstanding beauty close to Rievaulx Abbey and Old Byland. Farmhouse cooking recommended by the Daily Telegraph. Speciality home baked bread. Riding, walking from farmyard. Central for touring countryside, 1 hour from York or coast. 1 en-suite, 1 family with private bathroom, tea/coffee-making facilities. Open all year. Map ref: 253 184

Cringle Carr Farm, Hawnby, Helmsley, North Yorkshire YO6 5LT

Susan Garbutt
☎ 043 96 264
BB From £14
EM From £9
Sleeps 5
🐎
👑

Cringle Carr is a dairy farm situated in glorious scenery with the River Rye running along the edge of the farmland, ideal for peaceful walks and nature observation. The comfortable CH accommodation comprises of 1 twin, 1 family bedroom with washbasins, shower room for guests' exclusive use, tea/coffee-making facilities, dining/sitting room with colour TV. Home produce where possible. Open Feb–Nov. Map ref: 252 184

Easterside Farm, Hawnby, Helmsley, North Yorkshire YO6 5QT

Mrs Sarah Wood
☎ 04396 277
BB From £16
EM From £10
Sleeps 7
🐎
👑

A large 18th century Grade II listed farmhouse, nestling on Easterside Hill and enjoying panoramic views. Ideal base for walking, touring, the coast and the city of York. Enjoy good food and a warm welcome in comfortable surroundings. All rooms have en-suite facilities. Open all year (closed Christmas). Map ref: 252 184

Hill End Farm, Chop Gate, Bilsdale, North Yorkshire TS9 7JR

Brenda Johnson
☎ 043 96 278
BB From £14.50
EM From £9.50
Sleeps 5
🐕 🐎 ♘
👑 👑

Looking for a comfortable, peaceful break? Then come and join us in our 17th century farmhouse in picturesque Bilsdale. Eight miles from the market town of Helmsley. Guests are welcome to wander around our family run farm. Two comfortable bedrooms, one bathroom en-suite, one with washbasin. Tea/coffee making facilities. Comfortable lounge. Good home cooking with generous helpings. Open Mar–Nov. Map ref: 253 185

Low Northolme, Salton, York, North Yorkshire YO6 6RP

Diane Peirson
☎ 0751 32321
⌂⌂ From £16
EM From £8.50
Sleeps 5
☜
♨ ♨ Commended

Georgian farmhouse, 4 miles from Kirkbymoorside, close to North Yorkshire moors. Arable farm with breeding sheep. Bedrooms en-suite, TV lounge, snug and kitchenette with tea/coffee-making facilities. Central heating, log fires in winter. Enjoy excellent home cooking and hospitality. Private fishing, golf nearby. Ancient city of York within easy reach. Evening meal by arrangement. Open all year. Map ref: 254 183

Manor Farm, Old Byland, Helmsley, York, North Yorkshire YO6 5LG

Joyce Garbutt
☎ 043 96 247
⌂⌂ From £14
EM From £10
Sleeps 5
♂
♨

You are assured of a warm welcome at Manor Farm, situated in the picturesque village of Old Byland. Ideally placed for walking and touring the North York Moors. Guests welcome to browse around the family-run dairy and sheep farm. Two comfortable bedrooms with washbasins and tea/coffee-making facilities, guests' bathroom, lounge with log fires, central heating. Good home cooking. Open Mar–Nov.
Map ref: 253 184

Valley View Farm, Old Byland, Helmsley, York, North Yorkshire YO6 5LG

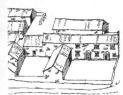

Sally Robinson
☎ 043 96 221
⌂⌂ From £22
EM From £10
Sleeps 10
♄ ♌ ⏢ Å ♣ (meeting room (8))
♨ ♨ Commended

A relaxed atmosphere and friendly family welcome await you. Situated on the edge of a small village, we still have an outstanding view. See the farm animals and enjoy the quiet. Ryedale has many attractions, please ask for brochure. Generous portions of home produced meat and delicious desserts are served at dinner. Bargain winter breaks available. Open all year (including Christmas). Map ref: 253 184

Wether-Cote Farm, Bilsdale, Helmsley, York, North Yorkshire YO6 5NF

Winnie Wood
☎ 043 96 260
⌂⌂ From £14
EM From £9.50
Sleeps 6
♄ ♌ ♂ ♔
Listed

A warm welcome awaits you at Wether-Cote Farm. A family-run working farm set amidst the beautiful North Yorkshire moors, 7 miles north of the market town of Helmsley. Outstanding views and central for hiking and touring. Highly recommended for good home cooking. Tea/coffee-making facilities, comfortable lounge and separate dining room. Open Mar–Nov. Map ref: 253 185

FARM HOLIDAY BUREAU

THE 1000+ BUREAU MEMBERS OFFER A UNIQUE LINK TO CUSTOMERS ACROSS THE UK

All Bureau members belong to a local Group. Each member can refer you to an equally high quality member within his Group . . . or across the UK: England, Northern Ireland, Scotland, Wales.

22 Yorkshire Coast & Moors

When you come to stay with us on our farms you have the opportunity to visit the seaside and enjoy the countryside inland as well.

The coast offers sandy beaches, secret caves, pretty fishing villages and 30 miles of Heritage Coast with bird sanctuaries and wildlife. The resorts of Scarborough, Whitby and Bridlington offer lively entertainment in the evenings for all tastes. There are over 1,000 miles of public footpaths and bridleways in the area and recognised walks like the White Rose Walk, the Cleveland Way and the Lyke Wake Walk. Or perhaps pony trekking through the National Park appeals to you. The North Yorkshire Moors steam railway provides superb nostalgia for railway enthusiasts and spectacular scenery for all who travel on it between Grosmout and Pickering. Those interested in historic heritage will find much to enjoy. At Pickering the parish church is famous for its unique 15th-century wall painting of St George and the Dragon. Whitby and Rievaulx Abbeys are examples of magnificent religious architecture of the area. Ancient castles can also be explored at Helmsley, Pickering and Scarborough.

Group Contact: Mrs M. Clark ☎ 0723 870249/870675

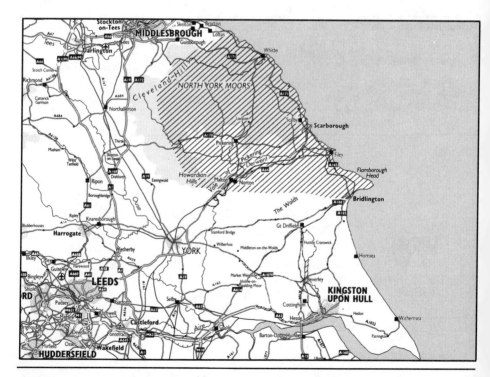

Bed and Breakfast (and evening meal)

Belmont, Ruswarp Bank, Whitby, North Yorkshire YO21 1NF

Eileen Morley
☎ 0947 60 2519
BB From £15
Applied

Adjoining our 300-acre dairy and mixed farm at Cross Butts, Eileen welcomes you to her lovely old manor house. Belmont is set in own grounds, furnished throughout in old furniture with a beautiful large four poster bed, overlooking the village of Rushwarp. Close to the River Esk for walks, fishing, boating, moors and beaches. Open Mar–Nov.
Map ref: 262 194

Cote Bank Farm, Egton Road, Aislaby, Whitby, North Yorkshire YO21 1UG

Barbara Howard
☎ 0947 85314
BB From £15
EM From £8.50
Sleeps 6
🐕 (3) 🛏 ♨ ✕
♨♨

Relax and eat well in the comfort of our 18th century farmhouse. Mullioned windows, log fires, period furniture, large garden, superb views. Good home cooking, special diets by arrangement. Local places on interest include historic Whitby 5 miles (sandy beaches), Robin Hood's Bay, Goathland (Heartbeat filmed here), steam railway, excellent walking in national park. Lambing March/April. Open all year (closed Christmas). Map ref: 258 192

Croft Farm, Fylingthorpe, Whitby, North Yorkshire YO22 4PW

Pauline Featherstone
☎ 0947 880231
BB From £14.50
Sleeps 6
✕ 🐕 (5)
♨♨ Commended

18th century farmhouse in lawned garden on small dairy farm overlooking the old smuggling village of Robin Hood's Bay. Tastefully furnished in the 'olde worlde' charm with open beams, staircase and fireplaces. Rooms with washbasins (1 en-suite) plus panoramic view of the sea, moors and countryside. Guests' lounge, bathroom. Ideal base for coastal resorts, walking and touring the beauty spots of North Yorkshire. Our speciality is a good hearty breakfast. Open Easter–mid-Oct. Map ref: 264 191

The Grange, Glaisdale, Whitby, North Yorkshire YO21 2QW

Heather Kelly
☎ 0947 87241
BB From £13
EM From £7
Sleeps 6
🛏 🐕 ☕ ♨ ♨
Listed

Beautiful stone manor house with magnificent hilltop view. It lies amidst our sheep/arable farm bordering the Esk river which boasts the best salmon fishing in the country. Home grown produce used in our generous meals. Excellent position for walks, steam railway and Whitby. Bathroom en-suite or shared between 2 rooms. Packed lunches and fishing by arrangement. Open Mar–Oct (incl.). Map ref: 256 193

The Grange, Bempton Lane, Flamborough, Bridlington, Humberside YO15 1AS

Joan Thompson
☎ 0262 850207
Fax 0262 851359
BB From £12
Sleeps 6
🛏 🐕 🧍 🏕 ♨
Listed

For a relaxing holiday come and stay in our Georgian farmhouse situated in 450 acres of stock and arable land on the outskirts of Flamborough village. Ideally situated for birdwatching at RSPB Sanctuary at Bempton, sandy beaches, cliffs and coves on our 'Heritage Coast'. Golf and sea fishing nearby. Open all year (closed Christmas & New Year).
Map ref: 261 168

Island Farm, Staintondale, Scarborough, North Yorkshire YO13 0EB

Mary Clarke
☎ 0723 870249
[BB] From £13
Sleeps 6
🐕 🚭 🐃
♨♨

Relax in our spacious and comfortable farmhouse and garden. Enjoy excellent home cooking. All bedrooms have en-suite facilities. Being close to coast and in open countryside, it is ideal for walking or visiting many places of interest. Our visitors always appreciate our large games room with toys and full size snooker table. Brochure on request. Open Easter–Nov. Map ref: 262 189

Newgate Foot, Saltersgate, Pickering, North Yorkshire YO18 7NR

Alison Johnson
☎ 0751 60215
[BB] From £13.50
EM From £7.50
Sleeps 5
🐃 🖾 🏕 🐉 🛎 🍴
♨♨ Commended

Just 1 mile off the A169, but in a world of its own in the middle of the moors with no neighbours in sight! Enjoy walking on the moors, through the forest, or trout fishing in our own lake. See the ewes and lambs and thoroughbred mares and foals. Whitby 14 miles, York 35 miles. One en-suite bedroom, 1 twin/3 bedded, 1 single. Open Jan–Nov. Map ref: 259 183

Plane Tree Cottage Farm, Staintondale, Scarborough, North Yorkshire YO13 0EY

Mrs Marjorie Edmondson
☎ 0723 870796
[BB] From £13
EM From £7
Sleeps 6
🐃 🐉
Listed

This 60-acre mixed farm is situated off the beaten track, between Scarborough and Whitby. We have rare breeds of sheep, pigs, cattle and free range hens. Also a very friendly cat called 'Danny' This small, homely cottage has character with its beams and low ceilings, and beautiful open views. Good wholesome home cooking. Open May–Oct. Map ref: 262 189

Seavy Slack, Stape, Pickering, North Yorkshire YO18 8HZ

Anne Barrett
☎ 0751 73131
[BB] From £12
EM From £9
Sleeps 6
🐃 🐉
Listed

A family dairy farm with comfortable farmhouse situated on the edge of the North Yorkshire Moors, offering good home cooking with mainly home produced food. Close to the market town of Pickering and North Yorkshire Moors Railway and only a short drive from the east coast or historic city of York. Open Easter–Oct. Map ref: 259 183

Self-Catering

Asp House Farm, Stainsacre, Nr Whitby, North Yorkshire YO22 4LR

Patricia Ward
☎ 0947 603997
[SC] From £130–£270
Sleeps 6 + cot

🏠 🏠 🏠 🏠 Approved

Asp House is a spacious, beamed cottage in an open rural position. Sleeps 6 comfortably. Beautiful views and delightful garden. Situated between the coast, moors and dales; many wonderful walks available. Storage heaters and log fire available for winter breaks. Whitby 3 miles. Open all year. Map ref: 264 192

Blackmires Farm, Danby Head, Danby, Whitby, North Yorkshire YO21 2NN

Gillian & Lewis Rhys
☎ 0287 660352
SC From £100–£250
Sleeps 2/6
Approved

Self-catering cottage for six with storage heaters and two bedroomed modern caravan. Adjacent to moors in an area of outstanding natural beauty. Central for touring North Yorks Moors National Park by road and rail. Good walking country. Fishing and seaside at Whitby. Visit Flamingo Park, Castle Howard, Rievaulx and other abbeys, folk museums, picturesque villages. Fishing in River Esk. Open Feb–Nov. Map ref: 263 192

Croft Farm Cottage, Croft Farm, Fylingthorpe, Whitby, North Yorkshire YO22 4PW

Pauline Featherstone
☎ 0947 880231
SC From £120–£240
Sleeps 4
Approved

Forget the pressures of everyday living! Come and relax in the cottage attached to our 18th century farmhouse on a working dairy farm, offering spectacular views, home comforts, peace and tranquillity. Overlooking Robin Hood's Bay, within easy reach of coastal resorts, Moors Railway and termination of well-known walks. 2 bedrooms, 1 double and 1 with built-in bunk beds. Fully equipped including linen. Colour TV and sun lounge. Open all year (closed Christmas). Map ref: 264 191

Island Farm, Staintondale, Scarborough, North Yorkshire YO13 0EB

Mary Clarke
☎ 0723 870249
SC From £100–£200
Sleeps 6
Approved

A cosy, two-bedroomed cottage with central heating, adjacent to farmhouse on hill farm between Scarborough and Whitby. Perfect base for varied holiday. It will take at least a week to see all the interesting places in the area. B&B and evening meal available. Open Easter–Nov. Map ref: 262 189

Pond Farm, Fylingdales, Whitby, North Yorkshire YO22 4QJ

FARM HOLIDAY BUREAU

Grace Cromack
☎ 0947 880441
SC From £100–£150
Sleeps 6

We offer a 6-berth caravan, situated on 400-acre mixed stock farm edging the North Yorkshire Moors and near to Robin Hood's Bay. It is situated in a walled garden with pleasing views and has all mains services including shower, toilet. TV, fridge, double and bunk-bedded rooms. Ideal for visiting historic towns, coastal resorts. Forest and moorland walks, pony trekking and clay pigeon shooting. Open Apr–Oct. Map ref: 268 185

FARM HOLIDAY BUREAU

FOLLOW THE COUNTRY CODE

Leave nothing but footprints,
Take nothing but photographs,
Kill nothing but time!

23 Vale of York and Wolds

When you come to stay with us on our farms you are within easy reach of Yorkshire's capital city with its beautiful Minster and a wealth of history; visit the Railway Muesum and Jorvik Centre. Whilst in the area see Castle Howard where Brideshead Revisited was filmed; and the abbeys of Rievaulx, Byland and Selby. The area is rich in market towns, Driffield the capital of the Wolds where reputedly King Alfred is buried, Beverley described as the most perfect of county towns with its cobbled streets and 'bars' or town gates. Beverley Minster is one of the finest churches. Explore the many country houses all rich in history and full of beautiful furniture.

Hull is a major port where sailing ships have given way to modern ferries and some of its docks to a yacht marina.

Horse racing takes place at York, Beverley, Ripon and Thirsk, all providing an exciting day out.

Group Contact: Mrs J. Brown ☎ 04395 233

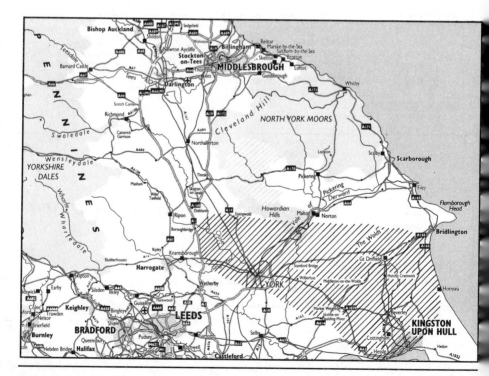

Bed and Breakfast (and evening meal)

Church Farm, Scackleton, York, North Yorkshire YO6 4NB

Mrs Cynthia Firby
☎ 0653 628403
BB From £13
EM From £9
Sleeps 6
Listed

A spacious, comfortable stone farmhouse on our sheep and arable farm in a quiet hamlet in the Howardian Hills. Designated Area of Outstanding Natural Beauty. 2 guest bathrooms, 1 en-suite. Family suite. Tea/coffee-making facilities in all bedrooms. Central heating, good home cooking, wonderful views. Ideal base for walking or visiting York, the moors and coast. Open Mar–Nov. Map ref: 252 171

Crow Tree Farm, Arram, Beverley, Humberside HU17 7NR

Mrs Margaret Hart
☎ 0964 550167
BB From £14
EM From £8
Sleeps 3
Applied

This peaceful smallholding with quiet gardens natural pond and secluded courtyards, supports various friendly animals – cows, horses, goats, chickens and offers excellent country fare. Set in an original farming hamlet with views across open meadows to Beverley Minister, while easily accessible to York and the coast. Open all year. Map ref: 268 168

High Catton Grange, High Catton, near Stamford Bridge, York, YO4 1EP

Sheila Foster
☎ 0759 71374
BB From £13.50
Sleeps 6
Listed

Stay in our lovely farmhouse in peaceful rural setting, yet only 8 miles east of historic York and convenient for many interesting locations, stately homes, coast, etc. Accommodation on our 300-acre farm offers a friendly welcome, relaxed atmosphere and attractive traditional furnishings, along with beautiful countryside and good home cooking. Open mid-Jan–early Dec. Map ref: 256 171

Kelleythorpe, Great Driffield, East Yorkshire YO25 9DW

Tiffy Hopper
☎ 0377 42297
BB From £13
EM From £10
Sleeps 6
Listed

Imagine peacocks strutting, ducks swimming and trout rising. Enjoy tea on the sun terrace overlooking a crystal clear shallow river, the friendly atmosphere of our lovely Georgian farmhouse with its mellow antique furniture, pretty chintz and new bathrooms, 1 en-suite, is sure to captivate you. Delicious country cooking. Children very welcome. Ideally placed for touring. Open all year (closed Christmas & New Year). Map ref: 266 173

Lund Farm Cottage, Lund Farm, Gateforth, Selby, North Yorkshire YO8 9LE

Chris & Helen Middleton
☎ & Fax 0757 228775
BB From £15.00
Sleeps 4
Commended

Join us for lambing-time or harvest in our cosy 18th century farmhouse, in the very centre of Yorkshire. Just half an hour from York. The ideal base from which to explore our beautiful county. Pine beams and log fires, patio, large enclosed garden and babysitting. Open all year. Map ref: 251 162

Prospect Farm, Marton-cum-Grafton, Boroughbridge, North Yorkshire YO5 9QJ

Rowena Naish
☎ 0423 322 045
BB From £15
Sleeps 4
🐴 🦮 🦮 🦮 ℀
♛

Prospect Farm has a beautiful 18th century farmhouse retaining many original features and traditional furnishings. This working farm is in a pretty village and has spectacular views over the Vale of York. Large family room with en-suite bathroom. Children welcome. Private carp lake. Easy access to York, Harrogate, Dales, Moors, Wolds and coast. Close to A1 and B6265 roads. Open all year. Map ref: 245 175

Rudstone Walk Farm, South Cave, Brough, North Humberside HU15 2AH

Mrs Pauline Greenwood
☎ 0430 422230/ Fax
0430 424552
BB From £18
EM From £12.50
Sleeps 8
🐓 🦮 ♿ ♿ 🦮 ℀
Listed Highly Commended

Stay with us in our beautiful 400-year-old farmhouse. Mentioned in the Domesday Book. Delicious home cooking, unrivalled views of Vale of York, Beverley, coast and moors. Licensed, ETB highly recommended. Free brochure available. Open all year. Map ref: 264 191

Sunley Court, Nunnington, York, North Yorkshire YO6 5XQ

Mrs Joan Brown
☎ 043 95 233
BB From £12.50
EM From £8
Sleeps 6
🐓 🦮
♛ ♛

Sunley Court is a comfortable modern farmhouse with open views in a quiet secluded area. The farm is arable with sheep and horses. All bedrooms have tea/coffee-making facilities, washbasins, electric blankets, one has shower/toilet en-suite. Good home cooking. Central for York, moors and coast. Open all year. Map ref: 252 185

Winifred Farm, Amotherby, Malton, North Yorkshire YO17 0TG

FARM HOLIDAY BUREAU

Carolyn Timm
☎ 0653 698165
BB From £12.50
EM From £10
Sleeps 4
▲ 🆑
Applied

Nestling in between the Howardian Hills and the moors and the coast in the heart of Ryedale, 25 miles from York. A traditional, comfortable farmhouse on a working farm with a large garden with private parking. Situated on the B1257 between Malton and Helmsley. Good variety of attractions in the area. Open Jan–Dec. Map ref: 258 179

Self-Catering

Lund Farm Cottage, Lund Farm, Gateforth, Selby, North Yorkshire YO8 9LE

Chris & Helen Middleton
☎ & Fax 0757 228775
SC From £135–£250
Sleeps 4
🐓 🦮 🆑 🦮 ℀
🏠🏠🏠 **Commended**

Pine beams and blackleaded fireside range are special features of the cosy cottage wing of our 18th century farmhouse just half-an-hour from York. Join us for lambing-time (December to March) or harvest. Fireside suppers on request. Also babysitting. Large enclosed garden, heating, linen and towels included. Open all year. Map ref: 251 162

Rudstone Walk Farm and Country Cottages, South Cave, Nr Beverley, Brough, Humberside HU15 2AH

Mrs Pauline Greenwood
☎ 0430 422230
Fax 0430 424 552
SC From £159–£441
Sleeps 2/6
🐕 ♿ 📺 £ 🚭 ⚒
🐾 🐾 🐾 🐾
Highly Commended

Thirteen superb cottages (7 new 1992), beautifully furnished to highest Tourist Board standards. Each has luxury spacious lounge with colour TV, modern kitchen with microwave, utility room. CH and linen included. Personal supervision. Set in 300 acres of unrivalled views on a site mentioned in the Domesday Book. Close to historic Beverley, York; ideal for moors and coast. Open all year. Map ref: 264 191

DISABLED VISITORS

members offering suitable accommodation to disabled/less able visitors. Please do check the extent of the facilities before booking.

THOSE LITTLE EXTRAS

For advice on farms that can offer 'extras' such as four-poster beds, special diets, farm trails, fishing rights – even stabling and trekking arrangements if you are bringing your own horse – ring the Farm Holiday Bureau on (0203) 696909.

THE 1000+ BUREAU MEMBERS OFFER A UNIQUE LINK TO CUSTOMERS ACROSS THE UK

All Bureau members belong to a local Group. Each member can refer you to an equally high quality member within his Group . . . or across the UK: England, Northern Ireland, Scotland, Wales.

24   Fylde and Wyre – Lancashire

Contrasting scenery beckons you to the Fylde and Wyre where the bracing coastline with its sand dunes, a National Nature Reserve at Lytham St. Annes, offers sanctuary for wild life. Travel up the coast to the hustle and bustle of Blackpool with its famous illuminations. Then on through Cleveleys finally resting at Fleetwood, an ancient fishing port, where the River Wyre meets the sea.

Travel east to Poulton-le-Fylde, an ancient market town, with its stocks and beautiful Norman church.

Inland from the coast the acres of rich farm land dotted with villages, some with weekly street markets, all have an individual character and charm of their own.

Move up to the hill country, excellent for walkers and explorers: Bleasdale Fell and Beacon Fell, adjoining the rolling hills of the Forest of Bowland, or enjoy a picnic at Brock, an area of outstanding beauty.

We have lots to offer everyone – including excellent theatres at both Preston and Blackpool.

Group Contact: Mrs Heather Smith ☎ 0253 836465

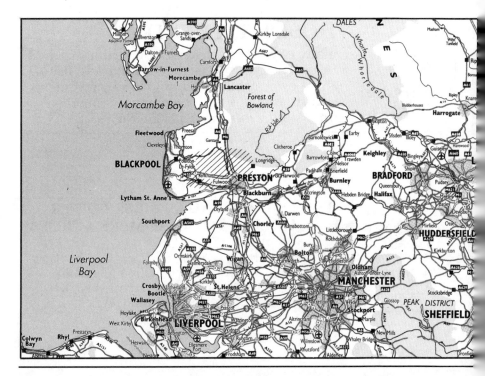

Bed and Breakfast (and evening meal)

Park Head Farm, Bilsborrow Lane, Inglewhite, Nr Preston, Lancashire PR3 2LN

Mrs Ruth Rhodes
☎ 0995 40352
BB From £12
Sleeps 6
ઝ
Listed

A 200-year-old oak-beamed farmhouse in a quiet setting on a 215-acre dairy farm making traditional farmhouse cheese. Family, double and twin bedrooms with washbasins, shaver points, colour TV, CH and tea/coffee-making facilities. Shower in bathroom. Ideal for walking/touring Forest of Bowland, Lake District, Yorkshire Dales, Blackpool. North of M6 J32. AA listed. Open all year. Map ref: 212 168

Swarbrick Hall Farm, Singleton Road, Weeton, Nr Kirkham, Lancashire PR4 3JJ

Mrs Heather Smith
☎ 0253 836465
BB From £15
Sleeps 4
ઝ ☞
👑

Relax and enjoy the peace and tranquility of rural Fylde within easy reach of the Fylde's coastal resorts. Good access to Lake District, Trough of Bowland and Yorkshire Dales. Our 200-acre working farm offers excellent accommodation in beautiful Georgian farmhouse. 1 family room with en-suite bathroom, colour TV, tea making facilities. Visitors' lounge. Open all year. Map ref: 201 167

Todderstaffe Hall Farm, off Fairfield Road, Singleton, near Blackpool, Lancashire FY6 8LF

Mrs Maureen Smith
☎ 0253 882537
BB From £15
Sleeps 4
ઝ 🐈
👑

Enjoy a friendly welcome at our 260-acre arable farm situated 4 miles from the attractions of Blackpool in a peaceful corner of the Fylde and within easy reach of Lake District. Oak beams and open fires maintain the charm of the old farmhouse but modern comforts, like central heating have been added. One twin/family room with en-suite bathroom, colour TV, and tea making facilities. Reduced terms early season. Map ref: 204 165

Self-Catering

Swarbrick Hall Farm Cottage, Singleton Road, Weeton, Nr Kirkham, Lancashire PR4 3JJ

Mrs Heather Smith
☎ 0253 836465
SC From £90–£275
Sleeps 5
ઝ ☞
🔑 🔑 🔑 🔑
Commended

Relax and enjoy the peace and tranquillity of rural Fylde, within easy reach of the Fylde's coastal resorts. Good access to Lake District, Trough of Bowland and Yorkshire Dales. Our 200-acre working farm offers excellent accommodation in cottage attached to main house. 2 twin rooms, bathroom, lounge, kitchen/diner, CH, linen, electric included. Shop and pub 1½ miles. Open all year. Map ref: 201 167

25 West Lancashire

A vast marshland until the early 18th century, West Lancashire is now one of the most fertile areas in Britain, the main industry being agriculture. In the middle of this 'garden' lies the ancient town of Ormskirk, where the market was first chartered in the 13th century. Henry VIII was responsible for the Parish Church's unusual appearance – after Burscough Prior was dissolved, a bell tower was built alongside the steeple to house the bells of the Priory.

People with an interest in history will find a visit to 15th-century Rufford Old Hall and its collection of Tudor furniture fascinating, and railway enthusiasts will enjoy Steamport Museum at Southport with its collection of railway memorabilia. Nearby, the Cedar Farm Gallery at Mawdsley has farm animals and a children's play area which enables mum and dad to enjoy the Craft Centre.

Bird lovers should head for the Wildfowl Trust Centre at Martin Mere where rare and exotic species come and go in an unspoilt area of natural wetland.

Both the Leeds and Liverpool Canal and the River Douglas are pleasant and intriguing to traverse whether you are walking along the banks or boating on the water.

A short distance away, across the boundary into Merseyside, Southport has excellent shops and miles of sandy beach, and at Knowsley Safari Park you can watch a wide variety of animals. The Pilkington Glass Museum at St Helens offers a chance to see how glass is made. Whatever your pleasure, you can find it in West Lancashire.

Group Contact: Mrs Wendy Core ☎ 0704 880337

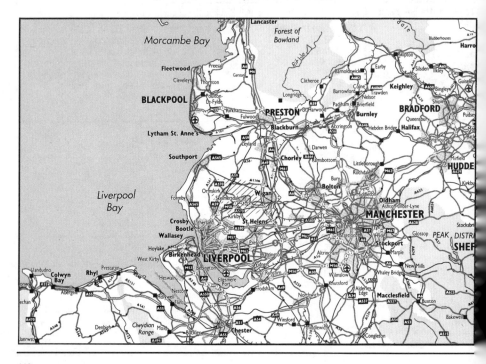

Bed and Breakfast
(and evening meal)

Brandreth Barn, Brandreth Farm, Tarlscough Lane, Burscough, Nr Ormskirk, Lancashire L40 0RJ

Mrs M Wilson
☎ 0704 893510
▦ From £18
EM From £4.50
Sleeps 14
☼ ઼ ▪
♨ ♨ ♨ Approved

Situated alongside the wildfowl trust Martin Mere, an 18th century brick-built barn conversion dated 1774. 5 minutes from A59, 15 mins from M6. All rooms fully centrally heated, with tea/coffee-making facilities. All rooms en-suite plus colour TV. Licensed restaurant. Also disabled facilities. Arable farm. Open all year. Map ref: 206 155

Sandy Brook Farm, Wyke Cop Road, Scarisbrick, Southport, Lancashire PR8 5LR

Mrs W E Core
☎ 0704 880337
▦ From £14
Sleeps 15
☼ ħ ᴪ ઼
♨ ♨

This small, comfortable arable farm is situated in the rural area of Scarisbrick, midway between the seaside town of Southport and the ancient town of Ormskirk. The A570 is only ½ mile away. The converted farm buildings are attractively furnished, and all bedrooms have en-suite facilities, colour TV and tea/coffee-making facilities. Disabled facilities available. Open all year. Map ref: 205 156

Self-Catering

Martin Lane Farmhouse Cottages, Martin Lane, Burscough, Lancs L40 8JH

Elaine Stubbs
☎ and fax 0704 893527
▧ From £175–£300
☼ ▪ ᴪ
ↄↄↄↄ Commended

Relax and enjoy yourself, in the heart of the peaceful West Lancashire countryside. Nestling among acres of green fields, are 'The Granary' and 'The Shippon'. Both are comfortably furnished and fully equipped to a very high standard. An excellent base for visiting the abundance of north west beauty spots. Open all year. Map ref: 207 155

NO ANSWER?
Farmers are mostly out and about during the day.
Try to telephone before 9.30am or after 4pm.

26 Lancashire Pennines

The Forest of Bowland, the largest area of unspoilt countryside in Lancashire, 1,827ft high Pendle Hill and the Pennines afford the visitor to the area a chance to appreciate Lancashire at its most beautiful. Complementing such countryside are a number of towns and villages, all with their own individual character: Clitheroe with its castle and museum; Whalley with its Cistercian Abbey (founded in 1296) and Georgian and Tudor houses; the old market towns of Colne, Skipton and Ribchester, with its Roman Museum; Barley, at the foot of Pendle Hill, with its connections with the Witch Trials of 1612; Slaidburn, the gateway to the Forest of Bowland, once a Royal hunting ground.

There is something here to suit all tastes. For example, places of historic interest, such as Browsholme Hall, the home of the Parker family, which houses a display of 13th-century domestic articles, can be contrasted with the new Preston Guild Hall with facilities for many social, cultural and educational activities. If you prefer a quiet, more sedate pace, you can enjoy one of the several country parks and picnic areas, such as Beacon Fell, Spring Wood, Barley or Wycoller. A holiday in the farms of the Lancashire Pennines will also leave you within easy reach of the Yorkshire Dales, the Lake District, Haworth and Brontë Country.

Group Contact: Mrs Carole Mitson ☎ 0282 865301

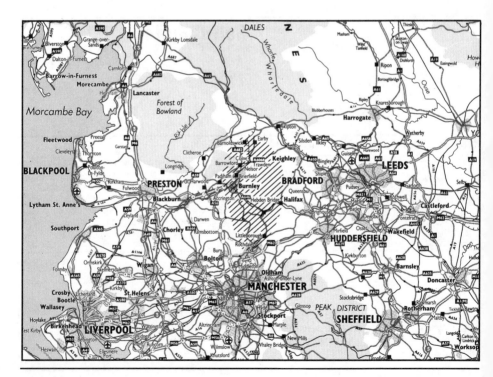

Bed and Breakfast (and evening meal)

Eaves Barn Farm, Hapton, Burnley, Lancashire BB12 7LP

Mrs M Butler
☎ 0282 771591/770478
BB From £18.50
EM From £8
Sleeps 5
Listed

Eaves Barn Farm is a mixed working farm. The accommodation comprises a spacious cottage attached to the main house, recently re-furbished to a high standard offering luxury facilities. Quality home cooking is provided using fresh local produce, home-made preserves a speciality. The farm is situated within close proximity of the local motorway network affording easy access to all Lancashire's tourist attractions and places of historic interest. Open all year. Map ref: 221 164

Higher Wanless Farm, Red Lane, Colne, Lancashire BB8 7JP

Carole Mitson
☎ 0282 865301
BB From £16
EM From £8.50
Sleeps 4
🐕 (3) 🛁 ⚔
♨ ♨

Ideally situated for visiting 'Pendle Witch' country, Haworth or Yorkshire Dales – the farm nestles peacefully alongside the Leeds/Liverpool Canal. Shire horses and sheep are reared on the farm, where the warmest of welcomes awaits you. Spacious and luxurious bedrooms (1 en-suite) offer every comfort for our guests. Several country inns nearby offering wide range of meal facilities. AA selected establishment. Open Jan–Nov. Map ref: 225 165

Lower White Lee, Fence, Burnley, Lancashire BB12 9ER

Helen Boothman
☎ 0282 613563
BB From £15
EM From £7.50
Sleeps 4
🐎 🐕 (2) ✿
♨ ♨

A 200-acre dairy farm, offering accommodation in beautifully furnished 18th century farmhouse. 2 bedrooms, each with tea/coffee-making facilities, central heating. Lounge and separate dining room. 25 mins from M6. Ideally situated for Brontë Country, Yorkshire Dales and the Lakes. Open Jan–end Nov. Map ref: 224 165

Parson Lee Farm, Wycoller, Colne, Lancashire BB8 8SU

Patricia Hodgson
☎ 0282 864747
BB From £11–£15
EM From £5
Sleeps 6
🐎 🐕 🐾 🛁
♨

There's a warm welcome at our 110-acre sheep farm situated on the edge of beautiful Wycoller Country Park. The 250-year old farmhouse, which has exposed beams and mullion windows, is peacefully located and perfect for walking, being on the Brontë, Pendle and Pennine Ways, or for visiting places of interest in Lancashire or Yorkshire. Pendle Way walking breaks and Flower Basket weekends. Both en-suite bedrooms, furnished in country style, have tea/coffee-making facilities. Open all year. Map ref: 225 167

Pasture Bottom Farm, Bacup, Lancashire OL13 9UZ

Ann Isherwood
☎ 0706 873790
BB From £13
EM From £6
Sleeps 4
🐕 🐎 ✂
♨ ♨ Approved

60-acre beef farm offering farmhouse bed and breakfast. Ideally situated for walking Rossendale and Lancashire Moors. Local attractions include a textile museum, skiing at Rossendale and hang gliding at Whitworth. Open all year. Map ref: 223 159

Self-Catering

Meadowtop Farm Cottage, Meadowtop Farm, Green Haworth, Accrington, Lancashire BB5 3SL

Miss Ruth Dawson
☎ 0254 232879
📺 From £80–150
Sleeps 4 (+ cot)
🐕 🐄
🐑 🐑 🐑 🐑 **Commended**

Cottage attached to farmhouse on 38 acres amid West Pennine moors. Mixed farm with goats, sheep, horses, free range poultry, golfing, riding, walking or touring. Ribble Valley, Yorkshire Dales, Lake District are within easy reach. Large kitchen diner, lounge, bathroom, 2 bedrooms (1 double and 1 adult bunk beds), cot, highchair, payphone, disabled facilities. Full central heating, electricity, colour TV, towels and linen are included. Open all year. Map ref: 221 162

FINDING YOUR ACCOMMODATION

FARM HOLIDAY BUREAU

The Group contacts at the beginning of each section can always help you find a vacancy in your chosen area.

FARM HOLIDAY BUREAU

GOOD FOOD

Nearly all Bureau members now hold a certificate in Essential Food Hygiene.

A warm and friendly welcome awaits visitors to this beautiful and dramatic countryside, still remarkably untouched by tourism. Holiday-makers will find unusual and interesting places to visit close by, with Blackpool, York and the Peak District less than an hour away. The Lake District and the North Yorkshire Moors are an easy two hours, whilst businessmen are well placed for work in Manchester, Liverpool, Leeds and Bradford and close to Manchester Airport and Intercity rail.

Walkers on the Pennine Way will experience stark moorland scenery blending with attractive valley towns like Delph, Uppermill, Marsden and Hebden Bridge and there are equally interesting routes over Blackstone Edge with the Roman Road, the Rossendale Way, the Calderdale Way and the Colne Valley Circular. There are canal trips at Uppermill, Sowerby Bridge and Littleborough, and water sports at Hollingworth Lake and Scammanden Dam, where flocks of wild fowl can be seen. The South Pennine textile heritage is magnificently illustrated in the Colne Valley Museum, Golcar, the Helmshore Museum at Haslingden, and the Saddleworth Museum at Uppermill. Craft centres and mill shops abound and traditional handweaving, clog and slipper making and dyeing and printing can be studied here. The National Museum of Film, Photography and Television at Bradford attracts visitors from all over the world, as does Castlefield, G-Mex and Granada Studios Tour in Manchester, not to mention the Piece Hall in Halifax originally a cloth market and now restored to house craft centres, markets, restaurants and the unique Heavy Horse museum. The Albert Dock and Wigan Pier are both within an hour's distance and the newly restored railway from Bury to Rawtenstall, where there is a fine artificial ski-slope and a trip on the Worth Valley Railway, are an unforgettable experience.

Group Contact: Mrs Jane Neave ☎ 0706 41116/7

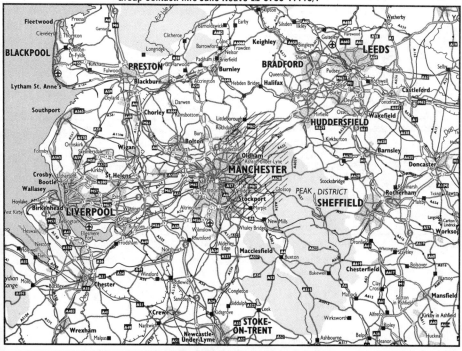

Bed and Breakfast (and evening meal)

Boothstead Farm, Rochdale Road, Denshaw, Oldham, Greater Manchester OL3 5UE

Mrs Norma Hall
☎ 0457 878622
From £17
Sleeps 4
Listed

An 18th century Pennine hill farm ideally situated within 3½ miles of M62 Junctions 21 and 22 (A640). Cosy lounge with TV, open fire and central heating throughout. Good walking country and touring base for neighbouring counties and beauty spots. Close to Saddleworth leisure amenities. Open 2 Jan–22 Dec. Map ref: 225 154

Globe Farm, Huddersfield Road, Delph, Nr Oldham, Greater Manchester OL3 5LU

Jean Mayall
☎ 0457 873040
From £16
EM From £6
Sleeps 10

Overlooking the picturesque valleys of Saddleworth but within easy reach of M62 junction 22, Manchester Airport, Yorkshire Dales and Peak District. Only ¼ mile from Pennine Way. Evening meal can be provided if required. Colour TV, CH, drying room, tea/coffee-making facilities. Good home cooking and real northern hospitality. Open all year (closed Christmas & New Year). Map ref: 227 155

Higher Quick Farm, Lydgate, Oldham, Greater Manchester OL4 4JJ

Annis Heathcote
☎ 0457 872424
From £15
EM From £5
Sleeps 4
Listed Highly Commended

Higher Quick Farm is a grade II listed farmhouse on a 40 acre beef farm, with magnificent views from all rooms. Warm and comfortable house, colour TV and tea-making facilities in each bedroom (1 twin, 1 double), visitors' own bathroom/toilet. Ideal area for walking, easy distance M62, 10 miles Manchester Airport, close to Uppermill with a craft centre, museum, golf, canal boat, swimming pool. Open all year (closed Christmas). Map ref: 227 153

Leaches Farm, Ashworth Valley, Rochdale, Lancashire OL11 5UN

Mrs Jane Neave
☎ 0706 41116/7 or 228520
From £18
Sleeps 5
Listed

1674 hill farm in 'The Forgotten Valley'. Magnificent unrestricted views of Yorkshire, Lancashire, Cheshire, Derbyshire hills, on a clear day to the Welsh mountains. Panoramic 'twinkling lights' of Greater Manchester at night. 18 inch stone walls, oak beams, log fires, central heating. Unique 'Rural Wildlife' in the heart of industrial East Lancashire. 10 mins M62 (J19) and M66, Edenfield, 30 mins Manchester Airport. Open 2 Jan–22 Dec. Map ref: 224 156

Needhams Farm, Uplands Road, Werneth Low, Gee Cross, near Hyde, Cheshire SK14 3AQ

Mrs Charlotte Walsh
☎ 061 368 4610
Fax 061 367 9106
From £18
EM From £7
Sleeps 12
Commended

Farmhouse accommodation dating back to the 16th century, offering 4 en-suite rooms. Evening meals available each evening. Residential licence. Surrounded by lovely views. Ideal for Manchester Airport and city centre. Courtesy service from airport and Piccadilly station for a small charge. Six bedrooms in all. Open all year. Map ref: 226 148

Shire Cottage, Benches Lane, Chisworth, Hyde, Cheshire SK14 6RY

Monica Sidebottom
☎ 0457 866536
or 061-427 2377
BB From £15–£18
Sleeps 6
🛏 🐾 ⚹ ⚹
♨ ♨ Commended

Real home from home accommodation in peaceful location. Magnificent views overlooking Etheroe Country Park. Convenient for Manchester Airport, city centre,Peak District, stately homes and numerous places of interest. Ground floor bedrooms and bathroom. All rooms have vanity units/shaver points/tea-making facilities/TV. Family room has own shower and toilet. Bathroom has shower and bidet. Early breakfast for businessmen and travellers. Open all year. Map ref: 228 147

White Cross Farm, Emley, Nr Huddersfield, West Yorkshire HD8 9QY

Marie Gill
☎ 0924 848339
BB From £14
Sleeps 5
🛏 🐾 ⚹
Listed Approved

Mixed working farm with listed farmhouse. Some buildings date from 12th century when monks from Byland Abbey lived here and dug for iron ore and kept sheep. Set in rolling Pennine countryside. Tea/coffee-making facilities, TV, central heating in all bedrooms. Close to Yorkshire Mining Museum, Yorkshire Sculpture Park and Holmfirth (Last of Summer Wine country). 3 miles from M1 (jct. 38/39). Open all year (closed Christmas). Map ref: 237 157

Self-Catering

Boardmans, Hawkshaw Lane, Bury, Lancashire BL8 4LD

Janice Barnes
☎ 0204 88 2844
SC From £110–£240
Sleeps 7
🐾 🐾 ⚹
Applied

17th century cottages with four poster beds, mullion windows, oak beams, inglenook style fireplaces, open fires and central heating, landscaped gardens. Situated in outstanding walking country yet near bustling market towns, mill shops and antique shops. Secluded yet convenient for the motorway network. All linen included. Shorter/longer lets by arrangement. Map ref: 220 156

Hollingworth Hall Farm Holiday Cottages, Hobson Moor Road, Mottram, via Hyde, Cheshire SK14 6SG

Don Parker
☎ 0457 766188
SC From £110
Sleeps 3/10
🐾 ⚹
♪ Commended

Grade II listed buildings renovated and converted to provide superb self-catering accommodation in 4 cottages and 2 flats, plus bunkers barn and hikers barn which have showers and laundry faciliites. Ideally situated at the edge of the Peak National Park with splendid walking and the Pennine Way approximately 3 miles away. Open all year. Map ref: 227 149

Lake View, Ernocroft Farm, Marple Bridge, Stockport, Cheshire SK6 5NT

Monica Sidebottom
☎ 0457 866536
SC From £150–£250
Sleeps 6
🐾 🐾 ⚹
♪ ♪ ♪ Commended

A new, self-catering farm bunglaow, 2 miles Marple Bridge, 4 miles Glossop. Overlooking Etherow Country Park. Ideal base for exploring Peak District, Marple locks and waterways, country parks and stately homes. Peaceful location. Accommodates 6 with all mod cons. TV. Cot available. Open all year. Map ref: 228 147

Roundhill Farm, Long Lane, Dobcross, Oldham, Lancashire OL3 5QH

Mrs R Lancashire
☎ **0457 875044**
🆂🅲 **From £150–£200**
Sleeps 6
🐕 🅔 🛖 ⚓
🔑 🔑 🔑 **Approved**

A welcome break in a comfortable, homely and beautifully-located 19th century stone-mullioned cottage on a working dairy farm. Panoramic views of Saddleworth villages and peaceful surroundings. Ideal location for walking, riding, Pennine Way, Yorkshire Dales and Peak District. Many local museums, craft centres and excellent eating places. Cottage fully modernised to accommodate 4–6, with central heating, log fire and bedding. Open all year. Map ref: 227 154

PRICES

Prices include VAT and service charge (if any) and are:
B&B per person per night
EM per person
SC per unit per week
Tents and caravans per pitch per night

FARM HOLIDAY BUREAU

FARM HOLIDAY BUREAU

CONFIRM BOOKINGS

Disappointments can arise by misunderstandings over the telephone. Please write to confirm your booking.

FARM HOLIDAY BUREAU

BUREAU ACCOMMODATION IS RELIABLE

This Guide lists **Farm Holiday Bureau** members only. They are all inspected by the National Tourist Board for standards (see introduction pages) and by fellow members to maintain a high quality.

28 Cheshire

Cheshire is one of England's undiscovered counties. Renowned for lovely black and white architecture and its superb cheese, it is a county of contrasts. From the majesty of the Peak District across the Cheshire Plain to the Dee estuary, from North Wales to Manchester, from the Shropshire Hills to Liverpool, Cheshire has something for everyone. The county has a rich history, well-documented for visitors, with Roman remains in Chester, Elizabethan towns like Nantwich, fine castles and country mansions and museums about the industrial revolution such as Styal Museum at Northwich or Paradise Silk Mill at Macclesfield.

Cheshire offers many peaceful country pursuits: there are canals, wonderful walking (from the Sandstone Trail to shorter farm walks), cycling and fishing. The county has many charming villages and towns, fine old churches, numerous antique shops. There are beautiful gardens in Cheshire – country house, botanical and municipal – plus two of Europe's largest garden centres, Bridgemere Garden World and Stapley Water Gardens.

Chester, the county town, is one of Britain's top tourist destinations. Situated on the River Dee with a splendid cathedral and unique Rows, it offers sophisticated shopping facilities as well as a fine heritage.

Group Contact: Mrs Veronica Worth ☎ 0260 224419

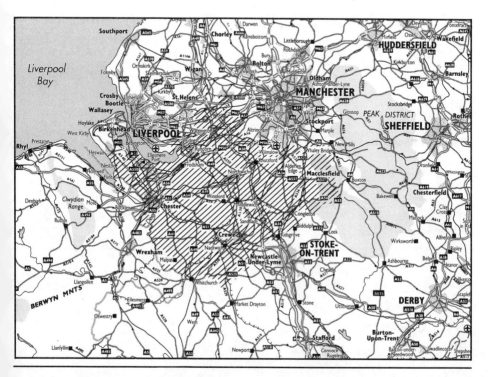

Bed and Breakfast (and evening meal)

Adderley Green Farm, Heighley Castle Lane, Betley, Nr Crewe, Cheshire CW3 9BA

Mrs Sheila Berrisford
☎ 0270 820203
BB From £14
Sleeps 6

Relax in our lovely Georgian farmhouse on a 250-acre dairy farm. Set in large garden along a pretty country lane near an old ruined castle. Fully centrally heated with colour TV, washbasins and tea trays in all bedrooms. En-suite available. Beautifully decorated in the Laura Ashley style. Ideally situated for Stapeley Water Gardens, Alton Towers and Chester, 10 mins M6 J16. Fishing available. Open all year. Map ref: 218 132

Beechwood House, 206 Wallerscote Road, Weaverham, Northwich, Cheshire CW8 3LZ

Janet Kuypers
☎ 0606 852123
BB From £12.50
EM From £6.50
Sleeps 4
Listed

Warm and comfortable 1830s farmhouse, on 19 acre stock farm in peaceful surroundings. One twin, 2 single bedrooms. Home cooking, adaptable mealtimes. Guests' dining room/lounge with tea/coffee-making facilities and colour TV. Within easy reach of M6 J19 or J20A, M56 J10; good half-way stop when travelling long distances. Good local sports facilities. Ideal weekly business accommodation. Open Jan–Nov. Map ref: 215 141

Bell Farm, 7 Bluebell Lane, Tytherington, Macclesfield, Cheshire SK10 2JL

Joan Worth
☎ 0625 423551
BB From £13
Sleeps 5
Listed

Comfortable farmhouse in a quiet lane of A538, 1 mile from Macclesfield town centre, and within easy reach of several stately homes. Close to the Peak National Park. Separate dining room and TV lounge. One single room (en-suite) one twin, and one double with washbasins. Full central heating. Open all year (closed Christmas). Map ref: 225 143

The Golden Cross Farm, Siddington, Nr Macclesfield, Cheshire SK11 9JP

Hazel Rush
☎ 0260 224358
BB From £12
Sleeps 6

Small organic dairy farm, 100 yards from the A34 on the B5392 in picturesque surroundings. Central for Macclesfield, Congleton, Holmes Chapel and Alderley Edge. Places of local interest include Capesthorne Hall, Gawsworth Hall, Tatton Hall, Styal Mill and Nether Alderley Mill. 2 double rooms, 2 single rooms, all with washbasins and tea/coffee-making facilities. Central heating, guests' lounge, colour TV. Open all year (closed Christmas & New Year). Map ref: 225 143

Goose Green Farm, Oak Road, Mottram St Andrew, Nr Macclesfield, Cheshire SK10 4RA

Dyllis Hatch
☎ 0625 828814
BB From £16
Sleeps 6
(6) Commended

Welcome to our beef/arable farm set in beautiful countryside with panoramic views. Just off A538 between Wilmslow and Prestbury, in easy reach of M6, M56 and Manchester Airport. Own fishing, horse riding nearby. Comfortable, homely with log fire in guests' lounge. Separate dining room. Pay phone. Double en-suite, twin and single rooms, all with washbasin, TV, CH and tea/coffee-making facilities. Open all year (closed Christmas). Map ref: 225 142

Laburnam House Farm, Hearns Lane, Faddiley, Nantwich, Cheshire CW5 8JL

Eddie & Sheila Metcalfe
☎ 0270 74 378
BB From £20
Sleeps 2
🐕 (2) 🐂 ✂ 🛋 🎿 🎯
👑 👑

Perfect for short breaks or mini holidays. Superbly appointed suite of rooms available for bed and breakfast. Spacious, warm, very comfortable, many extras. Double bedroom, bathroom, sitting room and south east facing fully equipped balcony. Our personal attention to detail guaranteed. Extra beds by arrangement. Brochure and discounts available. Map ref: 214 132

Lea Farm, Wrinehill Road, Wybunbury, Nantwich, Cheshire CW5 7NS

Allen & Jean Callwood
☎ 0270 841429
BB From £12.50
EM From £7
Sleeps 6
🐂 🐎 🎿 🛄
👑 👑

A charming farmhouse set in landscaped gardens where peacocks roam on a 150-acre dairy farm. Spacious, attractive bedrooms with washbasins, TV and tea/coffee-making facilities. 1 double en-suite, 1 family and 1 twin room. Luxurious lounge with open log fire, with dining room overlooking garden. Snooker, pool table, fishing available. Near to Stapeley Water Gardens and Bridgemere Garden World. M6 J16, Chester and Alton Towers. Open all year (closed Christmas & New Year). Map ref: 217 134

Little Heath Farm, Audlem, Nantwich, Cheshire CW3 0HE

Hilary Bennion
☎ 0270 811324
BB From £12
EM From £7
Sleeps 6
🐕
👑 👑 **Commended**

Relax and enjoy our warm hospitality in comfortable beamed farmhouse on the outskirts of lovely canalside village. A high standard of accommodation. Spacious bedrooms with H&C, tea-making facilities, one en-suite. TV lounge and dining room. Try our good home cooking. Near Bridgemere and Stapeley Water Gardens, Nantwich, Chester and Stoke (Wedgwood) on the A529. Our aim is to make your stay enjoyable. Open all year (closed Christmas). Map ref: 216 129

Lower Harebarrow Farm, Over Alderley, Macclesfield, Cheshire SK10 4SQ

Mrs Beryl Leggott
☎ 0625 829882
BB From £12
Sleeps 5
🐎 🐂
👑

Comfortable farmhouse within easy reach of many Cheshire beauty spots, stately homes and the Derbyshire hills. Situated on the B5087 midway between Alderley Edge and Macclesfield. Near M6, M56 and Manchester Airport. One twin and one single bedroom, both with HC and 1 double. Open all year. Map ref: 225 142

Newton Hall, Tattenhall, Chester, Cheshire CH3 9AY

Mrs Anne Arden
☎ 0829 70153
BB From £15
Sleeps 4
🐕 🐂 🐾 🎿 🛄
👑 👑

Part 17th century oak-beamed farmhouse set in large well kept grounds, with fine views of historic Beeston and Peckforton Castles and close to the Sandstone Trial. Six miles south of Chester off A41 and ideal for Welsh Hills. Rooms are en-suite or have adjacent bathroom. Fully centrally heated. Open all year. Map ref: 210 134

Oldhams Hollow Farm, Manchester Road, Tytherington, Macclesfield, Cheshire SK10 2JW

Brenda Buxton
☎ 0625 424128
BB From £15
EM From £8.75
Sleeps 6
🐂 🐕
Listed Commended

A 16th century listed farmhouse on a working farm, tastefully restored yet retaining its great character with oak beams throughout. 3 double bedrooms are comfortably furnished with CH, H/C, electric blankets, colour TVs, tea/coffee-making facilities. Large lounge and separate dining room. Nestling in the foothills of the Pennines 1 miles from the market town of Macclesfield, we are ideally located for visiting the many attractions of Cheshire. Evening meal by arrangement. Map ref: 225 143

Poole Bank Farm, Poole, Nantwich, Cheshire CW5 6AL

Caroline Hocknell
☎ 0270 625169
🅱️ From £12.50
Sleeps 6
🐎 🛏️
🏵️ 🏵️ **Commended**

A charming 17th century timbered farmhouse on 260-acre dairy farm set in quiet countryside 2 miles from the historic town of Nantwich. Ideal base for discovering the beautiful Cheshire countryside. Central for Chester and the Potteries. Comfortable and attractive rooms, all with period furnishings. TV and tea/coffee making facilities. A warm welcome and an excellent breakfast are assured. Open all year.
  Map ref: 216 133

Sandhole Farm, Hulme Walfield, Congleton, Cheshire CW12 2JH

Veronica Worth
☎ 0260 224419
🅱️ From £23
Sleeps 24
🍴 🐎 🐕 🍵 🛁
🏵️ 🏵️ **Commended**

The comfortable traditional farmhouse and delightful converted stable block are situated 2 miles north of Congleton on A34, 15 mins from M6 and 30 mins from Manchester airport. Most of our rooms have modern en-suite facilities and all have the usual extras, including hairdryers, remote control teletext TV plus trouser press and payphone. Large comfortable lounge, separate newly built conservatory/dining room. Open all year. Map ref: 224 137

Sandpit Farm, Messuage Lane, Marton, Macclesfield, Cheshire SK11 9HS

Irene Kennerley
☎ 0260 224254
🅱️ From £13
Sleeps 6
🐕 🍴 🐎 (2)
🏵️ 🏵️

A friendly welcome to our 100-acre arable farm in peaceful surroundings. Well maintained farmhouse with H/C in single/twin room. En-suite shower room in double and twin rooms. All bedrooms have tea/coffee and TV. Heated throughout. Separate dining room and TV lounge. Excellent touring centre for Peak District, Chester and Potteries. Manchester airport 14 miles. National Trust properties, stately homes and Jodrell Bank Science Centre nearby. Open all year. Map ref: 226 141

Snape Farm, Weston, Nr Crewe, Cheshire CW2 5NB

Mrs Jean Williamson
☎ 0270 820208
🅱️ From £12.50
EM From £6
Sleeps 4
🐎 🐕
🏵️ 🏵️

Enjoy a warm welcome to our centrally heated farmhouse on a 150-acre beef/arable farm set in rolling countryside. 3 miles from Crewe. A good centre for visiting Nantwich, Chester or the Potteries. Guests' lounge and snooker room. 1 twin (en-suite) and 1 double room, each with colour TV and tea/coffee-making facilities. 4 miles from M6 (jct. 16). Open all year. Map ref: 218 134

Stoke Grange Farm, Chester Road, Nantwich, Cheshire CW5 6BT

Georgina West
☎ 0270 625525
🅱️ From £15
Sleeps 6
🐕 🍴 🐎
🏵️ 🏵️

An attractive farmhouse dating from 1838 on a working dairy farm, with ponies, chickens, geese and lambs. Spacious en-suite bedrooms with colour TV and hot drink facilities. Comfortable guest lounge with TV, solarium, games and reading room. Guests can relax on the verandah and watch the canal boats passing the farmhouse. Vegetarians are catered for. Cheshire Tourism Development Award winner. Open all year. Map ref: 216 133

FARM HOLIDAY BUREAU

Please mention **Stay on a Farm** when booking

Self-Catering

Stoke Grange Mews, Stoke Grange Farm, Chester Road, Nantwich, Cheshire CW5 6BT

Georgina West
☎ 0270 625525
SC From £150–£300
Sleeps 2–6 + cot
♂
Applied

Holiday homes created from a fine old barn near the owner's canalside farmhouse and traditional dairy farm in lush heritage rich countryside some 15 miles south of the Roman town of Chester. Each has exposed beams, pine furniture, and offers fully equipped accommodation with all mod cons. Small rear patio with chairs, large shared garden with chairs and canal access. Children's play area and farm pets corner. Barbeque area. . Cheshire Tourism Development Award winner. Open all year. Map ref: 216 133

DISABLED VISITORS

members offering suitable accommodation to disabled/less able visitors. Please do check the extent of the facilities before booking.

FINDING YOUR ACCOMMODATION

The Group contacts at the beginning of each section can always help you find a vacancy in your chosen area.

29   Staffordshire's Vale of Trent

Situated in the heart of England, between the famous 'Potteries' and Peak District National Park in the north and Birmingham in the south, Staffordshire's Vale of Trent is a delightful area which, despite its easy accessibility, has remained largely unspoilt by development and is rich in local traditions.

At its heart the ancient hunting forests of Needwood and Cannock Chase dominate. Only remnants of Needwood have survived but Cannock Chase is today a lovely area of heath and forest providing the visitor with a multitude of outdoor pursuits.

In contrast to the peace and tranquillity of Cannock Chase there is fun for all the family at superb leisure parks. Drayton Manor Park and Zoo has an open plan zoo, lakes and amusement park and the award winning Alton Towers – Britain's premier Leisure Park – combines spectacular rides with magnificent gardens.

There is Stafford, the county town with its impressive timber-framed Ancient High House; Tamworth, once the capital of the ancient kingdom of Mercia, with its Norman castle; Burton-upon-Trent, home of the brewery industry; and the Vale's pride, Lichfield, a delightful cathedral city, birthplace of Dr Johnson and host to international music and folk festivals. Whether you explore the Vale by car, taking a leisurely driving route; by foot, walking the Staffordshire Way long distance footpath; or by traditional narrowboat – you can't fail to be impressed by Staffordshire's Vale of Trent.

Group Contacts: BB   **Mrs Lynette Bailey** ☎ 0889 562363
                 SC   **Mrs J. Hollinshead** ☎ 0543 262595

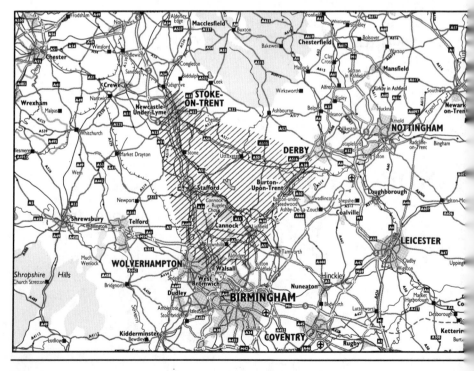

Bed and Breakfast (and evening meal)

Stramshall Farm, Stramshall, Uttoxeter, Staffordshire ST14 5AG

Lynette Bailey
☎ **0889 562363**
⬛ **From £13**
Sleeps 6
🛏 ⛫ ☞
Listed Commended

In the picturesque village of Stramshall you will find a welcome at our late Victorian home with spacious bedrooms, TV lounge/dining room and luxury bathroom. Attractive gardens. All bedrooms with H/C, towels, tea/coffee-making facilities. CH and electric blankets. Ample parking. Ten minutes to Alton Towers and convenient for Peak District and many other attractions. Open Mar–Nov. Map ref: 233 126

Self-Catering

Ashmore Brook Cottage, c/o Ashmore Brook Farm, Cross-in-Hand Lane, Lichfield, Staffordshire WS13 8DY

Helen Broome
☎ **0543 255753**
⬛ **From £85–£125**
Sleeps 5
🛏 ⛫ (2) 🎣
⚷ ⚷ ⚷ **Approved**

250-acre dairy farm close to city of Lichfield, birthplace of Dr Johnson, with good selection of shops and restaurants. In easy reach of Derbyshire and Dales. Many stately homes and museums, NEC and all Midlands attractions. Three bedrooms, sleeping 5 with linen provided. Fully equipped kitchen, dining room, lounge with colour TV, bathroom and cloakroom. Electricity by meter. Pets by arrangement. Open all year. Map ref: 234 116

Elmhurst Dairy Farm, c/o Curborough Hall Farm, Lichfield, Staffordshire WS13 8ES

Mrs Joan Hollinshead
☎ **0543 262595**
⬛ **From £125–£180**
Sleeps 4/6
🛏 ⛫
⚷ ⚷ ⚷ – ⚷ ⚷ ⚷ ⚷
Commended

Four cottages tastefully converted from farm buildings. Three sleeping 6, one sleeping 4, with bed linen provided. Situated in the small village of Elmhurst, 2½ miles from Lichfield city. A good selection of shops, restaurants and country pubs. Within easy reach of Derbyshire Dales, NEC, Alton Towers and all Midlands attractions. Ideal centre for holidays or business. Telephones available. Brochure on request. Open all year. Map ref: 234 116

Priory Farm Fishing House, c/o Priory Farm, Blithbury, Rugeley, Staffordshire WS15 3JA

Mr John Myatt
☎ **088 922 269**
⬛ **From £60–£110**
Sleeps 4
⛫ 🛏
⚷ ⚷ ⚷ **Approved**

Converted 18th century fishing house overlooking River Blithe, offering unique accommodation for up to 4 persons on secluded dairy farm. Ideal for lovers of the countryside and wildlife. Convenient for Abbots Bromley, Lichfield, Cannock Chase, Alton Towers and the Peak District. Comfortable, tastefully furnished accommodation includes large bed-sitting room with colour TV, modern kitchen and shower room. Brochure on request. Open all year. Map ref: 231 119

30 Peak District

Britain's first National Park offers variety and spectacular scenery, from the exhilaration of the wide, windswept moorlands in the north to the softer south where the Manifold and Dove rivers run parallel through water meadows, woodlands and rocky gorges.

As well as some of the best walking in the country, the Peak District offers numerous stately homes such as Chatsworth, Haddon and Hardwick, as well as the thrills of Alton Towers, Britain's first theme park.

Find a bargain in the Potteries seconds shops and at Gladstone Pottery Museum go back in time amongst the bottle kilns. Wedgwood shows a complete contrast by demonstrating modern production of fine china.

Wonderful contrasts in entertainment are to be found: the New Victoria Theatre at Stoke-on-Trent is 'theatre in the round' whilst the perfect Edwardian Opera House at Buxton offers a wide variety of entertainment including an International Opera Festival.

Leek and Bakewell markets transform sleepy country towns when farmers from miles around descend on them. At Matlock cable cars glide majestically across the Derwent; Castleton is famous for its show caves and Blue John stone. So, whether having afternoon tea at a stately home, admiring the Well Dressings or picnicking amongst the heather, you can be sure that the Peak District has something for you.

Group Contacts: ⓑⓑ **Joy Lomas** ☎ **062 985 250**
ⓢⓒ **Jean Salt** ☎ **0538 308331**

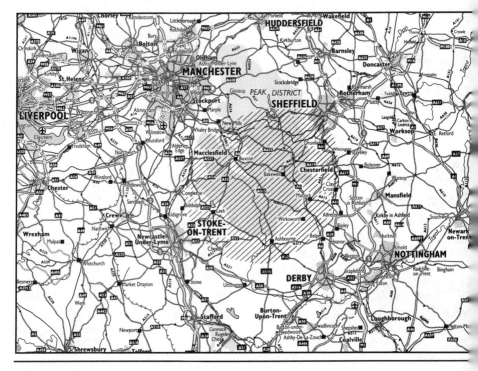

Bed and Breakfast (and evening meal)

Barms Farm, Fairfield, Buxton, Derbyshire SK17 7HW

Lorraine Naden
☎ 0298 77723
BB From £17
Sleeps 6
⚘ ☡ (5)
Listed

Luxury accommodation for non-smoking guests within our spacious home which overlooks the local 18-hole golf course. All bedrooms are en-suite, have colour TV and drinks facilities, and are furnished and decorated to a high standard. Inglenook fireplaces, exposed beams, etc are complemented by double glazing and full central heating. Open all year (closed Christmas week). Map ref: 233 142

Beechenhill Farm, Ilam, Ashbourne, Derbyshire DE6 2BD

Sue Prince
☎ 033527 274
BB From £16
Sleeps 5
⚘ ☡
♕ ♕ Commended

We live in one of the best places in the world! Our centrally heated farmhouse nestles on south facing hill (Dovedale). We take pleasure in sharing our home with our guests. We've 2 delightful rooms, wonderful views (tea/coffee-making facilities, washbasins, own lounge, shower/WC. Beautifully decorated (stencils, murals). After jolly good breakfast explore our farm – glorious walks lead from our door. Map ref: 234 133

Brook House Farm, Cheddleton, Leek, Staffordshire ST13 7DF

Elizabeth Winterton
☎ 0538 360296
BB From £15
EM From £9
Sleeps 10
⚘ ♿ ☡ ♥ ♖
♕ ♕ ♕ Commended

A 180-acre dairy farm situated in a picturesque valley with many pleasant walks. Convenient for Peak District, Pottery museums and Alton Towers. 2 spacious family rooms in a tastefully converted cowshed, 2 comfortable rooms in the farmhouse all with en-suite facilities and tea/coffee-makers. Dine in our attractive conservatory with magnificent country views. A warm welcome awith log fires and good food a speciality. Open all year. Map ref: 228 133

The Church Farm, Holt Lane, Kingsley, Stoke-on-Trent, Staffordshire ST10 2BA

Mrs Jane Clowes
☎ 0538 754759
BB From £12.50
Sleeps 4
⚘ ☡ ♥ ♖
♕

18th century farmhouse with beamed ceilings, traditionally furnished to give a country cottage atmosphere. Guests' own cosy TV lounge and dining room with log fires and central heating adding to the warmth of welcome. Bedrooms have wash-basins, shaver points and beverage making facilities. A 165 acre dairy farm in the small village of Kingsley, 5 miles from Alton Towers. Consall Nature Reserve 1 mile. The Staffordshire Way footpath runs through our land. Open all year (closed Christmas & New Year). Map ref: 229 131

Cordwell Farm, Cordwell Valley, Holmesfield, Nr Sheffield, Derbyshire S18 5WH

Janet Biggin
☎ 0742 890303
BB From £15
Sleeps 6
☡ ♖
Listed Approved

16th century listed farmhouse set on working dairy and poultry farm. This beautiful old house nestles in the charming Cordwell Valley, within easy reach of Chatsworth House (seat of Duke of Devonshire), Haddon Hall and the historic town of Bakewell. On fringe of Peak Park yet only 5 miles from Chesterfield and Sheffield. 2 double rooms, 1 family room. Open Jan–Nov. Map ref: 242 144

Fernydale, Earl Sterndale, Buxton, Derbyshire SK17 0BS

Joan Nadin
☎ 0298 83236
ⒷⒷ From £15
Sleeps 4
⚲
♨ ♨

Our luxury farmhouse is part of a 200-acre dairy /sheep farm and is ideally situated in a quiet rural setting within the Peak District National Park. The accommodation offers guests' dining room, lounge and conservatory. Two double bedrooms are furnished to a high standard offering en-suite, colour TV and central heating. Open Jan–Nov. Map ref: 233 139

Henmore Grange, Hopton, Wirksworth, Derbyshire DE4 4DF

John & Elizabeth Brassington
☎ 062 985 420
ⒷⒷ From £20
EM From £8.50
Sleeps 24
Ⓖ ⛅ & ⛄ ⚲
♨ ♨ ♨

Between Ashbourne and Matlock by Peak National Park overlooking Carsington Water, offering good old-fashioned hospitality in a beautifully converted barn in a garden planted to attract butterflies. Most rooms have private bath/shower rooms. All have tea/coffee-making facilities. Choice of menu. Fire certificate. Visited by HRH Duke of Gloucester. Certificate of Merit in Come to Britain Award. Open all year. Map ref: 239 134

Lane End Farm, Abney, Hathersage, via Sheffield, S30 1AA

Mrs Jill Salisbury
☎ 0433 650371
ⒷⒷ From £15
Sleeps 6
⚯ ⛅ ⚶
Listed Highly Commended

Are you looking for comfort and friendly hospitality in a traditional farmhouse? Lane End, a dairy/sheep farm with panoramic views in a hamlet above the lovely Hope Valley, offers a high standard of accommodation. Ideal area for most outdoor activities and touring the Peak District. Castleton caverns, Edale, Kinder Scout within easy reach. 3 bedrooms, (1 en-suite), with tea/coffee-making facilities. CH, washbasins, TV lounge. Own horse welcome. Farm trail. Open all year (closed Christmas). Map ref: 237 144

Ley Fields Farm, Leek Road, Cheadle, Stoke-on-Trent, Staffordshire ST10 2EF

Mrs Kathryn Clowes
☎ 0538 752875
ⒷⒷ From £15
EM From £8.50
Sleeps 6
⛅ ⚘
♨ ♨ ♨

Listed Georgian farmhouse amidst beautiful countryside with local walks offering abundant wildlife. Convenient for Alton Towers, Pottery museums and Peak District. Spacious, traditionally furnished accommodation includes guests' lounge and dining room. Luxury bedrooms with hot drink facilities, family suite, family en-suite, double en-suite. CH. Excellent home cooking and a warm welcome to our family home. Open Mar–Nov. Map ref: 229 129

Lydgate Farm, Aldwark, Grange Mill, Wirksworth, Derbyshire DE4 4HW

Joy Lomas
☎ 062 985 250
ⒷⒷ From £14
Sleeps 6
⚯
Listed Commended

A warm welcome, a high standard of accommodation and good food await you in our listed Grade II 17th century house on a 300-acre mixed farm in the Peak National Park. Ideally located for touring and walking the Derbyshire Dales and trails, Chatsworth, Haddon and other stately homes. Convenient for Matlock, Heights of Abraham, Gulliver's Kingdom, Tramway and Mining Museum etc. Central heating, tea/coffee-making facilities, some rooms with private bathroom. Map ref: 239 135

Middle Hills Farm, Grange Mill, Matlock, Derbyshire DE4 4HY

Mrs Linda Lomas
☎ 0629 650 368
ⒷⒷ From £15
Sleeps 6
⚯ ⛅ Å ⚘
♨ ♨

Five miles west of Matlock on the A5012, this small working farm with new limestone farmhouse and large garden is set amidst beautiful scenery. Ideal for touring Peak District, close to Chatsworth House, Dovedale and other places of interest. Spacious accommodation. All bedrooms with washbasins and tea/coffee facilities. Family rooms en-suite. Visitors lounge with colour TV/pool table. Open all year. Map ref: 237 135

The Old Bake & Brewhouse, Blackwell Hall, Blackwell in the Peak, Taddington, near Buxton, Derbyshire SK17

Mrs Christine Gregory
☎ 0298 85271
BB From £13.50
Sleeps 6
ॐ ⚹ ⊕ ⚘
Applied

Early 18th century farmhouse set in a peaceful, mature garden of 2 acres. Beyond the trees, gorgeous views of the Derbyshire Dales. Our 300-acre dairy/cereal/beef/sheep farm is midday way between Bakewell and Buxton, central for Chatsworth, Haddon, Derbyshire Dales, caves, etc. Private lounge/dining room, bathroom/shower. CH, washbasins, tea/coffee making facilities. Open all year. Map ref: 234 140

Old Furnace Farm, Greendale, Oakamoor, Stoke-on-Trent, Staffordshire ST10 3AP

Maggie Wheeler
☎ 0538 702442
BB From £18
Sleeps 6
ॐ ☞
Listed Commended

A beautifully furnished Victorian farmhouse, set in a superb position, with magnificent views, yet only two miles from Alton Towers. Three double/twin rooms, each with colour TV and en suite bathroom. Full central heating plus log fire in residents' lounge. Ideal location for walking or simply relaxing. Open all year. Map ref: 230 130

Shallow Grange, Chelmorton, near Buxton, Derbyshire SK17 9SG

Christine Holland
☎ 0298 23578
Fax 0298 78242
BB From £17.50
EM From £12
Sleeps 3
ॐ (5) Å ⊕ ⚘ ▪
≋ ≋ Commended

Shallow Grange is situated in the heart of the Peak District. Set amidst beautiful open views. This working dairy farm has numerous unspoilt walks. The 18th century farmhouse has your comfort in mind, offering high quality fixtures and fittings including all en-suite bedrooms with colour TV, tea/coffee making facilities. Full central heating and double glazing. Open all year. Map ref: 232 142

Wolfscote Grange Farm, Hartington, Nr Buxton, Derbyshire SK17 0AX

Jane Gibbs
☎ 0298 84342
BB From £14.50–£15.00
Sleeps 6
ॐ ✝ ⊞ ⊕ ⚘
Listed

'Away from it all' is the perfect way to describe Wolfscote Grange. Set high above Wolfscote Dale overlooking Berrisford Dale with Dovedale 1 mile downstream. This old 15th century farmhouse has great character; all 3 bedrooms, guest lounge and private bathroom, antique furnishing (tea/coffee-making facilities, washbasins, central heating), "tasty breakfast". Then explore our working beef/sheep farm and the beautiful hill/dale walks leading from our door. Open Mar–Nov. Map ref: 232 141

Self-Catering

Cote Bank & Cherry Tree Cottages, Buxworth, via Whaley Bridge, Derbyshire SK12 7NP

Pamela Broadhurst
☎ 0663 750566
SC From £140–£350
Sleeps 2/6
ॐ ✝ ⚘
ℯ ℯ ℯ ℯ Highly
Commended

Spacious and beautifully appointed cottages, with rear patios, in secluded farmyard of 150-acre working hill farm. Close to village amenities and excellent walks. Lounge with log fire, separate dining room, downstairs toilet, modern kitchen. Three bedrooms (1 double, 1 twin, with washbasins, third with adult bunk beds), bathroom, separate shower. Full CH. Towels, linen, TV, electricity and logs included. Laundry. Open all year. Map ref: 229 143

Ferny Knowle, Edge Top Farm, Sheen Road, Longnor, Buxton, Derbyshire SK17 0PS

Pauline Grindon
☎ 0298 83264
⌷SC⌷ From £150–£300
Sleeps 6
🐕 ✄ 🐎 🏛
🔑 🔑 🔑 🔑 Commended

A secluded farm cottage in the south of the Peak District, lying between the upper reaches of the Dove and Manifold Valleys with excellent views of the surrounding countryside. Recently renovated, the cottage comprises lounge (with open fire), kitchen/dining room, downstairs bathroom, 1 double, 1 twin bedded and 1 bunk room all with washbasins, shower and WC upstairs. Centrally heated throughout. Open Mar–Dec.
Map ref: 231 138

The Hayloft, Stanley House Farm, Great Hucklow, Derbyshire SK17 8RL

Margot Darley
☎ 0298 871044
⌷SC⌷ From £135–£205
Sleeps 4
🐕 ✄ 🐎
🔑 🔑 🔑 🔑 Highly
Commended

The accommodation is skilfully converted from the original hayloft and the interior is comfortably furnished, mainly with antiques. Comprises a lounge with open fire, colour TV and cottage suite, two twin-bedded rooms, kitchen/diner. The Hayloft offers an ideal centre for exploring the Peak District. All linen/towels at no extra charge. Electricity by 50p meter. Open all year. Map ref: 236 143

Lower Berkhamsytch Farm, Bottom House, Nr Leek, Staffordshire ST13 7QP

Edith & Alwyn Mycock
☎ 0538 308213
⌷SC⌷ From £85–£160
Sleeps 2/6 cot
🐕 🐎
🔑 🔑 Approved

Comfortable cottage adjoining farmhouse on dairy farm, comprising lounge/diner with colour TV and double bed-settee. Fully equipped kitchen area with electric cooker. One double bedroom, one twin, cot available. Shower room with toilet and washbasin. Ideally situated for visits to Alton Towers, Potteries, Peak District and moorland beauty spots. Electricity, heating, parking. Open all year. Map ref: 228 134

Northfield Farm, Flash, Nr Buxton, Derbyshire SK17 0SW

David & Elizabeth
Andrews
☎ 0298 22543
Fax 0298 23228
⌷SC⌷ From £50–£260
Sleeps 2/7
🐕 & 🐎 🔨
🔑 🔑 🔑 Approved

Situated in England's highest village. An ideal centre for outdoor activities or for the more leisurely holiday, close to the many attractions of the Peak Park and Potteries. The farm is also a BHS approved riding centre. 3 well-appointed flats with all facilities and CH. Linen and electricity inclusive. Games and laundry rooms. Ground floor flat suitable for the less able. Open all year. Map ref: 230 138

Old House Farm Cottage, Old House Farm, Newhaven, Hartington, Buxton, Derbyshire SK17 0DY

Sue Flower
☎ 0629 636268
⌷SC⌷ From £150–£250
Sleeps 6
🐕 🐎 🏛
🔑 🔑 🔑 🔑 Commended

Charming cottage conversion on 400-acre working dairy/sheep farm in the heart of the Peak District. Opportunity to watch farm activities. Highly recommended accommodation includes storage heaters and fitted carpets throughout, lounge /dining with colour TV, kitchen (electric cooker, fridge, microwave, washer and tumble dryer), bathroom including shower. 2 large bedrooms with washbasins (1 double, 1 family with twin beds and full size bunks). Cot and highchair. Brochure on request. Open all year. Map ref: 233 136

Pye Ash Farm, Leek Road, Bosley, Macclesfield, Cheshire SK11 0PN

Dorothy Gilman
☎ 0260 273650
⌷SC⌷ From £200–£375
Sleeps 10
🐎 &
🔑 🔑 🔑 🔑 Commended

Old beamed farmhouse near Peak District and Staffordshire's moorlands. Shop and pubs are short walk away. In beautiful . countryside farmed with beef and sheep. Many National Trust properties close by including Biddulph Grange Gardens. Alton Towers 15 miles. Ideal for two families. All heating, linen, etc inclusive. Open all year. Map ref: 226 138

Shatton Hall Farm, Bamford, Nr Sheffield, Derbyshire S30 2BG

Angela Kellie
☎ **0433 620635**
🆂 **From £95–£235**
Sleeps 2/6 + cot
🐴 🐎
🐾 🐾 🐾 **Commended**

Recently converted stone cottages on an Elizabethan farmstead: a superb setting in the Peak District. Lovely walking area, fishing, riding, cycle-hire nearby. Hard tennis court. Private terrace, safe play areas, ample car parking. Open plan living room, open fires, CH, colour TV, well-equipped kitchen, 2 double bedrooms. Linen included. Put-u-up and cot available. Full laundry facilities. Pets by arrangement. Open all year. Map ref: 240 147

Shaw Farm, New Mills, near Stockport, Derbyshire SK12 4QE

Mrs Nicky Burgess
☎ **061 427 1841**
🆂 **From £120–£240**
Sleeps 6
🐕 🐴 🎋 ♨
🐾 🐾 🐾 **Commended**

Come and enjoy our working dairy farm. Stay in an old stone built farmhouse with lovely views. Entrance hall leads to fully equipped kitchen diner. Large beamed sitting room. Upstairs 2 bedrooms with third by prior arrangement. Full carpeting and central heating throughout. South facing, pleasant gardens. Pets by arrangements. Open all year. Map ref: 229 145

Spring Cottage, c/o Old Furnace Farm, Greendale, Oakamoor, Stoke-on-Trent, Staffordshire ST10 3AP

Mrs Maggie Wheeler
☎ **0538 702442**
🆂 **From £150–£400**
Sleeps 4/9 cot
🐕 🐴 🐕
🐾 🐾 **Commended**

Set in a superb position at the head of the Dimminsdale Valley with magnificent views. The house is in a secluded position and only 1 mile from village shop and inns, with Alton Towers 2 miles away. The accommodation is suitable for two families with ample room for nine people. Complete freedom for children. Full central heating, log fire, cot and highchair available. Bed linen included. Also chalet sleeping four. Spacious parking. Open all year. Map ref: 230 131

FARM HOLIDAY BUREAU

FOLLOW THE COUNTRY CODE
Leave nothing but footprints,
Take nothing but photographs,
Kill nothing but time!

The countryside round the delightful old market town of Ashbourne, at the southern end of the Pennine Range in Derbyshire, is among the most beautiful in the whole of England. The spectacular scenery of Dovedale and the Manifold Valley, the rolling uplands with their scattered copses and stone walls and isolated traditional farmsteads are well known. Less dramatic but no less rewarding is the tranquil beauty of the unspoilt countryside and villages of the area.

These qualities have long been appreciated and there are strong literary connections, Izaak Walton and Samuel Johnson wrote in praise of the area and George Eliot based her novel Adam Bede on nearby Ellastone where her family lived. Handel wrote part of the Messiah while staying at Calwich Abbey near Ellastone.

Ashbourne itself is a small, historic country town of distinction, with shops, hotels, restaurants, a swimming pool and other facilities of a very high quality.

The whole area is crisscrossed with footpaths providing ideal conditions for walking and there are ample facilities for pony trekking and cycle hire.

Within easy access are many well known places of interest, great country mansions, the Blue John mines at Castleton, the fascinating industrial archaeology of Derbyshire and Staffordshire and the varied delights of Alton Towers.

Group Contact: Gillyan Prince ☎ 0335 324284

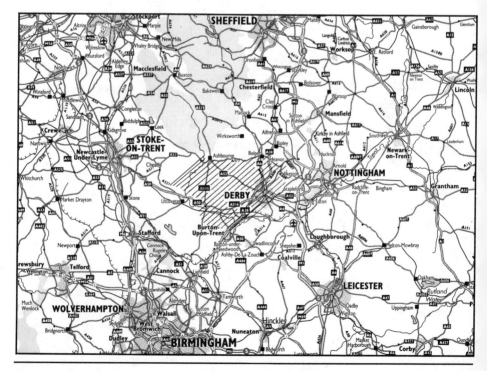

Bed and Breakfast (and evening meal)

The Beeches Farmhouse, Waldley, Doveridge, Derby, Derbyshire DE6 5LR

Barbara Tunnicliffe
☎ and fax 0889 590288
BB From £15
EM From £9.50
Sleeps 28
彡 & 🖼 🖴
🏵 🏵 🏵 Highly Commended

Winners of top national award for farm based catering 1992. Enjoy dining in our oak beamed licensed restaurant – after exploring the Derbyshire countryside or the thrills of Alton Towers. Excellent en-suite family rooms retain the character of our 18th century farmhouse. Children love feeding the animals on our working dairy farm. A warm welcome awaits you. Open all year. Map ref: 235 127

Chevin Green Farm, Chevin Road, Belper, Derbyshire DE56 2UN

Carl & Joan Postles
☎ 0773 822328
BB From £13
Sleeps 12
🐴 ⅄ 🐎 🦌
🏵 🏵 Approved

Relax and enjoy the peace, tranquillity and the beauty of the rolling Derbyshire countryside. Our beamed farmhouse offers single, twin, double and family bedrooms all en suite. Guests' own lounge with colour TV, dining room with separate tables and generous breakfasts. Ideal centre for the six stately homes, Alton Towers, the Dales, walking and business in the area. Meals available at local Inns and Restaurants. Open all year. Map ref: 242 131

Dannah Farm, Bowmans Lane, Shottle, Belper, Derbyshire DE5 2DR

Joan Slack
☎ 077 355 0273/0630
Fax 077 355 0590
BB From £24.50
EM From £13.50
Sleeps 18
& 彡 🐕 🖼 🛫 🖴
🏵 🏵 🏵 Highly Commended

Lovely Georgian farmhouse set amidst beautiful countryside on mixed working farm. All rooms en-suite. Colour TV, etc. Superb licensed restaurant, winners 1992 national award for farm catering, where we aim to serve the very best in farmhouse cooking. Set in large gardens. AA selected, RAC acclaimed. Johansens recommended. Current fire certificate. Four poster suite. Open all year. Map ref: 239 133

Denstone Hall Farm, Denstone, Uttoxeter, Staffordshire ST14 5HF

Mrs Joyce Boden
☎ 088 959 0253
BB From £12
Sleeps 6
彡 🐴 🐕
Listed

Stay on our dairy farm in the beautiful Churnet Valley. We are only ten minutes from Alton Towers and within easy reach of the Peak District and many stately homes. Absorb the rural atmosphere of market day at Ashbourne or Uttoxeter and visit the many pottery factory shops and museums. Trout fishing available. Open Mar–Nov. Map ref: 232 125

Home Fields, Norbury Lane, Ellastone, Ashbourne, Derbyshire DE6 2GY

Gillyan Prince
☎ 0335 324284
BB From £13
Sleeps 6
彡 ⅄
Listed

A warm welcome awaits you with tea and homemade cakes at this delightful smallholding close to the River Dove, Staffordshire and Derbyshire border. One family with wash basin, 1 double/twin with washbasins, tea making facilities. Central heating, lounge with TV, open fire. Easy access Dales, stately homes and Alton Towers. Sample our local pub bar meals, within walking distance. Map ref: 234 127

Lees Hall Farm, Boylestone, Ashbourne, Derbyshire DE6 5AA

Mavis Wilson
☎ 0335 330259
⌷ From £13
Sleeps 6
✄ ♨
👄 👄

Welcome to Lees Hall, a 100-acre beef and sheep farm. The 400-year-old house is set in an unspoilt, rural landscape amid quiet country lanes. 1 family, 1 twin bedded room, both en-suite. Tea/coffee-making facilities and central heating. Full English breakfast. Ideally situated for visits to Alton Towers, the Derbyshire Dales and several stately homes. Open all year (closed Christmas). Map ref: 237 127

Little Park Farm, Mappleton, Ashbourne, Derbyshire DE6 2BR

Joan Harrison
☎ 033529 341
⌷ From £12.50
Sleeps 6
♨ (2) 🍴
👄 Commended

Enjoy the peace and quiet at this 123-acre dairy farm, situated in the beautiful Dove valley. Nearby delightful walks, Alton Towers, NT houses and bike hire. The 300-year-old listed farmhouse features oak beams and is tastefully furnished. All bedrooms have washbasins. Comfortable visitors' lounge, TV. Good wholesome farmhouse food served. Open Mar–Nov. Map ref: 236 132

New Park Farm, Moorend, Bradley, Ashbourne, Derbyshire, DE6 1LQ

Carol Akers
☎ 0335 43425
⌷ From £13.50
EM From £10
Sleeps 12
♿ ✄
👄 👄 Commended

A very warm welcome to our comfortable farmhouse in quiet surroundings. Good home cooking with varied menu using wholesome local produce. Special diets by request. Children can feed the hens and ducks, collect the eggs. Well situated for all Derbyshire attractions and beautiful countryside. We offer guests en suite double, twin, family rooms, guests' own lounge and dining room. Open Mar–Nov. Map ref: 238 130

Parkview Farm, Weston Underwood, Derbyshire DE6 4PA

Mrs Linda Adams
☎ 0335 60352
⌷ From £18.50
Sleeps 6
✄ ♨ 🍴
👄 👄 Commended

Enjoy country house hospitality in our elegant farmhouse. The house is set in a large garden and has lovely views overlooking the National Trust's Kedleston Hall. All rooms are beautifully furnished and have washbasins and tea/coffee-making facilities. Guests' own bathroom, shower room, sitting room and delightful dining room. Country pubs and restaurants close by. 1 twin and 2 doubles with antique four-poster beds. Open all year (closed Christmas). Map ref: 241 129

Shirley Hall Farm, Shirley, Ashbourne, Derbyshire DE6 3AS

Mrs Sylvia Foster
☎ 0335 60346
⌷ From £14
Sleeps 6
✄ ♨ (6) ⚓ 🐟 ⌇
👄 👄 Commended

Our 200-acre family-run dairy/arable/sheep farm 4 miles from Ashbourne has a lovely old, part moated, timbered farmhouse in peaceful countryside. Excellent walks and private coarse fishing. Many stately homes, the Dales, Alton Towers nearby. One twin with handbasins and guests' bathroom, 2 double bedrooms en-suite. Guests' sitting room, TV, CH and drinks facilities all rooms. Superb English breakfasts. Local pubs, one within walking distance, for excellent evening meals. Open all year (closed Christmas). Map ref: 238 128

Sidesmill Farm, Snelston, Ashbourne, Derbyshire DE6 2GQ

Mrs Catherine Brandrick
☎ 0335 42710
⌷ From £13.50
Sleeps 5
✄ ♨ (6)
Listed Approved

Peaceful dairy farm on the banks of the River Dove, a rippling millstream flowing past the 18th century stone-built farmhouse. Good home cooking and a warm welcome guaranteed. Within easy reach of Alton Towers, Dovedale and many other places of interest. Double and twin-bedded rooms, guests' lounge, colour TV, hot drink facilities. Visitors' bathroom. Open Easter–Oct. Map ref: 235 129

South View Farm, Cubley, Ashbourne, Derbyshire DE6 2FB

Carol Walker
☎ 0335 330302/330029
BB **From £14**
Sleeps 6
☼ **(6 mths)**
🐾 🐾 **Commended**

This traditional farmhouse is situated on the A515 at the edge of the Peak District at Cubley. It provides an ideal base for any holiday, being close to Alton Towers, Matlock, Chatsworth House and many other places of interest. Guests have their own dining room and lounge with TV. Tea/coffee-making facilities in all rooms. Full English breakfast. Open all year (closed Christmas & New Year). Map ref: 236 131

Waldley Manor, Marston Montgomery, Nr Doveridge, Derbyshire DE6 5LR

Anita Whitfield
☎ 0889 590287
BB **From £14**
Sleeps 6
☼
🐾 **Commended**

A warm welcome awaits you in this delightful 16th century Manor farmhouse, with characteristic oak beamed rooms and inglenook fire. Come and help feed the animals and milk the cows on our working dairy and sheep farm, which is within easy reach of the Peak District. Traditional full English breakfast served every day. One family room with double bed and bunk beds, 1 double room with double bed. Open Feb–Oct (incl.). Map ref: 235 126

Yeldersley Old Hall Farm, Yeldersley Lane, Bradley, Ashbourne, Derbyshire DE6 1PH

Mrs Janet Hinds
☎ 0335 44504 or 344504
BB **From £13**
EM From £7.50
Sleeps 6
⊁ ☼
Listed

Yeldersley Old Hall Farm is a family-run dairy farm of 70 acres. The Grade II listed farmhouse is situated in pleasant and quiet rural surroundings just 3 miles from the market town of Ashbourne and within easy reach of Dovedale, Alton Towers, Matlock and many stately homes. Farmhouse breakfast provided. Lounge with log fire. Non-smokers only please. Open Mar–Nov. Map ref: 238 130

Self-Catering

Briar, Bluebell & Primrose Cottages, c/o Yeldersley Old Hall Farm, Yeldersley Lane, Bradley, Ashbourne, Derbyshire DE6 1PH

Mrs Janet Hinds
☎ 0335 44504 or 344504
SC **From £110–£220**
☼ ■
🔑 🔑 🔑 **Commended**

Situated on a working dairy farm the newly-converted Grade II listed barn now contains 3 self-catering units, each with 3 bedrooms, accommodating up to 5/6 people. Bathroom with bath and shower, fitted kitchen, fully carpeted. Night storage heating, colour TV. Ideal spot for touring Derbyshire. Ashbourne 3 miles. Open all year. Map ref: 238 130

Chevin Green Farm, Chevin Road, Belper, Derbyshire DE56 2UN

Carl & Joan Postles
☎ 0773 822328
SC **From £75–£230**
Sleeps 4/6
♿ ⊁ ☼ 📺 🐾
🔑 🔑 🔑 – 🔑 🔑 🔑 🔑
Commended

This attractive conversion of farm buildings provides a perfect setting for five bungalows of character in the peace and tranquillity of the beautiful rolling Derbyshire countryside. These superb bungalows are well equipped and provide a perfect base to explore the Peak District, the Dales, stately homes, Alton Towers and numerous other holiday attractions. Open all year. Map ref: 242 131

Culland Mount Farm, Brailsford, Ashbourne, Derbyshire DE6 3BW

Mrs Carolyn Phillips
☎ 0335 60313
🆂🅲 From £125–£250
Sleeps 4–7
🐄 ✄ ❀
⚘ ⚘ ⚘ **Commended**

A magnificent Victorian farmhouse with splendid views. A working dairy farm with opportunity to watch farm activities. Whilst retaining many original features the house is divided making a luxurious holiday home. Colour TV, full central heating, open log fire, cot, washing machine, drier, fridge/freezer, linen and electricity inclusive. T.B. commended. Map ref: 237 129

Hall Farm Bungalow, c/o Shirley Hall Farm, Shirley, Ashbourne, Derbyshire DE6 3AS

Mrs Sylvia Foster
☎ 0335 60346
🆂🅲 From £120–£250
Sleeps 6
🐎 🕭 🐎 🛆 ⚉ ❧
⚘ ⚘ ⚘ **Commended**

Our bungalow on edge of village and close to the farm has large lawned garden with excellent views. 3 double bedrooms suitable for 6 adults. Open plan living area, French window, fully carpeted, central heating, open fire, colour TV. Bathroom, kitchen with fridge, cooker, washing machine. Ample parking. Private coarse fishing, superb walking, convenient for Alton Towers, stately homes and Matlock. Ashbourne 4 miles. Open all year. Map ref: 238 128

Honeysuckle Cottage, c/o Park View Farm, Weston Underwood, Derbyshire DE6 4PA

Mrs Linda Adams
☎ 0335 60352
🆂🅲 From £90–£300
Sleeps 6
🐄 🕭
⚘ ⚘ ⚘ **Commended**

This is a truly delightful country cottage set in its own secluded garden with wonderful views over the Derbyshire countryside. Full of character and charm, furnished to a very high standard, with beamed sitting room and antique furnishings. Accommodation for 6 persons in 3 bedrooms. Linen provided. Colour TV, automatic washing machine and tumble dryer. Storage heating on Economy 7. Smaller village cottage also available. Map ref: 238 129

Merryfields Farm, c/o Little Park Farm, Mappleton, Ashbourne, Derbyshire DE6 2BR

Joan Harrison
☎ 033529 341
🆂🅲 From £90–£230
Sleeps 6
🐎 🐄 (3)
⚘ ⚘ ⚘ **Approved**

Merryfields Farm is situated near the village of Kniveton in the beautiful Derbyshire hills, ideal location for the Derbyshire Dales, Alton Towers and Carsington Waters 2 miles away. Pleasant walks and bike hire, 2 miles from Ashbourne. 2 double and 1 twin bedded rooms, bathroom. Lounge, dining/kitchen. Electric cooker, microwave and fridge, night storage heater and electric fires. Pleasant garden and car space. Open Easter–end Oct. Map ref: 238 132

The Mistle, The Saddlery, c/o Shirley Hall Farm, Shirley, Ashbourne, Derbyshire DE6 3AS

Mrs Sylvia Foster
☎ 0335 60346
🆂🅲 From £80–£150
Sleeps 2/4
🐄 🐎 🛆 ⚉ ❧
⚘ ⚘ ⚘ **Commended**

The Mistle in private grounds attached to pretty thatched cottage. Superb small barn conversion, well appointed. Lounge, dining room, fully equipped kitchen, cloaks, toilet, 1st floor double bedroom and bathroom, sleeps 2. *The Saddlery* 1st floor barn conversion on our farm. Old stone steps to entrance lobby, family bedroom, lounge/dining, kitchen, bathroom. Both have heat store radiators, electric fires. Open all year. Map ref: 238 128

LET THE TELEPHONE RING!
Some farmhouses are big places. Let the telephone ring long enough to give the owner time to answer it.

FARM HOLIDAY BUREAU

Sherwood Forest is nowadays much smaller than it used to be, but near Edwinstowe you can still find Robin Hood, at the Sherwood Forest Visitor Centre where his story is told in a walk-through exhibition. There are also films, guided walks in the forest and lots of other activities here together with a fair to enjoy at Edwinstowe or perhaps a village cricket match close to the church where Robin Hood is said to have married Maid Marion.

Worksop is a pleasant market town with a fine priory and 14th-century gatehouse – both well worth a visit. Retford has a small museum and some interesting Georgian buildings around its market square. The open-air markets at Newark and Mansfield are both popular with visitors as well as local residents and each town has its local museums. Newark's parish church has a fine spire and interesting treasury but the nearby Minster at Southwell is on a larger scale even though Southwell, home of the Bramley apple, is hardly more than a village.

In Nottingham, Robin Hood's statue stands outside the castle which houses the city's fine arts museum, and there's a small Robin Hood exhibition at the gatehouse. At the foot of Castle Rock, beside the ancient Trip to Jerusalem Inn, is the Brewhouse Yard Museum illustrating the city's social history, while nearby the Canal Museum and the Museum of Costume and Textile shows other aspects of the city's heritage. The Lace Centre, in an attractive timbered building, shows off a range of Nottingham's finest work, which you can buy as a souvenir.

Group Contacts: ⓑⓑ **Mrs Pat Haigh** ☎ **0777 870417**
ⓢⓒ **Mrs Jenny Esam** ☎ **0602 652039**

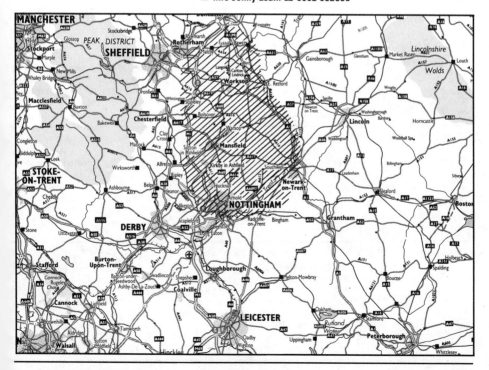

Bed and Breakfast (and evening meal)

Blue Barn Farm, Langwith, Mansfield, Nottinghamshire NG20 9JD

June Ibbotson
☎ 0623 742248
ⓑⓑ From £15
Sleeps 6 cot
🐾 🐕 🛶 🏕
♨ ♨ Approved

Welcome to our family-run 450-acre farm in peaceful surroundings on the edge of Sherwood Forest in Robin Hood country, 5 miles from M1 (J30) off A616. Many interesting places catering for all tastes only a short car journey away. Excursions with qualified guide can be arranged. 1 double, 1 twin, 1 family, all with tea/coffee-making facilities and washbasins. Cot available. Dining room, lounge, TV. Open all year (closed Christmas Day). Map ref: 250 138

Forest Farm, Mansfield Road, Papplewick, Nottinghamshire NG15 8FL

Mrs E J Stubbs
☎ 0602 632310
ⓑⓑ From £14.50
EM From £5
Sleeps 5
🐕 ✂ 🐕
Listed

Forest Farm is located on the A60 standing well back up the farm road away from traffic noise. Pleasant views from south-facing rooms, 1 double, 1 single, 1 twin, all with tea-making facilities. TV in lounge/dining room. Midway between Mansfield and Nottingham, and ideal touring or business base. Open all year (closed Dec). Map ref: 250 134

Hall Farm House, Gonalston, Nottinghamshire NG14 7JA

Mr & Mrs R C Smith
☎ 0602 663112/663338
Fax 0602 664644
ⓑⓑ From £20
EM From £12
Sleeps 6
🐕
♨ Commended

An idyllic 18th century farmhouse in one of Nottinghamshire's prettiest villages. Near the minster town of Southwell. Comfortable bedrooms overlook a lovely garden. Heated swimming pool, tennis court and games room; also aviary of exotic birds and loft of racing pigeons. By arrangement, Rosie your hostess will give you a generous dinner. No smoking in bedrooms. No pets. Open all year (closed Christmas). Map ref: 256 133

Home Farm, Cropwell Bishop, Nottinghamshire NG12 3BU

Mrs K. Barlow
☎ 0602 892598
ⓑⓑ From £14
Sleeps 4
🐕 (3) 🐕 🎿
Listed

Family-run arable farm and livery yard on the edge of the Vale of Belvoir, approx 9 miles SE of Nottingham and within 25 minutes' drive of Newark, Grantham and Melton Mowbray. The Grantham canal is close by, providing delightful country walks. Home Farm is in the centre of the village, opposite historic church and 1 mile from A46. Open all year
Map ref. 257 128

Jerico Farm, Fosse Way, Nr Cotgrave, Nottinghamshire NG12 3HG

Mrs Sally Herrick
☎ 0949 81733
ⓑⓑ From £15
Sleeps 6
✂ 🐕 (5) ☛ 🛶 🎿
♨ ♨ Commended

Jerico Farm offers warm, comfortable accommodation, surrounded by our own attractive farmland. Good firm beds and tea/coffee-making facilities in all bedrooms, one en-suite. Guests' own sitting room. Tourist information provided. Good pub food available nearby. Situated within easy reach of Sherwood Forest, Nottingham and Leicester. Find us on the A46, 1 mile north of A46/A606 junction, south of Cotgrave village. Open all year (closed Christmas). Map ref: 254 128

Manor Farm, Moorhouse Road, Laxton, Newark, Nottinghamshire NG22 0NU

Mrs Pat Haigh
☎ 0777 870417
⚏ From £12
EM From £6
Sleeps 6
🛏 ⅍ ☡
Listed

Manor Farm is a family-run dairy and arable farm of 137 acres, in the historic mediaeval village of Laxton, situated 10 miles north of Newark, and on the verge of the popular tourist area of Sherwood Forest in Nottinghamshire. 2 family rooms, 1 double room, tea/coffee-making facilities available. Visitors' lounge and dining room. Access to rooms at all times. Open all year (closed Christmas & New Year). Map ref: 256 139

Self-Catering

Blue Barn Cottage, c/o Blue Barn Farm, Langwith, Mansfield, Nottinghamshire NG20 9JD

June Ibbotson
☎ 0623 742248
🆂🅲 From £300–£350
Sleeps 8 + cots
🛏 ☡ 🐴 🐖
🐾 🐾 🐾 🐾 **Commended**

Do come and relax in peace and comfort on our family-run farm in Robin Hood country. Visit quiet villages, stately homes rich in history, ramble through country parks or hunt bargains in thriving market towns. Blue Barn is off the A616 near Cuckney. 4 bedrooms, bathroom, breakfast kitchen, dining room, lounge, TV, washing machine and dryer. CH and linen included. Open all year. Map ref: 250 138

The Loft House, Criftin Farm, Epperstone, Nottingham, Nottinghamshire NG14 6AT

Jenny Esam
☎ 0602 652039
🆂🅲 From £235–£275
Sleeps 4
☡ 💺 🛏
🐾 🐾 🐾 🐾
Commended

This 17th century converted granary is situated in the heart of Robin Hood Country, close to the historic town of Southwell. Comfortably furnished with original beams in lounge and kitchen. Central heating, colour TV, log fire, utility room with washer/dryer. Two twin bedded rooms, each with own bathroom. Use of heated swimming pool May/Sept and snooker room in walled garden. Open all year. Map ref: 254 132

The Willows, c/o Top House Farm, Mansfield Road, Arnold, Nottingham, Nottinghamshire NG5 8PH

Mrs Ann Lamin
☎ 0602 268330
🆂🅲 From £150–£250
Sleeps 6
🛏 (by arrangement) ⅍
☡ 🐴
🐾 🐾 🐾 **Commended**

The Willows is a self-contained unit, tastefully furnished. It has 3 bedrooms, well-equipped kitchen, open fireplace and night storage heater. Surrounded by large gardens, it is within easy reach of Nottingham, Newstead Abbey, Southwell Minster, the Dukeries, Sherwood Forest, Derbyshire and the National Watersports Centre. Open all year. Map ref: 256 129

Please mention **Stay on a Farm** when booking

Camping and Caravanning

Sherwood Forest Caravan Park, Nr Edwinstowe, Mansfield, Nottinghamshire NG21 9HW

Mrs Shaw-Browne
☎ **0623 823132**
Tents From £9
Caravans From £9
🛆 ⚏ ☺ 🛉 ♿ ⚞
✓ ✓ ✓ ✓ ✓

Award-winning park in Robin Hood Country, Immaculate shower/toilet/hair washing room and laundry. Large shop with off licence, TV room. Play areas, woodland walks, lakes for fishing and guests' own boats. Special pitches for guests with dogs. 70 electric hook-up points. Warm welcome for overnight halt, quiet weekend or long holiday. Resident warden. Bookings necessary Bank Holidays. Brochure on request. Open March/Easter–end Sept. Map ref: 252 138

PRICES

Prices include VAT and service charge (if any) and are:
B&B per person per night
EM per person
SC per unit per week
Tents and caravans per pitch per night

CONFIRM BOOKINGS

Disappointments can arise by misunderstandings over the telephone. Please write to confirm your booking.

33 Lincolnshire

Visit one of the market towns, especially on market day when you join the bustle and activity and bid at the auctions for country produce which is brought in from the surrounding villages. Buy some Lincolnshire sausages, pies and cooked meats from a local butcher to eat either on holiday or to take home.

Tennyson Country forms the southern part of the Lincolnshire Wolds that have been designated as an Area of Outstanding Natural Beauty.

Halt awhile to visit a Saxon church or a perfectly preserved 18th-century chapel, or go for a walk along part of the Viking Way which stretches the length of the county. Alternatively you can enjoy short walks in picnic places such as Tattershall, Stickney and Willingham Ponds near Market Rasen, along the Spa Trail – a disused railway line that runs between Horncastle and Woodhall Spa, and in a nature reserve as at Snipe Dales near Spilsby. All have signed walks and trails with interpretation boards that help you to understand and appreciate the surroundings.

You can get a taste of the countryside by visiting one of the five windmills that are still in working order in the county at Alford, Burgh le Marsh, Heckington, Lincoln and Sibsey. Then go on to either the Museum of Lincolnshire Life in Lincoln or the Church Farm Museum, Skegness, which vividly illustrates the agricultural and social life of old Lincolnshire.

And then there is Boston and its Stump, the nearby Memorial marking the spot where the Pilgrim Fathers tried to leave England, Springfields near Spalding which has acres of flowers and . . . sorry no more space – you'll just have to come and stay on our farms and see for yourself!

Group Contact: Mrs Gill Grant ☎ 0673 842283

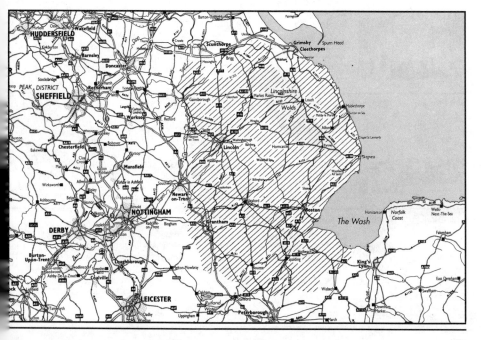

Bed and Breakfast (and evening meal)

Bleasby House, Legsby, Market Rasen, Lincolnshire LN8 3QN

Janet Dring
☎ 0673 842383
🅱 From £15
EM From £9–£10.50
Sleeps 5
🏃 ♡ ⌒
💐 💐 **Highly Commended**

Sample woodland and pastoral scenery on this arable and livestock farm situated at the foot of the Wolds, 4 miles SE of Market Rasen, with its golf course, racecourse and nature reserves. Fly fishing, hard tennis court and large garden. Comfortable rooms, 2 en-suite, one single with shower. Colour TV and tea/coffee-making facilities. Evening meal by arrangement. Open all year. Map ref: 272 146

East Farm House, Middle Rasen Road, Buslingthorpe, Market Rasen, Lincolnshire LN3 5AQ

Mrs Gill Grant
☎ 0673 842283
🅱 From £16
EM From £9
Sleeps 4
🔥 🏃 ⌒ ♿ ✂
💐 💐 **Highly Commended**

Peace and relaxation await you in beamed 18th century listed farmhouse on 410 acre conservation award-winning farm with farm trail and coarse fishing overlooking unspoilt countryside. Situated 4 miles SW of Market Rasen, ideal for rambling, touring beautiful Lincolnshire Wolds, coast, historic Lincoln and surrounding market towns. Wholesome farmhouse food, spacious bedrooms all with private facilities, TV and tea/coffee makers. 1 with shower and basin en suite, separate WC. Guests' lounge. Business people welcome. Open all year. Map ref: 269 146

Gelston Grange Farm, Nr Marston, Grantham, Lincolnshire NG32 2AQ

Janet Sharman
☎ 0400 50281
🅱 From £15
Sleeps 6
⌒ (5)
💐

Real country hospitality, comfortable warm rooms, one four poster bed, all having washbasins, tea/coffee facilities, TV. All rooms near guest bathroom which also has a shower. Separate dining/sitting room, log fires when chilly. Large, full English breakfast. Short and long stays welcome. Northwards on A1 take the first right turn (signposted Marston) after Grantham roundabout. Evening meal by arrangement. Open all year. Map ref: 264 128

The Grange, Torrington Lane, East Barkwith, Nr Wragby, Lincolnshire LN3 5RY

Anne Stamp
☎ 0673 858249
🅱 From £18
EM From £12
Sleeps 6
✗ ⌒ (8) 🏃 ⌂ ✂
💐 💐 💐 **Deluxe**

Welcoming Georgian house on family farm where Anne and Richard assure you of care and comfort. Twin/double rooms en suite. Colour TV, radio, tea/coffee-making facilities. Centrally heated. Guest sitting room. Wood fires (the Aga takes care of the cooking), conservatory, herb beds, lawn tennis, barbecue in extensive grounds. Quiet countryside. Central for Lincoln, Louth and the Wolds, Cadwell Park and Market Rasen races. Open all year. Map ref: 273 145

Greenfield Farm, Minting, near Horncastle, Lincolnshire LN9 5RX

Judith Bankes Price
☎ 0507 578457
🅱 From £16
Sleeps 6
⌒ 🏃 ✗ ♿ ✂
💐 💐

Judy and Hugh invite you to stay at their comfortable farmhouse set in a quiet location yet centrally placed for all the major Lincolnshire attractions. There are forest walks bordering the farm. We offer guests their own sitting room with woodburning stove, pretty en-suite shower rooms, heated towel rails, radios, tea/coffee making facilities, central heating. Open all year. Map ref: 275 143

The Manor, West Ashby, Horncastle, Lincolnshire LN9 5PY

Mrs Mary Chaplin
☎ 0507 523310
Fax 0507 522601
▧ From £19.50
Sleeps 5
ᗒ (8) ⛄ ⬅ ☂ ▪
Applied

Situated in 30 acres of Parkland with a well stocked trout lake, The Manor has superb views from every window. There is excellent pub grub and access to the Viking Way footpath within walking distance. Ideally placed to explore Tennyson Country and The Wolds. Lincoln, Louth and Cadwell Park are all close. Delightful spacious rooms all with washbasins, 1 twin, 1 double, 1 single and two bathrooms. Hard tennis court available. Map ref: 277 141

The Manor House, Manor Farm, Bracebridge Heath, Lincoln, Lincolnshire LN4 2HW

Mrs Jill Scoley
☎ 0522 520825
▧ From £14
Sleeps 6
ᗒ (12) ⤋
⬮ **Highly Commended**

Welcome to Lincolnshire. Stay in a lovely Georgian Farmhouse situated in large walled garden. 3 miles south of Lincoln. Comfortable bedrooms with washbasins, radio, tea/coffee facilities. Large lounge with log fire for cooler evenings. Open all year (closed Christmas and New Year). Map ref: 268 149

Skirbeck Farm, Panton Road, Benniworth, Lincolnshire LN3 6JN

Kay Olivant
☎ 0507 313682
▧ From £14.50
Sleeps 5
ᗒ ⤋
⬮ ⬮

Enjoy a stay on a working farm in a peaceful location within easy reach of historic Lincoln and market towns of Louth, Market Rasen and Horncastle. Surrounded by good walking country – fishing, clay pigeon shooting by arrangement. Farmhouse comfortably furnished with CH and log fires. All bedrooms have colour TV and Teasmaid, bathroom adjacent. Sunlounge overlooking secluded garden. Non-smokers only. Open Mar–Nov. Map ref: 274 144

Sycamore Farm, Bassingthorpe, Grantham, Lincs NG33 4ED

Mrs Sue Robinson
☎ 0476 85274
▧ From £13
Sleeps 6
ᗒ (6) ⤋
⬮

A warm welcome and comfortable accommodation is assured at Sycamore Farm. Our large peaceful Victorian farmhouse stands on a 450-acre farm, situated approximately 5 miles from the A1 and within easy reach of many historic houses. Spacious guest lounge with open fire on chilly nights, colour TV and piano. Accommodation is in 3 attractively decorated, bedrooms with lovely views across open countryside. Tea/coffee-making facilities. Open Mar–Nov. Map ref: 266 124

Self-Catering

Pantiles Cottage, c/o The Old Hall, Potterhanworth, Lincoln, Lincolnshire LN4 2DS

Mrs Susan Battle
☎ 0522 791338
ⓈⒸ From £130–£230
Sleeps 5
⛄ ᗒ ☂
⚷ ⚷ ⚷ **Commended**

A bottle of wine welcomes you to Pantiles. It is a charming oak-beamed cottage which has been tastefully decorated and furnished to accommodate 5 people. Its quiet garden and patio overlook fields and a duckpond. Situated 7 miles from Lincoln, it is within reach of many places of interest. Linen is provided and there is central heating, a log fire and TV. Open all year. Map ref: 267 138

Pingles Cottage, c/o Grange Farm, Broxholme, Nr Saxilby, Lincoln, Lincolnshire LN1 2NG

Pat Sutcliffe
☎ 0522 702441
ⓈⒸ From £160–£200
Sleeps 4
🏇 🐎 🐖
🔑 🔑 🔑 🔑
Commended

A 19th century farm cottage with its own lawn and garden, surrounded by sheep and corn fields, in the hamlet of Broxholme 6 miles from historic Lincoln. Pingles is comfortable and well-equipped for 4 people (extra bed by arrangement). Plenty of interesting things to do and see in the area or relax on the river bank and enjoy your own ½ mile of coarse fishing. Open all year. Map ref: 264 142

Stainton Manor Cottage, c/o Stainton Manor, Langworth, Lincoln, Lincolnshire LN3 5BL

Mrs L M H Bowser
☎ 0673 62423
ⓈⒸ From £100–£200
Sleeps 5 + cot
🏇 🐎
🔑 🔑 🔑 🔑 **Commended**

Tastefully decorated, semi-detached farm cottage set in a small picturesque village. It has a large garden with patio which looks onto scenic views of fields of horses and cattle. The cottage is well-equpped with fridge/freezer, washing machine, tumble dryer, highchair, cot, colour TV, full CH and an open fire. The city of Lincoln 7 miles, Market Rasen 7 miles, and only 5 miles to a 40 acre fishing reservoir. Open all year. Map ref: 270 143

FARM HOLIDAY BUREAU

BUREAU ACCOMMODATION IS RELIABLE

This Guide lists **Farm Holiday Bureau** members only. They are all inspected by the National Tourist Board for standards (see introduction pages) and by fellow members to maintain a high quality.

FARM HOLIDAY BUREAU

FOLLOW THE COUNTRY CODE

Leave nothing but footprints,

Take nothing but photographs,

Kill nothing but time!

FARM HOLIDAY BUREAU

THOSE LITTLE EXTRAS

For advice on farms that can offer 'extras' such as four-poster beds, special diets, farm trails, fishing rights – even stabling and trekking arrangements if you are bringing your own horse – ring the Farm Holiday Bureau on (0203) 696909.

34 North Shropshire

Shropshire is the largest county in the UK without a coastline and as Shrewsbury and Telford are the only towns of any real size, there are many miles of unspoilt countryside to enjoy and explore. Shropshire has its own lake district, comprising the meres centred around Ellesmere. For canal lovers there's the Llangollen Canal winding through delightful rural scenery.

Hodnet Hall and Gardens are well worth a visit and the National Trust has several properties in the area including Attingham Park, Benthall Hall, Dudmaston and Wilderhope Manor. It also owns the Long Mynd which includes the picturesque Carding Mill Valley and Wenlock Edge.

The Ironbridge Gorge (birthplace of the Industrial Revolution) is the setting for the Ironbridge Gorge Museum, a collection of historic sites which between them portray life as it was lived during the Industrial Revolution. One is the Blists Hill Open Air Museum which is a re-creation of a Victorian township. The world famous Iron Bridge is the focus of the Ironbridge Gorge Museum. Similarly the Acton Scott Working Farm Museum near Church Stretton recreates the past by practising 19th century farming techniques.

This area is rich in historic towns, crowned by Shrewsbury. Set in a loop of the River Severn, it has a castle, museum, the shuts or passageways and a wealth of old and historic buildings.

Group Contact: Mrs Sue Clarkson ☎ 0939 250289

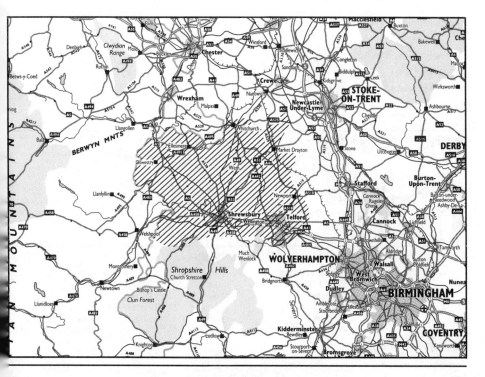

Bed and Breakfast (and evening meal)

Bradeley Green Farm, Tarporley Road, Whitchurch, Shropshire SY13 4HD

Ruth Mulliner
☎ 0948 3442
BB From £18
EM From £10
Sleeps 6
☼ ♞ ♥ ✶
♛ ♛ Commended

We assure our guests of a comfortable stay in our beautiful farmhouse. Central heating and open fires. All bedrooms have private bathrooms. This is a working dairy farm on a main north/south route, ideal for discovering Shropshire, Wales and Cheshire. We have a large collection of waterfowl, and extensive water gardens, all with open access to our visitors. Also a 'prize-winning' farm nature trail. Open all year (closed Christmas). Map ref: 212 128

Church Farm, Rowton, Wellington, Telford, Shropshire TF6 6QY

Virginia Evans
☎ 0952 770381
BB From £13.50
Sleeps 6
♞ ☼ Å ↩ static
caravans
♛

Come and enjoy a large country breakfast in our 300-year-old farmhouse peacefully set in quiet village, 6 miles from M54. A working dairy, pig, sheep farm where guests are welcome to join in. Family and four-poster bed with en-suite facilities. All bedrooms have washbasins, towels, tea/coffee-making facilities. Visitors' lounge with TV, dining room, CH. Central for Ironbridge, Shrewsbury. Children welcome. Weekly terms available. Open all year. Map ref: 216 117

Church Farm, Wrockwardine, Wellington, Telford, Shropshire TF6 5DG

Mrs Jo Savage
☎ 0952 244917
BB From £19
EM From £13
Sleeps 8
♞ ☼ ♿ ♠
♛ ♛ ♛ Commended

Our listed Georgian village farmhouse, with attractive gardens, built on the site of Wrockwardine's 12th century Manor, holds a warm welcome for all our guests. We have delightful bedrooms, some en-suite, oak beams, log fires and delicious traditional breakfasts and dinners. Near Ironbridge and Shrewsbury. One mile M54 and A5. Tempted? Please ask for brochure. Open all year. Map ref: 216 117

Elson House Farm, Elson, Ellesmere, Shropshire SY12 9EZ

Merle Sadler
☎ 069 175 276
BB From £14
Sleeps 5
☼ ✂
♛ ♛ Commended

A large farmhouse situated among the Shropshire Meres within easy reach of the Welsh border. Ellesmere is in easy reach of 3 golf courses, stately homes and castles. The attractive farmhouse has open fires and full central heating. Guests have their own lounge with colour TV, and separate dining room. One en-suite room, other bedrooms have washbasins. A family atmosphere welcomes you. Open March–Oct. Map ref: 206 127

Grove Farm, Preston Brockhurst, Shrewsbury, Shropshire SY4 5QA

Mrs Janet Jones
☎ 093 928 223
BB From £15
Sleeps 5
✂ ☼ ♠
♛ Commended

Enjoy our friendly village farmhouse set in 223 acres of lovely countryside, on A49. Quality accommodation and home cooking. Three delightful bedrooms with washbasins and 1 with shower en-suite. All have beverage trays. Guest bathroom. Central heating throughout. Ideally situated for Ironbridge World Heritage site, Shrewsbury, Chester, Potteries and Wales. Brochures available . Open all year. Map ref: 212 125

Haughmond Farm, Nr Shrewsbury, Shropshire SY4 4RW

Pearl Teece
☎ 0743 77244
[BB] From £15
Sleeps 5
Listed Commended

A 188-acre family dairy farm beautifully situated 4 miles NE of Shrewsbury on B5062. Ideal for exploring mediaeval town, Attingham Park, Haughmond Abbey and Hill. Spacious south-facing bedrooms have washbasins, tea/coffee-making facilities and colour TV. 1 family room, 1 twin-bedded room. Coarse fishing available on farm. Open March–Nov. Map ref: 209 118

Longley Farm, Stanton Heath, Shawbury, Shropshire SY4 4HE

Chris & Sue Clarkson
☎ 0939 250289
[BB] From £12.50
EM From £7
Sleeps 4
Listed Approved

A 15-acre smallholding set in beautiful countryside rearing sheep, some arable farming. The brick farmhouse is close to the historic towns of Shrewsbury, Chester, Ludlow and the Long Mynd Hills. Also Ironbridge Gorge and Museums. 1 double, 1 twin bedded room, guest bathroom. All rooms have tea/coffee-making facilities, TV, washbasins. Open all year (closed Christmas & New Year). Map ref: 213 123

Mickley House, Tern Hill, Market Drayton, Shropshire TF9 3QW

Mrs Pauline Williamson
☎ 0630 638505
[BB] From £20
Sleeps 5
Applied

Enjoy traditional farmhouse hospitality on our 125-acre working farm in unspoiled Shropshire countryside. Explore Medieval Shrewsbury , Roman Chester, Ironbridge Gorge Museums and Hodnet gardens. Relax by the inglenook fireplace or stroll leisurely through the garden down to our coarse fishing pools. Luxury ground floor en-suite bedrooms with central heating, colour TV, hospitality trays. Brochure on request. Closed Christmas. Map ref: 215 125

Mill House, Higher Wych, Malpas, Cheshire SY14 7JR

Chris & Angela Smith
☎ 0948 73362
[BB] From £15
EM From £7
Sleeps 4
🌑🌑🌑 Commended

Modernised Mill House on the Cheshire/Clwyd border in a quiet valley, convenient for visiting Chester, Shrewsbury and North Wales. The house is centrally heated and has an open log fire in the lounge. Bedrooms have washbasins, radios and tea-making facilities. 1 bedroom has an en-suite shower and WC. Reductions for children and senior citizens. Open Jan–Nov. Map ref: 211 129

Oulton House Farm, Norbury, Nr Stafford, Staffordshire ST20 0PG

Mrs Judy Palmer
☎ 0785 284264
[BB] From £17.50
Sleeps 6
🌑🌑 Commended

Oulton House is a 260-acre dairy farm situated on the Shropshire/Staffordshire border. Our large Victorian farmhouse offers warm, comfortable and well appointed en-suite bedrooms, all with tea trays. From your peaceful rural base discover our many local attractions. From the heritage of Ironbridge Gorge, the splendours of Shugborough to the bargains of the Potteries factory shops. As for dinner – we can recommend many local pubs and restaurants. Peace and quiet guaranteed. Open all year. Map ref: 222 122

The Sett, Stanton-upon-Hine Heath, Shrewsbury, Shropshire SY4 4LR

Brenda & Jim Grundey
☎ 0939 250391
[BB] From £23
EM From £15
Sleeps 14
🌑🌑🌑 Highly Commended

Converted barn offering high quality, comfortable 3 crown farmhouse accommodation on a working farm. 6 rooms en-suite with tea-making facilities. Visitors' lounge with colour TV, separate dining room, full central heating. Farm trail, conservation area. Central for Chester, Mid-Wales, Potteries and West Midlands. Close to Ironbridge and Shrewsbury (Home of Brother Cadfael). Ironbridge Breaks available. Open all year (closed Christmas and New Year). Map ref: 211 123

Soulton Hall, near Wem, Shropshire SY4 5RS

Ann Ashton
☎/Fax 0939 232786
🅱 From £21.50
EM From £13.50
Sleeps 6
🐕 🐎 🐈 ⛳ 🛥 ⚘
♛ ♛ ♛ **Commended**

Sample English country life in an Elizabethan manor house offering very relaxing holiday. Bird watching, fishing, riding. Good food, home produce where possible, super meals. Walled garden. Licensed bar. We welcome you. Open all year. Map ref: 212 125

Stoke Manor, Stoke-on-Tern, Market Drayton, Shropshire TF9 2DU

Mike & Julia Thomas
☎ 063 084 222
🅱 From £20
Sleeps 6
⚘ 🐎
♛ ♛
Highly Commended

A warm welcome awaits guests at Stoke Manor, a 250-acre arable farm with farm trail and vintage tractor collection. Ironbridge and Cosford Aerospace Museums, Wedgwood Potteries, ancient towns of Shrewsbury and Chester are only a few of many places to visit. Each bedroom has bathroom, colour TV, tea/coffee trays. Good eating places nearby. Residents' bar. AA listed. Open Jan–Nov. Map ref: 215 125

Self-Catering

SC

Bradeley Green Cottage, c/o Bradeley Green Farm, Tarporley Road, Whitchurch, Shropshire SY13 4HD

Ruth Milliner
☎ 0948 3442
🆂🅲 From £90–£150
Sleeps 4 + cot
🐎 🐎 ⛳ ⚘
♟ ♟ ♟ **Commended**

This comfortable cottage is set in glorious countryside, ideal for walking. Adjacent to waterfowl sanctuary, with open access to visitors. Double and twin rooms, all bedding and towels provided, bathroom with shower. Kitchen/diner with cooker, fridge, etc. Sitting room with colour TV. Electric meter (50p). Electric fires throughout. Cot available. Open fire, logs provided. Open all year. Map ref: 212 128

Church Farm, Rowton, Wellington, Telford, Salop TF6 6QY

Mrs Virginia Evans
☎ 0952 770381
🆂🅲 From £120–£250
Sleeps 4/6
🐎 🐎 ♿ 🏌 🚲 **(touring and static)** ⛳ 🛥
Applied

Two beautifully converted barn cottages, equipped and furnished to a high standard. Each sleeping 4/6 people. Linen and heating included. Patio area with barbeque. Guests welcome to help on our dairy/pig/sheep farm. Bicycles available. Ideal base for touring Ironbridge, Shrewsbury, Ludlow, Potteries, Wales, etc.. Open all year. Map ref: 216 117

The Granary, c/o Mill House, Higher Wych, Malpas, Cheshire SY14 8JR

Chris & Angela Smith
☎ 0948 73362
🆂🅲 From £75–£145
Sleeps 4/5 cot
⚘ 🐎
4 dragons

The Granary is a self-contained bungalow adjacent to Mill House. Sleeps 4/5 in 2 double bedrooms, kitchen/living area, shower and WC. TV. CH. Cot and babysitting available. Situated in a quiet valley with a small stream in the garden. Convenient for visiting Chester, Shrewsbury and North Wales. Open all year. Map ref: 211 129

Lloran Isaf, Llansilin, Oswestry, Shropshire SY10 7QX

Pat Jackson
☎ **069170 253**
SC **From £85–£220**
Sleeps 5
🐕 ♿ 🌾 🍴 🌲 🛄
Applied

Beautiful detached bungalow in enclosed garden on a farm in its own valley. Garden furniture, barbecue. Fully fitted kitchen, 3 bedrooms, WC, bathroom. Large lounge with dining area. Woodburning stove, colour TV, fitted carpets. Wonderful scenery, walks, trout fishing. Plenty of tourist attractions. Easy access North/Mid-Wales. Beautiful for a winter break. Linen hire and cot available. Open all year. Map ref: 202 125

Church Farm, Rowton, Wellington, Telford, Salop TF6 6QY

Mrs V Evans
☎ **0952 770 381**
SC **Static Caravans From £60–£160**
Sleeps 6/8
🌾 🍴 ✂ ⛺ 🚐
Applied

Two 6/8 berth caravans in garden setting with unspoilt views of the Wrekin. Well spaced on hard standing with parking. Each caravan is fully equipped with shower, toilet, spacious lounge, colour TV. Dining/kitchen area. Electric £1 meter plus gas. Barbeque, fishing, bicycles available. Touring caravans and tents welcome. Open all year. Map ref: 216 117

FINDING YOUR ACCOMMODATION

The Group contacts at the beginning of each section can always help you find a vacancy in your chosen area.

GOOD
FOOD

Nearly all Bureau members now hold a certificate in Essential Food Hygiene.

35 South Shropshire

If it's peace and quiet, unspoilt countryside, gently rolling hills, high desolate moorland and picturesque wooded valleys you are after – then South Shropshire is the place to come. Besides its exceptional countryside, there are bustling little market towns and a wealth of time-forgotten villages and historic buildings adding to South Shropshire's character.

Here on the Welsh border, the area forms a buffer between the English Plains and the Welsh Mountains and contains some of the finest scenery you will find in England. Part of the district is an 'Area of Outstanding Natural Beauty', so do not forget your camera.

There are many places to see, from the Brown Clee – which is the highest point in Shropshire – to the rugged moorlands of the Stiperstones, the gentle slopes of Wenlock Edge and the forested Clun Hills. For the steam enthusiast, a ride on the Severn Valley railway from Bridgnorth to Bewdley is a must. There are several National Trust properties in the area including a fine example of a fortified manor house at Stokesay and castles at Clun and Ludlow.

Ludlow has long been described as the most beautiful town in England and history is there for all to see in its old buildings and streets.

Bridgnorth, set on the banks of the River Severn and with its cliff railway, is full of interest. So too are Bishops Castle, Church Stretton and Cleobury Mortimer.

Group Contacts: ⓈⒸ **Mrs Christine Price** ☎ **054 74 249**

Bed and Breakfast (and evening meal)

Acton Scott Farm, Church Stretton, Shropshire SY6 6QN

Mary Jones
☎ 0694 781260
BB From £11.50
Sleeps 6
♿ ♘ Å ♞
Listed Approved

Situated in an area of outstanding natural beauty, the lovely old farmhouse has comfortable and spacious bedrooms, colour TV, lounge and a separate dining room. There is a popular Working Farm Museum in Acton Scott. The spectacular Long Mynd Hills and the valleys of Church Stretton are nearby. Central for visiting Shrewsbury. Ludlow and Ironbridge. We look forward to welcoming you. Open Feb–Nov. Map ref: 209 115

Batchcott Hall, Picklescott, Church Stretton, Shropshire SY6 6NP

Mr & Mrs J Lambie
☎ 0694 751 234
BB From £17.50
Sleeps 4
♿ ⛵ ♞
♛ ♛ Commended

We welcome you to stay on our farm situated amongst the beautiful South Shropshire hills. We have a double and twin bedroom, both with private bathrooms, a lounge, and sun room where we serve breakfast. Guests have the use of tennis court, trout pond and pleasant walks, or can relax in the garden enjoying the view. Open all year. Map ref: 207 112

Castle Farm, Longville, Craven Arms, Shropshire SY7 8DR

Mrs Varny Jones
☎ 0588 673255
BB From £13.50
Sleeps 5
♿ ♘ ♞
Applied

Castle Farm is steeped in history. First built in the 9th century, and rebuilt in the 13th century, it stands in its own courtyard surrounded by many ancient buildings. Close to Stokesay, Ludlow and Powys Castle, our farm is ideal for a walking holiday over Offa's Dyke or the Long Mynd. One family and one double room. Peace and quiet in abundance. Open Feb–Nov. Map ref: 206 106

Charlcotte Farm, Cleobury North, Bridgnorth, Shropshire WV16 6RR

Wendy Green
☎ 074 633 238
BB From £14
Sleeps 6
♿ ⅍ Å
♛ ♛ Approved

Charlcotte has a Georgian farmhouse set in pleasant grounds, midway between Ludlow and Bridgnorth at the foot of Brown Clee Hill. We are in close proximity to the Ironbridge Gorge, Shrewsbury and the Severn Valley Railway. Guests are welcome to relax at all times in the gardens or the drawing room which has a TV. All bedrooms have tea/coffee-making facilities. Open Mar–Nov. Map ref: 214 107

Court Farm, Gretton, Church Stretton, Shropshire SY6 7HU

Mrs Barbara Norris
☎ 0694 771219
BB From £19
EM £10
Sleeps 6
⅍ ♿ (14) ⊞ ♞
♛ ♛ ♛ Highly Commended

Stone Tudor farmhouse on 325-acre arable stock farm in peaceful countryside, 1 mile off B4371, equal distance to Ludlow, Shrewsbury, Bridgnorth, Ironbridge. Spacious rooms, inglenook fireplace, full central heating. 2 twin rooms, 1 double, all with private bathrooms, shaving points and tea/coffee-making facilities. Furnished to a high standard. A warm welcome and high quality cuisine using home produce whenever possible. Open Feb–Nov. Map ref: 211 113

The Glebe Farm, Diddlebury, Craven Arms, Shropshire SY7 9DH

Michael, Eileen or Adrian Wilkes
☎ 058 476 221
BB From £19
Sleeps 9
♿ (8) ♁ ⚹ ⚘ ✗
♛ ♛ **Highly Commended**

Relax amidst the leafy lanes and rolling hills that surround our 16th century farmhouse, part timbered, part mellow stone, nestling in the idyllic village of Diddlebury. 4 comfortable and individual bedrooms have private bathrooms, CTV, electric heating and tea/coffee. Table reservations for evening meals can be booked locally. South Shropshire is a delight. Why not come to stay for a break. Open Mar–Nov. Map ref: 207 106

The Hall, Bucknell, Shropshire SY7 0AA

Mrs Christine Price
☎ 054 74 249
BB From £15
EM From £8
Sleeps 6
✗ ♿ (7)
♛ ♛ **Commended**

The Hall is a working farm with spacious Georgian farmhouse and peaceful garden to relax in, after a day walking or exploring the Welsh Borderland with its historic towns and castles, also the black and white villages of North Herefordshire. Guest lounge, 1 twin en-suite, 2 double with washbasins, shaving points. Colour TV and tea-making facilities. Open 1 Feb–30 Nov. Map ref: 203 103

Hurst Mill Farm, Clunton, Craven Arms, Shropshire SY 0JA

Joyce Williams
☎ 0588 640224
BB From £13
EM From £7
Sleeps 6
♿ ♁ ⚹ ⚘ ⚘ ⚘
♛ ♛

Winner of "Shropshire Farm Breakfast Challenge". A warm welcome to this working farm where the "kettle's always on". Riverside farmhouse and spacious gardens. Nestling in the delightful Clun Valley, it lies between historic Clun and Clunton. Woodland and hills on either side. Two quiet riding ponies, kingfishers and herons. Pets welcome. Log fires. All facilities in rooms. Also 2 luxury cottages. AA listed. Open all year. Map ref: 204 105

Llanhedric, Clun, Craven Arms, Shropshire SY7 8NG

Mrs Mary Jones
☎ 0588 640203
BB From £13
EM From £7
Sleeps 6
♿ ♨
Listed

A friendly atmosphere and good food awaits you in this characteristic old farmhouse with spacious accommodation. Large gardens and lawns overlook the picturesque Clun Valley, surrounded by its hills. Near the Welsh border and Offa's Dyke. Ideal for walking or exploring the many places of historical interest, including Ludlow and Shrewsbury. Situated 2 miles off the A488 Clun to Bishop's Castle road; take turning for Bicton, then Mainstone. Open Apr–Nov. Map ref: 207 106

The Low Farm, Alveley, Nr Bridgnorth, Shropshire WV15 6HX

Patricia Lawley
☎ 029 97 206
BB From £13
EM From £7.50
Sleeps 6
♿ ⚘ ⚘
♛ ♛ **Approved**

The Low Farm is a peaceful, friendly working farm situated just off the Bridgnorth-Kidderminster A442 road. The farmhouse is Victorian. Guests have their own dining room and lounge with colour TV, log fires and central heating. Ideal for Severn Valley Railway and Ironbridge Museums. 1 family, 1 twin bedded room (both with washbasins). Open all year. Map ref: 222 107

Nethercott Farm, Neen Savage, Cleobury Mortimer, Kidderminster, Worcestershire DY14 8LA

Mrs Stroma Lennox
☎ 0299 270 304
BB From £15
♿ ✗
Listed

Relax in this attractive, half-timbered 16th century farmhouse with its lovely garden. Take leisurely walks around the farm, in the Wyre Forest, and on the Clee Hills. 1 double, 1 twin, 1 single bedrooms, all with tea/coffee-making facilities and H&C. Guests' bathroom, lounge with colour TV and log fires. Ideal touring centre for Ludlow, Shrewsbury, Ironbridge, Bewdley. Ample parking. Open all year. Map ref: 218 105

New House Farm, Clun, Shropshire SY7 8NJ

Miriam Ellison
☎ 0588 638314
🛏 From £14.50
EM From £8.50
Sleeps 5
🛏 🐕 🏕 🎣
♨ ♨ Commended

Peaceful isolated 18th century stone farmhouse set high in Clu hills. Farm of 325 acres including Iron-Age-fort. An E.S.A. area. Three major walks from the doorstep. Offa's Dyke, Shropshire Way and Kerry Ridgeway. Bedrooms furnished to high standard with scenic views. Tea/coffee-making facilities, TV. Twin-en-suite. Home cooking and a very warm welcome. Frequently featured and recommended in newspaper articles. Closed Dec. Map ref: 205 105

Rectory Farm, Woolstaston, Leebotwood, Church Stretton, Shropshire SY6 6NN

Jeanette Davies
☎ 0694 751306
🛏 From £18
Sleeps 6
🐕 (12) 🎣
♨ ♨ Highly
Commended

A half-timbered farmhouse, built around 1620. 1½ miles from the A49 Shrewsbury to Ludlow main road. It is situated at 750 feet on the lower slopes of the National Trust's Long Mynd Hills, in good walking country, and within easy reach of Church Stretton. All rooms have private bathrooms. QQQQ-AA selected. Winner of worldwide best B&B. Open Mar–Nov. Map ref: 209 114

Strefford Hall Farm, Strefford, Craven Arms, Shropshire SY7 8DE

Mrs Caroline Morgan
☎ 0588 672383
🛏 From £16
Sleeps 6
🍴 🐕 🛏 🎣
♨ ♨ Commended

Victorian farmhouse in quiet hamlet of Strefford nestling at the foot of the Wenlock Edge. A working farm of 350 acres keeping sheep, cattle and growing cereal. Spacious, traditionally furnished accommodation. Guests' lounge with TV, separate dining room, 2 double en suite, 1 twin, with private bathroom. All with tea/coffee-making facilities. Central base for walking and touring. Closed Dec & Jan. Map ref: 207 104

Self-Catering

SC

Eudon Burnell Cottages, Eudon Burnell, Nr Bridgnorth, Shropshire WV16 6UD

Margaret Crawford Clarke
☎ 074635 235
🅂🄲 From £150–£300
Sleeps 5/6
🛏 🐕 🎣 🍳
🐾 🐾 🐾– 🐾 🐾 🐾 🐾
Up to Commended

Eudon Burnell is a working dairy/arable farm of some 320 acres set in beautiful open countryside but only 3 miles from Bridgnorth and the Severn Valley Railway. Ironbridge 14 miles. Three comfortably furnished, well-equipped 3-bedroomed cottages. Economy 7 or gas central heating, washing machine, payphone in 2. Gardens with picnic tables, etc. A peaceful situation within easy reach of many interesting places. Open all year. Map ref: 218 110

Ryton Farm, Ryton, Dorrington, Shrewsbury, Shropshire SY5 7LY

Mrs Ann Cartwright
☎ 0743 718449
🅂🄲 From £125–£300
🐕 🛏 ♿ 🍴 🍳 🎣
🐾 🐾 🐾 Commended

Country cottages for 6 or converted barns for 2/4 (2 bedrooms, baths en-suite). All cottages are well equipped with microwaves, colour TVs, fitted carpets, linen and towels. Ample parking. Pets welcome. Coarse fishing available. Short breaks for 2 available. Six miles south of Shrewsbury. Open all year. Map ref: 209 114

---

36 Herefordshire

Herefordshire is a land of red earth, green meadows, quiet woods, streams and pretty black and white villages. This is the home of the world famous red and white Herefordshire cattle and a well-known centre for cidermaking. In the south are the spectacular gorges of the River Wye and the lovely woodland trails of the Forest of Dean; westward lies the tranquil Golden Valley leading into Offa's Dyke. To the east, Elgar country rises to the Malvern Hills with the finest ridge walk in England. Herefordshire is rich in history and within reasonable travelling distance of the Black Mountains, Brecon Beacons and Elan Valley in Wales and the Clee Hills, Carding Mill Valley, Long Mynd and Wenlock Edge in South Shropshire. The county itself has a range of sights that span every period in British history from Iron Age hill forts, Roman remains, Norman castles and mediaeval manor houses to stately homes and their gardens and heritage museums. In the village of Kilpeck there are renowned 12th-century Herefordshire carvings or pagan Celtic figures.

You may also like to wander through the street markets of the county which are at Tenbury Wells (Tuesday), Hay-on-Wye (Monday and Thursday), Leominster (Friday), Ross-on-Wye (Thursday and Saturday), Monmouth (Monday and Saturday) and Ledbury (Tuesday and Wednesday). Hay-on-Wye is famous for its secondhand bookshops and Hereford is the home of a very large cattle market on Wednesdays.

Group Contacts: 🆔 **Sylvia Price ☎ 056 886 388**
🆔 **Judy Wells ☎ 056 884 347**

Bed and Breakfast (and evening meal)

Aberhall Farm, St Owens Cross, Ross-on-Wye, Hereford, Herefordshire HR2 8LL

Freda Davies
☎ 098 987 256
BB From £14.50
Sleeps 6
✂ ☺ (10) ♠
♛♛

A quiet, secluded spot 200 yards off B4521. Relax in our 17th century farmhouse with lovely views of rolling countryside. We offer 1 twin, 2 double (one en suite), vanity units, tea/coffee-making facilities, CH, guests' own bathroom and toilet, lounge and dining room. Games room, tennis court. Excellent cuisine. 'Home from home'. Large garden. AA listed. Open all year (closed Christmas). Map ref: 213 085

The Barn Farm, Leinthall, Starkes, Ludlow, Shropshire SY8 2HP

Sylvia Price
☎ 056 886 388
BB From £14
EM From £11
Sleeps 6
☺ ♦

The Barn Farm is set in a peaceful secluded valley, near Ludlow on the Wigmore road. Former 'Shropshire Cook of the Year' provides a warm welcome and delicious home cooking. The comfortable bedrooms – 2 double en-suite, 1 twin with wash-basin – have tea/coffee-making facilities. Pets by arrangement. Map ref: 208 102.

Dinedor Court, Nr Hereford, Herefordshire HR2 6LG

Rosemary Price
☎ 0432 870481
BB From £15
Sleeps 4
☺ (10)
♛

Listed 16th century farmhouse beside the River Wye. Ideal for those seeking peace and quiet. Set in a large garden with views over rolling farmland and orchards. Elegant oak panelled dining hall, guests' own bathroom and TV lounge. Wood fires in season. Tea and coffee-making facilities. Only 3 miles from Hereford on B4399. Open Mar–Nov. Map ref: 211 090

Grafton Villa Farm, Grafton, Hereford, Herefordshire HR2 8ED

Jennie Layton
☎ 0432 268689
BB From £14
EM From £11
Sleeps 6
♦ ☺ ♣ ♠ ♣ ♈
♛♛ Commended

A farmhouse of great character and warmth set in an acre of lawns amidst the picturesque Wye Valley. Beautiful fabrics and antiques throughout, charming and comfortable bedrooms with vanity basins, TV and drinks tray. Guests' own bathroom, shower room or en-suite. We offer our guests a relaxing *holiday* on a 'real farm', enjoying a varied menu with farmhouse portions. Open all year (closed Christmas). Map ref: 214 098

Grange Farm, Newcastle, Nr Monmouth, Gwent NP5 4NX

Solveig Preece
☎ 0600 712636
BB From £11
EM From £8
Sleeps 6
♦ ☺ ✂ ♠
Listed

Wye Valley district. Stock rearing farm. The farmhouse is 16th century, peacefully situated in quiet countryside within easy reach of Forest of Dean, the ancient border town of Monmouth and South Wales. Farming family welcomes children and pets. Open Apr–Nov. Map ref: 209 084

Great House Farm, Stoke Prior, Leominster, Herefordshire HR6 0LG

Shirley Bemand
☎ 056882 663
BB From £13
EM From £10
Sleeps 6
Listed

Nestled in the quiet village of Stoke Prior we offer warm hospitality in our large 17th century farmhouse of immense character. Plenty to do – tennis court, swimming pool and many pleasant walks over 850 acres. Guests' own TV lounge, dining room and bathroom; 2 doubles, 1 twin bedroom. Tea-making facilities. Open all year. Map ref: 211 097

Haynall Villa, Little Hereford, Nr Ludlow, Shropshire SY8 4BG

Mrs Rachel Edwards
☎ 0584 711589
BB From £15
EM From £10
Sleeps 6
Commended

Enjoy a break at our 19th century home in the picturesque Teme Valley, close to A456 and Ludlow. Spacious bedrooms, (1 en-suite), vanity units/tea-making facilities. Guests' bathroom/shower room, dining room, lounge with colour TV, log fires. Large attractive gardens. Superb meals (incl. special diets). Herefordshire Hamper award winner featured in *Daily Telegraph*. Ideal for touring Middle Marches. Private fishing. Guests may participate on the farm. Open all year (closed Christmas). Map ref: 213 104

Hennerwood Farm, Pencombe, Bromyard, Herefordshire HR7 4SL

Anita Thomas
☎ 0885 400245
BB From £15
EM From £9
Sleeps 6

Get away from it all in the welcoming atmosphere of our delightful 17th century farmhouse with magnificent views. 250 acre family-run dairy/stock farm where you are welcome to take walks and view the animals. Comfortable bedrooms with wash basins, tea/coffee-making facilities. Guests' sitting room colour TV, and piano. Children welcome. Large enclosed garden. Traditional farmhouse food using own fresh produce and spring water. Open all year. Map ref: 215 096

The Hills Farm, Leysters, Leominster, Herefordshire HR6 9HP

Jane Conolly
☎ 056 887 205
BB From £19
EM From £14
Sleeps 6
Highly Commended

You will find scrumptious food – traditional or vegetarian – together with delightful accommodation at The Hills. Stunning views from the charming bedrooms, either en-suite or private bathroom, with colour TV and tea/coffee making facilities. For something different our third bedroom – The Tigeen – a cosy barn conversion offers the ultimate in seclusion with your own front door key. Open Mar–Oct. Map ref: 213 098

Holgate Farm, Kingsland, Leominster, Herefordshire HR6 9QS

Mrs Jenny Davies
☎ 0568 708275
BB From £13
EM From £9 (optional)
Sleeps 4
Listed

Traditional hospitality offered in this 300-year-old farmhouse on working family farm. Spacious rooms, tastefully furnished furniture, with polished floors and staircase. Situated in the beautiful north Herefordshire village of Kingsland. Within easy reach of Ludlow and The Welsh border country. Guests own bathroom and sitting room. Tea/coffee making facilities. Open Mar–Nov Map ref: 209 098

Home Farm, Bircher, Nr Leominster, Herefordshire HR6 0AX

Doreen Cadwallader
☎ 056 885 525
BB From £15
Sleeps 6

We welcome you to a traditional livestock farm offering you excellent service and accommodation. Set in a peaceful, secluded area on the Welsh Border, it's 4 miles north of Leominster, 7 miles south of Ludlow, and close to Croft Castle, Berrington Hall and other attractions. All rooms have tea/coffee-making facilities. TV and washbasins. Light evening meals by request. Open 1 Feb–30 Nov. Map ref: 208 098

Howton Court, Pontrilas, Herefordshire HR2 0BG

Nicholas & Helen Whittal-Williams
☎ 0981 240 249
BB From £20
EM From £14.50
Sleeps 6
🐕🐎🍴🍷♨🏊
♨♨♨ **Commended**

Amidst beautiful Herefordshire countryside, 17th century Howton Court offers food and accommodation of exceptional standard. Stone and timber frame family home, steeped in history and character, offers traditionally furnished oak-beamed bedrooms (en-suite or adjacent private bathrooms), oak-panelled, flagstoned dining room, spacious family drawing room, log fires. Secluded gardens, croquet lawn, covered swimming pool. Open all year. Map ref: 206 086

Knockerhill Farm, Callow, Herefordshire HR2 8BP

Beryl Davies
☎ 0432 268460
BB From £14
Sleeps 4
🐕(10)✂🏊
♨

Situated 3 miles from Hereford, 500 yds off A49. The house is of great charm with tasteful antiques and impressive entrance hall, set in beautiful gardens with large croquet lawn. We offer 1 twin and 1 double room, both fitted with basins, tea/coffee making facilities, colour TV, etc., with adjoining large bathroom. A welcome awaits with a pot of tea served in lounge or sun room. No smoking. Open all year. Map ref: 210 090

Lyston Smithy, Wormelow, Nr Hereford HR2 8EL

Shirley Handy
☎ 0981 540625
BB From £15
Sleeps 6
🐕(8)🐕♨
♨♨ **Commended**

Lyston Smithy is a fruit farm in Wormelow on the A466 Monmouth/Hereford road. Ideal for touring the Forest of Dean, Wye Valley and the beautiful Black Mountains of Wales. Accommodation includes residents' lounge with colour TV, dining room, twin bedrooms en-suite, and double room with shower. Drinks available. The welcome begins with afternoon tea while enjoying the view! Open all year. Map ref: 210 086

Marlbrook Hall, Elton, Ludlow, Shropshire SY8 2HR

Valerie Morgan
☎ 0568 86230
BB From £14
Sleeps 5
🐕(4)
♨

We welcome you to our traditional 18th century farmhouse accommodation on the Herefordshire/Shropshire border. Rooms have tea/coffee making facilities and washbasins. Lounge with colour TV. Dining room with oak beams and inglenook fireplace. Ideal for visiting historic Ludlow, Mortimor Forest and Offa's Dyke Open Mar–Nov. Map ref: 211 104

Moor Court Farm, Stretton Grandison, Nr Ledbury, Herefordshire HR8 2TR

Elizabeth Godsall
☎ 0531 670408
BB From £14
EM From £10
Sleeps 6
🐎🍴♨🏊
♨♨ **Commended**

Relax and enjoy our beautiful 15th century timber-framed farmhouse with adjoining oast houses in a peaceful location. It's a traditional working Herefordshire hop and livestock farm, in scenic countryside central to the major market towns. Easy access to the Malverns, Wye Valley and Welsh borders. Spacious bedrooms, en suite or private bathroom, tea/coffee-making facilities. Oak beamed lounge and dining room. Open all year. Map ref: 216 093

New House Farm, Much Marcle, Ledbury, Herefordshire HR8 2PH

Mrs Ann Jordan
☎ 0531 84 604
BB From £15
EM From £10
Sleeps 4
🐕(5)🐎♿🏊🐎

A friendly welcome awaits you at our delightful farmhouse enjoying panoramic views over Herefordshire, Worcestershire and Gloucestershire. Relax by a log fire on chilly evenings, or enjoy a swim in our outdoor pool during summer. We also welcome horses, for which a full livery service is provided. Open all year. Map ref: 216 093

Old Court Farm, Bredwardine, Herefordshire HR3 6BT

Sue Whittall
☎ 0981 500375
▦ From £18
EM From £13.50
Sleeps 4

Old Court is a 14th century mediaeval manor situated on the banks of the River Wye. It has been carefully restored to preserve a wealth of beams and a 15ft fireplace. Gardens enjoy beautiful views to the river. There are 2 four-poster bedrooms, 2 en-suite. Teamakers provided. Also evening meals and picnics. Phone for opening times. Map ref: 203 093

Orchard Farm, Mordiford, Nr Hereford, Herefordshire HR1 4EJ

Mrs Marjorie Barrell
☎ 0432 870253
▦ From £15.50
EM From £10.50
Sleeps 6
(10)　　　
Commended

Situated in the "Wye Valley Area of Outstanding Natural Beauty", guests return for the peace and quiet of our delightful farmhouse where we offer a warm welcome, superb views, delicious food cooked to exceptional standard, cosy bedrooms, with tea trays and washbasins. 2 guest bathrooms, large beamed dining room, two sitting rooms. Featured on Channel 4 Travelog. No smoking except one sitting room. Residential licence. Fishing. Open all year (closed Christmas). Map ref: 212 088

Paunceford Court, Much Cowarne, Nr Bromyard, Herefordshire HR7 4JQ

Jenny Keenan
☎ 0432 820208
▦ From £14
EM From £9
Sleeps 4
Listed

A warm friendly welcome awaits you at this old delightful farmhouse set in a quiet country location. Ideal for touring Malverns, Welsh Borders and Wye Valley. Bedrooms tastefully furnished to a high standard, separate bathroom/shower, tea-making facilities, dining room, TV lounge. Children welcome, evening meals available. Realistic prices, reduced for children Pets by arrangement. Open all year (closed Christmas & New Year). Map ref: 215 094

Pixhill Farm, Whitbourne, Worcester WR6 5ST

Gail & Richard Bellville
☎ 0886 21304
▦ From £12
EM From £8
Sleeps 2
(8)
Listed

A 16th century timber-framed farmhouse set in beautiful countryside amidst 200-acre deer and sheep farm and 120 acres of woodland. Walks, trout stream with fishing, bird-watching and gardens. Easy distance from Worcester and Hereford, historic Ludlow, market town Bromyard, and many country attractions.Swimming pool. Open Mar–Nov. Map ref: 219 097

Rowlestone Court, Pontrilas, Hereford, Herefordshire HR2 0DW

Mrs Margaret Williams
☎ 0981 240322
▦ From £13
Sleeps 5
Listed

Relax in this 14th century farmhouse set in 300 acres with panoramic views of the Black Mountains. 1 family room, 1 double. Guests' own bathroom, tea/coffee-making facilities. TV/large lounge with stone walls, dining room with inglenook and a Baby Grand to while away a few minutes. Rough shooting/fishing available. Hereford 12 miles, Abergaveny 12 miles. Evening meals by request. Open all year (closed Christmas). Map ref: 206 085

Sink Green Farm, Rotherwas, Hereford HR2 6LE

David Jones
☎ 0432 870223
▦ From £17

Sink Green awaits you with a warm, friendly welcome to its 16th century farmhouse overlooking the River Wye and picturesque Herefordshire countryside yet only 3 miles from the cathedral city of Hereford. Comfortable bedrooms, one with four-poster bed, all en-suite, tea/coffee making facilities and colour TV. Large oak-beamed lounge and traditional farmhouse fare. Children welcome, pets by arrangement. AA listed. Map ref: 211 089

The Upper House, Didley, Herefordshire HR2 9DA

Mrs Jane Manning
☎ 098 121212
⒝⒝ From £24.50
EM From £15.50
Sleeps 4
☺ ⋔
♛ ♛ Deluxe

A welcoming 17th century farmhouse offering exceptional accommodation. Very well appointed rooms, 1 double, 1 twin, each with en-suite Edwardian-style bathroom. Lounge, dining room, interesting garden. Large country breakfasts, 4-course dinners using home grown produce when available. Kennelling/stabling available. Ideal for visiting Kilpeck Church, Golden Valley, Black Mountains, Hay, Ross-on Wye. 7 miles south-west of Hereford. Open Apr–Nov. Map ref: 208 087

Upper Newton Farmhouse, Kinnersley, Herefordshire HR3 6QB

Pearl & Jon Taylor
☎ 0554 327727
⒝⒝ From £15
EM From £10
Sleeps 6
✕ ♒ ♨
Listed

17th century farmhouse. Pretty gardens overlooking the Black Mountains. Lovely fabrics, crafts and paint techniques abound coupled with traditional and tasty farmhouse fare, served with ample fresh garden produce – vegetarians welcomed! Ideally situated for touring.Honeymoon – four-poster/twin/double. Guests own bathroom/dining/lounge, plus extra comforts help to make your stay special. Open all year. Map ref: 205 094

Upper Pengethley Farm, Ross-on-Wye, Herefordshire HR9 6LL

Sue Partridge
☎ 0989 87687
⒝⒝ From £15
Sleeps 4
⋔ ✕ ☺ (8)
♛

Upper Pengethley is a family-run arable and stock rearing farm offering two delightful en-suite bedrooms in charming 18th century farmhouse. Situated 4 miles north of Ross-on-Wye on the A49. With magnificent views of the Welsh Hills and surrounding country, beautiful walks and opportunities to explore the locality. Open all year. Map ref: 214 084

The Vauld House Farm, Marden, Herefordshire HR1 3HA

Mrs Judith Wells
☎ 056884 347
⒝⒝ From £13.50
EM From £10
Sleeps 6
☺ ⋔ ♨
♛ ♛ ♛

Situated 6 miles north of Hereford in beautiful countryside, this 17th century farmhouse offers traditionally furnished, comfortable accommodation with guests' own lounge and dining room. Open log fires. All home cooking to a very high standard using fresh local produce. Guests may enjoy relaxing in the wooded and lawned gardens with carp ponds. Open all year. Map ref: 212 093

Self-Catering

SC

Bankside, Dilwyn, Hereford, Herefordshire HR4 8HD

Mrs Anna Wellings
☎ 0544 318329
⒮⒞ From £195–£300
Sleeps 6 + cot
☺ ⋔ ♒
♪ ♪ ♪ Commended

Spacious family house, overlooking unspoilt farmland with panoramic views of black mountains. Famous for black and white village trail. Two double bedded rooms (1 with four poster), 1 twin, nursery with cot, bathroom, 2 WCs. Large lounge, dining room, modern kitchen, shower room, secluded gardens with patio furniture. Linen included. Map ref: 207 097

Brooklyn, Marlbrook Hall, Elton, Ludlow, Shropshire SY8 2HR

Mrs Valerie Morgan
☎ 056 886 230
SC From £90–£170
Sleeps 6
🐕 🐂
🔑 🔑 🔑 🔑 **Approved**

Spacious three-bedroomed house with garden. Fitted carpets and furnished to a good standard. Colour TV, microwave oven and washing machine. Linen and towels included in price. Good touring area for exploring the market town of Ludlow, Mortimer Forest and the Welsh Borders. Open all year. Map ref: 211 104

Hallaston, Sarnesfield Weobley, Hereford HR4 8RE

Mrs Joanne Bright
☎ 0544 318182
SC From £120–£200
Sleeps 4
🐂
Applied

Listed 17th century farmhouse in a beautifully situation with spectacular views over the Wye Valley to the Black Mountains. Situated between Leominster and Eardisley on the picturesque black and white village trail. Very peaceful and ideal for children. Fully equipped unit with colour TV. Cot and linen provided. Map ref: 205 095

High House Farmhouse, c/o White House Farm, Preston Cross, Nr Ledbury, Herefordshire HR8 2LH

Mrs Gillian Thomas
☎ 053 184 231
SC From £120–£190
Sleeps 6
🐂 (6) 🐕
🔑 🔑 🔑 **Approved**

A 470-acre family farm on A449 3 miles Ledbury. Accommodation comprises two self-contained 13th century wing. Farmhouse beamed throughout with own garden. Ideal for touring Wye Valley, Malverns, Forest of Dean and Wales. Open all year. Map ref: 218 089

Mill House Flat, Woonton Court Farm, Leysters, Leominster, Herefordshire HR6 0HL

Mrs Elizabeth Thomas
☎ 056 887 232
SC From £120–£200
Sleeps 3/4 cot
🐂 🐕 🛠 🐖 🎋
🔑 🔑 🔑 – 🔑 🔑 🔑 🔑
Up to Commended

Half-timbered brick and stone detached mill, recently converted to provide comfortable first floor self-contained accommodation. Open plan kitchen/dining room/spacious sitting room, electric fire, colour TV. Night store heating and fitted carpets throughout. Linen/electricity included. Telephone. Sunny patio, parking, freedom to walk on the farm and enjoy a wealth of nature. Own farm produce. Short breaks. Open all year. Map ref: 209 098

The Vauld House Farm, Marden, Hereford, Herefordshire HR1 3HA

Judith Wells
☎ 056884 347
SC From £150–£195
Sleeps 5 cot/2 + cot
🐕 🐂 🎋 🛎
🔑 🔑 🔑 **Commended**

Set amidst beautiful countryside on family stock farm midway between Hereford and Leominster, this skilfully converted Victorian hop kiln is spacious and well-equipped. Sleeps 5 cot. Recently renovated 17th century Cider House, retaining character and charm. Ground floor sleeps 2. Lawned and wooded gardens with moat and ponds extend to over an acre. Open all year. Map ref: 212 093

West Wing and Bungalow Lodge, Bircher Hall, Leominster, Herefordshire HR6 0AX

The Lady Cawley
☎ 056885 218
SC From £50–£180
Sleeps 3
🐕 🐂 🛗 ✂
🔑 🔑 🔑 – 🔑 🔑 🔑
Approved

West Wing of 1759 old Manor House. Antique furnishings. Oil centrally heated throughout. Thermostats. Panelled lounge with fireplace. Modernised kitchen/diner, electric cooker, washing machine and tumble dryer. National Trust house, superb commons very close. Riding and fishing nearby. Heating metered. AA and Tourist listed. Sleeps 5. Hire cot, telephone, linen. Also Bungalow Lodge. Open all year. Map ref: 209 099

Wilden Cottage, c/o Wilden Farm, St Michaels, Tenbury Wells, Worcestershire WR15 8PL

Mrs Margaret Jones
☎ 056 887 255
🆂🅲 From £80–£205
Sleeps 5
🗢 🐕 🐾
🐾 🐾 🐾 **Approved**

Semi-detached cottage in own lawned garden, bordered by wooded brook and orchard. Idyllic setting for birdwatchers, naturalists and walkers, and exploring Herefordshire, Worcestershire and Shropshire. Conservation methods used on farm. Sleeps 5 in double, twin and single bedrooms. Sitting room with colour TV, open fire. Children and pets welcome. Open all year. Map ref: 213 099

PRICES

Prices include VAT and service charge (if any) and are:
B&B per person per night
EM per person
SC per unit per week
Tents and caravans per pitch per night

BUREAU ACCOMMODATION IS RELIABLE

This Guide lists **Farm Holiday Bureau** members only. They are all inspected by the National Tourist Board for standards (see introduction pages) and by fellow members to maintain a high quality.

37 Worcestershire

Worcestershire still has that flavour of Old England with flowering hedges, grazing pastures, rolling hills and bluebelled woodland, winding lanes and sleepy villages. To the north the Georgian town of Bewdley straddles the River Severn as it enters the county, fringed by the Wyre Forest where wild deer wander, and Droitwich, the historic spa town with its high street of timber-framed shops, is to be found. To the west discover Leominster and to the south Ledbury with their unforgettable black and white quaintness.

Follow the gentle flow of the Severn, Teme and Avon as they make their way through the county passing through such delights as Evesham, Pershore and Upton-on-Severn. Climb the rolling hills of Malvern, Abberley, Woodbury and Clee. Discover Malvern with its Priory Church and famous drinking water flowing freely at St Annes Well and Holy Well. At the south east tip of our county lies famous Broadway, the picturesque Cotswold village.

Worcestershire is steeped in history and where better to discover this than Worcester itself, the heart of our county. Dominated by its grand and beautiful cathedral, the city has many interesting museums, the Commandery with its civil war connections, the Royal Worcester Porcelain factory and museum and the Guild Hall.

Find true country hospitality by staying on a Worcestershire farm. Whether you choose self-catering cottages, a smallholding or fruit farm, arable or dairy farm, you will be sure of a warm country welcome and a high standard of accommodation.

Group Contacts: 🅱🅱 **Mrs Pauline Grainger ☎ 0299 404027**
🆂🅲 **Mr R. Goodman ☎ 0299 896500**

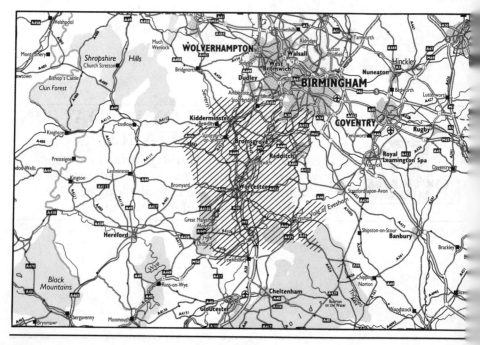

Bed and Breakfast (and evening meal)

Bullockhurst Farm, Rock, Nr Bewdley, Worcestershire DY14 9SE

Margaret Nott
☎ **0299 832 305**
🅱 **From £15**
Sleeps 4

Come and savour the peace and tranquility of our Georgian farmhouse set in large gardens and beautiful undulating countryside. En-suite facilities. Well situated for exploring the Wyre Forest, Bewdley with its Severn Railway and enjoying the panoramic views over the Worcestershire and Shropshire countryside. Excellent meals available in village. Children welcome. 1½ miles off A456. Map ref: 222 103

Chirkenhill, Leigh Sinton, Malvern, Worcestershire WR13 5DL

Mrs Sarah Wenden
☎ **0886 832205**
🅱 **From £15**
Sleeps 6

We welcome guests to our attractive farmhouse conveniently situated 4 miles from Malvern and 5 from Worcester. Its elevated position commands lovely views of the Malvern Hills and surrounding countryside and its rural location ensures a peaceful break. Excellent country walks or drive the Elgar Route. Dogs/horses can be housed by arrangement. Swimming pool (summer). Open all year. Map ref: 220 097

Church Farm, Abberley, Nr Worcester, Worcestershire WR6 6BP

Sally & Roy Neath
☎ **0299 896316**
Fax 0299 896773
🅱 **From £16**
Sleeps 6
🐴 **Commended**

Established 11 years, we are 12 miles west of Worcester in a setting that delights our visitors. Our farm nestles against the backdrop of the Abberley Hills and the beauty of the views is matched by the appeal and comfort of the bedrooms, all of which are en-suite. Evening meals are no problem as you can stroll from our door, across the fields, to the village inn. Open Easter–Oct. Map ref: 218 101

Church House, Shelsley Beauchamp, Nr Worcester, Worcestershire WR6 6RA

Gill & Arthur Moore
☎ **08865 393 or**
0886812 393
🅱 **From £15**
EM From £9.50
Sleeps 4

A warm welcome awaits you on our 200-acre family run cattle and sheep farm in the Teme Valley. Country cooking is our speciality with meat and vegetables home or locally produced. All bedrooms have bathrooms en-suite. Guests can relax in a large sitting room with colour TV after visits to the Welsh Borders, Shakespeare Country, the Malverns and many local attractions. Open March–Oct. Map ref: 218 101

Clay Farm, Clows Top, Nr Kidderminster, Worcestershire DY14 9NN

Mike & Ella Grinnall
☎ **0299 832421**
🅱 **From £15**
Sleeps 6
🐴 **(6)** **Commended**

Modern farmhouse with 98 acres with magnificent views – well stocked trout and coarse fishing pools – bedrooms en-suite with tea making facilities. TV lounge with spacious sun lounge. Central heating. Close proximity to Ludlow, Severn Valley Railway and Ironbridge Gorge. Brochures on request. On the B4202 Clows Top-Cleobury-Mortimer Road. Open all year (closed Christmas). Map ref: 221 102

Eden Farm, Ombersley, Nr Droitwich, Worcester WR9 0JX

Mrs Ann Yardley
☎ 0905 620244
🅱 From £16
Sleeps 5
🐕 🐈 ✿
♕♕ **Commended**

Come and enjoy our listed 17th century home with its lovely garden and fishing on the Severn. It's just off the A449 and the Wychavon Way, a wonderful centre for exploring the heart of England, with Worcester 7 miles, Droitwich 6 miles. Bedrooms are tastefully decorated, with bathrooms en suite, tea/coffee-making facilities. Homemade produce and preserves. 1 mile from Clacks Farm (TV garden). Open all year. Map ref: 223 098

Hill Farm, Bournheath, Bromsgrove, Worcestershire B61 9HU

Lillian Rutter
☎ 0527 72403
🅱 From £16.50
EM From £11.50
Sleeps 6
🐈 (3)
♕ **Approved**

Hill Farm has overlooked the peaceful village of Bournheath for 250 years. This Georgian listed building with mediaeval cruck barn makes an ideal base for touring the Heart of England. Explore on foot the beauty of the local countryside or drive to numerous surrounding market towns. 1½ miles to M5/M42 access with Birmingham Convention Centre, NEC, Birmingham airport 20 mins by car. Open all year. Map ref: 227 103

Hunt House Farm, Frith Common, between Tenbury Wells and Bewdley, Worcestershire WR15 8JY

Chris & Jane Keel
☎ 0299 832277
🅱 From £15
Sleeps 6
🐈 (8) 🐕 ☂
♕♕ **Highly Commended**

16th century timber framed farmhouse surrounded by breathtaking views. Our 180-acre farm is arable/sheep, and we offer comfort, peace and hospitality in a relaxing, friendly atmosphere. All bedrooms en-suite with tea trays. Visitors welcomed with tea and homemade cake in guest sitting room. Excellent local eating houses. Convenient for Worcester, Shropshire, Hereford, NEC, Ironbridge, Wales. Map ref: 220 099

Lightmarsh Farm, Crundalls Lane, Bewdley, Worcestershire DY12 1NE

Mrs Pauline Grainger
☎ 0299 404027
🅱 From £14.50
Sleeps 4
🐈 (10) 🐕 ☂
Listed

A small, pasture farm in an elevated position with fine views. Ideal location for walking, wildlife and exploring Heart of England. The house is approx 200 years old, full central heating, offers comfortable accommodation; TV lounge with inglenook fireplace. Truly rural setting, only 1 mile from Bewdley's shops and restaurants, Severn Valley Railway and West Midland Safari Park. Brochure on request. Open all year. Map ref: 222 103

Lower Doddenhill Farm, Newnham Bridge, Nr Tenbury Wells, Worcestershire WR15 8NU

Clifford & Joan Adams
☎ 058 479 223
🅱 From £14
Sleeps 4
🐈 (6) 🐕 🅰 ☂
♕

A warm and friendly welcome awaits visitors to our 17th century listed farmhouse standing high above the beautiful Teme Valley with exquisite views. The pretty bedrooms all have en-suite or private bathroom facilities together with colour TV, tea-making facilities, etc. Ideally situated for exploring the Heart of England. Past AA regional farmhouse of the year. Open Mar–Nov. Map ref: 217 106

Old House Farm, Tibberton, Droitwich, Worcestershire WR9 7NP

Pat Chilman
☎ 090 565 247
🅱 From £15
Sleeps 4
🐕 ✗ 🐈
♕♕

Family run 100-acre dairy farm set off B4084, in peaceful village of Tibberton but only 1 mile from M5, J6. The farmhouse is tastefully furnished for comfort and relaxation with large garden and splendid views of Malvern Hills. Central for the Heart of England including Worcestershire, Herefordshire, Warwickshire, Gloucestershire and the Cotswolds. Washbasins en-suite. Open Apr–Oct. Map ref: 226 099

Phepson Farm, Himbleton, Droitwich, Worcestershire WR9 7JZ

David & Tricia Havard
☎ 090 569 205
▧ From £15
Sleeps 10
🐕 🏇 ♨ 🛍
♨ ♨

In our 17th century oak beamed farmhouse we offer a warm welcome, good food and a relaxed and informal atmosphere. The recently converted Granary has two ground floor bedrooms with en-suite bathrooms and colour TV whilst the farmhouse has double, twin and family accommodation. Peaceful surroundings on family stock farm. Walking on Wychavon Way. Featured in 'Wish You Were Here'. Open Jan–Dec. Map ref: 226 099

Self-Catering

Blackhouse Farm, Suckley, Worcestershire WR6 5DW

Mrs Grace Mansell
☎ 0886 884234
▨ From £170–£425
Sleeps 7/9
🐕 🏇
✿ ✿ ✿ **Highly Commended**

The beauty of this 16th century timber-framed barn conversion complements the convenience of its fully equipped luxury accommodation. Ideal for a peaceful holiday in an area of outstanding natural beauty. Set in the heart of Elgar country, within easy reach of many places of interest and two cathedral cities. Good walking, large garden, garage, barbecue. Central heating, linen provided. Open all year. Map ref: 225 095

The Granary, c/o Phepson Farm, Himbleton, Droitwich, Worcestershire WR9 7JZ

David & Tricia Havard
☎ 090 569 205
▨ From £140–£210
Sleeps 2
🐕 🏇 ♨
✿ ✿ ✿ ✿ **Commended**

The recent conversion of the old granary is reached by an outside stone staircase. The light and airy flat is double-glazed and very comfortably furnished. Situated on working stock farm in peaceful surroundings. Entrance through stable door. Fitted kitchen, colour TV, double bedroom with en-suite bathroom. Linen, electricity, night storage heating included. Open all year. Map ref: 227 097

Old Yates Cottages, Old Yates Farm, Abberley, Nr Worcester, Worcestershire WR6 6AT

Sarah & Richard Goodman
☎ 0299 896500
▨ From £100–£230
Sleeps 2/4
🐕 ♿ 🏇
✿ ✿ ✿ ✿ **Commended**

Four cottages in peaceful, secluded positions with private gardens, situated on small farm between Abberley Hills and the Teme Valley. Cosy, fully equipped and heated, also log fires, colour TV. Launderette and table tennis room. 1 mile from village supermarket and garage. Many restaurants, leisure and recreational activities within easy reach. Ideal centre to explore the Midlands and Welsh Borders. Brochure available. Open all year. Map ref: 224 096

NO ANSWER?
Farmers are mostly out and about during the day.
Try to telephone before 9.30am or after 4pm.

---

38 Warwickshire

The native county of William Shakespeare has a lot to offer and with its mediaeval castles, historic towns of Warwick, Stratford-upon-Avon, Leamington Spa, Rugby and Kenilworth and its delightful countryside, the visitor is spoilt for choice.

Stratford-upon-Avon is the provincial home of the Royal Shakespeare Company who perform in the three theatres near the River Avon. There are many half-timbered buildings in the town, several of which have associations with the great bard himself and the shopping centre satisfies the most discerning shopper. A few miles up the River Avon lies the town of Warwick with its magnificent mediaeval castle brought to life by Madame Tussaud's vignettes.

At Kenilworth, a few miles away, the remains of Kenilworth Castle, one of the major English strongholds, can be seen. Close to Kenilworth is the Royal Showground which is the stage for the Royal Show every July and a year-round agricultural centre.

Royal Leamington Spa is an elegant Regency town with wide streets, crescents and fine gardens and famous for its healing waters; the Royal Pump Rooms are today the home of a Medical Treatment Centre.

There are also many pretty villages throughout the county waiting to be explored and the delights of stately homes such as Packwood House, Ragley Hall, Charlecote Park, Baddesley Clinton and Coughton Court will remain with the visitor for a long time.

Group Contact: Miss Deborah Lea ☎ 0295 770652

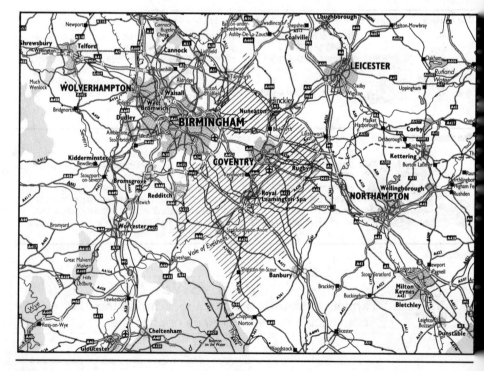

Bed and Breakfast (and evening meal)

Ascott House Farm, Ascott, Whichford, nr Long Compton, Shipston-on-Stour, Warwickshire CV36 5PP

Mrs Janet Haines
☎ 0608 84655
BB From £14
Sleeps 6
🐕 🐎
♨ ♨

Listed stone farmhouse in designated Area of Natural Beauty on edge of Cotswolds. 500-acre arable/sheep farm, attractive garden, outdoor swimming pool, snooker room, interesting walks. 2 double en-suite/family rooms, 1 twin with washbasin. Tea/coffee-making facilities, CH, TV lounge, traditional dining room. Golf/riding within 5 miles. Ideal for Stratford-upon-Avon/Cotswolds/Oxford, M40 Banbury 10 miles. Open all year. Map ref: 242 093

Bevington Hall Farm, Iron Cross, Salford Priors, Worcestershire WR11 5SJ

Theresa Bomford
☎ 0386 870 240
BB From £17
Sleeps 5
Listed

A quiet, spacious, comfortable Victorian farmhouse, with large garden and croquet lawn, surrounded by 240-acre farm on the Warwickshire/Worcestershire border. Perfectly situated for visiting Stratford-upon-Avon, National Agricultural Centre and National Exhibition Centre. Various sporting facilities nearby. Each room has its own bathroom. Drawing room with colour TV and piano. Numerous places for good evening meals. Open Easter–Oct. Map ref: 233 095

Church Farm, Dorsington, Stratford-upon-Avon, Warwickshire CV37 8AX

Mrs Marian J Walters
☎ 0789 720471
and 0831 504 194
BB From £13
Sleeps 14
♿ 🐎 🐕 🎾 💼
♨ ♨ **Commended**

A warm welcome awaits you at our mixed working farm with lakes, equestrian course and woodlands to explore. Situated on edge of quiet pretty village yet ideal for touring Stratford, Warwick, Cotswolds, NAC, NEC, Worcester and Evesham. Some bedrooms en-suite with TV. Stabling and fishing available. Open all year. Map ref: 238 096

Crandon House, Avon Dassett, Leamington Spa, Warwickshire CV33 0AA

Deborah Lea
☎ 0295 770652
BB From £17
EM From £11
Sleeps 6
🐕 🐎 (8) 🔲 🎾
♨ ♨
Highly Commended

A specially warm welcome at our farmhouse offering an exceptionally high standard accommodation and comfort. Set in 20 acres, beautiful views over unspoilt countryside. Small working farm, rare breeds cattle, sheep and poultry. Own produce, excellent food. Large garden. Full CH, log fire. 3 rooms with private facilities. Colour TV, tea/coffee tray. Peaceful, quiet, easy access to Warwick, Stratford, Cotswolds. Located between M40, J11/12 (4 miles). Open all year (closed Christmas). Map ref: 246 095

Glebe Farm, Exhall, Alcester, Warwickshire B49 6EA

John & Margaret Canning
☎ 0789 772202
BB From £14.50
Sleeps 5
🐕 🐎 🎾 🏹
♨ **Approved**

Shakespeare named our village 'Dodging Exhall' and it has somehow 'dodged' the passing of time, so if you want a true taste of rural England, come and relax in our quaint old farmhouse – parts of it dating from Tudor times – with its log fires, four-poster bed and country hospitality. 1 double, 1 twin, 1 single, tea/coffee trays, electric blankets. Smoking in lounge. Payphone. Laundry. Ample parking. Open all year (closed Christmas & New Year). Map ref: 234 095

Hill Farm, Lewis Road, Radford Semele, Leamington Spa, Warwickshire CV31 1UX

Rebecca Gibbs
☎ 0926 337571
BB From £15
EM From £12
Sleeps 10
🐴 Å 🚐 (and static caravans)
🏵 🏵 **Approved**

Hill Farm is a comfortable, friendly farmhouse situated in 350 acres of mixed farmland. Excellent food, large garden, attractive double/twin/single bedrooms, some en suite, with CH and tea/coffee-making facilities. Comfortable TV lounge, quiet room, guests' bathroom. Children welcome. AA and Farm Holiday Guide award winner. Caravanning/Camping Club certificated site. Ideal for Shakespeare Country. Open all year (closed Christmas). Map ref: 242 099

Irelands Farm, Irelands Lane, Henley-in-Arden, Solihull, West Midlands B95 5SA

Pamela Shaw
☎ 0564 792476
BB From £16
Sleeps 6
🐕 ⅔ 🐃
🏵 🏵 **Commended**

If a quiet, relaxing holiday is what you are looking for, then visit our late Georgian farmhouse. Large rooms all with own bath/shower, TV, tea/coffee-making facilities, radio, CH. Set in 220 acres of peaceful farmland. Close to National Exhibition Centre, Stratford-upon-Avon, Warwick, National Agricultural Centre. Looking forward to meeting you. Open all year (closed Christmas & New Year). Map ref: 235 099

Kirby Farm, Whatcote, Shipston-on-Stour, Warwickshire

Carol Fox
☎ 0295 680 525/223
BB From £10
Sleeps 6
🐃
Listed

Farmhouse bed and breakfast in spacious, attractive stone-built farmhouse. En-suite accommodation available. Magnificent views of the countryside, within easy reach of the Cotswolds, Stratford-upon-Avon, Warwick and Oxford. Situated close to the A422 Banbury–Stratford road, 1 mile from the village of Oxhill, 2 miles from Tysoe. Open Mar–Nov. Map ref: 243 091

Little Hill Farm, Wellesbourne, Warwick, Warwickshire CV35 9EB

Charlotte Hutsby
☎ 0789 840261
BB From £15
EM From £7.50
Sleeps 6
🐕 ⅔ 🐃 🐴 ❀
🏵 🏵

Set in 700 acres of beef/arable farmland, our rambling William & Mary farmhouse offers a warm, friendly relaxed atmosphere, with antiques and beams throughout the house. Each bedroom has private bathroom. Drawing room with colour TV. The farm is situated on A429 on Warwick Road from Wellesbourne, only 6 miles from Warwick and 6 miles from Stratford-upon-Avon. Open all year (closed Christmas & New Year). Map ref: 239 096

Lower Watchbury Farm, Wasperton Lane, Barford, Warwickshire CV35 8DH

Valerie Tole
☎ 0926 624772
BB From £19.50
Sleeps 3
⅔ 🐃 🐕 ❀
Listed

In the heart of Shakespeare Country, we offer you a warm welcome. Situated in 50 acres with outstanding views over rural Warwickshire, our recently refurnished accommodation includes 1 family/twin room with lounge area and en-suite bathroom. Colour TV, tea/coffe-making facilities. Excellent farmhouse breakfast. Large garden. Warwick, Stratford-upon-Avon, Kenilworth and Cotswolds nearby. Brochure available. Open Apr–Oct. Map ref: 239 097

Manor Farm, Willey, Nr Rugby, Warwickshire CV23 0SH

Mrs Helen Sharpe
☎ 0455 553143
BB From £16
Sleeps 6
⅔
🏵 🏵 **Commended**

Attention to detail ensures us many repeat bookings. Being on the borders of Warwickshire, Leicestershire, Northamptonshire makes us the perfect venue for north/south travellers or visitors to NEC, NAC, etc. We offer genuine hospitality, peace and tranquility combined with the convenience of being 5 miles from Midlands motorway triangle. Convenient A5, Fosse Way. AA Listed QQQ. Open all year. Map ref: 250 107

Maxstoke Hall Farm, Fillongley Road, Maxstoke, Nr Coleshill, Birmingham, Warwickshire B46 2QT

Mrs Heather Green
☎ 0675 463237
🛏 From £19.50
EM From £6.75
Sleeps 3
🔥 🍴 ⊞ 🏹 ⬳ 🎪 ⬛ 🎯
👑 👑 **Commended**

Elegant farmhouse, built in 1632, and set in beautiful countryside. Bedrooms have en-suite facilities, TV, hostess tray. Comfortable oak-beamed dining and sitting rooms for use by guests. Situated 3 miles from Coleshill, 5 mins from M6 and M42. 15 mins from National Exhibition Centre, Birmingham Airport and International Railway Station. Open all year. Map ref: 235 108

Newbarn Farm, Sibford Gower, Nr Banbury, Oxfordshire OX15 5RY

**Robin Wingate-
Routledge**
☎ 029 578 330
🛏 From £16.50
Sleeps 3
✂ 🍴 ⬛
Listed

A Swedish house built 3 years ago. Triple glazed, very warm and light. Traditionally furnished. Nice garden. 1 twin bedroom with TV. 1 single room with radio. Tea/coffee trays. Small working farm, pedigree Suffolk sheep, calves, Jersey cow and poultry. Situated on top of a hill, with beautiful, far-reaching views over open countryside. Lovely walks. Ideal for Oxford, Stratford-upon-Avon, Cotswolds. Open all year. Map ref: 246 091

Newfields, Shakers Lane, Long Itchington, Rugby, Warwickshire CV23 8QB

Rosemary Reeve
☎ 0926 632207
Fax 0926 632115
🛏 From £17–£25
Sleeps 4
🍴 ✂ 🏹 ⬳ 🎪 ⬛ 🎯
👑 👑

Rosemary and Richard Reeve offer a warm welcome to non-smokers to stay in their beautiful 17th century Manor House situated in the centre of their 450-acre farm. Centrally heated comfortable twin bedroom, en-suite shower and WC, and family triple room with own bathroom. Log fires in guests' dining/sitting room. Conservatory, garden and tennis court. Open all year. Map ref: 245 101

New House Farm, Brailes, Banbury, Oxfordshire OX15 5BD

Helen Taylor
☎ 060875 239
🛏 From £14
Sleeps 6
🍴 🐎
👑 👑

Quietly nestling under Brailes Hill, a Georgian farmhouse on 450-acre mixed farm in an area of outstanding natural beauty. In easy reach of Cotswolds, Oxford, Stratford. 1 family room en suite, 1 double en suite, 1 twin with washbasin. Large garden, 18-hole golf course within walking distance. Open all year. Map ref: 246 091

Park Farm, Spring Road, Barnacle, Shilton, Coventry, Warwickshire CV7 9LG

Linda Grindal
☎ 0203 612628
🛏 From £17.50
EM From £11
Sleeps 4
🐎 (12)
👑 **Commended**

A warm welcome awaits you at Park Farm, a listed building dating back to the Civil War and originally moated. Spacious, comfortable and quiet, it is near the M6/M69 motorways. Two bedrooms with washbasins, TV, electric blankets and tea/coffee-making facilities. Guests' own bathroom. Separate sitting and dining room. Full CH. Excellent food. Open all year. Map ref: 244 108

Sharmer Farm, Fosse Way, Radford Semele, Leamington Spa, Warwickshire CV31 1XH

Nora Ellis
☎ 0926 612448
🛏 From £15–£20
Sleeps 9
🐎
👑 👑 **Commended**

A warm welcome, comfort and good English cooking, using local produce, awaits guests at our recently extended and tastefully furnished farmhouse. Set in 120 acres, 4 miles from Royal Leamington Spa. An excellent base for touring Shakespeare Country or one-night-stop for travellers and business people. Fire certificate. Trout fishing nearby. Brochure available. Open all year (closed Christmas & New Year). Map ref: 242 099

Shrewley Pools Farm, Haseley, Warwickshire CV35 7HB

Mrs Cathy Dodd
☎ 0926 484315
BB From £17
EM From £6
Sleeps 6
🐶 ⅄ ♨ ♠
Listed Commended

Why not sample the delights of staying in a beautiful 17th century traditional farmhouse? Set in an acre of landscaped garden with 4-acre pool. Shrewley Pools has many interesting features, including timbered barn, huge fireplaces, and beamed ceilings. 2 bedrooms, one en-suite, with tea/coffee tray. Close to Warwick, Stratford-upon-Avon, the NEC and NAC. Open all year (closed Christmas). Map ref: 237 100

Snowford Hall, Hunningham, Nr Royal Leamington Spa, Warwickshire CV33 9ES

Rudi Hancock
☎ 0926 632297
BB From £15
EM From £12
Sleeps 6
🐶 ♔
👑👑 Commended

A warm welcome and peaceful surroundings in 18th century farmhouse on 250-acre mixed working farm in rolling countryside. Near the Roman Fosse Way, ideal for visiting Stratford, Warwick, Leamington, Cotswolds, NAC and NEC. 1 double room with washbasin; 1 twin room with shower/basin/WC; 1 twin room with shower/basin. Singles extra. CH, good home cooking. Open all year (closed Christmas & New Year). Map ref: 243 103

Thornton Manor, Ettington, Stratford-upon-Avon, Warwickshire CV37 7PN

Mrs Gillian Hutsby
☎ 0789 740210
BB From £16
Sleeps 6
🐶 (5) ♔ ♨
👑👑

A 16th century stone-built manor house, overlooking peaceful countryside on an 800-acre farm. Tennis, fishing and riding nearby. There is a log fire to relax by in the comfortable hall, plus a television and piano. Separate guest kitchen and breakfast room. Private showers/bathroom for each bedroom. Situated off the A429 Warwick road, from Ettington. Open all year (closed Christmas & New Year). Map ref: 239 094

Tibbits Farm, Nethercote, Flecknoe, Nr Rugby, Warwickshire CV23 8AS

Alison Mills
☎ 0788 890239
BB From £17
Sleeps 6
🐶 🐴 🙏 🖼 ♨ ♠ ♔
👑👑

Retreat from the trials of life to the seclusion and tranquillity of our 17th farmhouse idyllically situated within acres of rolling countryside, where we offer luxurious bed and breakfast accommodation. The spacious and pretty bedrooms have private bathrooms, colour TVs, tea/coffee making facilities. Tibbits is ideally situated for exploring the many places of historic, scenic and cultural interest in the area. (French spoken). Map ref: 249 099

Walcote Farm, Walcote, Haselor, Alcester, Warwickshire B49 6LY

Prim & John Finnemore
☎ 0789 488264
BB From £17
Sleeps 4
🐶 🐴 ⅄ ♔ ♨
👑👑

Stratford-upon-Avon is only 5 miles from a tranquil picturesque hamlet with our attractive 16th century listed oak-beamed farmhouse and its inglenook fireplaces. Ideal for Shakespeare properties, Warwick Castle, The Cotswolds, Ragley Hall, NEC, NAC or to relax and enjoy the idyllic countryside. Private fishing. Comfortable rooms. En-suite and tea/coffee making facilities. Open all year. Map ref: 234 097

Walton Farm, Walton, Nr Wellesbourne, Warwickshire CV35 9HX

Mrs A Hutsby
☎ 0789 841966
BB From £15
Sleeps 6
⅄ 🐶 (14)
Applied

A comfortable, friendly farmhouse situated in an unspoilt estate hamlet, nestling in wooded countryside. Large garden and pretty duck pond. 3 bedrooms, all en-suite. Ideally situated between Stratford-upon-Avon, Warwick and National Exhibition Centre. Open all year. Map ref: 237 095

Whitchurch Farm, Wimpstone, Stratford-upon-Avon CV37 8NS

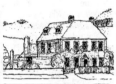

Mrs Joan James
☎ 0789 450275
🅱 From £14
EM From £8
Sleeps 6
🐴 🏠
Listed

Lovely Georgian farmhouse set in park–like surroundings in peaceful Stour Valley 4½ miles from Stratford. Very convenient for Warwick Castle and Shakespeare properties. Ideal for touring the Cotswolds by car or rambling. The bedrooms are large, well furnished with washbasins, two with en-suite bathroom, CH and tea/coffee-making facilities. Separate dining room and sitting room for guests. Open all year (closed Christmas Day). Map ref: 237 094

Yew Tree Farm, Wootton Wawen, Solihull, West Midlands B95 6BY

Mrs Janet Haimes
☎ 0564 792701
🅱 From £14
Sleeps 4 cot
🐴 🏠
🏵 🏵 Commended

Georgian farmhouse situated on A3400 in village of Wootton Wawen, 2 miles south of Henley-in-Arden, 6 miles north of Stratford-upon-Avon. Within easy reach of Warwick Castle, Royal Showground, NEC, and the Cotswolds. 700-acre dairy/arable farm with lake and woodland walks. 2 large double bedrooms, CH, en-suite, tea/coffee-making facilities. Cot available. Comfortable visitors' lounge with colour TV. Excellent pubs and restaurants nearby. Open all year (closed Christmas & New Year). Map ref: 235 098

Self-Catering

Furzen Hill Farm Cottage, c/o Furzen Hill Farm, Cubbington Heath, Leamington Spa, Warwickshire CV32 6QZ

Mrs Christine Whitfield
☎ 0926 424791
🆂 From £90–£250
Sleeps 4/7
🐴 🐴 🐎
🔑 🔑 🔑 Up to
Commended

Furzen Hill is a dairy and arable farm. The cottage is part of 17th century farmhouse with a large shared garden. Sleeping 7. The barn, recently converted, sleeps 4. Also 2 cottages on the Fosse Way at Radford Semele. Each equipped for 4. All situated within easy reach of NAC, NEC, Warwick and Stratford. Open all year. Map ref: 243 104

Glebe Farm Holiday Cottages, c/o Glebe Farm, Exhall, Alcester, Warwickshire B49 6EA

John & Margaret
Canning
☎ 0789 772202
🆂 From £125–£450
Sleeps 2/7
🐴 🐕 ♿ 🔥 🐎
Applied

Wanting to get away from it all? Leave the 20th century behind, come through our thatched archway into the farmyard and try one of our delightful cottages recently converted from the old farm buildings. Situated in picturesque Shakespearean village on working farm. Compact and fully equipped including towels, bedlinen, colour TV, CH and electricity. Payphone, laundry, ample parking, shop. 1 cottage suitable disabled. Open all year. Map ref: 234 097

The Granary, c/o Glebe Farm, Kinwarton, Alcester, Warwickshire B49 6HB

Susan Kinnersley
☎ 0789 762554
🆂 From £70–£125
Sleeps 2 cot
✂ 🐴 🔥 🏠 🐎
🔑 🔑 🔑 Commended

Off the beaten track, yet near the small market town of Alcester, this cottage retains many interesting features of the original granary combined with modern standards of warmth and comfort. The farm is bounded by the River Alne and there are a variety of attractive country walks in the area. Linen provided, colour TV. Cot available. Car space. Short breaks by arrangement. Open all year. Map ref: 233 097

Hipsley Farm Cottages, Hipsley Lane, Hurley, Atherstone, Warwickshire CV9 2HS

Mrs Ann Prosser
☎ 0827 872437
Fax 0827 872437
🆂🅲 From £185–£290
🐕 🐄 🍵 ⚓ 🚗 ♿
🔑 🔑 🔑 – 🔑 🔑 🔑 🔑
Highly Commended

Hipsley Farm is situated in beautiful rolling countryside only 3 miles from junction 10, M42/A5, so ideal for NEC, Birmingham, Warwick, Leicester. The barns and cowshed have been carefully converted into 6 comfortable, individually furnished cottages. Fully equipped including CH, colour TV, bed linen and towels, laundry, payphone, putting green, ample parking on site. One cottage suitable for disabled. ETB highly commended. Open all year. Map ref: 242 112

Irelands Farm, Irelands Lane, Henley in Arden, Warwickshire B95 5SA

Pamela Shaw
☎ 0564 792476
🆂🅲 From £120–£388
Sleeps 4
🐄 ♿ ✂ 🐕
🔑 🔑 🔑 🔑 **Commended**

Four attractively converted oak-beamed cottages in courtyard on 220-acre working farm. Very quiet location yet within 3 miles of M42/M40 junction. All cottages centrally heated and tastefully furnished, and equipped to a high standard. Linen provided. Private patios. Open all year. Map ref: 235 099

North & South Cottages, Edstone, c/o Yew Tree Farm, Wootton Wawen, Solihull, West Midlands B95 6BY

Mrs Janet Haimes
☎ 0564 792701
🆂🅲 From £100–£230
Sleeps 6 in each house
🐕 🍵
🔑 🔑 🔑 – 🔑 🔑 🔑 🔑
Approved

Leave the busy A3400 Birmingham to Stratford-upon-Avon road and a short drive through Edstone Park brings visitors to these two delightful semi-detached houses surrounded by lawned gardens. Each house is comfortably furnished, carpeted and equipped to Tourist Board standards. Central heating, colour TV, telephone. Four miles Stratford-upon-Avon, near Cotswolds, NEC and Royal Showground. Open all year. Map ref: 232 098

Snowford Hall Farm Cottage, c/o Snowford Hall, Hunningham, Nr Leamington Spa, Warwickshire CV33 9ES

Rudi Hancock
☎ 0926 632297
🆂🅲 From £100–£250
Sleeps 5/6
🐕 🐎
🔑 🔑 🔑 **Approved**

Fully centrally heated spacious 2–bedroomed cottage on a quiet country road surrounded by well maintained lawns and farmland. Capable of sleeping 5/6 people. A comfortable lounge with TV and fitted kitchen makes this cottage an ideal base for touring the Cotswolds, Shakespeare Country and exploring Warwick, Kenilworth and Oxford. The NAC is 5 miles and NEC 15 miles away. Open all year. Map ref: 243 103

FARM HOLIDAY BUREAU

CONFIRM BOOKINGS

Disappointments can arise by misunderstandings over the telephone. Please write to confirm your booking.

---

39 Northamptonshire

Northamptonshire, the county of 'squires and spires', has houses, monuments and fine churches too numerous to mention. There's Sulgrave Manor, home of George Washington's ancestors; Rockingham Castle which was 'Arnescote Castle' in the BBC TV series 'By the Sword Divided'; Boughton House, modelled on Versailles; and Althorp, the home of the father of the Princess of Wales.

At the castle remains, by the river in picturesque Fotheringhay, you may ponder upon the execution of Mary, Queen of Scots and the birth there of Richard III, and the Battle and Farm Museum will give you a taste of that decisive Civil War battle in 1645. A firm hold has been kept on our heritage and at Brixworth and Earls Barton you will be able to see possibly the country's finest examples of a Saxon church and tower. Many of the county's villages and towns have splendid churches dating from Norman times through to the 15th century.

Traditional methods of transport and entertainment are well preserved. The Waterways Museum at Stoke Bruerne gives you a fascinating insight into life on the canals, and there are boat trips along the Grand Union Canal. On the Nene Valley Steam Railway you can take a nostalgic trip down the line and study steam trains and rolling stock from all over the world.

Group Contact: Mrs M. Hankins ☎ 08015 614

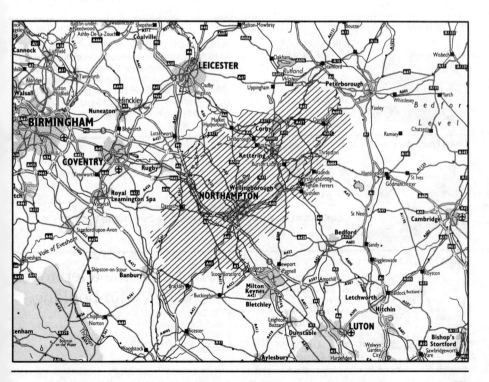

Bed and Breakfast (and evening meal)

Barewell Fields, Moreton Pinkney, Daventry, Northamptonshire NN11 6NJ

Margaret Lainchbury
☎ 0295 760754
From £15
EM From £10
Sleeps 5
(7)
Listed Highly Commended

A friendly welcome awaits you at Barewell Fields, situated in peaceful Moreton Pinkney in unspoilt countryside. 9 miles from M1, also M40 Banbury. Ideal touring centre for NT properties, Oxford and Stratford. Guests may relax in own drawing room, also use of own dining room and bathroom. Just 5 mins' walk through the village is Home Farm, a working farm run by Margaret's son, where you are welcome to visit. Open all year. Map ref: 253 094

Dairy Farm, Cranford St Andrew, Kettering, Northamptonshire NN14 4AQ

Audrey Clarke
☎ 053 678 273
From £18
EM From £10
Sleeps 6
Commended

Enjoy a holiday in a comfortable 17th century farmhouse with oak beams and inglenook fireplaces. Peaceful surroundings, large garden containing ancient circular dovecote. Dairy Farm is a working farm situated in a beautiful Northamptonshire village just off the A14 within easy reach of many places of interest or ideal for a restful holiday. Good farmhouse food and friendly atmosphere. Open all year. Map ref: 265 106

Drayton Lodge, Daventry, Northamptonshire NN11 4NL

Ann Spicer
☎ 0327 702449
Fax 0327 76365
From £20
EM From £12
Sleeps 8

Drayton Lodge is a secluded 18th century farmhouse set on the edge of Daventry to one side and rolling Northamptonshire countryside to the other. A warm, friendly welcome awaits you. Beautiful centrally heated bedrooms with en suite bathrooms and TVs. Championship golf course within ½ mile. Historical places of interest to visit. Full traditional English breakfast served. Open all year. Map ref: 252 099

Green Farm, Weedon Lois, Towcester, Northamptonshire NN12 8PL

P J Elkington
☎ 0327 860249
From £16
Sleeps 6
Listed Commended

Green Farm is a comfortable 18th century farmhouse set in rolling countryside on a 550-acre mixed farm. You can enjoy private coarse fishing or visit the many local attractions, including Sulgrave Manor, Canons Ashby, and Silverstone Grand Prix circuit to name but a few! The M1 and M40 are both within 10 miles. Open all year. Map ref: 256 094

Manor Farm, Adstone, Towcester, Northamptonshire NN12 8DT

Elisabeth Paton
☎ 0327 860284
From £15
EM From £8 (by arrangement)
Sleeps 6
Commended

Peace and quiet but plenty to see and do at this 430-acre farm. The farmhouse, built by an ancestor of George Washington in 1656, stands on the edge of a tiny village. Enjoy woodland walks, ponds, wildlife and flowers or explore nearby historic houses, the Cotswolds, Stratford-upon-Avon, Silverstone. Fun for all the family. Try our clay pigeon shooting instruction. Open all year. Map ref: 256 094

Pear Tree Farm, Aldwincle, Nr Kettering, Northamptonshire NN14 3EL

Mavis Hankins
☎ 080 15 614
BB From £15
EM From £9
Sleeps 7
🐕 🦆 👤 🎪
♨ ♨ Commended

Pear Tree Farm is a mixed 400-acre farm consisting of cattle, sheep, poultry and arable. Comfortably furnished with relaxed family atmosphere and good home cooking. Four bedrooms. Excellent for walking, birdwatching, fishing. Large garden for relaxing. Open all year (camping Feb–Sept). Map ref: 265 107

Quinton Green Farm, Quinton, Northamptonshire NN7 2EG

Mrs Margaret Turney
☎ 0604 862484
Fax 0604 862230
BB From £18
Sleeps 6
🐕 🐎 🎪
♨ ♨ Commended

The Turney family look forward to welcoming you to their comfortable, rambling 17th century farmhouse, only 10 mins from Northampton, yet overlooking lovely rolling countryside. We are close to Salcey Forest, with its wonderful facilities for walking. M1 (Jct. 15) is just 5 mins away; central Milton Keynes 20 mins. Open all year. Map ref: 259 097

Rifle Range Farm, Yielden, Bedfordshire MK44 1AW

Mrs Ann Paynter
☎ 0933 53151
BB From £15
EM From £7
Sleeps 3
🐕 🐎 🎪
Listed Commended

A quiet, comfortable farmhouse offering pleasant walks in open countryside. 4 miles from A45, between Kimbolton and Rushden. Centrally placed for a stopover north and south. EM by arrangement. Open all year. Map ref: 268 102

Walltree House Farm, Steane, Brackley, Northamptonshire NN13 5NS

Richard & Pauline Harrison
☎ 0295 811235
Fax 0295 811147
BB From £19
EM From £8
Sleeps 16
🐕 🐎 👶 ♿ 🎿
♨ ♨

A converted courtyard provides warm, comfortable accommodation, with most bedrooms having private bath, giving freedom, flexibility and independence. Traditional English breakfasts are served in the Victorian house, drinks in the drawing room or conservatory. Ideal base for touring Warwick, Stratford-upon-Avon, Blenheim, Cotswolds, London and National Trust properties. Evening meal by arrangement. Open all year (closed Christmas & New Year). Map ref: 253 089

West Lodge Farm, Pipewell Road, Desborough, Northamptonshire NN14 2SH

Margaret Dee
☎ 0536 760552
BB From £18
Sleeps 4
🐕 🐎 👤 🦆 🎣 🎪 🎿
♨ ♨ Commended

A spacious William IV farmhouse in hunting country, with abundant wildlife on view. Situated on a secluded working arable farm of over 500 acres. Farm walks available through woodland. Trout fishing close by. Also stately homes and canal network gives country-lovers plenty to do. Open all year. Map ref: 260 107

Wold Farm, Old, Northampton, Northamptonshire NN6 9RJ

Anne Engler
☎ 0604 781258
BB From £18
EM From £10
Sleeps 10
🐕 🐎 🎪 ♿
♨ ♨ ♨

A friendly, informal atmosphere is offered at this 18th century farmhouse on 250-acre beef/arable farm. Attractive bedrooms, some en-suite, overlook landscaped gardens with colourful pergola. Close to 7th century Brixworth Church, Pitsford Reservoir with trout fishing, sailing and nature reserve. Farmhouse breakfast in oak–beamed dining room with inglenook fireplace. Relax by log fire or at snooker table. Snacks or 4-course evening meal on request. Open all year. Map ref: 258 099

Woolleys Farm, Welford Road, Naseby, Northamptonshire NN6 7DP

Heather Jeffries
☎ 0858 575310
🛏 From £15
EM From £6
Sleeps 2

Comfortable Georgian farmhouse 1 mile west of Naseby, away from the road and overlooking garden and fields. Midway between Northampton and Leicester, and near the site of the Battle of Naseby 1645. Twin bedded room with shower en-suite and tea-making facilities. Map ref: 255 105

Self-Catering

Papley Farm Cottages, Papley Farm, Warmington, Peterborough PE8 6UU

Joyce Lane
☎ 0832 272583
🔲 From £100–£300
Sleeps 2/5

Commended

On our large mixed farm, peace and comfort are to be found in The Chestnut Tree, Slade House or The Bungalow, all sleeping 5, Tudor Cottage or Brook End sleeping 2. Luxuriously equipped, all are warm, spacious and prepared especially for you – including linen. Farm and nature walks. Near Oundle, Stamford and Peterborough. 5 miles from A1. Open all year. Map ref: 272 109

Rye Hill Farm, Holdenby Road, East Haddon, Northamptonshire NN6 8DH

Michael & Margaret Widdowson
☎ 0604 770990
🔲 From £120–£340
Sleeps 2/6

Highly Commended

7 miles NW of Northampton, 5 cottages in courtyard of smallholding surrounded by gently undulating countryside. Converted to a very high standard from barns and an old coach house, facilities include payphones, microwaves, dishwaters, bed linen, laundry room, games room and small shop. Friendly animals. Pretty, unspoilt villages, many local places of interest, good touring country. Althorp nearby. Open all year. Map ref: 255 103

FARM HOLIDAY BUREAU

GOOD FOOD

Nearly all Bureau members now hold a certificate in Essential Food Hygiene.

40 Bedfordshire

We invite you to spend some time in the County of Bedfordshire in the rural heartland of England. With riches ripe for discovery, it is ideally situated between Oxford and Cambridge. The Great Ouse, with its quiet backwaters together with the Lakes at Stewartby, Wyboston and Grafham make ideal venues for the fisherman and the watersports enthusiast. Cyclists will appreciate the ease with which they can travel throughout the area, while walkers will find the newly established Greensand Ridge Walk provides many routes. Golfers also have a wide choice of courses available.

Our stately homes include Woburn Abbey and Luton Hoo, plus pretty villages with thatched cottages and beamed Tudor buildings. The National Trust own the extraordinary 16th-century stone dovecote and stables at Willington, plus 422 acres of hill country at Dunstable Downs. Bedford Museum has a display relating to the history and natural history of the area, while the Cecil Higgins Art Gallery enjoys an international reputation for the quality of its collections. Luton Museum and Art Gallery exhibit local and natural history, archaeology and lace, while Stockwood Park Craft Museum has exhibits relating to rural life and crafts.

The Shuttleworth Collection of historic aeroplanes and road vehicles is open every day of the year, while for garden enthusiasts there is the Swiss Garden and Wrest Park Gardens.

For the naturalist there is the RSPB nature reserve and headquarters, or Stagsden Bird Gardens, with hundreds of rare birds from all over the world. For something more exotic, visit Whipsnade Zoo or the Wild Animal Kingdom at Woburn.

Bedfordshire is also the birthplace of market gardening – so guests might find themselves going home laden with fresh fruit and vegetables from a farm shop or a pick–your–own unit! Whatever your interests you'll enjoy your stay in Bedfordshire.

Group Contacts: BB **Mrs Janet Must** ☎ **0234 870234**
                        SC **Mrs Angela Little** ☎ **0525 712978**

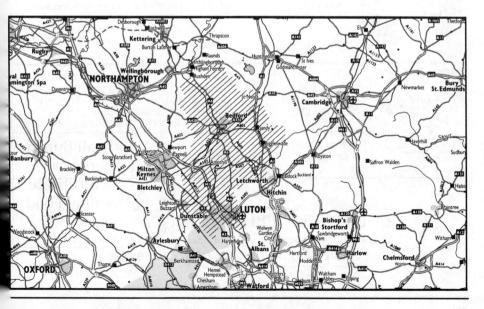

Bed and Breakfast (and evening meal)

Church Farm, Roxton, Bedford, Bedfordshire MK44 3EB

Janet Must
☎ 0234 870234
BB From £14
Sleeps 6
🛇 🐕 🐈 🌂 🛍
Listed

An attractive old farmhouse with a comfortable self-contained guest wing overlooking the garden and small orchard. Situated in a quiet village ½ mile from A1. Large bedrooms with tea and coffee-making facilities. Full English breakfast served in 16th century dining room. We offer double, single and family accommodation. Open all year. Map ref: 269 095

Firs Farm, Stagsden, Bedfordshire MK43 8TB

Mrs P Hutcheon
☎ 02302 2344
BB From £14.50
Sleeps 4
🛇 (5) 🐕 🛍
🐝

Firs Farm is a family run arable farm, set in quiet surroundings ¼ mile south of A422. The farmhouse is timber framed and set in a large garden with swimming pool. Accommodation consists of double rooms with tea/coffee making facilities and guests' lounge with colour TV. Many local tourist attractions. Open all year. Map ref: 267 094

Grovebury Farm, Grovebury Road, Leighton Buzzard, Bedfordshire LU7 8TF

Mrs Elizabeth Kinsey
☎ 0525 373363
BB From £14
Sleeps 6
🛇 (12) ✂
Listed

Grovebury Farm is an arable and beef farm of 400 acres, located 1 mile from Leighton Buzzard and within easy reach of Woburn Abbey, Whipsnade Zoo and several golf courses. Also situated mid-way between Oxford and Cambridge, and with a 40 min train service to London. Open all year. Map ref: 265 085

Highfield Farm, Sandy, Bedfordshire SG19 2AQ

Margaret Codd
☎ 0767 682332
BB From £14
Sleeps 6
🛇 🐕
🐝 🐝 Highly
Commended

Tom and Margaret Codd welcome guests to their comfortable farmhouse. Just 1 mile north of Sandy on the A1, Highfield Farm is excellently situated for visiting Cambridge, Shuttleworth, the RSPB, Grafham Water and for taking the Greensand Ridge Walk. Family, double and single bedrooms, some with en-suite bathroom. Guests' sitting room with log fire and colour TV. Open all year. Map ref: 275 095

LET THE TELEPHONE RING!
Some farmhouses are big places. Let the telephone ring long enough to give the owner time to answer it.

FARM HOLIDAY BUREAU

Self-Catering

'The Old Stone Barn', c/o Home Farm, Warrington, Olney, Buckinghamshire MK46 4HN

Mrs & Mrs G. Pibworth
☎ 0234 711655
SC From £140–£280
Sleeps 1/6
🐴 🐕 ⊞ ♿ ♨ ♣ ⚘
🏵 🏵 🏵 🏵 **Commended**

A charming combination of old character and modern facilities, the Old Stone Barn is 3 ground floor and 3 first floor spacious self-contained apartments peacefully positioned on an arable farm 1½ miles north of Olney. Relax in the gardens, make use of the outdoor heated swimming pool or take day trips to Oxford, Cambridge, London or the Cotswolds. Open all year. Map ref: 264 095

Priestley Farm, Church Road, off Temple Way, Flitwick, Bedfordshire MK45 5AN

Mrs Angela Little
☎ 0525 712978
SC From £125–£150
Sleeps 6
🐴 🐂
🏵 🏵 🏵 **Approved**

The Georgian farmhouse set in open countryside offers 3 double bedrooms (one twin bedded), bathroom, lounge, kitchen/diner. Central heating. Linen provided. A working family dairy farm with 90 Jersey cows and young stock. Visitors are welcome to watch the milking and other seasonal activities. Shopping facilities and main railway station etc 2 miles, M1, 4 miles. Plenty of footpaths to enjoy the Bedfordshire countryside. Open all year. Map ref: 269 090

FOLLOW THE COUNTRY CODE

Leave nothing but footprints,

Take nothing but photographs,

Kill nothing but time!

DISABLED VISITORS

members offering suitable accommodation to disabled/less able visitors. Please do check the extent of the facilities before booking.

41 Cambridgeshire

Cambridgeshire is a county of contrasts, a county of quiet waterways, gentle hills, lanes, busy towns, attractions great and small, all presented with a friendly welcome for the visitor.

Best known is Cambridge itself, one of Britain's oldest university cities where the colleges in their architectural splendour rest near tranquil rivers overhung with willows, the city that inspired Brooke and Byron.

As well as Cambridge the county has many other attractions. North of Cambridge lies the strikingly flat landscape of the Fens. This once barren marshland was home to the 'Fen Tigers' who lived by cutting reeds and catching eels. Today, the landscape is crisscrossed with dykes which have vastly improved the drainage of this peaty area and made the land a valuable asset for farming.

For contrast there is the hustle and bustle of the modern city of Peterborough with its excellent shopping or the stately grandeur of Ely Cathedral, so called 'Ship of the Fens'.

Wherever you go in Cambridgeshire it is a beautiful county to explore with large towns and small villages, cathedrals and tiny churches and cricket on the village green.

Group Contact: Mrs Hilary Nix ☎ 0353 778369

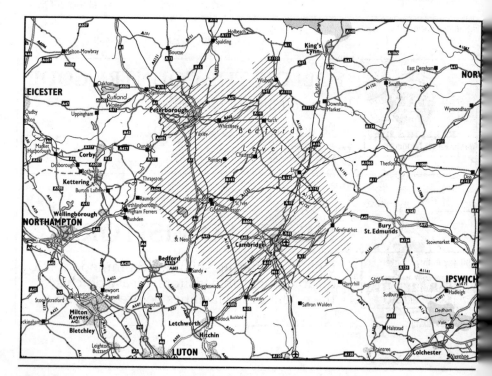

Bed and Breakfast (and evening meal)

Forge Cottage, Lower Road, Stuntney, Ely, Cambridgeshire CB7 5TN

Mrs Alison Morbey
☎ 0353 663275
0831 833932 mobile
🛏 From £20
Sleeps 4
🏕 ⛵ ♿
♿ ♿ Highly
Commended

A Shire horse and arable farm with a 17th century listed farmhouse situated in the centre of a quiet village. In an elevated position overlooking the Fens to Ely Cathedral. Furnished in antiques, the accommodation is in two luxurious bedrooms with en-suite facilities. 3-acre garden with tennis court for guests' use. Ideal base for touring. Ely 2 miles, Newmarket 12 miles, Cambridge 15 miles. Open all year (closed Christmas). Map ref: 287 107

Gransden Lodge Farm, Little Gransden, Sandy, Bedfordshire SG19 3EB

Mr & Mrs P Cox
☎ 0767 677365/677647
🛏 From £12.50
Sleeps 5
🐎 🐴 ✕ ♿
♿

A warm and friendly atmosphere awaits you at Gransden Lodge, where we have double, twin and single rooms with TV, clock-radio and tea/coffee-making facilities. Ample bathrooms and WCs. Dining room, also large lounge with TV. Many local pubs and restaurants for evening meals. Situated on the B1046, west of Cambridge. London 50 miles. Also convenient for Stansted Airport (M11, jct. 12). Open all year. Map ref: 275 095

Hill House Farm, 9 Main Street, Coveney, Ely, Cambridgeshire CB6 2DJ

Hilary Nix
☎ 0353 778369
🛏 From £16
EM From £13
Sleeps 6
✕ 🐎
♿ ♿ ♿ Commended

A warm and friendly welcome awaits you on this arable farm in unspoilt Fenland village, 3 miles west of historic Cathedral city of Ely. Victorian farmhouse has full central heating, comfortable, tastefully furnished, en-suite bedrooms with colour TV. Open views of surrounding countryside. Cambridge, Newmarket, Peterborough, Welney Wild fowl refuge, Wicken Fen nearby. Ideal for touring Cambridgeshire, Norfolk, Suffolk. Evening meal by arrangement. Regret no pets. No smoking. Map ref: 287 117

Manor Farm, Landbeach, Cambridgeshire CB4 4ED

Vicki Hatley
☎ 0223 860165
🛏 From £15
Sleeps 6
🐎 (3) ♿
♿ ♿ Commended

A comfortable and welcoming Georgian farmhouse surrounded by a large enclosed garden in which children are welcome to play. We are a 620-acre mixed farm in a quiet village only 5 miles from Cambridge and 10 miles from Ely. All rooms have washbasins, some en-suite, TV and tea/coffee-making facilities. A traditional English breakfast is served. Coarse fishing is available. Open all year. Map ref: 284 099

Spinney Abbey, Wicken, Ely, Cambridgeshire CB7 5XQ

Valerie Fuller
☎ 0353 720971
🛏 From £16
Sleeps 6
✕ 🐎 (5)
♿ ♿

Spacious Georgian farmhouse, standing in a large garden on our mixed dairy/arable farm which borders the National Trust nature reserve Wicken Fen. Two en-suite double rooms and twin with private bathroom. Central heating and electric blankets for colder months. All with TV and tea/coffee tray. Guests' sitting room. Open all year. Map ref: 288 105

---

42 Norfolk & Suffolk

Where better to spend your holiday than in this part of East Anglia, one of the driest and sunniest parts of England, within easy reach of the North, the Midlands, London . . . and Europe.

In the north of the area is Norwich, 'capital' of East Anglia, with its beautiful Norman cathedral. The coastline around Norfolk and North Suffolk is very beautiful and parts have been designated as Heritage Coast and an Area of Outstanding Natural Beauty. The holiday resorts, including Cromer and Great Yarmouth, provide all the entertainment one could wish for, and it is difficult to imagine them as formerly quiet fishing villages.

The coast and Broads are a haven for wildlife and there are many sanctuaries in the area, such as the Minsmere Nature Reserve and Bird Sanctuary, the Earsham Otter Trust and several farm and wildlife parks and museums. Alternatively, you may prefer to spend your time enjoying the countryside, visiting the churches (and pubs!) of the villages, exploring the small market towns and discovering their history – often closely linked with the wool trade. There are many places to spend a day, a few examples being Somerleyton Hall and maze near Lowestoft; 14th-century Winfield College, a centre for music and the arts; Bressingham Steam Museum and Gardens and, of course, Lavenham with its beautifully timbered houses and inns.

Group Contacts: BB **Rosemary Bryle** ☎ **0473 87253**
SC **Margaret Langton** ☎ **0473 87210**

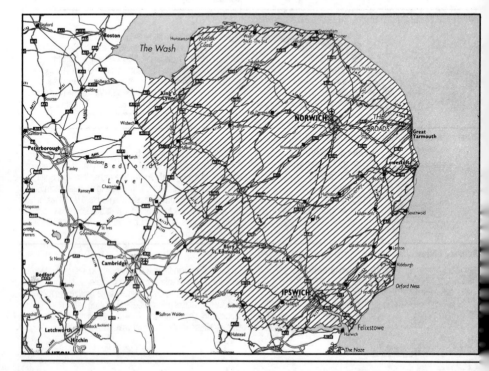

Bed and Breakfast (and evening meal)

Brighthouse Farm, Melford Road, Lawshall, near Bury St Edmunds, Suffolk IP29 4PX

Mr & Mrs Truin
☎ 0284 830385
🅱🅱 From £12
🔥 🐂 ✂ 🎄 ⚇
🏵🏵 **Commended**

Timbered Georgian farmhouse, set in beautiful surroundings of the Suffolk countryside, 3 acres of picturesque gardens. We offer homely accommodation. Centrally heated throughout, log fires in TV room in winter. Two double rooms, one twin with en-suite facilities. Historic Bury St. Edmunds/Lavenham close by. Good restaurants locally. Open all year.
Map ref: 300 099

Broad Oak Farm, Bramfield, Halesworth, Suffolk IP19 9AB

Mrs Patricia Kemsley
☎ 098684 232
🅱🅱 From £13
EM From £7
Sleeps 6
🔥 🐂 🎄 ⚇
🏵 **Commended**

A dairy farm with a spacious 16th century farmhouse, carefully modernised. Surrounded by meadowlands and attractive gardens with tennis court. 3 double bedrooms with H&C, 1 en-suite and separate guest bathroom. Sitting room with colour TV, dining room where good home cooked food is served (evening meal by arrangement). There's a friendly welcome waiting. Bramfield is 2 miles north west of the A12 on the A144. Southwold 7 miles. Open all year. Map ref: 321 104

Caravel, Pear Tree Farm, Hartest, Bury St Edmunds, Suffolk IP29 4EG

Mrs Rachel White
☎ 0284 830217
🅱🅱 From £15
Sleeps 4
🔥 (1) ✂
🏵

A warm welcome awaits you in our modern farm chalet bungalow on this arable farm. Ideally situated for exploring Lavenham, Constable country, and Cambridge. Accommodation comprises a comfortable guest lounge, twin, double rooms with washbasins, private bathroom, TV and coffee/tea facilities. Open April–Sept. Map ref: 301 095

College Farm, Hintlesham, Ipswich, Suffolk IP8 3NT

Mrs Rosemary Bryce
☎ 047387 253
🅱🅱 From £15
Sleeps 6
🔥 (5) 🎄
🏵🏵 **Highly Commended**

A warm welcome awaits you at this 600-acre arable/beef farm. The 15th century beamed farmhouse is in a quiet position with large garden. Double room with en-suite bathroom; family room and single room both with washbasin. Tea/coffee tray and central heating in all rooms. Guests' lounge with colour TV and log fire. Good food available locally. Close to Constable Country. Sorry, no pets. Open all year (closed Christmas & New Year). Map ref: 311 093

Colveston Manor, Mundford, near Thetford, Norfolk IP26 5HU

Wendy Allingham
☎ 0842 878218
🅱🅱 From £17
EM From £10
Sleeps 6
🔥 (12)
Listed

Enjoy a warm welcome at this comfortably furnished, spacious old farmhouse in the heart of Breckland. Rural setting. Visitors' lounge and dining room. One double en-suite, one double, 1 twin bedroom, sharing 2 bathrooms, all with tea/coffee-making facilities. Large farmhouse breakfasts, delicious dinners, using own produce where possible – recommended. Birdwatching, country walks, golf and fishing locally. Open all year. Map ref: 299 111

Earsham Park Farm, Harleston Road, Earsham, Bungay, Suffolk NR35 2AQ

Mrs Bobbie Watchorn
☎ 0986 892180
BB From £16
EM From £10
Sleeps 6
✔ ⌘ ⅋
♛ ♛ Commended

Come and enjoy rural luxury in our beautiful Victorian farmhouse. The large en-suite rooms have all facilities. Guests are welcome to help with the animals or wander around the gardens. Norwich and the coast are ½ an hour away. The Otter Trust and other attractions nearby. Children welcome, sorry no pets or smoking. Open all year. Map ref: 318 110

East Farm, Barnham, Thetford, Norfolk IP24 2PB

Margaret Heading
☎ 0842 890231
BB From £18
Sleeps 6
⌘ (3) ↟
⍟

Relax and enjoy the comfort and warm welcome at East Farm in the village of Barnham. We're a 1,000-acre arable farm with beef and sheep on the edge of Breckland on Norfolk/Suffolk border between Thetford and Bury St Edmunds. A grey flint-faced house in peaceful surroundings with superb views. Spacious heated rooms with en suite bathrooms. Full English breakfast from local produce. Open all year. Map ref: 302 105

Eastgate Farm, Great Walsingham, Norfolk NR22 6AB

Mary John
☎ 0328 820251
BB From £17
EM From £10
⌘ (12) ↟ ☞ ♠ ⅋
Listed

Eastgate is a working farm, 4 miles from the coast. The beautiful Georgian farmhouse is spacious and centrally heated. One twin-bedded, 2 double rooms, all with private bathrooms. Little Walsingham famous for its pilgrimages is ½ mile away. We can accommodate your horse or arrange riding locally. There are excellent eating places nearby. Evening meals by arrangement. Map ref: 303 127

Elm Lodge Farm, Chippenhall Green, Fressingfield, Eye, Suffolk IP21 5SL

Sheila Webster
☎ 037 986 249
BB From £15
EM From £9
Sleeps 6
✔ ↟ ⌘ (10)
♛ ♛ Approved

This 112-acre working farm with early Victorian farmhouse overlooks a large common (SSSI) where animals graze in summer – the perfect spot for an after-dinner stroll. Spacious bedrooms with washbasins, separate dining and sitting rooms, log fires and excellent food ensure that a comfortable, relaxing holiday is enjoyed by all those we warmly welcome to this attractive and peaceful corner of Suffolk. Open Mar–Nov. Map ref: 315 107

Highfield Farm, Great Ryburgh, Fakenham, Norfolk NR21 7AL

Mrs E Savory
☎ 032 878 249
BB From £14
EM From £8.50
Sleeps 6
⌘ (10) ⍟
Listed

Spacious and comfortable farmhouse on working farm 10 miles from the coast. Ideal for birdwatchers and country lovers, set well away from the road in 500 acres of rolling farmland. Twin with en-suite, double and twin with shared bathroom. Guests' sitting room and dining room. Clay pigeon shooting, farm walks, horse riding locally. Sorry, no pets. Open Mar–Nov (incl). OS ref: 947 279. Map ref: 305 125

Hillside Farm, Brooke, near Norwich, Norfolk NR15 1AU

Mrs Carolyn Holl
☎ 0508 50260
BB From £15
EM From £7.50
⌘ ↟ ⍟ ☞ ⍟ ⅋
Listed

This is a 350-acre arable and stock farm. A thatched and timber-framed house situated in a pretty village, 7 miles south of Norwich, within easy reach of coast and Broads. One twin/family room, 1 double/family room, both with private facilities. Large games barn with snooker, pool and table tennis. Five acre private lake for coarse fishing. Relaxed family atmosphere. Open all year. Map ref: 315 115

The Lodge Farm, Weston Road, Thelnetham, Diss, Norfolk IP22 1JL

Mrs Christine Palmer
☎ 0379 898203
BB From £15
EM From £8
Sleeps 6
♿ ⅟ ☕ ✿ ⅍
♨♨ **Commended**

Lodge Farm is a working farm of 200 acres with vineyard and Shire horses in a peaceful location 7 miles south of Diss. The thatched farmhouse has beams and inglenooks. 2 en-suite rooms and 1 with hand bason only, guests' own sitting room, and walled garden for guests' use. Excellent freshly cooked food – own garden produce used whenever possible. Table licence & off licence. Open all year. Map ref: 308 116

Malting Farm, Blo Norton Road, South Lopham, Diss, Norfolk IP22 2HT

Cynthia Huggins
☎ 037 988 201
BB From £16
Sleeps 6
⅟ ✿ ✿ ▬

Situated on Norfolk/Suffolk border amid open countryside. A working dairy farm where it is possible to see cows being milked, and there are farmyard pets. Farmhouse is Elizabethan timber-framed (inside) with inglenook fireplaces. Central heating. Some four poster beds, some en-suite. Easy reach Norfolk Broads, Norwich, Cambridge, Bressingham Steam Museum and Gardens. Cynthia is keen craftswoman in quilting, embroidery, spinning, weaving. Open all year. Map ref: 308 106

Old Coach House, Thursford, Fakenham, Norfolk NR21 0BD

Mrs Ann Green
☎ 0328 878273
BB From £16
EM From £7
Sleeps 8
♿ ⅋ ⅄ ✿ ⅍
Listed

Small peaceful working farm set in parkland with cows, sheep, ducks etc. Farmhouse is a converted 17th century coachhouse. Main bedroom has four-poster sharing bathroom with 1 twin-bedded room, also 1 twin-bedded room with en-suite bathroom. Farmhouse dining/kitchen, guests own sitting room with TV and sunroom. Children welcome, pets by arrangement. Close to Thursford collection and within easy reach of sandy beaches. Open all year (closed Christmas). Map ref: 306 127

Park Farm, Sibton, Saxmundham, Suffolk IP17 2LZ

Margaret Gray
☎ 072 877 324
BB From £12.50
EM From £9
Sleeps 6
⅋ ⅟ ✿ ✿ ⅍
♨♨

A friendly welcome, good food and comfortable accommodation await you at Park Farm. We have 1 double, en-suite, and 2 twin rooms for guests, each with washbasin. English breakfast and 3-course dinner are prepared from our own, or very local, produce and all tastes and special diets gladly catered for. Ideally situated for enjoying the unspoiled Suffolk countryside. Open all year (closed Christmas & New Year). Map ref: 320 103

Rymer Farm, Barnham, Thetford, Norfolk IP24 2PP

Sarah Rush
☎ 0842 890 233
Fax 0842 890 653
BB From £16
Sleeps 6
♿ ⅋ ☕
♨♨ **Approved**

17th century farmhouse on arable farm in centre of East Anglia. We have lounge with TV, log fire and dining room for full English breakfast. One double room with lounge, en-suite, 1 twin-bedded room and 1 double room with shared bathroom all centrally heated with tea/coffee-making facilities. Lovely farm walk, flower arrangers, garden, fishing in carp pond. Open all year (closed Christmas). Map ref: 302 105

Salamanca Farm Guest House, Stoke Holy Cross, Norwich, Norfolk NR14 8QJ

Mrs Barbara Harrold
☎ 0508 492322
BB From £14
Sleeps 8
♿ (6) ⅟
♨♨

"Real experience of English hospitality" – "All we could have asked for" – just two comments from our visitors' book. The Harrold family have welcomed guests to their farm for 20 years. 4 miles from the cathedral city of Norwich, the valley of the River Tas, with the mill where Colmans began producing mustard, provides an attractive holiday base. Open 15 Jan–15 Dec. Map ref: 315 115

Shelfanger Hall, Shelfanger, Diss, Norfolk IP22 2DE

Mrs Deborah Butler
☎ 0379 642094
🅱️ From £16
Sleeps 6
🍼 (8)
♛♛

Shelfanger Hall is a 16th century moated farmhouse, tucked away from busy roads overlooking large garden and farmland. Accommodation consists of 1 double and 1 twin bedroom with en-suite facilities and 1 double with private bathroom, all with tea/coffee-making facilities and TV/games room available for guests including full size snooker table. Open all year.
Map ref: 312 106

Shrublands Farm, Northrepps, Cromer, Norfolk NR27 0AA

Mrs Ann Youngman
☎ 0263 78297
🅱️ From £16
EM From £10
Sleeps 6
🍼 (13) ⅍ ♛ ⚘
♛♛ Highly
Commended

Shrublands Farm is an arable farm set in the village of Northrepps, 2½ miles SE of Cromer and 20 miles north of Norwich. The Victorian/Edwardian house has 1 twin and 1 double with washbasins, and 1 twin with private bathroom. Separate bathroom, sitting room and dining room for guests. Full central heating, log fires in chilly weather. Sorry, no pets. Open all year (closed Christmas & New Year).
Map ref: 315 130

Stratton Farm, Walton Highway, West Norfolk PE14 7DP

Derek & Sue King
☎ 0945 880162
🅱️ From £20
Sleeps 6
🍼 (5) ⅍ ♿ ⌚ ⚘
♛♛ Commended

Derek and Sue King invite you to stay on their peaceful farm which supports a prize winning herd of short horn cattle. All rooms are en-suite, have tea/coffee-making facilities, colour TV, and central heating. One room is specifically designed for wheelchair users. Free carp fishing and use of heated swimming pool. Full English breaked with home produced sausages, bacon, eggs and marmalade. Open all year (including Christmas). Map ref:285 118

Toll Barn, Norwich Road, North Walsham, Norfolk NR28 0JB

Annette Tofts
☎ 0692 403063
🅱️ From £15
Sleeps 12
🍼 (8) 🐴 ⅍ ⌚ ⚘
Listed Highly
Commended

Toll barn in farming country is a uniquely charming house, created within the shell of an 18th century Norfolk barn. Converted farm buildings form luxurious lodges around a central fountain in peaceful courtyard gardens. Each cosy room has en-suite facilities. Traditional farmhouse breakfast served in exposed brick and beamed dining room. The Weavers Way footpath runs past the house. Coast 6 miles; Norfolk Broads 5 miles; Norwich 12 miles. Open all year. Map ref: 279 284

Weaners Farm, Bears Lane, Lavenham, Sudbury, Suffolk CO10 9RX

Hazel Rhodes
☎ 0787 247310
🅱️ From £16
Sleeps 4
🍼 ♛
Listed

This modern farmhouse surrounded by cornfields but only 1 mile from historic village is easy reach for Constable country Cambridge and National Trust houses. Breakfast only served, featuring homemade sausages and free range eggs from the farm. It is a peaceful spot and there are some lovely walks close by. Open Mar–Nov. Map ref: 303 095

Woodlands Farm, Brundish, near Woodbridge, Suffolk IP13 8BP

Jill Graham
☎ 0379 384444
🅱️ From £14
EM From £12
Sleeps 6
🍼 (10) ⅍
♛♛ Highly
Commended

A friendly welcome and good home cooking assured in our comfortable, timber-framed farmhouse set in peaceful countryside near Framlingham. Within easy reach of the coast and numerous local attractions. One twin and 2 double bedrooms with en-suite bathrooms, and tea/coffee facilities. Separate dining and sitting rooms with inglenooks. Centrally heated with log fires in cold weather. Open all year (closed Christmas). Map ref: 318 105

Self-Catering

Dolphin Lodge, Roudham Farm, Roudham, East Harling, Norfolk NR16 2RJ

Mrs E. Jolly
☎ 0953 717126
SC From £140–£295
Sleeps 5/6
🐎
🗝 🗝 🗝 **Highly
Commended**

Pair of beautifully restored cottages on edge of Thetford Forest on a Breckland farm. Both spacious and well equipped; central heating, AGA, woodburning stove, washing machine, tumble drier, fridge, colour TV, cot and highchair available. Each cottage sleeps 5 in two bedrooms. Many local tourist attractions. Ideal for a quiet secluded holiday or a busy sightseeing one. Open all year. Map ref: 309 112

Hall Farm Cottage, Church Lane, Copdock, Ipswich, Suffolk IP8 3JZ

Mrs Yvonne Carr
☎ 04737 30287
SC From £120–£275
Sleeps 4
🐎 🐈 🗝 🌲
🗝 🗝 🗝 **Commended**

Part of period farmhouse on a 3 miles circular walk close to Constable country with easy access to A12 and A45. Open fireplace, fuel supplied, beamed ceilings, central heating, colour TV, washing machine. Linen and towels provided, electricity extra. Cot and high chair. 1 double and 1 twin bedroom. Open all year. Map ref: 311 092

Honeypot Cottage, Deben Lodge Farm, Fakenham, Ipswich, Suffolk IP10 0RA

Mrs Theresa Adams
☎ 03948 564
SC From £110–£180
Sleeps 4 + cot
🐎 🗝 🐈 🌲
🗝 🗝 🗝 **Commended**

Renovated cottage on mixed farm. Well-equipped and comfortable with superb views. 1 double, 1 twin bedroom, fitted kitchen, lounge/diner, bathroom with bath and shower. Facilities include washing machine, microwave, fridge, cooker, colour TV, storage heater and cot. Linen, towels and elctricity included. Enclosed garden with furniture and BBQ. Stables for guests' horses. Sea 5 miles, country and river walks. Fishing, golf nearby. Sorry no pets. Map ref: 318 091

Sid's Cottage, c/o The Grange, West Rudham, Kings Lynn Norfolk PE31 8SY

Mrs Angela Ringer
☎ 0485 528 229
SC From £120–£195
🐎 🐈
🗝 🗝 🗝 **Approved**

Sid's Cottage is semi-detached, surrounded by grass but has no enclosed garden. Overlooks a small orchard, patio at rear. Sleeps 4 in 3 bedrooms. Linen provided. Gas central heating, open fire, colour TV, auto washing machine, fridge/freezer. Cot and highchair available on request. Electricity 50p meter. Free carp fishing on farm. Good base for seeing Norfolk. Sandy beach in easy reach. Sorry, no pets. Open all year. Map ref: 292 122

Stable Cottages and The Granary, Chattisham Place, Nr Ipswich, Suffolk IP8 3QD

Mrs Margaret Langton
☎ 0473 87210
SC From £120–£295
Sleeps 2/8
🐎 ♿ 🐈 🌲
🗝 🗝 🗝 **Commended**

Restored stables and Tudor granary converted to 3 comfortable and well-equipped holiday cottages, one with wheelchair facilities. Situated in a SE facing courtyard with central heating, fitted kitchen, colour TV. Linen, towels, electricity included. Games, laundry room on site. Use of heated swimming pool and tennis court by arrangement. Quiet, rural village near Constable Country. Sea ½ hr, riding, windsurfing, fishing nearby. Open Mar–Nov. Map ref: 310 093

Wood Lodge, High House Farm, Cransford, near Framlingham, Woodbridge, Suffolk IP13 9PD

Tim & Sarah Kindred
☎ 072878 461
ⓈⒸ From £200–£340
Sleeps 8 + cot
⛄ 🐾 ⌁ 🏛
🔑 🔑 🔑 🔑 **Commended**

Beautiful country retreat. Spacious 3 bedroom house set with ½ acre of garden in 18 acres of woodland. Sleeps 6/8 plus cot in 2 family rooms with 1 double and 1 single bed in each and 1 twin-room. Lounge with central heating, woodburning stove, colour TV, fitted kitchen, fridge-freezer washer-drier etc. Large dining room, upstairs bathroom, downstairs shower room. Ideal for exploring rural Suffolk, Farmlingham Castle, Minsmere Bird Reserve, Snape Maltings and the heritage coast. Open all year. Map ref: 318 101

FARM HOLIDAY BUREAU

BUREAU ACCOMMODATION IS RELIABLE

This Guide lists **Farm Holiday Bureau** members only. They are all inspected by the National Tourist Board for standards (see introduction pages) and by fellow members to maintain a high quality.

FARM HOLIDAY BUREAU

THE 1000+ BUREAU MEMBERS OFFER A UNIQUE LINK TO CUSTOMERS ACROSS THE UK

All Bureau members belong to a local Group. Each member can refer you to an equally high quality member within his Group . . . or across the UK: England, Northern Ireland, Scotland, Wales.

43 Essex

Essex surprises – it is still a rural county yet just a short trip east from London. It is a land of rolling countryside and river valleys, creeks and estuaries with a scattering of villages and country towns.

While you are here take the opportunity to see for yourself all that Essex has to offer. Local farm produce, Essex wines and seafood, oak beamed country pubs serving real ale and traditionally cosy tea shops.

Explore the past in Colchester, the oldest recorded town in England, with a Norman castle built on the foundations of what was the largest Roman temple in Northern Europe. Lose yourself in the 6,000 acres of Epping Forest or wander through Hatfield Forest with its woodland, pasture, lake and nature reserve.

The Essex coastline is one of contrasts, from remote marshes to lively seaside resorts.

Essex is highly accessible by road and rail. The M25 and M11 motorways are on the western boundaries of the county with trunk roads linking the rest of the county to the motorway network.

There are regular train services from London Liverpool Street to 70 different destinations throughout Essex including Stanstead Airport, Port of Harwich and Felixstowe.

Group Contact: Joyce Withey ☎ 0277 362695

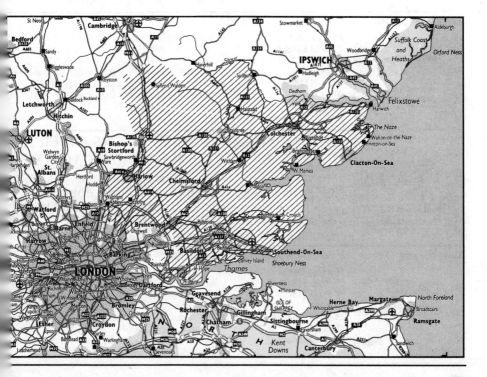

Bed and Breakfast (and evening meal)

Bonny Downs Farmhouse, Doesgate Lane, Bulphan, Nr Upminster, Essex RM14 3TB

Rose Newman
☎ 0268 542129
BB From £15
EM From £8
Sleeps 6
♿ ✗ ⛺ 🐕
Listed Approved

Large, comfortably furnished, pleasantly situated in large garden with lovely views. Close to Langdon Hills Country Park and Basildon New Town (modern shopping centre). Convenient for London, Southend, South East England via M25, A13, A127. Sheep/cattle kept on the farm. 2 twin, 1 family bedrooms, 1 bath with toilet/shower, 1 shower room with toilet. Tea/coffee trays. Good cooking. Open all year (closed Christmas). Map ref: 294 073

Bumbles Farm, Moreton Road, Ongar, Essex CM5 0EZ

Joyce Withey
☎ 0277 362695
BB From £13
Sleeps 6
⛺ (12) ✗ 🐎 🎿 💼 ✗
Listed

A warm welcome awaits you at Bumbles. This large cottage has inglenook and oak beams. Now run as a smallholding. Very comfortable with guests' lounge, TV, guests' bathroom and additional showerroom. Tea/coffee always available. Easy access to M11 and M25 East Anglia and London. Open all year. Map ref: 289 078

Duddenhoe End Farm, Nr Saffron Walden, Essex CB11 4UU

Peggy Foster
☎ 0763 838258
BB From £17.50
Sleeps 6
✗ ⛺ (12) ☜
👑 👑 Highly Commended

Duddenhoe End Farm is situated on the outskirts of the peaceful hamlet of Duddenhoe End. The house is 17th century and has a wealth of beams and inglenook fireplaces. Accommodation consists of 3 double bedrooms all en-suite. Tea/coffee-making facilities. Visitors' sitting room. Within easy reach of Cambridge, Duxford War Museum, London and Suffolk. Open all year (closed Christmas). Map ref: 288 091

'Greys', Ongar Road, Margaret Roding, Nr Great Dunmow, Essex CM6 1QR

Mrs Joyce Matthews
☎ 024 531 509
BB From £16
Sleeps 6
✗ ⛺ (10)
Listed

Formerly two cottages, 'Greys' is quietly situated on the family farm – arable and sheep. Beamed throughout and with large garden. Ideal for short breaks and exploring. Pretty villages, old towns etc. 2 double rooms and 1 with twin beds. Tea/coffee available. Just off the A1060, Bishops Stortford to Chelmsford road, at telephone kiosk in village. Open most of year. Map ref: 293 085

Kings Vineyard, Fossetts Lane, Fordham, near Colchester, Essex CO6 3NY

Mrs Inge Tweed
☎ 0206 240377
BB From £16
Sleeps 6
⛺ (2) 🚐 (touring and static) ♿ ⊞ 🎿 💼 ✗
👑 👑 Commended

Why not sample the delights of the Essex countryside while relaxing at this rural farmhouse overlooking the Colne Valley. Traditional or vegetarian breakfast in elegant conservatory. Twin and double rooms, CH, H/C. Tea/coffee facilities. Guest bath/showers, toilets. Ideally situated 5 mins from A12, Colchester 6 miles Harwich/Felixstowe 22 miles. SC caravan available. Ideal for walking/cycling. Friendly welcome. Also for business people. Open all year. Map ref: 303 085

New House Farm, Mutton Row, Stanford Rivers, Nr Ongar, Essex CM5 9QH

Mrs Beryl Martin
☎ 0277 362132
BB From £16
Sleeps 8
♿ ♨ 🏊 Å 🐎 🏇 ☜ 🍴
♨ ♨

An arable working farm of 150 acres offering accommodation in Tudor farmhouse, with beams and inglenooks. All rooms have H/C and CH. 2 bathrooms and a shower for guests. Accommodation for disabled guests in special unit. Three lakes and 10 acres of grass surround the house. A warm welcome awaits you in rural unspoilt countryside. Easy access to London, Cambridge and East Anglia. Open all year (closed Christmas & New Year). Map ref: 288 077

Parsonage Farm, Arkesden, Saffron Walden, Essex CB11 4HB

Daniele Forster
☎ 0799 550306
BB From £15
Sleeps 4
🐴 🐕
♨ ♨

Lovely Victorian farmhouse in centre of picturesque prize-winning village. 1 double room en-suite, 1 twin with private bathroom. TV. Tea/coffee-making facilities in bedrooms. The farm is arable but a few pets are kept. Hard tennis court in large garden. Good food at local pub. Close to Saffron Walden, Duxford War Museum. Cambridge 18 miles, London 50 mins, Stansted 25 mins. Open all year. Map ref: 286 088

Rockells Farm, Duddenhoe End, Saffron Walden, Essex CB11 4UY

Mrs Tineke Westerhuis
☎ 0763 838053
BB From £16
EM From £7
Sleeps 6
🐴 🐕 ♿ ☜ 🎾 🦊
♨ ♨

Rockells is an arable farm in a beautiful corner of Essex. The Georgian house has a large garden with a 3-acre lake for coarse fishing. All rooms have private facilities, one room is downstairs. On the farm are several footpaths, and beautiful villages in the area. Within easy reach of Audley End House, Duxford Air Museum and Cambridge. London is about 1 hour by car or train. Stansted airport 30 mins by car. Open all year. Map ref: 286 090

Spicers Farm, Rotten End, Wethersfield, Braintree, Essex CM7 4AL

Mrs Delia Douse
☎ 0371 851021
BB From £15
Sleeps 6
🐕 🐴 🍴 🦊
♨ ♨

Comfortable farmhouse with large garden in area designated special landscape value. Quiet with pleasant walks, yet convenient for Stansted, Harwich, Cambridge and Constable country. A working farm with animals. Accommodation offered in 1 double and 2 twin rooms (1 en-suite), all with tea/coffee-making facilities and colour TV and lovely views. Open all year. Map ref: 29 08

Self-Catering

SC

The Granary, c/o Rockells Farm, Duddenhoe End, Saffron Walden, Essex CB11 4UY

Mrs Tineke Westerhuis
☎ 0763 838053
SC From £140–£180
Sleeps 5
🐕 ☜ 🎾 🦊
🔑 🔑 🔑 Commended

The Granary is part of Rockells farmyard, an arable farm in a beautiful corner of Essex. A large lounge with kitchen area has original woodpanelling. The cottage is fully equipped to high standard. Garden with 3-acre lake for excellent fishing. In the area are several footpaths and beautiful villages with excellent pubs. Audley End House, Duxford Air Museum and Cambridge nearby. London is 1 hour by car or train. Stansted airport 30 mins by car. Open all year. Map ref: 286 090

The Holiday Cottages, Orsett, c/o Lorkins Farm, Orsett, Essex RM16 3EL

John & Marilyn Wordley
☎ 0375 891439
Fax 0375 891274
🆂🅲 From £295–£430
Sleeps 5/6
🛆 🔟
Applied

Two adjoining cottages, superbly equipped and maintained, quietly situated in an attractive village. Each sleeps 5/6 persons. Price includes gas, electricity, CH, linen. Superb local sports facilities and ideal for visiting London 22 miles (30 mins by train). The cottages won the AA Holiday Home of the Year Award for Southern England in 1988. Also a luxury self-catering caravan available at the farm (£80–£160 per week). Open all year. Map ref: 294 068

Keppolsmore, c/o Ashes Farm, Cressing, Braintree, Essex CM7 8DW

Mrs Moran Ratcliffe
☎ 0376 83236
🆂🅲 From £140–£200
Sleeps 4
✂ 🍴
🐾 🐾 🐾 🐾 Commended

A modern bungalow for mature holidaymakers in the quiet country town of Coggeshall. Easy rail access to London, or by M11 to Cambridge, or visit Constable Country and the coast. 15 antique shops, good provisions and eating places within 2 minutes walk. Payphone installed. Open Apr– Oct. Map ref: 297 085

PRICES

Prices include VAT and service charge (if any) and are:
B&B per person per night
EM per person
SC per unit per week
Tents and caravans per pitch per night

FARM HOLIDAY BUREAU

FARM HOLIDAY BUREAU

THOSE LITTLE EXTRAS

For advice on farms that can offer 'extras' such as four-poster beds, special diets, farm trails, fishing rights – even stabling and trekking arrangements if you are bringing your own horse – ring the Farm Holiday Bureau on (0203) 696909.

44 Thames Valley

The Thames Valley is at the heart of historical England.
Farms and homes are situated in the area stretching from the Chiltern Hills above Henley through the rich farmland of the Vale of Aylesbury and on to the west of Oxford and the Cotswolds.

Oxford is at the centre of the region and its dreaming spires and great buildings, including mediaeval colleges and Renaissance masterpieces such as the Sheldonian Theatre, can provide great historical interest. You can take guided tours of Oxford, Windsor and Burford or enjoy browsing in antique shops and bookshops.

Woodstock has many historical associations and is the site of Blenheim Palace, the magnificent home designed by Sir John Vanbrugh for the Dukes of Marlborough. Sir Winston Churchill was born there and is buried in the nearby churchyard of Bladon. The area includes the moated castle at Broughton near Banbury and many other Tudor and 18th-century manors and country houses.

Places of interest include the Cotswold Wildlife Park, Birdland, Cogges Farm Museum and a steam railway centre and activities such as boating, pony trekking and brass rubbing are available.

Group Contact: Mrs F. Emmett ☎ 0494 881600

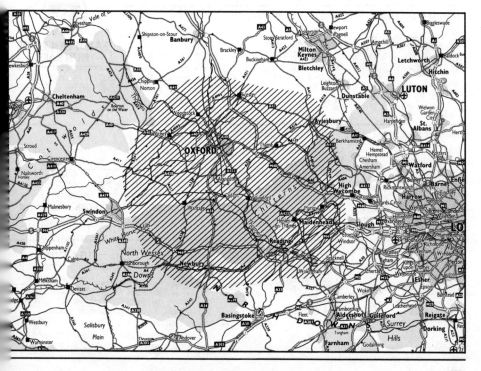

Bed and Breakfast (and evening meal)

Ashen Copse Farm, Coleshill, Highworth, Nr Swindon, Wiltshire SN6 7PU

Pat Hoddinott
☎ 0367 240175
BB From £15
Sleeps 6
✂ ☎ ☂

Ideal setting for peace and quiet, walking, visiting numerous attractions. 580-acre National Trust beef and arable farm in beautiful countryside. Spacious, comfortable accommodation in 17th century farmhouse (1bedroom en-suite). Small outdoor swimming pool. Meet our lambs, calves and pony. Children's toys and games available. Reduction for children sharing. Many pubs and restaurants. Near M4 (J15). Open all year (closed Christmas Day). Map ref: 237 073

Banbury Hill Farm, Enstone Road, Charlbury, Oxfordshire OX7 3JH

Angela Widdows
☎ 0608 810314
BB From £16
EM From £7
Sleeps 6
✂ ☎
☂ ☂ Commended

Natural Cotswold stone farmhouse commanding spectacular view in AONB overlooking the small township of Charlbury with the ancient Wychwood Forest nestling against the River Evenlode. Large variety of animals around the farm. Ideally centred – midway Oxford, Stratford-upon-Avon, near Blenheim, Burford and Bourton-on-the-Water. Dining room, lounge, daytime access. Friendly and peaceful atmosphere. Open all year. Map ref: 245 083

Bowling Green Farm, Stanford Road, Faringdon, Oxfordshire SN7 8EZ

Della Barnard
☎ 0367 240229
Fax 0367 242568
BB From £13
Sleeps 6
✂ ☎ ☂ ☂
☂

Attractive 18th century period farmhouse offering 20th century comfort situated in the Vale of the White Horse, just 1 mile south of Faringdon on the A417. Easy access to M4 for Heathrow Airport. A working farm breeding cattle and horses. Large twin/family room on ground floor en-suite. All bedrooms have colour TV, tea/coffee-making facilities and CH throughout. Open all year. Map ref: 241 074

Fords Farm, Ewelme, Wallingford, Oxon OX10 6HU

Marlene Edwards
☎ 0491 39272
BB From £15
Sleeps 4
✂ ☎
Listed

500-acre mixed farm, arable beef and sheep. Attractive farmhouse set in historic part of village with famous church almshouses and school. Peaceful surroundings with good walks and good selection of pubs nearby. Easy access to Henley, Oxford, Reading, Windsor, Heathrow and London. Friendly and comfortable atmosphere. 2 twin rooms. Open May–Mar. Map ref: 255 072

Foxhill Farm, Kingsey, Aylesbury, Buckinghamshire HP17 8LZ

Mary-Joyce Hooper
☎ 0844 291650
BB From £17
Sleeps 6
CH ✂ ☂ (5)
Listed

Foxhill is a spacious 17th century farmhouse listed as being of architectural interest. 3 quiet double/twin bedrooms with colour TV and tea making, 2 with shower. Guests' lounge, colour TV. Enjoy our large attractive garden with views to the Chiltern Hills or use our heated swimming pool. We recommend restaurants in nearby Thame and surrounding villages. Ideally positioned for Heathrow, Oxford, Windsor and London (1 hour). Open Feb-Nov (incl). Map ref: 259 077

Hill Grove Farm, Crawley Road, Minster Lovell, Oxfordshire OX8 5NA

Mrs Katharine Brown
☎ 0993 703120
🅱 From £16
Sleeps 4
✂ 🐎 🛏
🛏 **Highly Commended**

Hill Grove is a mixed, family-run 300-acre working farm situated in an attractive rural setting overlooking the Windrush Valley. Ideally positioned for driving to Oxford, Blenheim Palace, Witney (Farm Museum) and Burford (renowned as the Gateway to the Cotswolds and for its splendid Wildlife Park). We offer bed and a hearty breakfast in a friendly atmosphere. Children welcome. 1 double/private shower, 1 twin/double en-suite. AA listed. Open all year (closed Christmas). Map ref: 242 080

Little Parmoor Farm, Frieth, Henley-on-Thames, Oxfordshire RG9 6NL

Frances Emmett
☎ 0494 881600
🅱 From £17
Sleeps 6
🐎 🛏 ✂
Listed Commended

16th century brick and flint farmhouse with oak beam interior, log fires in winter and CH, on a 220 acre mixed farm in the Chilterns, an area of outstanding natural beauty. Convenient for Windsor, Marlow, Henley, Oxford and Heathrow. Taxi service available. Farmhouse breakfast including free range eggs and local honey, tea/coffee-making facilities. Good pubs and restaurant food in attractive villages nearby. Open all year. Map ref: 267 074

Lyford Manor, Lyford, Wantage, Oxfordshire OX12 0EG

Mary Pike
☎ 0235 868204
🅱 From £18
Sleeps 7
✂ 🐎 🐕 🛏
🛏 🛏 **Highly Commended**

Savour the peace and quiet of rural Oxfordshire on a 400 acre working dairy farm in our 15th century stone manor house which nestles on the banks of the River Ock. The rooms are spacious and comfortable with private facilities, CH and tea/coffee-making facilities. Many local attractions and excellent eating places within easy reach. Open all year. Map ref: 245 072

Manor Farm, Brimpton, Reading, Berkshire RG7 4SQ

Jean Bowden
☎ 0734 713166
🅱 From £16
Sleeps 4/5
🐎
Listed

Historic Georgian farmhouse on working dairy/arable farm in Kennet Valley. Norman chapel of St Leonard used by Knights Templars after Crusades adjacent. M4 and M3 within 10 and 15 minutes, Heathrow, Gatwick and south coast within easy reach. Ideal base for Windsor, Henley, Bath, Salisbury, Stonehenge and more. Only 50 miles west of London. Good pubs and restaurants locally. Open all year. Map ref: 250 064

Manor Farm, Chaddleworth, Newbury, Berkshire RG16 0EG

Mrs Margaret Cooper
☎ 048 82 215
🅱 From £17.50
Sleeps 4
🐕 (7) ✂ 🛏
🛏 🛏 **Commended**

Manor farm is a mixed farm with a Georgian farmhouse situated in the peaceful surroundings of the rolling Berkshire Downs. With lovely walks and super views, Ridgeway 3 miles. Easy access to main auto routes (A34/M4) 10 minutes. 1 double, 1 twin room available in a warm and friendly atmosphere. Good eating places locally. Open all year. Map ref: 247 067

Manor Farm, Kelmscott, Nr Lechlade, Gloucestershire GL7 3HJ

Anne Amor
☎ 0367 52620
🅱 From £16
EM From £10
Sleeps 6
✂ 🐕 🐖
🛏 🛏

315-acre dairy farm in beautiful, peaceful, unspoilt village of Kelmscott at foothills of Cotswolds, on banks of River Thames. 17th century Cotswoldstone farmhouse, with spacious, comfortable rooms all with washbasins, tea/coffee-making facilities, CH, guests' TV lounge. Within easy reach Oxford, Woodstock, Burford, Cheltenham, Bath. Easy access to M4, J15. Good pubs and restaurants locally. Dinners by arrangement. AA/Elizabeth Gundrey recommended. Open all year. Map ref: 239 074

Manor Farm, Shabbington, Aylesbury, Buckinghamshire HP18 9HJ

Joan Bury
☎ 0844 201103
BB From £15–£20
Sleeps 6
♿ ⏵ (8)
Listed

This 188-acre grazing farm is in a quiet pastoral setting with lovely views. Bounded by the River Thame. Twelve miles from Oxford, Manor Farm is conveniently situated for Chilterns, Cotswolds, Thames Valley and London. Accommodation in modern, well-equipped bungalow with lounge, kitchen, bathroom, colour TV, CH. Breakfast served in adjacent farmhouse. Many good pubs and restaurants in area. Open all year. Map ref: 259 079

Mead Close, Forest Hill, Nr Oxford, Oxfordshire OX9 1EB

Audrey Dunkley
☎ 0865 872248
BB From £15.20
EM From £8
Sleeps 5
⏩
Listed

450 acre mixed farm, dairy and cereals. Family farm, milking 80 cows. Warm and welcoming farmhouse, full CH, 5 miles to Oxford city centre, 5 minutes to Park and Ride. 10 minutes from 'Le Manoir' restaurant. Easy to find from A40. 2 traditional English pubs in village, both serving food. Enjoy visiting the Cotswolds, Blenheim Palace, Waterperry Gdns, Waddesdon Manor and Windsor. Open all year. Map ref: 250 079

Monkton Farm, Little Marlow, Buckinghamshire SL7 3RF

Jane & Warren Kimber
☎ 0494 521082
Fax 0494 443905
BB From £18
Sleeps 6
✂ ⏵ (5) 🐴 ⏩
Listed Commended

A 150-acre working dairy farm with 14th century 'Cruck' farmhouse set in the beautiful Chiltern Hills, yet only 30 miles from London and 27 miles from Oxford. Heathrow 20 mins, 1 single, 1 double and 1 family room available. English breakfast served in the farm kitchen. Large choice of pubs and restaurants nearby. Taxi service to Heathrow available. Open all year. Map ref: 264 073

Moor Farm, Holyport, near Maidenhead, Berkshire SL6 2HY

Mrs G Reynolds
☎ 0628 33761
BB From £17.50
Sleeps 4
⏵ ✂ 🐴 ⏩
👑 👑 Commended

In the pretty village of Holyport. Moor Farm is 4 miles from Windsor. The farmhouse is a timber-framed, 700-year-old 'listed' manor with charming en-suite rooms, furnished with antiques. It is well placed for touring the Thames Valley and visiting London. Also close to Heathrow. Suffolk sheep and horses kept on farm. Stabling, riding and tuition by arrangement. Open all year. Map ref: 263 067

'Morar', Weald Street, Bampton, Oxfordshire OX18 2HL

Janet Rouse
☎ 0993 850162
Fax 0993 851738
BB From £17
EM From £12.80
Sleeps 6
⏩ ✂ ⏵ (6)
👑 👑 Highly Commended

A non-smoking farmhouse (retired from farming) where meat, vegetables, bread are nearly all home-produced and cooked to perfection. Vegetarian dinners offered. Pet sheep and goats will love your fuss and attention. Cotswolds, Oxford, Woodstock, swimming, sailing, riding, fishing all close by. We Morris dance, bellring, garden – and laugh! 1 twins, 2 doubles en-suite. Elizabeth Gundrey recommended. Open all year (closed Christmas). Map ref: 241 078

Neals Farm, Wyfold, Reading, Berkshire RG4 9JB

Bridget Silsoe
☎ 0491 680258
BB From £15
Sleeps 6
🐴 ⏵ ✂ 🏕 ⏩ 🐴 ⏩
👑

Our spacious Georgian farmhouse, set high in the Chilterns, is approached through beech woods which open to reveal a wonderful view. Secluded, quiet and completely rural, this is a 100-acre livestock farm, set in an area of outstanding natural beauty. Guests treated as family. Relaxed, informal atmosphere. Heated swimming pool. Excellent home-produced food. Easy access Henley, Windsor, Heathrow and London. Open all year (closed Christmas). Map ref: 254 067

New Farm, Oxford Road, Oakley, Aylesbury, Buckinghamshire HP18 9UR

Binnie Pickford
☎ **0844 237360**
ⓑⓑ **From £16**
EM From £10
Sleeps 6
🔥 (6) 🐾 🌲
Listed Commended

Warm, friendly atmosphere in fully modernised farmhouse. Good food, comfortable bedrooms, views over 163 acres devoted to sheep, beef, arable. Situated on Oxfordshire/Buckinghamshire boundary in peaceful surroundings. Walks in adjacent Bernwood Forest Nature Reserve. 7 miles Oxford, close to Waterperry Gardens, Waddesdon Manor, Quainton Railway Centre, Blenheim Palace and M40 to Windsor and London. Pubs and restaurants nearby. Map ref: 252 080

North Farm, Shillingford Hill, Wallingford, Oxfordshire OX10 8NB

Hilary Warburton
☎ **086 732 8406**
ⓑⓑ **From £17.50**
Sleeps 4/6
✗ 🔥
🏵 🏵 **Commended**

Spacious and comfortable farmhouse on our 500 acres of farmland with sheep and pygmy goats. Enjoy walks by the River Thames and private fishing. Ideal for Oxford and Henley and within easy reach of Windsor and London. 2 double bedrooms with private bathrooms (1 en-suite), colour TV, tea/coffee-making facilities. Excellent local pubs. Open all year. Map ref: 252 073

The Old Farmhouse, Station Hill, Long Hanborough, Oxfordshire OX7 2JZ

Vanessa Maundrell
☎ **0993 882097**
ⓑⓑ **From £33**
Sleeps 4
☺ ✗ 🔥 (12) 🐎
🏵 🏵 **Highly Commended**

The Old Farmhouse is over 300 years old, full of period charm and character, inglenook fireplace, beams and flagstone floors. Only 15 minutes from Oxford, Woodstock and the Cotswolds. Friendly hospitality and tasteful accommodation. Delicious home cooking. Non-working farm, but husband a farmer. One double en-suite, one double with washbasin. French, German, Spanish, Italian spoken. Open all year (closed Christmas). Map ref: 246 081

Rectory Farm, Northmoor, Witney, Oxfordshire OX8 1SX

Mary Anne Florey
☎ **0865 300207**
ⓑⓑ **From £18.50**
Sleeps 4
✗
🏵 🏵 **Highly Commended**

Rectory Farm is a 16th century farmhouse retaining all the old charm alongside modern comforts. Both rooms have en-suite facilities, central heating, tea/coffee-making facilities. We are conveniently situated for Oxford, the Cotswolds, Blenheim and the Thames path. Fishing on the Thames available. We can assure you of a warm welcome and a peaceful and comfortable stay. Open 1st Feb–mid Dec. Map ref: 245 076

Wallace Farm, Dinton, Nr Aylesbury, Buckinghamshire HP17 8UF

Jackie Cook
☎ **0296 748660**
Fax: 0296 748851
ⓑⓑ **From £18**
Sleeps 6
🔥 🚲 🐾 🌲 🐎
🏵 🏵

This 16th century listed farmhouse is situated in a quiet, rural setting in the Vale of Aylesbury, yet within easy reach of London, Oxford and Heathrow. A small family farm, rearing beef cattle and sheep, plus chickens, ducks and geese. Plenty of opportunitites for country walks, coarse fishing or browsing through our extensive library. Comfortable accommodation with a warm welcome. Open all year. Map ref: 260 080

LET THE TELEPHONE RING!
Some farmhouses are big places. Let the telephone ring long enough to give the owner time to answer it.

Self-Catering

Hill Grove Cottage, c/o Hill Grove Farm, Crawley Road, Minster Lovell, Oxfordshire OX8 5NA

Mrs Katharine Brown
☎ 0993 703120
⑊ From £220–£250
Sleeps 2/6 cot
✂ ⌂
↝ ↝ ↝ ↝ **Commended**

Hill Grove Cottage is a large bungalow adjacent to our farmhouse. 2 double bedrooms, 1 twin, bathroom and shower, dining room, lounge, kitchen. Fridge/freezer, washing machine, tumble dryer, CH. Gardens. Situated above the Windrush Valley, excellent walks yet within driving distance of Oxford, Woodstock and Burford (Gateway to the Cotswolds). Cot and babysitting by arrangement. Electricity included. Linen free. Open June–Sept. Map ref: 242 080

Moor Farm, Holyport, near Maidenhead, Berkshire SL6 2HY

Mrs G Reynolds
☎ 0628 33761
⑊ From £200–£340
Sleeps 2/4
↝ ✂ ⌂
↝ ↝ – ↝ ↝ ↝ ↝

Highly Commended

In the pretty village of Holyport, courtyard cottages are on the 700-year-old manor of Moor Farm and are conversions from a Georgian stable block and two small barns. They retain many original features and are furnished with antique pine. The 4 cottages are well placed for touring the Thames Valley and are 4 miles from Windsor and convenient for visiting London. Sheep and horses are on the farm. Stabling and riding tuition by arrangement. Map ref: 263 067

Wallace Farm Cottages, c/o Wallace Farm, Dinton, Nr Aylesbury, Buckinghamshire HP17 8UF

Jackie Cook
☎ 0296 748660
Fax 0296 748851
⑊ From £140–£240
Sleeps 2/5
↝ ♿ ↝ ⌱ ↝ ⌂ ↝
↝ ↝ ↝ **Commended**

Adjacent to the Farmhouse are two fully furnished self-catering cottages. THE OLD FOALING BOX – 2 twin bedrooms, bathroom, dining, living rooms. KEEPERS COTTAGE – 1 double bedroom, bathroom, living/dining room. Both have fully fitted kitchens, washing machines, TV. Bed linen provided, and all on one level giving easy access. Many lovely country walks in quiet rural area. Open all year. Map ref: 260 080

FINDING YOUR ACCOMMODATION

FARM HOLIDAY BUREAU

The Group contacts at the beginning of each section can always help you find a vacancy in your chosen area.

45 Cotswolds & Royal Forest of Dean

The villages and scenic beauty of the Cotswolds are famed throughout the world. The many honey-coloured villages include Bibury, Broadway, Painswick and Lower Slaughter while some of the finest churches in the country are at Northleach, Fairford and Winchcombe which also has Sudeley Castle. Along the River Severn the villages have black and white half-timbered cottages and catle graze peacefully in the orchards and meadows. Gloucester with its cathedral, the elegant Regency town of Cheltenham and picturesque Tewkesbury with its 12th century abbey are in the Severn Vale. There are numerous visitor attractions in the main towns and villages while further afield are Berkeley Castle and Sir Peter Scott's Wildfowl Trust at Slimbridge.

Bordered by two rivers, the Severn and the Wye, is the beautiful and romantic Forest of Dean, ancient hunting grounds of kings and still covered by oak woodlands. Scattered through the Forest are mining towns such as Cinderford, Coleford and Lydney. Below Symonds Yat, the River Wye meanders dramatically in a most attractive wooded gorge.

Group Contact: Mrs Michelle Burdett ☎ 0452 812148

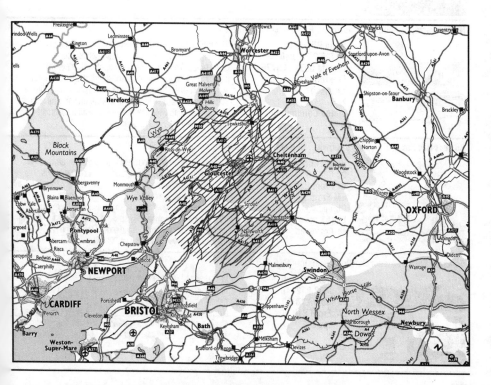

Bed and Breakfast (and evening meal)

Abbots Court, Church End, Twyning, Tewkesbury, Gloucestershire GL20 6DA

Bernie Williams
☎ 0684 292515
BB From £12.50
EM From £7.50
Sleeps 15
ᕁ ᕁ ᕁ ᕁ ᕁ
🏆 Approved

Lovely, quiet farmhouse in 350 acres between Cotswolds and Malverns. All bedrooms have colour TV, most en suite, tea-making facilities. Large lounge, separate dining room, excellent home cooked food. Licensed bar. 3 games rooms with pool table, table tennis, children's TV room, grass tennis court, bowling green, children's play area on lawn. Superb touring area. Open all year. Map ref: 226 089

Bould Farm House, Bould, Chipping Norton, Oxon OX7 6RT

Mrs Lynne Meyrick
☎ 0608 658850
BB From £15
Sleeps 6
ᕁ ᕁ ᕁ ᕁ ᕁ
Listed

Bould farm, 17th century cotswold farmhouse on 300-acre family farm set in beautiful countryside, 10 minutes drive from Stow-on-the-Wold and Bourton-on-the-Water and Burford, within easy reach of Blenheim Palace and the Cotswold Wildlife Park, children welcome. Map ref: 242 085

Brawn Farm, Sandhurst, Gloucester, Gloucestershire GL2 9NR

Sally Williams
☎ 0452 731010
Mobile 0831 260776
BB From £16
Sleeps 4
ᕁ
Listed Commended

Delightfully situated in an elevated and peaceful position with panoramic views across open countryside. The accommodation comprises a wing of this listed house. The bedrooms are very spacious and comfortable with a wealth of exposed beams. Separate guests' sitting room and dining room. An idyllic place to stay with superb walks through the Severn Vale and excellent base for touring the Cotswolds. Open all year. Map ref: 222 083

Butlers Hill Farm, Cockleford, Cowley, Cheltenham, Gloucestershire GL53 9NW

Bridget Brickell
☎ 0242 870455
BB From £15
EM From £7
Sleeps 6
ᕁ (6) ᕁ
🏆 Approved

A warm welcome awaits you on this mixed working farm between Cheltenham and Cirencester. Relax in this modern spacious farmhouse, in a quiet part of the Churn Valley with attractive walks and an ideal centre for exploring the cotswolds. All rooms have H & C and tea/coffee-making facilities, separate guests' sitting room with colour TV and separate dining room. Also self-contained cottage with 2 twin-bedrooms kitchen/living room and shower room. Open all year (closed Christmas and New Year). Map ref: 228 080

Damsels Farm, Painswick, Gloucestershire GL6 6UD

Michele Burdett
☎ 0452 812148
BB From £18.50
EM From £16.50
Sleeps 6
ᕁ ᕁ
🏆

Welcome to Damsels Farm where Henry VIII is reputed to have hunted with Ann Boleyn. Children may help feed the ducks, geese, chickens, calves and orphan lambs. The house is set in a quiet Cotswold Valley on the Cotswold Way. We are within easy reach of Cheltenham, Cirencester, Bath, Slimbridge and The Malverns. Open Mar–Oct (incl). Map ref: 226 076

Down Barn Farmhouse, The Camp, Stroud, Gloucestershire GL6 7EY

Anita Morley
☎ **0452 812853**
🏠 **From £14.50**
Sleeps 6
🏇 ♿ 🐎 🛦 ☂ 🐾
Listed

The farmhouse is on a smallholding with Pygmy and other goats ¼ of a mile off the Cotswold Scenic Leisure Drive (B4070), halfway between Stratford-upon-Avon and Bath. All accommodation is on the ground floor in a separate wing of the farmhouse and suitable for the immobile. Three bedrooms with washbasins, visitors' TV lounge with tea-making facilities. Lovely views and peaceful setting. Within easy reach of all Cotswold attractions. Open all Jan–Nov. Map ref: 225 079

Gilbert's, Gilbert's Lane, Brookthorpe, Nr Gloucester, Gloucestershire GL4 0UH

Jenny Beer
☎ **and fax 0452 812364**
🏠 **From £20**
Sleeps 6
🕭 🐕 🖢
🍃 🍃 **Commended**

Gilbert's which nestles beneath the Cotswolds close to Gloucester may have been Whaddon Manor 400 years ago. It is listed as an architectural gem. Whilst each room has modern comforts – private bathroom, TV, radio, telephone, etc. – the atmosphere is in keeping with the unpretentious nature of the house and organic smallholding, echoing a long history of living with this environment. Open all year. Map ref: 223 081

Hartpury Farm, Chedworth, Nr Cheltenham, Gloucestershire GL54 4AL

Peter & Peggy Booth
☎ **0285 720350**
🏠 **From £12.50**
EM From £7.50
Sleeps 6
🏇 🕭 ☂
Listed

Hartpury, lying centrally in the Cotswolds and in a quiet village, provides views across the valley. Good walking. Farm produce, provided by Jersey cows and organic gardening, cooked to traditional recipes. The beamed sitting room, vintage 1650, leads onto the garden where we often serve coffee. When we can, we help with excursions and local history. Open Mar–Nov. Map ref: 229 081

Home Farm, Bredons Norton, Tewkesbury, Gloucestershire GL20 7HA

Mick & Anne Meadows
☎ **0684 72322**
🏠 **From £16**
EM From £10
Sleeps 6
🏇 🕭 🛦 ☂
🍃 🍃 **Commended**

Mixed 150-acre family-run farm with sheep, cattle and poultry. Situated in an extremely quiet, unspoilt little village nestling under Bredon Hill. Superb position for walking, an excellent base for touring or relaxing. The 18th century farmhouse is very comfortably furnished. All bedrooms have en-suite bathrooms. Gas CH. Good home cooking, evening meal by arrangement. Lounge, TV. Children welcome. Open mid Jan–mid Dec. Map ref: 226 090

Hunting Butts Farm, Swindon Lane, Cheltenham, Gloucestershire GL50 4NZ

Jane Hanks
☎ **0242 524982**
🏠 **From £15–£17.50**
EM From £9
Sleeps 16
🏇 ♿ 🕭
🍃 🍃 🍃 **Commended**

Hunting Butts is a working 200-acre beef and arable farm on the edge of beautiful countryside overlooking the historic town of Cheltenham Spa, just 1½ miles from the town centre. Cheltenham Leisure Centre is a short walk away with swimming pools, squash courts, softland, etc. Children's playground, tennis courts, boating lake and golf course are again within easy walking distance. Open all year. Map ref: 226 089

Hydeaway, Hyde Lane, Newnham-on-Severn, Gloucestershire GL14 1HQ

Jennifer Dalton
☎ **0594 516788**
🏠 **From £17.50**
Applied

A short distance from the dairy farm, Hydeaway ia a recently built family farmhouse standing in 25 acres overlooking the river Severn and some 2 miles from the Forest of Dean. An en-suite double room with twin beds available throughout the year. Traditional farmhouse breakfast. Open all year. Map ref: 218 079

Kilmorie Guest House, Sings End, Gloucester Road, Corse, Staunton, Nr Gloucester, Gloucestershire GL19 3RQ

Sheila Barnfield
☎ 0452 840224
BB From £10
EM From £5.50
Sleeps 11
⌥ (5) 🧸 ♨ ⬛
Listed

Built in 1848 by the Chartists, Kilmorie is a Grade 2 listed smallholding keeping farm livestock, ponies and fruit. Children may help with animals. All accommodation on ground floor, tea/coffee trays and washbasins in all bedrooms, CH, large garden. Good home cooking, full English breakfast, 3 course evening meal. Some private facilities. Ideal for Cotswolds, Malverns, Forest of Dean, and places of natural and historic interest. Fire certificate. Kennels available for pets. Open all year (closed Christmas & New Year). Map ref: 222 085

Manor Farm, Manor Farm, Greet, Winchcombe, Cheltenham, Gloucestershire GL54 5BJ

Richard & Janet Day
☎ 0242 602423
BB From £20
Sleeps 4
⌥ 👤 ♨ ⬛
Listed

Luxuriously restored 16th century cotswold manor on mixed family farm, excellent views, near Sudeley Castle and steam railway. Convenient to Broadway, Cheltenham, Evesham, Tewkesbury and M5. 1½ miles from Cotswold Way and Wychavon Way. Large garden, croquet lawn, children welcome, horses can be accommodated. Open Jan–Nov. Map ref: 231 085

Nastend Farm, Nastend, Nr Stonehouse, Gloucestershire GL10 3RS

Jackie Guilding
☎ 0453 822300
BB From £12
EM From £8
Sleeps 6
⌥ ♨
♨♨

Enjoy that well-earned break in the friendly atmosphere of our small dairy farm set in pleasant surroundings. Watch (or help!) the daily running of our farm. For the more energetic, walk the 1½ mile farm trail. The spacious listed farmhouse boasts many modern conveniences, includingen-suite, CH, all blending in nicely with the traditional flavour of the oak-beamed residence, large garden with swimming pool. Open all year (closed Christmas & New Year). Map ref: 223 077

New House Farm, Aston Ingham, Longhope, Gloucestershire GL17 0LS

Mrs Betty Beddows
☎ 0452 830484
BB From £16
EM From £10
Sleeps 6
🧸 ⌥ ♨ ⬛
♨♨

Peaceful Georgian farmhouse set in 80 acres of farmland with beautiful views over the Malverns. All rooms have central heating, H/C, tea/coffee-making facilities and satellite TV. Family room en-suite, twin and double rooms with guests' own bathroom. Guests' dining room and lounge. Ideal for touring Cotswolds, Malverns and Forest of Dean. Open all year. Map ref: 217 084

Postlip Hall Farm, Winchcombe, Cheltenham, Gloucestershire GL54 5AQ

Mrs Valerie Albutt
☎ 0242 603351
BB From £14
Sleeps 4
⌥ 🧸 👤 ⊞ ♨ ♨
♨♨ Commended

A warm friendly welcome awaits guests on this family-run stock farm, set off B4632, amongst some of the most beautiful scenery in the Cotswolds – on side of Cleeve Hill. 1½ miles from Winchcombe. Great base for visiting Cotswolds, Stratford, Bath, Warwick Castle, Malverns. Superb walking, golf course nearby. 1 en-suite, 1 private bathroom, lounge, dining room, TVs, beverages. Idyllic surroundings. Open all year (closed Christmas). Map ref: 229 088

Ranbury Farm House, Poulton, Cirencester, Gloucestershire GL7 5HN

Rosemary Stallard
☎ 0285 851 279
BB From £14
Sleeps 4
🧸 ⌥ ♨
Listed

Welcome to Ranbury – a large Cotswold stone farmhouse, surrounded by a big walled garden in the village of Poulton, on the A417, between Cirencester and Lechlade. Ideal for touring the Cotswolds, Air Tattoo and within easy reach of Bath, Bristol, Cheltenham and Gloucester. Children welcome. Dogs by arrangement. Nearby local pubs serve good inexpensive lunches and evening meals. Open Easter–Nov. Map ref: 236 175

Saul Farm, Saul, Gloucestershire GL2 7JB

Mrs Wendy Watts
☎ 0452 740384
[BB] From £15
EM From £6
Sleeps 6

Take a break and relax in the comfort and homely atmosphere of our 17th century house overlooking a lake. Guests are welcome to lend a hand around the farm, which is situated between the River Severn and the Berkeley Canal. Many interesting places to visit nearby. TV lounge with open fire, spacious bedrooms with en-suite and home cooking are waiting for you and your family. 2 miles from M5 (jct. 13). Open all year. Map ref: 220 079

Sudeley Hill Farm, Winchcombe, Gloucestershire GL54 5JB

Barbara Scudamore
☎ 0242 602344
[BB] From £17.50
Sleeps 6

Highly Commended

Delightfully situated above Sudeley Castle with panoramic views across the surrounding valley, this is a 15th century listed farmhouse with a large garden on a working mixed farm of 800 acres. Ideal centre for touring the Cotswolds. Family/twin en-suite, 1 double, 1 twin, sharing guest bathroom. Comfortable lounge with TV and log fires. Separate dining room. Map ref: 229 088

Town Street Farm, Tirley, Gloucestershire GL19 4HG

Sue Warner
☎ 0452780 442
[BB] From £15
Sleeps 4

Approved

Town Street Farm is a typical working family farm close to the River Severn, within easy reach of M5 and M50. The farmhouse offers a high standard of accommodation with en-suite facilities in bedrooms and a warm and friendly welcome. Breakfast is served overlooking the lawns, flowerbeds and tennis court which is available for use by guests. Open all year. Map ref: 223 084

Wickridge Farm, Folly Lane, Stroud, Gloucestershire GL6 8JT

Gloria & Peter Watkins
☎ 0453 764357
[BB] From £15
EM From £12
Sleeps 5

Listed Commended

Wickridge Court Farm is situated 1 mile from the B4070 holiday route. A farm of 250 acres with cattle and horses. The historic farmhouse is a sympathetically converted Cotswold stone barn offering all en-suite rooms. It is a peaceful suntrap set in a fold of the beautiful Slad Valley offering excellent walks through National Trust woods; Stroud Leisure Centre with its heated pool is 1 mile, many places of interest within easy reach. Open all year. Map ref: 224 077

Windrush Farm, Bourton-on-the-Water, Cheltenham, Gloucestershire GL54 3BY

Mrs Jenny Burrough
☎ 0451 20419
[BB] From £15
Sleeps 4

Commended

We look forward to welcoming you to our family-run arable farm in a delightful setting. 2 miles from Bourton-on-the-Water. The Cotswold stone house has a lovely garden and panoramic views. Enjoy the beauty of the area, with its rolling hills, picturesque villages and places of interest. Our local 17th century pub is a stroll across the fields for evening meals. Open all year. Map ref: 236 084

Please mention **Stay on a Farm** when booking

Self-Catering

Bangrove Farm, Teddington, Tewkesbury, Gloucestershire GL20 8JB

Pat Hitchman
☎ 0242 620223
[SC] From £190–£250
Sleeps 2/8
🐾
🔑 🔑 🔑 Approved

An attractive self-contained property part of 17th century oak-beamed farmhouse on arable/livestock farm in quiet rural setting near Cheltenham. Ideal for walking and touring Cotswolds. Comfortably furnished, fitted carpets throughout. 3 double bedrooms (1 with washbasin), large bathroom. Downstairs cloakroom, kitchen/diner, large lounge, TV. Linen/electricity/use of washing machine included. Children welcome. Garden, hard tennis court, barbecue. Golf/riding available. Open Apr–Oct. Map ref: 098 088

Cornerways, Home Farm, Bredons Norton, Tewkesbury, Gloucestershire GL20 7HA

Mick & Anne Meadows
☎ 0684 72322
[SC] From £180–£230
Sleeps 6 cot
🐕 🐎 🛗 🎪
🔑 🔑 🔑 🔑
Approved

Cornerways is situated in a lovely small and peaceful village under Bredon Hill with superb views of the Avon and Severn valleys. Excellent base for touring, walking or relaxing. Comfortably furnished with fitted carpets, well equipped kitchen, lounge with woodburner, TV, dining room, 3 double bedrooms, bathroom, storage heaters, washing machine, cot. Large garden. Riding can be arranged locally. Open all year. Map ref: 097 090

Court Close Farm, Manor Road, Eckington, Pershore, Worcestershire WR10 3BH

Eileen Fincher
☎ 0386 750297
[SC] From £150–£190
Sleeps 4/6
🐾 🔀 🛗 🎪
🔑 🔑 🔑 Approved

A self-contained wing of our lovely 18th century farmhouse and garden on village edge, bordering Gloucestershire. Outstanding views of Bredon Hill. Attractive set dairy farm with meadows sloping to the Avon. Fishing by arrangement. Central for Shakespeare, Malvern and Cotswold jaunts. Convenient kitchen/diner and comfortable sitting room with TV, storage heat and electric fire. 3 bedrooms, linen provided. Open Apr–Oct. Map ref: 227 090

Damsels Mill Cottage, Damsels Farm, Painswick, Gloucestershire GL6 6UD

Michele Burdett
☎ 0452 812148
[SC] From £150–£360
Sleeps 8 + cot
🐾 🐓
🔑 🔑 🔑 Approved

An attractively renovated, comfortably furnished, detached stone cottage of great charm and character with many original features including beams and inglenook. The cottage stands in its own enclosed garden on a quiet lane in a pretty valley just 1 mile from the hillside market town of Painswick – often described as the Queen of the Cotswolds. Open all year. Map ref: 226 076

Folly Farm Cottages, Malmesbury Road, Tetbury, Gloucestershire GL8 8XA

Julian Benton
☎ 0666 502475
Fax 0666 502 358
[SC] From £132–£624
Sleeps 2/10
🐓 🛗 🐾
🔑 🔑 🔑 – 🔑 🔑 🔑 🔑
Up to Commended

Close to Royal Tetbury, 9 superior farm courtyard cottages. Well furnished and fully equipped throughout. Central heating CTV, microwave. Linen, logs provided. Laundry. Large gardens, barbecue and play area. Meals to order. Riding, fishing, golf nearby. Pubs 2 mins walk. Resident hosts; ideal accommodation for disabled and family reunions. Civilised pets and children welcome! Close to M4 and M5 motorways. Open all year. Map ref: 228 088

Hollytree Bungalow, Ermin House Farm, Syde, Cheltenham, Gloucestershire GL53 9PN

Mrs Catherine Hazell
☎ 0285 821255
[SC] From £230–£250
Sleeps 5 + cot
🐾 🕭 ⅍ ⌨ ⅋
⚷ ⚷ ⚷ **Approved**

Comfortable three bedroomed bungalow peacefully situated on arable farm near Cirencester. Well equipped with colour TV, fridge/freezer, washing machine and tumble drier. Garage, ample parking and lawns. Ideal centre for touring and walking in the Cotswolds. Within easy reach of Oxford, Bath, Stratford-upon-Avon and Cotswold Water Park. Under personal supervision of owner. Open July, Aug, Sept. Map ref: 228 081

The Lodge Barn, Bredons Hardwick, Tewkesbury, Gloucestershire GL20 7EB

Judith Pearman
☎ 0684 295556
[SC] From £200–£380
⅍ ⊱ ⚊
Applied
⚷ ⚷ ⚷ ⚷ ⚷ **Highly Commended**

A delightfully restored 17th century brick and timber barn, situated within the peaceful grounds of a Grade II listed Georgian farmhouse. 2 miles from Bredon village. Fully equipped kitchen, two twins (one can be zip-linked 6 ft), colour TV, fitted carpets, central heating. Tastefully furnished. Garden, coarse fishing on farm. Windsurfing ½ mile. Easy access to Cotswolds. Open all year. Map ref: 226 087

Manor Farm, Greet, Winchcombe, Cheltenham, Gloucestershire GL54 5BJ

Richard & Janet Day
☎ 0242 602423
[SC] From £150–£400
Sleeps 3/7
⅍ ⅄ ⌨ ⌱ ⚊
⚷ ⚷ ⚷ ⚷ **Highly Commended**

Beautifully restored 15th century tithe house and newly restored 'Shuck's Cottage' and 'Boot hole cottage', on family farm. Central for Tewkesbury, Broadway, Evesham, Cheltenham. Sleep 3–7, cot and high-chair available. Horses accommodated. Croquet lawn. Close to Cotswold Way and Wychavon Way, in sight of steam railway. Full central heating, every modern convenience. Open all year. Map ref: 231 085

New House Farm Cottages, New House Farm, Aston, Ingham Lane, Longhope, Gloucestershire GL17 0LS

Mr C Beddow
☎ 0452 830484
[SC] From £200–£380
Sleeps 4/5
⅍ ⌱
Applied

Newly converted cottages in peaceful surroundings. Well equipped with dishwashers, microwaves, satellite TV, gas central heating, linen and electric all inclusive. Beautiful walking country. Open all year. Evening meal available. Map ref: 217 084

No. 1 & 2 Cottages, Poulton Fields Farm, Cirencester, Gloucestershire GL7 5SS

Andrew & Gaby Wigram
☎ 0285 851388/851830
Fax 0285 850210
[SC] From £190–£340
Sleeps 6/12
⅍ ⅄ ⌱ ⌨ ⚊
⚷ ⚷ ⚷ ⚷ **Commended**

Two cottages recently modernised (1991), fully furnished and equipped to luxury standard. The accommodation sleeps 6/12 and consists of sitting room, dining room, kitchen, 3 bedrooms and bathroom including shower. Situated within walled garden in centre of farm 5 miles east of Cirencester. Electricity meter read, payphone, carpeted and double-glazed throughout. Open Mar–Oct. Map ref: 230 076

Old Mill Farm, nr Cirencester, c/o Ermin House Farm, Syde, Cheltenham, Gloucestershire GL53 9PN

Mrs Catherine Hazell
☎ 0285 821 255
[SC] From £125–£295
⚷ ⚷ ⚷ ⚷ **Commended**

Four superior barn conversions featuring Cotswold stone pillars and beams. Situated 4 miles from Cirencester on mixed farm beside River Thames and Cotswold Water park for walking, birdwatching, fishing, sailing and jet skiing. Trains to London 1¼ hrs. Prices include full central heating, electricity, bed-linen, colour TV. Separate laundry room with pay-phone. Convenient for Stratford-upon-Avon, Oxford, Stonehenge, Bath and Tetbury. Open all year. Map ref: 231 075

Peach Tree Cottage, c/o Hartpury Farm, Chedworth, Nr Cheltenham GL54 4AL

Mr & Mrs Booth
☎ 0285 720350
SC From £130–£160
Sleeps 3/6 cot

A 17th century cottage in the straggling unspoilt village of Chedworth with nearby footpaths leading to the Roman villa. The studio accommodates 3 with a studio couch in the large sitting room. Beautiful views and French windows onto garden. The cottage has 1 double room with washbasin and a communicating twin and double. South-facing. Cot and washing machine. Open July, Aug, Sept. Map ref: 232 081

Warrens Gorse Cottages, Home Farm, Warrens Gorse, Cirencester, Gloucestershire GL7 7JD

John & Nanette Randall
☎ 0285 831261
SC From £95–£170
Sleeps 3/4/5
 Approved

2½ miles from Cirencester between Daglingworth and Perrotts Brook, these attractive whitewashed cottages are ideally situated for touring the Cotswolds. The cottages are personally attended by the owners and are comfortably furnished and well equipped. 100-acre sheep, cattle and corn farm. Pottery and craft workshop with or without instruction. Golf club nearby. Water sports 5 miles. Open Mar–Oct. Also Christmas holidays. Map ref: 231 077

Westley Farm, Chalford, Stroud, Gloucestershire GL6 8HP

Julian & Liz Usborne
☎ 0285 760262
SC From £120–£250
Sleeps 2/5
 Approved

Steep meadows of wild flowers and beech woods are the setting for this old fashioned 80-acre hill farm with breathtaking panoramic views over the Golden Valley. Children especially enjoy the donkey, calves, lambs and foals. Adults may prefer the complete tranquillity and abundant wildlife. Horseriding. Nearby golf, gliding, watersports. Midway Cirencester – Stroud. Four cottages, two flats. Brochure available. Open Apr–Oct. Map ref: 225 076

FARM HOLIDAY BUREAU

GOOD FOOD

Nearly all Bureau members now hold a certificate in Essential Food Hygiene.

46 Bath & Wells

This area has a wealth of history going back to prehistoric times. The Druid Stones near Pensford are 600 years older than Stonehenge and there's always been a touch of magic and mystery in the air around Glastonbury, the ancient town and legendary Isle of Avalon, where it is rumoured King Arthur and his queen were buried.

The visitor is within easy striking distance of the beautiful city of Bath with its Regency architecture and older vestiges of civilisation like the Roman Baths. The whole town is alive with shops and pavement cafés. Another city within easy reach is Bristol, renowned as one of the world's leading ports. With Clifton Zoo, museums, theatres and marvellous shops, it's a vistor's delight. At the famous Wookey Hole Caves you can see the Witch of Wookey and visit a cave chamber in which the acoustics are said to be near perfection. Looking from Ebbor Gorge you will see what must be one of the grandest views in the world.

Interested in wine? There are two vineyards at Pilton and North Wooton where you can taste the local brew. And, of course, if you fancy something stronger, there is always the famous Somerset cider.

With the famous Gorge and caves at Cheddar, the lovely cathedral city of Wells, and the Mendip hills, you will be spoilt for choice.

Group Contacts: 🄱🄱 **Mrs Judi Hasell ☎ 0272 332 599**
🅂🄲 **Jo Smart ☎ 0761 490281**

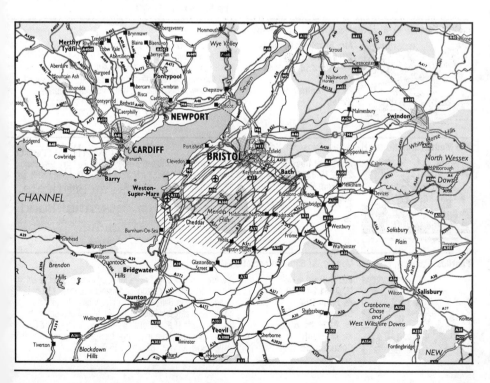

Bed and Breakfast (and evening meal)

Barrow Vale Farm, Farmborough, Bath, Avon BA3 1BL

Cherilyn Mary Langley
☎ 0761 470300
🅱 From £14
Sleeps 6
✄ ♨ ☙ (3)
🦢🦢

Barrow Vale is a family-run dairy farm, situated between the historic cities of Bath and Wells. The farmhouse, which has been comfortably modernised, offers central heating, well furnished bedroms (1 en-suite and 1 with private bathroom) and guests' lounge with TV. It is within easy reach of places of interest with local pubs and restaurants close by. Open Mar–Oct. Map ref: 217 260

Herons Green Farm, Compton Martin, Bristol, Avon BS18 6NL

Mrs Sandra Hasell
☎ 0275 333372
🅱 From £13
Sleeps 6
☙ ♨
Listed

A natural stone-built farmhouse by the side of Chew Valley Lake. Enjoy freedom and peace walking the fields with beautiful views of surrounding Mendip Hills and Lakes. A warm, friendly atmosphere awaits you. Attractive oak beamed dining room featuring the original water well. Double and family room with washbasins, razor points, tea/coffee-making facilities. Guests' own shower room. Large breakfasts. Open Mar–Nov. Map ref: 213 061

Icelton Farm, Wick-St-Lawrence, Weston-super-Mare, Avon BS22 0YJ

Mrs Elizabeth Parsons
☎ 0934 515704
🅱 From £14
Sleeps 6
☙ (6 months) 🈺
Listed

Icelton is a working dairy/sheep farm, just off the M5 (jct. 21). Ideal for touring Wells, Cheddar, and Mendip Hills. This listed farmhouse offers double room with H/C, family-room with H/C and shower. Tea/coffee-making facilities. Oak-beamed dining room and lounge, both with inglenook fireplaces. English breakfast. Good pubs and restaurants close at hand. No dogs. Open Mar–Nov. Map ref: 205 060

The Model Farm, Norton Hawkfield, Pensford, Bristol, Avon BS18 4HA

Margaret Hasell
☎ 0275 832144
🅱 From £14
Sleeps 6
☙
🦢🦢

The farmhouse is situated 2 miles off the A37 in a peaceful hamlet, nestling under the Dundry Hills. A working arable and beef farm in easy reach of Bristol, Bath, and many other interesting places. The accommodation consists of 1 family room en-suite and 1 double room with washbasin. Guests' lounge and dining room. Open Feb–Nov. Map ref: 214 064

Pantiles, Bathway, Chewton Mendip, Nr Bath, Somerset BA3 4ND

Pat Hellard
☎ 0761 241519
🅱 From £14
Sleeps 6
🄲 ♞ ✄ ☙ ⚲
🦢🦢 Highly
Commended

A warm welcome awaits at Pantiles, an attractive house set in 2 acres of garden and paddock situated in a small Mendip village. 15 miles Bath/Bristol, 5 miles Wells. Our aim is quality B&B at reasonable prices. We offer 3 bedrooms, 1. double, 2 twin (1 en-suite) all with hospitality tray. H &C. Colour TV, central heating. Large lounge with wood fires in winter. Open all year. Map ref: 215 057

Redhill Farm, Emborough, Nr Bath, Somerset BA3 4SH

Jane Rowe
☎ **0761 241294**
🅱 **From £14**
Sleeps 6
🛏 ✕ 🏕 ⬚
Listed

Our listed farmhouse built in Cromwellian times is situated high on the Mendips between Bath,and Wells. It is the perfect centre for outdoor activities and sightseeing. We are a working smallholding with a variety of animals to delight the children. CH. Guests' private bathroom. Fresh home produce. Tea/coffee-making facilities and washbasins in bedrooms. No dogs. Bath and West show ground 7 miles. Open all year. Map ref: 214 056

Southway Farm, Polsham Wells, Somerset BA5 1RW

Anita Frost
☎ **0749 673396**
🅱 **From £15**
Sleeps 6
🛏
🏵 🏵 **Commended**

A Georgian listed farmhouse situated halfway between Wells and Clastonbury overlooking Somerset levels and cider orchard. Accommodation is 3 comfortable and attractively furnished bedrooms, 1 with private bathroom, a delicious full English breakfast is served. Guests may relax in the cosy lounge or pretty garden. Ideal location for touring the glorious west country. Open Feb–Nov. Map ref: 211 054

Tor Farm, Nyland, Cheddar, Somerset BS27 3UD

Mrs Caroline Ladd
☎ **0934 743710**
🅱 **From £15**
Sleeps 20
🛏 ⬚ 🏂 ♨
Listed Commended

Tor Farm is situated on the beautiful Somerset levels and has open views from every window. The farmhouse is licensed and is fully centrally heated, with tea/coffee-making facilities in all rooms. Some rooms have full en-suite and private patios. From Cheddar, take A371 towards Wells. After 2 miles, turn right, signposted Nyland. Tor Farm is on the right, after 1½ miles. Open all year (closed Christmas). Map ref: 209 058

Woodbarn Farm, Denny Lane, Chew Magna, Bristol, Avon BS18 8SZ

Mrs Judi Hasell
☎ **0275 332599**
🅱 **From £13**
Sleeps 6
✕ 🛏
Listed

Woodbarn is a working beef/arable farm. Only 5 minutes from Chew Valley, lake-trout fishing, birdwatching, etc. Chew Magna has a Norman church and 16th century church house and is central for touring. There is 1 double room with washbasin and 1 family room with en-suite. Both have tea trays. Guests' own lounge and dining room. Cream teas Sundays June–September. Open Marc–Dec (Closed Christmas). Map ref: 214 062

FARM HOLIDAY BUREAU

BUREAU ACCOMMODATION IS RELIABLE

This Guide lists **Farm Holiday Bureau** members only. They are all inspected by the National Tourist Board for standards (see introduction pages) and by fellow members to maintain a high quality.

47 Bath & Wiltshire

Easily accessible within 100 miles of London the Midlands and the sea, Wiltshire offers the best of rural England, the marvellous scenery is its biggest surprise. Almost half the county is designated as an 'Area of Outstanding Natural Beauty'. The wide peaceful downland is rich in historic interest: Stonehenge, Avebury and Silbury Hill stand out on the rolling green plain, with picturesque villages hidden away along the chalk stream valleys. Castle Combe and the National Trust village of Lacock are well known, but there are scores more waiting to be discovered.
Wiltshire's rich heritage dates back to 4000 BC, prehistoric remains number no fewer than 4500 plus countless Roman and Medieval sites. Six hundred years of building are displayed in the magnificent collection of historic homes, ranging from Longleat, Bowood House and Corsham Court to smaller manor houses such as Sheldon Manor which have the atmosphere of a family home.
Walk the ancient Ridgeway Path, an important nomadic and trading route, or the Kennet and Avon Canal now restored along much of its route, and once the fastest means of transport from London to Bristol via Bath. Just over the county border the Romans built their city around the hot springs, and eleven centuries later Georgian architects did the same. Bath can rightfully claim to be one of the most beautiful cities in England.
Whether you just stop for a short break or decide to stay longer on a farm or go Self-Catering the people of Wiltshire will welcome you.

Group Contacts: 🅱🅱 **Mrs Shirley Bull ☎ 0672 515225/515166**
🆂🅲 **Mrs Janet Tyler ☎ 0380 850523**

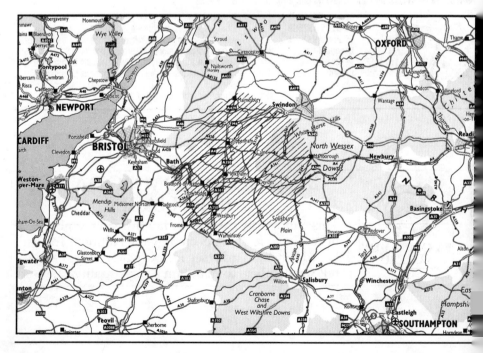

Bed and Breakfast (and evening meal)

Bayardo Farm, Clatford Bottom, Nr Marlborough, Wiltshire SN8 4DU

Mrs Shirley Bull
☎ 0672 515225/515166
BB From £15
Sleeps 4
🛏 ⚥ ⟡ (8) ⌂ 🏠
♨ ♨ Commended

255-acre mixed farm in beautiful, peaceful setting 3 miles from Marlborough and 5 miles from pre-historic Avebury. A warm welcome is assured in our 18th century tastefully renovated farmhouse, open log fires in winter. Full CH. Guest lounge, seperate dining room. Double/twin rooms with H/C, shaver points. Tea/coffee facilities. Bathroom and shower. Glorious walks from the door. Spacious garden. Open end Jan–end Nov. Map ref: 235 064

Boyds Farm, Gastard, Nr Corsham, Wiltshire SN13 9PT

Dorothy Robinson
☎ 0249 713146
BB From £14.50
Sleeps 6
🛏 ⚥ 🕱
♨ ♨ Commended

Enjoy a relaxing stay on our arable farm situated in the peace and tranquillity of the unspoilt Wiltshire countryside. Our delightful 16th century farmhouse, as featured by the *Daily Express*, accommodates families, couples and individuals, CH, H/C, tea/coffee-making facilities. Guests' own lounge with woodburning stove. Easy access to M4, Bath, Lacock, Castle Combe, Stonehenge, Bradford-on-Avon. Excellent pub food close by. Open all year. Map ref: 225 063

Frying Pan Farm, Broughton Gifford Road, Melksham, Wiltshire SN12 8LL

Barbara Pullen
☎ 0225 702343
BB From £15
Sleeps 6
⚥ ⟡ (2)
♨ ♨

Frying Pan Farm is a stock rearing farm which is situated 1 mile from Melksham, making it ideally positioned for visiting Bath, Bradford-on-Avon, Lacock and many National Trust properties. The house is a 17th century Grade 2 listed building, with cosy accommodation consisting of 2 double rooms, 1 en-suite, 1 double, 1 twin with tea/coffee-making facilities. Guests' own lounge with colour TV. Open all year (closed Christmas & New Year). Map ref: 226 062

Hatt Farm, Old Jockey, Box, Nr Bath, Wiltshire SN14 9DJ

Mrs Carol Pope
☎ 0225 742989
BB From £15
Sleeps 4
⚥ ⟡
Listed Commended

We warmly invite you to enjoy the peace and comfort of our family home. Hatt farm was built in the 18th century overlooking magnificent views of the rolling Wiltshire countryside, only 5 miles from Bath. Ideal for visiting many NT properties, picturesque villages and ancient historical sites. One twin, one double/family room all with private facilities. Tea/coffee facilities. CH, TV lounge. Log fire in Winter. Open Jan–Nov. Map ref: 222 063

Higher Green Farm, Poulshot, Devizes, Wiltshire SN10 4RW

Marlene & Malcolm Nixon
☎ 0380 828355
BB From £14
Sleeps 6
🛏 ⚥ ⟡
Listed

Listed 17th century timbered farmhouse facing south onto village green close to a traditional inn. This is a 140 acre working dairy farm situated between Bath and Salisbury, 3 miles from Devizes and within easy reach of many National Trust properties. Tea-making facilities, guests' lounge, colour TV. Double, twin and 2 single rooms, 2 bathrooms, 2 toilets. Open Mar–Nov. Map ref: 224 059

Hillside Farm, Edington, Westbury, Wilts BA13 4PG

Carol Mussell
☎ 0380 830437
BB From £14
Sleeps 4
Listed

A friendly welcome awaits you on our small working farm, nestled under the edge of Salisbury Plain in a secluded position off the B3098. We have panoramic views towards Bath and Devizes from our large garden. Close to many NT properties. Accommodation comprises 1 twin/family room, 1 double with washbasins, colour TVs and tea/coffee-making facilities. Open all year (closed Christmas & New Year). Map ref: 227 057

Little Cotmarsh Farm, Broad Town, Wootton Bassett, Swindon, Wiltshire SN4 7RA

Mary Richards
☎ 0793 731322
BB From £15
Sleeps 6
Listed

17th century farmhouse in quiet hamlet of Cotmarsh. Comfortable attractive bedrooms with washbasins, one with toilet/shower en-suite. All have tea/coffee-making facilities and electric heating. Colour TV on request. Beams throughout, flagstone dining room with inglenook fireplace and wood burning stove. Close to Avebury, Marlborough, Oxford and Cotswolds. Bath 26 miles, M4 (J16) 4 miles. Good pub food 2 miles. Open all year (closed Christmas). Map ref: 231 066

Longwater, Lower Road, Erlestoke, Nr Devizes, Wiltshire SN10 5UE

Pam Hampton
☎ 0380 830095
BB From £19
EM From £10.50
Sleeps 10
🐴 ♿ 🐂 🏃 ⚙ 🐾 🎪 ⛴
🐚 🐚 🐚 **Commended**

A peaceful retreat overlooking our own lakes and parkland with 2½ acre waterbird area. 160-acre organic farm with rare sheep & cattle. Family suite, double/twin rooms all en-suite, TV and tea-making facilities, CH. 2 ground floor bedrooms. Spacious lounge, large conservatory, separate dining room. Traditional farmhouse fayre using local produce. Special diets. Local wines. Coarse fishing. Erlestoke Sands Golf Course adjacent. Open all year. Map ref: 229 060

Lower Foxhangers Farm, Rowde, Devizes, Wiltshire SN10 1SS

Cynthia & Colin Fletcher
☎ 0380 828254
BB From £14.50
Sleeps 6
🐴 🐕 🐂 🏃 🏀 ⚙ **(touring & static)** 🍴 🎪
🐚 🐚

Visit the newly restored flight of 29 locks alongside our canalside mixed farm. Superb for boating, fishing and walking. Quietly situated 18th century spacious farmhouse offers double, family, twin bedded rooms with washbasins, tea/coffee-making facilities. Guest lounge with TV. Situated in centre of Wiltshire, easy reach of Stonehenge, Avebury & Bath. Open Apr–Oct. Map ref: 227 061

Manor Farm, Corston, Malmesbury, Wiltshire SN16 0HF

Mrs Ross Eavis
☎ 0666 822148
BB From £14
Sleeps 12
🐂 🖎
🐚 🐚 **Commended**

A friendly welcome awaits you at our unique 17th century farmhouse on a working dairy/arable farm of 436 acres. Single, twin, double and family rooms all with washbasins and tea/coffee-making facilities, one room en-suite. Guests' lounge with colour TV. Full fire certificate. Good pub food within walking distance. Credit cards accepted. Open all year. Map ref: 227 069

Manor Farm, Wadswick, Box, Corsham, Wiltshire SN14 9JB

Carolyn Barton
☎ 0225 810700
BB From £16
Sleeps 6
🗲 🐂 🖎 🏇 🎪 ⛺
🐚 🐚 🐚

Visit us at Wadswick, a peaceful hamlet close to the National Trust village of Lacock, yet only 6 miles from Bath. Our 16th century farmhouse has large, spacious rooms, en-suite with tea/coffee-making facilities and colour TV. Open Mar–Nov. Map ref: 224 064

Oakwood Farm, Upper Minety, Malmesbury, Wiltshire SN16 9PY

Mrs Katie Gallop
☎ 0666 860286
⌂ From £13
EM From £7
Sleeps 6
Listed Commended

A friendly farming couple welcome you to their working dairy farm close to the quiet village of Upper Minety. Situated off the B4040, overlooks Minety church on the edge of the Cotswolds. Ideal for touring the Cotswolds and surrounding National Trust properties. 2 double rooms and 1 twin. Guests' lounge/dining room with colour TV. Also tea/coffee-making facilities. Open all year. Map ref: 227 069

Pickwick Lodge Farm, Corsham, Wiltshire SN13 0PS

Gill Stafford
☎ 0249 712207
⌂ From £15
Sleeps 6
Listed Commended

A warm welcome awaits at Pickwick Lodge Farm, situated in peaceful surroundings ½ mile off the A4 between Chippenham and the Georgian city of Bath. Many footpaths, NT properties to visit, quiet villages to explore, or just relax in the garden. 2 double, 1 twin, with colour TV, tea/coffee facilities, H/C. Full CH. 2 private bath, 1 private showers. Children welcome. Open Feb–Nov. Map ref: 225 065

Poulshot Lodge Farm, Poulshot, Devizes, Wiltshire SN10 1RQ

Diana Hues
☎ 0380 828255
⌂ From £15
Sleeps 4
Listed

Friendly, working mixed farm in the picturesque village of Poulshot. Ideally situated for easy access to Lacock, Bath, Avebury and many other places of interest. Two twin rooms with tea/coffee making facilities. Own lounge with TV. Close to Kennet and Avon Canal. Excellent pub food close by. Open all year. Map ref: 224 059

Saltbox Farm, Drewetts Mill, Box, Corsham, Wiltshire SN14 9PT

Mary Gregory
☎ 0225 742608
⌂ From £15
Sleeps 4
Commended

Saltbox is a dairy farm, quietly located 1 mile off A4, 6 miles from Bath and centrally situated for touing the west country. Our listed 18th century farmhouse is set inthe beautiful Box Valley, offering scenic walks in a wildlife and conservation area.
Guests' lounge with colour TV, double and twin bedrooms with washbasins and tea/coffee-making facilities, central heating throughout. Closed Christmas and New Year. Map ref: 222 063

Sevington Farm, Yatton Keynell, Castle Combe, Chippenham, Wiltshire SN14 7LD

Judith & Roger Pope
☎ 0249 782408
⌂ From £14
Sleeps 6
Listed Commended

Listed 18th century farmhouse offering a warm welcome, comfortable beds and a hearty breakfast. Large lounge, colour TV and a separate dining room. 300 acres of former arable land are now in "Set-a-Side" offering interesting farm walks, seeing wildlife and countryside in its natural state. Private fishing in our two lakes. All our rooms have tea/coffee-making facilities. American Express accepted. Open Jan–Nov. Map ref: 227 067

Smiths Farm, Bushton, Swindon, Wiltshire SN4 7PX

Dee Freeston
☎ 0793 731285
⌂ From £14
Sleeps 6
Listed Commended

Uneven floors, old latch doors, beams in and out, history throughout. A garden to browse, fields for to roam – most important of all, Smiths Farm is our home. Welcome to our dairy and beef farm, to cosy double and family rooms, CH, H & C, tea/coffee trays. Excellent pub food 5 minutes' walk; easy drive to M4, Cotswolds, Bath, Marlborough, Swindon. Open all year. Map ref: 232 067

Spiers Piece Farm, Steeple Ashton, Nr Trowbridge, Wiltshire BA14 6HG

Jill Awdry
☎ 0380 870266
BB From £14
Sleeps 6
♿ ☇ ♞ ⚷ ♨
♛ ♛ Commended

Follow a treasure trail and find a warm welcome to our spacious Georgian farmhouse with its fantastic views and family-run arable and stock farm. Take A350 from Melksham, follow the Keevil Airfield signs and find us within easy reach of many tourist attractions. Two doubles and a twin-bedded room with washbasins. Tea/coffee-making facilities and CH. Guests' lounge and bathroom. Open Feb–Nov (incl). Map ref: 226 057

Stonehill Farm, Charlton, Malmesbury, Wiltshire SN16 9DY

Mrs Edna Edwards
☎ 0666 823310
BB From £14
Sleeps 6
♞ ⚷
Listed

Large 15th century Cotswold stone house on 180-acre dairy/sheep farm in a quiet location 3 miles from the ancient borough of Malmesbury and 8 miles from the M4. Ideally situated for days in Bath, Cirencester, Stonehenge and the Cotswolds. 3 bedrooms available, 1 with en-suite facilities. Friendly hospitality and comfort are assured. Open all year. Map ref: 229 071

Self-Catering

Bannerdown View Farm Cottages, Ashley Road, Bathford, Bath, Avon BA1 7TS

Heather Sully
☎ 0225 859363
SC From £150–£300
Sleeps 4/5
⚷
Applied

Beautifully stone barn converted to very high standard. Laundry/payphone, large shared garden with furniture, B-B-Q set in lovely countryside, easy reach of Bath, approx 3½ miles, Bradford-on-Avon with its Saxon church and tythe barn, also Kennet canal, many National Trust properties within 10 miles. Good selection of pubs to eat out, stabling for own horse, logs for winter lets. Baby sitting by prior arrangement. Regret no pets. Map ref: 221 062

The Derby, Court Farm Stables, Heddington, Nr Calne, Wiltshire SN11 0PL

Mrs Janet Tyler
☎ 0380 850 523
SC From £130–£195
Sleeps 2
♿ ♞ ⚷
♟ ♟ ♟ ♟ Commended

The Derby is a bungalow-style stable conversion set in idyllic surroundings on a secluded and level site, approached over a paved courtyard with Victorian lamp and wishing well. Traditionally furnished, ideal for two people. Full central heating, open fireplace, colour TV, microwave, washing machine and dryer. Garage. Linen included. Open all year. Map ref: 230 065

Home Farm Barn, Home Farm, Heddington, Nr Calne, Wiltshire SN11 0PL

Mrs Janet Tyler
☎ 0380 850523
SC From £150–£325
Sleeps 5
♿ ♨
♟ ♟ ♟ ♟
Commended

Home Farm is a dairy and arable farm with its own private lake, panoramic views and unbeatable downland walks in small village. Riding school and golf course adjoins farm. The 17th century barn retains all its original roof timbers and beams thus providing immense character, 3 bedrooms, colour TV, wood burning stove. Full CH. Linen included. Washing machine, dryer and microwave. Open all year. Map ref: 230 065

Lower Foxhangers Farm, Rowde, Devizes, Wiltshire SN10 1SS

Cynthia & Colin Fletcher
☎ 0380 828254
sc From £130–£190
Sleeps 4/5
🐕 🐈 ♿ 🏃 ⚤ (touring & static) 🏧 ❤ ☂
✿ Approved

Situated in a tranquil setting by the canal in the centre of Wiltshire. Within easy reach of Bath, Stonehenge and Avebury. The four mobile homes comprise 2/3 bedrooms, separate lounge, kitchen and flush bathroom, with patios and garden furniture. Ideal for walking and fishing. Boat hire by arrangement. Open Apr–end Oct. Map ref: 227 061

Stonehill Farm, Charlton, Malmesbury, Wiltshire SN16 9DY

Mrs Edna Edwards
☎ 0666 823310
sc From £110–£230
Sleeps 2/3
🐕
✿ ✿ ✿ Commended

Stonehill is a working dairy/sheep farm on the Wilts/Glos border and 3 miles from Malmesbury. The cow Byre and Bull Pen are converted cowsheds and each sleeps 2/3 people plus cot or small bed. Ideal for days in the Cotswolds, Bath and Stonehenge also watersports at the Cotswold parks. Open all year. Map ref: 229 071

Salisbury

Swaynes Firs Farm, Grimsdyke, near Coombe Bissett, Salisbury, Wiltshire SP5 5RF

Arthur Shering
☎ 0725 89240
BB From £16
Sleeps 6
🐕 🐎 ☂ 🏹
♔ Approved

Swaynes Firs Farm is a small active farm with horses, steers, poultry and oranmental duck ponds. The rooms are spacious with en-suite, TV and nice views. Ideal for touring or visiting the many historic sites in area, an ancient roman ditch is on the farm. A warm welcome awaits all our guests. Open all year. Map ref: 235 048

FARM HOLIDAY BUREAU

FOLLOW THE COUNTRY CODE

Leave nothing but footprints,

Take nothing but photographs,

Kill nothing but time!

48 Hampshire

Hampshire is a beautiful county of contrasts . . . of creeks, harbours and beaches, grand rivers and sparkling streams, forests, and lush farmland with picturesque villages and hamlets.

The main centres of the county have all played an important role in history: the Saxons made Winchester their capital; Southampton bears witness to the Norman invasion, and Portsmouth is especially famous for its naval heritage with Nelson's HMS Victory, Henry VIII's Mary Rose and the first ironclad warship, HMS Warrior, on display.

Hampshire has numerous other links with the past and its people. You can visit Jane Austen's house at Chawton or Charles Dickens' birthplace in Portsmouth, for example, or enjoy the many rich treasures on show in the museums of the county's towns and cities.

In the New Forest there are plenty of quiet picnic spots and lots of ponies.

Hampshire is served by a network of footpaths and bridleways and many country parks. There are long distance walks and guided walks which can take you round the towns and cities, along the Solent coastline or perhaps inland along the famous Test Valley taking in Romsey and Stockbridge. The country mansions of Broadlands, Breamore, Stratfield Saye and Highclere Castle are among several Hampshire homes open to the public and there are gardens galore.

Group Contact: Mrs Melanie Bray ☎ 0705 631597

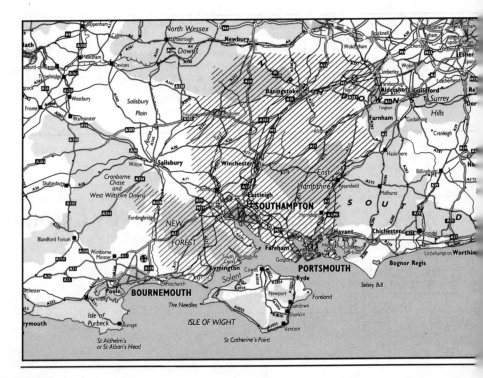

Bed and Breakfast (and evening meal)

Acres Down Farm, Minstead, Nr Lyndhurst, Hampshire SO43 7GE

Mrs Annie Cooper
☎ 0703 813693
📟 From £13
Sleeps 6
🐂 🏕 ⏏
Listed

Homely New Forest farm keeping cattle, sheep, pigs and ponies according to the ancient laws of the New Forest. Situated on the west of the picturesque village of Minstead, opening directly onto the open forest with its heathlands and wooded dales. Ideal centre for walking and touring holiday. Own stocked trout lake. Farmhouse cream teas. Open all year. Map ref: 241 043

Brocklands Farm, West Meon, Petersfield, Hampshire GU32 1JN

Sue Wilson
☎ 0730 829228
📟 From £15.50
Sleeps 6
🐂 👫 ✕ ⏏ 🛄 🕱 🕱
Listed

Brocklands Farm in the famed Meon Valley has good views of the countryside and is within easy reach of the coastal ports and also the ancient towns of Winchester, Petersfield and Chichester. The light and airy farmhouse is furnished traditionally with a homely atmosphere. An old railway line and grass headlands provide farm walks. Day sailing in the Solent. Afternoon tea available. Open all year (closed Christmas). Map ref: 258 047

The Bungalow, c/o Oakdown Farm, Dummer, Basingstoke, Hampshire RG23 7LR

Mrs Elizabeth Hutton
☎ 0256 397 218
📟 From £15
Sleeps 6
🐂 (12) 🕱 🕱
♨

Oakdown Farm Bungalow is on a secluded, private road, next to junction 7 on the M3, 3 miles south of Basingstoke and close to the village of Dummer. Very good road communications to London, Winchester, Southampton, Oxford, the South-West and the Midlands. Wayfarer's Walk within 200 metres. Open all year. Map ref: 254 055

Compton Farmhouse, Compton, Nr Chichester, West Sussex PO18 9HB

Mrs Melanie Bray
☎ 0705 631597
📟 From £15 (children £5)
Sleeps 6
🐂 🕱
Listed

Children are especially welcome at our old, flint family farmhouse. We are 200 yards up a track from the village square, next door to the church and are bordered by fields and woods. Lovely walks and plenty to do in our enclosed, child-orientated garden. Own sitting/dining room with drink-making facilities, fridge, TV, video. Chichester and Portsmouth nearby. Open all year. Map ref: 258 045

Corhampton Lane Farm, Corhampton, Southampton, Hampshire SO3 1NB

Mrs Barbara Hall
☎ 0489 877506
📟 From £14–£16
Sleeps 4
✕ 🕱
Listed

Our 600-acre arable farm is on the B3035 Bishops Waltham/Corhampton road within easy reach of Winchester, Southampton and Portsmouth. The 17th century farmhouse is warm and comfortable with modern conveniences, surrounded by lovely countryside and many places of historic interest and enjoyment. Local hostelries offer excellent facilities. Tourist Guide's helpful assistance is available. Open Apr–Oct. Map ref: 255 048

Park Farm, Stoneham Lane, Eastleigh, Hampshire SO5 3HS

Angela Fright
☎ **0703 612960**
🏠 From £13
EM From £10
Sleeps 6
🐟
Listed

Converted coaching stables in a beautiful rural setting. Close to Southampton, Romsey, Winchester and New Forest (15 mins). 800 yards off M27 (jct. 5). Coarse fishing in own small, secluded lake and in adjacent, 200-year-old Capability Brown landscaped lakes, both well stocked. Tea/coffee facilities, CTV in all bedrooms. Packed lunches and evening meals by arrangement only. Diets catered for. Water purifier installed. Open all year. Map ref: 248 045

Pyesmead Farm, Plaitford, Romsey, Hampshire SO51 6EE

Mrs C Pybus
☎ **0794 23386**
🏠 From £12
EM From £6
Sleeps 4
🚶🐟🐴🐕
Listed

Come and stay on a small, family-run stock farm bordered by the New Forest and by the River Blackwater, a tributary of the well-known River Test. Guests are welcome to walk around the farm. Fishing available on our attractive, private lakes. Many activities locally, including horse riding, golf, swimming and forest walks. Open all year (closed Christmas).
Map ref: 243 045

Self-Catering

SC

Acres Down Farm, Minstead, Nr Lyndhurst, Hampshire SO43 7GE

Mrs Annie Cooper
☎ **0703 813693**
SC From £140–£170
Sleeps 4/5
🐟🐕🐴
🔑 🔑 🔑 Approved

Two 2-bedroom self-catering cottages on a working New Forest commoners farm set in the heart of the forest on the edge of Minstead Village. Shopping centre of Lyndhurst 2½ miles. The 19th century cottages are fully equipped with linen included, and CH in winter months. Ideal for walking and touring, coast within easy reach. Open all year.
Map ref: 241 043

Meadow Cottage, c/o Farley Farm, Braishfield, Romsey, Hampshire SO51 0QP

Mrs Janice Graham
☎ **0794 68265/68513**
SC From £130–£210
Sleeps 5
🐴🐟🏇
🔑 🔑 🔑 🔑 Commended

Well equipped, semi-detached cottage on a 400-acre beef and arable farm. Outstanding views of beautiful surrounding countryside. Ideal for walking or riding (own horse welcome), or touring historic centres of Romsey, Winchester, Salisbury, New Forest and coast. Cottage has CH, log fire, colour TV, downstairs WC, washer/dryer, cot. Garden with barbecue. Phone for brochure. Open Easter–end Oct. Map ref: 245 048

Please mention **Stay on a Farm** when booking

---

49 Sussex & Surrey

You've probably heard of 'Sussex by the Sea' so perhaps to you Sussex means the traditional attractions of the popular seaside resorts such as Brighton, Eastbourne, Hastings, Bognor Regis, Littlehampton and Worthing. What you may not know is that just inland there is a vast area of lovely downland punctuated with tiny villages and the occasional old market town. Further north busy towns such as Horsham, Crawley, East Grinstead and Reigate are surrounded by lush green countryside. There is also a rich history here – Chichester with its famous Roman cross, nearby Fishbourne with the remains of a palace once ruled by a King Cogidubnus . . . really; and Hastings – 1066 and all that.

In Surrey, the North Downs provide dramatic wooded hillsides with small, attractive towns and villages nestling in the valleys.

Here you can walk along the track claiming to be the Pilgrim's Way which connects Winchester to Canterbury; clamber up famous heights like Leith Hill – just short of 1,000ft – or its neighbour Box Hill, coming down via the intriguingly named Zig Zag Hill.

Yet nowhere in these counties are you ever more than a couple of hours from Central London should you wish to make a day trip there.

Group Contacts: Sussex: Brenda Gough ☎ 0273 478680
Surrey: Mrs Gill Hill ☎ 0306 730210

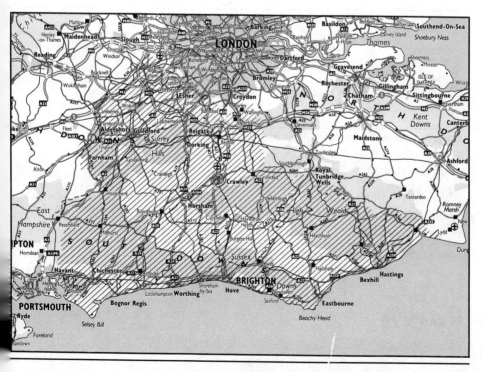

Bed and Breakfast (and evening meal)

Ashlands Cottage, Burwash, East Sussex TN19 7HS

Mrs Nesta Harmer
☎ 0435 882207
BB From £15
Sleeps 4
ħ
Listed Commended

Pretty period cottage in quiet Wealden farmland, within designated Area of Outstanding Natural Beauty. Glorious views, gardens and picnic spots on site. Kipling's "Batemans" only 5 mins walk across the fields, and many more places of interest nearby. Ideal for walking, touring, country pubbing or just sitting under a tree. Open all year. Map ref: 295 047

Borderfield Farm, Rowledge, Farnham, Surrey GU10 4EP

Mrs Pamela Simpson
☎ 025125 3985
BB From £16
Sleeps 4/5 + cot
ॐ Å ॐ ħ ॐ
Applied

A mixed farm on the outskirts of the village. Bedrooms with TV, tea/coffee-making facilities. Lounge with TV and log fire. Lovely walks, easy reach of London, New Forest and coast. Horse-driving available. Open 1 Feb–30 Nov.
Map ref: 262 055

Bulmer Farm, Holmbury St Mary, Dorking, Surrey RH5 6LG

Gill Hill
☎ 0306 730210
BB From £16
Caravans £3
Sleeps 6
ħ ॐ (12) ॐ ॐ ■ ॐ
ॐ ॐ

17th century beamed farmhouse, with inglenook fire. 3 twin-bedded rooms with washbasins, or en-suite double/twin bedroom with TV in tastefully converted barn, all with tea/coffee tray. 30-acre beef farm in picturesque Surrey Hills village, large garden, woodland walk to lake. Ideal walking/birdwatching. Homemade preserves. Good pubs nearby. Recommended by Elizabeth Gundry '*Staying off the Beaten Track*'. Overnight grazing for horses by arrangement. Open all year (caravans Easter–Oct). Map ref: 274 056

Camoys Farm House, Mill Road, Barcombe, Lewes, East Sussex BN8 5BH

Mrs Hedley Cornwell
☎ 0273 400662
BB From £16
Sleeps 6
У ॐ ħ ॐ ॐ ॐ ॐ
ॐ ॐ

A modern, spacious farmhouse in quiet surroundings enjoying outstanding views. 4 miles north of Lewes, close to Barcombe village. Ideally situated for visiting this part of Sussex with its historic buildings gardens, coast and South Downs. Downstairs twin bedded room en-suite suitable for disabled guests. Upstairs twin bedded room with basin and family room with basin and bathroom adjacent. All rooms with colour TV and tea/coffee making facilities. Cot available. 'A home from home' No smokers please. Open Jan–Nov. Map ref: 285 043

Crossways Farm, Raikes Lane, Abinger Hammer, Nr Dorking, Surrey RH5 6PZ

Sheila Hughes
☎ 0306 730173
BB From £14
Sleeps 6
ħ ॐ ॐ ■ ॐ
ॐ ॐ ॐ

Welcome to our 17th century listed farmhouse (book and TV setting) amidst the oustanding beauty of the Surrey hills. Good walks. Near A25 and Dorking/Guildford bus stop. Easy reach Gatwick, Heathrow, London, S Coast, Wisley. Large, comfortable rooms, washbasins, tea/coffee-making facilities, inglenooks, log fires, beams, colour TV. Walled garden, croquet. Laundry facilities. Good home cooking. Elizabeth Gundry recommended. Open all year. Map ref: 274 056

Goffsland Farm, Shipley, Horsham, West Sussex RH13 7BQ

Mrs Carol Liverton
☎ 0403 730434
[BB] From £14
Sleeps 5

Listed 17th century farmhouse on a 260-acre working farm with sheep, cattle and dairy herd. Situated in the Sussex Weald central to Gatwick and the South coast. Family room has double bed and bunk beds with washbasin and tea/coffee-making facilities. Own bathroom with WC and use of family sitting room with TV. Open all year. Map ref: 275 049

Lannards, Okehurst Lane, Billingshurst, West Sussex RH14 9HR

Betty & Derek Sims
☎ 040378 2692
[BB] From £15
Sleeps 5

Listed

Comfortable bungalow with view and walks in Sussex Weald. Surrounded by fields, dairy herd 14 mile. Attached to Fine Art Gallery. Sotheby's Auction Rooms ½ mile, Petworth and its antique shops and galleries 7 miles. Easy reach of London, M25 ½ hour, Gatwick 20 minutes, Chichester, Arundel, Goodwood and Brighton. Many historical gardens and theatres to visit; golf courses, riding schools, racing all within easy reach. Open all year. Map ref: 272 047

Manor Farm, Poynings, Nr Brighton, East Sussex BN45 7AG

Mrs Carol Revell
☎ 0273 857371
[BB] From £18
EM From £8
Sleeps 6

260-acre family run sheep/arable farm with charming old manor house resting quietly in a green valley under the South Downs. An area of outstanding natural beauty, ideal for riders, walkers and country lovers. Plenty of country pubs and eating houses nearby. A23 5 mins, Hickstead 10 mins, Gatwick 30 mins, Brighton and Hove 15 mins. Evening meal by request only. Open Mar–Dec. Map ref: 280 044

Manor Farm, Ripe, Nr Lewes, East Sussex BN8 6AP

Peter Benning
☎ 0323 811425
[BB] From £18
EM From £10
Sleeps 10

Highly Commended

Manor Farm is situated at the foot of the South Downs in the unspoilt village of Ripe. Accommodation is of the highest quality, and most bedrooms have bathrooms en suite. Facilities include a full size billiards room, coarse fishing and horse riding. Excellent golf courses within easy reach. Eastbourne, Brighton and Glyndebourne a few minutes drive away. Open all year. Map ref: 285 043

Moonshill Farm, The Green, Ninfield, Battle, East Sussex TN33 9LH

Mrs June Ive
☎ 0424 892645
[BB] From £15
Sleeps 6
(4)

In the heart of the '1066 Country' in the centre of Ninfield opposite pub. Farmhouse in 10 acres of garden, orchard, stables. Enjoy beautiful walks, golf and riding arranged. Comfortable rooms, 3 en-suite, CH and electric fires, hospitality tray, TV, lounge, parking and garage, babysitting service. Every comfort in our safe, quiet and peaceful home. Reduced rates for weekly bookings. Open Jan–Nov. Map ref: 299 042

New House Farm, Broadford Bridge Road, West Chiltington, Nr Pulborough, West Sussex RH20 2LA

Alma Steele
☎ 0798 812215
[BB] From £18
Sleeps 6
(10)

Commended

Listed 15th century farmhouse with oak beams and inglenook fireplace, in the centre of the village, close to local inns which provide good food. A new 18 hole golf course, open to non-members, is only ¼ mile away. Many places of historical interest in the area including Goodwood House, Petworth House, Parham House, Arundel Castle. Gatwick 40 minutes. En-suite facilities and colour TV in bedrooms. Open Jan-Nov. Map ref: 273 046

Ousedale House, Offham, Lewes, East Sussex BN7 3QF

Roland & Brenda Gough
☎ 0273 478680
BB From £20
EM From £10
Sleeps 6
✗ ✕ (10) ⊡ ▪
♨ ♨ ♨ **Highly
Commended**

Spacious Victorian country house with luxury accommodation. 3½ acre garden and woodland situated on a hillside plateau with panoramic views over the Ouse river valley. Country cooking, four poster bed, modern heating. Central for touring. About 1 mile from Lewes station – courtesy car. University 6 miles, Brighton 9 miles. Low season activity and other weekend breaks. Open all year.
Map ref: 284 043

The Stud Farm, Bodle Street Green, Nr Hailsham, East Sussex BN27 4RJ

Philippa & Richard Gentry
☎ 0323 833201
BB From £17
EM From £8.50 (by arrangement)
Sleeps 6
✕ (10)
♨ ♨ **Commended**

Situated in peaceful surroundings and beautiful countryside, ideal for walking. 8 miles from sea, Eastbourne, Hastings, South Downs in easy reach. Upstairs, family unit of double bedded room/twin bedded room both with handbasins and bathroom. Downstairs twin bedded room with shower, toilet, handbasin en-suite. Tea/coffee-making facilities. Guests' sitting room, colour TV. Sunroom. Good eating places nearby. Open all year (closed Christmas). Map ref: 294 095

Stud Farm House, Telscombe Village, Lewes, East Sussex BN7 3HZ

Tim & Nina Armour
☎ 0273 302486
BB From £15
EM From £7.50
Sleeps 6
✗ ✕ ✿ ✲ ▪ ✗
Applied

300-acre sheep farm in quiet hamlet on the South Downs Way. The sea is 1½ miles away, London 50 minutes by train, 10 minutes Newhaven/Dieppe 'Sealink Ferries'. Caravan parking, horse riding, cycling, golf, fishing, sailing, walking. Treat your horse to first class stables, grazing, downland riding. Winter breaks by log fires, farmhouse cooking, or join in the action in our family farming year. Open all year.
Map ref: 284 040

Sturtwood Farm, Partridge Lane, Newdigate, Dorking, Surrey RH5 5EL

Bridget MacKinnon
☎ 0306 631308
BB From £17
EM From £8.50
Sleeps 6
✗ ✿
♨ ♨

An attractive 18th century farmhouse in lovely countryside yet within 12 mins of Gatwick Airport. Many National Trust properties and gardens nearby. Also London, Brighton and several country towns. Map ref: 267 054

Self-Catering

SC

"Badgersholt" and "Foxholme", c/o Bulmer Farm, Holmbury St Mary, Dorking, Surrey RH5 6LG

Gill Hill
☎ 0306 730210
SC From £110–£260
Sleeps 2/4
♿ ✗ ✿ ✿ ▪ ✗
✗ ✗ ✗–✗ ✗ ✗
Commended

Two delightfully cosy, single-storey cottages, sympathetically converted from a Surrey barn, forming a courtyard with the farmhouse. Fully carpeted, electric CH, colour TV and linen (beds made up). Communal laundry room, use of 2-acre farmhouse garden. Situated in picturesque, quiet valley. Ideal walking country. "Badgersholt" sleeps 2 (also suitable disabled); "Foxholme" sleeps 4 in 2 bedrooms. Open all year. Map ref: 274 056

Black Cottage, c/o Newells Farm House, Lower Beeding, Horsham, West Sussex RH13 6LN

Vicky Storey
☎ 0403 891326
ⓈⒸ From £95–£150
Sleeps 4
🐕 🐖 🐄 🛶 🐎
🏌 🏌 🏌 Approved

A delightful secluded cottage in the centre of a sheep and arable farm, with views to the South Downs. Surrounded by woods and lovely walks. Sleeps 4 in comfort. Recently modernised, it is 40 mins from Brighton, 20 mins from Gatwick, with fishing, golf and beautiful Sussex, Surrey and Kent gardens within easy reach. The ideal holiday cottage. Open 2 Jan–20 Dec. Map ref: 277 048

Boring House Farm, Vines Cross, Heathfield, East Sussex TN21 9AS

Mrs Anne Reed
☎ 043 53 2285
ⓈⒸ From £120–£160
Sleeps 6
🐕 🐖 🐄 🛶
🏌 🏌 🏌 🏌 Commended

Peaceful farm cottage on sheep and beef farm. Marvellous views and walks, fishing available. Traditional local, good atmosphere/food in easy walking distance. Many beautiful places to visit. Beach within 15 miles. Accommodation (portion of farmhouse) comprises utility room, hall, WC, kitchen, dining room, sitting room, 3 bedrooms, 1 with shower, 1 with washbasin, bathroom and WC. Large garden. Open Mar–Sept and Oct ½ term. Map ref: 292 047

---

2 Highweald Cottages, Chelwood Farm, c/o Sheffield Park Farm, Nr Uckfield, East Sussex TN22 3QR

Mrs Nicky Howe
☎ 0825 790235/790267
ⓈⒸ From £140–£260
Sleeps 5 + cot
🐄 🐎
🏌 🏌 🏌 🏌
Commended

Picturesque semi-detached farm cottage with garden on dairy farm adjacent Ashdown Forest. Comfortable accommodation comprises 1 double, 1 twin, 1 single room, bathroom, WC, sitting room (log fire, colour TV, phone), kitchen (fridge/freezer, auto washing machine, tumble dryer, electric cooker). Close Sheffield Park Gardens, Bluebell Railway. Easy reach Downs and coast. Cot/high chair available. Beds made up. No towels or cot linen. Open all year. Map ref: 287 047

Park Farm, Arundel, Sussex BN18 0AG

Janet Seller
☎ 0903 882582
ⓈⒸ From £150–£265
Sleeps 5 + baby
🐄 🛶
🏌 🏌 🏌 Highly
Commended

A quietly situated, well equipped and attractively furnished semi-detached Victorian farm cottage. Large garden, 3 bedrooms. Downstairs has bathroom with shower, separate WC, sitting room, dining room, kitchen. Reductions for 3 or less excluding July/August. Ample parking. Beds made up. Ideally sited for sandy beaches, walking, fishing and places of historical and wildlife interest. Open Easter–end Oct. Map ref: 270 040

---

2 Victoria Cottage, c/o Hole and Alchorne Farm, Bell Lane, Nutley, East Sussex TN22 3PD

Pauline & Peter Graves
☎ 082 571 2475
ⓈⒸ From £135–£250
Sleeps 5
🐄 🛶 📦
🏌 🏌 🏌 🏌 Highly
Commended

A warm welcome awaits you at our comfortable, well-appointed semi-detached cottage, with lovely garden on our dairy farm. Near Ashdown Forest. 3 bedrooms (1 double, 1 twin, 1 single), bathroom, separate WC, sitting room with TV and phone, dining room, kitchen with electric cooker, fridge, washing machine, tumble dryer. Price includes electricity. Beds made up. Ideal for visiting South Downs, castles and coast. Open all year. Map ref: 286 049

Tipsy Oast, Brown's Farm, Robertsbridge, Sussex, TN32 5JG

Mr & Mrs Roy Palmer
☎ 0580 881184
Fax 0580 881863
ⓈⒸ From £165–£395
Sleeps 2/4
🐄 🐕 🛶 🔋 📦
Applied

Three pretty cottages in the grounds of oast house overlooking 1000-acre estate of the Rother Valley. Two bedroomed with en-suite and 1 larger 2 bedroomed. Fully equipped to high standard, communal laundry ¼ mile from olde worlde village and main line station also 1 bedroomed self-contained wing of oast house. Open all year. Map ref: 295 047

---

50 Kent

Kent is very much farming country, but the distinctive features are the many orchards, hop gardens and oast houses to be found in the aptly named 'Garden of England'. The hilly areas like the North Downs and the High Weald contrast with more lowlying parts such as the Low Weald and Romney Marsh. Each area has a distinct character which makes the Kent countryside very varied and attractive. Complementing the countryside are many historic towns and villages, among them the mediaeval port of Sandwich, Tenterden in the Weald with its wide tree-lined High Street, the traditional market town of West Malling, Cranbrook dominated by its splendid windmill, Rochester with its castle and cathedral and the hilltop village of Chilham built around a square and dominated by its castle.

Kent has a wealth of attractions for the visitor. Some of these, such as Dover Castle and Canterbury Cathedral, are well known. But there is much more – Roman remains, castles such as Leeds, Walmer and Deal, fortifications like the series of coastal Martello Towers built as a defence against Napoleon, historic houses like Hever Castle, where Henry VIII courted Anne Boleyn, Churchill's home at Chartwell, Penshurst Place and Knole set in a deer park on the outskirts of Sevenoaks. There are several vineyards open to the public, wildlife parks like Howletts and Port Lympne, the Whitbread Hop Farm, a working farm museum, three steam railways, numerous gardens and various country parks and picnic sites, all ideal for walks or family picnics.

**Group Contacts: Mrs Rosemarie Bannock ☎ 0622 812570/Fax 0622 814200
Mrs Diana Day ☎ 0622 831207/Fax 0622 831786**

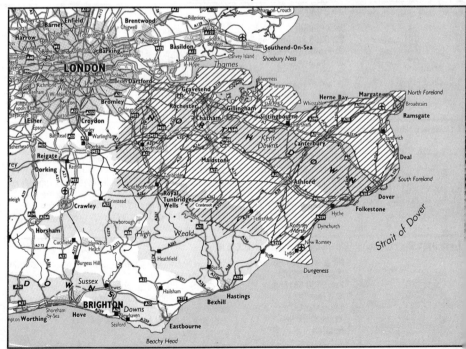

Bed and Breakfast (and evening meal)

Barnfield, Charing, Ashford, Kent TN27 0BN

Mrs Phillada Pym
☎ 0233 712421
BB From £18
EM From £11.50
Sleeps 6
🐕 🐏 ✂ 👤 🐴 ⬅ 🎋
Listed Commended

Charming Kent Hall farmhouse built in 1420 with a wealth of character amidst 500 acres of peaceful farmland. Convenient for the popular sights of Leeds Castle, Canterbury, Chilham, Sissinghurst and Channel ports. A warm welcome assured with good home cooking. 2 single rooms, 1 double, 1 twin. Open all year. Map ref: 308 055

Beachborough Park, Newington, Nr Folkestone, Kent CT18 8BW

Gordon & Jan Wallis
☎ 0303 275432
Fax 0843 45131
BB From £17.50
EM From £12.50
Sleeps 10
🐎 🐕 🐏 🐴 ⬅ 🛁
👑 👑 👑 👑 **Commended**

A period barn in the grounds of a listed Regency country house converted to provide 5 extremely comfortable en suite bedrooms. Excellent location for sightseeing, shopping, visiting the Continent, etc. Beach 4 miles, golf 1 mile. Coarse fishing in our own lake, heated swimming pool May–Sep. Excellent food, lovely grounds, rare farm animals, very peaceful and tranquil setting. Open all year. Map ref: 314 053

Blackmoor Farm, Sheephurst Lane, The Beech, Marden, Tonbridge, Kent TN12 9NS

Mrs J. Lutener
☎ 0622 831385/832999
BB From £16.50
Sleeps 4
🐕 (5) ✂ 🛁 🎋
Applied

Listed 16th century barn attractively converted to high standard, retaining interesting features, family run farm growing strawberries, apples and pears, come and enjoy them. Guest lounge with beams and TV. Many places of interest nearby. 1 hour from London, air and sea ports. Two twin rooms, private bath. Open all year (closed Christmas). Map ref: 298 055

Bletchenden Manor Farm, Headcorn, Kent TN27 9JB

Mrs Gill Waters
☎ 0622 890228
BB From £17.50
Sleeps 6
🐕 (10) 🎋 🛁
👑 👑

A warm welcome for guests at our attractive 15th century farmhouse surrounded by own farmland. 2 miles south of Headcorn village, peaceful location inthe Weald of Kent. Ideal base for visiting numerous National Trust properties, beautiful gardens, golf courses and excellent pubs in the area. 1 hour train journey to London. 1 double and 2 twin rooms with tea/coffee-making facilities and private bathrooms. Guests' sitting room with TV and a large beamed dining room. Open Jan–Nov. Map ref:: 310 054

Conghurst Farm, Hawkhurst, Kent TN18 4RW

Mrs Rosemary Piper
☎ 0580 753331
BB From £16.50
EM From £10
Sleeps 6
🐕 🐏 ✂ 🎋 🎋
👑 👑 **Highly Commended**

Conghurst Farm is a 500-acre mixed farm on the Kent/Sussex border in beautiful unspoilt countryside. This is an excellent centre for walking, touring and holiday-making. We offer a friendly welcome and every comfort in our peaceful Georgian farmhouse, and good English cooking using locally grown produce. Open Feb–Nov. Map ref: 297 049

Court Lodge, Court Lodge Farm, The Street, Teston, Maidstone, Kent ME18 5AQ

Mrs Rosemarie Bannock
☎ 0622 812570
Fax 0622 814200
BB From £15
Sleeps 6
⊕ ⅄ ⌇ (10) ▣ ♨
♨ ♨ ♨

16th century Tudor house with an enchanting garden, has lovely views of hop gardens and orchards. The house with oak beams, inglenook fireplaces and leaded windows has 3 attractive furnished rooms, 2 with en-suite facilities. Just 4 miles from Maidstone and M20. Ideally centred for visiting Leeds Castle and Ightham Moat, yet London, Heathrow, Gatwick Sheerness and Dover are approx 1 hour by car. Open all year (closed Christmas and New Year). Map ref: 294 057

Drylands Farm, Molash, Nr Canterbury, Kent CT4 8HP

Martin & Sally Holmes
☎ 0233 740205
BB From £20
Sleeps 5
⌇ ⅄ ♞ ♨
♨ ♨

With delightful views across the North Downs, this lovely farmhouse is situated in the midst of our 1200-acre working farm. All rooms with en-suite bathrooms, colour TV, tea/coffee-making facilities, overlooking miles of unspoilt countryside. Ideal touring base. Ancient village of Chilham 5 mins, Canterbury 15 mins. Within easy reach of the Channel ports. Open all year. Map ref: 308 058

Great Cheveney Farm, Great Cheveney, Marden, Tonbridge, Kent TN12 9LX

Mrs Diana Day
☎ 0622 831207
Fax 0622 831786
BB From £18
Sleeps 3
⅄ ⌇ (5) ♨
Listed Highly Commended

A warm welcome awaits you at Great Cheveney, a 16th century timber-framed farmhouse. Situated on a 300-acre fruit and arable farm, midway between Marden and Goudhurst villages on the B2079. Excellent base for touring the south east, with its many places of historical interest. 1 double with bath, 1 single with bath. Guests' lounge, TV, large garden, parking. Open all year. Map ref: 298 055

Hallwood Farm, Cranbrook, Kent TN17 2SP

Ann & David Wickham
☎ 0580 713204
BB From £18
EM From £12
Sleeps 6
♞ ⌇ (7) ♨
Listed

Hallwood Farm is a 15th century yeoman's farmhouse situated in heart of Weald of Kent. Nearby is Cranbrook, a typical Wealden town with its architecture of local timber, brick. Centre of an area rich in mediaeval churches, cathedrals, castles, manor houses, offering the visitor a wide range of interesting sightseeing. Sitting room, TV, 1 double, 2 twins, 3 course evening meal by arrangement. Spacious garden, ample parking space. Open Apr–Nov. Map ref: 297 052

Hazel Tree Farm, Hassell Street, Hastingleigh, Ashfold, Kent TN25 5JE

Christine Gorell Barnes
☎ 0233 750324
BB From £16
Sleeps 6
⌇ ⌗
Listed

A warm welcome is offered to guests in this beautiful 15th century farmhouse with beamed ceilings, inglenook fireplace and surrounded by a charming old garden. Bedrooms are attractively decorated and have lovely views. Situated in a tiny hamlet and yet only 9 miles from Canterbury. Ideal for walking and close to two nature reserves. Weekend painting courses. Open Apr–Oct (incl). Map ref: 310 054

Hoads Farm, Sandhurst, Cranbrook, Kent

Anne Nicholas
☎ 0580 850296
BB From £16
EM From £10
Sleeps 5
⌇
Applied

Bed and breakfast available in 17th century farmhouse on hop vine and sheep farm. Comfortable furnishings, sitting room with colour TV. Good centre for the coast, Bodiam Castle, Sissinghurst Castle, Scotney Castle and other National Trust properties. Excellent train service to London from Etchingham or Staplehurst. Dinner by arrangement. Dropside cot available on request. Open all year (closed Christmas).
Map ref: 299 049

Home Farm, Riverside, Eynsford, Nr Dartford, Kent DA4 0AE

Mrs Sarah Alexander
☎ 0322 866193
Fax 0322 868600
[BB] From £16
Sleeps 6
✂ ☜ (10) ⚠ ☂ ♨ ✗
♨ ♨ **Highly Commended**

Our 18th century farmhouse is set in the Darenth Valley, an area of outstanding natural beauty, ideal for London, Gatwick and the Channel ports, being only 2 miles from the M25/M20 junction. Leeds Castle, Brands Hatch and many NT properties within easy reach. There is a good selection of places to eat in the village. All bedrooms have en-suite facilities. Open Mar–Nov. Map ref: 289 063

Leaveland Court, Leaveland, Faversham, Kent ME13 0NP

Mrs Corrine Scutt
☎ 0233 740596
[BB] From £16.50
Sleeps 6
☜ ☂ ⚠ ☂ ✗
Applied

Impressive 15th century timbered farmhouse on 300-acre downland farm. Easy access, 3 miles south of M2 junction 6, Faversham 5 minutes, Canterbury 20 minutes. Situated in a quiet setting between 13th century Leaveland church and woodlands. All rooms have en-suite facilities, colour TV and tea/coffee trays. Traditional farmhouse food and warm welcome assured. Brochure available. Open all year. Map ref: 307 058

Manor Court Farm, Ashurst, Tunbridge Wells, Kent TN3 9TB

Julia Soyke
☎ 0892 740279
[BB] From £16
Sleeps 6
☂ ☜ ⚠ ⚙ ✿ ☂ ♨ ✗
♨ ♨

Georgian farmhouse with spacious accomodation on a sheep/arable farm extending to the River Medway and in beautiful countryside. On A264, 5 miles west of Tunbridge Wells. Guests are welcome to explore the farm. Many houses, castles and gardens in vicinity, including Hever, Penshurst, Sissinghurst. London 45 mins by train (from Tonbridge). Good food at a large choice of local pubs. Open all year. Map ref: 291 054

Pheasant Farm, Oare, Faversham, Kent ME13 0QB

Lorna & Neville Huxtable
☎ 0795 535366
[BB] From £15
EM From £10.50
Sleeps 4
☜ (5) ✂ ☂ ✗
Applied

14th century farmhouse on 130-acre working farm, next to nature reserve and Swale estuary. All rooms are en-suite with colour TV, tea/coffee-making facilities. Delightful sheltered garden with heated swimming pool. Ideal for visits to the continent and London. Historic cinq port town of Faversham 1½ miles Canterbury 8 miles. A warm relaxing home from home. Open all year. Map ref: 307 062

Pullens Farm, Lamberhurst Road, Horsmonden, Kent TN12 8ED

Sally Russell
☎ 089 272 2241
[BB] From £17
Sleeps 6
✂ ☜ ♨ ✿
♨ **Commended**

Our picturesque black and white timbered farmhouse is found midway between Horsmonden and Lamberhurst on B2162. Set in a large garden by a stream it offers a warm welcome. 2 double, 1 twin rooms. All have washbasins, tea/coffee-making facilities and radio/clock alarms. Visitors welcome to try their hand at fly fishing in the trout lake. Open Mar–Nov. Map ref: 295 053

Sissinghurst Castle Farm, Sissinghurst, Cranbrook, Kent TN17 2AB

James & Pat Stearns
☎ 0580 712885
[BB] From £19
EM From £12
Sleeps 6
✂ ☜ (5) ☂ ⚠
♨ ♨

This Victorian farmhouse with spacious rooms and beautiful views is delightfully situated within the grounds of the famous Sissinghurst gardens. Ample parking and it only takes a minute to walk to the gardens. Surrounding farm is largely arable with cattle and sheep. Evening meals available except weekends, a guests' sitting room, lovely garden, reduction long stay. Prices rise from April. Open all year. Map ref: 297 057

Tanner House, Tanner Farm, Goudhurst Road, Marden, Tonbridge, Kent TN12 9ND

Lesley Mannington
☎ 0622 831214
Fax 0622 832472
🅱🅱 From £16.50
EM From £12
Sleeps 6
✂ 🐕 🎴 ← ☂
🍺 🍺 🍺

For a restful break, holiday or stop over, we are ideally placed in the beautiful Weald countryside. Our Tudor farmhouse in the centre of our working farm offers high standards of accommodation and cuisine. All our rooms are en-suite, one with a genuine four-poster bed, and have colour TV, radio, tea/coffee-making facilities. We specialise in a countryside welcome. Visa/Access/Amex. Open all year. Map ref: 298 055

Vine Farm, Waterman Quarter, Headcorn, near Ashford, Kent TN27 9JJ

Mrs Jane Harman
☎ 0622 890203
🅱🅱 From £17.50
EM From £12
Sleeps 5
🐕 (10) ✂ ⛓ 🏇 ← ☂
♨ ✂

Charming Kent farmhouse, beamed and full of character over 400 years old. Peacefully situated along private drive, surrounded by farmland, ponds and garden. Attractively furnished with guests sitting-room; bedrooms all have private bathrooms. Centrally situated, an ideal base for visiting the County's Historic sites. Every comfort and a war welcome. Open Feb–Nov inclusive. Map ref: 298 054

Self-Catering

SC

Ash Place Farm, Ash, Sevenoaks, Kent TN15 7HD

Mrs J Scott
☎ 0474 872238
🆂🅲 From £140–£270
Sleeps 1/4
🎴 🎴 🎴 🎴 Commended

Luxury upstairs flat in converted Victorian farmhouse on 500-acre working farm. It comprises of large sitting room, ktichen, bathroom and 2 bedrooms, 1 with double bed, 1 with twin beds. At the top of a quiet road leading only to the farm. There is a large garden and splendid views. Many varied attractions locally and only 28 miles from Central London. P.Y.O. produce in season. Open all year. Map ref: 289 059

Beachborough Park, Newington, Nr Folkestone, Kent CT18 8BW

Gordon & Jan Wallis
☎ 0303 275432
Fax 0843 45131
🆂🅲 From £130–£350
Sleeps 4 cot
🕢 🐓 🐕 🏇 ←
🎴 🎴 🎴 🎴 Commended

East Wing (illustrated) and four other cottages all very comfortably furnished and equipped. Situated in lovely grounds and ideally located for sightseeing, shopping, visiting the Continent, etc. Beach, golf and other facilities very close. We have available coarse fishing, heated swimming pool May– Sep, licensed dining room, rare farm animals. Superb setting, very peaceful. Cot available. Special short break rates Nov–Mar. Open all year. Map ref: 314 053

"Birdwatchers Cottage", c/o Newhouse Farm, Leysdown-on-Sea, Sheerness, Isle of Sheppey, Kent ME12 4BA

Sally Marsh
☎ 0795 510201
Fax 0795 880379
🆂🅲 From £130–£300
Sleeps 8 + cot
✂ ⛓ 🐕 🕸
🎴 🎴 🎴 🎴 Highly
Commended

Idyllic, well-equipped, comfortable cottage on a cattle, sheep and arable farm for views, walks and sightseeing. Four bedrooms, CH, large garden. Should suit everyone. Situated between two nature reserves with several local places of interest. Under an hour to Canterbury, Maidstone and Rochester. About fifty miles to London. Ideal touring base and a quiet hideaway. Detailed leaflet available. Open all year. Map ref: 304 068

Bramley Cottage, Harts Heath Farm, c/o Huggins Farm, Staplehurst, Kent TN12 0HS

Daphne Tipples
☎ 0622 831269
⚃ From £90–£230
Sleeps 6/8
🛌 ✗ ⌂
🔑 🔑 🔑 **Approved**

Modern 3 bedroom house with fenced-in lawn, garage and hard parking area, on a 300 acre fruit/hop/sheep farm in pleasant wooded area in the Kentish Weald. Many interesting places to visit, including National Trust properties, Romney Marsh and the coast. Good train service to London (1 hour). Own transport essential. Situated between Staplehurst, Marden and Goudhurst. Open Apr–Sept (incl).
Map ref: 297 055

Golding Hop Farm Cottage, c/o Golding Hop Farm, Bewley Lane, Plaxtol, Kent TN15 0PS

Jacqueline Vincent
☎ 0732 885432
⚃ From £100–£220
Sleeps 5 + cot
🛌 ✗ ⌂
🔑 🔑 🔑 🔑
Highly Commended

13-acre farm producing Kent cobnuts for London markets. Surrounded by orchards and close to attractive village of Plaxtol. Secluded cottage, but not isolated. Sleeps 5, 2 double and 1 single, CH, colour TV, washer dryer and fridge/freezer. Horse riding, golf nearby. Car essential. Ample parking. Local station 2 miles with frequent trains to London. Motorway 4 miles. Dogs by arrangement only. Open all year.
Map ref: 292 058

Hazel Tree Cottage, Hassell Street, Hastingleigh, Ashford, Kent TN25 5JE

Christine Gorell Barnes
☎ 0233 750324
⚃ From £125–£225
Sleeps 4 + cot
⌂ ✗
🔑 🔑 **Commended**

A recently converted barn by a lovely old farmhouse is now an attractive and comfortable cottage for holidaymakers. Surrounded by fields, it has its own garden and terrace, and is ideally situated for sightseeing and exploring coast and countryside, and for day trips to France. Canterbury 9 miles, Folkestone 14 miles. Open all year. Map ref: 310 054

Markbeech Country Cottages, Falconhurst, Markbeech, Edenbridge, Kent TN8 5NR

Nicola Bain
☎ 0342 850526
Fax 0342 850940
⚃ From £135–430
Sleeps 2/14
🛌 ⌂ ♨
🔑 🔑 🔑 **Approved**

Picturesque hamlet in High Weald (Tunbridge Wells 9 miles), fine views north and south. Nearby Hever, Penshurst, Chartwell, Knole, bird sanctuaries, vineyards. 5 well-equipped Victorian cottages with tall chimneys and open fires. Adjacent to 600-acre dairy farm, lovely walks over fields. Two 17th century farmhouses outside village, washing machines, storage heating. Holidays and longer lets. Dogs by arrangement only. Open all year. Map ref: 287 054

Owls Nest, Kingsnoad Farm, Pye Corner, Ulcombe, Nr Maidstone, Kent ME17 1EG

David & Doreen Roe
☎ and Fax 0622 858966
⚃ From £130–£275
Sleeps 6 + cot
🛌 ♿ ✗ ⌂ ♨ ▪ 🍽
🔑 🔑 🔑
Approved

Converted Victorian milking parlour in truly secluded peaceful farm setting, ½ mile along track between grazing sheep and ripening corn. Fully equipped with continental quilts, colour TV, shower/WC, new kitchen, night storage heaters for year round occupation. Cot available. Sit awhile in large, comfortable withdrawing area beneath original oak beams and in front of blazing log fire. An ideal walking/touring base. Open all year. Map ref: 302 056

Pheasant Farm, Oare, Faversham, Kent ME13 0QB

Lorna & Neville Huxtable
☎ 0795 535366
⚃ From £189–£235
EM From £10.50
Sleeps 2
⌂ (5) ✗ ▪ 🍽
Applied

Attractive comfortable well-equipped beamed 14th century annexe to main farmhouse, bedroom, lounge shower, WC and kitchen, all with modern equipment. 130-acre working farm next to nature reserve and Swale estuary. Delightful sheltered garden with heated swimming pool. Ideal for visits to continent and London, Faversham 1½ miles, Canterbury 8 miles. A warm relaxing home from home. Map ref: 307 062

The Shire, Manor Farm, West Malling, Maidstone, Kent ME19 5NA

Mrs Richard Lambert
☎ 0732 842091
SC From £100–£375
Sleeps 4/6 cot
🐾 ♿ 🛏
♟ ♟ ♟ ♟ ♟
Commended

Stable conversion. 5 minutes walk from Saxon village, within easy reach of historic castles and houses and gardens. Good access to London, channel ports by road and rail, restaurants, country park, swimming and sports complex nearby, tennis court and table tennis. Cot available. Open all year. Map ref: 296 059

Spring Grove Oast, Spring Grove Farm, Wye, Ashford, Kent TN25 5EY

Charles & Liz Amos
☎ and fax 0233 812425
SC From £250–£650
Sleeps 5/9
🐾 ♿ 🛏 ☎ ☂ ♣
♟ ♟ ♟ ♟
Commended

6 spacious well appointed flats in a converted Oast House in the countryside. Wye village – 10 minute walk – pubs, cafés, restaurant and station. Situated in centre of Kent, M20 (A20) 10 minutes. Ashford 4 miles (fast rail link to London). Canterbury and Folkestone 10 miles. 1½ acres grounds, tennis court, heated swimming pool, fishing on farm, riding locally. Open all year. Map ref: 308 056

Whitehill Cottages, c/o Bramble Hall, Bushey Close, Boughton, Faversham, Kent ME13 9AE

Mrs M S Berry
☎ 0227 751203
SC From £150–£280
Sleeps 5 cot
🐾 🛏 ☂
♟ ♟ ♟ ♟ **Commended**

2 Victorian farm cottages. 1½ miles from the ancient town of Faversham and 6 miles from the historic city of Canterbury. Situated on a 400-acre working farm of hops, fruit and cereals Well-equipped with 3 bedrooms, sitting room and kitchen/dining room. Central heating and large garden. Prices fully inclusive of electricity, linen and towels. Map ref: 308 062

---

1 Wingham Well Cottages, Wingham Well Farm, Wingham, Canterbury, Kent CT3 1NW

Georgina Maude
☎ 0227 720253
SC From £150–£200
Sleeps 4/5
🐾 🛏 ☂ ☂ 🐦
♟ ♟ ♟ **Approved**

Situated in the small hamlet of Wingham Well, the Victorian semi-detached cottage has a pleasant view over the farm. Sleeps 5 (1 double, 1 twin, 1 single), simply and attractively furnished. Canterbury (cathedral), Sandwich (golf) 5–6 miles away. Channel ports 30 mins' drive. Dogs by arrangement only. Open all year. Map ref: 315 062

Camping and Caravanning

Tanner Farm Touring Park, Tanner Farm, Goudhurst Road, Marden, Tonbridge, Kent TN12 9ND

FARM HOLIDAY BUREAU

Phyllis Fuller
☎ 0622 831214/832399
Fax 0622 832472
Tents £5.50
Touring caravans
£5.50 per night
🛖 🐦 🐾 ♿ 🛏 ☂ ☂ ☎
✓ ✓ ✓ ✓

Newly developed touring park amidst beautiful rural countryside in the centre of working family farm where Shire horses are also bred. Well-equipped centrally heated shower block and laundry facilities. Specially equipped for the disabled. Electric hook-ups. Park shop for groceries, gifts and local crafts. Beautifully landscaped setting. Ideal for the country lover, birdwatcher or angler. A rural experience not to be missed. Visa/Access/Amex. Open all year. Map ref: 298 055

51 Isle of Wight

The Isle of Wight with its sandy beaches and small secluded coves, and the sea never more than 15 minutes from wherever you may be, has a wide variety of holiday activities.

With Cowes and the Royal Yacht Squadron, an international symbol of all that is finest in yachting, the Island is famous for its seafaring activities with something for everyone who enjoys messing about in boats.

For the rambler, the birdwatcher, the angler and for those who merely wish to relax beside the splendours of ancient lighthouses or towering chalk cliffs, the Isle of Wight is the ideal holiday retreat with an internationally acclaimed network of well marked footpaths. For the more adventurous, the Island is a haven for hang-gliders, windsurfers, water skiers, canoe enthusiasts and deep sea fishermen.

Attractions for both children and adults include, nature reserves, Butterfly World, the I.O.W. Rare Breeds Park, Blackgang Chine with its history of smuggling and shipwrecks, a steam railway featuring some of the earliest steam engines, Roman remains, historic manors, mills, craft centres, and vineyards open for guided tours and wine tasting. Above all, the Island boasts a climate that is regularly top of the Sunshine League in the British Isles and is particularly attractive in Spring or Autumn, favourite seasons for short break holidays.

Group Contact: Mrs Judy Noyes ☎ 852582

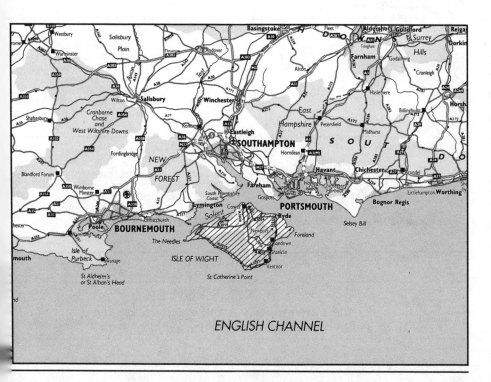

Bed and Breakfast (and evening meal)

Cheverton Farm, Shorwell, Newport, Isle of Wight PO30 3JE

Sheila Hodgson
☎ 0983 741017
🅱 From £13
Sleeps 4
🛏 ⚘ 🐕 🐎
Listed

Enjoy a relaxed and peacefulatmosphere in our listed farmhouse on a sheep, beef and arable farm set in a valley with walks straight onto downland. Pony trekking for children and light adults, clay pigeon shooting and dogs, cats, ponies and poultry to see. large garden, spacious rooms and good local food. Open Mar–Nov. Map ref: 250 033

Great Park Farm, Betty Haunt Lane, Carisbrooke, Isle of Wight PO30 4HR

Mrs Sheila Brownrigg
☎ 0983 522945
🅱 From £15
Sleeps 6
🛌 (8)
😋🍽 Commended

Come and stay on our arable farm with its lovely old Georgian farmhouse in peaceful surroundings with magnificent views over the solent and downs. Central to all main resorts and good eating places nearby. 3 bedrooms en-suite, dining, sitting room for guests, colour TV, tea/coffee-making facilities. Map ref: 248 034

Lisle Combe, Bank End Farm, Undercliff Drive, St Lawrence, Ventnor, Isle of Wight PO38 1UW

Hugh & Judy Noyes
☎ 0983 852582
🅱 From £14.50
Sleeps 5
🛌
Listed

Listed Elizabethan style farmhouse overlooking English Channel, home of the late Alfred Noyes (poet and author) and his family. 5 acre coastal garden with rare waterfowl and pheasant collection (over 100 species). Surrounded by farmlands for owner's herd of pedigree Friesians, free entry to owner's rare breeds park. Superb sea views, coves and small beaches in area of outstanding natural beauty. Open all year (closed Christmas & New Year). Map ref: 253 029

Youngwoods Farm, Whitehouse Road, Porchfield, Newport, Isle of Wight PO30 4LJ

Judith Shanks
☎ 0983 522170
🅱 From £12
Sleeps 4
⚘ 🛌 (8) 🐎 ↬
Listed

A grassland farm set in open countryside. The 18th century stone farmhouse, recently renovated, retains its original character. The guest rooms are spacious and enjoy magnificent views of the West Wight (H/C in each room. CH throughout). Close to Newtown Nature Reserve, an ideal base for the naturalist. Wild flowers. Red squirrels, owls and butterflies locally. Cowes sailing centre 4 miles. Open all year. Map ref: 249 034

FARM HOLIDAY
BUREAU

NO ANSWER?

Farmers are mostly out and about during the day.
Try to telephone before 9.30am or after 4pm.

Self-Catering

The Brewhouse and Barn Cottage, Knighton Farm, Newchurch, Sandown, Isle of Wight PO36 0NT

Anne Corbin
☎ 0983 865349
[SC] From £120–£330
🖊
🖊 🖊 🖊 🖊 **Approved**

Ideally situated in good downland walking country on small sheep farm, 3 miles from sea. Self-contained wing of listed 17th century farmhouse, 2 interconnecting bedrooms, spacious accommodation for 5. Also 2 bedroom cottage conversion in listed barn for 4. Both are well equipped and have large secure lawned gardens, with sandpits. Electricity included, Saturday and Sunday bookings. Linen hire available. Open all year. Map ref: 253 034

The Byre, Bucks Farm, Shorwell, Newport, Isle of Wight PO30 3LP

Mrs A Cecil
☎ 0983 551206
[SC] From £250–£450
Sleeps 11
🐾 🐴 🐕 ♿ 🏕 ✗
🖊 🖊 🖊 **Commended**

The Byre, Bucks farm in area of outstanding natural beauty on Shepherds Trail. Wonderful walks. 500-acre sheep/arable farm. Converted stables sleeps 11 + baby. Enclosed garden, spacious beamed sitting room. Stone fireplace. Dining room, 2 bathrooms, shower room, modern kitchen, dishwasher etc., central heating, logs and electricity included. Open all year. Map ref: 248 031

Cheverton Farm, Shorwell, Newport, Isle of Wight PO30 3JE

Sheila Hodgson
☎ 0983 741017
[BB] From £80–£300
Sleeps 4
🐕 ✗ 🐴 🏕
🖊 🖊 🖊 **Commended**

Old 'character' cottage with beamed ceilings throughout attached to main farmhous. Large garden and car parking area. Walking straight onto downs, and pony trekking for children and light adults. Clay pigeon shooting, and dogs, cats ponies and poultry to see. Good food locally, 10 minutes in car to nearest Beach. Open all year. Map ref: 250 033

Harbour Farm Cottage, Harbour Farm, Embankment Road, Bembridge, Isle of Wight PO35 5NS

Mrs D Hicks
☎ 0983 872610
[BB] From £100–£350
Sleeps 4
🖊 ✗
🖊 🖊 🖊 **Highly Commended**

Situated in a nature conservation area 2 miles from the harbour. Close to sandy beaches (5 minutes). The cottage faces South East with attractive views over lake and woodland. Sleeps 4 plus baby in two twin bedded rooms. Own small garden, car parking. Sorry no pts. Sailing/windsurfing, sea fishing nearby. Horses welcome. Good stabling. Friday bookings. Prices from £100 to £350 per week. Open all year. Map ref: 258 034

Lisle Combe Cottage, Lisle Combe, Bank End Farm, Undercliff Drive, St Lawrence, Ventnor, Isle of Wight PO38

Hugh & Judy Noyes
☎ 0983 852582
[SC] From £120–£220
Sleeps 5/6
🖊
🖊 🖊 **Approved**

Listed cottage overlooking English Channel. Own garden within grounds of Lisle Combe. Large pheasant and waterfowl collection, free entry to owner's rare breed park. Many small beaches and coves for swimming or sunbathing. Colour TV, everything provided except linen. Fine coastal walks in area of outstanding natural beauty. Surrounded by 180-acre family farm with pedigree Friesian herd. Open all year. Map ref: 251 027

52 Heart of Dorset

The Heart of Dorset Group offers you a range of holiday accommodation in the Dorset countryside. It is an area of outstanding natural beauty renowned for its beautiful villages, magnificent hills and lovely valleys.

Wherever you stay, the coast is but a short distance away with excellent swimming, sailing and fishing. For the country lover, the area has a wide choice of forest trails, coastal and inland walks, ancient monuments, historic houses and gardens. Dorset's mild climate makes it an ideal location for a holiday all year round.

Dorset's most famous son, Thomas Hardy, was born within three miles of Dorchester; his rambling cottage, Higher Bockhampton is open to the public. Most of his books were based on villages and towns in the area, many of which still retain the rural atmosphere of Hardy's Wessex.

A romantic figure of more modern times is Lawrence of Arabia, who spent a number of reclusive years in his remote and rather bleak cottage, Clouds Hill, near Bovington Camp.

Corfe Castle, Brownsea Island, Lulworth Cove, Durdle Door . . . even the Tolpuddle Martyrs' Museum are all here – you'll need more than a few days to discover Dorset!

Group Contact: Rosemary Coleman ☎ 0305 848391

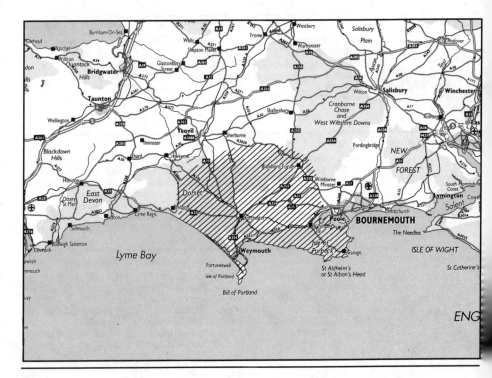

Bed and Breakfast (and evening meal)

Lamperts Farmhouse, 11 Dorchester Road, Sydling St Nicholas, Dorchester, Dorset DT2 9NU

Mrs R Bown
☎ 0300 341790
BB From £15
EM From £8.50
Sleeps 6

Enjoy home comforts in our 400-year-old thatched family farmhouse in the quiet unspoilt village of Sydling St Nicholas. Ideal for walking, touring or staying at home, relaxing or meeting the farmyard animals. 1 family, 1 twin room, both with washbasins and tea/coffee-making facilities, guests' bathroom and lounge. Children welcome. Evening meal by arrangement. Open all year. Map ref: 216 034

Lower Lewell Farmhouse, West Stafford, Dorchester, Dorset DT2 8AP

Marian Tomblin
☎ 0305 267169
BB From £15
Sleeps 6

Situated in the Frome Valley, four miles from Dorchester, this old historic farmhouse is reputed to be the Talbothays Dairy of Hardy's novel '*Tess of the D'Urbervilles*'. Ideally situated for exploring the beautiful countryside and coast. Three bedrooms, washbasins, tea/coffee-making facilities. Guests' sitting room. Central heating. Ample parking. A warm welcome awaits you at Lower Lewell. Open all year. Map ref: 220 034

Newlands Farm, West Lulworth, Wareham, Dorset BH20 5PU

Mrs Lesley Simpson
☎ 0929 41376
BB From £18
Sleeps 6
Listed

Newlands was built in the early 19th century and the farm has beautiful views of the sea and the distant Purbeck Hills. The beach is within walking distance. Well placed for coastal footpaths with water sports available within 15 miles and horse riding nearby. 2 double/family rooms with tea/coffee-making facilities and colour TV. Showers and washbasins en suite. Breakfast is served in the dining room. Regret no dogs. Open all year (closed Christmas). Map ref: 224 030

FARM HOLIDAY BUREAU

DISABLED VISITORS

members offering suitable accommodation to disabled/less able visitors. Please do check the extent of the facilities before booking.

Self-Catering

Birch Tree Cottage, c/o Travellers Rest Farm, Blandford Forum, Dorset DT11 0QG

Mrs Anne Hosford
☎ 0258 452641
🆂🅲 From £155–£250
Sleeps 5/6
☌
ⅇ ⅇ **Commended**

Charming traditional flint and brick semi-detached, fully modernised former farm cottage, set in attractive garden. Situated on large arable/sheep farm, 3 ½ miles from Blandford Forum in secluded rural area above village of Durweston. Cosy but spacious, comfortably furnished. Excellent for family holidays, keen walkers and those seeking a peaceful retreat. Ample car parking. Open all year. Map ref: 225 041

Dairy Cottage, c/o Trigon House, Wareham, Dorset BH20 7PD

Sandy Sturdy
☎ 0929 552097
🆂🅲 From £100–£290
Sleeps 2/7
🏌🐕🖽🛋👌
ⅇ ⅇ ⅇ **Commended**

An attractive, fully modernised 3 bedroomed cottage in a picturesque row of terraced cottages on a 1400 acre working farm/estate. 3 miles north west of Wareham. It comprises farmland, heathland, forestry and the River Piddle. Good birdwatching and walking, perfect for active families or restful retreat. Hardy country and sea nearby. Fenced gardens, parking, CH, colour TV and phone. Dogs by arrangement. Open all year. Map ref: 227 033

Glebe Cottage, c/o Glebe House, Moreton, Dorchester, Dorset DT2 8RQ

Carol Gibbens
☎ 0929 462468
🆂🅲 From £90–£220
Sleeps 4
♿☌
ⅇ ⅇ **Commended**

Glebe Cottage is set in an old rectory garden in the peaceful farming village of Moreton, famous for its church windows engraved by Laurence Whistler and burial place of Lawrence of Arabia. It is a wildlife haven. The cottage is detached, is on one floor with 2 double bedrooms, kitchen, living room, bathroom, night storage heating and has its own garden. Open all year. Map ref: 223 034

Gore Cottage, West Milton, Bridport, Dorset DT6 3SN. c/o Wingham Well Farm, Wingham, Canterbury, Kent CT3

Georgina Maude
☎ 0227 720253
🆂🅲 From £160–£250
Sleeps 5
🏌☌
ⅇ ⅇ **Approved**

Listed Grade II detached stone-built thatched cottage in own secluded garden on the edge of the village of West Milton. 1 double, 1 twin, 1 single, sitting room, dining/kitchen, tiny bathroom, separate WC and washbasin. The sea is about 5 miles away. Among other attractions are the Swannery at Abbotsbury and the Tropical Garden, Maiden Castle, Cerne Abbas (The Giant), Athelhampton and RAF Yeovilton. Open all year. Map ref: 212 035

Mill Cottage, Bramblecombe Farm, Melcombe, Bingham, Dorchester, Dorset DT2 7QA

Mrs Noel Hosford
☎ 0258 880248
🆂🅲 From £100–£350
Sleeps 7 + cot
☌🏌🏻
ⅇ ⅇ **Approved**

Eastfield is set in beautiful rolling country on large dairy farm 4 miles North A354 in mid-Dorset. The farm and surrounding area is rich in wildlife, ideal for naturalists, walkers and families with young children. Secluded detached farm bungalow, central heating and comfortable furnishings. Sleeps 7. Fenced garden with swing and sandpit. Ample parking. Open all year. Map ref: 223 037

Newmans Drove, c/o East Farm, Hammoon, Sturminster Newton, Dorset DT10 2DB

Angela Hughes or Fiona Idda
☎ 0258 860339/860284
⁣sc From £95–£245
Sleeps 6
♿ 🐌 👜 ♨
ℒ ℒ – ℒ ℒ ℒ
Up to Commended

3 self-contained bungalows, 1 specifically designed for wheelchair users, representing a tasteful conversion of an old farm building within a farming complex, easily accessible. Working dairy farm in the Blackmore Vale close to the River Stour with beautiful views of the surrounding countryside. Carpeting throughout, colour TV, sleeps 4–6. Electricity 50p meter. Birdwatching, walking and coarse fishing. Regret, no pets. Farm shop. Open all year. Map ref: 224 044

Old Dairy Cottage and Rose Cottage, c/o Eweleaze Farm, Tincleton, Dorchester, Dorset DT2 8QR

Rosemary Coleman
☎ 0305 848391
⁣sc From £100–£285
Sleeps 6/5
🐌 ⏳ ♨ ♦
ℒ ℒ ℒ Commended

Two attractively furnished character cottages, 1 with beams and inglenook fireplace, the other, open fires and large garden. The mixed farm has cows, calves, horses and beautiful woodland walks. Ducks and wildlife on the pond and streams. Tennis and fishing. Easy reach coast, golf, trekking, leisure centre. Excellent value low seasonwith OAP. Reductions and winter breaks. Open all year. Central heating. Map ref: 223 034

Whistley Waters, Milton-on-Stour, Gillingham, Dorset SP8 5PT

Mr & Mrs Campbell
☎ 0747 840666
⁣sc From £130–£330
Sleeps 6
🐌 ♿ ⏳ ♨ ♣
ℒ ℒ Commended

Two Scandinavian style lodges overlooking our 4 acres of trout and carp lakes in secluded quiet farmland. Very comfortably equipped with TV, microwave heating, double glazing. Each have 3 bedrooms, 1 double, 2 twins, bathroom, living room and kitchenette, 1 has extra WC and basin. B-B-Q, bicycles, fishing. Excellent National Trust visiting centre. Map ref: 222 048

FARM HOLIDAY BUREAU

THE 1000+ BUREAU MEMBERS OFFER A UNIQUE LINK TO CUSTOMERS ACROSS THE UK

All Bureau members belong to a local Group. Each member can refer you to an equally high quality member within his Group . . . or across the UK: England, Northern Ireland, Scotland, Wales.

53 Dorset

Come and explore Dorset with its delightful villages in the west of the county, the dairy pastureland of Blackmore Vale in the north, scenic Cranborne Chase in the east and the Purbeck Hills around Corfe Castle in the south.

The unspoilt countryside so vividly described by the author, Thomas Hardy is still unchanged in places – rolling downland and fertile valleys with picturesque villages of mellow stone and thatched cottages.

For a day out, travel to Salisbury and Winchester Cathedrals, or the theatres and other attractions of major resorts like Bournemouth and Poole. Dartmoor lies to the west and the New Forest to the east, both within easy reach. Sea trips for fishing or pleasure can be made from many of the ports along the coast.

Summer is not the only season in which to savour this delightful area. Winters are mild on the South Coast and spring and autumn are particularly good times for a Dorset holiday. The footpath network is unsurpassed, both inland and along the coast. The Coastal Way, in particular, offers dramatic and exciting scenery, as safe and sandy beaches give way to shifting banks of shingle and rugged cliffs teeming with birds. Historic houses, famous gardens, exciting coastline – you name it, Dorset has it!

Group Contacts: BB **Mrs Sally Wingate-Saul** ☎ **0258 817348**
SC **Mrs Sarah Gulliford** ☎ **0747 811433**

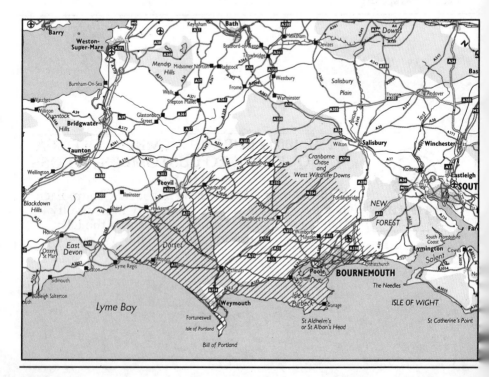

Bed and Breakfast (and evening meal)

Almshouse Farm, Hermitage, Sherborne, Dorset DT9 6HA

Mrs Jenny Mayo
☎ 0963 210296
🅱️ From £15
Sleeps 6
🐂 🐚

This charming old farmhouse – formerly a 16th century monastery – was restored in 1849. Surrounded by 140 acres, overlooking the Blackmore Vale. Accommodation in three double rooms with tea/coffee-making facilities. Dining rooms with inglenook fireplace, comfortable sitting room. Garden available to guests at all times. Sherborne 6 miles, Dorchester 14 miles. Open Jan–Dec. Map ref: 215 040

Barnsley Farm, Wimborne, Dorset BH21 4HZ

Mrs Barbara Priddle
☎ 0258 840296
🅱️ From £16
Sleeps 6
✂ 🐂 (8)
Listed

18th century farmhouse set in quiet and secluded river valley on 250 acre dairy and arable farm. 3 miles north of Wimborne Minster. An ideal base for exploring Dorset and New Forest. Many local pubs and restaurants for evening meals. Guest lounge with colour TV, central heating, twin and double rooms with tea/coffee-making facilities. Regret no pets. No smoking. Open Apr–Oct. Map ref: 231 038

Fossil Farmhouse, Winfrith Newburgh, Dorchester, Dorset DT2 8DB

Liz Sealey
☎ 0305 853355
🅱️ From £14
EM From £10
Sleeps 4
🐂 (2) ✂ 🎪 ▪ 🎿
Listed

Enjoy the traditions of farmhouse hospitality in the comfort of a new farmhouse in peaceful setting, on 370-acre dairy/arable farm. Rooms decoratively furnished, hot drinks facilities, lovely views. Breakfast menu. Guest lounge with colour TV. Convenient to Lulworth Cove and coastal walks. Regret no pets. Open all year. Map ref: 220 033

Gorwell Farm, Abbotsbury, Weymouth, Dorset DT3 4JX

Mrs Mary Pengelly
☎ 0305 871401
🅱️ From £16
Sleeps 6
🐂 ✂ 🎪 🎿
🐚

Our 17th century farmhouse is in its own quiet scenic valley only 2 miles from the coastal village of Abbotsbury. The coast path crosses our family dairy and sheep farm and we are within easy reach of Bridport, Dorchester and Weymouth, so ideal for a relaxing touring, walking or activity holiday. All rooms are centrally heated with washbasins and tea/coffee-making facilities. Local eating places recommended. Map ref: 215 032

Henbury Farm, Dorchester Road, Sturminster Marshall, Wimborne, Dorset BH21 3RN

Sue & Jonathan Tory
☎ 0258 857306
🅱️ From £16.50
Sleeps 6
🐂 ·
🐚

300-year-old farmhouse facing large front lawn and pond, situated on 200-acre dairy and arable farm. Guests' lounge with colour TV, heated outdoor pool. Near to New Forest and fifteen minutes from sandy beaches. Numerous local restaurants to meet your evening requirements. Many local attractions and country walks. Ideally situated for a great holiday. En-suite facilities available. Map ref: 228 038

Higher Langdon, Beaminster, Dorset DT8 3NN

Judy Thompson
☎ 0308 862537
BB From £15.10
EM From £10
Sleeps 4
⯌ 🛏 ⛺ ⬛
Applied

A spacious and homely working farm, set in acre's of rolling countryside. The informal atmosphere combined with traditional farmhouse cooking, ensure our guests enjoy all the country has to offer. Judy will start your day with a sizzling breakfast, she is also happy to cook an evening meal. Open all year. Map ref: 211 038

Holebrook Farm, Lydlinch, Sturminster Newton, Dorset DT10 2JB

Sally & Charles Wingate-Saul
☎ 0258 817348
BB From £19
EM From £9.50
Sleeps 11
♿ ⯌ ⬛ ⚑
Listed Commended

Situated in heart of Blackmore Vale and ideal as a central base for exploring Dorset, this is a family farm of 125 acres. Accommodation in 18th century farmhouse and delightfully converted stables, each with own sitting room, kitchen, shower, WC en-suite. Swimming pool, clay pigeon shooting, pool/table tennis room, mini-gym. Comfortable, friendly atmosphere. Good home cooking. AA listed. Open all year. Map ref: 220 047

Huntsbridge Farm, Leigh, Nr Sherborne, Dorset DT9 6JA

Mrs Su Read
☎ 0935 872150
BB From £17
Sleeps 6
⯌ ⯌
🌊 🌊 **Highly Commended**

Our stone farmhouse stands in a quiet position in the middle of Thomas Hardy's 'Woodlanders' countryside on a dairy and sheep farm. We have available 1 double en-suite, 1 double with H and C, 1 twin with H and C, dining room, TV lounge. All bedrooms have colour TV, radio alarms and tea/coffee-making facilities. Riding, fishing and golf are available locally. Open Apr–Dec. Map ref: 215 040

Knitson Old Farmhouse, Corfe Castle, Wareham, Dorset BH20 5JB

Rachel Helfer
☎ 0929 422836
BB From £13.50
EM From £10
Sleeps 6
Tents/Caravans £4
🛏 ⯌ (5)
Listed

15th century Purbeck stone farmhouse, snug and modernised, on 200-acre dairy and sheep farm. 2 miles from Swanage, 4 from Studland. Superb walking – downland, heathland, cliffs, beaches. Homegrown wholefood expertly prepared, log fire in flagstoned TV lounge. Golf, riding, aquatic sports nearby. Far-reaching views, lovely big garden. Open Jan–Nov. Map ref: 231 030

Maiden Castle Farm, Dorchester, Dorset DT2 9PR

Hilary Hoskin
☎ 0305 262356
BB From £16
EM From £10
Sleeps 6
⯌ ⯌
🌊 🌊 🌊 **Commended**

Our large working farm, 1 mile from Dorchester and 7 miles from Weymouth in the heart of Hardy country, enjoys magnificent views of Maiden Castle and the surrounding countryside. En-suite bedrooms with CH, TV and tea-making facilities, a telephone for guests' use and a licensed dining room combine to offer comfort, peace and quiet – ideal for the perfect holiday. Map ref: 218 034

Manor Farmhouse, High Street, Yetminster, Sherborne, Dorset DT9 6LF

Ann Partridge
☎ 0935 872247
BB From £27.50
EM From £13.50 (incl wine)
Sleeps 6
♿ ⯌ ⯌ ⛺ ⬛
🌊 🌊 🌊

Modernised 17th century farmhouse with oak panelling beams, inglenook fireplaces, luxuriously furnished. 1 double, 2 twin, 1 single bedrooms (all en-suite). Ann offers intimate knowledge of Dorset, historically and geographically, and cooks fresh local produce to traditional recipes. Village described as 'Best stone-built village in South of England'. Featured on BBC2 'House and Home' and *Sunday Times* August 1989. Electric chair lift. Open all year (closed Christmas). Map ref: 215 044

Priory Farm, East Holme, Wareham, Dorset BH20 6AG

Mrs Venn Goldsack
☎ 0929 552972
▣ From £16
Sleeps 4
✂ ➳ Å ▪
➽ Commended

16th century farmhouse on 400-acre dairy and fruit farm. Thick walls and thatch make it cosy in winter. Ideal for both coastline and countryside. One twin-bedded room with en-suite, WC and basin and separate showerroom, 1 twin-bedded room with sole use of bathroom. large book-lined guest's room with colour TV. Good selection of restaurants nearby. Regret no pets. Open most of the year (closed Christmas, New Year, mid-June to mid-July). Map ref: 227 033

Rudge Farm, Chilcombe, Bridport, Dorset DT6 4NF

Sue Diment
☎ 0308 482630
▣ From £16
EM From £10
Sleeps 6
➳ (14) ⚓ ❀
➽ ➽ Commended

Peacefully situated in the beautiful Bride Valley, just 2 miles from the sea. After a day spent exploring the lovely West Dorset countryside, relax in our comfortably furnished farmhouse and enjoy dinner prepared mainly from local produce, or try one of the many good local restaurants. All rooms are en-suite and have far reaching views. Open all year (closed Christmas). Map ref: 213 033

Toomer Farm, Henstridge, Templecombe, Somerset BA8 0PH

Ethelend Doggrell
☎ 0963 250237
▣ From £13–£16
Sleeps 6
➳ Å ⊄
➽➽

250-year-old stone-built house with charming walled garden surrounded by 380 acres of dairy/arable land. Splendid rural setting in the Blackmore Vale, 6 miles east of Sherborne. One family room, double bed and bunk beds with washbasin and TV, one twin bedroom with H/C and TV, one double with en-suite facilities. Lounge and dining room. Open all year. Map ref: 219 048

Yalbury Park, Frome Whitfield Farm, Frome, Whitfield, Dorchester, Dorset DT2 7SE

Ann Bamlet
☎ 0305 250336
▣ From £18
Sleeps 6
➳ (3) ↳
Applied

Stone farmhouse with large garden in parkland to River Frome, warm and welcoming for all country lovers, all rooms en-suite have TV, tea/coffee-making facilities, 1 double with french wndows to garden. 1 family room. Traditional farmhouse breakfasts. ½ mile on A352 Dorchester/Sherborne Road. Turn right past 'Sun Inn'. Map ref: 218 034

Self-Catering

SC

Dove Cottage & Buddens Farmhouse, c/o Buddens Farm, Twyford, Shaftesbury, Dorset SP7 0JE

Sarah Gulliford
☎ 0747 811433
▣ From £150–£400
Sleeps 4/6 + cot
✂ ➳
♟ ♟ ♟ ♟

Approved

HARRASSED? Have a real farm holiday, guests welcome to help feed pigs, sheep, chickens, goats, ponies and watch cows being milked. Relax in spacious farmhouse or 2 bedroomed cottage, overlooking patchwork fields and rolling hills. Both tastefully furnished, central heating, log fires, dishwasher, TV, laundry room, swimming pool. Fully equipped for babies and children. Open all year.
Map ref: 220 047

Courtyard Cottages, Holebrook Farm, Lydlinch, Sturminster Newton, Dorset DT10 2JB

Charles & Sally Wingate-Saul
☎ 0258 817348
SC From £130–£400
Sleeps 2/4
🏕 ⛳ ♿ 🐾
🔑🔑🔑🔑
Highly Commended

Our cottages are part of a delightful courtyard conversion. Come for a summer or winter break on a working farm, approx 2 hours London. Peaceful, quiet, well off the beaten track. Each cottage comfortably furnished, TV, microwave, oil CH. Swimming pool, laundry room, large gardens. Clay shooting arranged. Ideal base for exploring Dorset. Golf, tennis, fishing locally. Open all year.
Map ref: 220 047

The Granary, Luccombe Farm, Milton Abbas, Blandford, Dorset DT11 0BE

Murray & Amanda Kayll
☎ 0258 880558
SC From £150–£300
Sleeps 2 + cot
🏕 ⛳ 🧍 ♿ 🐾 🚲 ☕ 🎾
Applied

The Grandary, standing on Saddlestones for 200 years, has two beds, with space for children, colour TV and modern appliances should make your stay comfortable. The conversion standard is high, the countryside beautiful, walks/plentiful and other country pursuits such as riding fishing and sailing are available. Open Feb–Nov.
Map ref: 222 036

Higher Langdon, Beaminster, Dorset DT8 3NN

Judy Thompson
☎ 0308 862537
BB From £122–£168
EM From £10
Sleeps 2
🏕 🧍 🎾 ♿
Applied

Situated on the 1st floor of Higher Langdon farmhouse, this delightful flat is decorated and equipped to the highest standard. Sleeping 2 people, the flat includes microwave as well as usual kitchen equipment. Historic houses and gardens nearby, and heritage coast only 9 miles away. Situated in Hardy Country. Use of garden. Open all year.
Map ref: 211 038

Higher Waterston Farm Cottages, Higher Waterston Farm, Dorchester, Dorset DT2 7SW

Mrs Carol Hammick
☎ 0305 848208
Fax 0305 848894
SC From £175–£420
Sleeps 4/6
🐾 ♿ 🎾
🔑🔑🔑🔑 – 🔑🔑🔑🔑🔑
Commended

Four superb courtyard cottages on sheep farm, one for disabled. 3/3/2/2 bedrooms sleeping 6/6/4/4. Each has terrace, TV, video, washing machine, tumble dryer, dishwasher, microwave, etc. Telephones. Big games barn. Tennis court. large, safe central lawn. Lovely country, beautifu walks. Centre of Hardy's Wessex. Sea 8 miles, Dorchester 4. Minimum one week summer, winter breaks. Open all year.
Map ref: 218 034

Rudge Farm, Chilcombe, Bridport, Dorset DT6 4NF

Sue Diment
☎ 0308 482630
SC From £110–£410
Sleeps 3/4/6
🏕 ♿ 🎾 🐾

Peacefully situated on 108-acre farm in the beautiful Bride Valley, just 2 miles from the sea. Six superbly comfortable, newly converted courtyard cottages, 1 designed for wheelchai access. Log fires, colour TV, linen supplied, launderette. Lovely country walks. Short winter breakfs. Open from March 93 onwards. Map ref: 213 033

Tamarisk Farm, West Bexington, Dorchester, Dorset DT2 9DF

Arthur & Josephine Pearse
☎ 0308 897784
SC From £120–£380
Sleeps 3/6
🐾 🏕 🎾
🔑🔑 –🔑 🔑🔑
Approved

One 3-bedroomed and two 2-bedroomed cottages in delightfu setting, beautiful views of sea. Set in large garden above village, sloping down to Chesil Beach. 150-acre organic farm vegetables, fruit, sheep, beef cattle, horses. Safe for children, pets. Fishing, walking, touring Hardy Country, Abbotsbury Gardens, Swannery. Cottages sleep 3/6; washing machine, CTV, etc. Open Mar–Nov. Map ref: 213 033

Yew House Cottages, c/o Yew House Farm, Marnhull, Sturminster Newton, Dorset DT10 1NP

Gil Espley
☎ **0258 820412**
Fax 0258 821044
🆂 **From £120–£245**
Sleeps 4/5 cot
♿ 🛏 ♨
🔑 🔑 – 🔑 🔑 🔑 🔑
Commended

Three timber cottages equipped to highest standard of comfort for summer or winter holidays. Situated in a secluded rural setting overlooking Blackmore Vale. Central heating, colour TV, linen inclusive. Cot available. Outdoor swimming pool. Excellent centre for sightseeing. Coarse fishing in Stour. Many good pubs for local beer and food. One cottage designed for disabled visitors. Colour brochure. Open all year.
Map ref: 223 046

FARM HOLIDAY BUREAU

CONFIRM BOOKINGS

Disappointments can arise by misunderstandings over the telephone. Please write to confirm your booking.

FARM HOLIDAY BUREAU

BUREAU ACCOMMODATION IS RELIABLE

This Guide lists **Farm Holiday Bureau** members only. They are all inspected by the National Tourist Board for standards (see introduction pages) and by fellow members to maintain a high quality.

54 Somerset

Welcome to Somerset; we hope that your stay with us will be truly enjoyable. There's so much to do and see. For walking visit the Quantocks and the Brendon Hills or the National Park. Taunton is a town well worth visiting; it was the scene of Judge Jeffries' Bloody Assizes in 1685, and the County Museum will tell you all you need to know. But don't forget Wells and its Cathedral and Glastonbury with its Tor. For those who wish to explore our history, Somerset offers a tremendous range of National Trust properties such as Dunster, with its Castle (often used in films), Barrinton Court, Muchelney and its thatched 14th-century Priest House, the superb gardens of Hestercombe House or the journey to the centre of the earth at Cheddar Gorge and Wookey Hole.

For the steam enthusiast, there's the West Somerset Railway and the East Somerset Railway. Museums of all sorts are spread all over this hidden jewel in a crown.

Sport we cannot forget, cricket at the County Ground, golf, horseriding, polo or a day at the races.

And two final items most certainly not to be overlooked; cider and cheese – the basic items of a ploughman's lunch! Tempted? Then give us a ring and come and stay for a few days or rent a cottage and really explore Somerset.

Group Contacts: BB Jane Sedgman ☎ 0458 223 237
SC Geraldine Hunt ☎ 027864 228

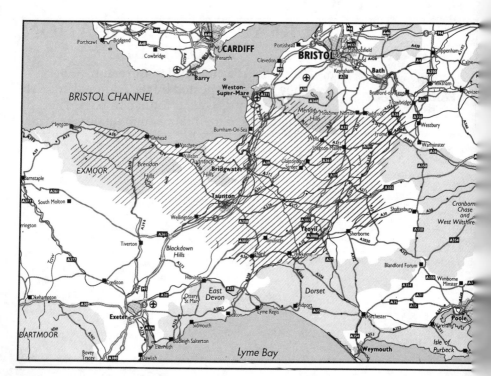

Bed and Breakfast (and evening meal)

Binham Farm, Old Cleeve, Minehead, Somerset TA24 6HX

Mrs S Bigwood
☎ 0984 40222
▦ From £13
Sleeps 6
🛏 ⚹ 🐕 🐈
Listed

Predominantly 17th-century Jacobean farmhouse on a working family farm in an idyllic setting close to the Exmoor National Park and Quantock Hills. A few minutes walk across our fields to Blue Anchor sea front and the West Somerset Steam Railway. Comfortably furnished bedrooms with en-suite facilities available, private lounge with colour TV, mediaeval dining hall. Full CH. Open all year. Map ref: 191 055

Blackmore Farm, Cannington, Bridgwater, Somerset TA5 2NE

Mrs Ann Dyer
☎ 0278 653442
Fax 0278 653442
▦ From £16
Sleeps 6
⚹ 🐕 🐈
🏆 🏆 **Commended**

A tastefully restored and furnished mediaeval manor house dating back to the 14th century, set in rolling countryside with views to the Quantock Hills. Traditional farmhouse bed and breakfast includes rooms with oak bedsteads and four poster bed. Within easy reach of Exmoor, West Somerset coast, Taunton, Wells and Glastonbury. Good selection of local eating places. Open all year. Map ref: 202 052

Bushfurlong Farm, Isle Brewers, Taunton, Somerset TA3 6QT

Michael & Judith Glide
☎ 0460 281219
▦ From £16
Sleeps 6
⚹ 🐕 🐈
🏆

A family-run arable farm with unique 300-year-old listed farmhouse built of local golden hamstone. It commands lovely country views. Large, pine-furnished bedrooms with washbasins and beverage making facilities. Lounge with colour TV, breakfast room, bathroom, shower room, CH throughout. Garden, fishing, bicycle hire. Substantial English breakfast. Pleasant local pubs for evening meal. Open all year. Map ref: 207 045

Cokerhurst Farm, 87 Wembdon Hill, Bridgwater, Somerset TA6 7QA

Diana Chappell
☎ 0278 422330
▦ From £16
Sleeps 6
🐕 ⚹ 🛏
🏆 🏆

A warm welcome awaits you at this farmhouse situated in quiet countryside. The peaceful garden overlooks the lake and 100-acre family run 'pick your own' soft fruit and arable farm. Good central location for exploring Somerset. Log fires, CH, tea/coffee facilities, TV, lounge, H and C all rooms, one en-suite. Good pub food 1½ miles. Open Easter–end Sept. Map ref: 202 052

Hale Farm, Cucklington, Wincanton, Somerset BA9 9PN

Pat & Jim David
☎ 0963 33342
▦ From £16
EM From £8
Sleeps 6
🛏 🐕 (6)
🏆 🏆

A friendly welcome awaits you in our old 17th century farmhouse the moment you walk in the door. Three attractive bedrooms with en-suite showers, toilets, washbasins, tea/coffee-making facilities. Comfortable lounge with colour TV, separate dining room serving delicious home cooking. Set in peaceful surroundings yet only 2 miles A303 London – Exeter road. Ideal touring centre country and coast. Open Apr–Oct. Map ref: 220 047

Halsdown Farm, Waerrow, Taunton, Somerset TA4 2QU

Mrs Ann James
☎ 0984 23493
BB From £13.50
EM From £7.50
Sleeps 6
🐎 🐕
Listed

Halsdown is a working dairy farm with many small animals. Ideal for family holidays, offering a friendly relaxed atmosphere. The lovely 15th century farmhouse is set in a secluded position high on the edge of Exmoor, close to Wimbleball and Clatworthy reservoirs for excellent fishing. The perfect setting for a restful holiday. Open Mar–Sep. Map ref: 193 047

Lower Church Farm, Rectory Lane, Charlton Musgrove, Wincanton, Somerset BA9 8ES

Alicia Teague
☎ 0963 32307
BB From £12
Sleeps 6
🐎 ✕ 🐕 (6)
🐴 🐴

Relax at our 18th century beamed house on dairy farm, 2 miles from A303 on Wiltshire/Dorset border surrounded by lovely countryside. Ideal touring. Quiet, pleasant, homely atmosphere. One twin, 1 double en-suite, 1 double with private downstairs bathroom. Full central heating. Dining room/lounge, colour TV. Tea/coffee-making facilities. Cottage garden, patio. Small tithe barn. AA listed. Open all year except Christmas. Map ref: 218 048

Lower Farm, Kingweston, Somerton, Somerset TA11 6BA

David & Jane Sedgman
☎ 0458 223237
BB From £18.50
Sleeps 5
🐕 🐎 ✕ 🍴
🐴 Commended

This Grade II listed farmhouse, sited in a conservation area and overlooking a wide stretch of open country, was formerly a coaching inn and retains many of its original features. The attractively furnished rooms are all en-suite, with tea/coffee-making facilities, colour TV and full central heating. Wells, Glastonbury, Cheddar, Wookey, Bath and Yeovil are within easy reach. Open all year. Map ref: 211 050

New House Farm, Burtle Road, Westhay, Nr Glastonbury, Somerset BA6 9TT

Mrs M Bell
☎ 0458 860238
BB From £13
EM From £9
Sleeps 6
🐎 🐕
🐴 🐴

Large Victorian farmhouse on dairy farm. Glastonbury 5 miles. Central for touring Wells, Cheddar etc. Accommodation comprises 2 double rooms with washbasin and one en-suite, all with colour TV, tea/coffee facilities. Lounge with colour TV, separate dining room and sun lounge. Central heating throughout. Open all year (closed Christmas). Map ref: 212 052

North Down Farm, Wiveliscombe, Taunton, Somerset TA4 2BL

Mrs Lucy Parker
☎ 0984 23730
BB From £13.50-£15
EM From £8
Sleeps 6
🐕 🐎 🐴 💺 ✕ 🍴
🐴 Commended

Family dairy farm set on the edge of Exmoor and Lorna Doone Country, 10 miles from Taunton, 1 mile from Wiveliscombe. Facilities for horse riding, fishing and sailing locally. Pleasant walks around the farm and locality. Picnic basket available on request. Magnificent views of the nearby Quantocks and Vale of Taunton. Open all year (closed Christmas). Map ref: 195 047

Northwick Farm, Mark, Highbridge, Somerset TA9 4PG

Mrs Geraldine Hunt
☎ 0278 641228
BB From £16
EM From £10.50
Sleeps 6
🐕 (5) 🐎 🏕 🚐
🐴 🐴 Commended

A warm and friendly welcome awaits you at Northwick Farm, situated on the Somerset levels in an area of outstanding natural beauty. An ideal base for touring Cheddar, Wells, Glastonbury, Peat Moors and coast. Golf, riding and fishing nearby, and within 2 miles of M5 (J22). Excellent local inns and restaurants. Open all year. Map ref: 204 055

Orchard Farm, Cockhill, Castle Cary, Somerset, BA7 7NY

Olive Boyer
☎ 0963 50418
BB From £13.50
EM From £8.50
Sleeps 5
ㅏ ㅎ ㄲ 시 ▦
✿ Commended

A 170-acre beef and vegetable-growing farm in area of outstanding beauty, yet only 1½ miles from Castle Cary. Centrally-heated farmhouse with 2 en-suite rooms, TV lounge. Traditional farmhouse meals served. Bath, Taunton, Longleat, Stourhead and coasts at West Somerset and Dorset within driving distance. Open all year. Map ref: 215 048

Orchard Haven, Langford Budville, Wellington, Somerset TA21 0QZ

Mrs Jenny Perry-Jones
☎ 0823 672116
BB From £15
Sleeps 5
◉ ⊬ ㅎ (5)
✿✿

Orchard Haven is the ideal place to enjoy the delights of Rural Somerset. It nestles in idyllic countryside standing by the River Tone. Lovely accommodation tastefully and comfortably furnished with a friendly atmosphere. The dining room has separate tables where a good full English breakfast starts the day. Having only a small number of guests assures first class attention. Good inns ¾ and 2 miles distance. Wellington 4 miles. Open Easter–Oct. Map ref: 198 046

Pinksmoor Millhouse, Pinksmoor, Wellington, Somerset TA21 0HD

Mrs Nancy K M Ash
☎ 0823 672361
BB From £16
EM From £10.50
Sleeps 6
ㅏ ㅎ ▦
✿✿✿
Commended

Take a stroll along the old millstream, haunt of kingfisher, snipe and mallard, go badger watching or just wander where you please around this family-run dairy farm. Period millhouse adjacent to old mill and stream. Cosy lounges, log fire, spacious en-suite bedrooms, tea/coffee-making facilities, CH, colour TV, farmhouse hospitality and cooking. AA listed. Close to coasts and moors. 10 minutes M5 J26. Open all year (closed Christmas and New Year). Map ref: 198 046

Quiet Corner Farm, Henstridge, Templecombe, Somerset BA8 0RA

**Patricia & Brian
Thompson**
☎ 0963 63045
BB From £17
Sleeps 6
ㅎ
✿✿ Commended

Secluded old farmhouse and barns in lovely garden and orchard setting with sheep and tiny Shetland ponies, with all of Somerset and Dorset to explore. Two double rooms, one en-suite, twin bedded room with space for the children. CH, log fires, sitting room with TV. Excellent breakfast menu includes fruit and yoghurt, real coffee. Henstridge lies twixt Shaftesbury & Sherborne at junction of A30/A357. Open all year. Map ref: 220 045

Townsend Farm, Sand, Wedmore, Somerset BS28 4XH

Sarah Willcox
☎ 0934 712342
BB From £13.50
EM From £9
Sleeps 6
ㅏ ㅎ (5)
✿✿

Townsend Farm is a working dairy farm, set in peaceful countryside with views of the Mendip hills, close to Wells, Cheddar and Glastonbury, 6 miles from M5 (jct 22). The spacious Victorian farmhouse offers comfortable accommodation and a friendly atmosphere, traditional English breakfast served in dining room, relaxing separate TV lounge. All bedrooms have TV, en-suite available. Open all year. Map ref: 209 055

Wembdon Farm, Hollow Lane, Wembdon, Bridgwater, Somerset TA5 2BD

Mrs Mary Rowe
☎ 0278 453097
BB From £16.50
ㅎ ⊬ ㅉ
Applied

Enjoy a carefree break at our 17th century family farmhouse. Situated near the Quantock hills, therefore an ideal base for visiting coastlines, Exmoor, Glastonbury and oustanding National Trust properties. The farmhouse is tastefully decorated, central heating throughout offering separate lounge, dining room, bedrooms are full en-suite, tea/coffee-making facilities, TV. Excellent local eating palces. We are also easy to find. Open Easter–Dec. Map ref: 202 052

Self-Catering

The Courtyard, c/o New House Farm, Burtle Road, Westhay, Nr Glastonbury, Somerset BA6 9TT

Mr & Mrs P Bell
☎ 0458 860238
SC From £150–£300
Sleeps 4–6
♘ ☙
🎣 🎣 🎣 🎣 **Commended**

The Courtyard is a converted barn which sleeps up to 4 adults and 2 children. Its situation on a dairy farm on the Somerset Levels makes it central for touring Wells, Cheddar, Bath, etc. Superbly equipped, including colour TV, washing machine, tumble dryer. Bed-linen, electricity and heating included. Open all year. Map ref: 212 052

Dykes House, Stoke-St-Gregory, Taunton, Somerset TA3 6JH

Mrs M J House
☎ 0823 490349/490619
SC From £110–£240
Sleeps 5 + cot
☙ 🎣
🎣 🎣 **Approved**

Dykes House is a self-contained spacious wing of thatched listed farmhouse with panoramic views. Comfortable and fully equiiped. Woodburner in lounge, kitchen/diner, 1 twin, 1 family room, bathroom, 2 toilets. Own drive and garden. Pay phone. Linen, towels and 5 storage heaters included. Exceller touring base. 8 miles M5, junction 25. Open all year. Map ref: 206 048

Hale Farm, Cucklington, Wincanton, Somerset BA9 9PN

Mrs Pat David
☎ 0963 33342
SC From £50–£150
Sleeps 4
☙ 🎣
🎣 🎣 🎣 **Approved**

Set in a peaceful, but not isolated, position on edge of village only 2 miles from A303. Ideal touring. Period converted former cowshed, comfortable and fully equipped. 2 twin-bedded rooms, bathroom, kitchen, sitting room. All electric (coin meter). Linen supplied. Open all year. Map ref: 220 048

Pear Tree Cottage, Northwick Farm, Mark, Highbridge, Somerset TA9 4PG

Mrs G Hunt
☎ 0278 641228
SC From £150–£280
Sleeps 4/6
☙ 🎣
🎣 🎣 🎣 🎣 **Commended**

Situated on the Somerset Levels in an area of outstanding natural beauty. Recent barn conversion. Luxurious and comfortable with beautifully co-ordinated fabrics and furnishings. Perfect for a peaceful relaxing holiday and an ideal base for touring this part of the West Country. Excellent facilities nearby for golf, fishing and riding and only 4 miles from coast. Map ref: 204 055

Rull Farm, Otterford, near Chard, Somerset TA20 3O

FARM HOLIDAY BUREAU

Mrs Pauline Wright
☎ 0460 234398
SC From £100–£160
Sleeps 5/6
☙ 🏕 ⊞ ⛲
🎣 🎣 **Approved**

We would like to welcome you to our family farm in the beautiful Blackdown hills with splendid scenic views. This accommodation is part of the farmhouse within easy reach of 5 local towns and coastal resorts. Open all year. Map ref: 203 043

55 Exmoor

This area is the Exmoor National Park which is situated on the north coast of Devon and Somerset. The park has miles of moorland which are ideal for country pursuits such as walking and riding, but also has many beautiful villages in the folds of the countryside.

On a journey of 10 miles, you could pass through narrow valleys dominated by beech woods, then suddenly you are on to the bleak moor. A mile or so on, you are surrounded by rich green farmland and then suddenly you hit the coast – with some of England's highest cliffs towering over the sea.

Exmoor is famous for its wild herds of ponies and red deer. The Rivers Exe and Barle rise high on the moors creating attractive moorland valleys. This is also the country that Blackmore made famous with 'Lorna Doone', and you can still find places described in the book.

Apart from excellent inland attractions like the famous Tarr Steps (an ancient clapper bridge), there are bustling and delightful resorts like Minehead, Porlock, Lynmouth and Lynton dotted along the glorious coastline, with rocky coves and small sandy beaches.

Group Contacts: 🔲 **Mrs Rosemary Pile 059 87 236**
🔲 **Mrs Ann Durbin 064 383 255**

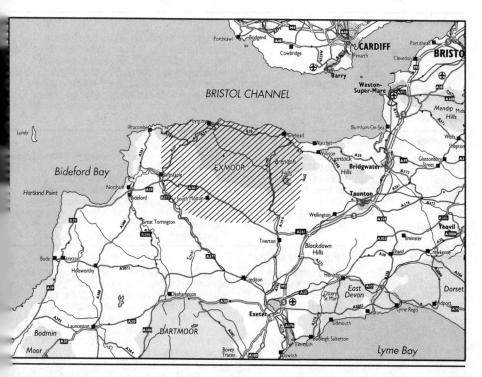

Bed and Breakfast (and evening meal)

Ashott Barton, Exford, Minehead, Somerset TA24 7NG

Mrs Jackie Thorne
☎ 064 383 294
BB From £16
EM From £11
Sleeps 4
Listed Commended

Comfortable farmhouse with lots of old pine and Laura Ashley furnishings, on 400-acre sheep and beef farm. Excellent central location for walking, touring, hunting. North Devon coast nearby. Children welcome – high chair, cot and high teas available. 1 double-bedded room with king size bed and colour TV. 1 twin-bedded room, 1 guest bathroom. Stabling available. Dogs by arrangement. Open May–Oct (incl). Map ref: 188 054

Bridwick Farm, Kentisbury, Barnstaple, Devon EX31 4NN

Mrs Marilyn Purchase
☎ 059 83 416
BB From £15
Sleeps 6
Commended

A warm, friendly atmosphere and homely welcome at this family livestock farm. Spacious accommodation, many extras included. TV Lounge, dining room. 2 bathrooms, separate shower room, H&C, hot drinks facilities. Pony rides. Excellent restaurant ½ mile (take-away available, use our dining room if you wish). Ideal for sandy beaches, moors, market towns and fishing. Reduction for children or stays over 3 days. Open May–Oct. Map ref: 177 053

Coombe Farm, Countisbury, Lynton, Devon EX35 6NF

Rosemary & Susan Pile
☎ 059 87 236
BB From £16
EM From £12.50
Sleeps 14
Commended

Comfortable old farmhouse set on a hillside between picturesque Lynmouth and the legendary Doone Valley. Coast path runs through the farm. Riding and fishing nearby. Beamed dining room, lounge with colour TV. 2 bedrooms with shower en-suite, 3 with H/C, all with hot drinks facilities. Licensed. Wholesome breakfasts and four course dinners. Dogs by arrangement. Weekly terms available. AA listed. Open Mar–Nov. Map ref: 182 057

Cutthorne Farm, Luckwell Bridge, Wheddon Cross, Somerset TA24 7EW

Anne Durbin
☎ 064 383 255
BB From £17.50
EM From £9.50
Sleeps 6

18th century yeoman farmhouse totally secluded in heart of Exmoor. A working farm, spacious and comfortable accommodation with log fires and CH. Luxury en-suite bathrooms. 4-poster bed. Candlelit dinners, high teas for children. For extra privacy – beautifully appointed mediaeval stone cottages on side of farmhouse overlooking pond and cobbled yard. Stabling. We are 2½ miles from 'The Rest and Be Thankful', Wheddon Cross, travelling on the B3224 towards Exford. Open Feb–Dec. Map ref: 188 053

Edgcott House, Exford, Nr Minehead, Somerset TA24 7QG

Gillian Lamble
☎ 064383 495
BB From £17
EM From £10
Sleeps 6

Country house of great charm and character amidst beautiful countryside in the heart of Exmoor National Park, 14 mile from village of Exford. Peaceful and quiet. All bedrooms have basins, private bathroom available. Excellent home cooking using fresh local produce is served in the elegant 'longroom' with its unique murals. Large garden, stabling. Comfortable, friendly centre for relaxing, walking, riding and fishing. Open all year. Map ref: 188 054

Emmetts Grange Farm, Emmetts Grange, Simonsbath, Minehead, Somerset TA24 7LD

Julia Brown
☎ 064 383 282
⒝⒝ From £20
EM £13
Sleeps 6
🐕 ⌕
🐝 🐝 🐝 Commended

This listed farmhouse stands in a quiet position on a 1200 acre stock farm. All rooms furnished to a high standard. A relaxed friendly atmosphere. The resident's lounge with log fire has a spectacular view. All bedrooms have CTV, tea/coffee-making facilities. Two with en suite bathrooms. Renowned for our delicious country cooking. Table licence. Ideal for exploring Exmoor. Open Mar–end Oct.
Map ref: 183 055

Glasses Farm, Roadwater, Watchet, Somerset TA23 0QH

Mrs Sheena White
☎ 0984 40552
⒝⒝ From £16.50
Sleeps 6
🐕 ⌕ (10) ⚊ ♞
🐝

This delightful thatched 16th century farmhouse is situated on the edge of Exmoor, at the foot of the Brendon Hills. Ideal for seeing the many local beauty spots. We are a working farm of 220 acres, dairy and arable. The farmhouse is beautifully decorated and comfortable, yet retains its original beams and character. Tea/coffee facilities, washbasin in all rooms. Open 5 Jan–15 Dec. Map ref: 195 054

Headgate Farm, Twitchen, South Molton, Devon EX36 1BD

Mrs Judy Hayes
☎ 059 84 481
⒝⒝ From £14
EM From £12
Sleeps 3
⌕ 🐕
🐝 🐝 Approved

Comfortable en-suite accommodation on working farm in a very pretty position close to open moorland and adjoining woodland. Quiet farm animals to interest children. An abundance of home cooked food and a warm, friendly atmosphere, log fire. Tea/coffee/squash-making facilities plus many little extras. Beaches and varied attractions within easy driving distance. Stabling available. Open May–Oct.
Map ref: 183 047

Highercombe, Dulverton, Somerset TA22 9PT

Barbara Marchant
☎ 0398 23451
⒝⒝ From £16
Sleeps 6
⌕ 🐕
🐝 🐝 Commended

Situated in Exmoor National Park close to open moorland. Grade II listed large country house originating from 14th century. Set in 8 acres of land with beautiful gardens. Comfortable double twin or family rooms with en-suite or private bathrooms. Tea/coffee-making facilities. Large TV lounge with far reaching views and from which wild deer can often be seen. Excellent area for country sports. Stabling.
Map ref: 188 047

Hindon Farm, Nr Minehead, Somerset TA24 8SM

Penny & Roger Webber
☎ 0643 705244
⒝⒝ From £16–18
EM From £12
Sleeps 6
🐕 ⌕ ⌕ ♞ ⚱ 🏺
Listed Commended

Superbly situated in secluded valley (Minehead 3 miles) – Selworthy (1 mile) find our friendly working National Trust Farm – 500 acres and direct access to moors. Spotty pigs, donkey, horses, goats, poultry and many sheep – come and help! Riding/stabling/grazing. Large lawn and stream, picnic area. Games barn. Own produce. Lovely 17th/18th century farmhouse with relaxed atmosphere and big breakfasts. Central heating. Pretty bedrooms all H & C and drinks tray. Guests sitting room. Child and weekly (off-peak) reductions. Open Easter –Oct. No smoking upstairs. Map ref: 191 055

Landacre Farm, Withypool, Minehead, Somerset TA24 7SD

Mrs P Hudson
☎ 064 383 223/487
⒝⒝ From £15
Sleeps 3
⌕ 🐕 ⌕ 🏺
Listed Approved

Large ground floor bedroom (1 double, 1 single) with sitting/breakfast area, colour TV, kitchenette and bathroom en-suite. Well equipped and comfortable. B&B or self-cater. Private fishing on River Barle. Riding available locally. Weekly terms. Situated on Exford/N. Molton Road. Open April–Oct.
Map ref: 193 052

Little Brendon Hill, Wheddon Cross, Nr Minehead, Somerset TA24 7DG

Mrs Shelagh Maxwell
☎ 0643 841556
ᴮᴮ From £15
EM From £8.50
Sleeps 6
⌇ ⌂ (5) 🐾 ▪
Listed Highly
Commended

A very comfortable country house offering a high standard of furnishings, set in the beautiful unspoilt surroundings of the Exmoor National Park. 2 twin rooms, 1 double room all with tea-making facilities. Two guest bathrooms. Central heating and log fires and good food a speciality. Horse riding, fishing and shooting are available locally. A truly relaxing place to pursue country pastimes. Open all year. Map ref: 191 055

Springfield Farm, Dulverton, Somerset TA22 9QD

Tricia Vellacott
☎ 0398 23722
ᴮᴮ From £14
EM From £9
Sleeps 5
🐾 ⌂
👑 👑 Commended

A warm welcome awaits you at our 270-acre working farm. Peacefully situated between Tarr Steps and Dulverton, overlooking the River Barle with magnificent moorland and woodland views. Very comfortable accommodation and delicious farmhouse meals. Guests' bathroom, 1 double and 1 single with H and C, 1 twin with private shower suite. Dining room with tea-making facilities, sitting room with colour TV. Open Easter–Nov. Map ref: 188 049

Wood Advent Farm, Roadwater, Watchet, Somerset TA23 0RR

Diana Brewer
☎ 0984 40920
ᴮᴮ From £16.50
EM From £10
Sleeps 10
🐾 ⌂
👑 👑 👑 Commended

Nestling at the foot of the Brendon Hills. Listed spacious farmhouse set in 340 acres of working farm. Relaxing en-suite rooms with hospitality trays. Chintzed lounge with log fires, inglenook heats the licensed dining room, where wonderful country dishes can be assured. Grass tennis court, heated outdoor pool, clay pigeon and pheasant shooting all available on the farm. Open all year. Map ref: 195 054

Self-Catering

Croft Cottage, c/o Higher Burrow Farm, Timberscombe, Minehead, Somerset TA24 7UD

Diana Rusher
☎ 0643 841427
ˢᶜ From £130–£250
Sleeps 7 cot
🐾 ⌂
ᵒ ᵒ Approved

Attractive, converted, stone built cottage situated 200 yds from farm, with own garden, and lovely views. Croft is spacious with one double room, 2 twin, 1 single, cot available. Large bathroom upstairs, second WC downstairs, washing machine Colour TV, log fire and small library. Horses or other animals accommodated by arrangement at farm. Electricity extra. Friday change-over. Open all year. Map ref: 191 055

Cutthorne Farm, Luckwell Bridge, Wheddon Cross, Somerset TA24 7EW

Ann Durbin
☎ 064 383 255
ˢᶜ From £95–£395
Sleeps 2/6
⌂ 🐾 ⚐ ⊕ ⊂ 🐾 ⅔
ᵒ ᵒ ᵒ ᵒ
Highly Commended

Situated in the heart of glorious Exmoor, two luxuriously appointed mediaeval barn conversions on side of farmhouse. Overlooking 14th century pond and cobbled yard. Self-catering or with meals in the farmhouse. Both furnished and equipped to the highest standard with antique pine, fitted kitchens and CH. Baby listening. Inclusive of linen, towels an electricity. Open all year. Map ref: 188 053

Dunsley Farm, West Anstey, South Molton, Devon EX36 3PF

Mrs Mary Robins
☎ 03984 246
SC From £90–£300
Sleeps 5
ᎭᏅᏗᎿᏘᏘ
ᏹᏹᏹᏹ **Commended**

Self-contained cottage forming part of 16th century farmhouse, overlooks meadows and woodland valley. Access off a quiet country road. 2 bedrooms (accommodate 5 people), bathroom, large lounge/diner with colour TV. Large modern equipped kitchen, electric heating (£1 meter). Linen provided, pets welcome. Coarse fishing available on farm. Dulverton 6 miles. Open all year. Map ref: 185 045

Emmetts Grange Farm, Emmetts Grange, Simonsbath, Minehead, Somerset TA24 7LD

Julia Brown
☎ 064 383 282
SC From £112–£353
Sleeps 4/8
ᎭᏅᏗ
ᏹᏹ–ᏹᏹᏹᏹ
Up to Commended

Two farm cottages sleeping 6, one spacious modern bungalow for 8 and self-contained flat for 4. All well equipped with CH and TV. Calor Gas cooking and microwave ovens. Dinners available in farmhouse by arrangement. All on a 1200-acre working moorland farm. Beautiful quiet position. 2½ miles out of Simonsbath on South Molton road. Open Mar–New Year. Map ref: 183 055

Highercombe, Dulverton, Somerset TA22 9PT

Barbara Marchant
☎ 0398 23451
SC From £135–£365
Sleeps 2/6
ᏅᏗ
ᏹᏹ **Commended**

Situated in Exmoor National Park, cottage to sleep 6, and 1st floor wing of large country house to sleep 2 +2 chidren. Close to open moorland in excellent area for walking, hunting, shooting, fishing. Both properties are warm, comfortable furnished and very well equipped. Peaceful setting with beautiful gardens. Pets welcome. Stabling available. Map ref: 188 047

Little Quarme Country Cottages, Wheddon Cross, Nr Minehead, Somerset TA24 7EA

Tammy Cody-Boutcher & family
☎ 0643 841249
SC From £80–£365
Sleeps 2/6
ᏗᏅᏘ
ᏹᏹᏹ **Up to Highly Commended**

Six stone cottages furnished and equipped to the highest standards in the heart of Exmoor. All have microwaves, colour TV, bed linen and towels. Standing amid 18 acres and large informal gardens, direct access to footpaths and bridlepath. Traffic free tranquillity with panoramic southerly views. Ample parking, free laundry room, childrens' play area, pay phone, stabling. Brochure available. Map ref: 191 055

Pembroke, Wheddon Cross, Minehead, Somerset TA24 7EX

Jennifer Escott
☎ 0643 841550
SC From £125–£300
Sleeps 6
ᏅᏗ
ᏹᏹᏹ **Approved**

Set off the road in a peaceful position with parking, private garden and relaxing scenic views, a detached bungalow in the heart of the Exmoor National Park, 2 minutes from village of Wheddon Cross. Well equipped with microwave automatic washing machine, colour TV etc. Linen included. Comfortably furnished. Open Mar–Dec. Map ref: 189 052

Ruggs Farm Bungalow, c/o Ruggs Farm, Brompton Regis, Dulverton, Somerset TA22 9NY

Jill Scott
☎ 039 87 236
SC From £115–£250
Sleeps 5 cot
ᏗᏅᏗᏅᎰ
ᏹᏹᏹ **Approved**

Farm bungalow close to the edge of Wimbleball Lake. Comfortable and well equipped, with deep freeze, washing machine, colour TV. Linen inclusive. Cot available. Beautiful walks, fishing and sailing on the lake. Fenced garden for dogs and children. A working farm of 365 acres with dairy cows and sheep. Open all year. Map ref: 194 051

Westermill Farm, Exford, Nr Minehead, Somerset TA24 7NJ

Jackie Edwards
☎ 064 383 238
🆂 From £135–£340
Sleeps 4/8
🐴 🐃 🛆 🐈 🏕 🍺 🐾
🐾 – 🐾 🐾 Commended

Six delightful log cabins of superior quality. Various sizes, well equipped. In small grassy paddocks on side of valley by a river. Also bright, comfortable cottage adjoining the farmhouse overlooks the river. Patio, double garage. Four waymarked walks over 500-acre farm in centre of Exmoor. 2½ miles shallow river, fishing, bathing. Laundry, payphone, information centre, seasonal small shop. Map ref: 188 052

West Ilkerton Farm, Lynton, North Devon EX35 6QA

Chris & Victoria Eveleigh
☎ 0598 52310
🆂 From £170–£360
Sleeps 6
🐴 🍴 🐃 🛆 🐎 🐈 🏕 🍺
🐾 🐾 🐾 Approved

Luxurious semi-detached cottage on secluded hill farm bordering open moor. Sheep, cattle, carthorses. Coast 3 miles, riding ½ mile. 3 bedrooms (2 king size, 1 twin) 2 bathrooms, living/dining room, kitchen (Rayburn, dishwasher, washing machine/tumble drier, microwave). CH. TV, video. Baby equipment and evening babysitting. Children, dogs and horses welcome. Special "Exmoor Farmer" holidays in winter. Ideal for walking, riding, family farm holidays. Open all year. Map ref: 183 055

Yelland Cottage, Challacombe, Barnstaple, Devon EX31 4TU

Jean Kingdon
☎ 059 83 433
🆂 From £100–£250
Sleeps 6
🐴 🍴 🐃
🐾 🐾 🐾 Approved

Semi-detached cosy farm cottage on working hill farm amidst beautiful countryside within easy reach of village pub and shop. Log fire, Rayburn plus electric conveniences. Relaxing lounge, colour TV. Linen provided. Friendly, relaxed atmosphere with farm animals and children love the pony rides. Spacious garden with ample parking. Ideal for beaches, walking, fishing, riding and touring North Devon. Open all year. Map ref: 179 053

Camping and Caravanning

Westermill Farm, Exford, Nr Minehead, Somerset TA24 7NJ

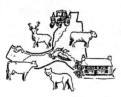

Jackie Edwards
☎ 064 383 238
Tents: adult £3/child £1
Car: 50p
2 adults + vehicle £6.50
(all prices per night)
🛆 🐴 🐃
✓ ✓ ✓

Beautiful secluded site for 60 tents and dormobiles beside upper reaches of River Exe. Centre of Exmoor National Park. Four waymarked walks over 500-acre working farm. 2½ miles shallow river, fishing and bathing. Loo block, showers, laundry, washing up. Information centre, small shop, payphone. A site and farm to enjoy in the most natural way. Children's paradise. Open Apr–Oct (incl). Map ref: 188 052

Please mention **Stay on a Farm** when booking

56 North Devon Coast & Country

North Devon is a warm, friendly and still largely unspoilt area of Britain. It is an area of tremendous contrast with dramatic cliffs, small coves and miles of golden, sandy, surf-washed beaches.

The coast offers miles of sand and surf at Westward Ho!, Saunton, Croyde, Putsborough and Woolacombe. Typical seaside towns and villages abound such as Instow, Ilfracombe, Combe Martin and the twin villages of Lynton and Lynmouth where Exmoor reaches the sea and the famous cliff railway runs between the two.

The countryside of inland North Devon still preserves the rural life of England which many people think has disappeared. The rolling hills and patchwork of small fields and family farms are still a predominantly livestock area. In the spring and early summer the hedgerows are massed with wild flowers. There is an abundance of wildlife with red deer, badgers, foxes, hares, rabbits, buzzards and many more species commonplace.

Nearby Exmoor offers magnificent scenery with rolling heather-clad hills and steeply wooded combes. Whatever sort of holiday you prefer you can find it here. It is a wonderful place for a quiet touring holiday or perfect for a family seaside holiday with many tourist attractions should the weather be less than perfect. Sporting people are well catered for with windsurfing, golfing, sailing, riding and much more available. Short breaks out of season are particularly rewarding with the area almost to yourself.

Group Contacts: BB **Mrs Andrea Cook** ☎ **0271 850543**
SC **Mrs Sandra Gay** ☎ **076 93 259**

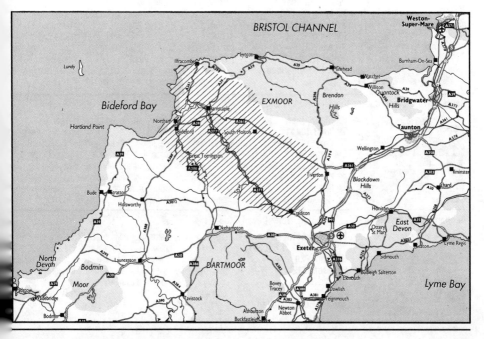

Bed and Breakfast (and evening meal)

Bocombe Farm, Parkham, Nr Bideford, North Devon EX39 5PH

Marian Scambler
☎ 0237 451 255
BB From £16
EM From £9 (by arrangement)
Sleeps 5
Listed

Family-run 107-acre dairy farm with 17th century listed farmhouse nestling in a peaceful secluded valley. Oak beams, log fires. Rooms en-suite, tea-making facilities. Close to picturesque Clovelly. Delightful coastal and country walks. Watch the milking and enjoy our 6-acre conservation area with trout ponds and abundant wildlife. Convenient to RHS Rosemore, Marwood Hill and Docton Mill gardens. Open all year (closed Christmas). Map ref: 169 045

Capitol Farm, Bishops Nympton, Nr South Molton, North Devon EX36 4PH

Mrs Cheryl Woollacott
☎ 0769 550435
BB From £13
EM From £7
Sleeps 5
Listed Commended

'Capitol' is a family-run sheep and cattle farm to which Robert, Cheryl and family welcome you. Friendly atmosphere and homely accommodation with traditional breakfasts and evening dinners. Children welcome, pony rides available. Separate TV lounge. Pleasantly situated on outskirts of village, near church and green. Ideal touring base for Exmoor and North Devon coast. Open all year. Map ref: 184 045

Combas Farm, Croyde, North Devon EX33 1PH

Mrs Gwen Adams
☎ 0271 890398
BB From £14.50
EM From £6.50
Sleeps 12
Listed Commended

Combas Farm, a 140-acre stock farm, nestles in its own secluded valley, just 15 mins' walk from miles of golden sands (5 mins from the village pub!). Many repeat bookings confirm claims to a warm welcome and high standard of home cooking using home produce including unusual fruit and veg. Wisteria rambles over this 17th century longhouse overlooking a lovely garden and unspoiled view. Colour brochure. Open Mar–Nov (incl).Map ref: 171 052

Court Barton, Lapford, Crediton, Devon EX17 6PZ

Sheila Mather
☎ 0363 83441
BB From £12.50–£15
EM From £9
Sleeps 6 cot
Approved

Treat yourself. Delightful mediaeval manor farmhouse. Delicious fresh food and Devonshire specialities, with free glass local wine/cider. Refurbished bedrooms with H&C, electric blankets, beverage facilities, 2 shower/bath/toilets. TV lounge. Lovely walks, stream, abundant wildlife to watch. Seasonal work. Baby calves. Daily milking. Ideally central ($\frac{1}{2}$ mile north A377). Dartmoor, Exmoor, National Trust, RHS Gardens, many attractions. Reductions for children. Map ref: 183 038

Denham Farm, North Buckland, Braunton, North Devon EX33 1HY

Mrs Jean Barnes
☎ and fax 0271 890297
BB From £20
EM From £12
Sleeps 24
Commended

There is always a warm welcome in this beautiful farmhouse situated near the golden sand of Croyde and Woolacombe. Come and sample Jean's delicious food. Relax in our lounge-bar and let Tony explain life on the farm. Use our games room or walk our country lanes. Childrens paradise with trailer rides, small pets, birds and farm animals. 10 en-suite rooms with TV, central heating throughout and log fires for out of season breaks. AA, RAC acclaimed. Open all year (except Christmas). Map ref: 173 053

Down Farm, Brayford, Barnstaple, North Devon EX32 7QQ

Celia Long Howell
☎ 0598 710683
🛏 From £14
Sleeps 4
🛇 🐕 🐾 ⚓
Listed

A small farm set in a sheltered corner of the Bray Valley. We offer a warm welcome to all comfortable bedrooms with a choice of four poster or brass bed, both with tea/coffee-making facilities and colour TV. Children welcome. Situated on the edge of Exmoor, good beaches nearby. Excellent pubs for evening meals. Open all year (closed Christmas). Map ref: 183 050

Fairlinch, Braunton, North Devon EX33 1JE

Mrs Elizabeth Dyer
☎ 0271 812508
🛏 From £14
🛇 🛆 🏠
Applied

Fairlinch is a truly impressive 17th century mansion house, original features of historical interest include moulded ceilings, an oak panelled breakfast room and antique furnishings. We enjoy a superb position providing extensive coastal views across Barnstaple Bay. A wide selection of local restaurants and pubs offer good value evening meals. Relax and enjoy a special holiday on this unqiue farm. Open Apr–Nov. Map ref: 175 050

Giffords Hele, Meeth, Okehampton, Devon EX20 3QN

Mrs Linden Draper
☎ 0837 810009
🛏 From £18.50
EM From £11
Sleeps 6/7
🛇 ⚓ 🛆 🛆
🛆 🛆 🛆 **Highly Commended**

Superb indoor swimming pool offering tropical temperatures all year. Acclaimed farmhouse food served in poolside restaurant. New luxury en-suite bedrooms with colour TV and beverage facilities. A beamed bar with a real fire. All this in the peaceful atmosphere of a traditional 175-acre farm. Ducks on the pond and badgers in the wood. Own Torridge fishing on farm. Ring for brochure. Open all year. Map ref: 174 039

Greenhills Farm, Yeo Mill, West Anstey, South Molton, North Devon EX36 3NU

Mrs Gillian Carr
☎ 039 84 300
🛏 From £14.50
EM From £7
Sleeps 5
🛇 🐕 🐾 🛆
Listed Commended

Relax and enjoy a holiday at Greenhills. The charming old farmhouse, the working dairy farm is nestled in the foothills of the Exmoor National Park. Guests have own lounge with colour TV, separate dining room. One double/family room, one twin-bedded room, both with tea-making facilities. All rooms are tastefully furnished to give a warm cosy atmosphere for you to relax. We take pride in our excellent home cooking using own and local produce. Map ref: 181 045

Maxton Down Farm, Bratton Fleming, Barnstaple, Devon EX32 7JL

Mrs Pat Burge
☎ 0598 710275
🛏 From £13.50
EM From £7
Sleeps 6
🛇 🐕
Listed

Be assured of a warm welcome at this beef and sheep farm set in peaceful countryside close to Exmoor. Enjoy the freedom of the fields, look at the animals or relax in the comfortable farmhouse. Guests have their own entrance and key. Large loung with colour TV, separate dining room, 3 bedrooms, bath/shower room, 2 WC's. Good plentiful food, tea/coffee-making facilities, we aim to give you a happy holiday. SAE brochure. Open Apr–Nov. Map ref: 183 050

Higher Churchill Farm, East Down, Nr Barnstaple, North Devon EX31 4LT

Mrs Andrea Cook
☎ 0271 850543
🛏 From £15
EM From £7
Sleeps 6
🐾 🛇 🛆 🏠 🌿
Listed Approved

Friendly family welcome to our lovely old farmhouse, on a working farm, part of a National Trust estate, in beautiful countryside between beaches and Exmoor. We have dairy cows and sheep and many pet animals. Children most welcome. Good food, mostly home or locally produced. Private or en-suite facilities. Peaceful shorts breaks, early and late. Lot to do in the area. Open Apr–Nov. Map ref: 176 054

Higher Clifton Farm, East Down, Nr Barnstaple, North Devon EX31 4LX

Mrs Elizabeth Smyth
☎ 0271 850372
🅱🅱 From £14
EM From £8
🅱🅱 & EM From £120 (weekly)
Sleeps 6
🐴 ⅍ 🐾
🍺 Approved

A warm welcome awaits on our family-run working farm. Large variety of farm animals. 17th century farmhouse stands at the end of its own drive. Very peaceful village, lovely view and walks, near all local attractions, beaches and Exmoor. Few minutes walk to pub. 3 bedrooms, all with H/C. Bathroom and 2 toilets. Lounge/dining room with tea/coffee-making facilities, TV. Children welcome. Babysitting. Good farmhouse cooking using own produce when available. Open May–Sept. Map ref: 176 054

Home Park, Lower Blackwell, Muddiford, North Devon EX31 4ET

Mrs Mari Lethaby
☎ 0271 42955
🅱🅱 From £15
EM From £6
Sleeps 6
🐴 🐕 🐾 ▪
🍺 🍺 Commended

70-acre sheep and beef farm set in glorious Devonshire countryside just off the beaten track. All rooms en-suite and with colour TV and teatrays. Childrens' play area outside open all the year. Guests may stay in if they wish. Numerous beaches, Exmoor, Dartmoor, Lynton and Lynmouth within easy reach. 2 miles from Barnstaple, 7 miles from Ilfracombe. SAE Brochure. AA QQQ. Open all year. Map ref: 176 052

Huxtable Farm, West Buckland, Barnstaple, North Devon EX32 0SR

Jackie Payne
☎ 0598 760254
🅱🅱 From £18
EM From £11
Sleeps 12
♿ 🐴 🐾 🖾
🍺 🍺 🍺 Commended

Relax in a mediaeval longhouse and barn carefully restored and furnished with antiques. Secluded sheep farm (2 miles from M5 link) ideally situated for Exmoor and North Devon coast. 4 course candlelit dinners of farm/local produce served with homemade wine. 3 en-suite bedrooms with colour TV. Winner 'Taste of Exmoor', log fires, games room, private baths/shower, sauna, reductions children, short/long breaks out of season. Open all year (closed Christmas & New Year). Map ref: 179 047

Waytown Farm, Shirwell, Barnstaple, North Devon EX31 4JN

Hazel Kingdon
☎ 0271 850396
🅱🅱 From £16
EM From £7
Sleeps 6
🐴 🐾 ▪
🍺 🍺 Commended

A family run beef and sheep farm, set in beautiful countryside 3 miles from historic town of Barnstaple, Exmoor and sandy beaches of Saunton and Woolacombe are within easy reach. Good farmhouse cooking, relaxed atmosphere. All children welcome, 2 en-suite bedrooms, twin bedroom all with colour TV tea/coffee-making facilities, bathroom, dining room, lounge with colour TV. Brochure. Weekly terms available. Map ref: 176 051

Self-Catering

SC

Barley Cottage and the Old Granary c/o Denham Farm, North Buckland, Braunton, North Devon EX33 1HY

Jean Barnes
☎ and fax 0271 890297
🆂🅲 £150–£550
Sleeps 4/8
🐾 🐴 🖾 ♿ 🐾
🐾 🐾 🐾 – 🐾 🐾 🐾 🐾
Commended

For a large party choose 'Barley Cott' with 4 bedrooms and 2 bathrooms or for a small party, the 'Old Granary' with 1 family size bedroom. Each is homely with good quality furnishings, extremely well equipped with everything you need. Visit nearby sandy beaches, walk our country lanes, picnic beside our lake. Enjoy the small pets corner, aviary, play area and games room. Book a farmhouse dinner, make friends in our bar. Come to Denham for holiday to remember. Open all year. Map ref: 173 053

Beech Grove, East Westacott, Riddlecombe, Chulmleigh, Devon EX18 7PF

Joyce Middleton
☎ 076 93 210
SC From £135
Sleeps 5/7 cot
⚓
♪ ♪ ♪ ♪ **Commended**

Set in pretty gardens overlooking beautiful countryside, between Dartmoor and Exmoor, our spacious bungalow, has a lovely atmosphere of warmth, peace and comfort. Situated on family-run beef and sheep farm. A happy friendly place to stay. Tempting meals and markets, in local towns and delightful villages. Superbly equipped, central heating, log fires, linen provided. Large games room, golf, riding, fishing, nearby beach 30 minutes. Open all year. Map ref: 180 044

Cleave Country Cottages, c/o Cleave Farm, Weare, Giffard, Nr Bideford, North Devon EX39 4QX

Elizabeth Moore
☎ 0805 23671
SC From £250–£550
Sleeps 5/6
⚓ 🐎 🚲 🐎
♪ ♪ ♪ ♪ **Commended**

A warm welcome awaits you at our working dairy farm. Luxury accommodation with en-suite facilities, central heating, free linen and a retired pony for small children! Automatic washing machine, tumble dryer. Cot available. Patio and barbecue. Situated in the countryside with panoramic views. Lovely walks, within easy reach of coast or Exmoor. Open all year. Map ref: 172 045

Drewstone Farm, South Molton, North Devon EX36 3EF

Ruth Ley
☎ 0769 572337
SC From £100
Sleeps 6
🐎 ⚓ 🐕 🐎 📺
♪ ♪ ♪ ♪ **Commended**

Escape to farm tranquillity on edge of Exmoor, 16th century luxury converted barn with beams, woodburner, colour TV, fitted carpets, washing machine. 3 bedrooms, bath-shower room. Fully equipped oak kitchen/diner and lounge upstairs to enjoy panoramic country views. Enclosed lawn, children's facilities, games room, animals to see, freedom to explore the farm. Country walks, clay-pigeon shooting, trout lake, and pony riding. Open all year. Map ref: 182 047

Giffords Hele, Meeth, Okehampton, Devon EX20 3QN

Mrs Linden Draper
☎ 0837 810009
SC From £200–£450
Sleeps 5/10
🐎 ⚓ 🐎 📺 📺
♪ ♪ ♪ ♪ **Up to Highly Commended**

Garden and courtyard cottages, part of old Devon longhouse. Lovely old beams, low windowsills, a huge inglenook and 4-poster bed. Pretty walled garden and play area, plus full access to our superb indoor swimming pool, farmhouse restaurant and bar. Each cottage sleeps up to 5 in 2 bedrooms which can interconnect to accommodate a party of up to 10 + cot. Own Torridge fishing. Ring for brochure. Open all year. Map ref: 174 039

Great Whitstone Farm, Meshaw, South Molton, Devon EX36 4NH

Sally Anne Meikle
☎ 0884 860914
SC From £120–£180
Sleeps 8
🐎 ⚓ 📺 🏕
♪ ♪ **Approved**

A friendly family run farm, a large traditional kitchen brings a warm welcome all year round with a rayburn and all mod cons. Spacious bedrooms accommodation up to eight people. Cot included. Guests welcome to hlep feed animals and look around the farm and watch the milking. Come and get away from it all. Open all year. Map ref: 183 045

Hollacombe Barton, Hollacombe, Chulmleigh, Devon EX18 7QG

Christine Stevens
☎ 0837 83385
SC From £150–£380
Sleeps 6
🐎 ⚓ 🐕 🐎 📺 📺
♪ ♪ ♪ ♪ **Commended**

Friendly folks and animals, come and meet them all. Very comfy farmhouse having washer/dryer, dishwasher, freezer, linen and towels. Log fire and central heating. Phone/fax. Relax in magnificent sun lounge, enjoy an involved farm experience or exciting activities. Guided walks, evening meals, taxi service, nothing too much trouble. Rural central position in Tarka country. Brochure. Map ref: 177 041

Manor Farm, Riddlecombe, Chulmleigh, North Devon EX18 7NX

Eveline Gay
☎ 076 93 335
SC From £115
Sleeps 7/8 + cot
🐕 🐴 ⚑
🔑 🔑 🔑 🔑 **Commended**

You are assured a friendly welcome at manor farmhouse, which has a self catering wing with garden and lovely views. Children can bottlefeed baby lambs, watch the milking, make friends with Poppy our tame sheep, see baby calves etc on our working dairy and sheep farm. There is an extremely well equipped, games room, catering for all ages, 3 bedrooms, washer/dryer, fridge/freezer, microwave, heating throughout. Open all year. Map ref: 177 042

Nethercott Manor Farm, Rose Ash, South Molton, North Devon EX36 4RE

Carol Woollacott
☎ 0769 550483
SC From £85–£300
Sleeps 4/8
🐕 🐴 ⚓ 🐟 🐈 🎋
🔑 🔑 – 🔑 🔑 🔑
Approved

Denis and Carol assure a warm welcome at Nethercott, a 17th century thatched house on a 200-acre working farm. Two comfortable self-contained wings sleeping 4/8. Pleasant views overlooking woods and trout pond. Pony rides, extensive games room and laundry. Also barbecuing facilities. 6 miles from the market town of South Molton, ideal for touring Exmoor and coast. Open all year. Map ref: 187 045

Norwood Farm, Hiscott, Barnstaple, North Devon EX31 3JS

Belinda Richards
☎ 0271 858 260
SC From £175–£400
Sleeps 5
🐕 🐴 ✂
🔑 🔑 🔑 🔑
Highly Commended

The old stable has been sympathetically converted to provide luxury accommodation, comprising full central heating, fully equipped kitchen with dishwasher, microwave and washing machine. A log burner sits in a cosy sitting room amongst well chosen furniture and soft furnishings. In all, a country cottage with charm and atmosphere. Terms include all linen, duvets and electric. Open all year. Map ref: 174 048

Northcott Barton Farm, Ashreigney, Chulmleigh, Devon EX18 7PR

Mrs Sandra Gay
☎ 076 93 259
SC From £110
Sleeps 8 + cot
🐕 🐈 🐴 🐟 🐈 🎋
🔑 🔑 🔑 **Approved**

Come and explore the farm, meet the animals and enjoy our beautiful countryside, children especially welcome 'help' feed lambs, calves, hens, collect eggs and watch milking. 3 bedroomed farmhouse wing offers 'home from home' comfort cosy oak-beamed lounge, log fire, heating throughout, automatic washing machine and linen provided. Large south facing garden, riding, fishing, golf nearby, warm welcome assured. Open all year. Map ref: 178 043

The Old Barn, Bocombe Farm, Parkham, Nr Bideford, North Devon EX39 5PH

Marian Scambler
☎ 0237 451 255
BB From £100
Sleeps 6 + cot
✂ 🐕 🐈 🎋
Applied

Charming, barn conversion on family run, dairy farm. Peacefully situated overlooking 6-acre conservation area with ponds and abundant wildlife. Delightful coastal and country walks. Close to picturesque Clovelly. 1 double en-suite, 2 twin. Fully equipped kitchen, lounge with log burner and colour TV. Separate dining room, enclosed patio, linen logs and electricity included in price. Open all year. Map ref: 169 045

The Old Coach House, Densham, Ashreigney, Chulmleigh, Devon EX18 7NF

Mrs Cole
☎ 07693 273
BB From £95–£245
🐕 🈶 🐈 🎋
🔑 🔑 🔑 **Approved**

Originally a barn adjoining our farmhouse, this single storey conversion has been carefully renovated with every comfort, 2 double bedrooms + cot. Bathroom with shaving point, open plan living room with dining and kitchen areas, woodburning stove, sun lounge, own garden with barbeque, visitors are welcome to watch the farming activities, milking cows, feeding lambs, calves, fishing in private brook, linen included, full central heating. Open all year. Map ref: 178 043

Pickwell Barton Holiday Cottages, Pickwell Barton, Georgeham, Braunton, North Devon EX33 1LA

Mrs Sheila Cook
☎ 0271 890987
⑤Ⓒ From £100–£300
Sleeps 7/9
⼞ ⽝ ⽞ ⽧
⚘ Approved

Sunnyside and Pickwell Barton cottages are two spacious, well equipped farm holiday cottages on a beef, sheep and arable farm. Pickwell is a small hamlet close to Putsborough and Woolacombe's golden sandy beach. Ideal for surfing and gorgeous coastal walks across our farm with breathtaking views of the sunset over Lundy Island. Golf, horse-riding, fishing nearby. Solid fuel Rayburn. available out of season. Open all year. Map ref: 171 052

Pitt Farm, North Molton, North Devon EX36 3JR

Mrs Gladys Ayre
☎ 05984 285
⑤Ⓒ From £95
Sleeps 4/6
⼞ ⽞
⚘ ⚘ ⚘ ⚘ Commended

Enjoy peaceful surroundings at our charming cottage, set in unspoilt Exmoor countryside, 1 mile from village shops, pubs, garage, equipped to high standard with night storage heating throughout 3 bedrooms. Bath/shower/beamed lounge. Colour TV, oak fitted kitchen/diner. Autowasher, fridge, microwave, etc. Own patio. Barbeque. Pond with ducks and geese. Freedom to explore our 230 acre sheep farm. Open all year. Map ref: 187 045

Sandick Cottage, c/o Sandick Farm, Swimbridge, Barnstaple, North Devon EX32 0QZ

Margaret Bartlett
☎ 0271 830243
⑤Ⓒ From £140–£290
Sleeps 6 cot
⽞ ⼧ ⽧
⚘ ⚘ ⚘ Commended

Enjoy a stay at our pretty pink cottage with its own lovely garden in tranquil surroundings near our dairy farm, only 5 miles from Barnstaple. It is central for beaches and Exmoor. Walk the adjoining Tarka trail or explore the farms, own woodland and fishing ponds. The spacious cottage accommodates 6, with linen provided, and is fully equipped. The cosy oak-beamed lounge with log fire provides home from home comfort. Open all year. Map ref: 179 048

Welcombe Farm, Charles, Nr Barnstaple, North Devon EX32 7PU

Margaret & Malcolm Faulkner
☎ 0598 710440
⑤Ⓒ From £100–£250
Sleeps 4/5
⼞ ⽞ ⽧
⚘ Commended

Just sit and enjoy the view, or use our central position for touring moors, beaches and gardens, from our lovely holiday home. Situated on a traditional dairy/sheep farm, it has panoramic views to Exmoor. Imaginative private setting in enclosed garden. Furnished to a high standard, with two bedrooms, bathroom/shower fully-fitted kitchen. Heating throughout for comfort. Duvet, linen for main bedroom included. Good walking and touring. Open Mar–Oct. Map ref: 180 050

Willesleigh Farm, Goodleigh, Barnstaple, North Devon EX32 7NA

Anne Esmond-Cole
☎ 0271 43763
⑤Ⓒ From £145–£590
Sleeps 2/6
⼞ ⼬ ⽨ ⽞
⚘ ⚘ ⚘ ⚘ Commended

Glorious countryside, warm welcoming farmhouse wing, 3 bedrooms, 4 poster, 2 bathrooms, wood fire, walled garden, swimming in enclosed heated pool May–Oct. Family run dairy farm. Two miles A361, ∂ mile from village, pub and shop. 10 miles Exmoor, beaches, RHS Rosemoor. Walking, riding. Electricity, bed linen, towels, all included in price. Detailed illustrated brochure. Open all year. Map ref: 177 049

FARM HOLIDAY BUREAU

LET THE TELEPHONE RING!
Some farmhouses are big places. Let the telephone ring long enough to give the owner time to answer it.

57 Heart of Devon

If you are undecided about which part of Devon to take your holiday, why not opt for the heart of the county . . . you can then tour and explore in all directions to get a taste of all that's best.

The Heart of Devon with its thatched cottages, lush meadows, steeply wooded valleys, rivers and streams, is unspoilt and rather special.

This is an area of traditional sheep and cattle farming. A visit to one of the local towns on market day will give you the chance to get the full flavour of the occasion, plus the opportunity to sample the produce itself . . . cheese, smoked trout, clotted cream and farmhouse cider.

As always in Devon there is much to see and do. There is a hint of nostalgia as well. Take Tiverton for example: the town's museum is one of the best folk museums in the West Country with its large railway gallery complete with restored GWR loco.

The Great Western Canal, 11 miles long, offers trips by horse-drawn barge.

There is, of course, much more – and all within easy reach. Exmoor, Dartmoor, the south coast resorts and dramatic seascapes of the north.

Group Contacts: ⓑⓑ Mrs Ann Boldry ☎ 039 85 347
                 ⓢⓒ Mrs Sylvia Hann ☎ 0884 256946

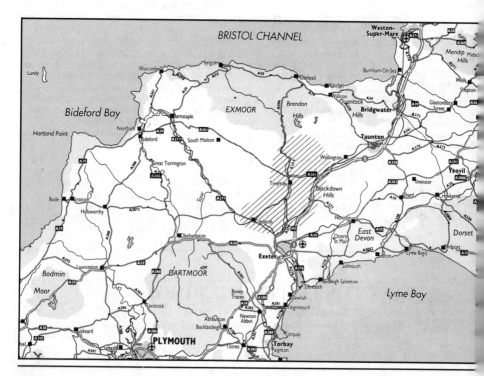

Bed and Breakfast (and evening meal)

Brindiwell Farm, Cheriton Fitzpaine, Crediton, Devon EX17 4HR

Doreen Lock
☎ 0363 866357
BB From £12
EM From £7
Sleeps 5
Listed

Delightful old farmhouse with oak beams and panelling. Tea/coffee-making facilities in all rooms. Situated between Tiverton and Crediton, and midway between north and south coasts and moors. Outstanding views to Dartmoor. 120-acre sheep farm with two doubles and one single. AA listed. Open all year. Map ref: 185 038

Great Bradley Farm, Withleigh, Tiverton, Devon EX16 8JL

Mrs Sylvia Hann
☎ 0884 256946
BB From £16
Sleeps 4
✄ ☡ (8) ☂
♨ ♨ Commended

Great Bradley is the perfect place to relax.Lovely 16th century farmhouse, with original panelling, offering comfort, peace and quiet. Attractive bedrooms with central heating, washbasins, htea/coffee trays and private bathrooms. Guests' lounge with log fire, TV, overlooking the garden and beautiful view beyond. Delicious home cooking and generous hospitality. Non-smokers only please. Open Mar–Oct (inclusive). Map ref: 188 044

Harton Farm, Oakford, Tiverton, Devon EX16 9HH

Mrs Lindy Head
☎ 03985 209
BB From £11
EM From £5
Sleeps 6
🐂 ✄ ☡ (4) ☂
Listed

Welcome to our comfortable stone-built farmhouse dating from 17th century, situated in secluded but accessible position near Exmoor. 1 family, 1 twin room with washbasins. Hearty, traditional home baking using additive-free home-produced meat and organically grown vegetables. Vegetarian menu on request. Tea-making facilities, home-spun wool available. Farm walk with nature notes, friendly animals. Reduction for children. Open all year (closed Christmas & New Year). Map ref: 187 045

Hele Barton Farm, Black Dog, Credition, Devon EX17 4QJ

Mrs Gillian Gillbard
☎ 0884 860278
BB From £13
EM From £8.50
Sleeps 6
☡ ✄
♨

Relax in peaceful surroundings with lovely views from our listed 17th century thatched farmhouse on family-run 236-acre mixed farm, 2 miles off Tiverton – South Molton Road nr Witheridge. 1 family, 1 twin/double with H and C plus 1 children's twin room tea/coffee-making facilities, central heating, 1 guest bathroom, guests' dining room and lounge with colour TV, evening meal by arrangement. Brochure. Open all year (closed Christmas). Map ref: 185 046

Hornhill, Tiverton, Devon EX16 4PL

Barbara Pugsley
☎ 0884 253352
BB From £15
EM From £10
Sleeps 6
✄ ☡ (8) ☂ ♨
♨ ♨ Commended

Overlooking the lovely Exe Valley, 5 mins from Tiverton, Hornhill, with its friendly family atmosphere, is perfect for exploring Devon or just relaxing. Double (4-poster) and twin-bedded rooms with en-suite/private bathrooms, colour TV, tea/coffee facilities, heating, electric blankets. Comfortable drawing room, log fires. Excellent home cooking. Large garden, ample parking. Moors, coasts within easy reach. AA QQQ. Open Mar–Oct. Map ref: 190 044

Lower Collipriest Farm, Tiverton, Devon EX16 4PT

Mrs Linda Olive
☎ 0884 252321
BB From £16.50
EM From £9.50
Sleeps 4
✄ ⌂ ♨
♨ ♨ ♨ **Highly Commended**

Come and relax and enjoy the beauty of the Exe Valley in our 17th century thatched farmhouse. Comfortable lounge with inglenook fireplace and oak beams. Colour TV. Central heating throughout. Twin bedded rooms with bathroom en-suite, tea/coffee-making facilities. Delicious, traditional fresh cooking with our/local produce. Lovely walks over 220-acre dairy farm, conservation pond/woodland area. An AA award-winning farm. Open Easter–Oct. Map ref: 190 044

Newhouse Farm, Oakford, Tiverton, Devon EX16 9JE

Mrs Anne Boldry
☎ 03985 347
BB From £14.50
EM From £9
Sleeps 6
☎ (10) ⌂ ✾
♨ ♨

A perfect base for discovering Devon, our livestock farm is close to Exmoor. A 400-year-old longhouse, tastefully and comfortably furnished featuring oak beams and inglenook. Bedrooms have washbasins, CH, tea trays, en-suite available. We aim to provide the best of farmhouse cooking – original recipes, 13 varieties of marmalade, home-baked bread, delicious puddings our speciality. AA listed. Detailed brochure. Open all year (closed Christmas). Map ref: 188 045

Oburnford Farm, Cullompton, Devon EX15 1LZ

Mrs Gillian Pring
☎ 0884 32292
BB From £17.50
EM From £9.50
Sleeps 14
✄ ☎ ♨ ⌂ ♨
♨ ♨ ♨ **Commended**

Beautiful Georgian farmhouse on peaceful 120-acre mixed farm, comfort and friendly family welcome guaranteed. Superb accommodation and lashings of home-produced fare – award winning. Special diets welcome. Family, double, twin rooms, all en-suite, with tea/coffee-making facilities. Lovely walks over farm, watch the milking and the making of clotted cream! A relaxing break any time of the year. Reductions for children. Open all year. Map ref: 190 040

Palfreys Barton, Cove, Tiverton, Devon EX16 7RZ

Mrs Eileen Babbage
☎ 0398 331 456
BB From £15
EM From £7
Sleeps 4
✄ ☎ ♨ Å ♞ ⌂ ♨
Listed Approved

Palfreys Barton is a working farm with a 17th century farmhouse set in 290 acres of glorious countryside with marvellous views. Facilities locally for golf, riding, fishing, tennis and swimming. Food is a speciality, fresh from the garden. 1 double room, 1 family room, both with washbasin. 1 single room. Dining room and lounge with colour TV. No pets. Open Mar–Oct. Map ref: 190 044

Quoit-at-Cross Farm, Stoodleigh, Tiverton, Devon EX16 9PJ

Mrs Linda Hill
☎ 03985 280
BB From £15
EM From £8
Sleeps 6
☎ ♨ ✾
♨ ♨ ♨

Charming 17th century farmhouse in conservation village. Excellent accommodation, family/double rooms, en-suite, colour TV and tea/coffee-making facilities, delightful inglenook dining room and relaxing lounge. Full English breakfast. Superb dinners. Large garden, ample parking. Easy reach National Trust properties, Exmoor safaris, swimming etc. A361 2½ miles. Open from April. Map ref: 190 044

Stockham Farm, Thelbridge, Crediton, Devon EX17 4SJ

Mrs Carol Webber
☎ 0884 860308
BB From £14
EM From £8
Sleeps 6
✄ ☎ ♞ ♨
♨ ♨

A warm welcome awaits you on our family-run 150-acre working farm 2½ miles off Tiverton-South Molton road near Witheridge. 14th century farmhouse, separate lounge, dining room, games room with information area. All bedrooms have H/C, one with en-suite bathroom, guest bathroom and shower room. Tea/coffee-making facilities, good food, lovely walks. Lots of animals, children especially welcome. Open Easter–Nov. Map ref: 185 046

Wishay Farm, Trinity, Cullompton, Devon EX15 1PE

Mrs Sylvia Baker
☎ 0884 33223
⒝ From £13
EM From £8
Sleeps 6
🐴
👑 👑

Comfortable and spacious 17th century farmhouse, set amid the peace and seclusion of the countryside. Ideal base for touring. Comfortable lounge with colour TV. Central heating. 1 family room with en-suite bathroom, double with separate guests' bathroom, both with colour TV and fridge and a single room. All with tea/coffee-making facilities. Children welcome. Golf and indoor bowls rink nearby. Open Feb–Nov.
Map ref: 190 039

Self-Catering

Brindiwell Farm, Cheriton Fitzpaine, Crediton, Devon EX17 4HR

Doreen Margaret Lock
☎ 0363 866357
⒮Ⓒ From £100–£120
Sleeps 3
🐴
🔑 🔑 Approved

Self-contained wing of delightful old farmhouse in peaceful countryside with outstanding views. One double, one single bedroom and Z bed. Colour TV. Midway between north and south coasts and moors. Close Dartmoor and Exmoor. Open all year. Map ref: 185 038

Cider Cottage, c/o Great Bradley Farm, Withleigh, Tiverton, Devon EX16 9JL

Mrs Sylvia Hann
☎ 0884 256946
⒮Ⓒ From £125–£320
Sleeps 5
🐴 ♨
🔑 🔑 🔑 🔑
Commended

Charming cottage, originally 17th century cider barn, on 155-acre dairy farm. Beautiful views, spacious accommodation for 5. 3 pretty bedrooms. Bed linen included. Comfortable oak-beamed lounge, superb new kitchen with dining area. Washing machine available. All tastefully furnished and equipped to provide a high standard of comfort and convenience. Large garden with picnic table. Walk our country lanes. Explore moors and coasts, or stay and enjoy the farm. Open all year. Map ref: 189 004

Hele Payne Farm, Hele, Exeter, Devon EX5 4PH

Mrs Maynard
☎ 0392 881530/881356
⒮Ⓒ From £80–£275
Sleeps 3/5/6
🐴 ☕ ♨ 🐾
🔑 🔑 🔑 🔑 Commended

Relax in our large swimming pool and enjoy the beautiful gardens. Children welcome to help feed the baby calves. Walking, private game and coarse fishing. Convenient moors/coast. Furnished, cleaned and decorated to a high standard. All units (Honeysuckle Cottage, The Wheat Loft, and Horseshoe Lodge) have colour TV, bed linen, microwave, laundry room, cot, highchair and central heating. Open all year. Map ref: 192 038

Palfreys Barton, Cove, Tiverton, Devon EX16 7RZ

Mrs Eileen Babbage
☎ 0398 331456
⒮Ⓒ From £120–£265
🔑 🔑 🔑

Delightful cottage with marvellous views across the Exe Valley and Dartmoor. Golf, fishing, riding, tennis and swimming within easy reach. 1 double room and 1 family room two single beds. Bathroom, fitted kitchen central heating, gas cooker, washing machine and lounge/diner, colour TV. No pets. Open all year. Map ref: 190 044

Swallowfield, c/o Hornhill, Tiverton, Devon EX16 4PL

Mrs Barbara Pugsley
☎ 0884 253352
SC From £200–£500
Sleeps 8 + cot
✗ ☎
♪ ♪ ♪ ♪ ♪ ♪
Commended

A 5 bedroom luxury modern house overlooking beautiful Exe valley and furnished to a high standard. Central heating. Large kitchen/diner with Aga, electric cooker, dishwasher, fridge freezer and microwave. Utility with washing machine. Large lounge, TV, open gas fuelled fire. 2 bathrooms (1 en-suite) and shower room. Linen provided. Come and explore Devon, the moors and coasts within easy reach or just relax in this peaceful place. Open Apr–Nov. Map ref: 190 044

Wonham Auchengree and Wonham Barton Flat, c/o Wonham Barton, Bampton, Tiverton, Devon EX16 9JZ

Anne McLean Williams
☎ 0398 331312
SC From £110–£235
Sleeps 6; 4/6
♪ ✗ ☎ ♔ ♟ ♠ ✾
♪ ♪ ♪ Approved

In the beautiful Exe Valley near Exmoor, Wonham Barton's generously-equipped, fully heated bungalow and flat, each with own garden, enjoy panoramic views. Cots, highchairs provided. Children welcome, dogs by arrangement. Visitors can enjoy a working farm and 300 acres of pasture and woodland with cattle, sheep, wildflowers, birds and deer. Riding, fishing, swimming, golf nearby. Village 2 miles. Map ref: 191 045

Camping and Caravanning

Palfreys Barton, Cove, Tiverton, Devon EX16 7RZ

Mrs Eileen Babbage
☎ 0398 331 456
⊕ static From
£110–£200 per week
☎ ✗ Å ⊕
✓ ✓ ✓

Two 6-berth static caravans on 290-acre working farm. Beautifully situated in paddock adjacent to the farmhouse, with marvellous views. Quiet, peaceful, lovely walks. Golf, fishing, riding, tennis and swimming within easy reach. Both caravans have shower, flush toilet, H & C water, gas cooker, electric fires, fridge, colour TV. Linen not provided. No pets. Open Mar–Oct. Map ref: 190 044

FARM HOLIDAY BUREAU

THE 1000+ BUREAU MEMBERS OFFER A UNIQUE LINK TO CUSTOMERS ACROSS THE UK

All Bureau members belong to a local Group. Each member can refer you to an equally high quality member within his Group . . . or across the UK: England, Northern Ireland, Scotland, Wales.

58 East Devon

East Devon has picturesque villages and miles of sandy and pebble beaches. This is the country of the old sea dogs of Elizabethan times, such as Sir Francis Drake and Sir Walter Raleigh. East Devon Farm and Country Holiday members offer a choice of farmhouse bed and breakfast, and self-catering accommodation all of a high standard.

Wherever you stay you are not far from the coast where you can enjoy peaceful clifftop walks and spectacular seascapes. Inland a little way you can wander over moors and common land or down winding country lanes. For the more active there's swimming, riding, sailing, fishing and windsurfing.

If it's places of interest you want, East Devon won't let you down – there are craft centres, churches, markets and museums. Exeter alone boasts a cathedral with a 300ft nave – the longest span of unbroken Gothic vaulting in the world, plus priceless manuscripts; a Maritime Museum with more than 100 craft from all over the world, and the Royal Albert Memorial collection of lace, glass and china.

If all that leaves you hungry, you can choose to take meals in village inns, thatched cottage cafés or seaside restaurants. Whatever your choice you will find excellent fare . . . at very fair prices.

Group Contacts: 🅱🅱 **Mrs Kerstin Farmer** ☎ **0404 813385**
🆂🅲 **Mrs Dorothy Glanvill** ☎ **0395 32185**

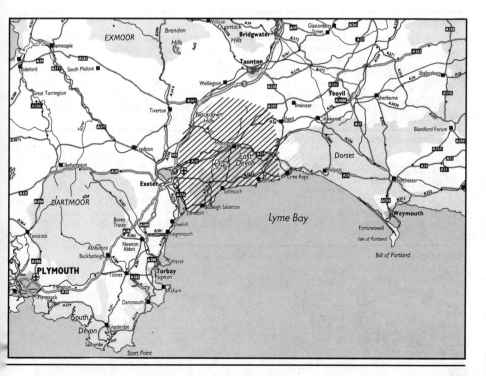

Bed and Breakfast (and evening meal)

Claypits Farm, East Hill, Ottery St Mary, Devon EX11 1QD

Jayne Burrow
☎ 0404 814599
🅱 From £16–£18
EM From £8.50
Sleeps 6
✗ ☡ (3)
♨♨

Relax on our mixed farm in the beautiful Otter Valley. Lovely walks and many attractions nearby, including Sidmouth 4½ miles. Double en-suite, twin and double with washbasins, guests' toilets/bathroom, tea/coffee facilities. Excellent comfortable accommodation, beamed ceilings, CH, large lounge, log burner, dining room. Good farmhouse cooking. Large garden, children's play area, many small animals (chickens, ducks and geese). Open Mar–Nov. Map ref: 196 035

Godford Farm, Awliscombe, Honiton, Devon EX14 0PW

Sally Lawrence
☎ 0404 42825
🅱 From £13
EM From £8.75
Sleeps 6
☡ ♔
♨♨

We invite you to stay on this family-run dairy farm, set in a beautiful river valley. Listed farmhouse with large sitting and dining rooms. Central heating. Colour TV. Drinks facilities in bedrooms. Large garden, play area, games barn for all ages. Families with children especially welcome. Cots and highchairs provided. Family and twin rooms, private bathrooms. Children reduced rates. Brochure. Open Easter–Sept. Map ref: 197 038

Great Houdbeare Farmhouse, Nr Aylesbeare, Exeter, Devon EX5 2DB

Mrs A Spanton
☎ 0404 822 415
🅱 From £17.50
EM From £8
Sleeps 6
✗ ☡ ☡ ☞ ▪
♨♨♨

Attractive 150-year-old farmhouse in totally secluded, peaceful situation. Ideal getaway from noise and bustle of everyday life. Pretty walks through farm woods with wild flowers, wildlife, but within easy reach of places of interest – Exeter, Dartmoor, Exmoor, Budleigh Salterton, Sidmouth. We offer every comfort, log fires, friendly atmosphere. Senior citizens welcome. Car essential. Open most of the year. Map ref: 193 035

Higher Bagmores Farm, Woodbury, Exeter, Devon EX5 1LA

Myrtle Glanvill
☎ 0395 32261
🅱 From £12
Sleeps 6
☡
♨

A working beef, sheep and arable farm, set in delightful Devon countryside. Exmouth 5 miles with sandy beaches and sailing facilities. Exeter 7 miles, the cathedral city of Devon, offers an excellent shopping centre. Bedrooms are equipped with tea/coffee-making facilities, H/C, shaver points. CH, lounge with colour TV. A full English breakfast is served. Ample parking, transport essential. Open Jan–Nov. Map ref: 194 034

Higher Coombe Farm, Tipton St John, Sidmouth, Devon EX10 0AX

Kerstin Farmer
☎ 0404 813385
🅱 From £13
EM From £9
Sleeps 6
☡ ♔ ⚘
♨♨

The Farmer family invite you to a relaxing stay on their sheep and beef farm, peacefully situated in the beautiful Otter Valley yet only 4 miles from Sidmouth seafront. Family, double, single rooms all have washbasins and tea/coffee-making facilities. (no smoking in bedrooms). Lounge with colour TV, separate dining room. Children welcome. Good, mainly home produced, farmhouse food. Full English breakfast. Open Mar–Nov. Map ref: 195 035

Higher Weston Farm, Nr Sidmouth, Devon EX10 0PH

Shirley Macfadyen
☎ 0395 513741
⬚⬚ From £14
Sleeps 6
♿ ✄ ⥅ (5) ⚡
♛ ♛ Commended

Family mixed farm in rural hamlet 2½ miles from Sidmouth. Pretty bedrooms with basins, hot drink facilities, TV, heating, beautiful views to the sea. Comfortable lounge with TV, books, games. We offer a wholesome breakfast with our own produce. Relax in our sunny garden with badminton and croquet areas. Walk along the cliffs, beach or coastal paths. Riding, golf and windsurfing nearby. Stabling and parking available. Open Feb–Nov. Map ref: 197 038

Lemprice Farm, Yettington, Budleigh, Salterton EX9 7BW

Mrs Hanneke Coates
☎ 0395 67037
⬚⬚ From £15–£18
Sleeps 5
⥅ ✄
Listed

This listed old farmhouse is surrounded by an area of outstanding natural beauty and scientific interest. Overlooking marshes abundant with wildlife. Home of the rare barn owl. Eceptional walking area, 3 miles from a blue flag beach. 8 miles from M5 junction 30. All bedrooms have bathroom en suite, tea/coffee-making facilities. Open all year. Map ref: 195 030

Lochinvar, Shepherds Park Farm, Woodbury, Nr Exeter, Devon EX5 1LA

Dorothy Glanvill
☎ 0395 32185
⬚⬚ From £13.50
Sleeps 6
⚡ ⥅ ⥅
♛

Dairy farm situated on the outskirts of Woodbury, with panoramic views of surrounding countryside. Accommodation is 1 double room with shower and washbasin en-suite, 1 family and 1 twin room with washbasin and hot drinks facilities, electric blankets, hair dryers, full CH. Separate toilet and bathroom. English breakfast served. Access to rooms at all times. Ample parking. Local inns and restaurants nearby. Open all year. Map ref: 194 034

Lower Pinn Farm, Peak Hill, Sidmouth, Devon EX10 0NN

Elizabeth Tancock
☎ 0395 513733
⬚⬚ From £16
Sleeps 6
⚡ ⥅ ⥅ ☂
♛ ♛

A friendly welcome and comfortable, spacious rooms await you at Lower Pinn. 2 miles west of the unspoilt coastal resort of Sidmouth. Two double/twin en-suite, one double with washbasin. All rooms have colour TV, tea/coffee facilities, electric blankets. Access at all times. Dining room in which a full English breakfast is served. Ample parking. Several local pubs and restaurants. Open Easter–Nov. Map ref: 196 033

Marianne Pool, Clyst St George, Exeter, Devon EX3 0NZ

Janet Bragg
☎ 0392 874939
⬚⬚ From £13.50
Sleeps 6
⥅
Listed

Situated in a peaceful rural location, 2 miles from M5 J30, and midway between the seaside town of Exmouth and the historic city of Exeter, this thatched Devon longhouse offers spacious family and twin-bedded rooms, with H&C, tea/coffee-making facilities, a comfortable lounge with colour TV and a dining room in which a full English breakfast is served. Large lawned garden ideal for children. Car essential. Open Mar–Nov. Map ref: 192 033

Newcourt Barton, Langford, Cullompton, Devon EX15 1SE

Mrs Sheila A Hitt
☎ 088 47 326
⬚⬚ From £13.50
Sleeps 6
✄ ⥅ (11) ⚓ ⬚ ⬚
Listed

Newcourt Barton is an ideal base for touring the Devon coast and countryside. It is a working farm with sheep. The red brick farmhouse is surrounded by a large garden with grass tennis court. Situated in a quiet position 4 miles Cullompton, M5 J28. Coarse fishing on farm. 1 twin, 1 double, 1 family, H/C, toilet and shower. Tea/coffee-making facilities, TV, lounge, dining room, full English breakfast. Local inn and restaurants for evening meal. Map ref: 193 038

Pinn Barton Farm, Pinn Lane, Peak Hill, Sidmouth, Devon EX10 0NN

Betty Sage
☎ **0395 514004**
BB **From £17**
Sleeps 6
🐎 🐕 🚲
♨ ♨ **Commended**

Enjoy a warm welcome on our 330 acre farm by the coast, 2 miles from Sidmouth seafront. Lovely walks in Area of Outstanding Natural Beauty. Comfortable bedrooms (all en-suite) with CH, colour TV, hot drink facilities, electric blankets, access at all times. TV lounge and dining room with separate tables. Substantial breakfast, bedtime drinks. Many restaurants, inns and places to visit nearby. Open all year. Map ref: 196 033

Pitt Farm, Fairmile, Ottery St Mary, Devon EX11 1NL

Susan Hansford
☎ **0404 812439**
BB **From £13.50**
EM From £8
🚲
Listed

A warm family atmosphere awaits you at this 16th century thatched farmhouse which nestles in the picturesque Otter Valley ½ mile from A30 on B3176. Within easy reach of all East Devon resorts and pleasure facilities. Good home cooking using fresh local/own produce. A working beef/arable farm surrounded by lovely countryside and rural walks. Family, double and twin rooms. Lounge with colour TV. Fire certificate. Open Feb–Nov. Map ref: 196 035

Rydon Farm, Woodbury, Exeter, Devon EX5 1 LB

Sally Glanvill
☎ **0395 32341**
BB **From £15**
Sleeps 6
🐎 💺 🚲 ♨
♨ ♨

Come and enjoy the peaceful tranquillity of our 16th century Devon longhouse on a working dairy farm. Ideal for exploring coast, moors and the historic city of Exeter. Exposed beams and inglenook fireplace. Bedrooms have central heating, washbasins, hair dryers and tea/coffee-making facilities. En-suite available. Full English breakfast with free range eggs. Several local pubs and restaurants. Open all year. Map ref: 194 034

Smallicombe Farm, Northleigh, Colyton, Devon EX13 6BU

Maggie Todd
☎ **040 483 310**
(0404 831310 Spring '93)
BB **From £15**
EM From £8
Sleeps 6
🚲 ♿
♨ ♨

Children are welcome at our small farm set in an area of outstanding natural beauty, but convenient for all East Devon coastal resorts. Friendly animals include Jersey cows, pigs, sheep, goats and numerous poultry. Family suite and ground floor twin bedded rooms all en-suite with tea/coffee-making facilities and colour TV's. Cots, highchairs and baby sitting provided. Children's play area and games room. Children and weekly rates reduced. Open all year. Map ref: 200 036

Wiscombe Linhaye, Southleigh, Colyton, Devon EX13 6JF

Sheila Rabjohns
☎ **040 487 342**
BB **From £15**
EM From £6
Sleeps 6
♿ 🚲 (5) 🐎 🍴
♨

A small working farm in the quiet countryside of East Devon but in reach of Sidmouth and Branscombe. A friendly atmosphere on this family farm with good home cooking from home/local produce. Two ground floor bedrooms with private bathroom. Drink facilities, TV and hair dryers in all bedrooms. Colour TV in lounge and separate dining tables. 1 double, 1 twin en-suite, 1 family room. Open Mar–Nov. Map ref: 202 034

Please mention **Stay on a Farm** when booking

Self-Catering

Bodmiscombe Farm, Blackborough, Nr Cullompton, Devon EX15 2HR

Mrs Brenda Northam
☎ 08846 315
SC From £100–£240
Sleeps 2/5
☼ ⌖ ⅄
⚷ ⚷ ⚷ **Commended**

A warm welcome assured on our 200-acre family run farm set in the Blackdown Hills. Lovely views from self-contained part of listed Devon longhouse with beamed ceilings. Private coarse fishing and woodland nature trail. Central north/south coasts and moorland. Large garden. All linen supplied. Electricty not metered. Pets by arrangement. Colour TV, microwave. Short breaks, brochure. Open Mar–Dec (incl). Map ref: 194 037

Court Brook Farm, Clyst St George, Devon EX3 0NT

Jenny Broom
☎ 0392 877710
Fax 0392 873378
SC From £95–£235
Sleeps 2/5 cot
☼ ⌖
⚷ ⚷ **Approved**

Relax in our comfortably furnished cottage in the small village of Clyst St. George. An ideal touring base only 5 miles from Exmouth and 5 miles to Exeter's Cathedral City. IN easy reach of Dartmoor. Well equipped kitchen/diner, lounge with colour TV, bathroom with bath/shower. 3 bedrooms, 1 twin, 1 double, 1 single. Garden with picnic furniture and ample parking, full details available. Open Mar–Nov. Mapr ref: 192 033

Lee Ford, Budleigh Salterton, Devon EX9 7AJ

Mrs N Lindsay-Fynn
☎ 0395 445894
Fax 0395 446219
SC From £120–£600
☼ ⅋
⚷ ⚷ ⚷ – ⚷ ⚷ ⚷ ⚷
Commended to Highly Commended

Near the seaside town of Budleigh Salterton, Lee Ford is a romantic 40-acre estate which offers holiday accommodation in two cottages each sleeping 5/6 and a studio flat for 2+2. All with colour TV, microwave ovens, self-dial phones, cot and linen available, barbecues. Some with central heating, washer-dryer, freezer, dishwasher, video. Tennis court. Golf, riding, sub-aqua, wind-surfing and country pursuits nearby. Open all year. Map ref: 195 030

Lemprice Farm, Yettington, Budleigh, Salterton EX9 7BW

Mrs Hanneke Coates
☎ 0395 67037
SC From £100–£390
Sleeps 5
☼ ⅄
⚷ ⚷ ⚷ ⚷

Three south-facing stone barn cottages. Purpose designed for disabled and elderly. Exceptional walking area of outstanding natural beauty and scientific interest. All cottage gardens overlook small lake and marshes with abundant wildlife; open countryside beyond. Bed linen, etc., heating, TV included. Dogs by arrangement only. Laundry room. Three miles to beach, 8 miles M5 junction 30. Brochure. Open all year. Map ref: 195 030

Odle Farm, Upottery, Honiton, Devon EX14 9QE

Linda Wyatt
☎ 0404 86272
SC From £90–£290
Sleeps 2/7
⌖ ☼
⚷ ⚷ ⚷ ⚷
Approved

Peacefully sheltered in the picturesque Otter Valley, where the Wyatt family assure you a warm welcome. Odle Farm is secluded, yet accessible for all activities. Choose from the farmhouse annexe or farm bungalow, both fully equipped and well furnished. Dining service available in farmhouse. Open all year. Map ref: 190 068

The Old Dairy, Courtmoor Farm, Upottery, Honiton, Devon EX14 9QA

Sally Cooke
☎ 0404 86316
SC From £95–£255
Sleeps 6
Commended

Relax and enjoy picturesque views of the Otter Valley on our 200-acre working family farm. Secluded yet ideal touring centre, Honiton only 5 miles. Spacious, comfortable furnished self-contained wing of farmhouse, 3 bedrooms. Bathroom, lounge with colour TV, large kitchen/diner with washing machine, tumble dryer, microwave, fridge, freezer, linen provided. CH. Garden play area plus barbecue. Brochure. Open all year. Map ref: 199 038

Otter Holt and Owl Hayes, c/o Godford Farm, Awliscombe, Honiton, Devon EX14 0PW

Sally Lawrence
☎ 0404 42825
SC From £80–£265
Sleeps 4 cot

Commended

Come and see where the hayracks are in our beautiful barn cottages, one of the many features that make them unique. Each cottage comprises beamed lounge with colour TV, pine kitchen/diner with washer/dryer, microwave, fridge/freezer. CH. 2 bedrooms (linen included). Shower room. Relax in the garden and games barn, or watch the cows being milked. Children welcome, large play area. Cot available. Brochure. Open all year. Map ref: 197 038

Smallicombe Farm, Northleigh, Colyton, Devon EX13 6BU

Maggie Todd
☎ 0404 83310
(0404 831310 Spring '93)
SC From £90–£375
Sleeps 2–8 + cots

Commended

Small farm in superb rural setting yet close to coast. Large variety of friendly farm animals including Jersey cows, pigs, sheep, goats and poultry. Chidlren's play area and games room. Recently converted barns retaining original features sleep 2/4, 4/5 and 6/8. One specially designed for wheelchair users. All units have automatic washing machines, microwaves, cots, linen. Open all year. Map ref: 200 036

The Stable, Heathstock Farm, Stockland, Honiton, Devon EX14 9EU

Mrs N Patch
☎ 0404 88267
SC From £100–£210
Sleeps 2/4

Approved

Set in a pretty hillside hamlet, The Stable is on one level and situated on a working family farm. Well furnished, with large lounge with bed settee, colour TV, storage heaters, kitchen with washer/dryer, bathroom, double bedroom. Relax in grounds or on patio, and watch hens roaming and cows coming for milking. Enjoy wonderful Devon views. 9 miles coast. Open Mar–Dec. Map ref: 199 038

BUREAU ACCOMMODATION IS RELIABLE

This Guide lists **Farm Holiday Bureau** members only. They are all inspected by the National Tourist Board for standards (see introduction pages) and by fellow members to maintain a high quality.

FARM HOLIDAY BUREAU

59 Dartmoor & South Devon

If you enjoy the outdoor life, this area offers unlimited opportunities in the 365 square miles of Dartmoor National Park, with its contrasting open moorland, wooded valleys and the coast. Walking, horseriding, climbing, birdwatching and golf, or alternatively coarse, game and sea-fishing, sailing and windsurfing, are all within approximately half an hour's drive.

Also easily accessible are many places of interest. Dartington Hall, centre of culture and the arts, Buckfast Abbey, the Dart Valley Steam Railway and the Shire Horse Centre. You may also visit historical sites from the Bronze Age onwards, country mansions, busy markets, antique and craft shops, country parks, National Trust properties, museums and resorts of all kinds from bustling Torquay to tranquil villages.

Food and drink can be a special delight in this part of the world. No visit would be complete without sampling a traditional cream tea . . . and the best of this delicacy should come with a yellow crust and be thick enough to stand your spoon in. Then there's the local cider!

And for appetites of a different kind you can spend your evenings enjoying the theatre, concert and show life on offer in Torquay, Paignton, Plymouth and Exeter.

Group Contacts: BB **Sue Wills ☎ 0364 661506/ Fax 0364 661516**
  SC **Mrs Angela Bell ☎ 036 42 391**

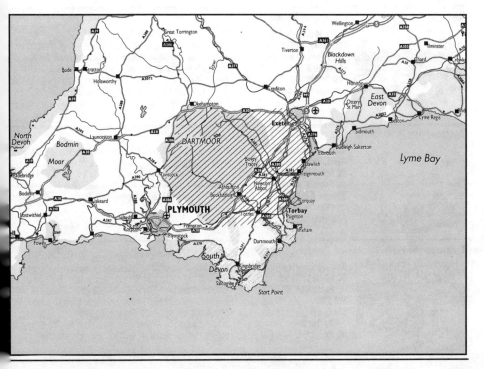

Bed and Breakfast (and evening meal)

Adams Hele Farm, Ashburton, South Devon TQ13 7NW

Dorothy Dent
☎ 0364 52525
🅱 From £13.50
EM From £6.50
Sleeps 6
🐴 🛏

This 16th century listed farmhouse with oak beams and log fires nestles on a south facing hill overlooking the Dart valley and moors. It is a comfortable base from which to explore Dartmoor and the South Devon coast. 90 acres stocked with ponies, cattle and sheep. Peace, comfort and good home cooking with farm and local produce. 3 spacious double rooms all with H/C, tea/coffee-making facilities. Open Feb–Nov. Map ref: 184 026

Berry Farm, Berry Pomeroy, Totnes, Devon TQ9 6LG

Mrs Geraldine Nicholls
☎ 0803 863231
🅱 From £13
Sleeps 6
🚫 🛏 (3)
Listed Commended

Family working farm, warm welcome. Clean comfortable and good food accommodation as features in the Daily Telegraph magazine. Spacious rooms, well appointed. Bathrrom with seperate shower, separate WC, lounge, TV, good local eating places recommended, close to coast and within easy reach of Dartmoor. Open all year. Map ref: 182 022

Budleigh Farm, Morehampstead, Devon TQ13 8SB

Mrs Judith Harvey
☎ 0647 40835
🅱 From £13
Sleeps 5
🛏 🐴 ♞
🛁 **Commended**

Lovely old thatched farmhouse, a listed building, set in the Wray Valley, part of the Dartmoor National Park, ½ mile from Moretonhampstead. Just off the A382 which makes Budleigh easy to find and a good base for exploring the area. Pretty garden. Fishing, riding and golf nearby. Target shooting and archery on site. Open Feb–Dec. Map ref: 184 032

Coombe Farm, Kingsbridge, South Devon TQ7 4AB

Beni & Jonathan Robinson
☎ 0548 852038
🅱 From £16.50
Sleeps 6
🛏 (12) 🐴 🚫 ♣
Applied

Come and enjoy the peace and beauty of Devon in our lovely 17th century farmhouse. Wonderful breakfast, large elegant rooms each with own bathroom, colour TV, hot drink facilities. Artists have the use of an art studio, and fishermen the well known Coombe Water fishery. Open all year. Map ref: 183 01£

Crannacombe Farm, Hazlewood, Loddiswell, Nr Kingsbridge, South Devon TQ7 4DX

Shirley Bradley
☎ 0548 550256
🅱 From £14.50
EM £8
Sleeps 6
🚫 🛁 🐴 ♞

In an area of outstanding natural beauty near Kingsbridge. Working farm, Georgian farmhouse, comfortable, informal, absolutely peaceful. We have family/double bedrooms with private bathrooms and TV and a separate children's room sleeping 2. Lovely views, walks and a clean river to paddle, play and picnic by. Wholesome food, prize winning cider, children's pool. Hot drink facilities. Map ref: 183 018

Dodbrooke Farm, Michelcombe, Holne, Newton Abbot, Devon TQ13 7SP

Judy Henderson
☎ 0364 3461
[BB] From £11–£14
Sleeps 6
🐕 🐎 🐾
Listed

Dodbrooke Farm is a listed 17th century former longhouse in an idyllic valley at the foot of Dartmoor. Food is mostly home produced and the rooms are warm and comfortable. There are sheep and goats on the farm and a lovely garden for guests to explore. Come and enjoy a friendly atmosphere with local walking, riding and carriage driving. Open all year (closed Christmas). Map ref: 182 025

Foales Leigh, Harberton, Totnes, Devon TQ9 7SS

Carol Chudley
☎ 0803 862365
[BB] From £13
EM From £9
Sleeps 6
🐎 🎪 🐾 💬
🏆 Commended

A charming 16th century farmhouse in traditional courtyard setting this 250-acre family farm is situated in peaceful surroundings within attractive unspoilt countryside but within easy reach of beaches, moors and towns. Comfortable accommodation includes large oak-beamed lounge with woodburner, games room, spacious family double en-suite, double room, twin room with luxury bathroom. Open Jan–Nov. Map ref: 185 022

Frenchbeer Farm, Chagford, Devon TQ13 8EX

Christine Malseed
☎ 0647 432427
[BB] From £15
Sleeps 6
🐕 ✂ 🐎
🏆

Thatched 16th century Devon longhouse situated in beautiful unspoilt countryside in Dartmoor National Park. Enjoy the friendly informal atmosphere on our working sheep and beef farm. Ideal base for walking, riding, fishing, touring or simply to relax and unwind. Basins in bedrooms with tea/coffee facilities. Lounge with colour TV. Good local eating places recommended in and around Chagford. Open Jan–Nov (incl). Map ref: 181 033

Frost Farm, Hennock Road, Bovey Tracey, South Devon TQ13 9PP

Linda Harvey
☎ 0626 833266
[BB] From £15
EM From £9
Sleeps 6
🐎 ✂ 🚾 ▪
🏆 Commended

A pretty, pink-washed thatched farmhouse by old cider orchards. Two double rooms en-suite, 1 twin bedded with private bathroom, pine-furnished with beverages and colour TV. Good wholesome breakfast. At the close of the day, enjoy a Devonshire supper with local meats, produce and delicious Devonshire cream – "perfick"! 1 ½ miles Bovey Tracey, 10 minutes from A38. Ring for brochure. Open all year. Map ref: 185 028

Great Court Farm, Weston Lane, Totnes, Devon TQ9 6LB

Janet Hooper
☎ 0803 862326
[BB] From £13
EM From £8
Sleeps 6
✂ 🐎
🏆

A warm welcome, views of Totnes and comfortable, friendly accommodation awaits you at our 400-acre dairy farm running down to the River Dart. Colour co-ordinated spacious bedrooms with tea/coffee-making facilities, washbasins, central heating, 1 family/twin, 2 doubles, 2 bathrooms/shower, separate toilet. Guest lounge with colour TV. Dining room to enjoy good food. Evening meal by arrangement. Playroom, garden. Plenty of inns and restaurants nearby. Open Jan–Nov. Map ref: 185 022

Great Sloncombe Farm, Moretonhampstead, Newton Abbot, Devon TQ13 8QF

Mrs Trudie Merchant
☎ 0647 40595
[BB] From £15
EM From £9
Sleeps 6
🐕 🐎 ✂
🏆 🏆 Commended

Share the magic of Dartmoor all year round whilst staying in our lovely 13th century farmhouse. A working dairy farm set amongst meadows and woodland, abundant in wild flowers and animals. A welcoming place to relax and explore Devon. Comfortable double and twin rooms with en-suite or private bathrooms and central heating. Plenty of delicious home-cooked Devonshire food. Open all year. Map ref: 183 033

Greenwell Farm, Nr Meavy, Yelverton, Plymouth, Devon PL20 6PY

Bridget Cole
☎ 0822 853563
BB From £20
EM From £11
Sleeps 6

Fresh country air, breathtaking views and scrumptious country cuisine set the scene at Greenwell. This busy farming family welcomes you to share the countryside and wildlife. Set in the Dartmoor National Park is ideal for the walking enthusiasts and for visiting National Trust properties. Plymouth, Cornwall and South Devon coast only 8 miles. 2 double rooms en-suite, 1 twin. Private facilities. Wine licence. Weekly discounts. Open all year (closed Christmas). Map ref: 175 025

Higher Michelcombe Farm, Holne, Nr Ashburton, Devon TQ13 7SP

Mrs Jacqueline Parsons
☎ 03643 483
BB From £15
EM From £7.50
Sleeps 5

Listed

Stone-built, fully modernised and well appointed farmhouse accommodation. Relaxed friendly atmosphere, good food. Comfort guaranteed. Beautiful and peaceful valley setting extending into the hills of southern Dartmoor. The ideal base for walking, riding, golfing, fishing and touring. Within easy reach of beaches, historic towns and pretty villages. 3 miles from A38. Stabling. Open all year (closed Christmas). Map ref: 182 025

Higher Venton Farm, Widecombe-in-the-Moor, Newton Abbot, South Devon TQ13 7TF

Mrs Betty Hicks
☎ 0364 2235
BB From £13
EM From £7
Sleeps 6

Listed

A friendly welcome awaits you at Higher Venton Farm, a 16th century thatched Devon longhouse and working farm. Peaceful and relaxing, ideal for touring Dartmoor, coast 16 miles. Riding stable nearby. 1 double en-suite and 1 twin all with washbasins and CH. Car spaces. Good home cooking and local produce. The farmer, Peter, takes the part of Uncle Tom Cobbleigh on Widecombe Fair Day. Open all year. Map ref: 183 026

Kellinch Farm, Bickington, Newton Abbot, Devon TQ12 6PB

Frances Pike
☎ 0626 821252
BB From £15, weekly £95
EM From £8.50
Sleeps 4

🐾 🏆 Commended

Secluded working livestock farm set in beautiful, rolling landscape central for Dartmoor, coast and many places of interest. Enjoy a warm, friendly atmosphere, good country cooking, fresh farm produce. TV lounge with inglenook, separate dining room. 1 twin, 1 double, both with en suite. Cot and highchair available. Children's play area. Games and laundry room. Many tame animals. Open all year. Map ref: 184 026

Lower Southway Farm, Widecombe-in-the-Moor, Devon TQ13 7TE

Dawn Nosworthy
☎ 0364 2277
BB From £12
EM From £10
Sleeps 6

Listed

Situated in the lovely valley of Widecombe-in-the-Moor within the Dartmoor National Park with superb views. Ideal for walking, riding or touring Dartmoor. Excellent farmhouse food. 1 family, 1 twin, each with H/C, tea/coffee-making facilities and heating. Lounge with colour TV. Open all year. Map ref: 183 026

Marridge Farm, Ugborough, Nr Ivybridge, South Devon PL21 0HR

Fiona Winzer
☎ 0548 82 469
BB From £15
EM From £8
Sleeps 6

Traditional, family-run dairy farm in the heart of peaceful countryside. Local unspoilt sandy beaches and the beautiful scenery of Dartmoor. Good home cooked food, cream and fresh vegetables. Children welcome. Baby-sitting available. Open all year. Map ref: 181 021

Mill Farm, Kenton, Exeter, Devon EX6 8JR

Delia Lambert
☎ 0392 832471
[BB] From £14
Sleeps 12
🛏 🍴
Listed Commended

One mile from the picturesque village of Kenton and historic Powderham Castle, beside the River Kenn discover Mill Farm. We offer very comfortable accommodation in lovely rural setting with plenty of excellent local eating places to sample. Dartmoor 20 minutes – M5 Exeter, Birdwatching, forest walks, beaches all 4 miles. So many different aspects of our beautiful county to explore. Open Mar–Oct. Map ref: 191 030

Mill Leat Farm, Holne, Ashburton, Newton Abbot, Devon TQ13 7RZ

Dawn Cleave
☎ 0364 3283
[BB] From £13
EM From £7.70
Sleeps 6
🛏
Listed Approved

120-acre hill farm situated on the edge of Dartmoor, an ideal place for touring Devon's beautiful countryside, moorland or beaches. Comfortable accommodation in 18th century farmhouse with large spacious bedrooms. Very peaceful surroundings, just right for relaxing. Open all year. Map ref: 182 025

Narracombe Farm, Ilsington, Newton Abbot, Devon TQ13 9RD

Sue Wills
☎ 0364 661506
Fax 0364 661516
[BB] From £14
Sleeps 6
🐴 🛏 ✂
Listed Commended

Come and relax and enjoy the hospitality and informality that are always assured at Narracombe. Lovely home, mostly dating back to 16th century, surrounded by beautiful countryside and spectacular views. Spacious and well appointed twin and double rooms, CH, family lounge with colour TV, bathroom with shower and delicious farmhouse breakfasts. A large rambling garden. Reductions for children. Open Jan–Nov. Map ref: 183 024

New Cott Farm, Poundsgate, Newton Abbot, Devon TQ13 7PD

Margaret Phipps
☎ 0364 3421
[BB] From £16
EM From £9.50
Sleeps 6
♿ ✂ 🛏 (3) ☛ ♨
♨♨ Commended

A friendly welcome, beautiful views, pleasing accommodation await you at New Cott. The farm adjoins Dr Blackall's Drive on Two Moors Way. Come letterboxing, trout fishing, bird watching, walk the farm trail, experience the peace and quiet in open moorland and in the Dart Valley. All bedrooms en-suite with tea/coffee, heating. Lots of lovely home made food. Free range eggs and clotted cream. Short breaks welcome, weekly reductions. Open all year. Map ref: 182 025

Peek Hill Farm, Dousland, Yelverton, Devon PL20 6PD

Justine Colton
☎ 0822 852908
[BB] From £12
EM From £5.50
Sleeps 6 + cot
🐴 🛏 ✂ ♨
Listed

Children especially welcomed on our mixed farm. Easily located on B3212 Yelverton – Princetown road. Walk on the moor, visit local historic market towns, good sporting, leisure facilities and night life near by. Family cycle hire on farm. High tea and packed lunch on request. Open Jan–Nov. Map ref: 175 025

Penlee Farm, Postbridge, Yelverton, Devon PL20 6TJ

Mrs Felicity McMurtrie
☎ 0822 88207
[BB] From £17
Sleeps 5
🐴 🛏 (8) ✂ 🧍 🐴
♨♨ Approved

Penlee Farm is a Grade II listed Edwardian house standing above the East Dart Valley at Postbridge, in the centre of Dartmoor. Enjoy this working mixed farm which includes rare breeds of animals and offers excellent livery stabling for horses. Spacious and well appointed south-facing bedrooms. 1 double, 1 twin-bedded, 1 single. Lounge with colour TV. Open Easter–Oct. Map ref: 185 034

Smallacombe Farm, Dawlish, Devon EX7 0PS

Mrs Alison Thomson
☎ 0626 862536
🛏 From £13.50
EM From £7
Sleeps 6

Smallacombe Farm is a 120-acre working farm with sheep and free-range hens, surrounded by peaceful country views yet only 2 miles from Dawlish and the Blue Flag beaches. Enjoy an evening barbecue, relax in the garden while children play safely with no busy road. With Dartmoor, Exeter and Torquay only 30 mins drive away, Smallacombe is an ideal base from which to enjoy south Devon. Open all year (closed Christmas). Map ref: 191 028

Strashleigh, Ivybridge, Devon PL21 9JP

Mrs Paula Salter
☎ 0752 892226
🛏 From £13
Sleeps 6

Listed

A comfortable bed and a delicious, farmhouse breakfast awaits you. Strashleigh is a working farm, situated on the A38 near Ivybridge. The house provides an interesting history and wide views of beautiful Devonshire countryside. Perfect base for touring, beaches. City entertainment, sports facilities and tourist attractions. 1 double room with H&C, 1 family room, 1 twin, all with tea-making facilities. Lounge with CTV. Open April–Oct. Map ref: 180 019

Venn Farm, Ugborough, Ivybridge, Devon PL21 0PE

Pat Stephens
☎ 0364 73240
🛏 From £16
EM From £9
Sleeps 12

🐾🐴 🛁

🐚 🐚 **Commended**

Working farm amid peaceful scenery in the South Hams on edge of Dartmoor. Easy access to Plymouth, Exeter and many beaches. Children encouraged to take an interest in farm life. The speciality of the house is 'carve your own roasts' and the atmosphere is friendly and relaxed. Large garden with pretty streams help you unwind. Most rooms en-suite. Open Jan–Nov. Map ref: 180 019

Wellpark Farm Bungalow, Dean Prior, Buckfastleigh, Devon TQ11 0LY

Mrs Rosemarie Palmer
☎ 0364 43775
🛏 From £12
EM From £5
Sleeps 6 cot

🌿🐴

Listed Commended

Wellpark dairy farm is set onthe edge of the Dartmoor National Park. Comfortable/relaxing and friendly atmosphere. Ideal base for touring/beaches. Tea/coffee-making facilities, afternoon teas with homemade Devon scones. Wood burning fires in colder months. Plus many excellent local eating places. Open Feb–Nov. Map ref: 183 023

Wellpritton Farm, Holne, Ashburton, South Devon TQ13 7RX

Sue Townsend
☎ 0364 3273
🛏 From £15
EM From £8
Bedrooms 4

🐴♿🐕🛁

🐚🐚 **Highly Commended**

A beautiful farmhouse on the edge of Dartmoor, where goats, donkeys, rabbits and chickens are kept and sometimes sheep and cattle. Only ½ hour drive from Exeter, Plymouth and Torbay with riding, fishing, walking, sailing and golf nearby. Modernised to high standard – most rooms en-suite, games room and swimming pool. Caring personal attention. Farm produced food. Weekly rates B&B & EM From £133. Open all year (closed Christmas). Map ref: 182 025

West Cannamore Farm, Wrangaton, South Brent, Devon TQ10 9HA

Mrs P E Wakeham
☎ 0364 72250
🛏 From £12
EM From £7
Sleeps 6

♿🐴

Listed

Spacious farm bungalow on 80-acre mainly arable farm. Easy access from A38, close to moors, golf, horse riding and Ivybridge leisure centre. Local beaches within easy reach. 2 double, 1 twin with H & C and tea-making facilities. Full English breakfast and good home cooking. No dogs in house. Open all year. Map ref: 186 023

Whitemoor Farm, Doddiscombsleigh, Nr Exeter, Devon EX6 7PU

Mrs Barbara Lacey
☎ 0647 52423
BB From £13.50
EM From £7.50
Sleeps 6

Listed 16th century thatched farmhouse, set in seclusion of its own garden and farmland within easy reach of Exeter, coast, Dartmoor and forest walks. The Cobb House has exposed beams, log fires. Home made preserves. Good meals at local inn. Evening meal on request. Children and pets welcome. Open all year. Map ref: 188 031

Wooston Farm, Moretonhampstead, Newton Abbot, Devon TQ13 8QA

Mary Cuming
☎ 0647 40367
BB From £14
EM From £8
Sleeps 6
(3)
Commended

Wooston Farm is situated above the Teign Valley in the Dartmoor National Park with views over open moorland. The farmhouse is surrounded by a delightful garden. There are plenty of walks on the moor and wooded Teign Valley adjoining farm. Good home cooking and cosy log fires await you at Wooston. 2 double en-suite, 1 with four-poster, 1 family room. Also mountain bikes available. Open all year except Christmas. AA listed. Map ref: 183 032

Self-Catering

Budleigh Farm, Morehampstead, Devon TQ13 8SB

Mrs Judith Harvey
☎ 0647 40835
SC From £70–£290
Sleeps 6

Up to
Commended

Six cottages and flats, converted from barns, each with its own character, on a sheep farm tucked into the end of the Wray Valley ½ mile from Moretonhampstead. Outdoor swimming pool, barbecue; table tennis and darts; target shooting and archery on site; golf, fishing and riding nearby. Excellent centre for exploring the area. Open Jan–Dec. Map ref: 184 032

Crownley, c/o Mill Combe, Ilsington, Newton Abbot, Devon TQ13 9RT

Mrs Sue Retallick
☎ 0364 661430
SC max £190
Sleeps 5/7

Commended

Crownley bungalow is fully furnished with 3 bedrooms and a sofa bed in the sitting room, kitchen/diner, garden and parking. Set in a lovely valley with woods and fields and the moor just over the hill. Ideal for touring Dartmoor and South Devon. Plymouth, Exeter, Torquay within easy reach. Sea approx 14 miles away. Linen included. Children and pets welcome. Open Easter–Oct. Map ref: 184 028

Murtwell Farm Cottage, Murtwell Farm, Diptford, Totnes, Devon TQ9 7NQ

Nicola de Pulford
☎ and fax 05488 2207
SC From £223–£458
Sleeps 6 + cot

Applied

Enjoy the relaxed atmosphere of our small working farm, set in an area of outstanding beauty. Close to both coast and moors. Converted threshing barn. 3 en-suite bedrooms, large lounge/dining room, fitted kitchen, all beautifully furnished. Central heating, log burning fire, stabling and grazing available. Open all year. Map ref: 184 022

Narramore Farm Cottages, Narramore Farm, Moretonhampstead, Devon TQ13 8QT

John & Sue Bennett
☎ 0647 40455
SC From £121–£398
♨ 🐾 🐕 ♿
🔑 🔑 🔑 🔑 **Highly Commended**

Narramore is a 107-acre farm favouring conservation and traditional farming methods. The land is blessed with flower and fauna, wildlife ranges from foxes to badgers and buzzards. Our luxury barn converted cottages make an ideal haven to relax from the stresses of life in peace and quiet of the countryside. Evening meal available. Open all year.
Map ref: 184 032

Seale Stoke, Holne, Newton Abbot, Devon TQ3 7SS

Pat & Charles Hill-Smith
☎ 03643408
SC From £160–£300
♨ 🐕
🔑 🔑 🔑 🔑 **Approved**

Traditional stone-built organic stock farm, situated above River Dart valley and woods on the edge of Dartmoor. Magnificent views and good walking. One mile from Holne village at the end of a quiet lane. Comfortable and equipped to highest standards, for 6. Three bedrooms, open plan kitchen/sitting room and bathroom. Linen, towels, colour TV provided. Open Easter–Oct. OS ref: SX695708. Map ref: 182 024

Shippen and Dairy Cottages, c/o Lookweep Farm, Liverton, Newton Abbot, Devon TQ12 6HT

Averil Corrick
☎ 0626 833277
SC From £115–£340
Sleeps 4/5 cot
🐕 🐈
🔑 🔑 🔑 – 🔑 🔑 🔑 🔑
Commended

Come and relax in the peace and tranquillity of these two delightful barn converted cottages. Set within the Dartmoor National Park with easy access to the coast, golf, riding, walking and fishing locally. Sleeps 4/5, fully equipped and well furnished throughout. Own gardens with beautiful views. Ample parking. Use of outdoor heated swimming pool. High chairs, cots and linen available. Open all year.
Map ref: 186 026

Stickwick Farm Holiday Homes, c/o Frost Farm, Bovey Tracey, South Devon TQ13 9PP

Linda Harvey
☎ 0626 833266
SC From £125–£345
Sleeps 2/12
🐕 🍴 🐈 ▪
🔑 🔑 🔑 🔑 –
🔑 🔑 🔑 🔑 🔑
Commended

Our holiday homes are delightful with lots of pictures, pottery and pretty bed linen. Wonderful wildlife and walks. Enjoy a fine selection of homemade fayre. Gardens, games room, children's farmyard. Georgian House (8 bedrooms) Farmhouse (3 bedrooms) Cottage (2 bedrooms). Dishwashers, laundry facilities, microwaves and more . . . ring for brochure today. Open all year. Map ref: 185 029

Strashleigh Farm, Ivybridge, Devon PL21 9JP

Mrs Paula Salter
☎ 0752 892226
SC From £110–£200
Sleeps 2 + cot
🐕
🔑 🔑 🔑 **Approved**

Peacefully set with views of Dartmoor, Strashleigh annex is a 1 level self-contained wing of the farmhouse. Double bedroom with en-suite bathroom; newly fitted kitchen with dishwasher and a cosy open plan living area with a beautiful granite mullion window, woodburner and colour TV. Being near A38 its a perfect base for many attractions and activities. Brochure available. Open all year. Map ref: 179 020

Wooder Manor, Widecombe-in-the-Moor, Newton Abbot, Devon TQ13 7TR

Mrs Angela Bell
☎ 03642 391
SC From £90–£460
Sleeps 2/12
♿ 🐕 🐈 ▪
🔑 🔑 🔑 **Commended**

Cottages and converted coachhouse on 108-acre family farm, nestled in picturesque valley surrounded by unspoilt woodland, moors and granite tors. Central for touring Devon and exploring Dartmoor by foot or on horseback. Clean and fully equipped. Colour TVs, laundry facilities, central heating. Gardens, courtyard for easy parking. Good food at local inn (¾ mile). Choose a property to suit you from our brochure. Open all year. Map ref: 182 028

60   Moor to Shore in Devon

The South Hams in South Devon is a unique part of the West Country, catering for a wide variety of tastes. The area lies between Plymouth and Torbay, is easily accessible from the A38 and is renowned for its beauty and variety of countryside. Not just the countryside either – it has such towns as Elizabethan Totnes with its castle, or the historic seaport of Dartmouth scattered around the Dart estuary and plenty of attractive villages.

The coastline, which is truly spectacular, has sheltered harbours and estuaries at Yealm, Salcombe and Dartmouth.

Fishing, riding and golf can be enjoyed in many places and if you could ever possibly tire of the area, turn north and the Dartmoor National Park is just a stone's throw away. The mild climate of the area makes it particularly attractive for out-of-season visits.

The area also includes wildlife and country parks, a Shire Horse centre at Dunstone near Yealmpton and a wide variety of interesting museums. For those fans of steam, the area boasts two steam railways on the Dart Valley Railway, one of which connects with Totnes main line.

Group Contact: Mrs Jill Balkwill ☎ 0548 550312

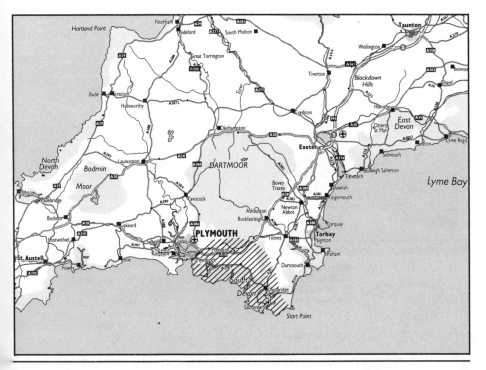

Bed and Breakfast (and evening meal)

Burton Farm, Galmpton, Kingsbridge, South Devon TQ7 3EY

David & Anne Rossiter
☎ 0548 561210
[BB] From £17
EM From £7.95
Sleeps 17
✠ ⛟ 🐎 🏕 🛌 🐑 ☂
♨ ♨ Commended

Working dairy and sheep farm situated in the valley running towards Hope Cove. 3 miles from famous sailing haunt at Salcombe. Walking, beaches, sailing, windsurfing, bathing, diving, fishing. Guests welcome to enjoy the farm's activities according to season. Traditional farmhouse cooking, home produce (clotted cream, etc). 4 course dinner. Access to rooms at all times. En-suite available and washbasins. Tea-making facilities. Welcome assured. Map ref: 185 013

Court Barton Farmhouse, Aveton Gifford, Kingsbridge, Devon TQ7 4LE

John & Jill Balkwill
☎ 0548 550312
[BB] From £16
Sleeps 18
🐎 ☕ ♿ ✗
♨ ♨ Commended

Delightful 16th century listed manor farmhouse situated in 40-acre farm. Accommodation in 7 bedrooms, mostly en-suite, tea/coffee-making facilities. Comfortable TV lounge with lots of books, sunny breakfast room to enjoy delicious country farmhouse breakfasts. Full central heating and log fires in colder weather. Close to moorland, beaches, ideal centre for walking, sailing, fishing, birdwatching. Open all year (closed Christmas). Map ref: 181 016

Gabber Farm, Down Thomas, Plymouth, Devon PL9 0AW

Margaret MacBean
☎ 0752 862269
[BB] From £13
EM From £7
Sleeps 12
⛟ 🏕 ☂
Listed

A warm welcome is assured on this working dairy farm in an area of outstanding natural beauty. Situated on the coast near Plymouth, with the beaches of Wembury and Bovisand nearby. Good home cooking, tea-making facilities in the double, family and twin bedded rooms. Children's room available. Open Mar–Nov. Map ref: 173 020

Helliers Farm, Ashford, Aveton Gifford, Kingsbridge, Devon TQ7 4ND

Christine Lancaster
☎ 0548 550689
[BB] From £15.50
Sleeps 9
✠ ⛟ ☕ ♿
♨ ♨

A small sheep farm set on a hill overlooking a lovely valley, an ideal centre for touring the coasts, moors and Plymouth. Recently modernised accommodation comprises family, double, twin and single rooms, all with washbasins and tea/coffee facilities. Double or family en-suite. 2 bathrooms, lounge, TV, games room. Trout pond. Full farmhouse breakfasts with local produce. Fire certificate held. Open all year. Map ref: 181 016

Higher Torr Farm, East Allington, Totnes, Devon TQ9 7QH

Susan Baker
☎ 0548 52248
[BB] From £15
EM From £7
Sleeps 6
🏕 ✠ ⛟
Listed Approved

Mixed working farm in lovely area offering comfortable accommodation in homely atmosphere. Good home-produced cooking. Quiet, peaceful walks to spot the wildlife. Close to moors and coast. Family room with en-suite facilities, twin room with washbasin, single room. Tea/coffee-making facilities in all rooms. TV lounge. Babysitting by arrangement. Open Mar–Oct. Map ref: 184 016

Reveton Farm, Loddiswell, Kingsbridge, South Devon TQ7 4RY

Mr & Mrs J Star
☎ 0548 550265
BB From £15
Sleeps 4
🕏
🏆 Commended

Traditional working farm set in outstandingly beautiful valley, 3 miles from Kingsbridge. Rolling fields run down to the river where you can fish for salmon/trout or simply enjoy the peaceful scenery. You can dine/breakfast on our veranda overlooking this lovely valley. Fresh, generous farmhouse cooking. Accommodation: 1 double, 1 twin, both with TV, sharing private bathroom. Open all year. Map ref: 184 016

Sherford Down, Sherford, Kingsbridge, Devon TQ7 2BA

Mrs Heather Peters
☎ 0548 531208
BB From £17.50
Sleeps 6
✕ 🕏 (3) 🐎
Listed

Elegant, beautifully appointed Georgian farmhouse in lovely setting on 280-acre farm, 3 miles to sea and Kingsbridge. Friendly family home, very warm welcome. 2 large comfortable rooms with tea trays and en-suite shower/WC or private bathroom. Stupendous breakfasts, local produce. Own children kept – over 3s welcome! Dozens of super pubs 1–5 miles. Dogs and smokers outside only please. Illustrated brochure. Open Easter–Oct. Map ref: 184 017

South Allington House, Chivelstone, Kingsbridge, South Devon TQ7 2NB

Barbara & Edward Baker
☎ 0548 51272
BB From £15
Sleeps 24
🕏 🍵
🏆 🏆 Commended

Country house and working farm in 4 acres of beautiful grounds on the South Devon coast. Ideal for walking the coastal path. All rooms have H/C, tea-making facilities, 5 en-suite. Access at all times. High tea for children, babysitting. TV lounge. Pay phone. We have bowls, croquet and coarse fishing. Midday snacks should you tire of the beach. Open Apr–Nov. Map ref: 185 013

South Huish Farm, South Huish, Kingsbridge, South Devon TQ7 3EH

David & Jill Darke
☎ 0548 561237
BB From £12
EM From £8
Sleeps 6
🕏 🏠
Listed

We welcome guests to our attractive 17th century mixed working farm (cows, sheep and arable). Situated in a lovely valley 1 mile from Thurlestone Sands with windsurfing, sailing, golf, horseriding and many coastal walks. Arrangements can be made to watch the milking and lambing. Enjoy the locally produced farmhouse fare. Children welcome. Babysitting. Open Mar–Oct (incl). Map ref: 183 015

Tunley Farm, Loddiswell, Kingsbridge, South Devon TQ7 4ED

Paul & Joy Harvey
☎ 0548 550279
BB From £14
Sleeps 6
✕ 🕏 🏠 🐎
🏆 🏆

Enjoy a happy farmhouse holiday in our listed early 17th century home. The dairy farm nestles in a tranquil valley. Loddiswell village ½ mile, Kingsbridge 4 miles. Beautiful beaches, water sports, horse riding. Dartmoor nearby. Double en-suite, double adjoining childrens room plus bathroom. Comfortable friendly and relaxing. Choice of breakfast, timed to suit you. Child reductions, babysitting, many local eating places recommended. Open Mar–Oct. Map ref: 183 017

LET THE TELEPHONE RING!
Some farmhouses are big places. Let the telephone ring long enough to give the owner time to answer it.

Self-Catering

The Laurels, c/o South Allington House, Chivelstone, Kingsbridge, South Devon TQ7 2NB

Barbara & Edward Baker
☎ 054851 272
⚲ From £90–£360
Sleeps 5 cot
✂ ☡ ✿
⚷ ⚷ ⚷ ⚷ **Commended**

The Laurels is the east wing of the house which has been designed to give you home comforts in relaxing surroundings. Set in 4 acres of grounds, safe for children. Close to beaches. Kitchen/lounge/dining room, all equipped to a high standard. Washer/dryer, dishwasher, colour TV. Bed-linen, towels and electric inclusive. Short breaks off-season. Open all year. Map ref: 185 013

Oldaport Farm Cottages, Modbury, Ivybridge, Devon PL21 0TG

Miss C Evans
☎ 0548 830 842
⚲ From £124–£348
☡ ✝
⚷ ⚷ ⚷ – ⚷ ⚷ ⚷ ⚷
Highly Commended

Oldaport is a small sheep farm of 60 acres, lying in the Erme Valley, and offering lovely views of the countryside. The four cottages, which sleep 2/6, were redundant stone barns which have been carefully converted into comfortable holiday homes. All fully equipped, heating in all rooms. Sandy beaches nearby, Dartmoor 8 miles. Excellent birdwatching. Brochure available. Open all year. Map ref: 179 018

Stone Barton, c/o Court Barton Farmhouse, Aveton Gifford, Kingsbridge, Devon TQ7 4LE

John & Jill Balkwill
☎ 0548 550312
⚲ From £200–£450
Sleeps 8
☡ ✿ ⚑ ⚕
⚷ **Approved**

Come to stay here for a real family holiday. Stone Barton is a modern, 4-bedroomed house sleeping up to 8 and is attached to the main farmhouse, 100 yards from village. Games rooms and lovely walks across the farm. Barbecue in garden is very popular in summer. Full central heating and open fire for colder months. Linen and electricity are inclusive. Open all year. Map ref: 181 016

Widland Farm, Modbury, Ivybridge, South Devon PL21 0SA

Ian & Bridgette Anthony
☎ and Fax 0548 830719
⚲ From £140–£357
Sleeps 5 + cot ⁻
✂ ☡
⚷ ⚷ ⚷ ⚷ **Commended**

Peacefully sheltered between Dartmoor and Bigbury Bay, three immaculate cottages face south over the small sheep and grass farm. Personal attention and high standards of maintenance are assured. Carefully equipped and furnished, each cottage has 3 bedrooms and 2 bathrooms. With short breaks off season, an ideal family holiday all year. Bed linen, CH, electricity and CTV inclusive. Open all year. Map ref: 181 018

Withymore Farm, Malborough, Kingsbridge, South Devon TQ7 3ED

Mrs Jo Hocking
☎ 0548 561275
⚲ From £150–£350
Sleeps 6 cot
⚑ ☡ ✿ ⚕
⚷ ⚷ ⚷ **Commended**

Recently modernised cottage nestling in a peaceful valley on a family-run dairy farm within a short distance of Salcombe. Very comfortable and furnished to a high standard throughout. Colour TV, bed linen, CH. Well equipped kitchen. Large enclosed garden. Ideal centre for family holiday with many beaches, sailing, fishing, golf, horse riding and spectacular coastal walks. Open all year. Map ref: 184 014

61 West Devon Welcome

West Devon, with its sheltered valleys, rugged hills and picturesque villages, offers you a chance not just to visit the countryside but to be a part of it . . . on our working beef, sheep and dairy farms. A chance to enjoy a real family holiday, taking your time, enjoying the peace of the countryside, joining in the local activities, travelling out to enjoy the beautiful beaches, entertainments, sights and attractions. A year-round delight.

There are many varieties of animals, birds and wild flowers for you to see. Walks and trails have been established in many forests and around a number of reservoirs. More active pursuits include riding and fishing or the more leisurely crafts of pottery, spinning or jewellery-making to learn.

For those interested in history or literature there are many ancient churches, Bronze Age settlements and the home of Sir Francis Drake plus the setting for the 'Hound of the Baskervilles'. Morwellham Quay and other National Trust properties are within easy reach . Resist, if you can, the locally made cheese, yoghurt, chocolate, fudge, cider or the famous Devon Cream Tea.

West Devon has so much to offer . . . why not come and share a little bit of "our heaven down in Devon".

Group Contact: Mrs Mary Pyle ☎ 0837 85279

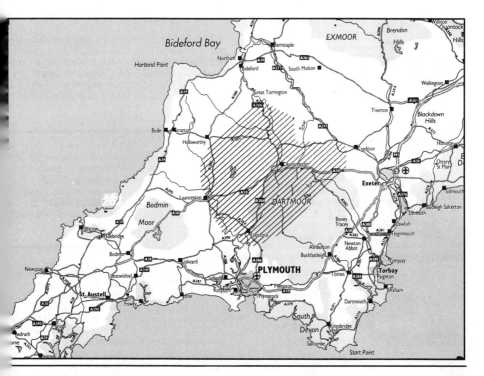

Bed and Breakfast (and evening meal)

Eastown Farm, Honeychurch, North Tawton, Devon EX20 2AG

Mrs Mary Pyle
☎ 083 785 279
🅱 £13
EM £8
Sleeps 6
♿ 🐕 🅰 ⛺ ♨
Listed

Come and relax in our Georgian farmhouse, warm and friendly atmosphere awaits you. Beautiful peaceful Devon countryside centrally situated for touring Dartmoor and Exmoor. Riding, fishing, swimming 'Tarka trail' nearby. Delicious farmhouse cooking, lounge, TV, dining room, centrally heated, 1 double, 1 twin, 1 family, 2 bathrooms. Reductions weekly stays and children. Open Feb–Nov. Map ref: 176 036

Hartleigh Barton, Petrockstowe, Okehampton, Devon EX20 3QJ

Angela Jones
☎ 040 923 344
🅱 From £14
EM £11
Sleeps 6
♿ 🅰 🛏 ⛺ ♨
Listed Highly
Commended

Discover a recipe for relaxation – true peace, exceptional surroundings and delightful food with every need anticipated we aim to ensure our guests leave revived and thrilled with our beautiful old house and the attention given to the details that really count. Central touring, fishing, Tarka Trail close by. Open Feb–Nov. Map ref: 175 040

Higher Cadham Farm, Jacobstowe, Okehampton, Devon EX20 3RB

John & Jenny King
☎ 083785 647
🅱 From £12
EM From £7
Sleeps 7
♿ (3) 🅰 ⛺
🍽 Commended

Pack your sun hat and wellies for a relaxing break on our 16th century secluded family-run farm. Plenty of activities for the more energetic – you may even sleep in our four-poster bed! Licensed and AA listed. One week's stay costs just £115 inclusive and as we have two children we offer special rates for yours. Detailed brochure available. Open Mar–Nov. Map ref: 175 034

Lower Nichols Nymet Farm, North Tawton, Devon EX20 2BW

Mrs Jane Pyle
☎ 0363 82510
🅱 From £16
EM From £8
Sleeps 6
♿ 🛏 ⛺ ♨
🍽 Highly
Commended

We offer a haven of comfort and rest on a modern working dairy farm and provide the perfect base for exploring the beauties of the West Country. Residents' lounge, colour TV. All rooms en-suite, plus tea/coffee-making facilities. An ideal holiday centre – beaches, golf, good walks, riding, fishing, fine houses and gardens nearby to visit. Open Mar–Oct (incl) Map ref: 176 036

Lower Oak Farm, Inwardleigh, Okehampton, Devon EX20 3AS

Rosemary Banbury
☎ 0837 810412
🅱 From £12
EM From £7
Sleeps 6
♿ (3)
🍽 Approved

Spring, summer, autumn, come enjoy a peaceful holiday in our attractive 16th century farmhouse on 172-acre working farm, near Okehampton. Friendly atmosphere, good farmhouse cooking, cream a speciality. Ideal for touring coasts of Devon and Cornwall, and Dartmoor. Short distance for golf, fishing, sailing, swimming, walking and riding. Weekly terms B&B from £80. Reductions for children. Short long breaks welcomed. Open Apr–Oct. Map ref: 175 034

Middlecott Farm, Broad Woodkelly, Winkleigh, Devon EX19 8DZ

June Western
☎ 0837 83381
BB From £14
EM From £8
Sleeps 6
🐎 🦮

The real farmhouse accommodation offered at Middlecott Farm in the heart of rural Devon will guarantee you a relaxing holiday away from the hurly-burly of everyday life. To see Devon at its best come and sample the delights of the unspoilt countryside, walk on Dartmoor, visit nearby fishery, walk the Tarka Trail, enjoy our delicious food. Weekly terms at reduced rates. Open Jan–Nov. Map ref: 174 033

Oaklands Farm, North Tawton, Devon EX20 2BQ

Winifred Headon
☎ 0837 82340
BB From £13
EM From £7
Sleeps 6
🐎 🦮

A warm welcome awaits you at Oaklands, a 130-acre farm in the centre of Devon. Easy to find on a level drive from a good road. Traditional farmhouse cooking with ample of everything. Heating and electric blankets in bedrooms. Lounge with colour TV. Pleasant gardens. Reductions for children. Open all year. Map ref: 176 036

Rubbytown Farm, Gulworthy, Tavistock, Devon PL19 8PN

Mary Steer
☎ 0822 832493
BB From £16.50
EM From £10
Sleeps 6
🦮 🐎 (5) 🐿 ⚓
🏵 🏵 **Highly Commended**

Stay in our lovely old farmhouse and sleep in four-poster beds. Enjoy woodland walks. There is abundant wildlife, you may see deer if you are lucky and at dusk the foxes and badgers at play. Help with feeding the calves. Good farmhouse cooking with evening meals served by candlelight. St Mellion Golf and Country Club nearby. Upholstery classes are held locally. Open all year. 2 double, 4 posters, en-suite, 1 twin with private bathroom, games room. Evening meal served by candlelight by prior arrangement. Map ref: 173 027

Seldon Farm, Monkokehampton, Winkleigh, Devon EX19 8RY

Mary Case
☎ 0837 810312
BB From £13
EM From £8
Sleeps 6
🐎 🦮
🏵 **Commended**

Relax in our delightful 17th century farmhouse situated in a beautiful unspoilt part of the Devonshire countryside. Abundant wildlife and in the spring time we have a carpet of bluebells. Warm relaxing atmosphere delicious food, homemade soups, garlic mushrooms, pheasant in red wine, chicken in mushroom sauce and for dessert we have memorable sticky toffee pudding with plenty of Devonshire clotted cream. Open Mar–November. Map ref: 176 034

Week Farm, Bridestowe, Okehampton, Devon EX20 4HZ

Margaret Hockridge
☎ 083786 221
BB From £14
EM From £9.50
Sleeps 10
🐎 🦽 🦮 📺 ⚓
🏵 🏵 **Commended**

Guests return annually to our 17th century farmhouse. Set in peaceful countryside 3 4 mile from A30. Good home cooking assured. Central for Dartmoor and coast. Lounge with colour TV and log fires. 1 single, 2 doubles, 3 family rooms, 3 en suite (1 ground floor). En-suite £3 extra per day. All have tea/coffee-making facilities, razor points, night storage heaters. 3 rooms with TV. Birthdays, anniversaries catered for. AA listed. Come and spoil yourselves. Fire certificate held. Open all year (closed Christmas). Map ref: 173 033

Woodcroft, Broadwoodkelly, Winkleigh, Devon EX19 8EN

Jean Skinner
☎ 0837 83405
BB From £11.50
EM From £7
🐎 🦮 🦴 ⚓
Listed

A friendly family atmosphere awaits you on our family-run mixed farm in the heart of lovely unspoilt Devonshire countryside. Enjoy a delicious 4-course meal in the dining room, then view our prize-winning cattle or relax in the lounge with colour TV or family games. Weekly terms BB & EM £120. Reduction for children under 14. Open 1 Mar–31 Oct. Map ref: 174 033

Self-Catering

The Granary, Higher Town Farm, Sampford Courtenay, Okehampton, Devon EX20 2SX

Marion Pratt
☎ 0837 82285
🆂🅲 From £140–£270
Sleeps 2/6
🐾 🛇 🐕
🔑 🔑 🔑 **Commended**

Where the rabble wielded bill hooks in 1549, the villagers now wield hoes in Britain's prettiest village. Sampford Courtenay is famous for the Prayer Book rebellion, Britain in Bloom, and Entente Florale. Soak up the history, the bouquet and the colours while relaxing at The Granary, a home from home from which to explore all Devon has on offer. Open all year.
Map ref: 177 036

FOLLOW THE COUNTRY CODE

Leave nothing but footprints,

Take nothing but photographs,

Kill nothing but time!

FARM HOLIDAY BUREAU

DISABLED VISITORS

members offering suitable accommodation to disabled/less able visitors. Please do check the extent of the facilities before booking.

FARM HOLIDAY BUREAU

62 Upper Tamar, North West Devon

This area covers the North Cornwall/Devon border area with its glorious coastline and miles of sandy beaches, sheltered coves and rugged cliffs, friendly resorts and quiet villages, country market towns and wide open spaces peacefully set in undulating countryside.

The coastline from Hartland to Crackington Haven is as dramatic as it is beautiful. Bude, once described by the late Sir John Betjeman as 'the least rowdy resort in the country' has retained its atmosphere of easy-going charm while catering for the most discerning of modern day tourists. Another resort which tourists are advised to visit is Clovelly with its steeply cobbled streets. Holsworthy and Launceston have weekly cattle and pannier markets. Both have a golf course and sports hall and Launceston also has a heated swimming pool. There are several pony trekking centres in the area and facilities for fishing at sea, on the lake or by the river.

This area has been recommended as a restful, comfortable base for touring the whole of Devon and Cornwall. There are many tourist attractions including the moors, National Trust properties, steam railways, leisure parks, museums and the cities of Exeter, Plymouth and Truro all within easy driving distance.

Group Contact: Marlene Heard ☎ 0409 253339

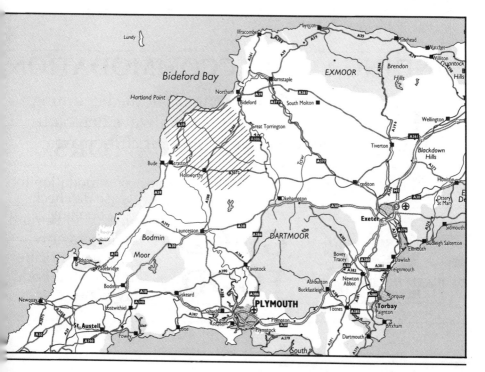

Bed and Breakfast (and evening meal)

Elm Park, Bridgerule, Holsworthy, Devon EX22 7EL

Sylvia Lucas
☎ **028881 231**
🅱 **From £12**
EM From £6
Sleeps 12

Elm Park is 6 miles from Cornish surfing beaches at Bude an ideal for touring both Devon and Cornwall. Children are especially welcomed with pony and tractor and trailer rides. Twin and family rooms with en-suite and tea/coffee making facilities ample 4-course dinners with freshly produced fare and delicious sweets. B&B and EM from £115 weekly. Games room. Open Mar–Nov. Map ref: 162 038

Thorne Park, Holsworthy, Devon EX22 7BL

Marlene Heard
☎ **0409 253339**
🅱 **From £12**
EM From £7
Sleeps 15

Listed Commended

A warm welcome, beautiful views and delightful accommodation await you at this working dairy/sheep farm. Wander through fields and pretty valley with stream, watch activities, including milking. 5 bedrooms (3 en-suite), delicious home cooking. Riding, fishing, golf nearby. Pony rides, play area. Holsworthy 1 ½ miles, coast 10 miles. Great for touring. Weekly BB & EM from £112; child reductions. Open all year (closed Christmas). Map ref: 167 038

FINDING YOUR ACCOMMODATION

FARM HOLIDAY BUREAU

The Group contacts at the beginning of each section can always help you find a vacancy in your chosen area.

FARM HOLIDAY BUREAU

GOOD FOOD

Nearly all Bureau members now hold a certificate in Essential Food Hygiene.

63 Cream of Cornwall

Cornwall is a unique part of this country with a coastline of 326 miles. The north coast has wonderful stretches of firm golden sands and soaring cliffs. Many beaches offer excellent surfing, and further north you can visit the harbour of Boscastle and the clifftop castle at Tintagel with Arthurian connections.

Newquay with its beaches stretching for seven miles, sheltered coves, and shops is a premier attraction in the north. St. Ives is another surfing honeypot which has great charm and has attracted artists for many years.

The south coast is a complete contrast with wooded estuaries, picturesque fishing ports and popular resorts. Penzance with its vivid colours has wonderful views across the bay to St. Michael's Mount.

Here are excellent facilities for sailing and deep-sea fishing, as there are at Fowey which overlooks its busy estuary harbour. St. Mawes is a charming, unspoilt village across the Fal from Falmouth and Mevagissey, Polperro and Looe are fine examples of traditional Cornish fishing villages.

Inland, Cornwall has its attractions. To the east of Bodmin, the county town, are the open uplands known as Bodmin Moor with the county's highest peaks at Rough Tor and Brown Willy. The historic market town of Launceston is dominated by its ruined castle.

Group Contacts: 🆎 **Judith Nancarrow** ☎ **0726 67111**
🆂🅲 **Kathy Woodley** ☎ **0872 510555**

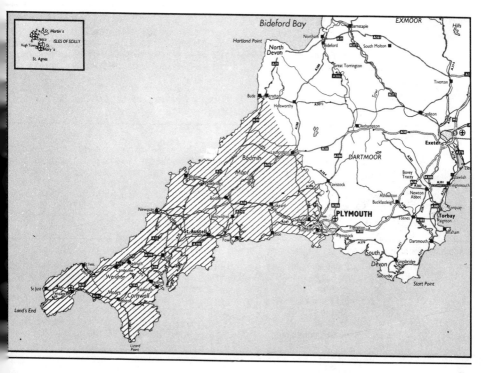

Bed and Breakfast (and evening meal)

Arrallas, Ladock, Truro, Cornwall TR2 4NP

Mrs Barbara Holt
☎ 0872 510379
BB From £14
EM From £8
Sleeps 6
🐕 🍴 🛡 🎾
🏵 🏵 🏵 **Commended**

Arrallas is part of the Duchy of Cornwall enjoying a "heart of the country" peaceful atmosphere. We are adjacent to 400 acres of Duchy woodlands, offering wonderful walks and superb views from the house. 15 minutes drive from the North coast. Centrally situated for touring. All bedrooms en-suite (2 double, 1 twin) with TVs. Quality menus. Choice of 2, 3 or 4 courses. Full central heating. Parking. Beverage facilities. Phone for directions. Open Jan–Nov (incl). Map ref: 148 015

Bucklawren Farm, St Martin-by-Looe, Cornwall PL13 1NZ

Mrs Jean Henly
☎ 05034 738
BB From £14
EM From £8
Sleeps 12
🐕 🛏 🛡
🏵 🏵 🏵 **Commended**

Bucklawren is situated deep in unspoilt countryside yet only 1 mile from the beach, 2½ miles from Looe and 1 mile from Woolly Monkey Sanctuary. It is a large working farm with a spacious, comfortable farmhouse which enjoys beautiful sea views and a large garden. We offer excellent accommodation with family and en-suite rooms. Farmhouse cooking in a friendly and relaxed atmosphere. Open Mar–Nov (incl). Map ref: 165 018

Caduscott, East Taphouse, Liskeard, Cornwall PL14 4NG

Lindsay Pendray
☎ 0579 20262
BB From £12
EM From £7.50
Sleeps 4/5
🍴 🐕 🛡
Listed

Down the lane wild flowers nod in passing; to relax and unwind in this 17th century listed farmhouse peeping over the valley where streams converge to make the 10 mile journey to the sea at Looe. Double room (en-suite, toilet/shower), adjoining twin bedded room. Personal attention, facilities for children. Explore the wealth of gardens, houses and coastal paths, many protected by the National Trust. Open Apr–Sept. Map ref: 162 023

Carglonnon Farm, Dulog, Liskeard, Cornwall PL14 4QA

Mrs Ann Bray
☎ 0579 20210
BB From £12.50
Sleeps 6
🐕 🐕 🌴
🏵 🏵

A lovely 18th century Georgian farmhouse which is part of the Duchy of Cornwall Estate. A working mixed farm of 230 acres, situated 4½ miles from fishing port of Looe. Forestry walks from farm. Golf, horse-riding, Theme Park, coastal walking, moors all nearby. All rooms have H&C, tea-making facilities, central heating. Open all year. Map ref: 162 023

Degembris Farmhouse, St Newlyn East, Newquay, Cornwall TR8 5HY

Kathy Woodley
☎ 0872 510555
BB From £15
EM From £8
Sleeps 12
🐕 🌴 🛡
🏵 🏵 **Commended**

Degembris is a listed Cornish farmhouse built in the 18th century on the site of the old manor. The house is set on a 165-acre farm overlooking a beautiful wooded valley where pleasant walks may be enjoyed on our country trail. All rooms have H/C, tea/coffee-making facilities and colour TV. We will provide you with comfort, home cooking and a taste of country life. Open Easter–Oct. Map ref: 149 020

Ennys, St Hilary, Penzance, Cornwall TR20 9BZ

Sue White
☎ 0736 740262
BB From £20
EM From £12.50
Sleeps 10
🐴 🎍

🏵 🏵 🏵 Commended

Beautiful 16th century manor farm in idyllically peaceful wooded surroundings. Excellent suppers by candlelight. Bread baked daily! Log fires. 3 en-suite bedrooms, 1 with romantic four-poster overlooking walled gardens and tennis court. Self-contained family suite. Near to beaches and the famous St Michael's Mount. Gourmet weekend winter breaks. Featured in *Country Living* magazine and *The Daily Telegraph*. Open all year (closed Christmas). Map ref: 136 010

Hendra Farm, Polbathic, Torpoint, Cornwall PL11 3DT

Mrs A Hoskin
☎ 05035 225
BB From £12.50
Sleeps 6
🍴 🐴 🏕 🐕 🖤

Listed Commended

Hendra is a working farm situated in an area of outstanding natural beauty. The fishing port of Looe is 6 miles, and safe bathing beaches of Downderry and Seaton only 2 miles. The main shopping centre of Plymouth is within ½ hours travelling. TV lounge. Family room with en-suite shower and WC. Babysitting. Open Apr–Oct. Map ref: 167 019

Higher Kergilliack, Budock, Falmouth, Cornwall TR11 5PB

Jean Pengelly
☎ 0326 372271
BB From £15
EM From £8
Sleeps 6
🐴 🐎 🏕

🏵

18th century Georgian listed farmhouse, former residence of Bishop of Exeter, 1 mile Falmouth on B3291 to Constantine and Seal sanctuary. Poppy our friendly dog will show you round our 130-acre dairy farm to see the cows and calves. Near many lovely sandy beaches. 1 double with en-suite, WC and shower, 1 double 1 single can be booked as suite with private bathroom. Open Jan–Nov. Map ref: 148 010

Kerryanna Guest House, Treleaven Farm, Mevagissey, Cornwall PL26 6RZ

Linda Hennah
☎ 0726 843558
BB From £19
EM From £10
Sleeps 12
🐴 (5) 🖤

🏵 🏵 🏵 Commended

The Hennah family invite you to enjoy the peace and tranquility at Treleaven Farm, a working farm overlooking the quaint fishing village of Mevagissey. All bedrooms en suite with colour TV and tea-making facilities. Beautiful countryside surrounding with abundant wildlife and flowers. Creative and traditional farmhouse cooking with choice of menus. Games barn, large gardens, licensed bar, outdoor heated pool. Open Easter–Oct. Map ref: 155 016

Longstone Farm, Trenear, Helston, Cornwall TR13 0HG

Gillian Lawrance
☎ 0326 572483
BB From £13
EM From £7
Sleeps 12
🐴 ♿ 🐎

🏵 🏵 Approved

A warm welcome awaits you at Longstone Farm, a 62-acre dairy farm situated in the centre of peaceful countryside in West Cornwall. Ideal for touring, beaches and visiting many holiday attractions including Poldark Mine, Triple Theme Park and Leisure Centre. Also horseriding nearby. Modernised farmhouse, all bedrooms have H/C. Good farmhouse fare served, separate tables in dining room. Large sun lounge/play area. Open Mar–Nov. Map ref: 141 009

Loskeyle Farm, St Tudy, Bodmin, Cornwall PL30 3PW

Mrs Sandra Menhinick
☎ 0208 851005
BB From £12.50
EM From £7.50
Sleeps 6
🐴
🏵

Loskeyle is an 85-acre dairy farm forming a part of the Duchy of Cornwall. Situated in a peaceful part of mid-Cornwall, close to Bodmin Moor but within easy reach of the north and south coasts. We offer you comfortable accommodation in a relaxed and friendly atmosphere. Children especially welcome, free babysitting by arrangement. Beverage facilities. Open Mar–Oct. Map ref: 157 024

Manuels Farm, Quintrell Downs, near Newquay, Cornwall TR8 4NY

Mrs Jean Wilson
☎ 0637 873577
BB From £14
EM From £8.50
Sleeps 12
♈ ⚞ ☙ ♨
☙ ☙ Highly
Commended

A listed 17th century farmhouse situated in a sheltered valley, 2 miles from Newquay's magnificent beaches. Relax in peaceful countryside in this traditional Cornish farmhouse. Beautifully furnished, delicious plentiful farmhouse cooking. Log fires. Award winning garden. Children especially welcome. Nursery teas, free babysitting, play area, pony rides. Meet a whole variety of pets and farm animals on this friendly working farm. Open all year (closed Christmas). Map ref: 147 022

Polhormon Farm, Polhormon Lane, Mullion, Helston, Cornwall TR12 7JE

Alice Harry
☎ 0326 240304
BB From £15
Sleeps 8
♈ ☙
☙

Polhormon is a working dairy farm with magnificent coastal and country views, overlooking sandy Poldhu Cove. Situated ½ mile from charming Mullion Village on 'The Lizard'. The Victorian farmhouse has old fashioned comfort and relaxed family atmosphere. Bathroom and separate WC. Central heating. Access at all times. Tea/coffee-making facilities in bedrooms. Babysitting by arrangement. Ponyriding, golf, fishing trips nearby, plus glorious NT cliff walks. Open Easter–Nov. Map ref: 142 006

Polsue Manor Farm, Tresillian, Truro, Cornwall TR2 4BP

Geraldine Holliday
☎ 087252 234
BB From £15
EM From £7
Sleeps 14
♈ ☙ ♨
☙

The farmhouse on this 190-acre working farm, set in glorious countryside, overlooks the tidal Tresillian River and one of the prettiest parts of Cornwall. Only minutes from the beautiful cathedral city of Truro. Centrally situated between north and south coasts, ideal centre for touring the county. Delightful country walks. All bedrooms have H/C. Traditional home cooking, comfortable, relaxed friendly atmosphere. Open most of year. Map ref: 148 016

Poltarrow Farm, St Mewan, St Austell, Cornwall PL26 7DR

Judith Nancarrow
☎ 0726 67111
BB From £16
EM From £8
Sleeps 6
☙ ⊕ ♞ ♨
☙ ☙ Commended

Our charming wisteria clad farmhouse set in peaceful farming countryside is well placed to spend time discovering Cornwalls heritage, beaches and harbours, National Trust coastal walks and properties. Famous gardens and moor. The bedrooms have private facilities/TV. Traditional Cornish fare with table licence together with an invitation to explore our small working farm are all here to make your farm holiday most enjoyable. Open most of the year. Map ref: 155 0189

Rescorla Farm, Rescorla, St Austell, Cornwall PL26 8YT

Mrs Judith Clemo
☎ 0726 850168
BB From £12.50
EM From £8.50
Sleeps 6
♞ ⓔ
☙

Rescorla is a working dairy farm set in a small hamlet centrally situated for touring both north and south coasts. The spacious bedrooms have a commanding view of the open countryside. There is a guest bathroom and seperate WC. A friendly relaxed atmosphere to enjoy the farmhouse fare. Open Apr–Oct inclusive. Map ref: 155 018

Rose Farm, Chyanhal, Buryas Bridge, Penzance, Cornwall TR19 6AN

Mrs Penny Lally
☎ 0736 731808
BB From £16.50
Sleeps 6
☙ ♨
☙ ☙ Commended

Rose Farm is a small working farm in a little hamlet close to the picturesque fishing villages of Mousehole and Newlyn and 7 miles from Lands End. The 200-year-old granite farmhouse is cosy with pretty, en suite rooms. 1 double, 1 family suite and a romantic 15th century four poster room in barn annexe. We have all manner of animals, from pedigree cattle to pot-bellied pigs! Open all year (closed Christmas). Map ref: 130 010

Trebah Farm, Mawnan Smith, Falmouth, Cornwall TR11 5JZ

Jean Kessell
☎ 0326 250295
[BB] From £11.50
EM From £7
Sleeps 4
⚤ ⛷ ⚹
Listed

Guests receive a warm welcome at our comfortable and peaceful farmhouse set in 150 acres of beautiful countryside. Adjoining National Trust garden and the renowned Helford River where a variety of watersports are available. There are miles of scenic coastline to walk with numerous watering holes. Access at all times. TV lounge. Babysitting. Open Feb–Nov. Map ref: 147 010

Treffry Farm, Lanhydrock, Bodmin, Cornwall PL30 5AF

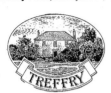

Pat Smith
☎ 0208 74405
[BB] From £18
EM From £9
Sleeps 6
⚤ ⛷ (6) ⚹ ▪ 🐎
🏵 🏵 Highly
Commended

Historic, listed Georgian farmhouse (1720) on 200 acre dairy farm adjoining National Trust Lanhydrock. Guaranteed warm welcome and home cooking in generous quantities! Ideal for touring Cornwall, within easy reach of many beaches. Visitors welcome to explore farm and meet animals. 3 pretty bedrooms with colour TV and en-suite facilities, 1 with four-poster bed. Open Easter–Oct. Map ref: 157 024

Tregaswith Farmhouse, Tregaswith, near Newquay, Cornwall TR8 4HY

John & Jacqui Elsom
☎ 0637 881181
[BB] From £15.95
EM From £7
Sleeps 6
⛷ 🐎 🐕 ▪
🏵 🏵 🏵 Highly
Commended

Tregaswith is a small hamlet just outside Newquay, 4 miles to beaches and several National Trust properties near. The farmhouse built over 250 years ago, now a smallholding breeding rare poultry and horses. Pony rides and an introduction to carriage driving can be arranged. We have a reputation for delicious food. 3 beautiful bedrooms, all en-suite. Antiques and oak beams throughout. Open all year. Map ref: 150 023

Tregidgeo, Grampound, Truro, Cornwall TR2 4SP

Mrs Sally Wade
☎ 0726 882450
[BB] From £14
EM From £7.50
Sleeps 6
⛷
🏵 🏵 Commended

Tregidgeo is a mixed farm of 216 acres. The spacious farmhouse is tastefully furnished with a friendly family atmosphere, found in a beautifully secluded and peaceful setting. Well situated for beaches and touring bedrooms have H and C, beverage facilities and TV, 1 en-suite, good home cooking with the emphasis on fresh farm and local produce, large walled garden and play area. Open all year (closed Christmas). Map ref: 148 015

Treglisson, Hayle, Cornwall TR27 5JT

Carole Runnalls
☎ 0736 753141
[BB] From £15
Sleeps 14
⛷
🏵 🏵 Commended

Treglisson is an ideal holiday base from which to explore and discover the delights of West Cornwall. All rooms are en-suite with hair driers and tea/coffee-making facilities. There is also an indoor-heated swimming pool. Guests are welcome to wander around the farm and along the lanes to the woods which are especially beautiful in the spring. Open all year. Map ref: 138 013

Tregonan, Tregony, Truro, Cornwall TR2 5SN

Sandra Collins
☎ 087253 249
[BB] From £12
Sleeps 6
⛷
🏵 Commended

Come and enjoy the peaceful tranquility of this secluded farmhouse, situated at the end of a ½ mile private lane on a 300 acre arable and sheep farm. Lying 6 miles west of Mevagissey at the head of the renowned Roseland Peninsula. 2 beaches within 3 miles. Spacious, comfortable accommodation. All bedrooms H/C, beverage-making facilities. Good selection of eating places locally. Open Mar–Oct. Map ref: 153 015

Tregondale Farm, Menheniot, Liskeard, Cornwall PL14 3RG

Stephanie Rowe
☎ 05779 342407
BB **From £15**
EM From £8.50
Sleeps 6
🐴 🐎

♨ ♨
Highly Commended

Come and join our family with the peace of the countryside, near the coast amidst wildlife, flowers and woodland walks on a 180-acre mixed farm. Pedigree animals being naturally reared, pony rides, tennis court and play area. The characteristic farmhouse with en-suite/private facilities, beautifully set in original walled garden, home grown produce tastefully presented. Idyllic for exploring Cornwalls' holiday attractions. Open all year. Map ref: 165 024

Trehane Farm, Trevalga, Boscastle, Cornwall PL35 0EB

Mrs Sarah James
☎ 0840 250510
BB **From £14.50**
Sleeps 6
🐴 🐎 🐕 ♞ 🌿
♨

Welcome to Trehane, a sheep and dairy farm on the spectacular North Cornwall heritage coast. Farmhouse set in magnificent position overlooking sea, superb coastal views. We offer a comfortable friendly atmosphere and excellent food using fresh farm produce and home baked bread. Enjoy fine walks along the coast or inland on to Bodmin Moor. New spring/autumn breaks. Learn to spin from fleece to fibre in this very lovely place. Open all year. Map ref: 158 033

Trewellard Manor Farm, Pendeen, Penzance, Cornwall TR19 7SU

Mrs Marion Bailey
☎ **and fax 0736 788526**
BB **From £14**
Sleeps 6
🐕

♨ ♨ **Commended**

The farm is situated in a superb coastal position between Lands End and St Ives. We offer a friendly, relaxed atmosphere with seasonal log fires and CH. 3 bedrooms (1 en-suite) all with tea/coffee facilities. Use of swimming pool (May–Sep) with good beaches within easy reach. Horse riding and coarse fishing available nearby. This is an outstanding area for walking, either inland or on the coast path. Open all year (closed Christmas). Map ref: 131 012

Treworgie Barton, Crackington Haven, Bude, Cornwall EX23 0NL

Pam Mount
☎ 08403 233
BB **From £16**
EM From £11
Sleeps 6 + 6
🐎

♨ ♨ ♨ **Highly commended**

Enjoy personal attention and friendly atmosphere at our 106-acre farm with 25 acres of woodland, 2 miles from Crackington Haven. The 16th century farmhouse has 3 bedrooms, all with private or en-suite facilities and TV. Also romantic barn room with four poster bed, and newly created family suite. Excellent freshly cooked, carefully presented food our speciality. Open Apr–Sep (Nov, Feb, Mar advance bookings only). Map ref: 161 035

Wheatley Farm, Maxworthy, Launceston, Cornwall PL15 8LY

Valerie Griffin
☎ 056681 232
BB **From £17**
EM From £9.50
Sleeps 12
🐕 🐎

♨ ♨ ♨
Highly Commended

Discover the delights of our Cornish heritage at Wheatley. Amble through farm lanes, enjoy peace and tranquility amid beautiful Cornish countryside, explore rugged coastline, search out sandy coves nearby. Absolute comfort in spacious bedrooms, tastefully decorated all with en-suite facilities, TV. Working farm animals to visit, pony rides, play area for children. We pride ourselves in offering a tempting menu. Enjoy personal attention and friendly atmosphere. Open Easter–Sep. Map ref: 163 035

Please mention **Stay on a Farm** when booking

Self-Catering

Bucklawren Farm, St Martin-by-Looe, Cornwall PL13 1NZ

Mrs Jean Henly
☎ 050 34 738
SC From £100–£400
Sleeps 4/6
♘ ⤳ ⌬ ▪
⚘ ⚘ ⚘ ⚘ **Commended**

Three attractive stone cottages recently tastefully converted from farm buildings, furnished to high standard, and set in a large garden. Bucklawren is situated deep in unspoilt countryside, yet only one mile from the beach and three miles from the fishing village of Looe. Ideal position for coastal paths, National Trust properties, fishing trips, beaches and Plymouth. Open all year. Map ref: 164 019

Cadson Manor Farm, Callington, Cornwall PL17 7HW

Mrs Brenda Crago
☎ 0579 83187
SC From £150–£350
♂ ⚞
⚘ ⚘ ⚘ **Commended**

A fully self-contained wing of the Old Manor, with picturesque views of the Lynher Valley. Traditionally furnished, comfort and style combined with old world charm. 3 miles from Callington, off the A390. Delightful river walks amidst splendid Cornish countryside. 2 bedrooms both with H&C, sleeps up to 4. Shower room with washbasin and WC. Electricity and bedlinen inclusive. Brochure available. Open all year. Map ref: 168 025

Cherry Hills and Golden Meadows, c/o Kerryanna, Treleaven Farm, Mevagissey, Cornwall PL26 6RZ

Mrs Linda Hennah
☎ 0726 843558
SC From £180–£400
Sleeps 4
♞
⚘ ⚘ ⚘ ⚘ **Commended**

The Hennah family welcome you to Treleaven Farm, overlooking the quaint fishing village of Mevagissey. Surrounded by rambling countryside, wildlife and flowers. Cherry Hills and Golden Meadows are two luxuriously converted barns equipped and furnished to a very high standard. Each sleeps 4. Use of outdoor pool May–Sept. Games barn and putting green. Meals can be taken in the guest house nearby. Open all year. Map ref: 155 016

Coach House, c/o Lantallack Farm, Landrake, Cornwall PL12 5AE

Nichola Walker
☎ 0752 851281
SC From £160–£405
⚒ ⤳ ⚞ ⚘
⚘ ⚘ ⚘ ⚘ **Commended**

A Georgian farm coach house, beautifully converted to provide the utmost holiday comfort. Outstanding views across undulating countryside and wooded valleys. The perfect retreat for a relaxing holiday. Close to many National Trust properties, Dartmoor and Bodmin Moor. The nearest beach is only 20 mins away. 2 bathrooms, colour TV, dishwasher, log fire, CH, phone, games room. Electricity and bedlinen inclusive. Open all year. Map ref: 168 022

Glynn Barton Farm Cottages, Glynn Barton, Cardinham, Bodmin, Cornwall PL30 4AX

Diana Mindel
☎ 020882 375
SC From £100–£390
♂ ♘ ♿ ▪
⚘ ⚘ ⚘ ⚘ **Commended**

Tastefully converted stone and slate farm buildings in 12 picturesque acres enhanced by the surrounding farmland and forestry, with superb views along the Glynn Valley. A designated area of outstanding natural beauty. A landscaped heated swimming pool has been carefully sited to provide seclusion and shelter. Peace and quiet. Central to Moors and north and south coasts. Open all year. Map ref: 159 025

Lodge Barton Farm, Liskeard, Cornwall PL14 4JX

Rosanne Hodin
☎ 0579 344432
SC From £80–£340
Sleeps 2/5 cot

Commended

Lodge Barton is set in a beautiful river valley flanked by woodland. We keep a milking herd of goats and also have calves, ducks, hens and geese. Everyone can help milk, feed and collect eggs. Our character cottages are luxuriously equipped including heating, woodburners, video, linen, laundry room, private gardens and playground. We are close to sea, moors, sailing, windsurfing, riding, fishing, golf. Open all year. Map ref: 164 023

Lower Trengale Farm, Liskeard, Cornwall PL14 6HF

Louise Kidd
☎ 0579 21019
Fax 0579 21432
SC From £100–£350
EM From £5
Sleeps 4/5

Commended

A small farm, set in beautiful countryside, offering three comfortable and well equipped cottages which have been carefully converted from a stone barn. Children love helping with the cows, sheep, pigs, hens and their young. There is a pony to ride, a sandpit, swings and table tennis. Lovely views from the garden. All linen suplied, laundry, meals and babysitting available. Open all year. Map ref: 164 023

Manuels Farm, Quintrell Downs, near Newquay, Cornwall TR8 4NY

Alan & Jean Wilson
☎ 0637 873577
SC From £95–£390
Sleeps 2/4 cot

Commended

Imagine a family holiday close to Newquay's magnificent beaches but tucked away in your own quiet valley. Secluded from the crowd but perfectly placed for touring, walking and riding. Your own character cottage in the country, on the farm, with gardens, flowers, pets and farm animals around you. The children will enjoy the calves, tractor and ponies while you relax. Open all year (closed Christmas). Map ref: 147 022

Menaburle Farm, Boconnoc, Lostwithiel, Cornwall PL22 0RT

Vicki Alderman
☎ 0208 873703
SC From £150–£350
Sleeps 4

Approved

Off the beaten track, down quiet lanes ideal for strolling, yet only a few miles from main roads, Menaburle is perfectly situated for relaxing or exploring Cornwall. Sheep and cattle graze by the stream which runs through our 260 acres. Walk over the fields, befriend the pigs, chickens, dogs and cats. A self-contained farmhouse wing, sleeps 4. Open all year. Map ref: 169 022

Nancolleth Farm Caravan Park, Newquay, Cornwall TR8 4PN

Joan Luckraft
☎ 0872 510236
SC From £95–£250
Sleeps 6/6

Nancolleth a 250-acre farm, 5 miles from Newquay. Central for touring Cornwall. Secluded caravan park with 6 deluxe 6-berth caravans in garden setting, well spaced, on hard standings with parking. Each caravan has 2 bedrooms, shower room with toilet, colour TV, fridge, spacious lounge, dining and kitchen areas. Laundry. Phone. Country trail. Families and couples welcomed. ETB Rose Award Caravan Holiday Park Award 1993. Open May–Oct. Map ref: 148 022

Poltarrow Farm Cottage, c/o Poltarrow Farm, St Mewan, St Austell, Cornwall PL26 7DR

Judith Nancarrow
☎ 0726 67111
SC From £100–£390
Sleeps 6

Commended

Poltarrow farm cottages, converted from old traditional buildings are set in peaceful farming countryside and are well placed to see quaint harbours, beaches, famous gardens and Cornwalls heritage. The well appointed accommodation include modern kitchen conveniences, linen and central heating to make your farm holiday very enjoyable. 1 cottage designed for the less abled visitors. Map ref: 155 018

Rescorla Farm, Rescorla, St Austell, Cornwall PL26 8YT

Mrs J Clemo
☎ 0726 850168
SC From £160–£330
Sleeps 5
🏠 🐕 🐎 🅴
🔑 🔑 🔑
Up to Commended

At Rescorla Farm, egg collecting, feeding pigs and calves are part of the daily routine which you are more than welcome to participate in. Relax by a log fire in our cosy cottages, where high standards are guaranteed. Games room and babysitting available for the children. Set in the country, but central for touring both coasts. Flowers and a welcome tray await you. Open all year. Map ref: 155 018

Treffry Farm, Lanhydrock, Bodmin, Cornwall PL30 5AF

Pat Smith
☎ 0208 74405
SC From £85–£510
Sleeps 2/8
🐕 🐎 🐎 🐎
🔑 🔑 🔑 🔑
Highly Commended

Imagine country cottages, rambling roses, chintzy sofas, rocking chairs, pot pourri, log fires on winter days, honeysuckle perfume on summer nights – they're here at Treffry. Our dairy farm adjoins the National Trust at Lanhydrock where you can walk for miles in glorious parkland. Search out rugged cliffs and hidden sandy coves, or relax and meet our farm animals and pony. A warm welcome awaits you. Open all year. Map ref: 157 024

Tregevis Farm, St Martin, Helston, Cornwall TR12 6DN

Julie Bray
☎ (0326) 231265
SC From £150–£350
Sleeps 7 + cot
🗲 🐕
🔑 🔑 🔑 🔑 **Approved**

Tregevis is situated on a dairy farm in the heart of the countryside, only 2 miles from the beautiful Helford River and ½ mile from the little village of St Martin. The accommodation is a self-contained part of the farmhouse, it is spacious and, having three floors, gives the children plenty of scope on a rainy day. Modern kitchen with automatic washer/dryer and a games room. Visitors are welcome to look around the farm. Open Easter–Oct. Map ref: 145 007

Tremadart Farm, Duloe, Liskeard, Cornwall PL14 4PE

Evelyn Julian
☎ 05032 62855
SC From £100–£420
Sleeps 12
🐎
🔑 🔑 🔑 🔑 **Approved**

Tremadart farm offers spacious half of farmhouse set in large garden on 330-acre mixed farm which is part of the Duchy of Cornwall. It is situated in village of Duloe, 3 miles Looe and daily travelling distance of all Cornwall. Accommodation offers 4 bedrooms, bathroom, shower room, 2 toilets. Forestry walks, golf, horse riding, indoor swimming and sports complex close by. Open all year. Map ref: 164 022

Trevalgan Farm, St Ives, Cornwall TR26 3BJ

Jean Osborne
☎ 0736 796433
SC From £90–£350
Sleeps 2/6
🐕 🐎
🔑 🔑 🔑 **Commended**

Trevalgan is a coastal stock-rearing farm surrounded by magnificent scenery, just 2 miles from St Ives. Enjoy walking our farm trail to the cliffs overlooking the sea, a paradise for nature lovers. Traditional granite barns have been carefully converted into 7 lovely holiday homes around an attractive courtyard. Land's End, St Michael's Mount, Mousehole and Lamorna within easy reach by car. Open all year (closed Feb). Map ref: 136 015

Trewalla Farm Cottages, Trewalla Farm, Minions, Liskeard, Cornwall PL14 6ED

Cheryl van der Salm
☎ 0579 342385
SC From £150–£320
Sleeps 2/4
🐎 🏠 🐎
Applied

Our small, traditionally-run farm on Bodmin Moor has rare breed pigs, hand milked sheep, hens, geese and ponies, all free-range and v ery friendly. Our three cottages are beautifully furnished and very well equipped. Their moorland setting offers perfect peace, wonderful views, ideal walking country and a good base for exploring – if you can tear yourself away! Open Mar–Dec. Map ref: 165 025

Trewithen Country Lodges, Trewithen Farm, Laneast, Launceston, Cornwall PL15 8PW

Mrs Margaret Colwill
☎ 0566 86343
⒮⒞ From £120–£320
Sleeps 6
☖ ↑ ☂
↗ ↗ ↗ **Commended**

A warm and friendly welcome awaits you at our Scandinavian style lodge, peacefully situated in a garden with swings on our mixed farm, say hello to the pony and enjoy panoramic views of the surrounding Bodmin Moor. Centrally heated, luxuriously furnished, well equipped kitchen washer/drier, 2 upper floor bedrooms, duvets and bed linen provided. Open all year. Map ref: 160 033

Wheatley Farm, Maxworthy, Launceston, Cornwall PL15 7LY

Valerie Griffin
☎ 056681 232
⒮⒞ From £90–£440
Sleeps 2/7
☖ ☌
↗ ↗ ↗ ↗
Commended

Discover the delights of our Cornish heritage, amble through country lanes. Explore the rugged coastline, search out sandy coves nearby. Simply relax in one of our two idyllic country cottages, absolute comfort, chintzy sofas, curtains and quilts in delicate country prints. Enjoy warmth of log fires at Wheatley farm you can visit the animals, pony rides and play are for children, a warm welcome awaits you. Open all year. Map ref: 163 035

Wooldown, Rowbarton and Cyder Cottage, c/o Wooldown, Marchamchurch, Bude, Cornwall EX23 0HP

Mrs S Blewett
☎ 0288 361 216
⒮⒞ From £200–£600
⅃ ☌
↗ ↗ ↗ ↗ **Commended**

Wooldown, a spacious wing of 20th century farmhouse with 4 bedrooms. Cyder Cottage with 1 double bedroom and children's room, 1 twin and conservatory. Rowbarton with 2 bedrooms and conservatory. All properties have gardens, barbecue, kitchen with dishwasher, microwave, fridge, washing machine, bathrooms with shower and toilet. CH; electricity and bed-linen inclusive. Panoramic views. Open Apr–Oct (Wooldown), others all year. Map ref: 163 039

FARM HOLIDAY BUREAU

BUREAU ACCOMMODATION IS RELIABLE

This Guide lists **Farm Holiday Bureau** members only. They are all inspected by the National Tourist Board for standards (see introduction pages) and by fellow members to maintain a high quality.

FARM HOLIDAY BUREAU

FOLLOW THE COUNTRY CODE

Leave nothing but footprints,

Take nothing but photographs,

Kill nothing but time!

64 Llŷn Peninsula

With more than 70 miles of coastline, backed by the dramatic mountains of Snowdonia, this is an Area of Outstanding Natural Beauty where the warm waters of the Gulf Stream give a mild climate all year round. The Welsh language and way of life still flourish here and while you struggle with the seemingly impossible Celtic names, you will appreciate the very Welshness of it all.

It is also an area compact enough to travel around and get to know – and one that you will want to come back to time and time again.

No-one comes to this part of Wales without setting foot on mighty Mount Snowdon; and even if you only clamber for a relatively short distance you will be rewarded with views the like of which you will never have seen before. And you could always walk one way and take the famous narrow gauge railway the other!

Right at the foot of the Peninsula lies Bardsey Island – a bird sanctuary, place of pilgrimage and the legendary resting place of 20,000 saints.

Nestling on its own wooded peninsula you will find Portmeirion, the Italianate extravaganza created by the late Sir Clough Williams Ellis, full of delightful surprises in the shape of statues, follies and fake facades.

Group Contact: Mrs Annwen Hughes ☎ 0758 612621

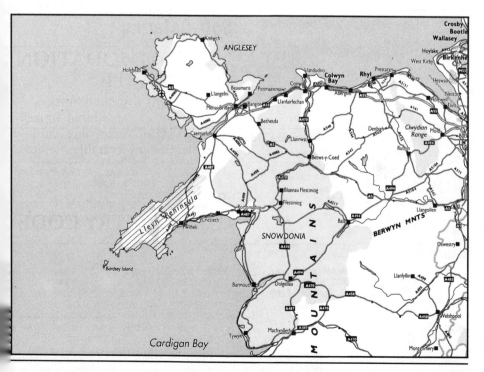

Bed and Breakfast (and evening meal)

Mathan Uchaf Farm, Boduan, Pwllheli, Gwynedd LL53 8TU

Mrs Jean Coker
☎ 0758 720487
BB From £14
EM From £8
Sleeps 5
🐕 🐈 👤
Listed

A 190-acre dairy farm, situated off the main Pwllheli to Nefyn Road. Centrally position for northern and southern beaches of peninsula. Guests can participate in farm activities. Large garden provides safe play area. We have 2 dogs who play ball and a Shetland pony. 1 double room, 1 family room with washbasins, 1 twin bedded room. Dining room, sitting room with colour TV. Good food and friendly atmosphere are our aim. Open Mar–Nov. Map ref: 163 126

Yoke House Farm, Pwllheli, Gwynedd LL53 5TY

Annwen Hughes
☎ 0758 612621
BB From £15
Sleeps 4
🐎 (10) 🌲
♨ 👑

A beautiful wooded drive welcomes you to this Georgian farmhouse on a 290-acre working dairy farm, where guests can watch the milking, calf feeding, etc. Exciting natural trail on farm. We offer comfortable, tastefully furnished accommodation and all bedrooms have washbasins, shaver points, tea/coffee-making facilities. Beach 5 mins by car. Open Easter–Sept. Map ref: 167 126

Self-Catering

Castellmarch, Abersoch, Pwllheli, Gwynedd LL53 7UE

Mrs H M Jones
☎ 0758 712242
SC From £90–£300
Sleeps 6
🐈 🐕
Approved

Castellmarch, a traditional family run beef and sheep farm, lies one mile from the yachting village of Abersoch and only a few minutes walk from nearest sandy beach. Castellmarch a listed 16th century farmhouse, was once the home of fabled March Ap Meirchion- a man with horses ears. Accommodation comprises of Cegin-isa (wing of farmhouse) sleeps 4. All rooms have exposed beams. The Granary (converted 18th century outbuilding) sleeps 5. A chalet set on elevated position sleeps 4-6. All enjoy sea views. Linen, cot and high chair available. 50 p meter. Brochure. Open all year. Map ref: 168 127

Cefnamwlch, Tudweiliog, Pwllheli, Gwynedd LL53 8AX

Mrs Wynne-Finch
☎ 075 887 209
SC From £90–£200
Sleeps 4/6 + cot
🐈
Approved

Houses 1 & 2 sleep 6 in 3 double bedrooms. Cot available. Converted from wing of owner's 17th century manor farmhouse on ancient Welsh estate. Situated in beautiful woodland setting 1 mile from village of Tudweiliog, along rhododendron drive. Easy reach sandy beaches, golf course. Ideal touring centre. Colour TV, tumble dryer and spindryer. Play area. Electric 50p meter. Ty Thimble Cottage sleeps 4 in 2 double bedrooms. Open Easter–end Oct. Map ref: 162 127

Gwynfryn, Gwynfryn Farm, Pwllheli, Gwynedd LL53 5UF

Sian B Ellis
☎ 0758 612536
sc From £75–£450
Sleeps 2/8
4–5 Dragons

Organic dairy farm, 2 miles sandy beaches, 25 miles Snowdon, castles, railways, slate mines. Playroom, adventure playground, animals and helping farmer keeps children occupied. Wellies a must! Sheets, storage heaters, central heating included, takeaway dishes, babysitting by arrangement.. Open fires. Dishwashers in 3 houses. Romantic couples, families, all are welcome. Map ref: 167 126

Penllechog, Llanaelhaearn, Caernarfon, Gwynedd LL54 5BH

Sydna Ellis
☎ 0758 85232
sc From £150–£300
Sleeps 6 + cot
Approved

Beef and sheep farm positioned on a hillside with panoramic views of Caridgan Bay and St Tudwal Islands,1 mile from Llanaelhaearn off the A499 Pwllheli to Caernarfon road. A tranquil base within easy distance of Anglesey, Snowdonia and the Lleyn Peninsula. 3 double bedrooms, comfortable spacious lounge with colour TV, kitchen/dining area with electric cooker and refrigerator and washing machine if required. Double glazing, fitted carpets, safe play area, elec extra. Open Easter–Oct. Map ref: 169 129

Rhydolion, Llangian, Abersoch, Pwllheli, Gwynedd LL53 7LR

Catherine Morris
☎ 075 881 2342
sc From £95–£245
Sleeps 8
Approved

A charming self-contained wing of this 16th century farmhouse situated in unspoilt countryside, only ¾ mile from beach. 3 bedrooms, one with an attractive four poster bed. Sitting/dining room with original beams and inglenook fireplace. Modern kitchen and laundry room, 50p electric meter. Private garden with barbecue and furniture. Children's play area. Free linen. Join in farm activities. Warm Welsh welcome assured. Open Mar–Oct. Map ref: 165 123

Tai Gwyliau Tyndon Holiday Cottages, c/o Penlan, Rhos Isaf, Caernarfon, Gwynedd LL54 7NG

Mrs Elizabeth Evans
☎ 0286 831184
sc From £75–£410
Sleeps 5/8
(touring & static)
3 Dragons

120 acre sheep farm on the beautiful Lleyn heritage coast. Peaceful and relaxing self-contained cottages and bungalows. 1 mile from Llanengan with its village shop, country pub and 16th century church. Boating resort of Abersoch only 2 miles away, beautiful sandy beach of Porthneigwl within 200 yards (with private access). All cottages have glorious views of the bay. Ideal family holiday. Personal supervision. Free brochure. Open all year. Map ref: 171 137

Towyn Farm, Tydweiliog, Pwllheli, Gwynedd LL53 8PD

Iona Wynne Owen
☎ 075887 230
sc From £100–£300
Sleeps 6/8 + cot
4 Dragons

Enjoy a relaxing holiday in unspoit area of outstanding natural beauty. 200 yds from renowned Towyn beach. Ideal fishing, surfing, boating. Nefyn golf course 3 miles. A 300-year-old modernised farmhouse, carpeted throughout, colour TV, 4 bedrooms sleeping 8, continental quilts and heaters. Open fire in autumn/winter. Bathroom with bath and shower. Fitted kitchen, washing machine, tumble dryer, microwave oven. Sheltered lawn garden with barbeque. Free babysitting. Cot and high chair. Also ground level cottage sleeping 6. Map ref: 162 127

Please mention **Stay on a Farm** when booking

65 Snowdonia

In Snowdonia those interested in history have a wealth of locations to visit, from the early 12th century Welsh fortresses at Dolbadarn and Dolwyddelan to the magnificent castles of Edward 1st at Caernarfon, Beaumaris, Harlech and Conwy. The National Trust's historic houses include Plas Newydd on Anglesey and Penrhyn Castle near Bangor. Segontium Fort at Caernarfon is witness to the four hundred years of Roman occupation and there is an interesting museum nearby.

Take a boat trip along the Menai Strait, a ride on a steam train into the mountains with the Talyllyn or Ffestiniog Railways, alongside Llanberis Lake or even up Mount Snowdon itself. Visit the heart of a Welsh slate quarry, take a trip to the theatre at Bangor or Harlech, or see craftsmen at work – some of the many choices available. Add to this the Sports Council's excellent centres near Caernarfon and Capel Curig, heated swimming pools at Caernarfon, Bangor and Harlech, golf at one of the many courses with superb sea views, some really excellent restaurants and pubs and walks in the mountains or forests, and often a week is all too short a time to stay with us.

Most of us are Welsh speaking as Snowdonia is the heartland of the Welsh language and we will be very happy to teach you a few Welsh greetings or tell you more about our ancient language.

**Group Contact: Mrs Jane Pierce, Ty Mawr Farm, Llanddeiniolen, Caernarfon,
Gwynedd LL53 3AD ☎ 0248 670147 or 0248 670336**

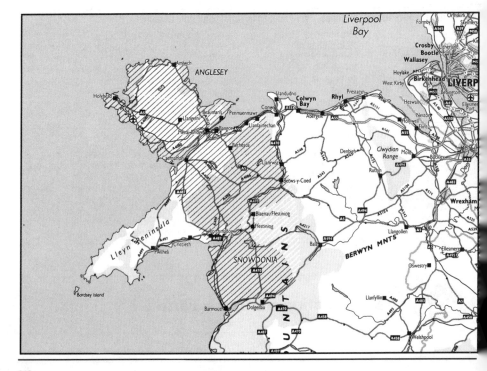

Bed and Breakfast (and evening meal)

Cae'r Efail, Llanfaglan, Caernarfon, Gwynedd LL54 5RE

Mrs Mari Williams
☎ 0286 76226 or 2824
BB From £14
EM From £8
Sleeps 6
ᗑ ⋔ ♨

In its grounds of 20 acres enjoying perfect peace, seclusion and magnificent views of Snowdpnia and Anglesey. A trip on one of the great little trains is not to be missed. Built at turn of the century, recently modernised, Cae'r Efail offers comfortable, tastefully furnished accommodation. Good food is of prime importance, using home/local produce, 2 doubles (1 en-suite), 1 twin. Reduced rates for children. Open Easter–Oct. Map ref: 461 602

Llwydiarth Fawr, Llanerchymedd, Isle of Anglesey, Gwynedd LL71 8DF

Mrs Margaret Hughes
☎ 0248 470321/470540
BB From £17.50
EM From £10
Sleeps 6
ᕘ ⤝ ᗑ

Highly Commended

Secluded Georgian mansion set in 800 acres of woodland and farmland. Ideal touring base for island's, coastline, Snowdonia and North Wales coast. Nearby is Llyn Alaw for trout fishing. Reputation for excellent food using farm and local produce. Bedrooms with en-suite bathrooms. TV, CH, log fires. A warm Welsh welcome to guests who enjoy walks and private fishing. Welsh Farmhouse Award. Brochure available. Open Jan–Nov. Map ref: 170 163

Pengwern, Saron, Llanwnda, Caernarfon, Gwynedd LL54 5UH

G & J Lloyd Rowlands
☎ 0286 830717
BB From £15
EM From £8.50
Sleeps 6
⤝ ᗑ ♨ ⚘

Highly Commended

Charming, spacious farmhouse of character, situated between mountains and sea. Unobstructed views of Snowdonia. Well appointed bedrooms, all en-suite or with private facilities. Set in 130 acres of land which runs down to Foryd Bay. Jane has a cookery diploma and provides the excellent meals with farmhouse fresh food, including home-produced beef and lamb. Excellent access. Open Feb–Nov. Map ref: 173 122

Plas Tirion Farm, Llanrug, Caernarfon, Gwynedd LL55 4PY

C H Mackinnon
☎ 0286 673190
BB From £16
EM From £8.50
Sleeps 6
ᕘ

Highly Commended

Welcome to our working dairy farm with comfortable, heated accommodation. All en-suite bedrooms with beverage facilities, TV and panoramic views. Recommended for breakfast and dinners using fresh produce. Special diets available; residential licence; packed lunches. Rough shooting. 4 miles Llanberis and Caernarfon, 10 miles Anglesey, 8 miles beach. Wales Farmhouse Award; Open May–Oct. Map ref: 174 137

Plas Trefarthen, Brynsiencyn, Anglesey, Gwyneed LL61 6SZ

Marian Roberts
☎ 0248 430379
BB From £16
EM From £10
Sleeps 14
⋔ ᕘ

Highly Commended

A large Georgian house in 200 acres of land on the shore of the Menai Straits. Outstanding views of Snowdonia and Caernarfon Castle, ideal base for touring Anglesey and Snowdonia, walking and local National Trust properties. Small groups catered for, excellent home cooking. Large en-suite bedrooms, tea/coffee-making facilities, colour TV, full size snooker table. Welsh welcome. Map ref: 173 137

Tre'r Ddol Farm, Llanerchymedd, Isle of Anglesey, Gwynedd LL71 7AR

Ann Astley
☎ 0248 470278
🅱 From £16
EM From £9
Sleeps 6
🐕 🐄 🐎
♨ ♨ ♨
Highly Commended

If you are looking for freedom and relaxation this family farm of 200 acres can oblige. Its historic 17th century house and country antiques add to the mystery and character of the past. Ornithologists' paradise, plus excellent fishing at Llyn Alaw and sport activities. Spacious en-suite bedrooms. Guests' comfort a priority and food a speciality. Children enjoy sandy rocky beaches. Pony rides and participate in farm activities. Wales Farmhouse Award. SAE for brochure. Open Jan–Nov. Map ref: 168 144

Ty Mawr Farm, Llanddeiniolen, Caernarfon, Gwynedd LL55 3AD

Jane Llewelyn Pierce
☎ 0248 670147
🅱 From £15
Sleeps 6
🐎 🖴
Applied

Ty Mawr is a working farm with easy access off the B4366 road. Making it an ideal base for touring Snowdonia. We have 3 double rooms all with en-suite bathrooms and tea/coffee-making facilities. Robert and Jane Pierce welcome you to their farm and to enjoy the cows, hens, horses and the rare Welsh badger faced sheep. Plenty of good wholesome traditional food in comfortable warm surroundings. Open all year. Map ref: 174 138

Ty Mawr Farmhouse, Saron, Llanwnda, Caernarfon, Gwynedd LL54 5UH

Carol Mills
☎ 0286 830091
🅱 From £14
Sleeps 6
🐕 🍴 🐄 (4) 🖴 🍽
♨ ♨ ♨
Highly Commended

Character farmhouse, parts date from 1600s, interesting blend of country antiques and modern comfort. Pretty bedrooms with colour TV, tea/coffee, CH, en-suite shower, bath, WC. Delicious breakfasts, traditional grill, wholefood or vegetarian. Light suppers available 6.30pm to 9.30pm at reasonable prices. Tranquil, sunny position, easy to find, good access. Smallholding with friendly goats, calves, poultry. Open Jan–Nov. Map ref: 173 122

Self-Catering

SC

Llys Bennar, Dyffryn Ardudwy, Gwynedd LL44 2RX

Catrin Rutherford
☎ and fax 0341 247316
🆂�🅲 From £183–£370
Sleeps 4/7
🐕 ♿ 🐄 Å 🐎
4 Dragons

Attractive 18th century farm buildings converted into charming cottages, within a courtyard setting. They have retained the original charm of the oak beams, one with inglenook fireplace. Both have nightstore heating. Laundry facility available. Ten minutes to village or to sandy beach. One mile from station. In Snowdonia National Park. Many attractions in the area. Open all year. Map ref: 177 124

Ynys, Ystumgwern, Dyffryn Ardudwy, Gwynedd LL44 2DD

Jane & John Williams
☎ 0341 247249
🆂🅲 From £125–£420
Sleeps 2/8
🐕 🐄 Å 🐎 ♿ 🕯 🖴 🍽
5 Dragons

A taste of luxury with a cosy, relaxed atmosphere in quiet setting, 1 mile from sandy beach, shops and station. Kitchen/diner with dishwasher, microwave, Aga, oak beams. Lounge has electric or open fire in inglenook fireplace and NSH. Each bedroom is tastefully furnished and heated. Laundry room. Barbecue and picnic tables. Ample parking via private drive. Welcome from owners close at hand if required. Farmhouse award. Open all year. Map ref: 177 124

66 Calon Eryri – Heart of Snowdonia

A choice of quality, traditional welsh farmhouses, in an Area of Outstanding Natural Beauty. All our farms are centrally located within the Snowdonia National Park, making them an ideal base for exploring the whole of North Wales.

Most of us have en-suite bedrooms, tea and coffee trays, colour TV's and provide full farmhouse breakfasts with optional evening meals. There are numerous attractions within this area including narrow gauge railways – the spectacular Ffestiniog Railway, Bala Lake railway and the Welsh Highland at Porthmadog. Slate is the theme at Blaenau Ffestiniog, where the Llechwedd Slate Caverns and Gloddfa Ganol Mountain Centre welcome thousands of visitors, and where you can journey into victorian working conditions. Stroll through the unique Italianate village of Portmeirion near Porthmadog. Dry slope skiing at Trawsfynydd. Pony trekking near Porthmadog and Ffestiniog. Bala Lake is renowned for it's watersports, sailing and windsurfing. Keen fishermen can fish at Bala Lake, Llyn Celyn and Trawsfynydd. Bodnant Garden in the Conwy valley is world acclaimed and not to be missed! There are many National Trust properties to visit. Also a great choice of historic and roman ruins. All this plus the mountains, lakes, waterfalls and fine beaches await you. Hear our language, listen to local choirs practising, above all relax, find peace and tranquility in the resplendent beauty that surrounds you.

Group Contact: Carol Bain ☎ 0766 87397

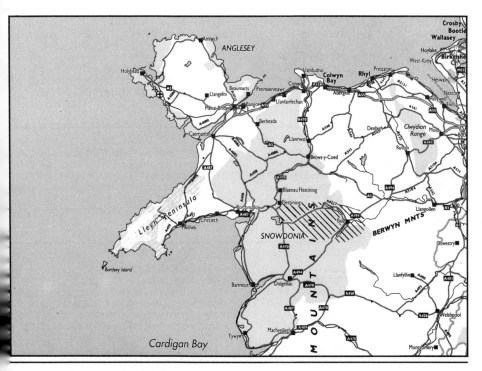

Bed and Breakfast (and evening meal)

Bryn Celynog Farm, Cwm Prysor, Trawsfynydd, Gwynedd LL41 4TR

Mrs G E Hughes
0766 87378
From £14
EM From £7
Sleeps 6
Commended

A true Welsh welcome awaits you on this beef, sheep farm. 3 miles from Trawsfynydd village. Stonbuilt farmhouse centrally heated throughout. Choice of spacious twin, double, or family bedrooms with washbasins, tea/coffee-making facilities, guests' bathroom, lounge with colour TV, log fire, seperate tables in dining room, reputation for excellent food and friendliness. Optional evening meal. Open all year. Map ref: 186 127

Fferm Fron-Gôch, Frongoch, Bala, Gwynedd LL23 7NT

Carys Davies
0678 520483
From £13
EM From £7.50
Sleeps 6
(9)
Highly Commended

A beautiful stone built farmhouse with interesting historical links with Abraham Lincoln's ancestors. Set in 600 acres of unspoilt countryside, situated 3 miles from Bala on the A4212. Traditionally furnished with antiques, log fires and oak beams. Relax in a friendly Welsh atmosphere. 2 double en-suite, 1 twin bedroom. Open all year. Map ref: 188 127

Old Mill Farmhouse, Fron Oleu Farm, Trawsfynydd, Gwynedd LL41 4UN

Carol Bain
0766 87397
From £15
EM From £7.50
Listed

It's our aim to provide a relaxing friendly atmosphere for guests visiting our character farmhouse (circa. 1700), overlooking the lake and mountains. Adjacent level access bedrooms in stonebuilt converted farmbuildings. All en-suite with TV, central heating, tea/coffee-making facilities. Ample portions of fresh wholesome food, guest lounge, log fires, child reductions. Help feed various friendly animals. Escape and unwind! SAE please for brochures. Open Mar–Dec.

Rhydydefaid Farm, Frongoch, Bala, Gwynedd LL23 7NT

Olwen Davies
0678 520456
From £13
Sleeps 6
Listed Commended

A true Welsh welcome awaits you at our traditional Welsh stone farmhouse. 3 miles from Bala near A4212 road. 100-acre working farm. Oak beamed lounge with inglenook fireplace. 1 oak beamed en-suite, family bedroom, twin/single bedrooms with wash basin, both with tea/coffee-making facilities. Ideal for touring Snowdonia. Map ref: 188 128

Tyddyn Du Farm, Gellilydan, Ffestiniog, Gwynedd LL41 4RB

Paula Williams
0766 85281
From £14, EM From £7.50,D, B&B From £133
Sleeps 6
Highly Commended

This beautiful old farmhouse is centrally located for the spectacular walks, numerous attractions and beaches of North Wales. Our 17th century farmhouse has charm and character, inglenook, antiques and exposed stonework. One superb cottage suite, all have beverage trays. Home cooking with homemade soups, buns etc. Vegetarians welcome. Ponies, ducks and bottle-fed lambs on farm. Open Jan–Nov. Map ref: 180 129

67 Warm Welsh Welcome Clwyd

Clwyd – its northern boundary strung with seaside resorts – comes up with some surprising contrasts, from the sandcastle and holiday atmosphere of the coast to the fortresses left behind from mediaeval times. It is a splendid area of Wales which, away from the necklace of sea towns, is relatively unvisited.

St Asaph, at the head of the Vale of Clwyd, might be just a village, but it is also a cathedral city – even if the cathedral is the smallest in the country and one of the oldest in Wales. It dates back to the 15th century and houses treasures like William Morgan's Welsh translation of the Bible.

Further into the county lies Ruthin, a mediaeval market town famous for its curfew bells, rung every night at 8pm since the 11th century. Ruthin also boasts a castle where you can enjoy a mediaeval banquet and the Maen Huail stone where King Arthur is said to have beheaded his rival in love, the unfortunate Huail. The craft centre in Ruthin is worth a visit, as are the ones at Nannerch and Llanasa. Crafts of a different nature are to be found in Llangollen where horse-drawn barges glide along the Shropshire Union Canal and the International Musical Eisteddfod is held annually in early July.

For a faster pace, what about a trip along the restored section of the Great Western Railway from Llangollen to Fford Junction? To the west is Llyn Brenig, a fishing and sailing centre, with nearby forests full of inviting trails and picnic sites.

Group Contact: Mrs Del Crossley ☎ 097 888 270

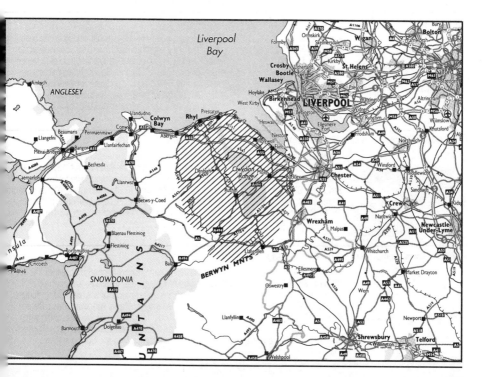

Bed and Breakfast (and evening meal)

Bach-y-Graig, Tremeirchion, St Asaph, Clwyd LL17 0UH

Anwen Roberts
☎ 0745 730627
BB From £16
EM From £9
Sleeps 6
⚡ 🐎
🐛 🐛 🐛 Highly
Commended

A 16th century listed farmhouse nestling at the foot of the Clwydian Range with beautiful views of the surrounding countryside. Highest standard of traditional furnishings and decor, en suite, TVs, tea/coffee-making facilities in bedrooms, full CH, beamed inglenook fireplace with log fires. Central for North Wales, Chester coast 9 miles. Games room. 40 acre woodland trail on farm. WTB Farmhouse Award. AA selected award. Open all year. Map ref: 195 140

Bodangharad, Llanfwrog, Ruthin, Clwyd LL15 2AH

Enid Jones
☎ 0824 702370
BB From £12.50
Sleeps 6
🐓 🐎 🏛
Listed Approved

Bodangharad is a 100-acre dairy/sheep farm in unspoilt countryside, with a wealth of wild flowers and hedgerows. Panoramic views of Vale of Clwyd. We are a few minutes' drive from historic market town of Ruthin, with easy access to Chester, coast and Snowdonia. House with interesting interior with exposed beams, open fires and spacious rooms for guests. It offers peace and tranquility and plenty of farmhouse fresh food. Open Mar–Nov. Map ref: 195 134

Bryn Awel, Bontuchel, Ruthin, Clwyd LL15 2DE

Beryl J Jones
☎ 082470 2481
BB From £14.50
EM From £6
Sleeps 4
🐓
🐛 🐛
Highly Commended

This 35-acre working farm is situated in the beautiful hamlet of BONTUCHEL where you can relax in peace to enjoy wonderful walks and wildlife. Convenient base for Chester, North Wales coast and Snowdonia. Beryl was awarded a medal for the FHB 'British Main Meal' competition in 1989 and holds the WTB Farmhouse Award. Two rooms en-suite, twin and double. Open all year. Map ref: 194 134

Cae Madoc Farm, Llandegla, Nr Wrexham, Clwyd LL11 3BD

Mrs Del Crossley
☎ 0824 790423
BB From £14
EM From £8.50
Sleeps 6
🐓 🐎 🏃 ⚓
🐛

A short break or a long stay to re-charge your batteries? 'Cae Madoc', quiet cosy old centrally heated farmhouse. Situated on A5104 Chester/Corwen road close to beautiful Horseshoe Pass. Central for visiting Mold (Theatr Clwyd), Wrexham (Erddig NT), Chester (Zoo). Walking, pony trekking, carriage rides, fishing nearby. Home-made produce. Children reduced rates. Brochure available. Open all year (closed Christmas). Map ref: 198 137

College Farm, Peniel, Denbigh, Clwyd LL16 4TT

Helen Parry
☎ 074 570 276
BB From £13
EM From £7.50
Sleeps 5
🐓 🐓 ⚡ 🐎
🐛 Highly Commended

We invite you to our 140-acre farm set in a peaceful location 2½ miles from Denbigh. Farmhouse is centrally heated, bedrooms have washbasins and tea/coffee-making facilities. Central for coast and mountains. Nearby is Brenig Reservoir for fishing, sailing and walking. Evening meal by arrangement. WTB Farmhouse Award. A warm Welsh welcome is assured by the bilingual Parry family. Map ref: 193 134

lainwen Ucha, Pentre Celyn, Ruthin, Clwyd LL15 2HL

Elizabeth Parry
☎ 097 888 253
[BB] From £12
EM From £7
Sleeps 5
☿
Listed

Our 130 acre farm overlooks the beautiful Vale of Clwyd. Centrally situated to coast, Snowdonia, Chester and Llangollen. Modern house with 2 pleasant bedrooms to accommodate 5 persons. CH and good home cooking, a warm welcome to visitors throughout the year. Take A525 from Ruthin towards Wrexham; after 4 miles turn left after college, we are a mile up this road. Open Jan–Nov. Map ref: 196 133

---

hewl Farm, Waen, St Asaph, Clwyd LL17 0DT

Eirlys Jones
☎ 0745 582287
[BB] From £11–£13
EM From £8
Sleeps 6
✂ ☿ ✿
♛ ♛ Commended

Enjoy Welsh hospitality on our 180-acre farm, conveniently situated ½ mile from A55 expressway in a peaceful and beautiful setting. Comfortable bedrooms with radiators and tea/coffee-making facilities. Double has en-suite facilities, twin and family HC. Spacious lounge with inglenook fireplace and colour TV. Evening meal by arrangement. Convenient for Chester, coast and Snowdonia. Free fishing. Games room. Reductions for children. Map ref: 193 141

---

aith Daran Farm, Llandegla, Wrexham, Clwyd LL11 3BA

Pat Thompson
☎ 097 888 685
[BB] From £16
Sleeps 4
☿ ⚔ 🔌 💼
♛ ♛

Beautifully situated near the top of the breathtaking Horseshoe Pass at the junction of the A5104 and A542. Near Llangollen and mediaeval Ruthin, ideal for touring the N. Wales coast, Snowdonia and Chester. 85-acre dairy/beef farm. Conservatory to relax and enjoy the lovely views. Bedrooms en suite with tea/coffee-making facilities, electric blankets, radio and TV. Riding and shooting nearby. Open Mar–Nov. Map ref: 198 137

Coch Farm, Llangynhafal, Denbigh, Clwyd LL16 4LN

Anne L Richards
☎ 0824 790423
[BB] From £11
EM From £6
Sleeps 5
☿
♛ Commended

Working dairy and sheep farm, beautiful views, pleasant walks, five miles of historic towns of Ruthin and Denbigh. Ideal base for Chester and North Wales. Wash basins and tea/coffee-making facilities. Good home cooking, local produce, special diets catered for. A war Welsh welcome awaits you. Open all year (closed Christmas). Map ref: 195 137

[SC] # Self-Catering

---

ddyn Isaf, Rhewl, Ruthin, Clwyd LL15 1UH

Elsie Jones
☎ 0824 703367
[SC] From £95–£210
Sleeps 6 + cot
☿
3–4 Dragons

A warm welcome is assured on this 80-acre mixed farm with lovely views, 3 miles from market town of Ruthin. Within easy reach of Chester, the coast and Snowdonia. The comfortably furnished accommodation in the spacious self-contained part of farmhouse with oak beams has 1 double, 1 family bedroom, bathroom, separate toilet, kitchen, lounge/diner, colour TV, radio, highchair, cot available, central heating winter months. Linen provided. No pets. Open all year. Map ref: 194 135

68 Llangollen

A romantic town on the salmon-filled Dee. It is hard to imagine a more idyllic location. The discerning visitor can browse around the shops, St Collens Church, and the European Centre for Traditional and Regional Cultures, cross the 14th century bridge which is one of the seven wonders of Wales, take a horse-drawn boa along the canal or a steam train ride through the Vale. Plas Newydd – home of the Ladies of Llangollen, Valle Crucis Abbey, The Pillar of Eliseg and the Horseshoe pas are all within a short distance.

In the eighth century Offa, King of Mercia, built Offa's Dyke. Part of this legendary dyke runs parallel to the river Dee beneath the Eglwseg rocks past Castell Dinas Bran, which is well worth the climb for a spectacular view of the town. You can also enjoy the Panoramic Walks down to Trevor and Thomas Telford's famous aqueduct crossing high above the Dee.

In early July the surrounding hills really do come alive to the sound of music when the International Musical Eisteddfod welcomes singers and dancers from all over th world. This was first held in 1947 to heal the wounds of war, and the same welcome continues throughout the year.

Come and see what other hidden delights Llangollen has to offer and perhaps you may discover more wonders of Wales.

Group Contact: Mrs Shelagh Roberts ☎ 0978 823 403

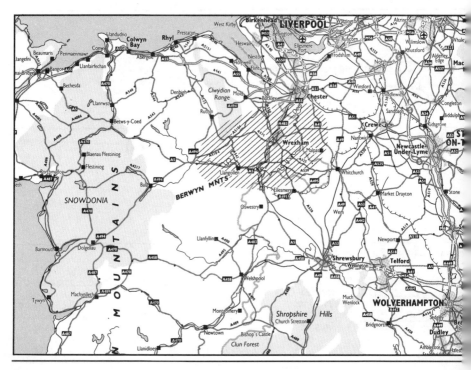

Bed and Breakfast
(and evening meal)

Cefn Y Fedw Farm, Garth, Llangollen, Clwyd

Mrs Shelagh Roberts
☎ 0978 823 403
BB From £15
EM From £7
Sleeps 6
🐕 🐈 ✄
♨ ♨

Cefn Y Fedw stands high above Garth village in the hills behind Llangollen. A working farm, offering good food, comfortable accommodation in spacious rooms. Guests' private bathrooms. A private walk for guests interested in rock formation, historical sites or birdwatching has been designed. Close to panorama walk, Offa's Dyke path. Ring for brochure. Open May–Oct. Map ref: 205 134

Pen-Lan Farm, Llangollen, Clwyd LL20 7BU

Myra Jones
☎ 0978 860 745
BB From £13
EM From £6
Sleeps 6
🐕 🐈 ♨
Applied

Gwilym, Myra, Mari and Huw, invite you to stay at Pen-Lan. The farm overlooks the beautiful valleys around Llangollen. We keep sheep and beef cattle, and a pony for free rides. Guests are welcome to walk about or help. We aim to provide friendly, peaceful holidays, with comfortable accommodation, and good food prepared by a Cordon Bleu cook. Open May–Oct. Map ref: 199 128

FINDING YOUR ACCOMMODATION

FARM HOLIDAY BUREAU

The Group contacts at the beginning of each section can always help you find a vacancy in your chosen area.

FARM HOLIDAY BUREAU

GOOD
FOOD

Nearly all Bureau members now hold a certificate in Essential Food Hygiene.

69 Croeso Cader Idris

A true Welsh welcome 'croeso' is offered by the farming families around Cader Idris, one of the highest peaks in Wales; from the farms you can explore the coast and the countryside of this lovely area of Wales.

A vast area of green valleys and mountains criss-crossed by long distance footpaths, old drover's lanes and mountain paths which provide some of the finest hill walking country in Britain. For the explorer and adventurer, fishing, golfing, riding, pony trekking, climbing, canoeing and a mountain bike safari ensure a wealth of activity. Dolgellau, beneath the majestic peak of Cader Idris, and Fairbourne, with its beautiful beach, combined with a visit to a real gold mine at Ganllwyd is a day out to remember. The fascination of watching working demonstrations of wind, water and solar power at the National Centre for Alternative Technology near Machynlleth or a visit to Trawsfynydd Power Station give an insight into the power of nature and man's sympathetic harnessing of it.

An exciting area of contrasts, from the golden beaches of the coast to the high mountains of the National Park, there is something for everyone, from craft workshops to forest visitor centres, towering castles to deep slate caverns.

The Welsh language is heard frequently; the farmers of Cader Idris have roots deep in the area, their forefathers having worked the land before them for generations.

A warm welcome is extended to visitors to share the language, history, culture and hospitality of one of the loveliest areas of Wales.

Group Contact: Mrs Meirwen Pughe ☎ 0654 761235

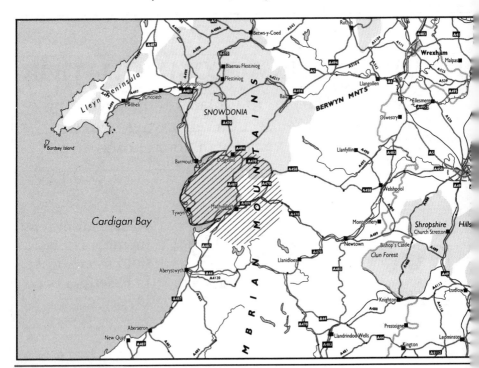

Bed and Breakfast (and evening meal)

Cynfal Farm, Bryncrug, Tywyn, Gwynedd LL36 9RB

Mrs Carys Evans
☎ 0654 711703
BB From £13
EM From £7
Sleeps 6
🐕 🛏
🦆 🦆

"Croeso" to Cynfal, a 340-acre farm run by a Welsh-speaking family. A Victorian period farmhouse of great charm and character, magnificently situated, with the pleasure of the Talyllyn narrow gauge railway running 150 yards below the house. Spacious bedrooms are tastefully decorated and have the use of two private bathrooms. Open Mar–Oct. Map ref: 175 113

Glynn Farm, Fairbourne Road, Dolgellau, Gwynedd LL40 1YA

Mrs E Wyn Price
☎ 0341 422286
BB From £12.50
Sleeps 6
🐕 🛏 🍵 ♨
Listed

Glyn Farm stands on a hill with all double rooms overlooking the picturesque Mawddach estuary, 1 mile from Dolgellau on old Fairbourne road, before junction for by-pass. TV and teasmade in all rooms. Spacious lounge with individual tables in dining room when possible. Fire certificate held. Children welcomed also well behaved dogs. Most years we have pet lambs. A.A. listed. SAE for colour leaflet. Map ref: 180 121

Gogarth Hall Farm, Pennal, Machynlleth, Powys, SY20 9LB

Mrs Deilwen Breese
☎ 0654 791235
BB From £12
EM From £6.50
Sleeps 6
🐕 🐕 🍵 🛏
🦆 🦆

Let Ron and Deilwen welcome you to Gogarth Hall, built around 1747. This working farm commands magnificent views of the Dovey Estuary, 4 miles from Aberdovey Beach. Come walking, birdwatching, fishing or shooting. Two traditionally furnished bedrooms sleeping 2–4, with washbasins and tea-making facilities. Guests' dining and sitting rooms. Evening meals and babysitting service. Also self catering. Open all year. Map ref: 181 112

Tanycoed Ucha, Abergynolwyn, Tywyn, Gwynedd LL36 9UP

Gweniona Pugh
☎ 0654 782228
BB From £12
EM From £7
Sleeps 5
🛏 🐕 🛏
Listed

Relax and enjoy your holiday on our farm with its beautiful views of Dolgoch Valley and Talyllyn narrow gauge railway. Sample true Welsh hospitality with generous home cooking. See sheep, cattle and many more on our 1100 acre family farm. Double, twin-bedded and single bedroom with washbasins and tea facilities. Shower in bathroom, CH and TV. Log fires when needed. Open Mar–Nov. Map ref: 178 115

Tyddyn Rhys Farm, Aberdovey, Gwynedd LL35 0PG

Mrs Mair Jones
☎ 0654 767533
BB From £13.50
Sleeps 5
🛏 🍴 🐕 🛏
🦆 🦆

A warm Welsh welcome awaits you at Tyddyn Rhys with its fantastic panoramic view of the Dovey Estuary and Cardigan Bay. Only ½ mile from the centre of Aberdovey with its beautiful sandy beaches. Full central heating with colour TV, tea/coffee making facilities in bedrooms. Also static caravan to let. Very nice walks in the area. Open Mar–Nov. Map ref: 176 119

Self-Catering

Carn y Gadell Uchaf, c/o Henblas, Llwyngwril, Gwynedd LL37 2QA

Mrs Swancott Pugh
☎ 0341 250350
🆂🅲 From £125–£350
Sleeps 6
⤸ ⤳
5 Dragons

An historic 16th century farmhouse situated 1 mile from A493, a perfect retreat with panoramic views of Cardigan Bay. Stone spiral staircase, inglenook fireplace with log fire, 3 bedrooms, 2 bathrooms, colour TV, video, dishwasher, washing machine, fridge/freezer, microwave, games room, drying room. Excellent accommodation, ideal for exploring Snowdonia National park. Welsh speaking family. Brochure. Open all year. Map ref: 176 114

Glynn Farm, Fairbourne Road, Dolgellau, Gwynedd LL40 1YA

Mrs E Wyn Price
☎ 0341 422286
🆂🅲 From £60–£220
Sleeps 4/8
⤳ 🐾 🐈 ▪
Approved

15th century farm cottage on working farm, 600 acres, 1 mile from Cross Foxes Inn, 4 miles Dolgellau at food of Cader Idris, a field from A487 Machynlleth road. Sleeps 8, cot, highchair. Free fishing, Sky TV. Ample parking. Inglenook with open fire. Also separate wing to sleep 4. SAE please for brochure. Map ref: 183 123

FARM HOLIDAY BUREAU

THOSE LITTLE EXTRAS

For advice on farms that can offer 'extras' such as four-poster beds, special diets, farm trails, fishing rights – even stabling and trekking arrangements if you are bringing your own horse – ring the Farm Holiday Bureau on (0203) 696909.

70 Montgomeryshire

The Heart of Wales has unspoilt villages, bustling little towns, and marvellous scenery – hills and mountains, sparkling streams, superb woodlands, tranquil lakes and reservoirs.

It is also surprisingly compact, with plenty to do and see without travelling far from your base. Roads are relative traffic free and none of the properties is much more than one hour's drive from the sandy beaches and rugged cliffs of the coast. There are plenty of country pubs for a lunchtime snack and the food we serve is largely fresh local produce, often from our own gardens. English is understood everywhere, but you will hear Welsh spoken, particularly in the north and west. You will soon become accustomed to the seemingly difficult sounds of our place names and personal names (we are all used to advising guests on pronunciation!) We also make a point of having information in our houses about events and places of interest, to help you enjoy your stay.

There are reminders of border struggles years ago; and the 8th century rampart built by King Offa is now a 170-mile public footpath. Among other man-made attractions, the area is renowned for its unique black-and-white buildings, including cruck houses, box-framed houses and their many variations.

Group Contact: Mrs Gwyneth Williams ☎ 0551 6285

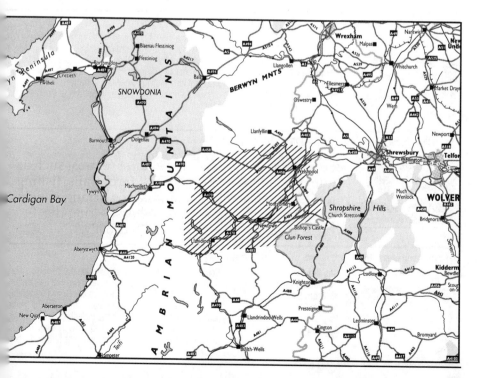

Bed and Breakfast (and evening meal)

Cwmllwynog, Llanfair, Caereinion,Welshpool, Powys SY21 0HFE

Joyce Cornes
☎ 0938 810791
BB From £12
½ ⌂
👑 👑 👑
Highly Commended

Built in the early 17th century Cwmllwynog is a traditional long farmhouse of character on a working dairy farm. We have a spacious garden with a stream at the bottom and a lot of unusual plants. All bedrooms have colour TV and drink making facilities. Double room en-suite, twin with hot and cold and private bathroom. Delicious home-cooked meals cooked. Just for you! We can help you with routes so that you can enjoy your countryside. Map ref: 195 115

Cyfie Farm, Llanfihangel-yng-Ngwynfa, Llanfyllin, Powys SY22 5JE

Mrs Lynn Jenkins
☎ 0691 648 451
BB From £16.50
EM From £9
Sleeps 6
⌂
👑 👑 👑
Highly Commended

A warm welcome awaits at Cyfie. A working hill farm close to scenic Lake Vyrnwy. The well featured farmhouse sits high with delightful views from the patio and colourful garden. Funished to a very high standard. 1 stable suite. Attractive bedrooms all with private facilities, beverage trays, TV, radio, hair dryers. Comfortable loungs with open log fires. Superb traditional meals served in our new dining room with conservatory feature. Awarded Wales Tourist Board Northmace Hospitality Award 1992. Open all year. Map ref: 195 116

Dol-Llys Farm, Llanidloes, Caernarfon, Powys SY18 6JA

Olwen S Evans
☎ 05512 2694
BB From £12
EM From £7
Sleeps 6
⌂ Å ⌨
👑 👑 **Commended**

Dol-Llys is a 17th century farmhouse intriguing because it has so many levels and small staircases. Situated on the banks of the river Severn one mile from the market town of Llanidloes. Visitors are free to wander the fields and watch the working farm activities. Fishing and childs pony on farm. Tea and coffee-making facilities. 2 en-suite bedrooms. Open all year. Map ref: 188 105

The Drewin Farm, Churchstoke, Montgomery, Powys SY15 6TW

Mrs Ceinwen Richards
☎ 0588 620325
BB From £13
EM From £7
Sleeps 6
⌐ ½ ⌂ Å ⌨
👑 👑 👑
Highly Commended

Relax in our friendly family run 17th century farmhouse retaining original character with oak beams and inglenook fireplace. 2 pleasant bedrooms with TV and drinks facilities, 1 en-suite both overlook magnificent unspoilt countryside. Games room with snooker table, good home cooking is served in the oak beamed dining room, vegetarian by request. Offas Dyke footpath runs through our mixed farm kennels for dogs. A warm Welsh welcome awaits you. AA WWBBA WTB 3 Crowns and farmhouse award. Map ref: 200 112

Dyffryn, Aberhafesp, Newtown, Powys SY16 3JD

Sue Jones
☎ 0686 688817
BB From £14
Sleeps 6
⌂
Applied

Come stay with us in our lovingly restored 17th century barn set in the heart of a 200 acre working sheep and beef farm. Luxury en-suite bedrooms all with colour TV and teamaking facilities. Separate guests loung and dining room. Full centrl heating. Traditional farmhouse fare including vegetarian – evening meals optional. Golf, fishing, pony trekking, glorious walks and lakes nearby. Guests are welcome to wlak the farm Map ref: 194 110

Gungrog House, Rhallt, Welshpool, Powys SY21 9HS

Eira Jones
☎ 0938 553381
BB From £16
EM From £9
Sleeps 6

Highly Commended

Off the A483 opposite its junction with the A458, just east of Welshpool, Gungrog House is located at Rhallt. A spacious 16th-century farmhouse, inside you will find traditional finishings. An oak staircase leads up to the well-appointed bedrooms, 2 with shower/toilet en-suite. The house is fully centrally heated. There is a large lounge with colour TV. Home cooking is a speciality served in our large dining room. Open Apr–Oct. Map ref: 199 115

Little Brompton Farm, Montgomery, Powys SY15 6HY

Gaynor Bright
☎ 0686 668371
BB From £14
EM From £8
Sleeps 6

Highly Commended

Robert and Gaynor warmly welcome you to their charming 17th century farmhouse. A working farm situated on B4385 2 miles east of the Georgian town of Montgomery. Many rooms have a wealth of oak beams. Family, double or twin bedrooms, some en-suite. Good traditional cooking. An ideal place to explore Mid Wales and the Border Country. Offa's Dyke passes through the farm. WTB Farmhouse Award. AA listed. Open all year. Map ref: 199 113

Llettyderyn, Mochdre, Newtown, Powys SY16 4JY

Mrs Margaret Jandrell
☎ 0686 626131
BB From £14
EM From £7
Sleeps 4

Highly Commended

Llettyderyn – a restored 18th century farmhouse with exposed beams, inglenook fireplace and traditional parlour. A working farm rearing sheep and beef. 2 miles from Newtown; an ideal base for touring Mid-Wales. Excellent farmhouse cooking, with home-made bread. Vegetarians catered for. Double and twin-bedded rooms with showers, washbasins, tea-making facilities and TV. Full central heating. Ample parking. Open Mar–Nov. Map ref: 195 108

Lower Gwerneirin Farm, Llandinam, Powys SY17 5DD

FARM HOLIDAY BUREAU

Mrs A Brown
☎ 0686 688286
BB From £13
Sleeps 6

Applied

Lower Gwerneirin is beautifully situated farm in the Severn valley. The farmhouse is a spacious Victorian dwelling offering comfortable accommodation. All rooms central yeated with hadbasins and tea-making facilities, 2 double and 1 twin. Guests own lounge with colour TV and log fire, fishing available in own trout pool. We have a wealth of wild life, ideally located for exploring mid-Wales. Delcious home cooking. Map ref: 192 108

Lower Gwestydd, Newtown, Powys SY16 3AY

Iris Jarman
☎ 0686 626718
BB From £15.50
EM From £7.50
Sleeps 6

Highly Commended

Lower Gwestydd is a listed half-timbered farmhouse set on a quiet hillside 2 miles north of Newtown just off the B4568 road. Guests have own lounge and dining room with exposed beams. All rooms centrally heated and bedrooms have shower and toilet en-suite. WTB Farmhouse Award and offers 'A Taste of Wales'. Finalist in the Best British Breakfast 1991 competition by *In Britain* magazine BTA. Large garden with beautiful views. Open all year. Map ref: 195 109

Moat Farm, Welshpool, Powys SY21 8SE

Gwyneth Jones
☎ 0938 553179
BB From £17
EM From £8
Sleeps 6

Highly Commended

Moat Farm is a 260-acre dairy farm set in the beautiful Severn Valley. The 17th century farmhouse offers warm and comfortable accommodation with good home cooking served in a fine timbered dining room, traditionally furnished with Welsh dresser. TV and tea facilities in all rooms, all en-suite. Quiet lounge, pool table and spacious garden. Good touring centre. Near Powis Castle. Open Mar–Nov. Map ref: 200 116

Self-Catering

Cwm Y Gath, Trewythen, LLandinam, Powys SY17 5BQ

Ceinwen & Ann Davies
☎ 0686688 444
SC From £70–300
Sleeps 4
🐾 ♿
Applied

Delightful shepherds cottage, refurbished to a high standard, overlooking a working beef and sheep farm with magnificent views in peaceful surroundings with a wealth of oak beams and inglenook fireplace. The cottage has one double bedroom and one twin bedroom. An ideal spot for nature lovers and walkers. Golfing, fishing, ponytrekking and lakes nearby. Enquiries welcome. Open all year. Map ref: 192 108

Gungrog Cottage, c/o Gungrog House, Rhallt, Welshpool, Powys SY21 9HS

Mrs Eira Jones
☎ 0938 553381
SC From £120–£200
Sleeps 6
🐾 ♿
Approved

Off the A483 opposite its junction with the A458, just east of Welshpool, Gungrog Cottage is located at a place called Rhallt, standing in an elevated position giving magnificent views of the Severn Valley. Set in 21 acres of farmland, the cottage is fully centrally heated and well-equipped. Kitchen/diner, bathroom with shower. The cottage was converted from a 16th century barn and retains much of its original charm and character. Open Apr–Oct. Map ref: 199 115

Red House, Trefeglwys, Nr Caersws, Powys SY17 5PN

Gwyneth Williams
☎ 05516 285
SC From £60–£200
Sleeps 2/6
🐾 Ⓔ
4 Dragons

Situated on a mixed family farm, overlooking the idyllic Trannon Valley, it is a comfortable self contained part of the farmhouse. Comprising of fully equipped kitchen with dining facilities and automatic washing machine, carpeted lounge with colour TV, 2 double, 1 twin, bathroom and a wealth of oak beams upstairs. Ideal touring area with an abundance of bird and animal life in unspoilt scenery. Open all year. Map ref: 191 109

FARM HOLIDAY BUREAU

THE 1000+ BUREAU MEMBERS OFFER A UNIQUE LINK TO CUSTOMERS ACROSS THE UK

All Bureau members belong to a local Group. Each member can refer you to an equally high quality member within his Group . . . or across the UK: England, Northern Ireland, Scotland, Wales.

71 Hills and Vales of Mid-Wales

Mid-Wales is an area of outstanding natural beauty; with rugged mountain scenery, lakes, gentle hills and beautiful valleys.

It is an area abounding in wildlife and natural history, providing a habitat for rare birds and flowers. It is still possible to see the Red Kite in its last stronghold in Wales.

This breathtaking scenery is perfect for walkers; from gentle rambles to exploring the long distance footpaths of Glyndwr's Way and the Upper Wye Valley; for the more experienced and adventurous, the remote areas of the vast Elan Valley watershed.

The area is steeped in history and includes Roman encampments, castles, caves, old mine workings, churches and monuments. It also offers practically every sport or pastime that requires an outdoor or country environment. This is a place to come to relax, to enjoy the peace, tranquillity and solitude of George Borrow's 'Wild Wales' and *the* place to recharge your batteries.

Group Contact: Mrs Ann Edwards ☎ 0597 810211

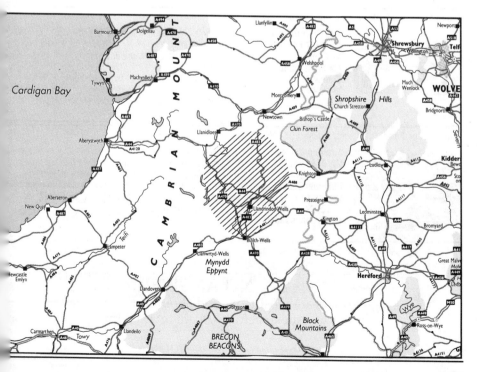

Bed and Breakfast
(and evening meal)

Beili Neuadd, Rhayader, Powys LD6 5NS

Mrs Ann Edwards
☎ 0597 810211
BB From £15
EM From £9.50
Sleeps 6
🐕 🐈
👑 👑 **Highly Commended**

An attractive 16th century stone-built farmhouse set amidst beautiful countryside in a quiet, secluded position approx. 2 miles from small market town of Rhayader. Guests are assured of every comfort with CH, log fires and spacious accommodation in single, double and twin bedded rooms, all with private facilities. WTB Farmhouse Award winner, good food and comfortable surroundings. Open all year (closed Christmas & New Year). Map ref: 190 101

Dyffryn Farm, Llanwrthwl, Llandrindod Wells, Powys LD1 6NP

Freddie Duffell
☎ 0597 811017
BB From £15
Sleeps 3
🐕 🐈
👑

Idyllically situated high in the Cambrian mountains, above the river Wye, Dyffryn Farm is surrounded by the Elan Valley, National Trust and R.S.P.B. reserves. A 17th century farmhouse with beams, slate floors, paintings, books, flowers and herbs. Good food, pretty bedrooms, magnificent views, relaxing garden. Many friendly animals welcome you to this very special place. Open all year. Ref: 090 100

Gigrin Farm, South Road, Rhayader, Powys LD6 5BL

Mrs Lena Powell
☎ 0597 810243
BB From £13
EM From £8.50
Sleeps 4
🐈 🏃 ⚡ ✂ 🍴 🎾
Listed

Gigrin is peacefully situated, with beautiful views overlooking the Wye Valley, ½ mile south of Rhayader, 3 ½ miles from the famous Elan Valley, 1 hour's drive from the sea. RSPB reserve farm and nature trail and fly-fishing (trout) on farm. 2 double bedrooms with washbasins and shaver points. Bathroom with shower. Separate dining room and sitting rooms. Colour TV. Evening meal by arrangement. Open all year. Map ref: 190 10

Willey Lodge Farm, Presteigne, Powys LD8 2NB

Mrs Ann Davies
☎ 0544 267341
BB From £13
EM From £7.50
Sleeps 4
🐈 (2) 🐕 ✂ 🏃 🎾
👑 👑 **Commended**

Relax in our small 16th century black and white farmhouse in beautiful Border country. The heart of the Marches close to Offa's Dyke. Historic Ludlow Cathedral City of Hereford. Perfect for walking or touring. Private facilities beverage trays home cooking from the garden. Children welcome. Open Mar–Nov. Map ref: 335 692

FARM HOLIDAY
BUREAU

NO ANSWER?
Farmers are mostly out and about during the day.
Try to telephone before 9.30am or after 4pm.

72 Ceredigion

Through the ages travellers have come to Ceredigion – the Romans built roads here, the Celtic saints had churches along the coast. Eight centuries ago Gerald Cambrensis wrote about the warm hospitality and, three centuries later, Henry Tudor stayed on his way to Bosworth. Somewhat later, the Victorians enjoyed a day's outing beside the fine beaches.

The 'Cardis' as the district's native inhabitants are known have guarded their heritage well – many still speak Welsh, Europe's oldest living language.

Ceredigion's 52-mile coastline, much now owned by the National Trust, looks out on the expanse of Cardigan Bay. Yachts and dinghies sail from small harbours like Aberaeron and New Quay, and the many sandy beaches, among them Aberporth and Llangrannog, are a haven for sunbathers and swimmers.

Inland, around Tregaron you might spot rare birds like the Red Kite, whilst the River Teifi produces some fine catches of salmon and sewin. Between the mountains and sea is an unspoilt patchwork of farmland; small market towns have market days well worth experiencing.

Other places of interest include woollen mills, unusual museums, the narrow gauge railway to Devil's Bridge, the National Library of Wales and the Camera Obscura at Aberystwyth.

Group Contact: Mrs Carole Jacobs ☎ 023 975 261

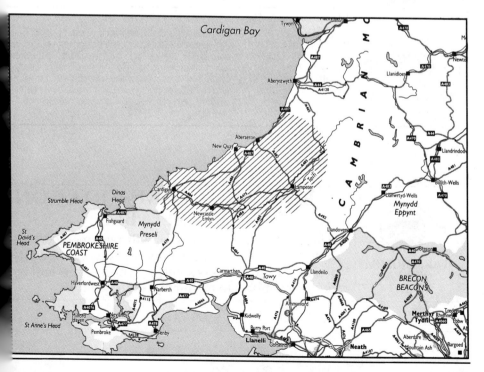

Bed and Breakfast (and evening meal)

Broniwan, Rhydlewis, Llandysul, Dyfed SA44 5PF

Carole Jacobs
☎ 0239 851261
🅱 From £16
EM From £8.50
Sleeps 6
🕊 ✂ 🐕 (5) 🎯 🍴
🐤🐤
Highly Commended

Relax in the peace of our Victorian farmhouse with its collection of books and paintings. Long vistas of the Preselli hills. Coast 10 minutes away. Enjoy birdwatching, walking (maps provided), pony trekking, fishing, studio facilities for painters, talking to your hosts. Generous home cooking includes vegetarian. 3 pretty bedrooms, 1 en-suite, quiet pets welcome. Open all year. Map ref: 167 092

Bryncastell Farm, Llanfair Road, Lampeter, Dyfed SA48 8JY

E A Beti & Sian Davies
☎ 0570 422447
🅱 From £14.50
EM From £7
Sleeps 4
♿ 🐎
🐤🐤 **Highly Commended**

'Croeso' to our 140-acre family farm commanding panoramic views over the Teifi Valley. All modern facilities with unrivalled hospitality and excellent cuisine. Access to farm activities, hillside walks or gentle strolls along the river bank in an area of unspoilt natural beauty. 3/4 mile fishing and shooting, 1 mile from University market town of Lampeter. WTB Farmhouse Award. Open all year. Map ref: 175 094

Penrhiw, Pontsian, Llandysul, Dyfed SA44 4UB

FARM HOLIDAY BUREAU

Faith Flower
☎ 054 555 614
🆂🅲 From £150–£296
Sleeps 4 + 2
🐕 (10) ✂
4 Dragons

Traditional Welsh long-house providing a peaceful retreat overlooking the Clettwr valley. Beamed sitting room with log fire and colour TV, dining room, pine furnished kitchen, dishwasher, hob, microwave/convection oven. Utility room, washer/dryer. 1 double, 1 twin adult bedrooms and 1 twin childrens' room up a steep staircase. Bathroom. Garden, fruit trees, barbeque, games and books. Logs, bed linen and water/storage heating included. Open all year. Map ref: 171 092

FARM HOLIDAY BUREAU

BUREAU ACCOMMODATION IS RELIABLE

This Guide lists **Farm Holiday Bureau** members only. They are all inspected by the National Tourist Board for standards (see introduction pages) and by fellow members to maintain a high quality.

73 Brecon

The Brecon Beacons welcome you to the great outdoors. This unspoilt countryside of mountains and forests, hills and valleys with rivers and lakes, caves and waterfalls, offers a great variety of country pursuits. Canoe on Llangorse Lake, visit Dan-yr-Ogof Showcaves, take a trip on the beautiful Monmouthshire and Brecon Canal or narrow gauge mountain railway.
The hills delight climbers, walkers and pony trekkers. Fish in the famous Rivers Wye and Usk or the many reservoirs. Lovely walks start from the Brecon Beacons Mountain Centre and Craig-y-Nos Country Park. Visit craft centres, castles and historic sites in the region; not to mention the many spas within easy reach. Browse round museums and secondhand bookshops and listen to the local choirs. Wherever you go you will meet friendly, helpful people in the country towns and villages.

Group Contact: Mrs Mary Adams ☎ 0874 636505

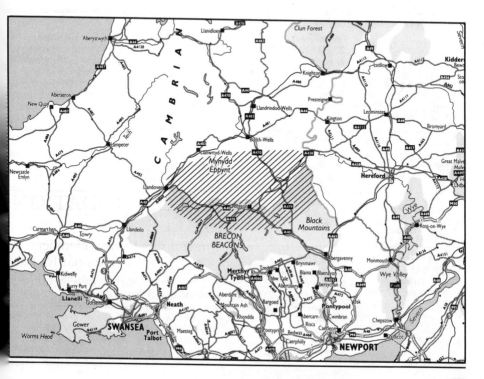

Bed and Breakfast (and evening meal)

Brynfedwen Farm, Trallong Common, Sennybridge, Brecon, Powys LD3 8HW

Mrs Mary Adams
☎ 0874 636505
BB From £16
EM From £9
Sleeps 6
♿ 🐎 ☇
🍴🍴🍴
Highly Commended

Brynfedwen, situated between Brecon and Sennybridge, is a hill livestock farm with lovely views over the Brecon Beacons and Usk River Valley. Excellent facilities for walking and all country pursuits. Traditional stone farmhouse. Central heating. TV lounge with log fire. 2 family and 1 twin bedded flat (equipped for disabled), all en suite. Personal attention and good home cooking. Children welcome. Farmhouse Award. Open all year. Map ref: 188 086

Cwmcamlais Uchaf Farm, Cwmcamlais, Senny Bridge, Brecon LD3 8TD

Mrs Jean Philips
☎ 0874 636376
BB From £15
EM From £8
Sleeps 6
🐾 (5) 🐈 ☇
🍴🍴🍴

Cwmcamlais Uchaf is a working farm situated in the Brecon Beacons National Park. 1 mile off the A40 between Brecon and Sennybirdge. Our spacious 16th century farmhouse has exposed beams, log fires and 3 tastefully decorated bedrooms, 1 double en-suite and 1 double and 1 twin with private bathrooms. Tea/coffee-making facilities. The River Camlais with its waterfalls flows through the farm land. Map ref: 189 085

Llwynneath Farm, Sennbyridge, Powys LD3 8HN

Val Williams
☎ 0874 636641
BB From £14
EM From £6
Sleeps 5
🐎 🐕
🍴🍴

Llwynneath is a 100-acre mixed hill farm with wonderful views of the Brecon Beacons and Usk Valley. A very warm welcome is extended to all who use it as a base for exploring the lovely countryside, market town and show caves. Plenty of pony riding, fishing, watersports and dry skiing nearby. 1 room en-suite. TV lounge. Open all year. Map ref: 188 086

Lodge Farm, Talgarth, Brecon, Powys LD3 0DP

Mrs Marion Meredith
☎ 0874 711244
BB From £15
EM From £9
Sleeps 6
🐎 🐕 ☇
🍴🍴

Enjoy the peace and tranquility on this working farm, nestling in the black mountains in eastern part of the National Park yet only 1½ miles from Talgarth. Attractively furnished bedrooms, tea-making, 2 en-suite. Varied menu, including vegetarian of freshly prepared real food and a warm welcome of prime importance, central base, walking, touring, pony trekking. Hay-on-Wye, Brecon 8 miles. Marked farm walk. Open all year. Map ref: 197 088

Trehenry Farm, Felinfach, Brecon, Powys LD3 0LN

Mrs Teresa Jones
☎ 0874 754312
BB From £16
EM From £9
Sleeps 6
🐾
🍴🍴🍴
Highly Commended

Trehenry is a 200 acre mixed farm situated east of Brecon, 1 mile off A470. The impressive 18th century farmhouse with panoramic views, inglenook fireplaces and exposed beams offers comfortable accommodation, good food and cosy rooms. TV lounge, separate dining tables, central heating, tea-making facilities. All rooms en-suite. Brochure on request. Farm House Award winner. Open Mar–Dec. Map ref: 195 087

Wermfawr, Pewpont, Brecon, Powys LD3 8ET

Linda Price
☎ **0874 636429**
🛏 **From £13.50**
EM From £9.99
Sleeps 6
🐕 🐴 ⚓ ☞
Listed

Working family farm peacefully situated in picturesque countryside with lake, walks and wildlife from badgers to buzzards. 18th century farmhouse offers log fire, exposed beams, traditional furniture and country-style bedrooms. Evening meals available. Toys/cot for children. Ideal base for touring. Many National Park amenities. Please ring for brochure. Warm welcome and personal service assured. Open all year. Map ref: 192 085

FARM HOLIDAY BUREAU

BUREAU ACCOMMODATION IS RELIABLE

This Guide lists **Farm Holiday Bureau** members only. They are all inspected by the National Tourist Board for standards (see introduction pages) and by fellow members to maintain a high quality.

FARM HOLIDAY BUREAU

DISABLED VISITORS

members offering suitable accommodation to disabled/less able visitors. Please do check the extent of the facilities before booking.

74 Gwent

To the north of the county are the Black Mountains and the Brecon Beacons with majestic peaks and deep sheltered valleys. This area contains part of the Brecon Beacons National Park which provides opportunities for pony trekking, walking and many other activities.

Eastern Gwent is very different – the countryside is pastoral with undulating, wooded hills and the river valleys of the Usk and Wye. Ancient market towns and picturesque villages are dotted throughout this part of the county. Part of the Welsh Marches falls within this region and there are a number of strategically placed castles, including Raglan and Chepstow, reminders of less peaceful times. Tintern Abbey, immortalised by Wordsworth, shows a more tranquil face of the county. Western Gwent can boast bracing, beautiful mountainsides, spectacular views and lovely walking country. It also has a rich industrial heritage with a wealth of attractions for those fascinated by the way we used to live.

Apart from its own attractions. Gwent is an ideal base from which to explore Cardiff, the South Wales Valleys, the Gower Peninsula, the Black Mountains, the Brecon Beacons National Park, the Forest of Dean, the Mendip Hills, the Cotswolds, Bristol and Bath . . . all within 60 miles of its borders.

Group Contacts: Mrs Gloria Powell ☎ 029 17 382

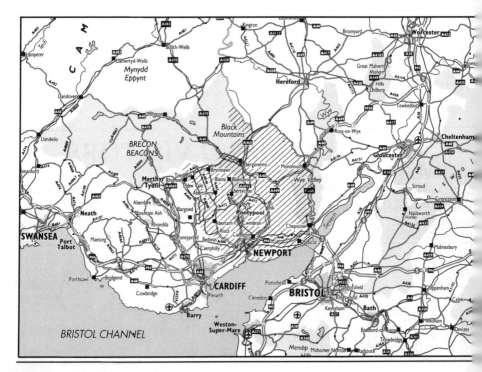

Bed and Breakfast (and evening meal)

Chapel Farm, Blaina, Gwent NP3 3DJ

Mrs Betty Hancocks
☎ 0495 290888
BB From £15
EM From £8.50
Sleeps 6
⌒ (4)
👑👑 Approved

Lovely renovated farmhouse with its original oak beams and inglenook fireplace. H&C, private showers for each room. Home cooking (evening meals by booking). Farming Welsh mountain sheep. Ideal base for touring many attractions over about 9-mile radius. A warm welcome assured. Open all year. Map ref: 203 081

The Grange, Penruos, Raglan, Gwent NP5 2LQ

Joyce Thom
☎ 060085 202
BB From £16
EM From £8
Sleeps 6
🐕🐕🎺💼
👑👑

Traditional mixed farm in quiet countryside with fantastic views between Abergavenny and Monmouth. 115 acres with trees, streams, animals. Walk or picnic on farm or on Offa's Dyke Path. Visit castles, take mountain drives. Bring pets or ponies. Large rooms, newly converted, 2 en-suite. Really good suppers. Come and share this beautiful place! Open all year. Map ref: 208 077

Little Treadam, Llantilio, Crossenny, Abergavenny, Gwent NP7 8TA

Beryl Ford
☎ 060 085 326
BB From £15
EM From £8
Sleeps 6
🐕
👑👑👑 Highly
Commended

Relax and enjoy comfort and peace in our 16th century beamed farmhouse. Delicious food. Restaurant licence. Centrally situated for Brecon National Park, Wye Valley and Black Mountains. Offa's Dyke Path long distance walk passes through the farm with White Castle a 2 mile walk away. All rooms en-suite. WTB Farmhouse Award. Open Mar–Nov. Map ref: 205 080

Parsons Grove, Earlswood, Nr Chepstow, Gwent NP6 6RD

Gloria Powell
☎ 02917 382
BB From £16
Sleeps 6
🅲🅷🐕♿⌒
👑👑 Highly
Commended

On edge of Wye Valley, peaceful and traffic-free, yet only 15 minutes Chepstow and M4. Large, centrally heated, country house, beamed lounge, log burner. Sunny conservatory in which to enjoy breakfast, overlooks swimming pool, and 2-acre vineyard. Magnificent views of Wentwood forest and picturesque Earlswood Valley. All rooms en-suite, furnished to very high standard. Tea/coffee-making facilities. Some with colour TV. Open Mar–Nov. Map ref: 208 073

Pentwyn Farm, Little Mill, Pontypool, Gwent NP4 0HQ

Stuart & Ann Bradley
☎ 049 528 249
BB From £13.50
EM From £10
Sleeps 6
⌒ (4) 🧍🛏🎺
👑👑👑 Highly
Commended

A 125-acre farm on the edge of the Brecon Beacons National Park where good food and hospitality are of prime importance. The 16th century Welsh longhouse has 20th century comforts without losing its traditional character and stands in a ½ acre garden with a swimming pool. 4 bedrooms (2 en-suite) with tea-making facilities. Restaurant licence. Rough shooting. WTB Farmhouse Award. Map ref: 205 076

Tŷ-Gwyn Farm, Gwehelog, Usk, Gwent NP5 1RT

Jean Arnett
☎ 0291 672878
BB From £14
EM From £9
Sleeps 6
✄ ✿ (14) ⚐ ▪
♨ ♨ ♨ Highly
Commended

Extensive views of Brecon Beacons National Park. 3 bedrooms (2 bath en-suite) with tea/coffee-making facilities. Spacious comfortable house which combines 'olde' charm inglenook fire place with new conservatory leading to garden and lawns. Centrally situated for touring, easy access M5, M50, M4. Quality meals. Vegetarians welcome. Xmas and New Year breaks. WTB Farmhouse Award. Good Room Gude Award. Brochure available. Open all year. Map ref: 206 077

The Wenallt Farm, Gilwern, near Abergavenny, Gwent NP7 0HP

Janice Harris
☎ 0873 830694
BB From £14.50
Sleeps 17
♨ ♜ ♉ ⚘ ⚓ ▪ ♔
♨ ♨ ♨ Commended

A 16th century Welsh longhouse set in 50 acres of farmland in the Brecon Beacons National Park commanding magnificent views over the Usk Valley. Retaining all its old charm with oak beams, inglenook fireplace, yet offering a high standard with en-suite bedrooms, good food and a warm welcome. An ideal base from which to see Wales and the surrounding areas. Licensed. AA listed. Brochure available. OPen all year. Map ref: 202 080

Self-Catering

SC

Granary & Coach House, Upper Cwm Farm, Llantilio Crossenny, Abergavenny, Gwent NP7 8TG

Ann Ball
☎ 0873 821236
SC From £155–£325
♨ ♜ ♉ ⚓ ♔
4 Dragons

Holidays and short breaks in beautifully converted old barn on working sheep farm. Family accommodation with central heating, TV, electricity, bed linen, towels included. Peaceful superb views, ideal for walking, birdwatching, exploring Welsh castles, Brecon Beacons, Wye and Usk Valleys. The Granary (upper) and coach house (ground) each have 3 double bedrooms lounge/dining/ kitchen, bathroom with shower. Brochure available. Open all year. Map ref: 204 080

Parsons Grove, Earlswood, Nr Chepstow, Gwent NP6 6RD

Gloria Powell
☎ 02917 382
SC From £80–£250
Sleeps 4/6
♜ ⚓ ✿
5 Dragons

Close to Wye Valley, set in 20 acres of peaceful countryside with heated swimming pool. Three cottages, furnished to very high standard. Fully carpeted with colour TV, fitted kitchen, refrigerator, cooker, small washing machine. All linen included. Overlooking vineyard with panoramic views of beautiful valley and Wentwood Forest. Riding nearby. 10 minutes St Pierre Golf Club. Open all year. Map ref: 207 073

Pentwyn Stable Cottages, Little Mill, Pontypool, Gwent NP4 0HQ

Stuart & Ann Bradley
☎ 049 528 249
SC From £120–£220
Sleeps 4
♜ ✿ ♔
Approved

Relax in rural tranquillity in our delightfully converted stable cottages. Enjoy the castles, museums and water sports. Walk in the Black Mountains or along the canal bank. Each cottage has 2 bedrooms, a fully fitted kitchen and a large beamed sitting room with wood burner and wonderful views over the large garden with swimming pool and barbecue. Linen, electricity and logs included in price. Meals available in farmhouse. Open all year. Map ref: 205 076

Worcester House, Castle Farm, Raglan, Gwent NP5 2BT

Mrs Vivien Jones
☎ **0291 690492**
🆂🅲 **From £100–£250**
Sleeps 6/7
🛏 🐎
4 Dragons

Part of a 17th century manor house. The oldest brick building in Gwent. Close to dual carriageway leading to Wye Valley, Brecon Beacons and Forest of Dean. Raglan Castle 20 yards, beautiful views. A 200-acre working dairy/arable farm with 3 bedrooms, bathroom, living/dining room leading to large lawn. Modern kitchen, shower room, everything except linen/towels. Open most of year. Map ref: 208 077

BUREAU ACCOMMODATION IS RELIABLE

This Guide lists **Farm Holiday Bureau** members only. They are all inspected by the National Tourist Board for standards (see introduction pages) and by fellow members to maintain a high quality.

THOSE LITTLE EXTRAS

For advice on farms that can offer 'extras' such as four-poster beds, special diets, farm trails, fishing rights – even stabling and trekking arrangements if you are bringing your own horse – ring the Farm Holiday Bureau on (0203) 696909.

75 Pembrokeshire

Pembrokeshire is the south western corner of Wales, now part of the larger modern county of Dyfed. A large portion of Pembrokeshire is covered by the Pembrokeshire Coast National Park, including most of the coastal strip and Preseli Hills. The countryside is unspoilt with an abundance and variety of wild flowers everywhere from the coast to the banks that skirt the miles of narrow country lanes.

The beaches vary from long sandy stretches to small rocky coves – but you could see them all if you walked the coastal footpath from St. Dogmael's in the north to Amroth in the south – 180 miles! You would also see the islands off the coast including Skomer and Skokholm which are nature reserves; and Caldy, inhabited by Cistercian monks. Some of these islands can be visited and you may see seals here or indeed off any part of the coastline.

The variable terrain from coast to hill, moorland to marsh provides an agreeable habitat for a wide variety of birds, insects and animals. The area is full of historical relics from ancient to modern, with Iron Age settlement remains, cromlechs and standing stones right up to those of more recent times with many castles and, of course, the fine cathedral of St. David's.

Group Contact: Mrs O Evans ☎ 0437 721382
Mrs Nesta Thomas ☎ 0437 731279

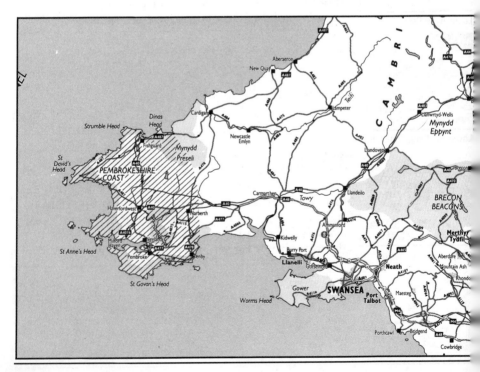

Bed and Breakfast (and evening meal)

Berry-Hill, Goodwick, near Fishguard, Pembrokeshire SA64 0HG

Mrs Mayrid Rees
☎ 0348 872260
🅱 From £15
Sleeps 4
✂
♕ ♕ Highly
Commended

Join us at our small holding where a warm Welsh welcome and good country cooking awaits you. Magnificently positioned overlooking Fishguard Harbour and Preseli Hills. Bedrooms have sea views and en-suite, tea/coffee-making facilities. Full central heating. Coastal path, 2 mins walk. Details and brochure available. Open Apr-Sep.
Map ref: 152 088

Gilfach Goch Farmhouse, Fishguard, Pembrokeshire, Dyfed SA65 9SR

June Devonald
☎ 0348 873871
🅱 From £16
EM From £9
Sleeps 12
✂ ♿ ☕
♕ ♕ ♕ Highly
Commended

Enjoy peace and tranquillity at our farmhouse in National Park. From pretty bedrooms sit and gaze at magnificent views over rolling countryside down to the sea. Be pampered – tea in bed, by log fires in winter, in our attractive gardens in summer. Sample 'real' food – fresh fruit and vegetables from our 10-acre smallholding, with a glass of wine. Fire certificate. Food hygiene certificate. Farmhouse award. Open 1 Mar–15 Nov. Map ref: 152 088

Lochmeyler Farm, Pen-y-Cwm, Llandeloy, Nr Solva, Haverfordwest, Dyfed SA62 6LL

Mrs Morfydd Jones
☎ 0348 837724
🅱 £20
EM £9
Sleeps 12
🐕 ♿ ☕ (10) ☯ 📱
♕ ♕ ♕ ♕
Deluxe

Lochmeyler is a 220-acre dairy farm in the centre of St David's Peninsula, 4 miles from Solva Harbour. Six en-suite bedrooms (no smoking in bedrooms), TV. 4-poster beds available. Two lounges, 1 non-smokers. Choice of menus, traditional and vegetarian. RAC highly acclaimed, AA selected. Member of Taste of Wales, WTB Farmhouse award. Licensed, credit cards accepted. Open all year. Map ref: 146 084

Lower Haythog, Spittal, Haverfordwest, Pembrokeshire SA62 5QL

Nesta Thomas
☎ 0437 731279
🅱 From £15
EM From £8.50
Sleeps 10–12
🐕 ☕ 🎣 ❤ 📱
♕ ♕ Highly
Commended

Get away from it all to the welcoming atmosphere of our delightful 200 year old farmhouse, where good food and laughter can be enjoyed. Set in idyllic countryside on a working farm, 5 miles north of Haverfordwest with wooded walks, private fishing, pony rides, attractive gardens. En-suite and private facilities, all bedrooms – hospitality trays. Centrally situated for beaches and places of interest. WTB Award. Fire and basic food hygiene certificates. Open all year. Map ref: 153 084

Penycraig, Punchestown, Haverfordwest, Pembrokeshire SA62 5RJ

Betty Devonald
☎ 0348 881277
🅱 From £13
EM From £7
Sleeps 6
☕ 🐕 ❤
♕ ♕

A warm welcome awaits you at Penygraig, a working farm, situated near the picturesque Preseli Hills, with plenty of walks, natural trails and places of unspoilt beauty to be enjoyed. The rugged coastline of North Pembrokeshire being not far away. In the spacious dining room good wholesome cooking is served. There is 1 double room en-suite, 1 family room. All rooms have tea trays, reductions for children sharing. Open Apr–Oct. Map ref: 154 088

Spittal Cross Farm, Spittal Cross, Haverfordwest, Dyfed SA62 5DB

Mrs Susan Evans
☎ 0437 87 206
BB From £12
EM From £8
Sleeps 4
⌂ ★
✺✺ Highly
Commended

A family run 200-acre dairy farm in the heart of the beautiful Pembrokeshire countryside, making it a convenient touring base for the many local activities, beaches and places of historical interest. We offer hearty breakfast, imaginative dinners and comfortable accommodation. Reduced rates for children. Dining/sitting room with colour TV, games and books available. Central heating throughout. Open May–Sep. Map ref: 154 083

Trepant Farm, Morwil, Rosebush, Pembrokeshire SA66 7RE

Marilyn Salmon
☎ 0437 532491
BB From £13
EM From £8
Sleeps 6
⌂
✺✺ Commended

A warm Welsh welcome on our mixed dairy farm in the beautiful Preseli hills, sandy beaches and hidden covers. Pony trekking, fishing are all nearby. Relax in the evening with excellent home cusine using best local produce. Vegetarians welcome. Open Apr–Oct. Map ref: 155 088

Torbant Farm Guest House, Croesgoch, Haverfordwest, Pembrokeshire, Dyfed SA62 5JN

Barbara Charles
☎ 0348 831276
BB From £16
EM From £9
Sleeps 14
♿ ⌂ ▪
✺✺ Commended

Torbant is a 110-acre dairy farm, near St David's, peacefully situated in spacious grounds, and just 1½ miles from the spectacularly beautiful Pembrokeshire coast with its abundance of wildlife and sandy beaches. Although modernised, the farmhouse retains its traditional character. 6 bedrooms, 3 en-suite. Fully licensed bar and restaurant.. Children welcome. AA/RAC listed. Open Easter–end Oct. Map ref: 152 080

Yethen Isaf, Mynachlogddu, Clynderwen, Pembrokeshire SA66 7SN

Mrs Ann Barney
☎ 0437 532256
BB From £13.50
EM From £7.50–£8.50
Sleeps 6
⌂ ★ ▪ ✂
✺✺

Yethen Isaf sits right in the midst of the Preseli Hills, offering superb walking, yet only 10 miles from the coast. The farm is approx 100 acres, breeding pedigree Welsh Black cattle and Beulah Speckleface sheep. The 250-year-old farmhouse offers superb, comfortable accommodation with home cooking, central heating and log fires. One room with en-suite facilities. Visits and activities arranged. Open all year. Map ref: 159 085

Self-Catering

[SC]

Torbant Farm Apartments, Croesgoch, Haverfordwest, Pembrokeshire, Dyfed SA62 5JN

Barbara Charles
☎ 0348 831276
SC From £150–£320
Sleeps 4 & 6
⌂

4 Dragons

Torbant Farm apartments are ideally situated on the St Davids Peninsula near spectacular coast with beautiful beaches and coastal walks. Completely self-contained, warm and comfortable, new fitted kitchens with washer/dryer, freezer etc yet with all guest house facilities available – evening dinners, quiet bar, large garden, play area. Open May–Sep. Map ref: 152 080

---

76 County Londonderry

This is a fertile agricultural county with small farms scattered across the broad sweeping land and long Atlantic beaches.

The city of Londonderry (also known as Derry) is best known for its massive ring of fortified walls and singing pubs. In the county's north-east corner is Coleraine (with one of the main campuses of the University of Ulster), conveniently close to the seaside resorts of Portstewart and Castlerock for sea angling, golf and children's amusements. For rewarding scenic drives the Sperrin Mountains are best approached from Limavady and the beautiful Roe Valley Country Park. The Bann river is noted for trout and salmon.

Group Contact: Mrs Margaret Moore ☎ 026 5868 229

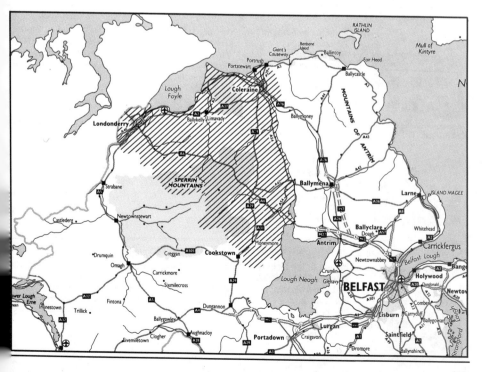

Bed and Breakfast (and evening meal)

Ballycarton Farm, Bellarena, Limavady, Co Londonderry BT49 0HZ

Mrs Emma Craig
☎ 05047 50216
BB From £12
EM From £6
Sleeps 12
Approved

Farmhouse (central heating) on 50 acre farm. Gliding, climbing, fishing. 1 single, 1 double, 1 twin, 2 family rooms (3 H/C). Dogs allowed outside. On coast road. Coleraine 14 miles, Limavady 5 miles. Open all year. Map ref: 107 219

Ballyhenry House, 172 Seacoast Road, Limavady, Co Londonderry BT49 9EF

FARM HOLIDAY BUREAU

Mrs Rosemary Kane
☎ 05047 22657
BB From £14
EM From £8.50
Sleeps 8
Approved

Tourist award winning large Victorian farmhouse on 300 acres of arable land. Working farm. Fully centrally heated, TV lounge and snooker room. 1 twin, 1 family room (both H/C), 1 double with shower. Situated on A2, 3 miles north of Limavady with views of Binevenagh and Donegal hills. Fishing, gliding, golf. Country and farm walks, water skiing all within 6 mile radius. Open all year. Map ref: 107 219

Greenhill House, 24 Greenhill Road, Aghadowey, Coleraine, Co Londonderry BT51 4EU

Mrs Elizabeth Hegarty
☎ 0265 868241
BB From £20
EM From £12
Sleeps 14
Grade A

Georgian country guest house (with central heating). Good views across wooded countryside in the Bann Valley and the Antrim hills. Convenient to North coast. Fishing nearby. 3 double, 2 twin, 2 family all H/C, 6 rooms with private bath/shower and toilet. Garvagh 3 miles. Coleraine 7 miles. 1 km on A29 from Coleraine and then B66 (Ballymoney). Map ref: 116 222

Heathfield, 31 Drumcroon Road, Garvagh, Co Londonderry BT51 4EB

Mrs Heather Torrens
☎ 026 65 58245
BB From £14
EM From £8
Sleeps 4
Approved

18th century farmhouse in spacious gardens. Mixed farm. 1 double, 1 twin bedded. Both with H/C. Central heating. TV lounge. Babysitter available. Close to fishing, shooting, golf, country walks. On A29 Gervagh 2 miles, Coleraine 8 miles, Portrush 12 miles. Open all year. Map ref: 114 216

Inchadoghill House, 196 Agivey Road, Aghadowey, Coleraine, Co Londonderry BT51 4AD

Mamie & Ann McIlroy
☎ 0265 868250/868232
BB From £12
EM From £6
Sleeps 6
Approved

Georgian farmhouse with central heating. Situated on 150 acre mixed farm, colour TV. Home cooking. River fishing on farm, golf nearby, 1 single, 1 double and 1 family room. All with H/C. Babysitting available. Farm off A54. Coleraine 9 miles. Ballymoney 6 miles. Kilrea 5 miles. Map ref: 116 222

Killeague House, Blackhill, Coleraine, Co Londonderry BT51 4HJ

Margaret Moore
☎ 0265 868229
BB From £15
EM From £9
Sleeps 6
✗ ☞
Approved

Georgian farmhouse built 1783. Central heating, tea-making facilities, colour TV. On dairy farm, stabling available. Outdoor riding arena. Riding instruction given by arrangement. Fishing in river on farm. 2 double, 1 family, both with H/C, 1 with shower. On A29. Garvagh 5 miles, Coleraine 6½ miles. Convenient to golf courses, Giant's Causeway and Bushmills Distillery. Good food, good fun, good fellowship is our motto. Open all year. Map ref: 116 219

The Poplars, 352 Seacoast Road, Limavady, Co Londonderry BT49 0LA

Mrs H McCracken
☎ 050 47 50360
BB From £13
EM From £7
Sleeps 10
Tents £2
⊛ Å ☎ ☞
Approved

Ten bed bungalow in gardens, views of Binevenagh, Dongeal Hills. Fishing 14 mile, golf 6 miles, Roe Valley Country Park 7 miles, Ulster Gliding Club ½ mile. H/C and shower in 2 bedrooms, bathroom and shower and 3 toilets. All home cooking. All ground floor. Babysitter available. Limavady 6½ miles, Coleraine 10 miles, Londonderry 24 miles. Map ref: 108 219

31 Ballylagan Road, Coleraine, Co Londonderry BT52 2PQ

FARM HOLIDAY BUREAU

Mrs Joyce Lyons
☎ 0265 822487
BB From £12.50
Sleeps 6
Approved

Traditional farmhouse (central heating) on working dairy farm. Home cooking and baking. TV lounge. 1 family room, 1 double room (both H&C). Fishing, golf, bowling nearby. Dogs allowed (outside). Portrush 2½ miles, Coleraine 3 miles, Giant's Causeway 5 miles. Situated off B17. Map ref: 115 223

Tullan's Farm, 46 Newmills Road, Coleraine, Co Londonderry BT52 2JB

FARM HOLIDAY BUREAU

Mrs Diana McClelland
☎ 0265 42309
BB From £12.50
Sleeps 7
Grade A4

1 family room with shower, 2 double rooms. Farmhouse (central heating) 1 mile from Coleraine. Nearby fishing, swimming pool, bowling, ice-skating, horse riding and bird watching. Babysitter. Dogs allowed outside. Portstewart/Portrush 5 miles. Golf and sandy beaches 5 miles. Turn off A29 Coleraine bypass (Cookstown–Portrush), ½ mile past roundabout (junction A26) into Newmills Road. Open all year. Map ref: 116 223

Tully Farm, 109 Victoria Road, Newbuildings, Co Londonderry BT47 2RN

FARM HOLIDAY BUREAU

Mrs Elizabeth Henderson
☎ 0504 42832
BB From £11.50
Sleeps 10
Grade A4

Farmhouse in the Foyle Valley with panoramic views. Golf course, pony trekking and fishing nearby. LOndonderry 4 miles, 1 single bedroom, 2 double bedrooms, 1 twin bedroom, 1 family room, all with H&C and on ground floor. Dogs allowed outside. On A5 Londonderry–Strabane road. Vouchers not accepted. Open all year. Map ref: 097 217

FARM HOLIDAY BUREAU
Please mention **Stay on a Farm** when booking

77 **County Antrim**

To the south east of the county, Belfast provides six-day shopping and city entertainment while to the north west lies the Causeway Coast, a playground of holiday resorts, with the Giant's Causeway the dominant feature. Between lie the nine glens of Antrim and their quaint waterfoot villages, the spectacular coast road, Carrickfergus Castle, and inland towns like Antrim with its ancient round tower and splendid park. There's a lakeside steam railway at Shane's Castle, pony trekking near Ballycastle, golf at Royal Portrush, as well as bathing, boating and fishing along the hundred miles of shore.

Group Contacts: North: Mrs Ria Johnston ☎ 026 57 31611
South: Mrs Eileen Duncan ☎ 084 94 22768

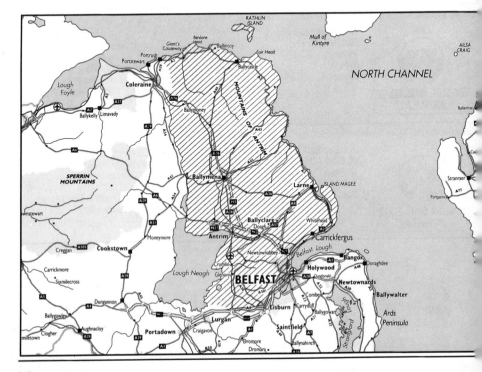

Bed and Breakfast
(and evening meal)

Beechgrove, 412 Upper Road, Trooperslane, Carrickfergus, Co Antrim BT38 8PW

Betta Barron
☎ 09603 63304
BB From £11.50
EM From £5
Sleeps 8
🐕 ♿ ⌂
Approved

A warm welcome awaits you at Beechgrove farmhouse (central heating) on 16 acre mixed farm near sea. Fishing, golf, riding. Knochagh monument, Belfast zoo, leisure centre nearby. 3 single, 1 double 2 family rooms, 1 twin (all H/C). Babysitter. Dogs allowed (outside). Off A2, 1 mile south of Carrickfergus. Larne 10 miles. Belfast 10 miles. Carrickfergus 3 miles. Map ref: 134 205

Breezemount, 27 Ballylig Road, Cloughmills, Dunloy, Ballymean, Co Antrim BT44 9DS

Mrs May O'Mullan
☎ 026563 468
BB From £13
EM From £6–£8
Sleeps 6
⌂
Approved

Modern country bungalow (central heating) with separate dining room and TV lounge. 2 double with bath and WC, 1 twin (shower and WC). 10 miles Ballymena on Coleraine road A26, 8 miles Ballymoney, 16 miles Ballycastle. Close to Logan's Fashions. Scenic drives through Glens of Antrim. Fishing locally. Open all year. Vouchers not accepted. Map ref: 124 211

Brown's Country House, 174 Ballybogey Road, Coleraine, Co Londonderry BT52 2LP

Mrs Jean Brown
☎ 02657 31627
BB From £15
EM From £9
Sleeps 13
Grade B

A bungalow with spacious lawns. Central heating. Home baking. On Ballymoney – Portrush road (B62). Safari Park 4 miles. 4 double bedrooms, 1 twin-bedded room, 1 family room, 4 ground floor (all H&C). Small dinner parties welcome. Babysitter. Dogs allowed (outside). Bushmills 4 miles, Coleraine and Portrush 5 miles. Open all year. Map ref: 114 222

Carnside Farm Guest House, 23 Causeway Road, Giants Causeway, Bushmills, Co Antrim BT57 8SU

Frances Lynch
☎ 02657 31337
BB From £16
EM From £12.50
Sleeps 15
🐕 ⌂
Grade B

Farmhouse (central heating) on 200-acre dairy farm. Magnificent coastal view. Fishing, golf, water sports. Old Bushmills Distillery 2 miles has weekday tours. 1 single, 4 double, 1 twin, 2 family rooms, 2 ground floor (all H/C). Babysitter. Dogs allowed (outside). Bushmills 2 miles, Ballaycastle 12 miles, Giants Causeway 14 mile. Open Mar–Oct. Map ref: 116 216

Country Guest House, 41 Kirk Road, Ballymoney, Co Antrim BT53 8HB

Dorothy Brown
☎ 02656 62620
BB From £15
EM From £8
Sleeps 8
© ♿ 🐕 ⌂
Grade B

Modern bungalow (central heating) in 1 acre of alpine and rare plants, near Antrim Glens Recreation Centre 1 mile. 3 double and 1 family, all rooms have private shower, toilet, etc. Supper available at no extra charge. Lounge with colour TV for guests. Babysitter available. Safari park 3 miles. Giant's Causeway 10 miles. From Ballymoney by-pass (A26) 50 yards along B147. Ballymoney 1 mile. Map ref: 118 218

Craigs Farm, 90 Hillhead Road, Ballycarry, Co. Antrim BT38 9JF

Mrs J Craig
☎ 09603 53759
[BB] From £12
Sleeps 7
Grade A4

3 rooms. 1 twin, 1 family, both H&C, 1 double. Centrally heated farmhouse located in quiet rural surrounds. Convenient for golf, fishing, horseriding, walking. Ample parking. Pack lunch available. Washing and ironing facilities. From Larne take the A2 towards Carrickfergus. Take 2nd right when you come through Glen village. Follow the signpost 'Ballycarry Farm guesthouse 3 miles'. Open all year. Map ref: 137 206

Hillview, 30 Middle Road, Islandmagee, Larne, Co Antrim BT40 3SL

Mrs Maureen Reid
☎ 09603 72581
[BB] From £12.50
EM From £7
Sleeps 6
Approved

Country bungalow (central heating) with panoramic views. Near sea. TV lounge, conservatory. Tea/coffee-making facilities. 1 double bed, 1 twin bed (both H&C), 1 twin bed with shower & wc. All ground floor. Open all year. Dogs allowed (outside). Horse riding, sea fishing, golf, open farm near by. Off A2, 7 miles south of Larne. Take B90 to Islandmagee. Carrickfergus 7 miles. Vouchers not accepted. Open all year. Map ref: 135 209

Hillvale, 11 Largy Road, Crumlin, Co Antrim BT29 4AH

Mrs Eileen P Duncan
☎ 08494 22768
[BB] From £12.50
Sleeps 6
ꝋ ⌇
Approved

Centrally heated farmhouse with sun porch, large gardens beside river, near Lough Neagh. 128-acre dairy farm. Near Antrim Forum sports centre. Tea/coffee making facilities. Babysitter. Dogs allowed outside. Vouchers accepted. Crumlin village 1 mile, Antrim 7 miles. Belfast International Airport 3 miles. Evening meal available if pre-arranged. Open all year. Map ref: 124 200

Kenbaan, 55 Bayhead Road, Portballintrae, Co Antrim BT57 8SA

Mrs Elizabeth Morgan
☎ 026 57 31534
[BB] £16
Sleeps 6
ꝋ
Approved

Country house (central heating) near Dunluce Castle. Bushmills Distillery, Giant's Causeway. Panoramic views of North Antrim Coast. 2 double beds, 1 twin bed (all H&C and tea/coffee-making facilities). Guests lounge with colour TV. Ample parking. Bushmills 1½ miles. Portrush 4 miles. Open Jan–Nov. Map ref: 117 226

Neelsgrove Farm, 51 Carnearney Road, Ahoghill, Ballymena, Co Antrim BT42 2PL

Mrs Margaret Neely
☎ 0266 871225
[BB] From £12.50
EM From £7
Sleeps 3
ꝋ ⌇ ⌇ Approved

Country house (central heating) in 1 acre of grounds on mixed farm. Home baking. Water skiing 2 miles. Sports complex 5 miles. 6 miles from Ballymena, 15 miles from International Airport. 1 double en-suite, 1 double, 1 twin room with H/C. Dogs allowed outside. Map ref: 124 207

Sprucebank, 41 Ballymacombs Road, Portglenone, Co. Antrim BT44 8NR

Mrs Thomasena Sibbett
☎ 0266 822150
[BB] From £13
Sleeps 10
ⴲ
Grade A3

Country house in spacious garden. 1½ miles from Portglenone on A54. Tea/coffee-making facilities in all rooms. En-suite room has its own entrance and is suitable for the partially disabled. Convenient to Glens of Antrim, Causeway coast, Sperrin mountains, fishing on River Bawn. Fishermen welcome – tacke space available. Dogs welcome outside. Open all year. Map ref: 119 211

White Gables, 83 Dunluce Road, Bushmills, Co Antrim BT57 8SJ

Mrs Ria Johnston
☎ 026 57 31611
🅱 From £18.50
EM From £11.50
Sleeps 6
😊 ⛱ (6)
Grade A

Modern country house on A2 coast road, near Dunluce Castle, Bushmills Distillery and Giant's Cuaseway. Panoramic views of North Antrim coast. All bedrooms with en-suite WC and shower. Tea/coffee-making facilities. Large comfortable guests' lounge with colour TV. Ample car parking space. Portballintrae 34 mile, Bushmills 2 miles. All Ireland Galtee Breakfast Award Winner. Open Apr–Sept. Map ref: 120 220

Ballynagashel House, 30 Cregagh Road, Ballymoney, Co Antrim BT53 8JN

FARM HOLIDAY BUREAU

Mrs Barbara Kirkpatrick
☎ 026 56 41366
🅱 From £15.00
EM From £7.50
Sleeps 9
Grade A2

Stone-built farmhouse of historical interest. 3 d/b (h&c), 1 family room with shower and wc. Health room with sauna, jacuzzi and sunbed. Private lake for trout fishing. Small rowing boat available. 6m Ballymoney on the B16 road. 9m Ballycastle (½m off A44 Ballycastle road). 11m Giant's Causeway. Open all year. Dogs allowed. Map ref: 119 219

FINDING YOUR ACCOMMODATION

FARM HOLIDAY BUREAU

The Group contacts at the beginning of each section can always help you find a vacancy in your chosen area.

FARM HOLIDAY BUREAU

GOOD FOOD

Nearly all Bureau members now hold a certificate in Essential Food Hygiene.

78 County Tyrone

Between the Sperrins in the north and the green Clogher Valley with its village cathedral in the south lies this region of great historical interest. The county's associations with the USA are recalled at the Ulster-American Folk Park near Omagh and Gray's old printing shop in Strabane still contains its 18th century presses. A mysterious ceremonial site of stone circles and cairns near Davagh Forest has recently been uncovered and there are other Stone Age and Bronze Age remains in the area. There are forest parks, Gortin Glen and Drum Manor, for driving or rambling, excellent trout and salmon waters near Newtownstewart, and market towns for shopping and recreation. Dungannon is notable for its fine glassware, Tyrone Crystal.

Group Contact: Mrs Nora Brown ☎ 086 87 84212

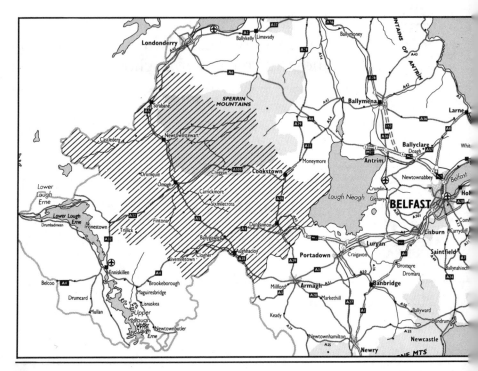

Bed and Breakfast (and evening meal)

Greenmount Lodge, 58 Greenmount Road, Gortaclare, Omagh, Co Tyrone BT79 0YE

Mrs F Louie Reid
☎ 0662 841325
📠 From £14.50
EM From £9.50
Sleeps 15
🐴 ✂ 🐕
Grade A

Farm guest house on 150-acre farm. Superb accommodation, excellent cuisine. Central for sightseeing. Fermanagh, Lakeland, the Sperrin Mountains. A5 from Ballygawley to Omagh, left before Traveller's Rest at Fintona sign 1 mile. Map ref: 098 201

Muleany House, 86 Gorestown Road, Moy, Co Tyrone BT71 7EX

Mrs Mary Mullen
☎ 08687 84183
📠 From £15
EM From £6–£8
Sleeps 14
@ 🐴 🐕
Grade A

Country house in 10 acres. Fishing, riding, golf, game shooting. 2 single, 2 double, 2 twin, 1 family room, 1 ground floor (all H/C). Dogs allowed outside. B106 sout of Moy, 14 mile, house on right. Dungannon 5 miles, Armagh 8 miles, Benburb 3 miles. Map ref: 113 194

FARM HOLIDAY BUREAU

BUREAU ACCOMMODATION IS RELIABLE

This Guide lists **Farm Holiday Bureau** members only. They are all inspected by the National Tourist Board for standards (see introduction pages) and by fellow members to maintain a high quality.

FARM HOLIDAY BUREAU

DISABLED VISITORS

members offering suitable accommodation to disabled/less able visitors. Please do check the extent of the facilities before booking.

79 County Fermanagh

Ulster's Lakeland spreads its web of waterways, islands, forest and glen, castles and abbey ruins, right across the county. Enniskillen, county town and shopping centre, strides the narrows between upper and lower Lough Erne. From here pleasure boats run daily cruises in summer. Golf, sailing, water-skiing and even pleasure flying are available nearby. Fishermen need no reminder that these are the waters where record catches are made. Two of Ulster's finest houses in National Trust care, Florence Court and Castle Coole, are in Fermanagh, too and there is an underground boat trip at Marble Arch Caves. Visitors to the old pottery at Belleek can watch craftsmen at work on fine porcelain.

Group Contact: Mrs Vera Gilmore ☎ 0365 521298

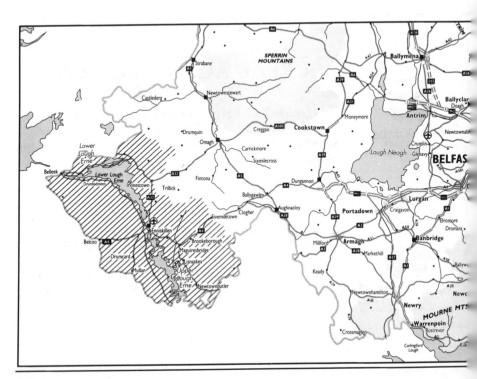

Bed and Breakfast (and evening meal)

Broadmeadows House, Cleenish Island Road, Bellanaleck, Enniskillen, Co Fermanagh

Lillian McKibbin
☎ **036582 395**
🅱 **From £12**
EM From £10
Sleeps 6
⊛ 🐕 ᵶ ⅄ ☺
Approved

Chalet bungalow (central heating). Close to Lough Erne. Angling, sailing near Florence Court (National Trust) and Marble Arch Caves. 1 single, 1 double, 1 twin, all ground floor. Suitable for elderly or disabled visitors. Babysitter. Personal attention to special needs. Owner qualified nurse. Dogs allowed outside. 1½ miles east of Bellanaleck on road to Cleenish Island. Enniskillen 6 miles. Map ref: 088 191

PRICES

Prices include VAT and service charge (if any) and are:
B&B per person per night
EM per person
SC per unit per week
Tents and caravans per pitch per night

CONFIRM BOOKINGS

Disappointments can arise by misunderstandings over the telephone. Please write to confirm your booking.

80 County Armagh

Northern Ireland's smallest county rises gently from Lough Neagh's banks, southward through apple orchards, farmland and hill forest to the rock summit of Slieve Gullion, mountain of Cuchulain. But the crown of Armagh is the city itself, a religious capital older than Canterbury, with two cathedrals, the Georgian Mall and a Planetarium and Observatory. Craigavon has a leisure centre and ski-slope, with lakes for water sports, and there is sailing on Lough Neagh and angling and canoeing on the Blackwater river.

Group Contact: Miss May Hanson ☎ 0861 525925

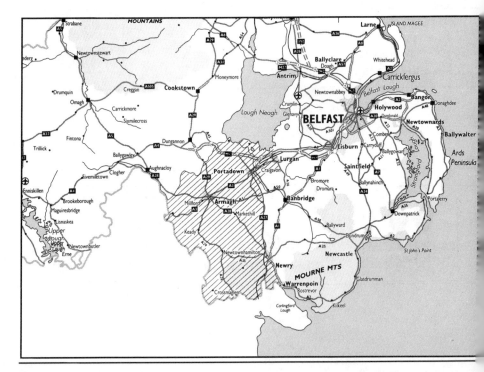

Bed and Breakfast (and evening meal)

Greenacres, 57 Red Lion Road, Portadown BT62 4HR

Mrs Florence Hampton ☎ **0762 352610** BB **From £13** **Sleeps 6** **Grade A3**	3 rooms. 2 twin, 1 double, all H&C. Bus stop 100 yards. Redbrick farmhouse (central heating) in 50 acres of orchard and mixed farming. Sailling, waterskiing in Craigavon Lakes, golf at Tandragee, fishing. Babysitter. Dogs allowed outside. 3 miles from Portadown on Loughgall road (B77), house on right after 12 cottages. Craigavon 5 miles. Open all year. Map ref:119 192

Heimat, Polnagh Road, Killylea, Co Armagh BT60 4NW

Doris McLoughlin ☎ **0861 568661** BB **From £11.50** **EM From £6** ⓖ 🛆 🕬 🐎 🐕 **Approved**	Modern chalet bungalow on mixed farm overlooking Killylea village. 2 double ground floor bedrooms. Fishing at Benburb, clay pigeon shooting. Navan Fort 3 miles. Babysitter available. Home cooking. 6 miles from Armagh city, halfway between Enniskillen and Belfast. Dogs allowed (outside). Open all year. Map ref: 114 189

Victoria, Cloughfin, Armagh, Co Armagh BT61 8HB

May Hanson ☎ **0861 525925** BB **From £12.50** **Sleeps 6** 🐎 🐕 **Approved**	3 rooms, 2 twin, 1 double. Open Easter–Nov (Christmas by arrangement). Country bungalow (central heating) National Trust Properties, golf fishing, walking, birdwatching nearby. Help with ancestor research at additional cost. Armagh 3 miles. From Armagh take B115 (Cathedral road), right at Teeraw Road, continue to T junction. Turn right along Tullysaran Road to the first left turn after Ballytroddan Road. Open all year. Map ref: 114 189

FARM HOLIDAY BUREAU

GOOD FOOD

Nearly all Bureau members now hold a certificate in Essential Food Hygiene.

81 County Down

This area includes the populous dormitory fringe along Belfast Lough (do not miss the Folk Museum at Cultra) and the ancient shrines of St. Patrick's Country round the cathedral hill at Downpatrick; the flat golden beaches of the Ards Peninsula and the mountainous Kingdom of Mourne; lively Newcastle with its seaside festival, and stately homes like Mount Stewart and Castle Ward open to visitors.

Horseriding, sailing, angling and golf are everywhere within reach, and there is motor racing at Kirkistown and sea angling in Strangford Lough.

Group Contacts: North: Mrs Joan McKee ☎ 0247 817526
South: Mrs Cissie Annett ☎ 03967 22740

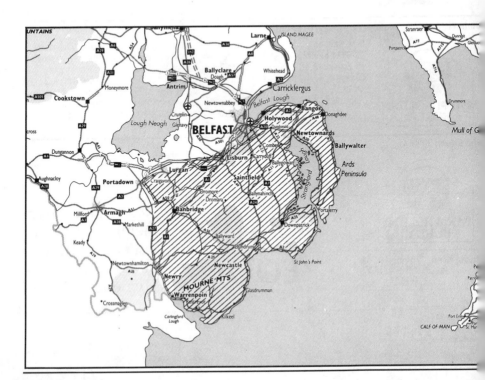

Bed and Breakfast (and evening meal)

Ballycastle House, 20 Mountstewart Road, Newtownards, Co Down BT22 2AL

Margaret Deering
☎ 024774 357
🅱🅱 From £14
Sleeps 6
🛆 ⚲ ⛺ ✂ 🐎
Approved

Ballycastle House is situated in a peaceful country setting overlooking Strangford Lough. Convenient to fishing, sailing, golfing, flying club, National Trust properties. Beside Mountstewart House and Gardens. Every comfort, hospitality assured. Winner of 3 tourism Awards. 3 double rooms (H/C), 1 en suite bathroom, 1 with WC. Dogs allowed (outside). Large vintage engine collection. Newtownards – A20 south 4 miles, Ballywalter signpost left 23 mile farmhouse left. Map ref: 137 198

Beechill, Loughries Road, Newtownards, Co Down BT23 3RN

Mrs Joan McKee
☎ 0247 817526
🅱🅱 From £13.50
EM From £10
Sleeps 6
⛺ 🐎
Approved

Farmhouse on the Ards peninsula on a working farm. 1 double, 1 single, 1 family room (all H/C). Dogs allowed outside. A20 south from Newtownards, 2 miles left at Millisle signpost, left at Loughries School. Newtownards 4 miles, Bangor 8 miles. Map ref: 137 198

Bella Vista, 107 Scarva Road, Banbridge, Co Down BT32 3QD

FARM HOLIDAY BUREAU

B F McDonnell
☎ 08206 27066
🅱🅱 From £12.50
Sleeps 4
Grade A3

Georgian country bungalow in rural setting, 1 mile from town centre on Scarva Road. Private car parking. Golf club and driving range, 1 mile. Fishing 3 miles. 1 double bedroom, 1 twin bedroom (both H&C). Dogs not allowed. From Belfast/Dublin dual carriageway, take Banbridge by-pass to Scarva Street Post Office. Continue for 1 mile on Scarva road (B10). Newry 14 miles, Portadown 13 miles, Rathfriland 10 miles. Vouchers not accepted. Open all year. Map ref: 120 189

The Briers, 39 Middle Tollymore Road, Newcastle, Co Down BT33 0JJ

FARM HOLIDAY BUREAU

Mary & David Bowater
☎ 03967 24347 or 24067
🅱🅱 From £16
EM From £12
Sleeps 6
Grade U

3 rooms, 1 twin, 2 double all en-suite. Located 500 yards from Tollymore Forest Park, 18th century stonebuilt residence restored with sympathy keeping the olde worlde charme. Excellent dinner menu, fresh garden produce used in cooking (jams, preserves, bread etc). 2 acres of quiet garden with squirrels, rabbits and birds. Open all year. Map ref: 133 183

Carrig Gorm, 27 Bridge Road, Helen's Bay, Bangor, Co Down BT19 1TS

Mrs Elizabeth Eves
☎ 0247 853680
🅱🅱 From £16–£18
Sleeps 6
⊜ 🐕 ✂ 🐎
Approved

Part Victorian, part 18th century house (central heating) in secluded gardens ½ mile from sea. Six golf courses within 5 miles. Coastal walks, fishing. 1 twin, 1 family room. A2 from Belfast, 8 miles, Helen's Bay turn left 114 mile turn right, 3rd house on left. Train ¼ mile. Map ref: 138 202

Cornerhouse, 182 Dunmore Road, Ballynahinch, Co Down BT24 8QQ

Mrs Mary Rogan
☎ 0238 562670
🅱 From £12
EM From £6–£8
Sleeps 6
⛷ ♨
Approved

Farmhouse on 30-acre farm near Mournes. Forest parks, fishing, golf. 1 single, 1 double, 1 family room (1 H/C). Dogs allowed outside. Off A24 near Spa. Ballynahinch 5 miles. Map ref: 133 190

Gordonall, 93 Newtownards Road, Greyabbey, Newtownards, Co Down BT22 2QJ

Angela Martin
☎ 024774 325
🅱 From £13
Sleeps 5
⛷ ♨
Approved

Centrally heated farmhouse on 160-acre mixed farm overlooking Strangford Lough and Mourne mountains. Birdwatching, fishing, golf, flying club close by. Dogs allowed outside. Vouchers accepted. 2 rooms, one twin, one family, all H&C. On A20, first farm on left after Mount Stewart (NT). Newtownards 6 miles, Greyabbey 1 mile. Bus stop at end of farm lane. Open April to September. Map ref: 133 190

Greenlea Farm, 48 Dunover Road, Ballywater, Newtownards, Co Down BT22 2LE

Evelyn McIvor
☎ 02477 58218
🅱 From £12
EM From £6.50–£8
Sleeps 10/12
⛷ ♨
Approved

Recently modernised to fire authority regulations, on 120-acre farm overlooking sea, ½ mile village, churches and A2. Convenient to National Trust folk museum, antique shops, pottery, Kirkston racing. CH and H/C in all rooms. 1 family, 2 twin, 1 double and 1 single. Guests' bathroom and shower, toilet facilities. Sun lounge. Home cooking. Strangford Portaferry 13 miles, Newtownards 10 miles, Bangor 11 miles, Belfast 20 miles. Map ref: 137 198

Havine Farm Guest House, 51 Bally Donnell Road, Downpatrick, Co Down BT30 8EP

Mrs Myrtle Macauley
☎ 039685 242
🅱 From £12–£12.50
EM From £7.50
Sleeps 6
⛷ ♨
Grade B

A modernised 18th century farmhouse situated on 125 acre working farm in the heart of St Patrick's country, with central heating, H/C running water in all bedrooms, yet retaining its ancestral distinctions throughout the house, with a stream meandering through the gardens on its way to the sea. Open all year. Map ref: 136 187

The Maggimin, 11 Bishopswell Road, Dromore, Co Down BT25 1ST

Wilson & Rhoda Mark
☎ 0846 693520
🅱 From £14
EM From £5
Sleeps 8
🌐 ♨
Approved

Country house (central heating) with view of Mournes. 1 double, 1 twin, 1 family room (en-suite bathrooms). Home cooking. Separate visitors' lounge. Sprucefield Centre 10 mins. Going north on A1 Dromore bypass take Milebush Road (left) then immediately left (Maypole Road), 2nd right. Lane to house on left after disused railway bridge. Hillsborough 4 miles. Map ref: 126 192

Morne Abbey Guest House, 16 Greencastle Road, Kilkeel, Co. Down BT34 4DE

Annabel Shannon
☎ 06937 62426
🅱 From £13
EM From £7
Sleeps 13
♨ ♨ (1)
Grade B

New farmhouse on mixed farm in magnificent setting 12 miles from Kilkeel. A warm welcome assured, home cooking a speciality. Fishing, riding, tennis, bowls and golf nearby. Sea 1 mile. Silent Valley 4 miles. Babysitter available. 1 single, 2 twin and 2 double rooms, all H&C. Open Apr–Sep. Map ref: 128 177

Sharon Farmhouse, 6 Ballykeel Road, Ballymartin, Co Down BT34 4PL

M. Bingham
☎ **06937 62521**
ⓑⓑ **From £13**
EM From £6
Sleeps 7
🐎 ⛪ ✕ 🐴
Approved

A modern farm bungalow – 1 family and 2 double with H/C and central heating. With excellent sea and mountain views. Situated ideally for mountaineering and 10 minutes from beach. 2 miles from Kilkeel town and fishing port. The area is rich in varied birdlife. Good wholesome home cooked food served in abundance. A warm and welcoming atmosphere. Your comfort is our pleasure. Open all year. Map ref: 127 177

The Strand, 231 Ardglass Road, Ardglass, Co Down BT30 7UL

FARM HOLIDAY BUREAU

Mrs Mary Donnan
☎ **0396 841446**
ⓑⓑ **From £11.50**
EM From £7
Sleeps 5
Grade A4

2 rooms, 1 twin, 1 family. Open all year. 18th century, modernised, farmhouse in 130 acre working farm. Warm hospitality and home baking. Convenient to Ardglass fishing village, with its five historical castles, scenic 19 hole golf course, fishing and shooting. Castle Ward, National Trust 3 miles and Coney Island beach 1½ miles. Map ref: 140 184

Trench Farm, 35 Ringcreevy Road, Comber, Newtownards, Co Down BT23 5JR

Marueen Hamilton
☎ **0247 872558**
ⓑⓑ **From £15**
EM From £10
Sleeps 6
🐎
Approved

Farmhouse (central heating) on 100-acre horticultural farm overlooking Lough Scrabo Tower and Forest Park. National Trust properties. Golf, driving ponies kept as hobby. 1 family and 1 twin room (H/C). Electric blankets. Babysitter. A21 Newtownards Road. From Comber first road on right. Comber 2 miles, Newtownards 4 miles. Open all year. Map ref: 137 198

Wyncrest, 30 Main Road, Ballymartin, Kilkeel, Co Down BT34 4NU

Mrs Irene Adair
☎ **06937 63012**
ⓑⓑ **From £15**
EM From £12
Sleeps 12
🐎
Grade A

BTA Commended Country Guesthouse (central heating and open fires). "Taste of Ulster" 1991. All Ireland Galtee Best Breakfast Award. Two double, 4 twin (4 en-suite). Electric blankets. Every comfort assured. On main Newcastle/Kilkeel road (A2), Kilkeel 3 miles, Newcastle 10 miles. Reductions for extended bookings. Map ref: 128 177

FARM HOLIDAY BUREAU

FOLLOW THE COUNTRY CODE

Leave nothing but footprints,

Take nothing but photographs,

Kill nothing but time!

Compliments and complaints

Many visitors write to the Farm Holiday Bureau saying how much they have enjoyed their stay. If you feel that something or someone deserves acknowledgement, or if you have a suggestion on how to improve the guide, please write to the Farm Holiday Bureau (UK) Ltd, National Agricultural Centre, Stoneleigh, Warwickshire CV8 2LZ, or ring (0203) 696909.

If you are dissatisfied, please make your complaint to the host there and then. This gives an opportunity for rectifying action to be taken at once. It is usually difficult to deal with a complaint if it is reported at a later date. If the host fails to resolve the problem, please write to the Farm Holiday Bureau who will be happy to help.

For information on farm holidays in various countries in Europe please contact the following:

GERMANY
Komm Aufs Land Nordrhein Westphallen
Postfach 5925 – Schorlemerstraße 26
D – 4400 MUNSTER
Tel. [49] 251/599-305
Fax [49] 251 599 362

Deutsche Landwirtschaft Gesellschaft
Zimmerweg 16
D – 6000 FRANFURT A.M. 1
Tel. [49] 69 7 16 80
Fax [49] 69 72 41 554

Arbeitsgemeinschaft fur Urlaub und Freizeit auf
eem Lande
Dürstermeichen
D – 2725 BOTHEL
Tel. [49] 4266 – 199
Fax [49] 4266 85 48

BELGIUM
Federation des Gîtes de Wallonie
Rue du Millénaire, 53
B – 6941 VILLERS SAINTE-GERTRUDE
Tel. [32] 86 49 95 31
Fax [32] 86 49 94 07

FRANCE
Federation Nationale des Gites de France
35, rue Godot de Mauroy
F – 75009 PARIS
Tel. [33] 1 47 42 20 92
Fax [33] 1 47 42 73 11

Agriculture et Tourisme
9, avenue Georges V
F – 75008 PARIS
Tel. [33] 1 47 23 55 40
Fax [33] 1 47 23 84 97

HUNGARY
Association of Village Farm Houses
H – 1126 Budapest
Szoboszalai u. Z-4
Tel. [36] 1 11 83 877
Fax [36] 1 11 83 855

IRELAND
Irish Farm Holidays
Ashton Grove – IR-Knockrama Co Cork
Tel. [353] 021 82 15 37
Fax [353] 01 764 764

ICELAND
Icelandic Farm Holidays
Hotel Saga – Hagatorg
IS – 107 REYKJAVIK
Tel. [354] 1, 19 200
Fax [354] 1 62 82 90

ITALY
Agriturist
C. SO Vittorio Emmanuelle, 101
I – 00186 ROMA
Tel. [39] 66 86 97 86
Fax [39] 66 54 85 78

PORTUGAL
Associacao Portugesa de Turismo de
Habitacao (Privetur)
Trav. de Cima Dos Quarteis n° 24 – 2°A
P – 1200 LISBOA
Tel. [351] 1 69 15 08
Fax [351] 1 65 49 53

Associacao das Mulheres Agricultoras de
Portugal (AMAP)
Calçada Ribeiro Santos 19 r/o
P – 1200 LISBOA
Tel. [351] 1 674 063/4/5
Fax [351] 1 677 309

LUXEMBOURG
Association pour la Promotion du Tourisme rura
au Grand-Duché du Luxembourg
48, route de Bastogne
L – 9176 NIEDERFEULEN – Luxembourg
Tel. [352] 8 27 20

Index

to farms offering
Accommodation for disabled visitors,
camping and caravanning facilities and business breaks

County		Farm	Page No.	Disabled facilities	Tents	Touring caravans	Static caravans	Business people welcome	Meeting room (capacity)
Bedfordshire	B&B	Church Farm	186					✓	
		Firs Farm	186					✓	✓ (8)
		Gransden Lodge Farm	189					✓	
	SC	The Old Stone Barn	187	✓				✓	
Buckinghamshire	B&B	Manor Farm	204	✓					
		Monkton Farm	204		✓	✓			
		Neals Farm	204		✓				
	S&C	Wallace Farm Cottages	206	✓					
Cambridgeshire	B&B	Forge Cottage	189	✓	✓			✓	✓ (20)
Cheshire	B&B	Adderley Green Farm	128					✓	✓ (6)
		Laburnam House Farm	129			✓			
		Lea Farm	129					✓	
		Newton Hall	129					✓	
		Sandhole Farm	130					✓	✓ (40)
		Shire Cottage	125	✓					
	SC	Lake View	125	✓					
Cornwall	B&B	Arrallas	300					✓	✓ (20)
		Bucklawren Farm	300		✓			✓	
		Degembris Farm	300					✓	
		Hendra Farm	301		✓	✓		✓	
		Kerryanna Guest Farm	301					✓	
		Longstone Farm	301	✓					
		Manuels Farm	302					✓	
		Polsue Manor Farm	302					✓	
		Treffry Farm	303					✓	
		Tregaswith Farmhouse	303					✓	✓ (8)
	SC	Bucklawren Farm	304			✓		✓	
		Glynn Barton Farm Cottages	305	✓				✓	
		Lodge Barton Farm	305	✓				✓	
		Lower Trengale Farm	305					✓	✓ (14)
		Manuels Farm	306					✓	
		Poltarrow Farm Cottage	306	✓					
Cumbria	B&B	Bessietown Farm	76	✓				✓	✓ (20)
		Cracrop Farm	68					✓	✓ (8)
		Cragend Farm	88					✓	
		Craigburn Farm	76					✓	✓ (50)

County		Farm	Page No.	Disabled facilities	Tents	Touring caravans	Static caravans	Business people welcome	Meeting room (capacity)
Somerset (continued)	B&B	Redhill Farm	217		✓	✓			
		Tor Farm	217					✓	✓ (25)
	SC	Cutthorne Farm	260		✓	✓			
		Emmetts Grange Farm	261	✓					
		Ruggs Farm Bungalow	261	✓					
		Rull Farm	256		✓	✓			
		Westermill Farm	262		✓			✓	
	CC	Westermill Farm	262		✓				
Staffordshire	B&B	Brook House Farm	135	✓					
Suffolk	SC	Stable Cottages and The Granary	196	✓					
Surrey	B&B	Borderfield Farm	228		✓	✓			
		Bulmer Farm	228			✓		✓	
		Camoys Farmhouse	228	✓					
		Crossways Farm	228					✓	
	SC	Badgersholt and Foxholme	230	✓				✓	
Warwickshire	B&B	Church Farm	175	✓				✓	✓ (12)
		Hill Farm	176		✓	✓	✓		
		Maxstoke Farm	177		✓			✓	✓ (30)
		Newfields	177		✓	✓		✓	
		Shrewley Pools Farm	177		✓			✓	✓ (8)
		Tibbits Farm	178		✓	✓		✓	✓ (10)
		Whitchurch Farm	178					✓	✓ (12)
	SC	Glebe Farm Holiday Cottages	179	✓					
		The Granary	179					✓	✓ (20)
		Hipsley Farm Cottages	179	✓				✓	
		Irelands Farm	180	✓					
West Sussex	B&B	Goffsland Farm	229			✓			
		New House Farm	229					✓	
West Yorkshire	B&B	Brow Top Farm	97					✓	
	SC	Bottoms Farm Cottages	98					✓	✓ (12)
		Hole Farm	99	✓	✓	✓		✓	✓ (15)
		Westfield Farm Cottages	99	✓				✓	
Wiltshire	B&B	Bayardo Farm	219			✓			
		Longwater	220	✓	✓	✓		✓	✓ (12)
		Lower Foxhangers Farm	220		✓	✓	✓		
		Oakwood Farm	221					✓	
		Spiers Piece Farm	222					✓	✓ (10)
	SC	Lower Foxhangers Farm	223	✓	✓	✓	✓		

County		Farm	Page No.	Disabled facilities	Tents	Touring caravans	Static caravans	Business people welcome	Meeting room (capacity)
Dyfed	B&B	Bryncastell Farm	332	✓					
		Gilfach Goch Farmhouse	341	✓					
		Lochmeyler Farm	341	✓				✓	
		Lower Haythog	341					✓	
		Torbant Farm Guest House	342	✓				✓	✓ (80)
		Yethen Isaf	344					✓	✓ (20)
Gwent	B&B	The Grange	337					✓	
		Parsons Grove	337	✓					
		Pentwyn Farm	337		✓	✓			
		Tŷ-Gwyn Farm	338			✓		✓	
		The Wenaclt Farm	338	✓	✓			✓	✓ (30)
	SC	Granary and Coach House	338	✓					
		Parsons Grove	338	✓					
Gwynedd	B&B	Cae'r Efail	313					✓	✓
		Fferm Fron-Gôch	316					✓	
		Glynn Farm	323					✓	
		Llwydiarth Fawr	313	✓					
		Mathan Uchaf Farm	310		✓				
		Old Mill Farmhouse	316	✓				✓	✓
		Pengwern	313					✓	
		Rhydydefaid Farm	316					✓	
		Tydoyn Du Farm	316					✓	
		Ty Mawr Farm	314					✓	
		Ty Mawr Farmhouse	314					✓	
	SC	Glynn Farm	324					✓	
		Gwynfryn Farm	311	✓	✓			✓	
		Llys Bennar	314	✓	✓	✓			
		Rydolion	311		✓	✓			
		Tai Gwyliau Tyndon Holiday Cottages	311	✓		✓	✓		
		Towyn Farm	311	✓					
		Ynys	314	✓	✓	✓		✓	
Powys	B&B	Brynfedwen Farm	334	✓					
		Dol-llys Farm	326		✓	✓			
		The Drewin Farm	326		✓				
		Gigrin Farm	330		✓	✓			
		Little Brompton Farm	327		✓	✓		✓	
		Moat Farm	327					✓	
		Wermfawr	335		✓				
		Willey Lodge Farm	330		✓				
	SC	Cwm y Gath	328					✓	

Index

County		Farm	Page No.	Disabled facilities	Tents	Touring caravans	Static caravans	Business people welcome	Meeting room (capacity)
NORTHERN IRELAND									
Antrim	B&B	Beechgrove	347	✓					
		Country Guest House	347	✓					
		Sprucebank	348	✓					
Armagh	B&B	Heimat	355		✓	✓			
Down	B&B	Ballycastle House	357		✓	✓			
		Sharon Farmhouse	359	✓					
Fermanagh	B&B	Broadmeadows House	353	✓					
Londonderry	B&B	The Poplars	345		✓